Advancing Hybrid Pedagogies Through AI and Intercultural Collaboration

Thi-Phuong Nguyen
Department of Science, Technology, and International Projects, Ho Chi Minh City University of Economics and Finance, Ho Chi Minh City, Vietnam

Jiaming Zhang
Vrije Universiteit, Amsterdam, The Netherlands

Anna Loseva
International Education Institute, UEH University, Vietnam

IGI Global
Scientific Publishing
Publishing Tomorrow's Research Today

Vice President of Editorial	Melissa Wagner
Director of Acquisitions	Mikaela Felty
Director of Book Development	Jocelynn Hessler
Production Manager	Mike Brehm
Cover Design	Jose Rosado

Published in the United States of America by
IGI Global Scientific Publishing
701 East Chocolate Avenue
Hershey, PA, 17033, USA
Tel: 717-533-8845 | Fax: 717-533-7115
Website: https://www.igi-global.com E-mail: cust@igi-global.com

Library of Congress Cataloging-in-Publication Data

Names: Nguyen, Phuong Thi, 1990- editor | Zhang, Jiaming, 1982- editor | Loseva, Anna, 1996- editor
Title: Advancing hybrid pedagogies through AI and intercultural collaboration / [edited by] Phuong Thi Nguyen, Jiaming Zhang, Anna Loseva.
Description: Hershey, PA : IGI Global Scientific Publishing, [2026] | Includes bibliographical references and index. | Summary: "This book plans to advance both scholarly and practical understanding of hybrid pedagogies in the age of artificial intelligence (AI)"-- Provided by publisher.
Identifiers: LCCN 2026005268 (print) | LCCN 2026005269 (ebook) | ISBN 9798337374628 hardcover | ISBN 9798337374635 paperback | ISBN 9798337374642 ebook
Subjects: LCSH: Blended learning | Artificial intelligence--Educational applications
Classification: LCC LB1028.5 .A277 2026 (print) | LCC LB1028.5 (ebook)
LC record available at https://lccn.loc.gov/2026005268
LC ebook record available at https://lccn.loc.gov/2026005269

British Cataloguing in Publication Data
A Cataloguing in Publication record for this book is available from the British Library.

Table of Contents

Detailed Table of Contents

Hybrid education is undergoing a decisive transformation as generative AI and global digital connectivity become embedded in education systems. Once a pragmatic response to crisis, hybrid learning now signals a long-term shift in how knowledge is produced, governed, and experienced across institutions and cultures. This chapter adopts a futures-oriented lens to move beyond mere technological adoption, stressing anticipatory, ethical, and human-centred design. Drawing on futures thinking, policy foresight, and global education frameworks from UNESCO and the OECD, it outlines three plausible futures: the Adaptive Future, the Ethical Future and the Regenerative Future. From these, the Hybrid Education Futures Framework (HEFF) is proposed as a strategic tool for institutional reflection and policy design. The chapter argues that the core challenge is not technological disruption but human reinvention, guided by ethical intelligence to advance equity, resilience, and collective progress.

This chapter explores how artificial intelligence (AI) and intercultural collaboration are transforming hybrid pedagogy into a globally connected and ethically grounded model of learning. Hybrid pedagogy has emerged to respond to digital disruption, and it has developed into a supportive framework, thereby integrating digital innovation with intercultural empathy. Hybrid education promotes key educational goals such as adaptability, inclusivity, and global citizenships, upon the incorporation of AI-powered individualization with intercultural knowledge. The chapter analyses historical tracks,

Pedagogy (CRHP). The integration of the four pillars of the CRHP framework, cultural awareness, pedagogical adaptivity, collaborative intelligence, and ethical integrity, is presented to keep hybrid education inclusive and human centred. Through the lens of global case studies and ethical principles, the chapter posits that the most valuable innovations come not from automation of processes but, from the ethically guided human and machine partnership where co-agency is possible. The chapter ends with the assertion that the future of education is dependent on the construction of intelligent bridges, or learning ecosystems, that can integrate multiple dimensions of diversity and creativity with technology to sustain a sense of belonging and shared understanding within a digitally connected society.

Intersecting of Artificial Intelligence (AI) and hybrid pedagogies has redefined the landscape of higher education. As universities increasingly engage in Collaborative Online International Learning (COIL) and Virtual Exchange (VE) initiatives, the development of digital literacy, intercultural competence, and ethical awareness has become foundational for equitable global learning. When purposefully integrated, AI can scaffold intercultural dialogue, automate administrative processes, and provide adaptive feedback that enhances engagement and inclusivity. Ethical implications surrounding privacy, data governance, algorithmic bias, and equitable access present critical challenges. Conceptual and practical framework for employing AI as a mediating tool within hybrid pedagogies support intercultural collaboration exploring interconnections among digital literacy, global competence, and ethical AI practice, emphasizing transparency, cultural responsiveness, and data integrity.

This chapter examines the integration of artificial intelligence (AI) into hybrid pedagogical environments for Teaching English for Intercultural Communication (TEIC), with a focus on film-based learning. Using selected Disney films as cultural texts, it introduces the Intergenerational Sensitizer, a digital tool that adapts film-based critical incidents to prompt reflection, dialogue, and meaning-making across generational and cultural standpoints. Drawing on Bhabha's (1994) theory of hybridity, intercultural competence frameworks, and human-centered AI design, the chapter conceptualizes hybrid pedagogy as a "third space" where digital mediation and classroom interaction intersect. Methodologically, it follows a design-based approach, outlining the co-creation and application of AI-enhanced activities in hybrid Teaching English as a Foreign Language (TEFL) and TEIC settings. By treating AI as a mediator, the chapter shows how technology can support a model of hybrid language education that is ethically informed, culturally sensitive, and dialogically appropriate.

This chapter discusses the change of Physical Science education in the time of Artificial Intelligence and hybrid learning. It theorizes the transition between the traditional classroom designs and inclusive technology enhanced learning ecologies incorporating physical and digital space. The chapter is based on constructivist, socio-cultural, inquiry based and intercultural theories of learning. It explains the use of AI based tools, including adaptive learning systems, virtual laboratories, intelligent tutoring systems and generative simulations as well as automated assessment in Physical Science. The chapter also discusses the changing professional identity of educators, highlighting the fact that AI literacy and intercultural competence should be included in the teacher preparation programs. In the future, the chapter tells about the potential transformations of generative AI for a world scientific collaboration. In the end, it states that the suitable integration of AI into hybrid pedagogies developing scientifically literate, ethically informed and globally competent students.

With the rapid advancement of technology, access to information has also become easier. Artificial intelligence is one of the technologies that has come to the fore in recent years. As digital transformation occurs at such a rapid pace around the world, schools are also trying to keep up with this pace. However, one of the fundamental goals of education is to teach students how to cope with the rapid development of technologies and adapt to this situation. With the emergence of artificial intelligence, many traditional sustainability practices have been developed and enriched with

Preface

1. BACKGROUND

Higher education is currently experiencing a period of rapid transformation driven by technological innovation, global connectivity, and the emergence of artificial intelligence (AI). Over the past decade, digital technologies have increasingly reshaped the ways in which knowledge is created, shared, and accessed within educational environments (Zawacki-Richter et al., 2019; Kamalov et al, 2023). Earlier phases of digital transformation focused largely on expanding access to digital platforms and learning management systems, enabling institutions to deliver educational content beyond the physical classroom. However, recent developments suggest that the role of technology in education is evolving beyond infrastructure and delivery mechanisms toward deeper changes in pedagogy and learning design. Scholars have increasingly recognized that artificial intelligence is becoming a central driver of this transformation, influencing how institutions design curricula, how educators facilitate learning, and how students engage with knowledge in digitally mediated environments (Zawacki-Richter et al., 2019; Adiguzel et al., 2023; Kamalov et al., 2023).

The acceleration of digital transformation in education became particularly visible during the COVID-19 pandemic, when universities worldwide were required to rapidly adopt online and hybrid learning approaches. While these emergency responses initially focused on maintaining continuity of instruction, they also revealed important limitations in simply transferring traditional classroom practices into digital formats. As a result, scholars and practitioners have increasingly emphasized the need to rethink pedagogy itself rather than merely digitize existing teaching models. Hybrid education, which combines face-to-face and digital learning environments, has therefore emerged as a promising framework for enabling more flexible and inclusive learning experiences while supporting global collaboration among learners and institutions (Bond et al., 2024; Eager & Brunton, 2023). In this context, digital technologies are no longer viewed merely as tools for content delivery but as components of broader learning ecosystems that reshape relationships between educators, learners, and knowledge.

At the same time, advances in artificial intelligence are creating new opportunities for transforming teaching and learning processes. AI-enabled systems can support adaptive learning pathways, generate educational content, analyze student engagement data, and facilitate multilingual communication among students from diverse cultural backgrounds. These capabilities allow educational institutions to experiment with new forms of personalized and collaborative learning that extend beyond traditional classroom boundaries (Dempere et al., 2023; Kurtz et al., 2024). AI applications such as intelligent tutoring systems, conversational agents, and generative language models are increasingly being explored as tools for supporting feedback, self-regulated learning, and knowledge construction within hybrid environments (Chang et al., 2023; Lin et al., 2023).

However, the growing integration of AI into higher education also raises important ethical and institutional concerns. Scholars have highlighted issues related to algorithmic bias, data privacy, academic integrity, and unequal access to digital technologies, all of which complicate the adoption of AI in educational contexts (Grassini, 2023). Research has also pointed out that technological innovation alone cannot guarantee meaningful educational improvement, particularly when institutional policies, teacher competencies, and pedagogical frameworks are not aligned with technological change (Abdulrahman, 2024). These debates highlight the importance of approaching AI in education not merely as a technological development but as a broader pedagogical and institutional transformation.

2. RESEARCH THEME

Despite the rapid growth of research on artificial intelligence in education, much of the existing literature continues to focus primarily on technological capabilities rather than on the deeper pedagogical and institutional transformations required to integrate AI effectively within higher education systems. Early studies frequently emphasized the efficiency gains offered by automated tutoring systems, learning analytics, and AI-generated educational resources. While such innovations provide valuable tools for supporting teaching and learning, they do not fully address the broader question of how educational systems should evolve in response to the emergence of intelligent technologies (Michel-Villarreal et al., 2023; Malik et al., 2024).

This book therefore addresses a central question: how can artificial intelligence support the development of hybrid learning environments that enhance educational quality while preserving the human, ethical, and cultural dimensions of education? Addressing this question requires examining the evolving relationships between educators, learners, institutions, and digital technologies within contemporary educational systems. In hybrid learning environments, teaching and learning increasingly take place within sociotechnical ecosystems in which human actors interact with algorithmic systems and digital platforms to co-create knowledge. Within such ecosystems, educators are no longer simply transmitters of information but designers of learning environments that integrate digital tools, collaborative networks, and AI-supported feedback mechanisms (Abbasnejad et al., 2025).

Another important dimension of this transformation concerns the relationship between human educators and intelligent systems. While AI technologies can automate certain routine tasks such as grading, data analysis, and content generation, they cannot replace the relational and interpretive roles that educators play in facilitating meaningful learning experiences. Research increasingly emphasizes the importance of hybrid human-AI collaboration, in which intelligent technologies augment rather than replace the expertise of educators (Molenaar, 2022; Slade et al., 2024). In this perspective, AI functions not as a substitute for human teaching but as a partner that can extend educators' capacity to support learners through personalized feedback, adaptive instruction, and expanded access to knowledge resources.

At the same time, integrating AI into education requires careful consideration of ethical governance and institutional responsibility. Questions related to transparency, fairness, data governance, and digital equity have become central concerns in contemporary debates about AI in education (Nguyen et al., 2022; Azman & Tümkaya, 2025). Without appropriate governance structures, the adoption of AI technologies risks reinforcing existing inequalities rather than improving educational opportunities (Bulathwela et al., 2024). As a result, scholars increasingly argue that successful AI integration must be accompanied by institutional frameworks that promote responsible innovation, digital literacy, and equitable access to emerging technologies (Chan, 2023).

3. CONTRIBUTION

This book contributes to the evolving discourse on artificial intelligence in higher education by presenting a multidimensional perspective on hybrid pedagogical transformation. Rather than approaching AI solely as a technological tool, the chapters in this volume conceptualize artificial intelligence as part of a broader educational ecosystem that reshapes pedagogical practices, institutional structures, and intercultural learning experiences.

First, the book advances conceptual discussions about the future of hybrid education in an era characterized by generative AI and global digital connectivity. The chapters explore how emerging technologies can support innovative approaches to teaching and learning that emphasize adaptability, collaboration, and learner autonomy. Second, the volume brings together interdisciplinary perspectives from fields such as educational technology, intercultural communication, learning sciences, and higher education policy. By integrating these perspectives, the book provides a more comprehensive understanding of how AI-enabled educational transformation unfolds across different institutional and cultural contexts. Third, the book highlights the importance of ethical and culturally responsive approaches to AI integration. Several chapters examine how digital literacy, intercultural competence, and responsible governance frameworks can help ensure that technological innovation aligns with broader educational values, including inclusivity, equity, and sustainability. Finally, the volume provides practical insights for educators, researchers, and policymakers who are navigating the challenges of AI-enhanced education. Through conceptual frameworks, case studies, and pedagogical examples, the chapters illustrate how institutions can design learning environments that integrate technological innovation while preserving the human-centered principles that remain fundamental to education.

4. STRUCTURE OVERVIEW

The chapters in this volume are organised into five interconnected parts that collectively examine the evolving relationship between artificial intelligence, hybrid pedagogy, and global learning. The book opens with a forward-looking perspective in *Future Pathways – Rethinking Hybrid Education in the Era of Generative AI and Global Connectivity*, which establishes the conceptual foundations for understanding hybrid education in an increasingly AI-mediated world. This is followed by *Transforming Hybrid Pedagogies: Harnessing AI and Intercultural Collaboration for Global Learning*, which extends this vision by exploring how hybrid learning can enable more globally connected and collaborative educational practices.

The second part of the volume develops the theoretical and conceptual foundations of the field. *Beyond Optimization: Learning Analytics, Cultural Intelligence, and Human Flourishing in Hybrid Education* highlights the role of data-informed and human-centered approaches, while *Reconceptualising Artificial Intelligence in Education: Ethical and Cultural Dimensions* examines the ethical and cultural implications of AI adoption. Complementing this, *Reframing Teaching in the Age of AI: Educators and Intelligent Systems in Hybrid Learning* explores how the role of educators evolves within AI-supported learning environments.

The third part focuses on pedagogical design and innovation. *Intelligent Bridges: Designing Culturally Responsive Hybrid Pedagogies Through AI Collaboration* and *Advising Hybrid Pedagogies through AI and Intercultural Collaboration: Fostering Digital Literacy, Global Competence, and Ethical Practice* both emphasize the importance of culturally responsive teaching, intercultural collaboration, and the development of digital competencies in hybrid learning contexts.

The fourth part presents applied pedagogical innovations across different disciplines. Chapters such as *Film, AI, and Hybrid Pedagogy: Designing Intercultural Learning Experiences*, *Designing Inclusive Hybrid Pedagogies in Physical Science with AI from Classroom to Cloud*, and *Design of Artificial Intelligence Supported Education Module: The Example of Environment and Climate Change* illustrate how AI-supported hybrid pedagogies can be implemented in diverse educational settings.

Finally, the fifth part addresses broader institutional and societal dimensions of AI integration in higher education. *Preparing Higher Education for the Era of Artificial Intelligence: A Multidimensional Framework for Institutional Readiness* provides a strategic perspective on institutional transformation, while *Sustainability, AI, and Hybrid Pedagogy: Building Eco-Responsible, Culturally Inclusive Learning Systems* highlights the intersection of sustainability and digital education. The volume concludes with *AI for Trust and Social Interaction: A Social Capital Perspective on Knowledge Sharing in Vietnam's Higher Education*, which offers an empirical lens on trust, collaboration, and knowledge exchange in AI-mediated environments.

Together, these five parts provide a coherent and multidimensional exploration of how artificial intelligence and hybrid pedagogies are reshaping contemporary higher education, offering both conceptual insights and practical implications for educators, researchers, and policymakers.

REFERENCES

Abbasnejad, B., Soltani, S., Taghizadeh, F., & Zare, A. (2025). Developing a multilevel framework for AI integration in technical and engineering higher education: Insights from bibliometric analysis and ethnographic research. *Interactive Technology and Smart Education*. Advance online publication. DOI: 10.1108/ITSE-12-2024-0314

Abdulrahman, A. (2024). Unveiling the shadows: Beyond the hype of AI in education. *Heliyon*, *10*(9), e30696. Advance online publication. DOI: 10.1016/j.heliyon.2024.e30696 PMID: 38737255

Adiguzel, T., Kaya, M. H., & Cansu, F. K. (2023). Revolutionizing education with AI: Exploring the transformative potential of ChatGPT. *Contemporary Educational Technology*, *15*(2), ep425. DOI: 10.30935/cedtech/13152

Azman, Ö., & Tümkaya, S. (2025). Navigating the ethical landscape of AI integration in education: Balancing innovation and responsibility. *F1000Research*. DOI: 10.12688/f1000research.160011.1

Bond, M., Khosravi, H., de Laat, M., Bergdahl, N., Negrea, V., Oxley, E., Pham, P., Chong, S. W., & Siemens, G. (2024). A meta-systematic review of artificial intelligence in higher education: A call for increased ethics, collaboration, and rigour. *International Journal of Educational Technology in Higher Education*, *21*(1), 20. Advance online publication. DOI: 10.1186/s41239-023-00436-z

Bulathwela, S., Pérez-Ortiz, M., Holloway, C., Cukurova, M., & Shawe-Taylor, J. (2024). Artificial intelligence alone will not democratise education: On educational inequality, techno-solutionism and inclusive tools. *Sustainability (Basel)*, *16*(2), 781. Advance online publication. DOI: 10.3390/su16020781

Chan, C. K. Y. (2023). A comprehensive AI policy education framework for university teaching and learning. *International Journal of Educational Technology in Higher Education*, *20*(1), 38. Advance online publication. DOI: 10.1186/s41239-023-00408-3

Chang, D. H., Lin, M. P., Hajian, S., & Wang, Q. Q. (2023). Educational design principles for AI chatbots that support self-regulated learning. *Sustainability*, *15*(7). Advance online publication. DOI: 10.3390/su151712921

Dempere, J. M., Modugu, K., Hesham, A., & Ramasamy, L. K. (2023). The impact of ChatGPT on higher education. *Frontiers in Education*, *8*, 1206936. DOI: 10.3389/feduc.2023.1206936

Eager, B., & Brunton, R. (2023). Prompting higher education toward AI-augmented teaching and learning practice. *Journal of University Teaching & Learning Practice, 20*(5). Advance online publication. DOI: 10.53761/1.20.5.02

Grassini, S. (2023). Shaping the future of education: Exploring the potential and consequences of AI and ChatGPT in educational settings. *Education Sciences, 13*(7), 692. Advance online publication. DOI: 10.3390/educsci13070692

Kamalov, F., Calonge, D. S., & Gurrib, I. (2023). New era of artificial intelligence in education: Towards a sustainable multifaceted revolution. *Sustainability (Basel), 15*(16), 12451. Advance online publication. DOI: 10.3390/su151612451

Kurtz, G., Amzalag, M., Shaked, N., Zaguri, Y., Kohen-Vacs, D., Gal, E., Zailer, G., & Barak-Medina, E. (2024). Strategies for integrating generative AI into higher education. *Education Sciences, 14*(5), 503. Advance online publication. DOI: 10.3390/educsci14050503

Lin, C.-C., Huang, A., & Lu, O. (2023). *Artificial intelligence in intelligent tutoring systems toward sustainable education*. Smart Learning Environments., DOI: 10.1186/s40561-023-00260-y

Malik, A., Khan, M. L., Hussain, K., Qadir, J., & Tarhini, A. (2024). AI in higher education: Academicians' perspectives on teaching, research, and ethics in the age of ChatGPT. *Interactive Learning Environments*. Advance online publication. DOI: 10.1080/10494820.2024.2409407

Michel-Villarreal, R., Vilalta-Perdomo, E., Salinas-Navarro, D., Thierry-Aguilera, R., & Gerardou, F. (2023). Challenges and opportunities of generative AI for higher education as explained by ChatGPT. *Education Sciences, 13*(9), 856. Advance online publication. DOI: 10.3390/educsci13090856

Molenaar, I. (2022). Towards hybrid human-AI learning technologies. *European Journal of Education, 57*(4), 637–648. DOI: 10.1111/ejed.12527

Ng, D., Leung, J., Su, J., Ng, R., & Chu, S. (2023). Teachers' AI digital competencies and twenty-first century skills in the post-pandemic world. *Educational Technology Research and Development, 71*(1), 137–161. Advance online publication. DOI: 10.1007/s11423-023-10203-6 PMID: 36844361

Nguyen, A., Ngo, H., Hong, Y., Dang, B., & Nguyen, B.-P. T. (2022). Ethical principles for AI in education. *Education and Information Technologies*. Advance online publication. DOI: 10.1007/s10639-022-11316-w PMID: 36254344

Slade, J. J., Byers, S. M., Becker-Blease, K. A., & Gurung, R. (2024). Navigating the new frontier: Recommendations to address the crisis and potential of AI in the classroom. *Teaching of Psychology*. Advance online publication. DOI: 10.1177/00986283241276098

Zawacki-Richter, O., Marín, V. I., Bond, M., & Gouverneur, F. (2019). Systematic review of research on artificial intelligence applications in higher education. *International Journal of Educational Technology in Higher Education*, *16*(1), 39. Advance online publication. DOI: 10.1186/s41239-019-0171-0

Chapter 1
Future Pathways: Rethinking Hybrid Education in the Era of Generative AI and Global Connectivity

Thinh Gia Hoang
http://orcid.org/0000-0001-5010-931X
Department of Science, Technology, and International Projects, Ho Chi Minh City University of Economics and Finance (UEF), Ho Chi Minh City, Vietnam

Nam Hai Vu
UCSI University, Malaysia

ABSTRACT

Hybrid education is undergoing a decisive transformation as generative AI and global digital connectivity become embedded in education systems. Once a pragmatic response to crisis, hybrid learning now signals a long-term shift in how knowledge is produced, governed, and experienced across institutions and cultures. This chapter adopts a futures-oriented lens to move beyond mere technological adoption, stressing anticipatory, ethical, and human-centred design. Drawing on futures thinking, policy foresight, and global education frameworks from UNESCO and the OECD, it outlines three plausible futures: the Adaptive Future, the Ethical Future and the Regenerative Future. From these, the Hybrid Education Futures Framework (HEFF) is proposed as a strategic tool for institutional reflection and policy design. The chapter argues that the core challenge is not technological disruption but human reinvention, guided by ethical intelligence to advance equity, resilience, and collective progress.

DOI: 10.4018/979-8-3373-7462-8.ch001

1. INTRODUCTION: FROM HYBRID RESPONSE TO HYBRID FUTURES

The rapid acceleration of digital technologies over the past decade, intensified by global disruption and the rise of generative artificial intelligence, has fundamentally altered the landscape of education. What began as an emergency response to crisis has evolved into a deeper structural transformation, reshaping how learning is designed, governed, and experienced. Hybrid education, once narrowly defined as a combination of online and face to face delivery, has emerged as a long term paradigm that reflects broader shifts in epistemology, institutional logic, and global connectivity. This chapter situates hybrid education within this transformative moment and argues that its future trajectory will be shaped less by technological capacity than by how societies choose to align innovation with human development, ethical responsibility, and collective purpose.

1.1. Hybrid Education Beyond Crisis

The global expansion of hybrid and online learning was initially driven by necessity rather than strategic intent. Emergency remote teaching, widely adopted during periods of crisis, prioritized continuity over quality and often replicated traditional instructional models in digital environments with limited pedagogical redesign. While these early implementations exposed significant inequalities in access, digital literacy, and institutional preparedness, they also revealed the potential for more flexible, inclusive, and adaptive learning systems. As education systems move beyond crisis management, hybrid education is increasingly understood not as a temporary solution, but as a structural transformation of educational ecosystems.

This shift reflects a broader rethinking of education's role in a rapidly changing world. UNESCO's Futures of Education report emphasizes that education must move beyond incremental reform toward transformative change, redefining learning as a shared social endeavor oriented toward sustainability, solidarity, and human flourishing (UNESCO, 2022). Similarly, the OECD Learning Compass 2030 frames learning as a dynamic process that integrates knowledge, skills, attitudes, and values, preparing learners to navigate complexity, uncertainty, and ethical dilemmas (OECD, 2019). Within this context, hybrid education is not simply a delivery model, but a manifestation of deeper systemic change.

Hybrid learning's evolution also coincides with growing recognition of education as a key driver of human development. The Human Development Report 2023/24 highlights that technological progress alone does not guarantee human advancement. Instead, development depends on institutions' capacity to align innovation with equity, agency, and well being (UNDP, 2023). Applied to education, this insight underscores the risk of viewing hybrid systems as technologically neutral. Hybrid education reflects normative choices about whose knowledge is valued, how learning is assessed, and which forms of participation are enabled or excluded.

As hybrid education matures, it increasingly represents a long term educational paradigm characterized by flexibility, modularity, and co-creation. Learning pathways are no longer confined to fixed spaces or linear trajectories but unfold across physical campuses, digital platforms, workplaces, and global networks. This paradigm shift challenges long standing assumptions about curriculum design, academic authority, and institutional boundaries. It also raises new questions about governance, quality assurance, and the evolving role of educators in environments where learners have greater autonomy and access to diverse sources of knowledge.

1.2. Generative AI and Global Connectivity as Systemic Forces

The rise of generative artificial intelligence and intensified global connectivity has accelerated and complicated the transformation of hybrid education. Unlike earlier digital tools that primarily supported content delivery or administrative efficiency, generative AI systems actively participate in knowledge production, interpretation, and creative processes. This represents a significant epistemic shift, as learners increasingly engage with AI not merely as a tool, but as a collaborator in writing, problem solving, and meaning making.

Recent scholarship highlights both the promise and the tension embedded in this transformation. Kasneci et al. (2023) argue that generative AI can enhance learning by supporting personalization, feedback, and accessibility, particularly for learners with diverse needs. At the same time, concerns persist regarding cognitive dependency, academic integrity, and the erosion of critical thinking. Dwivedi et al. (2023) further emphasize that the central question is no longer whether AI can produce educational content, but how institutions define authorship, responsibility, and value in AI mediated learning environments.

These challenges are not purely technical but institutional and ethical in nature. Haidemariam and Gran (2025) caution that the development and deployment of generative AI often prioritize technical optimization over social alignment, creating systems that are efficient yet misaligned with human values. Their call for hybrid alignment strategies that combine technical safeguards with institutional, cultural, and normative approaches is highly relevant to the future of hybrid education. Educational systems must therefore engage with AI not only as an innovation, but as a governance challenge that demands ethical literacy, participatory decision making, and contextual sensitivity.

Global connectivity further reshapes the spatial and cultural dimensions of learning. Digital platforms enable cross border classrooms, international research collaborations, and global knowledge exchange at unprecedented scale. However, connectivity also introduces new forms of exclusion. Unequal access to digital infrastructure, linguistic dominance embedded in AI systems, and platform driven standardization risk marginalizing local pedagogical traditions and reinforcing global hierarchies. The blurring of boundaries between human and machine, local and global, and formal and informal learning thus generates both opportunity and tension within hybrid education ecosystems.

In this context, hybrid education becomes a site where global technological forces intersect with local educational cultures. Decisions regarding platform adoption, curriculum design, and assessment practices are increasingly influenced by transnational actors and infrastructures. This raises critical questions about autonomy, cultural representation, and educational sovereignty. Addressing these tensions requires moving beyond instrumental adoption toward reflective and values driven educational design.

1.3. Chapter Purpose and Structure

Against this backdrop, this chapter adopts a futures oriented approach to examine how hybrid education may evolve in the era of generative artificial intelligence and global connectivity. Rather than offering predictions, it employs future thinking and scenario development to explore plausible pathways and their implications for pedagogy, governance, and human development. Futures oriented analysis is particularly suited to this context because it enables institutions and policymakers to engage with uncertainty, surface underlying assumptions, and make strategic choices aligned with long term societal values.

The chapter is structured as follows. It first situates hybrid education within the post digital condition, highlighting how generative AI and global connectivity are reshaping knowledge production and learning ecosystems. It then introduces a futures thinking methodology and develops three illustrative scenarios for hybrid education, namely an adaptive future focused on personalization and flexibility, an ethical future centered on governance and cultural diversity, and a regenerative future oriented toward sustainability and well being. Building on these scenarios, the chapter proposes a Hybrid Education Futures Framework to support strategic reflection and institutional readiness. Finally, it examines institutional and policy pathways that can enable ethically grounded and globally inclusive hybrid education systems.

By framing hybrid education as a site of human reinvention rather than technological disruption alone, this chapter contributes to ongoing debates on the future of education. It argues that the success of hybrid education in the age of generative AI will depend not on the sophistication of technologies deployed, but on the capacity of educational systems to integrate innovation with ethical intelligence, cultural awareness, and a renewed commitment to collective progress.

2. THE POST-DIGITAL CONDITION OF HYBRID EDUCATION

The evolution of hybrid education is unfolding within what scholars increasingly describe as a post-digital condition, where digital technologies are no longer perceived as external innovations but as embedded, normalized, and inseparable from everyday educational practice. In this context, the distinction between digital and non-digital learning loses analytical relevance, giving way to more complex questions about knowledge production, human agency, and social inclusion. This section examines how post-digital education reshapes learning epistemologies, how generative AI alters the conditions of knowledge creation, and how global connectivity reconfigures educational spaces and inequalities.

2.1. Post-Digital Education and New Learning Epistemologies

Post-digital education signals a departure from earlier debates that framed learning as a choice between online and offline modes. Rather than positioning technology as an add-on or substitute for traditional instruction, post-digital perspectives recognize that digital infrastructures, data systems, and algorithmic processes are now constitutive elements of educational environments. As a result, hybrid education cannot be understood merely as a technical blend of modalities, but as a reconfiguration of how learning is conceptualized, experienced, and valued.

Within this epistemic shift, knowledge is increasingly understood as fluid, co-created, and multimodal. Learners engage with information not only through text-based curricula, but through interactive simulations, audiovisual media, collaborative platforms, and AI-mediated feedback systems. Learning thus becomes a process of navigation, interpretation, and synthesis across multiple representational forms. This aligns with the OECD Learning Compass 2030, which emphasizes learner agency, co-creation, and the integration of cognitive, social, and ethical dimensions of learning (OECD, 2019). In hybrid environments, learners are no longer passive recipients of knowledge, but active participants in shaping learning trajectories that extend beyond institutional boundaries.

UNESCO's Reimagining Our Futures Together further reinforces this epistemological transformation by framing education as a common good grounded in collaboration, pluralism, and shared responsibility (UNESCO, 2022). From this perspective, post-digital hybrid education foregrounds relational learning, where meaning emerges through interaction among learners, educators, technologies, and communities. Knowledge is not fixed or authoritative, but provisional and contextually situated. This challenges traditional hierarchies of expertise and raises important questions about curriculum authority, assessment practices, and academic legitimacy.

At the same time, the post-digital condition introduces new tensions. While hybrid systems enable flexibility and personalization, they also demand higher levels of self-regulation, digital literacy, and cognitive load management from learners. The assumption that learners can seamlessly navigate complex learning ecologies risks reproducing inequalities for those without adequate support or prior exposure. Consequently, post-digital epistemologies require institutions to rethink not only pedagogical design, but also support structures, scaffolding mechanisms, and inclusive practices.

2.2. Generative AI and Knowledge Production

Generative AI represents a significant inflection point within post-digital hybrid education, particularly in relation to knowledge production, authorship, and creativity. Unlike earlier educational technologies that primarily facilitated access to information, generative AI systems actively generate text, images, code, and analytical outputs that resemble human-created knowledge. This capability fundamentally challenges conventional distinctions between learning, assistance, and authorship.

Research suggests that generative AI can support learning in meaningful ways when embedded within pedagogically sound frameworks. Kasneci et al. (2023) argue that AI systems such as large language models can enhance feedback quality, support differentiated instruction, and lower barriers for learners with diverse linguistic or cognitive needs. Similarly, Bauer et al. (2025) caution against both uncritical adoption and outright rejection, emphasizing the need to move beyond hype toward evidence-based understanding of how AI affects learning processes and outcomes.

However, the integration of generative AI also raises profound epistemic and ethical concerns. Dwivedi et al. (2023) highlight growing uncertainty around authorship and originality in AI-mediated learning environments. When students rely on AI-generated content for writing or problem-solving, traditional indicators of learning achievement become less reliable. This challenges long-standing assessment models that equate individual production with individual understanding. In response, institutions are increasingly revising guidelines and policies governing AI use in teaching, learning, and research (An et al., 2025).

Beyond assessment, generative AI reshapes the nature of creativity itself. Punziano (2025) characterizes this shift as an adaptive epistemology, where knowledge creation becomes a collaborative process between human judgment and machine-generated possibilities. In this model, creativity is less about producing original artifacts in isolation and more about curating, critiquing, and contextualizing AI outputs. While this opens new avenues for experimentation and innovation, it also risks cognitive offloading, where learners defer critical thinking to automated systems.

The risk of automation bias and cognitive dependency is particularly salient in hybrid education, where AI tools are deeply embedded in learning platforms. Haidemariam and Gran (2025) argue that many generative AI systems are developed with limited consideration of social alignment, leading to tools that optimize efficiency at the expense of human values. They advocate for hybrid alignment strategies that integrate technical safeguards with non-technical interventions such as institutional governance, ethical training, and cultural contextualization. Applied to education, this implies that AI literacy must extend beyond tool usage to include critical understanding of AI limitations, biases, and societal implications.

2.3. Global Connectivity and Transnational Learning Spaces

Global connectivity constitutes a third defining feature of the post-digital condition, transforming hybrid education into a transnational phenomenon. Digital infrastructures enable learners and educators to participate in cross-border classrooms, international research collaborations, and global knowledge networks with unprecedented ease. Hybrid education thus increasingly operates across spatial, cultural, and institutional boundaries, giving rise to new forms of transnational learning spaces.

These developments align with broader trends in global education and human development. The Human Development Report 2023/24 underscores that connectivity has the potential to expand human agency and collective problem-solving, but only if institutional arrangements ensure equitable access and meaningful participation (UNDP, 2023). In education, this translates into opportunities for intercultural learning, collaborative knowledge production, and exposure to diverse perspectives. Hybrid classrooms that connect learners across regions can foster global citizenship and shared responsibility for global challenges.

However, global connectivity also reproduces and reshapes inequalities. Access to reliable digital infrastructure, affordable connectivity, and AI-enabled platforms remains uneven across and within countries. The World Bank highlights persistent digital divides that disproportionately affect learners in low-income and rural contexts, limiting their ability to participate fully in hybrid and transnational learning environments (World Bank, 2023). Moreover, linguistic dominance and cultural bias embedded in digital platforms and AI systems risk marginalizing local knowledge traditions and non-dominant epistemologies.

These dynamics complicate the promise of global hybrid education. While connectivity enables inclusion at scale, it can also lead to standardization and homogenization if global platforms impose uniform pedagogical models. Webster

(2024) argues that post-digital digital citizenship education must address not only technical competencies, but also power relations, cultural representation, and ethical participation in networked societies. This perspective is particularly relevant for hybrid education, where learners navigate overlapping formal and informal learning spaces governed by diverse actors.

In response, institutions face the challenge of designing hybrid learning environments that are globally connected yet locally grounded. This requires intentional strategies to support multilingualism, contextual relevance, and participatory governance. It also demands recognition that inclusion is not solely a matter of access, but of voice, agency, and cultural legitimacy. Without such considerations, hybrid education risks reinforcing the very inequalities it seeks to overcome.

3. FUTURES THINKING AND SCENARIO DESIGN IN EDUCATION

The accelerating integration of generative artificial intelligence into hybrid education systems has exposed the limitations of traditional planning and policy approaches in education. Rapid technological change, shifting institutional norms, and evolving learner expectations have created conditions of uncertainty that challenge linear models of reform. In this context, futures thinking and scenario design offer valuable analytical and governance tools for navigating complexity, anticipating emerging risks, and aligning innovation with educational values. This section examines why future thinking is essential for hybrid education, outlines a methodological approach grounded in trend and uncertainty analysis, and positions scenario development as a strategic instrument for institutional and policy decision making.

Before exploring future pathways, it is essential to ground this transition in the established taxonomy of hybridity. While often used interchangeably, Blended Learning typically refers to the strategic integration of in-person and online synchronous activities within a single course, whereas Hybrid Education represents a broader structural shift in institutional delivery. A more flexible evolution is HyFlex (Hybrid-Flexible), which grants students the agency to choose their mode of participation in-person, synchronous online, or asynchronous online on a session-by-session basis (Beatty, 2019). Generative AI accelerates this evolution by automating the translation of content across these modes, yet it also risks widening the "digital divide" if the pedagogical design does not account for varying levels of student self-regulation and access to high-bandwidth tools.

3.1. Why Futures Thinking Matters for Hybrid Education

Conventional educational planning has often relied on linear assumptions, incremental change, and stable institutional environments. Such approaches presume that future conditions can be extrapolated from past trends and that reforms can be sequenced through predictable stages. However, the emergence of generative AI and platform based learning ecosystems has disrupted these assumptions. Hybrid education now operates within a landscape characterized by rapid technological evolution, regulatory ambiguity, and contested educational norms. Under these conditions, linear planning is increasingly insufficient.

Future thinking provides a framework for engaging with uncertainty rather than attempting to eliminate it. Rather than asking what will happen, futures oriented approaches explore what could happen and what should happen under different value commitments. This distinction is particularly relevant for hybrid education, where decisions about AI adoption, data governance, and pedagogical design have long term implications for equity, agency, and institutional identity. Research on AI readiness and faculty responses highlights that uncertainty around generative AI has already generated anxiety, resistance, and uneven adoption across higher education institutions (Ali, 2025; Verano Tacoronte et al., 2025). These findings suggest that technical capacity alone does not determine successful integration. Instead, institutions must grapple with cultural readiness, ethical clarity, and shared vision.

Education under uncertainty also raises fundamental epistemic questions. Punziano (2025) argues that generative AI represents a paradigm shift that requires adaptive epistemologies capable of accommodating provisional knowledge, human machine collaboration, and continuous revision. From this perspective, futures thinking is not only a strategic tool but also an epistemological stance. It acknowledges that knowledge systems are evolving and that educational institutions must remain reflexive and open to redefinition. Bauer et al. (2025) similarly caution against simplistic narratives of technological impact, emphasizing the need to understand how AI reshapes learning processes in context specific ways.

In hybrid education, uncertainty is amplified by the convergence of multiple forces, including technological acceleration, global connectivity, and shifting societal expectations. Future thinking enables institutions to move beyond reactive responses and toward anticipatory governance. By systematically exploring alternative futures, educators and policymakers can identify potential tensions, surface implicit assumptions, and make more informed choices about the direction of hybrid education.

3.2. Methodological Approach

The futures oriented approach adopted in this chapter combines trend analysis with the identification of drivers, tensions, and critical uncertainties. Trend analysis involves examining observable developments in technology, pedagogy, policy, and institutional practice. In the context of hybrid education, key trends include the normalization of generative AI tools, the expansion of platform mediated learning, and growing emphasis on digital citizenship and ethical AI education (Kasneci et al., 2023; Webster, 2024). These trends provide insight into the direction of change but do not, on their own, determine future outcomes.

To move beyond descriptive analysis, future methodologies emphasize the identification of underlying drivers and tensions. Drivers refer to structural forces that shape educational systems, such as technological innovation, demographic change, labor market transformation, and governance regimes. Tensions emerge where these drivers interact in conflicting ways. For example, the push for rapid AI adoption in higher education often conflicts with concerns about academic integrity, faculty autonomy, and ethical accountability. Studies examining institutional AI guidelines reveal significant variation in how universities define acceptable AI use, reflecting divergent values and levels of preparedness (An et al., 2025).

Critical uncertainties represent factors whose future trajectory is both highly impactful and difficult to predict. In hybrid education, such uncertainties include the pace of AI regulation, societal trust in automated systems, and the extent to which institutions prioritize human centered learning over efficiency driven models. Haidemariam and Gran (2025) highlight that misalignment between technical optimization and social values remains a central challenge in AI development. This insight reinforces the need to treat ethical alignment not as a fixed standard, but as an evolving process shaped by institutional choices and cultural contexts.

The methodological approach also draws on insights from change management and organizational studies. Al Sabbagh and Elgeddawy (2025) and Gering et al. (2025) demonstrate that institutional responses to AI driven transformation are shaped by leadership, communication, and organizational culture. Futures thinking therefore integrates both external trends and internal capacities, recognizing that educational futures are co produced by structural conditions and institutional agency.

3.3. Scenario Development as a Governance Tool

Scenario development plays a central role in translating futures thinking into practical governance tools for hybrid education. Unlike forecasting, which seeks to predict likely outcomes, scenarios are designed to support sense making under uncertainty. They present coherent and plausible narratives that illustrate how different combinations of drivers, tensions, and uncertainties may unfold over time. In education, scenarios function as reflective devices that help stakeholders explore consequences, trade offs, and strategic options.

In the context of generative AI and hybrid education, scenarios enable institutions to examine how different governance choices may shape learning ecosystems. For example, one scenario may emphasize efficiency, personalization, and data driven optimization, while another prioritizes ethical oversight, cultural diversity, and participatory governance. By comparing such scenarios, decision makers can assess not only technical feasibility but also alignment with institutional values and societal responsibilities. Yan and Liu (2025) argue that ethical frameworks for AI education must be embedded within broader governance structures rather than treated as standalone guidelines. Scenario design supports this integration by situating ethical considerations within dynamic institutional contexts.

Scenarios also provide a bridge between foresight and strategy. Rather than offering abstract visions, well designed scenarios inform concrete decision making by identifying early signals, capability requirements, and potential risks. Research on faculty readiness and anxiety underscores that uncertainty about AI policy and expectations can undermine trust and engagement (Verano Tacoronte et al., 2025). Scenario based discussions can help address these concerns by creating shared understanding and fostering dialogue among educators, administrators, and learners.

Importantly, scenario development reinforces the idea that the future of hybrid education is not predetermined. It is shaped by collective choices about governance, pedagogy, and institutional purpose. By using scenarios as governance tools, institutions can move from reactive adaptation to proactive design. This approach aligns with broader calls for educational systems to exercise ethical intelligence, defined as the capacity to integrate technological innovation with human judgment, cultural awareness, and moral responsibility.

Future thinking and scenario design offer critical resources for navigating the post digital transformation of hybrid education. They enable institutions to engage constructively with uncertainty, align AI adoption with educational values, and develop strategies that are resilient, inclusive, and ethically grounded. The following section builds on this methodological foundation to explore three illustrative futures for hybrid education, highlighting distinct pathways and their implications for pedagogy, governance, and human development.

4. THREE FUTURES OF HYBRID EDUCATION

The future of hybrid education in the era of generative artificial intelligence will not unfold along a single trajectory. Instead, it is likely to evolve through multiple, overlapping pathways shaped by institutional priorities, governance choices, cultural values, and societal needs. Futures thinking emphasizes that these pathways are not predictions but plausible configurations of social and technological forces. This section presents three illustrative futures of hybrid education: the Adaptive Future, the Ethical Future, and the Regenerative Future. Each scenario highlights distinctive opportunities and risks, offering a structured lens through which institutions and policymakers can reflect on strategic choices and long-term consequences.

4.1. The Adaptive Future

The Adaptive Future envisions hybrid education systems that prioritize personalization, flexibility, and responsiveness to individual learner needs. In this scenario, generative AI plays a central role in designing adaptive learning pathways that adjust content, pace, and assessment based on real-time data. Learning becomes increasingly modular, competency-based, and aligned with lifelong learning trajectories rather than fixed degree structures.

AI-driven personalization is often framed as a solution to long-standing challenges in education, including learner disengagement, heterogeneity in prior knowledge, and scalability. The Microsoft AI in Education Report 2025 highlights how AI-enabled platforms can provide tailored feedback, intelligent tutoring, and predictive analytics that support learner progression across diverse contexts. Similarly, the World Bank's analysis of digital transformation in education underscores the potential of adaptive systems to expand access and efficiency, particularly in resource-constrained environments.

Within the Adaptive Future, hybrid education ecosystems extend beyond traditional institutions to include workplaces, online platforms, and informal learning communities. Credentials become stackable and portable, enabling learners to continuously reskill in response to labor market shifts. This vision aligns with the OECD Learning Compass 2030, which emphasizes learner agency, adaptability, and lifelong learning as core educational goals. In this scenario, institutions reposition themselves as learning hubs rather than sole providers of knowledge.

However, the Adaptive Future also introduces significant risks. Data-intensive personalization relies on extensive learner monitoring, raising concerns about surveillance, privacy, and consent. Algorithmic bias may reinforce existing inequalities if adaptive systems are trained on unrepresentative data or designed without attention to social context. Dwivedi et al. (2023) warn that efficiency-driven AI adoption can obscure deeper questions about educational purpose and responsibility. Without robust governance frameworks, adaptive hybrid systems risk prioritizing optimization over human judgment.

Moreover, research on faculty readiness suggests that adaptive technologies may exacerbate professional anxiety and role ambiguity. Ali (2025) and Verano-Tacoronte et al. (2025) demonstrate that uneven AI literacy and unclear institutional expectations can undermine trust and engagement. The Adaptive Future therefore depends not only on technological sophistication but also on investment in human capacity, transparent governance, and participatory design.

4.2. The Ethical Future

The promise of AI-enhanced hybridity must be weighed against empirical evidence concerning faculty and student well-being. Recent studies indicate that while AI can personalize learning, the "double-burden" of managing simultaneous physical and digital environments has significantly increased faculty workload, leading to what some scholars term "digital burnout" (Verano-Tacoronte et al., 2025). Furthermore, student equity remains a critical barrier; data from the World Bank (2023) suggests that without intentional "inclusive design," AI-driven hybrid models may inadvertently privilege students with superior prompt-engineering skills and high-end hardware, creating a new tier of "AI-poverty."

The Ethical Future centers on the deliberate integration of ethical governance, cultural diversity, and digital citizenship into hybrid education systems. In this scenario, AI adoption is guided by normative frameworks that prioritize fairness, accountability, transparency, and respect for human dignity. Rather than treating ethics as an afterthought, institutions embed ethical reflection into curriculum design, platform selection, and organizational decision making.

This vision resonates strongly with the values articulated by UNESCO in Reimagining Our Futures Together, which frames education as a public good grounded in pluralism, solidarity, and shared responsibility. Ethical hybrid education emphasizes intercultural inclusion and recognizes that global AI systems often encode dominant linguistic and cultural norms. Yan and Liu (2025) argue that ethical frameworks for AI education must address not only technical risks but also cultural representation and epistemic justice.

Digital citizenship becomes a central learning outcome in the Ethical Future. Learners are equipped to critically engage with AI systems, understand their limitations, and participate responsibly in networked societies. Webster (2024) emphasizes that post-digital citizenship education must extend beyond technical skills to include ethical reasoning, civic engagement, and awareness of power relations in digital spaces. Hybrid classrooms, particularly those operating across borders, become sites for intercultural dialogue and collective sense-making.

Governance structures play a decisive role in this scenario. An et al. (2025) document wide variation in institutional AI policies, reflecting differing ethical priorities and levels of preparedness. The Ethical Future assumes greater policy coherence, supported by participatory governance models that involve educators, students, and external stakeholders. Haidemariam and Gran (2025) advocate for hybrid alignment strategies that combine technical safeguards with non-technical interventions such as ethical training, organizational norms, and cultural contextualization.

Despite its normative appeal, the Ethical Future faces significant challenges. Ethical frameworks often lag behind technological innovation, creating gaps between stated principles and operational practices. Cultural homogenization remains a risk if global platforms impose standardized norms under the guise of ethics. Furthermore, ethical governance can be perceived as slowing innovation, generating tension between regulatory caution and competitive pressures. The Ethical Future therefore requires sustained institutional commitment and global coordination to avoid becoming symbolic rather than transformative.

4.3. The Regenerative Future

The Regenerative Future envisions hybrid education as a catalyst for sustainability, well-being, and human flourishing. In this scenario, education systems align AI-enabled innovation with ecological responsibility, social care, and collective resilience. Learning is oriented toward addressing complex global challenges such as climate change, inequality, and social fragmentation.

This vision aligns closely with the human development perspective advanced by United Nations Development Programme in the Human Development Report 2023/24, which emphasizes that progress must be evaluated in terms of well-being, agency, and planetary boundaries rather than economic growth alone. Regenerative hybrid education integrates sustainability into curriculum content, pedagogical practice, and institutional operations.

AI plays a supportive rather than dominant role in this future. It is used to facilitate systems thinking, interdisciplinary problem solving, and collaborative learning for sustainability. Leal Filho et al. (2025) demonstrate how AI can enhance sustainability education by enabling scenario modeling, data analysis, and experiential learning. Similarly, Suryanarayana et al. (2024) highlight the potential of AI-enhanced digital systems to support sustainable education management.

Well-being and relational learning are central to the Regenerative Future. Hybrid environments are intentionally designed to foster connection, reflection, and care, countering the risk of emotional detachment associated with over-digitization. Learning is understood as a collective process embedded in communities and ecosystems. This perspective challenges instrumental views of education and reasserts its social and moral dimensions.

Nevertheless, the Regenerative Future confronts a critical paradox. Large-scale AI infrastructure carries significant environmental costs, including energy consumption and resource extraction. Spelda and Stritecky (2020) caution that the expansion of AI systems may undermine sustainability goals if environmental impacts are not addressed. Furthermore, there is a risk that sustainability discourse becomes aspirational rather than actionable if not supported by institutional change and resource allocation.

The Regenerative Future therefore demands a reorientation of priorities, shifting from efficiency and scalability toward care, sufficiency, and long-term resilience. It requires institutions to balance technological innovation with ethical restraint and ecological awareness.

Figure 1. Three Futures of Hybrid Education in the Era of Generative Artificial Intelligence (Author's own work)

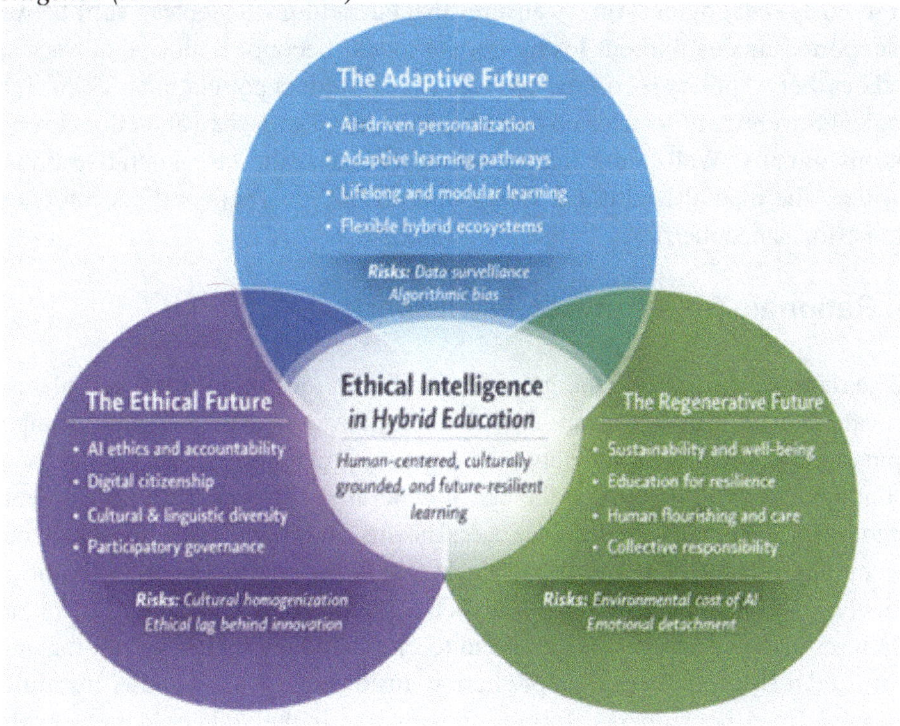

5. HYBRID EDUCATION FUTURES FRAMEWORK (HEFF)

As hybrid education enters a phase of structural consolidation shaped by generative artificial intelligence and global connectivity, institutions face increasing difficulty navigating complexity, uncertainty, and competing priorities. While many universities and education systems have developed digital strategies, AI guidelines, and quality assurance mechanisms, these instruments often remain reactive, fragmented, or narrowly compliance oriented. There is therefore a growing need for integrative frameworks that support long term reflection, anticipatory governance, and values based decision making. This section introduces the Hybrid Education Futures Framework (HEFF) as a conceptual and strategic tool designed to help institutions and policymakers engage proactively with the future of hybrid education.

The Hybrid Education Futures Framework (HEFF) synthesizes the three scenarios (Adaptive, Ethical, and Regenerative) into four strategic pillars for institutional action. First, Pedagogical Agility ensures that curriculum design can shift between AI-supported modes without losing human touch. Second, Inclusive Governance mandates that AI policy is co-created with diverse student populations. Third, Technological Sovereignty focuses on institutional control over data and ethical vendor relations. Finally, Well-being Integration ensures that the "Regenerative Future" prioritizes the mental health and flourishing of both learners and educators over mere performance metrics.

5.1. Rationale for a Futures Framework

The rationale for HEFF emerges from the limitations of conventional planning and evaluation tools in education. Traditional frameworks tend to emphasize inputs, outputs, and performance indicators that assume relatively stable environments. In contrast, hybrid education in the era of generative AI is characterized by rapid technological change, evolving pedagogical norms, and heightened ethical and social expectations. Linear planning models struggle to accommodate such conditions, particularly when innovation cycles outpace regulatory and institutional adaptation.

Futures oriented frameworks respond to this challenge by foregrounding anticipation and reflection rather than prediction. Instead of asking whether institutions meet predefined benchmarks, futures frameworks invite stakeholders to explore alternative pathways, examine underlying assumptions, and consider long term implications of present choices. This approach aligns with calls from UNESCO to rethink education as a shared societal project that must be continually redesigned in response to emerging global challenges. Similarly, the OECD Learning Compass 2030 emphasizes the need for education systems to cultivate foresight, agency, and responsibility rather than narrow forms of performance optimization.

Another motivation for HEFF is the growing recognition that compliance driven approaches are insufficient for governing AI enabled education. Studies of institutional AI policies reveal significant variation in scope, depth, and ethical clarity, often reflecting external pressure rather than internal consensus or capacity (An et al., 2025). While rankings and standards may incentivize adoption, they rarely capture contextual nuance or ethical trade offs. As a result, institutions risk pursuing technological legitimacy without meaningful alignment with educational values or human development goals.

HEFF is therefore conceived as a diagnostic and developmental framework rather than a ranking or accreditation tool. Its purpose is to support sense making across diverse institutional contexts and to enable dialogue among educators, leaders, policymakers, and learners. By integrating technological, ethical, human, and ecological considerations, the framework encourages institutions to move beyond short term adoption toward coherent, future oriented strategies.

5.2. Core Dimensions of HEFF

The Hybrid Education Futures Framework comprises five interrelated dimensions that together capture the key drivers and tensions shaping the future of hybrid education. These dimensions are not hierarchical and should be understood as mutually reinforcing components of institutional readiness and resilience.

The first dimension is technological intelligence. This refers not simply to the availability of digital infrastructure or AI tools, but to an institution's capacity to critically understand, select, and govern technologies in alignment with pedagogical goals. Technological intelligence includes data literacy, AI literacy, and the ability to evaluate the pedagogical and social implications of emerging tools. Research highlights that uncritical adoption of generative AI can amplify risks related to bias, automation, and academic integrity (Dwivedi et al., 2023; Bauer et al., 2025). HEFF therefore emphasizes informed decision making and continuous learning rather than technological determinism.

The second dimension is ethical and cultural governance. As AI systems increasingly shape learning processes, institutions must ensure that governance mechanisms address fairness, transparency, accountability, and cultural representation. Ethical governance extends beyond formal guidelines to include institutional norms, participatory processes, and ongoing ethical deliberation. Yan and Liu (2025) argue that ethical frameworks for AI education must be embedded within broader governance structures that reflect societal values. This dimension also recognizes the risk of cultural homogenization in globally connected hybrid systems and stresses the importance of linguistic diversity and epistemic pluralism.

The third dimension is human capability and agency. Hybrid education futures depend fundamentally on the capacity and confidence of educators, learners, and administrators to engage meaningfully with AI enabled environments. Studies on faculty readiness and anxiety demonstrate that technological change can undermine agency if roles, expectations, and support structures are unclear (Ali, 2025; Verano Tacoronte et al., 2025). HEFF foregrounds professional development, co creation, and shared ownership as essential conditions for sustainable innovation. Human agency is understood not only as individual competence, but as collective capacity to shape institutional futures.

The fourth dimension is sustainability and well being. This dimension reflects growing concern about the environmental and psychosocial impacts of large scale digitalization. While AI enabled hybrid education can contribute to efficiency and access, it also carries environmental costs associated with data centers, energy consumption, and electronic waste. Scholars caution that these costs may contradict sustainability goals if not explicitly addressed (Spelda and Stritecky, 2020). At the same time, over digitization can erode relational learning and emotional connection. HEFF therefore integrates sustainability and well being as core evaluative lenses, aligning with broader human development perspectives advanced by United Nations Development Programme.

The fifth dimension is global local collaboration. Hybrid education increasingly operates across borders, platforms, and sectors, creating opportunities for transnational learning and research. However, global connectivity also raises questions about autonomy, governance, and equity. HEFF emphasizes the importance of glocal strategies that balance global collaboration with local relevance and participation. This includes building partnerships that respect contextual knowledge, support inclusive access, and enable shared governance. Insights from global education initiatives and digital transformation studies highlight that collaborative capacity is a critical determinant of long term resilience (World Bank, 2023; Gering et al., 2025).

Together, these five dimensions provide a holistic lens for assessing and shaping hybrid education futures. They encourage institutions to consider not only what technologies they adopt, but how adoption interacts with ethics, people, sustainability, and global engagement.

5.3. Applications of HEFF

The Hybrid Education Futures Framework is designed for practical application across multiple levels of educational governance. One primary application is institutional strategy. HEFF can support universities and schools in aligning digital and AI strategies with long term educational missions. By mapping existing initiatives against the five dimensions, institutions can identify gaps, tensions, and areas for investment. This process supports strategic coherence and helps avoid fragmented or contradictory initiatives.

A second application is policy design. Policymakers can use HEFF to inform the development of AI and hybrid education policies that are anticipatory rather than reactive. Instead of focusing solely on risk mitigation or compliance, policies informed by HEFF can integrate ethical safeguards, capacity building, and sustainability considerations. This approach resonates with evidence from comparative studies showing that policy coherence and stakeholder engagement are critical for effective AI governance in education (An et al., 2025).

A third application is capacity building. HEFF provides a shared language and structure for professional development, leadership training, and organizational learning. By engaging educators and administrators in futures oriented reflection, institutions can build collective understanding and reduce anxiety associated with technological change. Change management research indicates that inclusive processes and clear communication enhance trust and adoption in AI driven transformation (Al Sabbagh and Elgeddawy, 2025).

Importantly, HEFF is intended to be adaptable rather than prescriptive. Institutions operating in different cultural, economic, and regulatory contexts may prioritize dimensions differently. The value of the framework lies in its capacity to facilitate dialogue, reflection, and iterative learning. In this sense, HEFF complements scenario based approaches introduced in the previous section by translating futures thinking into actionable institutional practice.

Figure 2. Hybrid Education Futures Framework (Author's own work)

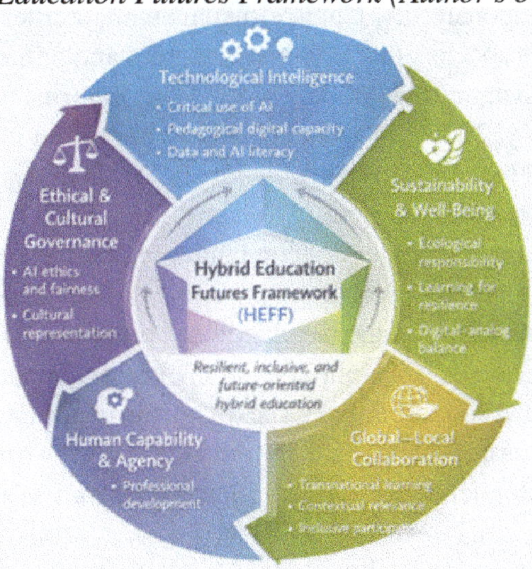

6. INSTITUTIONAL AND GLOBAL PATHWAYS FORWARD

The futures of hybrid education outlined in the previous sections cannot be realized through technology adoption alone. They require coordinated institutional transformation and global cooperation that align innovation with ethical responsibility, human development, and sustainability. This section translates the Hybrid Education Futures Framework into concrete pathways for action, focusing on institutional readiness, global collaboration, and policy and governance reform. Together, these pathways illustrate how hybrid education can move from experimental innovation toward resilient and inclusive systems.

6.1. Institutional Readiness for Future Hybrid Education

Institutional readiness for future hybrid education extends beyond infrastructure and platform availability. It encompasses leadership capacity, organizational culture, and the development of human capabilities that enable institutions to navigate uncertainty and complexity. Research on AI readiness consistently shows that institutions with similar technological resources often experience divergent outcomes due to differences in leadership vision, staff engagement, and governance coherence (Ali, 2025; Gering et al., 2025).

Leadership plays a pivotal role in shaping how hybrid education and generative AI are framed within institutional narratives. Leaders who present AI as a purely efficiency enhancing tool risk reinforcing instrumental and compliance driven adoption. In contrast, futures oriented leadership emphasizes purpose, ethical reflection, and shared responsibility. Change management studies demonstrate that inclusive leadership approaches that involve educators and administrators in decision making reduce resistance and anxiety while fostering trust and innovation (Al Sabbagh and Elgeddawy, 2025). This is particularly important given evidence that faculty uncertainty and fear surrounding generative AI can undermine pedagogical experimentation and professional identity (Verano Tacoronte et al., 2025).

Organizational culture constitutes a second pillar of readiness. Hybrid education flourishes in cultures that value learning, experimentation, and reflexivity. Such cultures encourage educators to adapt pedagogical practices, critically assess AI tools, and share insights across disciplinary and institutional boundaries. However, cultures shaped by rigid accountability regimes or performance metrics may discourage risk taking and reinforce superficial compliance. Futures oriented institutions therefore prioritize dialogue, ethical deliberation, and iterative learning over rigid standardization.

Capability development is equally critical. As generative AI reshapes teaching, assessment, and research practices, institutions must invest in sustained professional development rather than one off training initiatives. AI literacy in this context encompasses not only technical proficiency but also critical understanding of algorithmic bias, data governance, and pedagogical implications (Dwivedi et al., 2023; Bauer et al., 2025). Learner capability must also be addressed. Students require support to develop self regulation, critical thinking, and ethical judgment in hybrid environments where AI mediated assistance is readily available.

Institutional readiness thus emerges as a dynamic and relational process rather than a static condition. It depends on the alignment of leadership vision, organizational culture, and human capability with long term educational values. Without such alignment, hybrid education risks remaining fragmented and reactive.

6.2. Global Collaboration and "Glocal" Learning Ecosystems

The future of hybrid education is inherently global. Digital platforms and AI systems enable learning and research to transcend national boundaries, creating opportunities for cross border collaboration and shared knowledge production. At the same time, global connectivity intensifies disparities in access, voice, and influence. Effective pathways forward therefore require what may be described as glocal learning ecosystems that combine global collaboration with local relevance and agency.

Cross border partnerships are a central feature of these ecosystems. Universities increasingly participate in international consortia, joint degree programs, and shared digital platforms that support hybrid learning and research. Such partnerships can expand access to expertise, diversify curricula, and foster intercultural understanding. The World Bank's analysis of digital transformation in education highlights that collaborative models can enhance system resilience by pooling resources and sharing best practices, particularly in contexts with limited capacity (World Bank, 2023).

Virtual research and learning alliances represent a further evolution of global collaboration. These alliances leverage hybrid modalities to connect researchers, educators, and learners around shared challenges such as climate change, public health, and social inequality. When designed inclusively, they can democratize participation in knowledge production and reduce barriers associated with physical mobility. This aligns with human development perspectives advanced by the United Nations Development Programme, which emphasize collective agency and global cooperation as prerequisites for addressing complex global challenges (UNDP, 2023).

However, global collaboration also introduces risks. Platform dependency, linguistic dominance, and asymmetrical power relations can marginalize local knowledge systems and reinforce global hierarchies. UNESCO's vision of education as a common good underscores the importance of epistemic pluralism and cultural diversity in globally connected learning environments (UNESCO, 2022). Glocal ecosystems therefore require intentional governance mechanisms that ensure local participation, contextual adaptation, and shared ownership.

Institutions must also navigate tensions between standardization and diversity. While shared platforms and credentials can facilitate mobility and recognition, excessive harmonization risks eroding pedagogical autonomy and cultural specificity. Futures oriented hybrid education balances interoperability with flexibility, enabling global collaboration without imposing uniform models.

6.3. Policy and Governance Implications

Institutional transformation and global collaboration must be supported by coherent policy and governance frameworks. As generative AI becomes embedded in hybrid education systems, policymakers face the challenge of fostering innovation while safeguarding ethical, social, and environmental values. Evidence suggests that many existing policies remain reactive and fragmented, focusing on risk mitigation rather than long term system design (An et al., 2025).

One key policy priority is the integration of AI literacy into curricula at multiple levels. AI literacy extends beyond understanding how AI tools function to include ethical reasoning, critical evaluation, and civic responsibility. Webster (2024) argues that digital citizenship education in post digital societies must equip learners to engage with algorithmic systems as informed and responsible participants. Embedding AI literacy across disciplines supports the development of agency and resilience in hybrid learning environments.

Ethics by design constitutes a second critical governance principle. Rather than treating ethics as an external constraint, ethics by design integrates normative considerations into the development, procurement, and deployment of educational technologies. Yan and Liu (2025) emphasize that ethical frameworks for AI education should address fairness, transparency, accountability, and cultural representation throughout the system lifecycle. This approach aligns with calls for hybrid alignment strategies that combine technical safeguards with institutional and cultural mechanisms (Haidemariam and Gran, 2025).

Data governance is equally central. Adaptive and personalized hybrid education systems rely heavily on learner data, raising concerns about privacy, consent, and surveillance. Policies must therefore establish clear standards for data collection, use, and stewardship, ensuring that data practices respect human rights and institutional values. The Microsoft AI in Education Report 2025 highlights the importance of transparent governance structures and stakeholder engagement in building trust around AI enabled systems.

Policy coherence across institutional, national, and international levels is essential. Fragmented regulations can create uncertainty for institutions and exacerbate inequalities across jurisdictions. Futures oriented governance seeks alignment among educational, digital, and sustainability policies, recognizing that hybrid education operates at the intersection of multiple domains. International organizations and transnational networks play an important role in facilitating dialogue, sharing evidence, and promoting normative convergence while respecting contextual diversity.

7. CONCLUSION: TOWARD ETHICAL INTELLIGENCE IN HYBRID EDUCATION

The rapid integration of generative artificial intelligence and global digital connectivity has placed hybrid education at a pivotal crossroads. As this chapter has argued, the future of hybrid education is not predetermined by technological innovation alone, but shaped by choices made at institutional, cultural, and policy levels. The scenarios and frameworks presented throughout the chapter highlight both the transformative potential and the profound responsibility associated with redesigning education for an interconnected and intelligent world. This concluding section synthesizes key insights, articulates ethical intelligence as a guiding principle, and situates hybrid education within a broader vision of a global learning renaissance.

7.1. Key Insights from the Futures Scenarios

The three futures of hybrid education presented in this chapter reveal that no single pathway offers a complete solution to the challenges facing contemporary education. Instead, each future embodies distinct priorities, opportunities, and risks that must be understood in relation to one another.

The Adaptive Future foregrounds personalization, flexibility, and responsiveness. It demonstrates how AI driven systems can support diverse learner pathways, lifelong learning, and institutional agility. However, this future also exposes trade-offs between efficiency and autonomy, as data intensive personalization raises concerns about surveillance, algorithmic bias, and the erosion of professional judgment. Adaptation without ethical grounding risks reducing education to optimization rather than cultivation.

The Ethical Future emphasizes governance, cultural diversity, and digital citizenship. It highlights the necessity of embedding ethical reflection into AI adoption and hybrid learning design. This future complements the Adaptive Future by addressing its normative blind spots, yet it also faces its own tensions. Ethical governance can lag behind technological innovation, and global ethical frameworks may inadvertently privilege dominant epistemologies if not grounded in cultural plurality.

The Regenerative Future reframes hybrid education as a vehicle for sustainability, well being, and collective resilience. It challenges instrumental views of learning by reconnecting education to ecological responsibility and human flourishing. While this future offers a compelling normative vision, it also confronts practical constraints, including the environmental costs of AI infrastructure and the risk of aspirational rhetoric disconnected from institutional practice.

These futures illustrate that the central challenge is not choosing one pathway over another, but navigating their complementarities and tensions. Sustainable hybrid education emerges where adaptability is balanced with ethical governance, and where innovation is aligned with care, inclusion, and long term responsibility.

7.2. Ethical Intelligence as a Guiding Principle

In response to these insights, this chapter proposes ethical intelligence as a guiding principle for the future of hybrid education. Ethical intelligence refers to the capacity of individuals and institutions to integrate technological capability with empathy, moral imagination, and cultural awareness. It moves beyond technical proficiency or regulatory compliance to encompass reflective judgment, contextual sensitivity, and collective responsibility.

Ethical intelligence recognizes that generative AI is not a neutral tool but a socio technical system shaped by human values, assumptions, and power relations. Educators and learners operating in hybrid environments must therefore develop the ability to question how AI systems influence knowledge production, assessment, and participation. This aligns with broader calls from UNESCO to reimagine education as a common good grounded in human dignity and social solidarity.

At the institutional level, ethical intelligence manifests through governance structures that promote transparency, participation, and accountability. It requires leaders to articulate clear educational purposes and to engage stakeholders in ongoing dialogue about the implications of AI enabled transformation. Rather than delegating ethical responsibility to technical experts or policy documents, institutions cultivate shared ownership of ethical decision making.

Ethical intelligence also has a pedagogical dimension. Hybrid education must foster not only digital and AI literacy, but also ethical reasoning, empathy, and moral imagination. Learners should be supported to engage critically with AI generated content, to understand its limitations, and to reflect on their own responsibilities as creators and users of knowledge. This integrative approach resonates with the vision of learner agency advanced by OECD Learning Compass 2030, which emphasizes values, responsibility, and future oriented thinking as core educational outcomes.

Ultimately, ethical intelligence reframes the role of AI in education from replacement to augmentation. It positions technology as a partner in human development rather than a substitute for human judgment, care, and creativity.

7.3. Shaping a Global Learning Renaissance

The future of hybrid education must be understood within a broader global context marked by interdependence, inequality, and shared vulnerability. Global connectivity has expanded the reach of education, yet it has also intensified disparities in access, voice, and influence. In this context, shaping the future of hybrid education is inseparable from the pursuit of a more just and inclusive global learning order.

A global learning renaissance requires reimagining education as a shared human project rather than a competitive commodity. Hybrid education offers unprecedented opportunities for cross border collaboration, intercultural dialogue, and collective problem solving. When designed inclusively, hybrid learning ecosystems can connect learners and educators across regions to address global challenges such as climate change, public health, and social inequality.

However, realizing this potential depends on governance choices that prioritize equity and participation. As emphasized by the United Nations Development Programme, human development in the twenty first century hinges on collective agency and the ability to break systemic gridlock through cooperation and trust. Hybrid education systems that amplify dominant voices while marginalizing local knowledge risk reproducing global hierarchies rather than transforming them.

The global learning renaissance envisioned here is therefore grounded in ethical intelligence, cultural plurality, and mutual responsibility. It calls on institutions, policymakers, and educators to move beyond reactive adaptation toward deliberate design. By aligning technological innovation with human values, sustainability, and global solidarity, hybrid education can contribute to a future in which learning empowers individuals and communities to thrive together.

In conclusion, the era of generative AI and global connectivity presents education with both unprecedented opportunity and profound responsibility. Hybrid education stands at the center of this transformation. Its future will be shaped not by technology alone, but by the ethical intelligence with which societies choose to teach, learn, and connect in an increasingly intelligent and interconnected world.

REFERENCES

Al Sabbagh, M., & Elgeddawy, M. (2025). Change management and AI adoption for enhancing employee experience in higher education institutions, Oman. In *AI and IoT: Driving Business Success and Sustainability in the Digital Age* (Vol. 1, pp. 307–315). Springer Nature Switzerland., DOI: 10.1007/978-3-031-92240-4_28

Ali, A. M. (2025). Evaluating artificial intelligence readiness within faculty in the higher education sector. *Higher Education Quarterly*, *79*(4), e70061. DOI: 10.1111/hequ.70061

An, Y., Yu, J. H., & James, S. (2025). 'Investigating the higher education institutions' guidelines and policies regarding the use of generative AI in teaching, learning, research, and administration'. *International Journal of Educational Technology in Higher Education*, *22*(1), 10. DOI: 10.1186/s41239-025-00507-3

Bauer, E., Greiff, S., Graesser, A. C., Scheiter, K., & Sailer, M. (2025). Looking beyond the hype: Understanding the effects of AI on learning. *Educational Psychology Review*, *37*(2), 45. DOI: 10.1007/s10648-025-10020-8

Dwivedi, Y. K., Kshetri, N., Hughes, L., Slade, E. L., Jeyaraj, A., Kar, A. K., Baabdullah, A. M., Koohang, A., Raghavan, V., Ahuja, M., Albanna, H., Albashrawi, M. A., Al-Busaidi, A. S., Balakrishnan, J., Barlette, Y., Basu, S., Bose, I., Brooks, L., Buhalis, D., & Wright, R. (2023). Opinion Paper:"So what if ChatGPT wrote it?" Multidisciplinary perspectives on opportunities, challenges and implications of generative conversational AI for research, practice and policy. *International Journal of Information Management*, *71*, 102642. DOI: 10.1016/j.ijinfomgt.2023.102642

Gering, Z., Feher, K., Harmat, V., & Tamassy, R. (2025). Strategic organisational responses to generative AI-driven digital transformation in leading higher education institutions. *The International Journal of Organizational Analysis*, *33*(12), 132–152. DOI: 10.1108/IJOA-09-2024-4850

Haidemariam, T., & Gran, A. B. (2025). On the problems of training generative AI: Towards a hybrid approach combining technical and non-technical alignment strategies. *AI & Society*. Advance online publication. DOI: 10.1007/s00146-025-02445-0

Kasneci, E., Seßler, K., Küchemann, S., Bannert, M., Dementieva, D., Fischer, F., Gasser, U., Groh, G., Günnemann, S., Hüllermeier, E., Krusche, S., Kutyniok, G., Michaeli, T., Nerdel, C., Pfeffer, J., Poquet, O., Sailer, M., Schmidt, A., Seidel, T., & Kasneci, G. (2023). ChatGPT for good? On opportunities and challenges of large language models for education. *Learning and Individual Differences*, *103*, 102274. DOI: 10.1016/j.lindif.2023.102274

Leal Filho, W., Kim, E., Borsatto, J. M. L. S., & Marcolin, C. B. (2025). Using artificial intelligence in sustainability teaching and learning. *Environmental Sciences Europe*, *37*(1), 124. DOI: 10.1186/s12302-025-01159-w

Microsoft. (2025) *AI in Education Report 2025*. Redmond, WA: Microsoft. Available at: https://cdn-dynmedia-1.microsoft.com (accessed: 3 January 2026).

OECD. (2019) *OECD Learning Compass 2030*. Available at: https://www.oecd.org/education/2030-project/

Punziano, G. (2025). Adaptive epistemology: Embracing generative AI as a paradigm shift in social science. *Societies (Basel, Switzerland)*, *15*(7), 205. DOI: 10.3390/soc15070205

Spelda, P., & Stritecky, V. (2020). The future of human–artificial intelligence nexus and its environmental costs. *Futures*, *117*, 102531. DOI: 10.1016/j.futures.2020.102531

Suryanarayana, K. S., Kandi, V. P., Pavani, G., Rao, A. S., Rout, S., & Krishna, T. S. R. (2024). Artificial intelligence enhanced digital learning for the sustainability of education management system. *The Journal of High Technology Management Research*, *35*(2), 100495. DOI: 10.1016/j.hitech.2024.100495

UNDP. (2023) *Human Development Report 2023/24: Breaking the Gridlock*. Available at: https://hdr.undp.org

UNESCO. (2022) *Reimagining Our Futures Together*. Available at: https://www.unesco.org/en/futures-education

Verano-Tacoronte, D., Bolívar-Cruz, A., & Sosa-Cabrera, S. (2025). Are university teachers ready for generative artificial intelligence? Unpacking faculty anxiety in the ChatGPT era. *Education and Information Technologies*, *30*(14), 1–28. DOI: 10.1007/s10639-025-13585-7

Webster, J. (2024). Updating digital citizenship education for a postdigital society. *New Zealand Journal of Educational Studies*, *59*(1), 109–124. DOI: 10.1007/s40841-023-00305-3

World Bank. (2023) *Digital transformation in education: Evidence and policy implications*. Washington, DC: World Bank. Available at: https://documents1.worldbank.org (accessed: 3 January 2026).

Wu, C. H., Chien, Y. C., Chou, M. T., & Huang, Y. M. (2025). Integrating computational thinking, game design, and design thinking: A scoping review on trends, applications, and implications for education. *Humanities & Social Sciences Communications*, *12*(1), 1–12. DOI: 10.1057/s41599-025-04502-x

Yan, Y., & Liu, H. (2025). Ethical framework for AI education based on large language models. *Education and Information Technologies*, *30*(8), 10891–10909. DOI: 10.1007/s10639-024-13241-6

Chapter 2
Transforming Hybrid Pedagogies:
Harnessing AI and Intercultural Collaboration for Global Learning

Sovanna Huot
http://orcid.org/0009-0006-8335-442X
Department of Education, National Institute of Education, Phnom Penh, Cambodia

Kimyut Phin
http://orcid.org/0009-0009-5667-7313
Department of English, University of Delhi, New Delhi, India

ABSTRACT

This chapter explores how artificial intelligence (AI) and intercultural collaboration are transforming hybrid pedagogy into a globally connected and ethically grounded model of learning. Hybrid pedagogy has emerged to respond to digital disruption, and it has developed into a supportive framework, thereby integrating digital innovation with intercultural empathy. Hybrid education promotes key educational goals such as adaptability, inclusivity, and global citizenships, upon the incorporation of AI-powered individualization with intercultural knowledge. The chapter analyses historical tracks, theoretical backgrounds, and best practices across Asia and Europe, accentuating both opportunities and challenges in equalizing digitalization with human-centred education. It culminates that the integration of ethical AI and intercultural conversation can re-envisage hybrid education as a globally collaborative, inclusive, and equitable space bolstering Sustainable Development Goals (SDG 4 and SDG 17).

DOI: 10.4018/979-8-3373-7462-8.ch002

1. INTRODUCTION

Education systems in the 21st century around the world face an unparalleled transition and this change has brought about the integration of digitalization, artificial intelligence (AI), and international collaboration. People generally think that technology and culture are the two leading factors in reshaping how knowledge is made, disseminated, and experienced. For example, Marginson (2016) emphasizes that education links societies through knowledge transmission and cross-border collaboration and education plays a pivotal role as global public good. Furthermore, Garrison and Vaughan (2008) term the emerging phrase intentional integration of face-to-face and online learning as hybrid pedagogy and they emphasize that this model promotes learner autonomy, collaborative inquiry, and reflective engagement.

Given that a propelled necessity during the Covid-19 pandemic, hybrid education has evolved into a new teaching-learning model for 21st century learning skills (Bozkurt & Sharma, 2020). They articulate that compelling educators tend to adopt flexible, student-cantered, and technology-enhanced modalities as the pandemic catalysed a pedagogical paradigm shift. Likewise, Hodge et al. (2020) argue that the pedagogical paradigm has shifted as a remote teaching and purposefully designed hybrid learning, but they emphasize that the emerging paradigm represents an enduring reconfiguration of pedagogy rather than a crisis adaptation. However, Wayne Holmes et al. (2019) identify this shift as the most disruptive force in education since the invention of printing press even though the shift has been reinforced by the rapid maturation of AI technologies. AI-powered systems now facilitate reimagine how teachers and students co-create knowledge through the functions of adaptive learning, predictive analytics, automated feedback, and personalized instruction.

However, technology alone cannot be understood as a driving force to the transformation of pedagogy. One could suggest that intercultural collaboration is a growing body of a paramount dimension of educational reform and this enables learners to navigate complex global realities marked by diversity, inequality, and interdependence. According to Deardorff (2006), intercultural competence is no longer peripheral, but rather a core learning outcome for globally engaged institutions. Intercultural communication only fosters empathy and dialogic understanding, but also a sense of global citizenship in virtual learning environment (Huot & Em, 2025; O'Dowd, 2018). From this perspective, multilingual translation systems and adaptive communicative portals of AI-mediated tools play a pivotal role as bridges that surpass linguistic and cultural barriers (Byram, 2020; Huot & Hok, 2025a).

Moreover, when AI and intercultural collaboration have synergized together, it therefore expands the meaning of hybrid pedagogy beyond mere modality. W Holmes et al. (2019) vindicate that effective hybrid education lies in human-AI complementarity rather than technological sophistication because human-AI synergy is a balanced model where technology augments, rather than replaces, human interaction and cultural learning. Therefore, this chapter positions hybrid pedagogy as a glonacal (global–national–local) ecosystem that incorporates AI-driven efficiency with the intercultural collaboration of humanistic education (Huot, 2026b; Marginson, 2002). This incorporation advocates for digital transformation steered by inclusion, equity, and cultural diversity that respond to the outlook declared by the UNESCO Future of Education Report about learning to become (2021b).

Building on evolving landscape, the overall objective of this chapter attempts to examine three primary objectives. A first objective of this study attempts to examine how AI and intercultural cooperation within hybrid education are transformed across worldwide tertiary education. The purpose of investigation incorporates in investigating the ways in which institutions employ technology as an institutional tool and a vehicle for discussion, empathy, and cross-cultural engagement. A second aim is to understand how different countries adapt hybrid educational innovations to local and cultural contexts by synthesizing global scholarship and case studies from Asia especially ASEAN and India and Europe. Research found hybrid pedagogy achieves when localized practices adapted to global standards through culturally responsive frameworks (Makhija et al., 2025; Zhang et al., 2025). This study, third, sets out to pinpoint challenges that AI-assisted hybrid learning face while implementing them within the ethical, technological, and cultural contexts and propose adaptive strategies for inclusivity and sustainability. A number of studies have discussed the governing phenomena related to algorithmic transparency and the digital divide alongside cultural homogenizations in the global virtual classroom (Wayne Holmes et al., 2019; Williamson et al., 2023). This research focuses on the phenomena of hybrid pedagogy and the untapped possibilities in the cultural and technological innovations within artificial intelligence and intercultural communication. Although AI is famed as merely a technical intervention, it is now situated within wider moral and relational structure of education. To ensure fair, inclusive, and respective norms for human agency, Floridi (2023) argues that AI in pedagogy must be directed by an ethics of care.

This chapter also fosters the spirit of hybrid pedagogy as education as a form of diplomacy, fostering the relations of trust, mutual understanding and cooperative learning from diverse constellations. It is generally believed that hybrid pedagogy is a manifestation of a new global ethos of learning grounded in equity and empathy, not merely an outcome of digital modernization (Huot, 2026b; Makhija et al., 2025). In doing so, hybrid pedagogy not only supports the global education agenda enacted in UN Sustainable Development Goal 4 (Quality Education), but it also addresses SDG 17 (Partnerships for the Goals), which collectively substantiates the transformative potential of education as both a developmental and diplomatic organizations (ASEAN Secretariat, 2022; UNESCO, 2021b).

This introduction, in essence, constructs the ground-breaking space where the future of hybrid pedagogy is reshaping by the convergent AI and intercultural collaboration. This stems from a logical solution to a moral and intercultural movement, redefining how knowledge, culture, and technology, synergize to establish inclusive global educational communities.

2. LITERATURE REVIEW AND THEORETICAL–CONCEPTUAL FRAMEWORK

2.1. Hybrid Pedagogy and the Post-Digital Turn

One of the most magnificent educational models in the 21st century is hybrid pedagogy. This has emerged by blending the possibility of digital educational environments with the relational, communicative capacities of in-person education. Scholars like Garrison and Vaughan (2008) define hybrid learning or blended learning as a design system for inquiry and reflection. They continue to argue that this model emphasizes intentionality, interaction, and learner autonomy. Moreover, this model not merely extends the logistical convenience, but it also represents a pedagogical philosophy grounded in social constructivism, where it is known that learning is best acquired through engagement and critical dialogue.

Furthermore, Selwyn (2021) defines this shift as part of the post-digital turn in education since digital technology plays an important role in both an external supplement and a constitutive element of educational culture. Similarly, Jandrić et al. (2018) argue that the human and the technological, in post-digital learning, coexist symbiotically and this phenomenon shapes each other through reciprocal interaction. Likewise, Ross and Collier (2016) describe this paradigm as hybrid ecologies of learning. They mean these are spaces where physical presence, digital mediation, and affective engagement converge since hybrid pedagogy is neither purely online nor traditional operation.

Several studies found that hybrid learning environments not simply promote resilience and adaptability, but inclusivity through accommodating different learner needs (Bozkurt & Sharma, 2020; Liu et al., 2024). However, the increasing reliance on data-driven systems risks commodifying pedagogy if humanistic principles do not remain central to instructional design (Huot & Loch, 2025c; Knox, 2019). Consequently, within the paradigm of the post-digital zeitgeist, the present chapter contextualizes the hybridization of pedagogy for its complexities, as well as the ethical ideal for its application that seeks to promote and maintain a just and humane education for all in the world (Huot, 2026b; Makhija et al., 2025).

2.2. Artificial Intelligence in Pedagogy

Artificial Intelligence (AI) has become a striking means of mediums in forcing how teaching and learning transform now. According to research, AI's educational functions extend from adaptive learning systems and automated assessment tools to intelligent tutoring and linguistic translation engines (Huot & Loch, 2025b; Luckin & Holmes, 2016). It becomes apparent that while these technologies are designed responsively, they promote greater personalization, accessibility, and responsiveness in learning environments. Within this framework, Wayne Holmes et al. (2019) support for human-centric AI paradigm. They argue that this model seeks not to replace educators, but to enhance their competences, especially allowing educators to focus on creativity, mentorship, and empathy.

The integration of AI technology fosters pedagogical co-agency, where human instructors co-act with algorithms in scaffolding and guiding a cohort of learners (W Holmes et al., 2019; Huot, 2026a). Williamson et al. (2023) discuss adaptive learning systems such as Knewton and Coursera as having the capacity to customize more in course content because of predictive analytics, thus indicating a progression of learning environments from a more static state to a more fluid and flexible one. Yet, within these descriptions, however well-articulated they might be, there seems to be minimal recognition of the prospect of algorithmic decision-making as a form of surveillance and the discrimination that may stem from it, as well as the perceived inequities that may be deemed unjust (Knox, 2020; Selwyn, 2019).

In line with the above-mentioned principles, UNESCO's Recommendation on the Ethics of Artificial Intelligence (2021c) also responds to these challenges with the principles of transparency, accountability, and inclusiveness in regard to the governance of Artificial Intelligence in Education. In the same way, Floridi (2023) proposes an approach so called ethics of digital humanism, situating AI within moral frameworks which emphasizes human dignity and cultural diversity. Ethical AI integration in Cambodia, an emerging economic country with Southeast Asia, remains paramount for guaranteeing that technological development facilitates equitable access to quality education rather than reinforces existing socio-economic divides (ASEAN Secretariat, 2022).

2.3. Intercultural Collaboration and Global Citizenship

This further suggests that intercultural collaboration, in today's globalized learning landscape, plays a significant role in a pedagogical and ethical necessities. Based on research, Byram (2020) indicates that just because intercultural competence involve tolerance, it necessitates reflexivity, empathy, and critical awareness by means of one's own cultural heritages. Another perspective from Deardorff's (2006) *Pro-*

cess Model of Intercultural Competence illustrates a rotational process of attitude, knowledge, and skills that therefore turn out to effective and respectful interaction.

Intercultural collaboration, in digital and hybrid learning environment, takes new forms. O'Dowd (2018) terms virtual exchange as one form that emphasizes structured online dialogues between students in diverse cultural locations. Likewise, Helm (2024) declares that these dialogues augment both linguistic proficiency, and cross-cultural awareness and collaborative problem-solving. Technologies focusing on Collaboration without Borders do not consider the borderless nature of certain technologies such as AI systems with multilingual instantaneous translation, real time emotion recognition, adaptive conversational and interactive systems (Huot et al., 2024; Zawacki-Richter et al., 2019).

In the 21st Century, the learning framework, global citizenship has increased because of worldwide intercultural collaboration (Nussbaum, 2016; UNESCO, 2015). International educational collaboration enables students to understand their responsibility, interdependence, and global issues to be resolved. As a result of Intercultural Collaboration, ASEAN-India, especially the ASEAN Youth Intercultural Exchange Programs and the India-ASEAN Virtual Classroom Network exemplify Trust and Solidarity (ASEAN Secretariat, 2021; MEA, 2025)

2.4. Theoretical Frameworks

This study adopts a multi-theoretical framework to scrutinize how AI and intercultural collaboration interlock within hybrid learning paradigms by incorporating four contemporary perspectives:

Constructivism: According to Piaget (1952, 1970), learners learn best through experience and reflection since learning is a process of constructing knowledge. Based on this theory, hybrid learning is an innovative learning model to underpin learning environment that enable learners to cultivate abstracts concepts through multimodal engagement.

Connectivism: Goldie (2016) posits that knowledge, in the digital age, locates not merely in human minds but technological networks. Learning is best acquired through navigation, connection, and contribution to disparate networks of information. As Downes (2012) argues, connectivism, in hybrid learning and AI-enhanced education, elaborates how knowledge circulate through machine-human communication, a concept of "*learning ecologies of participation*."

Cultural–Historical Activity Theory (CHAT): Engeström (2001) proposes that learning happens not only in cultural but institutional environments, where learning is a goal-oriented and socially mediated activity. Hybrid learning, in this sense, constitute an activity system to intersect digital tools (AI technologies), communities (learners and educators), and cultural rules (intercultural norms) to communicate radically to produce intended learning outcomes. Within CHAT framework, hybrid pedagogy therefore communicates smoothly between local practices and global innovations.

Ethical AI in Education Framework: Floridi (2023) contextualizes digital ethics framework to substantiate how algorithmic transparency, accountability, and inclusivity are integrated. Hybrid learning, in this framework, is suggested to align with humanistic values in support of learner autonomy, and cultural integrity. Marginson (2010) terms a concept as a glonacal system, one that incorporates global innovation, national reform, and local cultural practice, when these frameworks are integrated to corroborate hybrid learning. These frameworks facilitate educators to situate hybrid learning not only as a socio-cultural transformation but as a technological synergy as well, as illustrated in **Figure 1**.

Figure 1. An integrated model illustrating the interplay of constructivism, connectivism, cultural-historical activity theory, and ethical AI principles within a hybrid pedagogy framework (Author's own work)

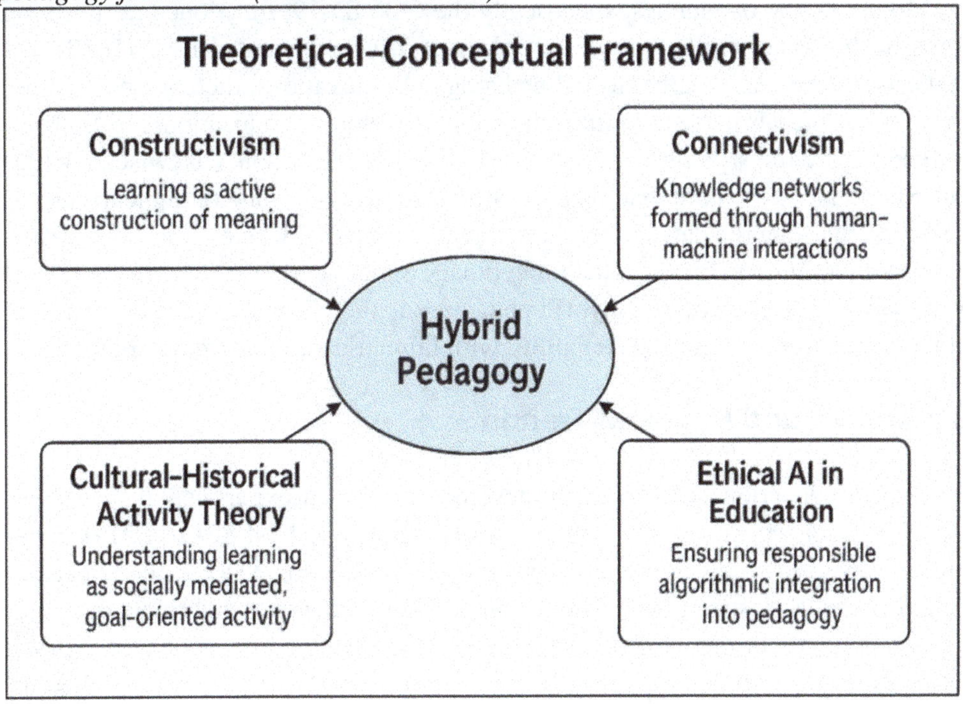

3. THE EVOLVING LANDSCAPE OF HYBRID PEDAGOGIES

3.1. Historical Development

During the past century, educational development witnessed the evolution of hybrid learning in response to educational philosophy, technological adaptation, and institutional reform. In the 19th-century correspondence education, knowledge was accessible through postal systems that constituted a first model of distance education (Huot et al., 2025; Peters, 2008). Up to the 20th-century education, open universities, particularly the UK's Open University and India's Indira Gandhi National Open University (IGNOU), emerged and combined printed materials, broadcast media, and face-to-face tutorials to approach disparate learners (Daniel, 2013). These innovations underlain the transformation for the present's hybrid systems, ones that incorporate synchronous and asynchronous pedagogy, digital applications, and AI-driven personalization.

Moreover, the pandemics, specifically the COVID-19, functioned as a driving force in this historical pathway. According to Zawacki-Richter et al. (2019), social crises have historically pushed pedagogical innovations, thereby accelerating transformations abruptly to online education that imposed educational institutions to reconfigure the structure and purposes of higher education. Likewise, Bozkurt and Sharma (2020) claim that the pandemic made ways of integrating learning experience, marking the dawn of the post-digital university, where online and offline modes of learning no longer function in binary opposition. Similarly, Garrison and Vaughan (2008) contend that hybrid pedagogy is therefore a significant model of global education, integrating flexibility with human-centred learning approach.

3.2. Global and Regional Trends

Hybrid education has obviously developed from an experimental, periphery and fringe stage to the innovative strategy of mainstream. UNESCO (2021a) names digital hybrid learning ecosystems as crucial to achieving SDG 4, the education goal. In Asia, and specifically in India and ASEAN countries, hybrid learning has become a policy priority to connect education, innovation, inclusion and regional integration. As a whole, India's study in India initiative, SWAYAM (Study Webs of Active–Learning for Young Aspiring Minds), and the National Education Policy (NEP) 2020 cumulatively drive hybrid and technology-enabled learning at national and transnational scales (MEA, 2025; Tilak et al., 2018). These efforts envisage education as a developmental instrument and as the diplomatic mezzo between South–Southeast Asian engagement.

These trends reflect the proportional developments within ASEAN countries. The ASEAN Work Plan on Education (2021-2025) accentuates open learning, digital transfiguration, and cross-border cooperation (ASEAN Secretariat, 2021). The evidence indicates that while countries such as Singapore, Malaysia, and Vietnam are in a leading position in incorporating hybrid and AI-driven learning ecosystems, Cambodia and Laos concentrate on infrastructural developments and policy adaptations (Huot, 2025; Huot & Tep, 2025). Nations commit to build educational resilience through different regional projects, namely, the ASEAN-India Virtual Classroom, and the ASEAN Cyber University to augment digital integration and knowledge exchange.

3.3. Case Illustrations

The hybrid learning development is finely elaborated through national and institutional case studies which manifest diverse levels of technological innovation, pedagogical reform, and cultural adaptation:

- **Vietnam:** According to Nguyen et al. (2023), Vietnamese institutions have incorporated AI-enabled adaptive learning into cross-cultural communication syllabi. Students involve in multilingual, multicultural conversations to improve global awareness through various platforms that integrate machine learning algorithms with human assistance. Such approach parallels with the *National Digital Transformation Program (2020 – 2030)* of Vietnam's broader education digitalization agenda.
- **India:** Hybrid pedagogy is a foundation stone that the National Education Policy (NEP) 2020 endeavours to enlarge access and internationalization. Indian universities deploy not merely virtual classroom and AI-driven assessment tools but MOOCs via platforms, namely, SWAYAM and NPTEL. Such systems stimulate creativity, inclusivity, international collaboration, for example with ASEAN partnership (Huot, 2026a; Knight, 2022). In parallel with hybrid augmentation in India, Nye (2004) designates knowledge diplomacy, a concept of utilizing education to promote trust and shared advancement.
- **Europe (Netherlands):** Vrije Universiteit Amsterdam is prominent for its AI-generated "Intercultural Competence Labs," in which AI translation and feedback platforms enable learners from different cultural backgrounds partake in collaborative projects. Such labs illustrate a hybrid learning model in Europe that integrates constructivist approach with ethical AI principles to substantiate empathy, collaboration, and contemplative practices.

The hybrid model, across these contexts, exemplifies a global coincidence toward inclusivity and creativity, yet it also emphasizes perpetual difference in infrastructure, digital literacy, and policy implementation. Therefore, the developing language of hybrid learning is not simply uniform but polycentric determined by local needs, global trends, and technological negotiation, as illustrated in Table 1. Education systems now operate as glonacal spaces, where global, national, and local dimensions communicate dynamically to develop hybrid pedagogy futures (Huot & Hok, 2025b; Marginson, 2016).

Table 1. The Evolving Landscape of Hybrid Pedagogies (Author's own work)

Aspect	Description
Historical Development	The 19th-century education was transformed to open institutions and AI-generated technological ecosystems. Hybrid education expedites a sustainable and institutionalized paradigm due to the COVID-19 pandemic.
Global and Regional Trends	Education increases equity and resilience due to hybrid pedagogy. Digital education policies in India and ASEAN are incorporated into national and regional frameworks, thereby underscoring access, innovation, and inclusion.
Case Illustration: Vietnam	AI-augmented education is adapted by Vietnamese institutions for intercultural interaction and language education, thereby corroborating national digital transformation and strategic plans.
Case Illustration: India	Initiatives like NEP 2020 and SWAYAM in India lie in hybrid pedagogy within tertiary education framework, connecting open and virtual education systems to innovation and diplomacy.
Case Illustration: Europe (Netherlands)	AI-powered Intercultural Competence Labs are utilized by Vrije Universiteit Amsterdam enables hybrid pedagogical contexts to promote collaboration and empathy.

4. OPPORTUNITIES AND BENEFITS

4.1. Pedagogical Innovation

Artificial Intelligence is integrated within hybrid learning frameworks that embody one of the most noteworthy transformations in 21st-century education. AI, for instance, accommodates cognitive scaffolding, while sustaining engagement through communicative instruction, thereby not only facilitating adaptive feedback loops, but also acknowledging learners to study at their own pace (Luckin & Holmes, 2016). Analogously, Wayne Holmes et al. (2019) argue that AI-driven learning analytics accumulate real-time monitoring of learner progress, energizing teachers to scaffold instruction in compliance with individual learning trajectories. In parallel, Trilling and Fadel (2009) suggest a concept of *21st-century learning skills*, where learner autonomy, problem-solving, and creativity formulate the foundation of educational excellence.

In addition, Bozkurt and Sharma (2020) maintain that hybrid learning that supports by intelligent tutoring systems produces pedagogical elasticity, a condition that learning contexts dynamically allocate to student needs and contextual demands. Such innovations augment formative assessment procedures and fill gaps between formal and informal education. For instance, AI-supported virtual assistants in blended learning contexts can emulate Socratic dialogue, thereby resonate critical inquiry while sustain human-like responsiveness (Zawacki-Richter et al., 2019). Educational innovations, in such case, grow not merely as a technological but epistemological shift, particularly revolutionizing instruction from content delivery to knowledge co-creation across physical and digital domains.

4.2. Intercultural Dimensions

AI and digital collaboration ameliorate hybrid learning to importantly enhance intercultural education and conversation. Intercultural competence, which enables effective and proper communication across cultural environments, is a core educational outcome, not an additional skill (Deardorff, 2006). Learners from different educational backgrounds, through AI-supported learning classrooms, involve in virtual exchanges, emulations, and cooperative projects in which surpass borders and time zones. These learning environments reflect the concept of virtual intercultural communication, in which students can both share knowledge and communicate meaning, identity, and empathy.

Nguyen et al. (2023) consideration is given to how, in the context of ASEAN-India relations and in other transregional contexts, there is the use of AI-tools in the form of sentiment analysis, virtual reality simulations and automated translators to work around the barriers of distance and culture to achieve engagement. Such communications create *glonacal learning ecologies*, in which interactions concurrently function at global, national, and local scopes (Marginson, 2010). This hybrid learning paradigm determines global citizenship education through the support of knowledge co-creation among different companions. Byram (2020) asserts that hybrid pedagogy transmutes students into cosmopolitan communicators, students who are competent in adapting intercultural reflection, cooperative problem-solving, and ethical thinking within globalization and digitalization.

4.3. Equity and Access

AI-driven hybrid learning has its potential to enhance educational accessibility, inclusivity, and equity. When ethically governed, digital transformation can fill gaps among systemic inequalities in response to quality education (UNESCO, 2021c). Geographic and physical barriers are resolved through assistive technologies, speech recognition, and AI-driven translation to strengthen inclusive education for learners with disabilities or marginalized groups (OECD, 2021). When open-access policies and localized educational programs are parallel to each other, AI can operate as an equity multiplier (Wayne Holmes et al., 2019).

Moreover, despite the infrastructural disparities in Southeast Asia, AI-enhanced tools accommodate spaces to bolster hybrid learning and revitalize higher education. According to ASEAN Secretariat (2021), learners can receive cost-effective access to high-quality resources through diverse open-source platforms, for example, SWAYAM in India and Open Distance Learning Network of ASEAN. Huot (2025) asserts also that the digital pedagogical reforms in Cambodia illustrate, not just how small countries can successfully regionally integrate and collaborate in AI, but also how they manage to overcome the capacity paradigms to engage in transnational education.

Floridi (2023) suggests one of the ethical AI frameworks to highlight the significance of establishing comprehensive algorithms that protect bias and augment cultural sensitivity. It is generally believed that AI in hybrid education that is responsively applied promotes epistemic justice to guarantee that all students from diverse settings, language, or socio-economic background can take advantage of and involve in the global common knowledge. Hybrid learning is therefore considered as a changing mechanism to strengthen learning efficiency, social equity, intercultural solidary, and global sustainability, as depicted in Table 2.

Table 2. Opportunities and Benefits of AI-Enhanced Hybrid Pedagogy

No.	Dimension	Description
1.	Pedagogical Innovation	AI authorizes versatile and individualized learning tracks, real-time monitoring, and perceptive tutoring systems. It strengthens engagement and learner autonomy through transfiguring education from content delivery to knowledge co-creation.
2.	Intercultural Dimensions	AI-supported hybrid learning stimulates universal virtual classrooms that augment intercultural communication, empathy, and cultural literacy. Translation and collaboration portals supported by AI enhance inclusivity and mitigate language barriers.
3.	Equity and Access	AI-powered translation, open learning frameworks, and supportive technologies improve availability for different students. Justice, transparency, and inclusivity, particularly in under-resource regions, confirmed by ethical AI frameworks.

To summarize, AI, hybrid education, and intercultural collaboration are convergent to establish a multidimensional opportunity for re-envisaging education not only as human but as technological initiative as well. The convergence of these enhances educational innovation, cultivates intercultural empathy, and increases access to learning as a global right in response to UNESCO's 2030 Agenda and ASEAN's commitment to an inclusive digital community.

5. CHALLENGES AND BARRIERS

Hybrid education introduces a range of complicated challenges, starting from technological, cultural, pedagogical to ethical, when incorporating it with AI and intercultural communication. Such obstacles do not merely exemplify logistical restraints; disclose unfathomable systematic inequalities and epistemic pressures included in universal education systems.

5.1. Technological Challenges

Although there are immediate developments in EdTech infrastructure, essential differences exist between technologically advanced and low-resource communities. According to Williamson et al. (2023), digital inequality is the current educational divide that highlights that the possibility for hardware, bandwidth, and AI-enhanced learning contexts stay imbalanced all over the Global South. For example, in ASEAN regions, country and distant institutions frequently endeavour with impoverished networking, old-fashioned devices, and inadequate digital literacy reinforcement

(ASEAN Secretariat, 2021). In Cambodia, Laos, and Myanmar, such broadband penetration persists below regional averages due to several infrastructural disparities that restrict the application of AI-powered hybrid education.

Furthermore, formula bias and the "Western epistemic hegemony" concealed within several AI systems debilitate inequality (Becker, 1975). Wayne Holmes et al. (2019) contend that data in most AI-generated platforms are trained by derivation from Euro-American environments where enhance their cultural adaptability but delimit linguistic and behavioural misinterpretation and paradigms of Asian students. Such cases cause culturally prejudiced feedback loops and uneven learning results. A localized and contextualized AI-powered education guarantees relevance and inclusion through culture-sensitive data training and human supervision (Luckin & Holmes, 2016).

5.2. Cultural and Pedagogical Barriers

Composite pedagogical ecosystems still receive unparalleled and inequitable developments in terms of intercultural and educational domains. Deardorff (2006) observes that deep intercultural qualification necessitates dialogical humility, a quality that is laborious to promote within virtual classrooms manipulated by AI-supported interactions, while intercultural communication intends to cultivate mutual understanding. While many ASEAN educational systems inherit teacher-centred approach and Western regions focus on student-centred principles, such diverse traditions of pedagogy can construct tightness in expectations, interaction styles, and participation patterns.

Despite efficacious in adaptive pedagogy, AI-generated patterns frequently neglect several cultural subtleties. As Wayne Holmes et al. (2019) admonish, overreliance on auto-operation can sabotage the connective and affective dimensions of instruction, thereby directing to what they delineate as pedagogical alienation. Education in contexts that is deeply embedded in cultural values of courtesy and community like India and Cambodia, when replaced educator authority with formulaic feedback, can establish resistance and disconnection among teachers and students.

Moreover, despite several advantages, digital literacy disparities worsen participation gaps. As Nguyen et al. (2023) claim, while learners from disadvantaged backgrounds strive to handle digital portals effectively, educators who are deficient in professional development training in AI technologies tend to feel disempowered. There is a digital divide that is created and that must be closed through the use of technology in upskilling and responsive education that creates a hybrid model of education that is grounded in the cultural traditions of the local area.

5.3. Ethical and Governance Issues

One of the most crucial challenges within AI adoption in education is the ethical dimension. Research found that unethical AI is not only a technological defect, but a social unfairness, especially when the breach of data privacy and informed consent are insufficiently prevented (Floridi, 2023; Huot & Loch, 2025a). Data collection from behavioural analytics to biometric tracking in several educational AI ecosystems elevate troubles about autonomy, surveillance, and learner rights. Algorithmic decision-making, as Selwyn (2021) criticizes the increasing educational technocracy, substitutes human evaluation in appraising learner performance, curriculum relevance, and even emotional commitment. Such trend jeopardizes demoting ethical roles of educators as facilitator and mentor. In addition, in ASEAN nations, delicate governance mechanisms allow private actors and state agencies to misuse educational information.

Despite the propagation for fair governance models highlighting data privacy, accountability, and algorithmic explanation to resolve these obstacles from UNESCO's Recommendation on the Ethics of Artificial Intelligence (2021c), the implementation remains imbalanced. Singapore and Malaysia have initiated AI ethics framework development for education, whereas states like Cambodia and Myanmar are shortage of thorough regulatory systems, keeping educational institutions prone to exploitation.

Taken together, AI-powered hybrid learning faces multifaceted and interdependent issues. It is generally evident that there exist not merely unequal opportunities accessible to technology and ineffective collaboration with cultural and pedagogical dichotomy, but deficient trust and accountability with ethics. A human-centred technological education, in view of future direction, can unify inclusive, empathetic, equitable development, and intercultural wisdom, not in renouncing AI (Wayne Holmes et al., 2019).

6. STRATEGIES AND PATHWAYS FOR TRANSFORMATION

AI-enhanced hybrid learning and cross-cultural communication necessitate the transformative innovation with systematic, organizational, and moral infrastructure. Educational goal of hybrid pedagogical paradigms strengthens technological efficiency, pedagogical sustainability, social equity, and cultural inclusion to respond to the educational prospects that increases digitized and universal interconnectivity. Based on international best practices, this stage delineates significant strategies for re-envisaging hybrid pedagogy across institutional, collaborative, and policy levels that align with the recommendations by the OECD (2023a), UNESCO (2021c) and regional educational frameworks (ASEAN Secretariat, 2021).

6.1. Institutional Strategies

Instructional improvement and institutional governance are, at the organizational level, central to educational restructuration and transformation. While developing curriculum and training educators, institutions must guarantee that human values embed in AI ethics, cultural knowledge and digital adoption. Within such a stage, as Wayne Holmes et al. (2019) contend, human-centred AI must be included to balance ethical and cultural responsiveness, and machine processes. Institutions should introduce teachers to adaptive frameworks and instruct them to critically assess AI technologies, decipher algorithmic feedback, and accommodate technology to distinctive learning environments.

In the course of educational transformation, curriculum development programs perform significant roles. AI-supported learning necessitates educators to serve not simply as knowledge transmitters, but as learning engineers who develop, evaluate, and individualize learning practices (Luckin & Holmes, 2016). Trainings facilitate educators to improve professional development, specifically enhancing key competencies to augment their digital fluency, intercultural understanding, and data literacy for functioning AI-enhanced classrooms.

Furthermore, promoting hybrid innovation is paramount when there have been inter-institutional collaborations between ASEAN and South Asian institutions. Regional partnerships have fostered, for example, historical connections between Vietnam National University and Nalanda University in India to develop a modern educational diplomacy as a result of AI-augmented hybrid programs. These collaborations empower co-designed curriculum development, exchange programs, and shared digital learning infrastructure, as Knight (2022) argues, accelerating regional education not as a competitive arena but as a collective good model.

6.2. Collaborative Models

Transformative hybrid education necessitates collaborative programs. Learners receive the opportunity to involve in global, peer-to-peer learning with flexibility through the reconfiguration of AI-powered digital exchange programs. Such intercultural exchanges cultivate key skills such as empathy, cultural competence, and global citizenship for the post-digital world (Deardorff, 2006; O'Dowd, 2018). Moodle AI and Microsoft's Global Learning Hub are learning models of adaptive feedback systems, collaborative learning portals, and AI-generated translation tools that can support seamless multilingual and multicultural cooperation.

Moreover, equitable hybrid paradigms that align with cross-border research consortia can shape academic knowledge production to increase inclusivity. Educational collaborations such as EU-ASEAN and ASEAN-India could collaboratively investigate best practices in AI learning, technological inclusion, and intercultural education. Such consortia would both enhance South-South collaboration and decentralize the world knowledge economy via broadening voices from developing spheres (Huot, 2025; OECD, 2023b).

An optimistic paradigm enhances technological literacy, data ethics, and cybersecurity across tertiary education universities such as the (EU in ASEAN, 2024). When incorporated with intercultural collaboration, AI education would function as a masterplan for other regional collaborations.

6.3. Policy and Ethical Frameworks

Balancing innovation with accountability is indispensable for healthy governance within policy level. Based on UNESCO's *Recommendation on the Ethics of Artificial Intelligence* (2021c) and the OECD's *AI Principles* (2019), governments and educational institutions must embrace national AI ethics charters for instruction. For any algorithmic systems that are utilized for admission, student engagement and assessment, these charters should determine explicability, transparency, and equity.

Stakeholders such as policymakers, technologists, educators, and civil society so called multi-stakeholders governance mechanisms are imperative for supervising AI application in education. According to research, ethical governance is a precondition, not a restriction on innovation (Floridi, 2023). AI-enhanced learning under such contributed approach facilitates human resources much more than interests of certain groups.

Coordination within geographical nations is equally paramount. The partnership between the ASEAN Secretariat and Ministry of Education of India have led to constitute a Regional Observatory on AI in Education to examine best practices, appraise ethical agreement, and support capacity-building plans. While preventing data sovereignty and cultural diversity, such coordination would standardize transnational collaboration.

6.4. Best Practices and Global Exemplars

Below are case studies that highlight hybrid education, artificial intelligence, and cross-cultural communication of a few influential universities and partnerships:

- **Open University (UK):** A renowned pioneer in online and hybrid pedagogy is the Open University, where utilizes AI-powered learner analytics to prognosticate student disentanglement and furnish untimely compromises (Ferguson et al., 2019). Such AI framework secures transparent decision-making and sustains learner autonomy.
- **Nalanda University (India) and Vietnam National University:** Having co-created cross-border hybrid programs, the universities incorporate AI translation and culturally personalized syllabi. Building on historical Southeast Asia-India connections, such cooperation sustains how cultural heritage to communicate digital-age education.
- **EU in ASEAN:** Regional partnership initiates to co-establish flexible frameworks for teacher education, digital inclusivity, and equitable access to AI technologies. This initiative intends to substantiate capacity-building collaboration and connects the North-South digital divide. Meanwhile, it nourishes intercultural cooperation through digital communication.
- **National Institute of Education (NIE), Singapore:** While sustaining ethical supervision and culturally communicative education, teachers are trained in NIE's *AI for Learning Lab* on how to consolidate adaptive AI tools into hybrid curricula.

The multitude of best practices enhance institutional infrastructure, partnerships, and good governance in support of hybrid learning transformation.

Achieving the goal set out in the vision of hybrid education also necessitates the use of empathy and technology and Selwyn (2021) refers to such partnership as the human-algorithmic partnership. Educational bodies must renovate technologically and promote intercultural understanding, social accountability, and ethical awareness. Such integration enables hybrid education to become a driving force for educational systems with inclusivity, equity, and global connectivity, especially when AI systems are employed in support of human creativity and intercultural understanding. The way forward for education must empower educators with thoughtful collaboration and ethical innovation, not replacing educators or hybrid education with algorithms.

7. CONCLUSION

Hybrid education has dynamically evolved from the integration of Artificial Intelligence and intercultural collaboration, and this approach has transformed education into a new instructional paradigm for the twenty-first century. Rather than replacing educators, AI strengthens their capacity to mentor, facilitate, and personalize learning, while intercultural collaboration imbues this process with empathy, ethical awareness, and global consciousness. These frameworks, together, enable education to bridge intercultural and regional boundaries, thereby connecting students and educators as a dynamical, human-centred ecosystem. The principles of AI ethics and intercultural communication direct hybrid education to go beyond the limitations of traditional education systems.

This pedagogy transforms to be a shared space of knowledge-based societies that cultivate collaboration, inclusion, and equity and such education functions as not merely a developmental but diplomatic bridge among distinctive societies. Hybrid pedagogy promotes both digital literacy and intercultural consciousness and social accountability through the evolution of technology and cultural collaboration:

- Construct AI-Intercultural Learning Labs across ASEAN-India institutions to strengthen experimentation, innovation, and teacher education in hybrid paradigms.
- Advance global hybrid education by establishing open-access database stores that accumulate and widely distribute best practices, case studies, and ethical principles.
- Link hybrid pedagogy programs to guarantee that learning innovation bestow directly to worldwide collaboration and equity in response to Sustainable Development Goal 4 (Quality Education) and SDG 17 (Partnerships for the Goals).

The investigation of this chapter, taken together, promotes a comprehensive framework that consolidates technological and intercultural awareness. The study envisages hybrid education, by localizing AI and intercultural communication as mutually strengthening pillars, as both a mode of effective education and as a driving force for equitable, shared human and sustainable development. Such synthesis enables education to function not only a moral but also a material foundation for worldwide coexistence in the digital era.

REFERENCES

Becker, G. S. (1975). *Human capital: A theoretical and empirical analysis.* National Bureau of Economic Research.

Bozkurt, A., & Sharma, R. C. (2020). Emergency remote teaching in a time of global crisis due to Corona Virus pandemic. *Asian Journal of Distance Education, 15*(1), i–vi. http://asianjde.com/ojs/index.php/AsianJDE/article/view/447

Byram, M. (2020). *Teaching and assessing intercultural communicative competence: Revisited.* Multilingual Matters.

Daniel, J. (2013). *Mega-universities and knowledge media.* Routledge. DOI: 10.4324/9780203045978

Deardorff, D. K. (2006). Identification and assessment of intercultural competence as a student outcome of internationalization. *Journal of Studies in International Education, 10*(3), 241–266. DOI: 10.1177/1028315306287002

Downes, S. (2012). *Connectivism and connective knowledge: Essays on meaning and learning networks.* National Research Council Canada.

Engeström, Y. (2001). Expansive learning at work: Toward an activity theoretical reconceptualization. *Journal of Education and Work, 14*(1), 133–156. DOI: 10.1080/13639080020028747

EU in ASEAN. (2024). *EU–ASEAN Sustainable Connectivity Package – Higher Education Programme (SCOPE-HE) 2024–2028* (2024–2028, Issue. EU-ASEAN – Global Gateway. https://euinasean.eu/scope-he

Ferguson, R., Coughlan, T., Egelandsdal, K., Gaved, M., Herodotou, C., Hillaire, G., Jones, D., Jowers, I., Kukulska-Hulme, A., & McAndrew, P. (2019). *Innovating pedagogy 2019: Open university innovation report 7.* The Open University.

Floridi, L. (2023). *The ethics of artificial intelligence: Principles, challenges, and opportunities.* Oxford University Press. DOI: 10.1093/oso/9780198883098.001.0001

Garrison, D. R., & Vaughan, N. D. (2008). *Blended learning in higher education: Framework, principles, and guidelines.* John Wiley & Sons.

Goldie, J. (2016). Connectivism: A learning theory fir the digital age. *Medical Teacher, 38*(10), 1–6. DOI: 10.3109/0142159X.2016.1173661 PMID: 27128290

Helm, F. (2024). *Intercultural communication in virtual exchange.* Cambridge University Press. DOI: 10.1017/9781009385589

Hodge, S. R. HAEGELE, J., HODGE, S., & SHAPIRO, D. (2020). *Routledge handbook of adapted physical education*. Routledge.

Holmes, W., Bialik, M., & Fadel, C. (2019). *Artificial intelligence in education promises and implications for teaching and learning*. Center for Curriculum Redesign.

Holmes, W., Bialik, M., & Fadel, C. (2019). *Artificial intelligence in education: Promises and implications for teaching and learning*. Center for Curriculum Redesign.

Huot, S. (2025). Digital tutors in the kingdom: Exploring ChatGPT's influence on Cambodian students' academic and cognitive growth. In Pandya, J. D., & Patel, K. C. (Eds.), *Interdisciplinary insights: Exploring multiple perspectives* (Vol. 2, pp. 36–54). Meadow Publication.

Huot, S. (2026a). Digital diplomacy in Cambodia: Embracing artificial intelligence for strategic engagement and national development. In Turan, A., & Ucuzal, H. (Eds.), *Diplomacy in the age of artificial intelligence* (pp. 307–330). IGI Global Scientific Publishing., DOI: 10.4018/979-8-3373-4937-4.ch013

Huot, S. (2026b). Emerging voices from Cambodia: International student journeys and educational aspirations in a globalized academic landscape. In Irham, I., Huda, M., & Yaqin, L. N. (Eds.), *International student narratives in globalized higher education* (pp. 365–400). IGI Global Scientific Publishing., DOI: 10.4018/979-8-3373-4212-2.ch014

Huot, S., & Em, S. (2025). Effective strategies of English teaching in Cambodia's underserved communities: Bridging digital divide to access education quality. [JEILT]. *Journal of Education Innovation and Language Teaching*, *1*(1), 53–77. DOI: 10.63381/jeilt.v1i1.38

Huot, S., & Hok, C. (2025a). Enhancing English language teaching for multilingual learners: Leveraging heritage languages in the classroom. *Journal of Social and Educational Research*, *4*(1), 87–95. DOI: 10.5281/zenodo.15698964

Huot, S., & Hok, C. (2025b). Unpacking the struggle: Linguistic, pedagogical, and cognitive barriers in Cambodian students' English essay writing. *Context (Ibadan)*, *12*(4), 149–168. DOI: 10.5281/zenodo.15807401

Huot, S., & Loch, S. (2025a). Digital practices in Cambodian EFL classrooms: Teacher narratives from remote learning. In K. Khette & Tayade (Eds.), *Proceeding of one day national conference on English language, literature, cultural studies and media studies* (Vol. 2, pp. 19–31). Centre for Learning, Research and Development, Savda, Maharashtra. DOI: 10.5281/zenodo.16921807

Huot, S., & Loch, S. (2025b). Educating in the age of AI: Preparing Cambodian teachers and students for an AI-augmented learning future. *Journal of Educational Technology and E-Learning Innovations, 1*(2), 31–38. DOI: 10.54536/jeteli.v1i2.5170

Huot, S., & Loch, S. (2025c). From rote to reflective: Integrating ChatGPT to transform learning outcomes in Cambodian education. *International Journal of Language and Literary Studies, 7*(4), 1–15. DOI: 10.36892/ijlls.v7i4.2188

Huot, S., Loch, S., Nget, R., & Em, S. (2025). Exploring multiliteracies in the digital era: A framework for 21st-century learning. [CJESS]. *Cambodian Journal of Educational and Social Sciences, 2*(1), 7–27. DOI: 10.69496/cjess.v2i1.50

Huot, S., Sam, R., & Nguon, T. (2024). Influencing factors in teaching career choices in Cambodia in teacher education colleges: A conceptual framework. *European Journal of Arts. Humanities and Social Sciences, 1*(6), 97–108. DOI: 10.59324/ejahss.2024.1(6).11

Huot, S., & Tep, P. (2025). Advancing ChatGPT for pedagogical innovation in Cambodia: Insight from global evidence and local implications. *The Context: Journal of English Studies, 12*(4), 115–135. DOI: 10.5281/zenodo.15806972

Jandrić, P., Knox, J., Besley, T., Ryberg, T., Suoranta, J., & Hayes, S. (2018). Postdigital science and education. *50*(10), 893–899. DOI: 10.1080/00131857.2018.1454000

Knight, J. (2022). Differentiating Knowledge Diplomacy from Soft Power and Cultural, Science, Education and Public Forms of Diplomacy. In Knight, J. (Ed.), *Knowledge diplomacy in international relations and higher education* (pp. 113–125). Springer., DOI: 10.1007/978-3-031-14977-1_9

Knox, J. (2019). What does the 'postdigital' mean for education? Three critical perspectives on the digital, with implications for educational research and practice. *Postdigital Science and Education, 1*(2), 357–370. DOI: 10.1007/s42438-019-00045-y

Knox, J. (2020). Artificial intelligence and education in China. *Learning, Media and Technology, 45*(3), 298–311. DOI: 10.1080/17439884.2020.1754236

Liu, M., Zhao, G., Zhong, Z., Ma, J., & Wang, W. (2024). Theoretical foundations for blended learning. In Li, M., Han, X., & Cheng, J. (Eds.), *Handbook of educational reform through blended learning* (pp. 1–44). Springer., DOI: 10.1007/978-981-99-6269-3_1

Luckin, R., & Holmes, W. (2016). *Intelligence unleashed: An argument for AI in education*. Pearson. https://www.pearson.com/content/dam/corporate/glob

Makhija, R., Aggarwal, S., & Jain, S. (2025). Hybrid learning, artificial Intelligence, and Indian indigenized values. In Makhija, R., Aggarwal, S., & Jain, S. (Eds.), *Indigenous Teaching Disciplines and Perspectives for Higher Education* (pp. 267–284). IGI Global Scientific Publishing. DOI: 10.4018/979-8-3693-9296-6.ch013

Marginson, S. (2010). Higher education in the global knowledge economy. *Procedia: Social and Behavioral Sciences, 2*(5), 6962–6980. DOI: 10.1016/j.sbspro.2010.05.049

Marginson, S. (2016). *The dream is over: The crisis of Clark Kerr's California idea of higher education*. University of California Press.

Marginson, S., & Rhoades, G. (2002). Beyond national states, markets, and systems of higher education: A glonacal agency heuristic. *Higher Education, 43*(3), 281–309. DOI: 10.1023/A:1014699605875

MEA. (2025). *Brief on India–Cambodia bilateral relations*. Ministry of External Affairs Government of India. https://www.mea.gov.in/Portal/ForeignRelation/Cambodia-2025.pdf

Nguyen, T. V., Cong Pham, H., Nhat Nguyen, M., Zhou, L., & Akbari, M. (2023). Data-driven review of blockchain applications in supply chain management: Key research themes and future directions. *International Journal of Production Research, 61*(23), 8213–8235. DOI: 10.1080/00207543.2023.2165190

Nussbaum, M. C. (2016). *Not for profit: Why democracy needs the humanities* (Updated ed.). Princeton University Press.

Nye, J. S. (2004). *Soft power: The means to success in world politics*. Public Affairs.

O'Dowd, R. (2018). From telecollaboration to virtual exchange: State-of-the-art and the role of UNICollaboration in moving forward. *Research-publishing. net, 1*, 1–23. DOI: 10.14705/rpnet.2018.jve.1

OECD. (2019). *OECD Principles on Artificial Intelligence*. Paris: Organisation for Economic Co-operation and Development. https://oecd.ai/en/ai-principles

OECD. (2021). *21st-century readers: Developing literacy skills in a digital world*. Organisation for Economic Co-operation and Development Publishing., DOI: 10.1787/a83d84cb-

OECD. (2023a). *OECD digital education outlook 2023: Towards an effective digital education ecosystem*. OECD Publishing., DOI: 10.1787/c74f03de-

OECD. (2023b). *Public governance review: Southeast Asia 2023*. OECD Publishing. https://www.oecd.org/en/publications/serials/oecd-public-governance-reviews_g1g1190c.html

Peters, G. P. (2008). From production-based to consumption-based national emission inventories. *Ecological Economics, 65*(1), 13–23. DOI: 10.1016/j.ecolecon.2007.10.014

Piaget, J. (1952). *The origins of intelligence in children.* International Universities Press. DOI: 10.1037/11494-000

Piaget, J. (1970). Science of education and the psychology of the child. Trans. D. Coltman.

Ross, J., & Collier, A. (2016). Complexity, mess, and not-yetness teaching online with emerging technologies. In Veletsianos, G. (Ed.), *Emergence and innovation in digital learning: Foundations and applications* (Vol. 80, pp. 50–70). ACUP.

Secretariat, A. S. E. A. N. (2021). *AADMER work programme 2021-2025.* ASEAN Secretariat., https://asean.org/wp-content/uploads/2021/08/AADMER-Work-Programme-2021-2025.pdf

Secretariat, A. S. E. A. N. (2022). *Digital policy action areas for a connected ASEAN: ASEAN best practice benchmarking and an action plan for regional harmonization.* ITU Publications Asia-Pacific Region. https://asean.org/wp-content/uploads/2024/03/Digital-Policy-Action-Areas-for-a-Connected-ASEAN.pdf

Selwyn, N. (2019). *Should robots replace teachers?: AI and the future of education.* John Wiley & Sons.

Selwyn, N. (2021). *Education and technology: Key issues and debates.* Bloomsbury Publishing.

Tilak, J. B., Tilak, J. B., & Ghosh. (2018). *Education and development in India.* Springer. DOI: 10.1007/978-981-13-0250-3

Trilling, B., & Fadel, C. (2009). *21st century skills: Learning for life in our times.* John Wiley & Sons.

UNESCO. (2015). *Quality physical education (QPE): Guidelines for policy-makers.* UNESCO. https://unesdoc.unesco.org/images/0023/002311/231101E.pdf

UNESCO. (2021a). *AI and education: Guidance for policymakers.* United Nations Educational, Scientific and Cultural Organization., DOI: 10.54675/PCSP7350

UNESCO. (2021b). *Futures of education: Learning to become.* Paris: UNESCO. https://unesdoc.unesco.org/ark:/48223/pf0000370801

UNESCO. (2021c). *Recommendation on the ethics of artificial intelligence.* Paris: UNESCO. https://unesdoc.unesco.org/ark:/48223/pf0000381137

Williamson, B., Macgilchrist, F., & Potter, J. (2023). Re-examining AI, automation and datafication in education. *48*(1), 1–5. DOI: 10.1080/17439884.2023.2167830

Zawacki-Richter, O., Marín, V. I., Bond, M., & Gouverneur, F. (2019). Systematic review of research on artificial intelligence applications in higher education–where are the educators? *International Journal of Educational Technology in Higher Education, 16*(1), 1–27. DOI: 10.1186/s41239-019-0171-0

Zhang, Q., Mohammad Ismail, M. I. R., & Zakaria, A. R. B. (2025). Enhancing intercultural competence in technical higher education through AI-driven frameworks. *Scientific Reports, 15*(1), 1–15. DOI: 10.1038/s41598-025-03303-1 PMID: 40594064

KEY TERMS AND DEFINITIONS

Artificial Intelligence (AI): Machine-based intelligence and self-reasoning override the learning capabilities of human beings. For instance, in a particular domain, a computer can undertake a myriad of tasks, all of which require human intelligence. In the context of education, AI enables the adjustment of learning, giving personalized feedback, and obtaining metrics to enhance the levels of teaching and academic improvement.

ASEAN–India Education: the educational cooperation and collaboration as established and supported in the Partnership Agreement between the Association of Southeast Asian Nations and India in the domain of education for developing educational structures and systems, and the transfer of knowledge and human capital within a particular region.

Ethical AI: Instructors, promoters, and policymakers' behaviors and values toward the development, implementation, and AI systems in the educational sector, and society in general, that incorporate equity, and justice, as well as the values of transparency, openness, inclusivity, and human rights.

Global Learning: Refers to educational experiences that enable learners to comprehend, participate in, and act within a globalized and interdependent setting and that incorporate cross-cultural understanding, global awareness and responsibility, as well as cooperative problem solving.

Hybrid Pedagogy: A blended educational approach that combines face-to-face and online learning environments to create flexible, interactive, and learner-centred experiences. It emphasizes the integration of digital technologies with human interaction to foster engagement, reflection, and collaboration across physical and virtual spaces.

Intercultural Collaboration: is fostering cooperation, learning, and sharing of knowledge among people or organizations of diverse cultural backgrounds. In cross-border education, it provides opportunities for participants to interact and engage meaningfully, thus developing empathy, cultural competencies, and global awareness.

Sustainable Development Goals (SDGs): In the year 2015, the United Nations established 17 particular goals as a framework to attain global peace, global growth, and global environmental sustenance. Within this study, SDG 4 (Quality Education) and SDG 17 (Partnerships for the Goals) are the main objectives of this study to provide equitable, inclusive, and collaborative hybrid education.

Chapter 3

Beyond Optimization: Learning Analytics, Cultural Intelligence, and Human Flourishing in Hybrid Education

Ngan Truong
https://orcid.org/0000-0002-8925-6226
University of Economics and Finance, Ho Chi Minh City, Vietnam

Muhammad Hasan
http://orcid.org/0000-0003-1112-2110
Universitas Negeri Makassar, Indonesia

ABSTRACT

The rise of learning analytics (LA) and artificial intelligence (AI) has enabled educators to personalize learning experiences at an unprecedented scale. This chapter explores how learning analytics can be ethically and intelligently applied to support learner autonomy, inclusivity, and well-being across intercultural hybrid learning environments. Drawing on frameworks from educational data science, humanistic psychology, and cultural intelligence (CQ), the chapter proposes a model of "Culturally Intelligent Analytics" (CIA) that integrates human judgment with AI precision. It highlights how data-informed decision-making can enhance not replace the emotional, ethical, and intercultural dimensions of learning. Through theoretical synthesis and real-world examples, the chapter redefines personalization as a process of nurturing potential and cultural belonging rather than optimizing performance metrics.

DOI: 10.4018/979-8-3373-7462-8.ch003

1. BACKGROUND AND RATIONALE

Learning analytics the collection, measurement, and interpretation of learner data for improving teaching and learning has evolved rapidly over the past decade. In hybrid education, AI-powered analytics systems now track participation, predict performance, and recommend personalized resources. Proponents argue that these technologies democratize education by offering adaptive learning pathways tailored to each student's needs. However, critics warn that excessive reliance on algorithmic decision-making risks reducing learners to data points, overlooking the human complexity that drives authentic learning.

Moreover, cultural and contextual differences profoundly influence how data should be interpreted. For instance, patterns of silence, turn-taking, or collaboration vary across cultures and may be misread as disengagement or underperformance by culturally blind algorithms. Similarly, the assumption that "more activity equals more learning" reflects a Western behavioral paradigm that may not apply globally. As such, learning analytics can unintentionally reinforce inequities rather than alleviate them.

This chapter addresses this critical tension by positioning learning analytics within the broader philosophy of human flourishing (Seligman, 2011; Nussbaum, 2013) and cultural intelligence (Ang & Van Dyne, 2015). It argues that hybrid pedagogy must move beyond performance optimization toward value-driven personalization where data serves as a mirror for reflection, not a mechanism of surveillance. The integration of AI in hybrid learning must thus preserve human dignity, ethical agency, and intercultural understanding.

2. THEORETICAL FOUNDATIONS AND LITERATURE REVIEW

While the potential for data-driven personalization in hybrid education is vast, its implementation must be grounded in established theoretical frameworks and a critical understanding of existing empirical evidence. This section provides a systematic review of the foundations of learning analytics (LA), its measured effectiveness, and its relationship with established learning theories.

The field of learning analytics emerged from a need to make sense of the vast amounts of data generated in digital learning environments. Siemens and Long (2011) provided the foundational definition that continues to guide the field: the "collection, measurement, analysis and reporting of data about learners and their contexts, for purposes of understanding and optimizing learning and the environments in which it occurs." This definition emphasizes that analytics are not merely about tracking, but about the *purpose* of improvement. Ferguson (2012) further established the field's origins by tracing its evolution from business intelligence and web analytics, arguing that for LA to be truly transformative, it must move beyond simple reporting toward predictive and prescriptive models that are deeply integrated into the pedagogical process. In the context of hybrid education, these foundations underscore the transition of analytics from institutional management tools to core components of the learning experience.

Despite the rapid adoption of LA systems, empirical evidence for their direct impact on learning outcomes remains mixed, necessitating a more cautious and evidence-based approach to implementation. A significant systematic review by Viberg et al. (2018) found that while LA is highly effective at identifying at-risk students, only 9% of studies showed a direct, measurable improvement in learning outcomes. This "effectiveness gap" suggests that data alone is insufficient; the impact of analytics depends heavily on how insights are translated into pedagogical interventions. Furthermore, Wong et al. (2019) argue that the field suffers from a publication bias toward successful pilot projects. They call for the inclusion of more "null or negative results" to build a more realistic and robust evidence base, preventing the "optimization" of systems based on incomplete or overly optimistic data.

For analytics to support human flourishing, they must be aligned with how humans actually learn, particularly through the lens of self-regulated learning (SRL). Zimmerman (2002) identifies three phases of SRL: forethought (goal setting), performance (monitoring), and self-reflection. Culturally intelligent analytics can support these phases by providing learners with "mirrors" for their own behavior, allowing them to adjust their strategies in real-time. However, Winne (2010) cautions that while analytics can provide the feedback loop necessary for monitoring and control, they can also hinder SRL if they are too prescriptive. If an AI system makes all the "monitoring" decisions for the student, it may inadvertently weaken the student's own metacognitive muscles. Therefore, the CIA Framework proposed in this chapter argues that analytics should function as decision-support tools that enhance, rather than replace, the learner's own self-regulatory processes.

Beyond theoretical concerns, large-scale empirical research has begun to document the tangible impact of cultural bias in educational technologies. Kizilcec et al. (2017) provided critical evidence of "completion bias" in Massive Open Online Courses (MOOCs). Their study demonstrated that learners' geographic and linguistic backgrounds are significant predictors of success, with non-native English speakers and individuals from developing countries, specifically those with a low Human Development Index (HDI) facing significantly higher barriers to course completion. This suggests that even supposedly "open" digital environments are often optimized for Western, native-English-speaking learners, inadvertently penalizing those from diverse cultural contexts. Such findings underscore the risk that learning analytics, if left "culturally blind," may reinforce existing structural inequities rather than alleviate them.

3. RESEARCH FOCUS / MISSION

The chapter will employ a conceptual synthesis approach, integrating insights from learning analytics research, intercultural education, and positive psychology. Case examples will include data-informed hybrid classrooms that have successfully applied ethical analytics for inclusivity such as multilingual engagement dashboards or culturally adaptive recommendation systems. The analysis will culminate in the proposal of a Culturally Intelligent Analytics (CIA) Framework for hybrid education, positioning analytics as a tool for ethical empowerment rather than control.

Figure 1. The CIA Framework (Author's own work)

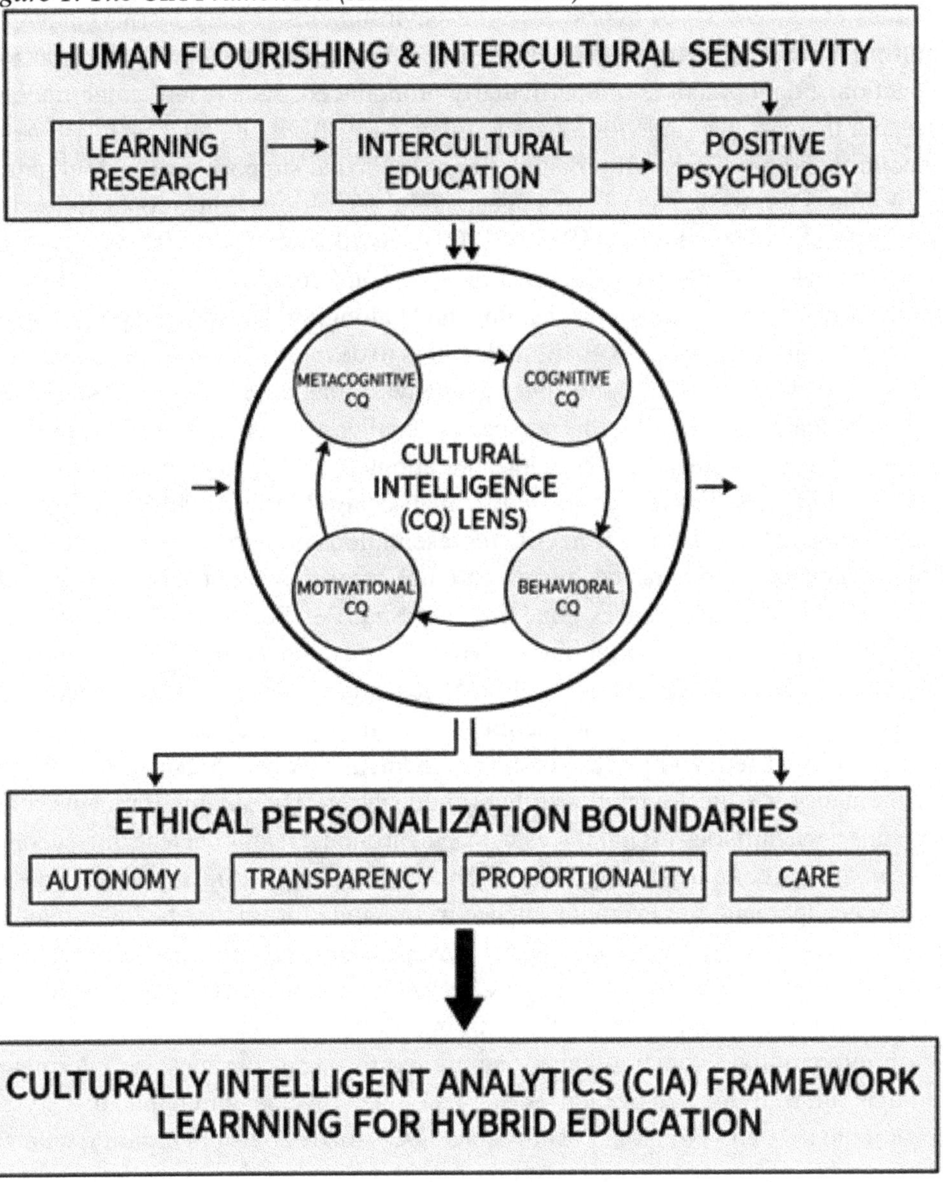

Over the past decade, learning analytics and artificial intelligence have become increasingly central to the design and governance of hybrid education. Initially framed as tools for improving efficiency, prediction, and performance optimization, these technologies have largely emphasized measurable outcomes such as retention, completion, and academic achievement. While such objectives remain institutionally important, a growing body of scholarship has highlighted the ethical, cultural, and humanistic limitations of narrowly predictive approaches (Ferguson et al., 2021; Holmes et al., 2023). In hybrid learning environments, where learners navigate multiple cultural, linguistic, and emotional contexts simultaneously, the risks of reductionist data practices are particularly pronounced. As a result, contemporary research increasingly calls for a paradigmatic shift: from analytics as instruments of control and prediction toward analytics as tools that support human flourishing, intercultural sensitivity, and learner agency (United Nations Educational, Scientific and Cultural Organization [UNESCO], 2021; Prinsloo & Slade, 2017).

Human flourishing in education extends beyond cognitive achievement to encompass well-being, autonomy, meaning, and belonging. Drawing on positive psychology, flourishing involves enabling learners to develop strengths, resilience, and a sense of purpose within supportive social environments (Seligman, 2011). When applied to learning analytics, this perspective challenges designers and educators to reconsider what is measured, how interpretations are made, and whose values are embedded in analytic systems. Recent human-centred learning analytics research emphasizes that data are never neutral representations of learners but are culturally situated constructions shaped by institutional priorities, epistemic assumptions, and technological affordances (Buckingham Shum & Ferguson, 2012). Without explicit ethical and cultural framing, analytics risk misinterpreting learner behaviour, marginalizing non-dominant cultural practices, and reinforcing deficit narratives, particularly for multilingual, international, or minority students.

Intercultural sensitivity is therefore not an ancillary concern but a foundational requirement for ethical analytics in hybrid education. Hybrid environments often combine asynchronous digital traces with synchronous, relational learning encounters, producing complex data ecosystems that capture only partial representations of learner engagement. For example, silence in an online forum may be interpreted as disengagement, despite cultural norms that value listening over verbal participation. Similarly, irregular login patterns may reflect time-zone differences, caregiving responsibilities, or infrastructural constraints rather than low motivation. Scholars in intercultural education have long argued that learning must be interpreted through culturally responsive lenses that recognize diverse communicative styles, epistemologies, and emotional expressions (Deardorff, 2020). Integrating cultural intelligence into learning analytics frameworks thus requires moving beyond surface-level behavioural metrics toward contextualized, reflexive interpretation.

Cultural intelligence, commonly conceptualized as comprising metacognitive, cognitive, motivational, and behavioural dimensions, provides a useful theoretical bridge between intercultural education and analytics design (Ang & Van Dyne, 2015). Metacognitive cultural intelligence involves awareness of one's assumptions and interpretive frameworks, a capacity that is equally relevant to educators and analytics designers. Cognitive cultural intelligence refers to knowledge of cultural norms and learning traditions, while motivational and behavioural dimensions concern openness, adaptability, and appropriate action across cultural contexts. Recent research suggests that analytics systems informed by cultural intelligence principles are better positioned to support inclusive pedagogies, particularly when they enable educators to interrogate data interpretations rather than accept algorithmic outputs uncritically (Li et al., 2025).

The ethical challenges of learning analytics intensify when personalization becomes a dominant design logic. Personalized learning pathways, adaptive recommendations, and predictive risk models promise tailored support but simultaneously raise concerns regarding surveillance, autonomy, and fairness. Idiographic learning analytics, which focus on individual learner trajectories, exemplify this tension by offering granular insights while potentially encroaching on privacy and self-determination (Wise et al., 2024). Ethical scholarship emphasizes that personalization must be bounded by humanistic principles that respect learners as agents rather than objects of optimization. Excessive reliance on automated recommendations can undermine learner autonomy, fostering dependency on algorithmic guidance and narrowing opportunities for exploratory learning (Porayska-Pomsta et al., 2024).

In hybrid education, these ethical boundaries are further complicated by uneven power relations between institutions, educators, and students. Learning analytics dashboards often privilege institutional perspectives, emphasizing metrics aligned with compliance and accountability rather than student-defined goals. From a human flourishing perspective, ethical analytics should instead support learners' capacity to make sense of their own learning data, reflect on progress, and exercise informed choice (Prinsloo & Slade, 2017). This aligns with calls for transparency, explainability, and participatory design in educational AI, where learners and educators are involved in shaping how data are collected, interpreted, and used (UNESCO, 2023).

Balancing data-driven insights with human judgment is therefore central to ethical analytics practice. While AI systems can detect patterns at scale, they lack the contextual sensitivity and moral reasoning required to interpret meaningfully complex human behaviour. Hybrid human–AI models have been proposed as a way forward, positioning analytics as decision-support tools rather than decision-makers (Holmes, 2025). In such models, educators retain interpretive authority, using analytics to inform professional judgment while remaining attentive to learners' lived experiences. This balance is particularly important in culturally diverse settings, where human educators are better equipped to recognize contextual nuances, relational dynamics, and emotional cues that data alone cannot capture.

Conceptual synthesis across learning analytics, intercultural education, and positive psychology reveals a shared emphasis on relationality, reflexivity, and empowerment. Learning analytics research contributes methodological rigor and technological innovation, intercultural education offers interpretive frameworks for cultural meaning-making, and positive psychology foregrounds well-being and growth. Together, these perspectives challenge instrumentalist uses of data and advocate for analytics that support ethical empowerment rather than behavioural control. Emerging case examples illustrate the practical implications of this synthesis. Multilingual engagement dashboards, for instance, allow educators to view participation patterns across languages without privileging a single linguistic norm, while culturally adaptive recommendation systems incorporate learner preferences and contextual constraints rather than relying solely on historical performance data (Buckingham Shum & Ferguson, 2012).

These developments suggest the need for an integrative framework that explicitly embeds cultural intelligence and ethical principles into learning analytics design and use. Rather than treating ethics as an external constraint, such a framework would position ethical reasoning as intrinsic to analytics practice. The proposed Culturally Intelligent Analytics (CIA) Framework responds to this need by reconceptualizing analytics as a mediating practice between data, culture, and human judgment. Before articulating this framework, it is necessary to examine more closely the humanistic boundaries of personalization and the practical strategies educators can employ to balance analytics with professional and ethical responsibility.

The promise of personalization in hybrid education rests on the assumption that data-driven insights can enhance learning relevance, efficiency, and support. However, ethical scholarship cautions that personalization, when implemented without cultural and humanistic safeguards, can exacerbate inequities and diminish learner agency. Predictive models often rely on historical data that reflect existing structural biases, thereby reproducing disadvantage for learners whose educational trajectories deviate from dominant norms (Kizilcec & Lee, 2020). In culturally diverse contexts, this risk is amplified, as algorithms trained on majority populations may misinterpret the behaviours and needs of learners from different cultural or linguistic backgrounds.

Ethical personalization therefore requires a shift from prescriptive adaptation to dialogic support. Rather than determining what learners should do next, analytics systems can provide options, insights, and reflective prompts that invite learner interpretation and choice. Research on explainable and human-centred AI in education emphasizes that learners are more likely to trust and benefit from analytics when systems are transparent and allow users to question or override recommendations (Buckingham Shum & Ferguson, 2012). This aligns with positive psychology's emphasis on autonomy as a core component of well-being, suggesting that ethical analytics should enhance, rather than constrain, learners' sense of control over their learning pathways.

Educators play a critical role in mediating the ethical use of analytics, particularly in hybrid environments where relational cues may be fragmented across modalities. Professional judgment enables educators to contextualize data within broader understandings of learners' circumstances, motivations, and cultural identities. Studies of hybrid human–AI decision-making indicate that educators are most effective when analytics are integrated into reflective pedagogical practices rather than used as authoritative indicators (Holmes, 2025). For example, rather than acting immediately on a risk alert, an educator might engage the learner in conversation, using the data as a starting point for mutual sense-making. Such practices foreground care, dialogue, and trust, which are essential for fostering well-being and intercultural understanding.

Case studies of inclusive analytics practices provide concrete illustrations of how ethical and culturally intelligent approaches can be operationalized. Multilingual engagement dashboards, for instance, have been used in hybrid classrooms to visualize participation across discussion forums, video contributions, and collaborative documents without imposing a single linguistic hierarchy. By allowing educators to view engagement holistically, these dashboards challenge deficit interpretations of language use and support culturally responsive pedagogy (Li et al., 2025). Similarly, culturally adaptive recommendation systems incorporate learner self-reports, contextual constraints, and cultural preferences alongside behavioural data, resulting in more nuanced and respectful forms of personalization.

These examples underscore the importance of participatory design in developing ethical analytics systems. When learners and educators are involved in defining what data matter and how insights are used, analytics become a shared resource rather than an external surveillance mechanism. UNESCO's guidance on human-centred AI emphasizes participation, inclusivity, and respect for human rights as foundational principles for educational AI governance (UNESCO, 2021, 2023). Embedding these principles into analytics design supports intercultural sensitivity by recognizing learners as co-constructors of meaning rather than passive data subjects.

The proposed Culturally Intelligent Analytics (CIA) Framework synthesizes these insights into an integrative conceptual model for hybrid education. At its core, the framework positions cultural intelligence as a mediating lens through which data are interpreted and acted upon. Metacognitive cultural intelligence encourages educators and designers to reflect on their assumptions about engagement, success, and risk. Cognitive cultural intelligence informs the selection and interpretation of indicators by foregrounding knowledge of diverse learning traditions and communication styles. Motivational and behavioural dimensions guide ethical action, emphasizing openness, adaptability, and respect in pedagogical responses to analytics insights.

Within the CIA Framework, ethical boundaries of personalization are articulated through principles of autonomy, transparency, proportionality, and care. Analytics should provide meaningful support without overwhelming learners or constraining choice. Data collection and use should be proportionate to educational purposes, avoiding intrusive monitoring that undermines trust. Transparency ensures that learners understand how their data are used and can contest interpretations, while care emphasizes the relational responsibilities of educators in acting on analytics insights. These principles align with broader ethical frameworks in AI and education, reinforcing the legitimacy and applicability of the CIA approach (Holmes et al., 2023; UNESCO, 2021).

Importantly, the CIA Framework does not reject predictive analytics outright but situates prediction within a broader ethical and cultural context. Predictive insights can be valuable when used reflexively and in combination with human judgment. For example, early warning systems may help identify learners who could benefit from additional support, but decisions about intervention should remain grounded in dialogue, cultural understanding, and professional care. In this way, analytics function as tools for ethical empowerment, enhancing educators' capacity to support diverse learners while respecting their dignity and agency.

Aligning learning analytics and AI with human flourishing and intercultural sensitivity requires a fundamental reorientation of purpose, design, and practice. Moving beyond predictive efficiency entails recognizing the cultural, emotional, and ethical dimensions of learning that data alone cannot capture. Through conceptual synthesis across learning analytics, intercultural education, and positive psychology, this chapter has argued for a culturally intelligent, human-centred approach to analytics in hybrid education. The proposed Culturally Intelligent Analytics Framework offers a pathway for positioning analytics as instruments of ethical empowerment rather than control, supporting inclusive, reflective, and flourishing learning communities in an increasingly hybrid and intercultural educational landscape.

4. EXPECTED CONTRIBUTIONS AND CONCERNS

This chapter makes a substantive theoretical and practical contribution to the fields of learning analytics (LA), artificial intelligence in education, and hybrid pedagogy by advancing the Culturally Intelligent Analytics (CIA) framework. While existing research has extensively examined the technical capabilities of analytics systems, far less attention has been paid to how educators interpret data across cultural contexts, how learners experience analytics emotionally, and how personalization intersects with human flourishing rather than performance optimization alone (Selwyn, 2020; Buckingham Shum & Luckin, 2019). The CIA framework responds to these gaps by reconceptualizing learning analytics as an interpretive, relational, and ethical practice embedded within culturally diverse educational environments.

The first major conceptual contribution of this chapter lies in its redefinition of data ethics within learning analytics. Traditional ethical discussions have often focused on compliance-oriented issues such as privacy protection, data security, and informed consent. While these remain critical, scholars increasingly argue that ethical analytics must extend beyond procedural safeguards to address questions of agency, power, and educational purpose. Prinsloo and Slade (2017) emphasize that learning analytics inherently shape how students are constructed as learners, influencing institutional responses and self-perceptions in ways that can either support or undermine agency. Building on this, the CIA framework reframes data ethics as an ongoing interpretive responsibility. Within this model, ethical analytics are understood as practices that require educators to continually evaluate how data interpretations affect learners' autonomy, dignity, and opportunities for growth. This aligns with human-centered AI principles, stressing that AI systems should augment rather than replace human judgment, particularly in contexts involving complex social and moral considerations (Miao et al., 2021).

The second conceptual contribution lies in the explicit integration of cultural interpretation into learning analytics. Despite growing recognition of diversity, much analytics research continues to rely on behavioral indicators such as frequency of online participation or timeliness of submissions that implicitly assume universal meanings of engagement and success (Cechinel et al., 2020). When applied uncritically, such metrics risk misrepresenting learners whose cultural backgrounds value reflective silence, collective responsibility, or indirect communication (Deardorff, 2020). The CIA framework addresses this by drawing on Cultural Intelligence (CQ) as a foundational lens. CQ offers a robust foundation for contextualizing learner data, encouraging educators to question what data signify rather than accepting algorithmic classifications at face value (Ang & Van Dyne, 2015). This responds directly to Wise and Shaffer's (2019) argument that analytics without theory risk becoming misleading or harmful, as data patterns are divorced from the social and cultural contexts that give them meaning.

The third conceptual dimension, human flourishing, extends learning analytics scholarship beyond its traditional focus on performance metrics and risk prediction. Drawing on positive psychology and self-determination theory, human flourishing is understood as a construct encompassing autonomy, competence, relatedness, and well-being (Ryan & Deci, 2020; Seligman, 2018). Recent studies highlight that analytics-driven interventions can have unintended emotional consequences, including anxiety and feelings of surveillance, particularly when learners perceive data use as punitive or controlling (O'Keeffe et al., 2023). By integrating human flourishing, the CIA framework reframes the purpose of personalization in hybrid education: rather than seeking only to optimize learning paths, it aims to support a learner's sense of agency and belonging.

The chapter advances significant pedagogical contributions by translating the CIA framework into concrete strategies. One such contribution involves the reconceptualization of learning analytics dashboards as reflective tools rather than monitoring mechanisms. While dashboards are common, their impact is highly dependent on design and pedagogical framing (Bodily et al., 2018). Dashboards that emphasize comparative rankings may inadvertently undermine motivation, particularly among students from marginalized backgrounds. The CIA framework advocates for reflective dashboards that prioritize sense-making over surveillance, designed to support learners in interpreting their own data within culturally meaningful contexts (Jivet et al., 2017).

Another pedagogical contribution lies in the promotion of co-design practices for data interpretation. Involving learners in defining what data matter fosters transparency, trust, and shared responsibility (Martinez-Maldonado et al., 2020). In culturally diverse hybrid classrooms, co-design serves an intercultural function by making explicit the values embedded in analytics systems. Furthermore, the framework proposes integrating intercultural reflection prompts within AI-driven feedback systems. Most AI feedback prioritize efficiency and task completion; however, by embedding prompts that invite learners to consider how cultural perspectives or group dynamics influenced their learning, AI systems can support deeper engagement and empathy (Li et al., 2025). This redefines analytics as a tool for ethical empowerment rather than behavioral control.

Beyond the classroom, this chapter addresses the systemic conditions under which CIA can be sustainably enacted. At the institutional level, the framework foregrounds the necessity of rethinking data governance through the lens of cultural plurality. Traditional governance often prioritizes compliance and risk mitigation (Slade & Prinsloo, 2013). CIA argues that institutions must adopt dynamic, dialogic consent models that recognize learners as active participants in the data ecosystem (Ifenthaler & Schumacher, 2016). Transparency is reconceptualized as an ongoing communicative process. Research indicates that student trust is strongly mediated by perceptions of fairness and respect (Drachsler & Greller, 2016; Tsai et al., 2021). Thus, CIA-informed institutions are encouraged to develop "explainable learning analytics" that include culturally accessible explanations of outputs and avoid deficit-oriented framings (Kizilcec, 2016).

The framework also challenges the epistemic assumptions embedded within analytics datasets, which often privilege dominant forms of engagement (Buckingham Shum & Crick, 2012; Gašević et al., 2015). CIA challenges institutions to examine whose learning behaviors are rendered visible and valuable, and whose are rendered anomalous. This shift requires intentional diversification of data sources, such as integrating qualitative narrative feedback and involving diverse stakeholders in model validation (Wise & Shaffer, 2015). Such a shift is consistent with decolonial critiques of educational technology, which caution against the uncritical exportation of Western epistemologies (Adam, 2019; Kizilcec & Lee, 2020).

Finally, the chapter contributes to professional development and policy regulation. CIA positions AI literacy as a form of ethical and cultural competence. Educators must be equipped to analyze cases involving cultural misinterpretation and representation harm (West et al., 2018; Viberg et al., 2020; Ferguson et al., 2016; Prinsloo et al., 2022). At the policy level, the chapter advances the discourse by grounding abstract ethical principles in lived intercultural realities (Miao et al., 2021; OECD, 2021). A key recommendation is the mandatory inclusion of Cultural Impact Assessments as part of institutional deployment. Similar to data protection assessments, these evaluate how analytics systems differentially affect learners from diverse cultural, linguistic, or socioeconomic backgrounds (Selwyn, 2019). By affirming student rights to contextual explanation and contestation, CIA aligns with emerging concepts of data justice, ensuring technology remains a space for ethical imagination (Eubanks, 2018).

5. CONCERNS AND LIMITATIONS

The chapter will also critically engage with several inherent challenges:

- **Data reductionism:** Overemphasis on quantifiable metrics can overlook emotional, social, and cultural aspects of learning.
- **Bias in data interpretation:** Analytics systems may misrepresent learners from minority or high-context cultures.
- **Privacy and consent dilemmas:** Students may lack agency over how their data is collected, interpreted, and shared.
- **Emotional detachment:** Over-personalization risks isolating learners in "algorithmic bubbles," reducing collective learning opportunities.

The chapter will argue that true personalization requires from human wisdom the capacity to interpret data through empathy, culture, and ethics. Learning analytics must therefore evolve from a tool of optimization to a medium of human connection and flourishing, where every data point becomes a dialogue about meaning, growth, and inclusion.

The rapid expansion of learning analytics and artificial intelligence within hybrid education has generated substantial optimism regarding the potential for personalized, data-informed learning. However, alongside these aspirations, a growing body of critical scholarship has identified deep-seated concerns that challenge the ethical, cultural, and pedagogical foundations of analytics-driven personalization. These concerns are not merely technical limitations that can be resolved through improved algorithms or more comprehensive datasets. Rather, they reflect structural tensions inherent in how data are produced, interpreted, and mobilized within educational systems shaped by power asymmetries, cultural diversity, and institutional imperatives. Within the Culturally Intelligent Analytics (CIA) framework, these tensions are understood as boundary conditions that define the limits of responsible analytics use, underscoring the necessity of embedding data ethics, cultural interpretation, and human flourishing as inseparable dimensions of analytics-informed practice.

One of the most pervasive limitations of learning analytics is its tendency toward data reductionism, whereby complex learning processes are translated into simplified, quantifiable indicators. Learning analytics systems predominantly rely on digital traces that are easily captured and processed, such as frequency of platform access, time-on-task, submission punctuality, and visible participation in online forums. While these indicators offer scalable means of monitoring activity, they risk conflating behavioral visibility with meaningful learning (Selwyn, 2019). As Biesta (2010) argues, educational systems increasingly governed by measurement frameworks are prone to valuing what can be counted rather than what truly counts, resulting in a narrowing of educational purpose. In hybrid environments, where learning unfolds across physical, digital, social, and emotional spaces, such reductionism becomes particularly problematic.

From an ethical standpoint, data reductionism constitutes more than an epistemological simplification; it represents a form of misrecognition that can shape how learners are perceived and acted upon. Gašević, Dawson, and Siemens (2015) caution that when analytics are decoupled from learning theory, they risk producing interpretations that are descriptively thin and normatively loaded. Metrics designed to signal engagement or risk may inadvertently encode assumptions about ideal learning behaviors that privilege speed, consistency, and constant interaction. Buckingham Shum and Deakin Crick (2014) demonstrate that dispositions central to lifelong learning, such as perseverance, ethical awareness, and reflective capacity, resist easy quantification and are therefore often excluded from analytics models. When such dimensions are rendered invisible, educational decision-making becomes skewed toward short-term performance optimization rather than holistic development.

Within the CIA framework, this limitation is situated squarely within the domain of data ethics. Ethical analytics are not defined solely by compliance with privacy regulations or data security standards, but by the responsibility to acknowledge what data cannot adequately represent. Wise and Shaffer (2015) argue that analytics systems lacking strong theoretical grounding invite overinterpretation, as educators may infer causality or intent from patterns that merely reflect surface behaviors. Research on analytics dashboards further illustrates this risk, showing that simplified visualizations can obscure contextual variability and reinforce deficit narratives, particularly when learners are compared against normative benchmarks (Knaflic, 2025). The CIA framework therefore insists that ethical analytics require interpretive restraint and reflexivity, recognizing data as partial representations that must be complemented by professional judgment and contextual knowledge.

Closely intertwined with data reductionism is the issue of cultural bias in data interpretation, which poses a significant challenge to inclusive analytics practices in culturally diverse hybrid classrooms. Learning analytics systems are typically developed within dominant educational paradigms that reflect particular cultural values regarding communication, participation, and achievement. Prinsloo and Slade (2017) argue that these systems often construct an implicit archetype of the "successful learner," against which all students are measured. Learners whose practices diverge from this archetype may be framed as disengaged, underperforming, or at risk, even when their behaviors are culturally meaningful and pedagogically appropriate.

Empirical research underscores the extent to which cultural norms shape observable learning behaviors. Sato, Haegele, and Foot (2017) illustrate that silence, frequently interpreted in Western contexts as passivity or lack of engagement, may signify respect, contemplation, or attentiveness in high-context cultures. Similarly, learners from collectivist traditions may prioritize group harmony over individual visibility, resulting in lower levels of overt participation without diminished cognitive engagement. When analytics systems equate learning with visible interaction, they risk systematically misrepresenting such learners. Kizilcec and Lee (2020) provide further evidence that algorithmic models trained on historical data can reproduce and exacerbate existing inequities, particularly when demographic and cultural variables are insufficiently accounted for.

These interpretive biases are not accidental but reflect broader sociotechnical dynamics. Williamson and Eynon (2020) argue that AI systems in education inherit the historical and institutional conditions under which data are produced, including patterns of exclusion and marginalization. Gilliard (2020) extends this critique by highlighting the cultural politics of educational platforms, noting that data infrastructures often prioritize institutional efficiency and scalability over cultural responsiveness. Within hybrid education, where learners from diverse linguistic, cultural, and socioeconomic backgrounds converge, such biases can become amplified, shaping analytics outputs that obscure rather than illuminate learner diversity.

The CIA framework addresses these challenges by positioning cultural interpretation as an essential mediating practice between data and pedagogical action. Rather than assuming that bias can be fully eliminated through technical fixes, the framework emphasizes the role of educators' cultural intelligence in interpreting analytics outputs. Cultural intelligence enables educators to recognize that data patterns are embedded within cultural contexts and to question the normative assumptions underlying analytic classifications. Holmes, Bialik, and Fadel (2019) argue that inclusive AI systems require human oversight capable of contextual judgment, particularly in educational settings characterized by diversity and complexity. In this sense, the CIA framework reframes analytics not as authoritative verdicts but as prompts for culturally informed inquiry and dialogue.

Another significant limitation of learning analytics concerns issues of privacy, consent, and learner agency, which are central to the data ethics dimension of the CIA framework. Although institutions increasingly emphasize transparency and compliance, research consistently demonstrates that students often lack meaningful control over how their data are collected, analyzed, and used. Slade and Prinsloo (2013) identify this imbalance of power as a defining ethical dilemma in learning analytics, noting that consent is frequently implicit, bundled into enrollment processes, or presented in opaque terms. In hybrid learning environments, where participation is mediated through digital platforms, opting out of data collection may be practically impossible without withdrawing from the learning experience altogether.

Empirical studies reveal that students' perceptions of privacy are characterized by ambivalence and resignation. Ifenthaler and Yau (2020) found that while students express concern about data misuse, they often accept analytics practices as inevitable, particularly when institutional expectations are unclear. Tsai et al. (2021) describe this dynamic as a privacy paradox, wherein learners recognize potential risks but feel unable to exercise agency. Prinsloo and Slade (2017) further argue that such conditions render students structurally vulnerable, as analytics-driven decisions may influence academic support, progression, or surveillance without learners' active participation in interpretive processes.

From the perspective of the CIA framework, these findings highlight the inadequacy of consent models that treat ethics as a procedural checkbox rather than a relational practice. Frameworks such as DELICATE offer valuable principles for privacy-aware analytics design, yet they do not fully address the lived experience of learners navigating opaque data ecosystems (Drachsler & Greller, 2016). UNESCO's (2021) guidance on AI in education reinforces the need to foreground learner rights, dignity, and autonomy, emphasizing that ethical AI must be transparent, explainable, and accountable. The CIA framework extends this position by advocating for participatory data practices in which learners are actively involved in decisions about data interpretation and use, transforming consent from a one-time transaction into an ongoing dialogue.

Beyond issues of ethics and culture, learning analytics also present significant challenges for human flourishing, particularly in relation to emotional engagement and social connection. While personalization is often promoted as learner-centered, excessive reliance on individualized analytics can inadvertently fragment learning communities. Kizilcec, Bailenson, and Gomez (2015) demonstrate that adaptive systems may reduce opportunities for social interaction by directing learners along personalized pathways that minimize peer engagement. In hybrid environments, where social presence is already mediated by technology, such tendencies risk exacerbating feelings of isolation and disconnection.

Rienties et al. (2020) caution that analytics-driven personalization can weaken collaborative learning when collective dynamics are subordinated to individual optimization. From a psychological perspective, this trend is troubling, as well-being and motivation are deeply relational phenomena. Seligman's (2011) work in positive psychology emphasizes that flourishing depends on belonging, shared meaning, and positive relationships, not merely on individual achievement. When analytics systems prioritize efficiency and prediction over relational depth, they risk undermining the very conditions that support sustained engagement and growth.

Zuboff's (2019) critique of personalization technologies further illuminates these risks, highlighting how predictive systems can shape behavior in ways that feel intrusive or controlling. Although her analysis extends beyond education, the logic of surveillance and behavioral modulation is increasingly evident in analytics-driven learning environments. When learners perceive analytics as mechanisms of monitoring rather than support, emotional detachment may ensue, eroding trust and intrinsic motivation. Within the CIA framework, human flourishing serves as a normative anchor that constrains the scope of personalization, insisting that analytics must enhance, rather than diminish, learners' sense of autonomy, connection, and meaning.

These interconnected concerns underscore a central argument of this chapter: that learning analytics, while powerful, are fundamentally limited in their capacity to capture the full complexity of human learning. Data reductionism, cultural bias, privacy dilemmas, and emotional detachment are not peripheral challenges but indicators of deeper tensions between technological rationality and educational values. As Biesta (2017) warns, when educational judgment is displaced by technical systems, education risks losing its ethical and democratic character. Selwyn (2022) similarly calls for resisting data determinism, urging educators to reclaim the moral purposes of education in an age of pervasive analytics.

These limitations collectively point toward a deeper, integrative concern: the gradual displacement of human judgment by algorithmic authority within analytics-informed education. As learning analytics systems become more embedded in institutional decision-making, there is a growing risk that educators defer interpretive responsibility to data-driven outputs, treating algorithmic classifications as neutral or objective truths. Biesta (2017) argues that such delegation represents a fundamental misunderstanding of education as a moral and relational practice rather than a technical process of optimization. When analytics are positioned as definitive arbiters of learner needs or potential, the space for professional discretion, ethical reflection, and pedagogical care is diminished.

Within the CIA framework, this tension is understood as a critical boundary condition that cuts across all three dimensions of data ethics, cultural interpretation, and human flourishing. From an ethical standpoint, uncritical reliance on analytics can obscure accountability, as decisions appear to be justified by "what the data say" rather than by explicit human reasoning. Slade and Prinsloo (2013) warn that analytics can function as instruments of power that normalize surveillance while diffusing responsibility across technical systems. When educators are encouraged to trust dashboards and predictive models without interrogating their assumptions, ethical agency is subtly eroded, and learners may be subjected to interventions they neither understand nor consent to.

Cultural interpretation is particularly vulnerable in such contexts, as algorithmic outputs often lack the explanatory depth required to account for cultural variability. Prinsloo and Slade (2017) emphasize that analytics classifications are not merely descriptive but performative; they shape how learners are seen and how they see themselves. A learner labeled as disengaged or at risk may internalize this categorization, even when it reflects a cultural mismatch rather than a lack of effort or ability. Williamson and Eynon (2020) note that such feedback loops can entrench inequality, as biased interpretations become self-reinforcing through repeated data-driven interventions.

The CIA framework responds to this risk by explicitly reasserting the primacy of human sense-making in analytics-informed education. Rather than positioning analytics as decision-makers, the framework conceptualizes them as dialogic artifacts that invite interpretation, questioning, and contextualization. Wise and Shaffer (2015) argue that analytics should support human inquiry rather than replace it, a position echoed in research showing that educators' pedagogical beliefs strongly influence how analytics are interpreted and used. Cultural intelligence, within this model, functions as a safeguard against over-automation by enabling educators to recognize when data patterns conflict with contextual knowledge and lived experience.

Another significant limitation arises from the institutional pressures that shape analytics deployment, particularly in contexts of accountability, efficiency, and performance management. Selwyn (2019) observes that learning analytics are often promoted as solutions to institutional challenges such as retention, completion rates, and resource allocation. While these goals are not inherently problematic, their prioritization can distort the ethical orientation of analytics systems. When institutional metrics become the primary drivers of analytics design, learner well-being and cultural inclusion risk becoming secondary considerations.

This institutional logic can exacerbate data reductionism by privileging indicators that align with managerial objectives rather than educational values. Gašević et al. (2015) caution that such misalignment between analytics and pedagogy undermines the legitimacy of data-informed interventions. Within the CIA framework, this tension highlights the importance of aligning analytics practices with explicit educational purposes grounded in human flourishing. Seligman's (2011) conception of well-being underscores that education should support not only achievement but also meaning, relationships, and personal growth. Analytics systems oriented solely toward efficiency may inadvertently undermine these broader aims.

Emotional dimensions of learning further complicate the ethics of personalization. While analytics-driven feedback is often designed to be timely and adaptive, it may lack the affective sensitivity required to support learners' emotional experiences. Rienties et al. (2020) demonstrate that analytics interventions can influence learners' motivation in unintended ways, particularly when feedback is perceived as impersonal or prescriptive. In hybrid environments, where opportunities for informal emotional support may already be limited, the emotional tone of analytics feedback becomes especially consequential.

Noddings' (2013) ethics of care offers a critical lens through which to examine this limitation. Care, in this framework, is relational and responsive, grounded in attentiveness to the needs and perspectives of others. Algorithmic systems, by contrast, operate through generalization and pattern recognition, making it difficult to respond to individual emotional contexts with genuine empathy. When analytics-driven personalization substitutes for human interaction rather than complementing it, learners may experience a sense of emotional detachment, perceiving education as a transactional process rather than a relational endeavor.

Zuboff's (2019) analysis of surveillance capitalism further illuminates the psychological implications of pervasive data monitoring. Although educational analytics are typically framed as supportive rather than extractive, the constant visibility of learner behavior can generate feelings of being watched or judged. Such perceptions may lead learners to adapt their behavior strategically to satisfy metrics rather than to engage authentically with learning tasks. From a human flourishing perspective, this dynamic undermines autonomy, as learners' actions become oriented toward algorithmic approval rather than intrinsic motivation.

The CIA framework explicitly resists this trajectory by defining personalization as an ethical practice bounded by respect for learner autonomy and dignity. Personalization, within this model, is not synonymous with prediction or behavioral steering but with the creation of conditions that enable learners to reflect, choose, and grow. UNESCO's (2021) guidance on AI in education reinforces the importance of explainability and learner involvement, emphasizing that systems should empower users to understand and question algorithmic processes. The CIA framework operationalizes this principle by advocating for analytics practices that foreground dialogue, transparency, and shared interpretation.

Taken together, these concerns underscore the argument that learning analytics must be approached with epistemic humility and ethical vigilance. Data, while valuable, are inherently incomplete representations of learning, shaped by cultural norms, institutional priorities, and technological affordances. Biesta (2010) reminds us that education is fundamentally concerned with questions of purpose and value that cannot be resolved through measurement alone. Selwyn (2022) similarly argues that reclaiming education in the age of data requires resisting narratives that frame analytics as inevitable or inherently beneficial.

The CIA framework positions these limitations not as reasons to abandon learning analytics but as imperatives to rethink their role within hybrid education. By integrating data ethics, cultural interpretation, and human flourishing, the framework offers a principled approach to navigating the tensions identified in this section. It insists that analytics should remain subordinate to human judgment, guided by empathy, cultural awareness, and ethical responsibility. In this vision, every data point becomes an invitation to dialogue rather than a trigger for automated control, and personalization becomes a means of supporting inclusive, meaningful learning rather than an end in itself.

Ultimately, the concerns and limitations outlined here converge on a central claim: that true personalization in hybrid education requires human wisdom. Wisdom, in this context, is not opposed to data but transcends it, encompassing the capacity to interpret information in light of ethical values, cultural contexts, and relational commitments. Learning analytics, when situated within such a framework, can contribute to human flourishing by supporting reflection, connection, and growth. Without this anchoring in human wisdom, however, analytics risk narrowing educational horizons, reinforcing inequities, and diminishing the relational foundations upon which meaningful learning depends.

REFERENCES

Ang, S., & Van Dyne, L. (2015). *Handbook of cultural intelligence: Theory, measurement, and applications*. Routledge. DOI: 10.4324/9781315703855

Bodily, R., Ikahihifo, T. K., Mackley, B., & Graham, C. R. (2018). The design, development, and implementation of student-facing learning analytics dashboards. *Journal of Computing in Higher Education*, *30*(3), 572–598. DOI: 10.1007/s12528-018-9186-0

Buckingham Shum, S., & Crick, R. D. (2012, April). Learning dispositions and transferable competencies: pedagogy, modelling and learning analytics. In *Proceedings of the 2nd international conference on learning analytics and knowledge* (pp. 92-101). DOI: 10.1145/2330601.2330629

Buckingham Shum, S., & Ferguson, R. (2012). Social learning analytics. *Journal of Educational Technology & Society*, *15*(3), 3–26.

Buckingham Shum, S., & Luckin, R. (2019). Learning analytics and AI: Politics, pedagogy and practices. *British Journal of Educational Technology*, *50*(6), 2785–2793. DOI: 10.1111/bjet.12880

Cechinel, C., Ochoa, X., Lemos dos Santos, H., Carvalho Nunes, J. B., Rodés, V., & Marques Queiroga, E. (2020). Mapping learning analytics initiatives in Latin America. *British Journal of Educational Technology*, *51*(4), 892–914. DOI: 10.1111/bjet.12941

Deardorff, D. K. (2020). *Manual for developing intercultural competencies: Story circles*. Taylor & Francis.

Drachsler, H., & Greller, W. (2016, April). Privacy and analytics: it's a DELICATE issue a checklist for trusted learning analytics. In *Proceedings of the sixth international conference on learning analytics & knowledge* (pp. 89-98). DOI: 10.1145/2883851.2883893

Ferguson, R., Hoel, T., Scheffel, M., & Drachsler, H. (2016). Guest editorial: Ethics and privacy in learning analytics. *Journal of Learning Analytics*, *3*(1), 5–15. DOI: 10.18608/jla.2016.31.2

Gašević, D., Dawson, S., & Siemens, G. (2015). Let's not forget: Learning analytics are about learning. *TechTrends*, *59*(1), 64–71. DOI: 10.1007/s11528-014-0822-x

Holmes, W. (2025, November). AI, education, and children's rights. []. Frontiers Media SA.]. *Frontiers in Education*, *10*, 1656736. DOI: 10.3389/feduc.2025.1656736

Holmes, W., Bialik, M., & Fadel, C. (2019). *Artificial intelligence in education promises and implications for teaching and learning*. Center for Curriculum Redesign.

Holmes, W., Bialik, M., & Fadel, C. (2023). *Artificial intelligence in education*. Globethics Publications.

Ifenthaler, D., & Schumacher, C. (2016). Student perceptions of privacy principles for learning analytics. *Educational Technology Research and Development, 64*(5), 923–938. DOI: 10.1007/s11423-016-9477-y

Ifenthaler, D., & Yau, J. Y. K. (2020). Utilising learning analytics to support study success. *Educational Technology Research and Development, 68*(4), 1961–1988. DOI: 10.1007/s11423-020-09788-z

Jivet, I., Scheffel, M., Drachsler, H., & Specht, M. (2017). Awareness is not enough: Pitfalls of learning analytics dashboards in the educational practice. In *European conference on technology enhanced learning* (pp. 82-96). Springer, Cham. DOI: 10.1007/978-3-319-66610-5_7

Kizilcec, R. F. (2016). How much information? Effects of transparency on trust in an algorithmic interface. In *Proceedings of the 2016 CHI Conference on Human Factors in Computing Systems (CHI '16)* (pp. 2390–2395). ACM.

Kizilcec, R. F., & Lee, H. (2020). Algorithmic fairness in education. *Educational Technology Research and Development, 68*, 1–20. DOI: 10.48550/arXiv.2007.05443

Kizilcec, R. F., Pérez-Sanagustín, M., & Maldonado, J. J. (2017). Self-regulated learning strategies predict learner behavior and goal attainment in Massive Open Online Courses. *Computers & Education, 104*, 18–33. DOI: 10.1016/j.compedu.2016.10.001

Knaflic, C. N. (2025). *Storytelling with data: A data visualization guide for business professionals*. John Wiley & Sons.

Martinez-Maldonado, R., Echeverria, V., Fernandez Nieto, G., & Buckingham Shum, S. (2020, April). From data to insights: A layered storytelling approach for multimodal learning analytics. In *Proceedings of the 2020 chi conference on human factors in computing systems* (pp. 1-15). DOI: 10.1145/3313831.3376148

Miao, F., Holmes, W., Huang, R., & Zhang, H. (2021). *AI and education: Guidance for policy-makers. United Nations Educational, Scientific and Cultural Organization*. UNESCO., https://unesdoc.unesco.org/ark:/48223/pf0000376709

OECD. (2021). AI and the future of skills, Volume 1: Capabilities and assessments. OECD Publishing. DOI: 10.1787/5ee71f34-en

Porayska-Pomsta, K., Holmes, W., & Nemorin, S. (2024). The Ethics of AI in Education. In du Boulay, B., Mitrović, A., & Yacef, K. (Eds.), *Handbook of Artificial Intelligence in Education*. Edward Elgar Publishing.

Prinsloo, P., & Slade, S. (2017). An elephant in the learning analytics room: The obligation to act. *Proceedings of the 7th International Learning Analytics & Knowledge Conference*, 46–55. DOI: 10.1145/3027385.3027406

Prinsloo, P., Slade, S., & Khalil, M. (Eds.). (2022). *Learning analytics in open and distributed learning: Potential and challenges*. Springer Nature. DOI: 10.1007/978-981-19-0786-9

Ryan, R. M., & Deci, E. L. (2020). Intrinsic and extrinsic motivation from a self-determination theory perspective: Definitions, theory, practices, and future directions. *Contemporary Educational Psychology*, *61*, 101860. DOI: 10.1016/j.cedpsych.2020.101860

Seligman, M. (2018). PERMA and the building blocks of well-being. *The Journal of Positive Psychology*, *13*(4), 333–335. DOI: 10.1080/17439760.2018.1437466

Seligman, M. E. P. (2011). *Flourish*. Free Press., DOI: 10.1007/978-94-017-9088-8

Selwyn, N. (2019). What's the problem with learning analytics? *Journal of Learning Analytics*, *6*(3), 11–19. DOI: 10.18608/jla.2019.63.3

Selwyn, N. (2020). Re-imagining 'learning analytics'… a case for starting again? *The Internet and Higher Education*, *46*, 100745. DOI: 10.1016/j.iheduc.2020.100745

Selwyn, N. (2022). The future of AI and education: Some cautionary notes. *European Journal of Education*, *57*(4), 620–631. DOI: 10.1111/ejed.12532

Slade, S., & Prinsloo, P. (2013). Learning analytics: Ethical issues and dilemmas. *The American Behavioral Scientist*, *57*(10), 1510–1529. DOI: 10.1177/0002764213479366

Tsai, Y. S., Whitelock-Wainwright, A., & Gašević, D. (2021). More than figures on your laptop:(Dis) trustful implementation of learning analytics. *Journal of Learning Analytics*, *8*(3), 81–100. DOI: 10.18608/jla.2021.7379

United Nations Educational, Scientific and Cultural Organization [UNESCO]. (2021). AI and Education: Guidance for Policy-Makers. (UNESCO Digital Library, https://unesdoc.unesco.org/ark:/48223/pf0000376709)

Viberg, O., Khalil, M., & Baars, M. (2020, March). Self-regulated learning and learning analytics in online learning environments: A review of empirical research. In *Proceedings of the tenth international conference on learning analytics & knowledge* (pp. 524-533). DOI: 10.1145/3375462.3375483

West, D., Tasir, Z., Luzeckyj, A., Na, K. S., Toohey, D., Abdullah, Z., & Price, R. (2018). Learning analytics experience among academics in Australia and Malaysia: A comparison. *Australasian Journal of Educational Technology*, *34*(3). Advance online publication. DOI: 10.14742/ajet.3836

Williamson, B. (2017). Big data in education: The digital future of learning, policy and practice. *Sage (Atlanta, Ga.)*. Advance online publication. DOI: 10.4135/9781529714920

Wise, A. F., & Shaffer, D. W. (2015). Why theory matters. *Journal of Learning Analytics*, *2*(2), 5–9. DOI: 10.18608/jla.2015.22.2

Zuboff, S. (2019). *The age of surveillance capitalism*. PublicAffairs., DOI: 10.2307/j.ctvbnm3gz

Chapter 4
Reconceptualising Artificial Intelligence in Education:
Ethical and Cultural Dimensions

Duy Le Anh Tran
http://orcid.org/0000-0001-9979-045X
Ho Chi Minh City University of Economics and Finance, Vietnam

Frederic Gautier
University Paris 1 Pantheon-Sorbonne, France

ABSTRACT

The growing integration of artificial intelligence (AI) in education has illuminated not only the transformative potential of technology but also its ethical vulnerabilities. As AI systems mediate learning processes, assessment, and decision-making, concerns about algorithmic bias, data privacy, and cultural representation have become central to discussions on hybrid pedagogy. This chapter explores how educators and institutions move beyond surface-level awareness of bias toward the development of an ethical and culturally responsive framework for AI use in education. It examines how biases embedded in data, design, and deployment stages affect learning equity across cultural contexts. Through a combination of ethical theory, intercultural analysis, and case-based evidence, the chapter argues for a paradigm of AI responsibility grounded in transparency, inclusivity, and human dignity. Ultimately, it supports educators, policymakers, and technologists to ensure that hybrid pedagogies not only leverage AI's capabilities but also uphold fairness, trust, and cultural respect..

DOI: 10.4018/979-8-3373-7462-8.ch004

1. INTRODUCTION

AI systems increasingly shape how learning content is delivered, how students are evaluated, and how educational institutions make strategic decisions. Yet, these systems are not neutral. They are trained on datasets reflecting social structures, economic disparities, and cultural norms, many of which reproduce historical inequities. In educational settings, algorithmic bias can manifest in predictive analytics for student performance, automated grading systems, or adaptive learning tools that misinterpret learners' behaviors due to cultural or linguistic differences.

As UNESCO (2023) and the OECD (2022) emphasized that ethical AI in education is not solely a technological concern but a cultural and social one. When algorithms privilege Western epistemologies or fail to represent non-dominant languages and cultural expressions, they risk creating new forms of digital colonization. For example, automated language feedback systems often penalize students for culturally specific rhetorical structures, while AI-based proctoring tools have been criticized for racialized facial recognition errors.

This chapter argues that addressing algorithmic bias requires a multi-level ethical framework, one that incorporates philosophical ethics, intercultural sensitivity, and institutional accountability. Ethical reflection must extend beyond compliance checklists to reimagine the fundamental question: What kind of humanity do we wish to cultivate through AI-enabled education? In doing so, hybrid pedagogy becomes a moral project, not merely a technical one grounded in equity, transparency, and respect for diverse human experiences.

2. RESEARCH FOCUS

2.1. Ethical Vulnerabilities of AI in Hybrid Education: Bias, Power, and Cultural Meaning

Adopting a critical interpretive approach, the chapter will analyze existing literature on AI ethics (Floridi, 2019; Boddington, 2021), intercultural communication, and responsible innovation. It will incorporate illustrative case studies such as AI proctoring controversies, automated essay scoring bias, and adaptive learning inequities to demonstrate how ethical lapses emerge in real educational contexts. The analysis will culminate in the proposal of a Culturally Responsive AI Ethics Framework (CRAEF) tailored for hybrid learning systems.

The rapid expansion of artificial intelligence in education has fundamentally altered how knowledge is delivered, assessed, and governed within hybrid and online learning environments. AI-driven systems now shape curriculum personalization, learner analytics, automated assessment, and institutional decision-making at scale. While these technologies promise efficiency and inclusivity, their integration has also exposed profound ethical vulnerabilities. Much of the existing discourse has focused on algorithmic bias as a technical flaw that can be corrected through improved data or fairness metrics. However, such an approach risks oversimplifying a deeply socio-cultural phenomenon. Bias in educational AI is not merely a computational anomaly, but a reflection of historical inequities, epistemological dominance, and value-laden design choices embedded within socio-technical systems (Barocas & Selbst, 2016; Floridi et al., 2018).

In hybrid pedagogical contexts, where digital systems increasingly mediate human interaction, ethical concerns cannot be disentangled from cultural meaning-making. AI systems are trained, deployed, and interpreted within specific cultural and institutional logics, often privileging dominant Western epistemologies and normative assumptions about learning, language, and assessment. As a result, ethical AI in education must be understood not only as a matter of technical fairness but as a moral and cultural project that interrogates whose knowledge is valued, whose identities are recognized, and whose agency is preserved (Williamson & Eynon, 2020). This chapter advances the argument that moving beyond algorithmic bias requires a shift toward culturally responsive ethical frameworks that foreground human dignity, pluralism, and institutional accountability in hybrid education.

Algorithmic bias has been extensively documented across domains, including education, healthcare, and criminal justice, where data-driven systems have been shown to reproduce and amplify existing inequalities (O'Neil, 2016; Noble, 2018). In educational settings, bias commonly manifests in predictive learning analytics, automated essay scoring, facial recognition-based proctoring systems, and adaptive learning platforms. These tools often rely on historical datasets that encode disparities related to race, socioeconomic status, language proficiency, and geographic location. When such data are treated as neutral representations of learner behavior, AI systems risk normalizing inequitable outcomes as objective predictions (Baker & Hawn, 2022).

Research in learning analytics demonstrates that predictive models used to identify "at-risk" students frequently correlate academic risk with demographic proxies rather than pedagogically meaningful indicators, thereby reinforcing deficit narratives about marginalized learners (Kizilcec & Lee, 2020). Similarly, automated essay scoring systems have been shown to favor dominant linguistic patterns and rhetorical structures, penalizing students whose writing reflects culturally distinct modes of argumentation or narrative organization (Perelman, 2014; Williamson et al., 2023). These examples underscore that algorithmic bias is not an isolated technical issue but a structural outcome of design decisions, institutional priorities, and cultural assumptions about what constitutes valid knowledge and performance.

Crucially, fairness in AI cannot be reduced to statistical parity or accurate metrics. Educational values such as formative learning, creativity, and epistemic diversity often conflict with narrow optimization goals embedded in algorithmic systems (Holmes et al., 2022). As Barocas, Hardt, and Narayanan (2019) argue, formal definitions of fairness inevitably involve normative trade-offs that must be negotiated through ethical and political deliberation rather than purely technical fixes. In education, these trade-offs are inseparable from cultural context, as notions of merit, success, and intelligence vary across societies and learning traditions.

While bias has received substantial scholarly attention, a growing body of research highlights additional ethical risks associated with AI adoption in education. These include threats to learner autonomy, privacy, transparency, and psychological well-being, all of which are intensified in hybrid learning environments where digital surveillance becomes normalized (Prinsloo & Slade, 2017; Zuboff, 2019). AI-driven monitoring tools, such as learning analytics dashboards and remote proctoring software, often collect granular behavioral data without meaningful informed consent, raising concerns about power asymmetries between institutions and learners.

Remote proctoring technologies provide a particularly salient example of ethical overreach. Studies have documented racialized errors in facial recognition, disproportionate stress among students with disabilities, and cultural misinterpretations of eye contact, body movement, or domestic learning spaces (Swauger, 2020; Gilliard, 2017). These systems not only risk false accusations of misconduct but also erode trust and psychological safety, transforming assessment into a surveillance-driven practice. Such outcomes reveal how ethical harm emerges not solely from biased algorithms but from broader institutional choices that prioritize control and efficiency over care and equity.

Transparency and explainability constitute another major ethical challenge. Many AI systems used in education operate as "black boxes," offering predictions or recommendations without intelligible explanations for educators or learners. This opacity undermines pedagogical judgment and limits learners' ability to contest or understand decisions that affect their academic trajectories (Burrell, 2016; Selbst & Barocas, 2018). In culturally diverse classrooms, the lack of explainability exacerbates misunderstandings, as learners may interpret AI feedback through different cultural frames, leading to confusion or mistrust. Ethical AI in education therefore requires not only technically interpretable models but also culturally meaningful explanations that align with local pedagogical practices.

In response to these challenges, scholars and international organizations have proposed ethical frameworks that situate AI within broader human-centered and rights-based paradigms. Floridi et al. (2018) articulate a foundational framework for AI ethics grounded in principles of beneficence, non-maleficence, autonomy, justice, and explicability. While influential, such principles must be operationalized within educational contexts that involve complex relational dynamics between learners, educators, institutions, and technologies. Education is not merely a service sector but a moral practice concerned with human development, socialization, and cultural transmission.

2.2. Toward a Culturally Responsive AI Ethics Framework for Hybrid Learning

UNESCO's Recommendation on the Ethics of Artificial Intelligence represents a significant advancement in this regard by explicitly linking AI ethics to cultural diversity, linguistic inclusion, and social justice (UNESCO, 2023). The Recommendation emphasizes that AI systems in education should support plural knowledge systems and avoid reinforcing epistemic hierarchies that marginalize non-dominant cultures. This position challenges technocentric narratives that frame AI as universally applicable and instead calls for contextualized ethical governance informed by local values and community participation.

Complementing this global perspective, Holmes et al. (2022) propose a community-wide ethical framework for AI in education that foregrounds participatory design, stakeholder engagement, and shared responsibility. Their work highlights that ethical AI cannot be achieved through isolated technical interventions but requires collective deliberation involving educators, learners, policymakers, and technologists. Importantly, this framework recognizes educators not as passive users of AI tools but as ethical agents whose professional judgment mediates how AI systems are interpreted and enacted in practice. Such an approach aligns with intercultural pedagogical theories that emphasize dialogue, reflexivity, and relational ethics in diverse learning environments.

A central limitation of many AI ethics frameworks is their insufficient engagement with culture as a constitutive dimension of learning. Culture shapes not only language use and communication styles but also epistemological assumptions about knowledge, authority, and learning processes. When AI systems are trained predominantly on data from the Global North and designed according to Western educational norms, they risk enacting what scholars describe as epistemic injustice, whereby certain ways of knowing are systematically devalued or erased (Fricker, 2007; Bhatt et al., 2023).

In hybrid education, epistemic injustice manifests when adaptive learning systems prioritize standardized content pathways that marginalize local curricula or indigenous knowledge systems. Similarly, natural language processing tools often struggle with code-switching, non-standard dialects, or culturally embedded metaphors, leading to misclassification or negative feedback for linguistically diverse learners (Blodgett et al., 2020). These limitations are not incidental but reflect broader power asymmetries in data production, model development, and market dominance within the global AI industry.

Intercultural communication research further demonstrates that learners' engagement with AI is mediated by culturally specific expectations about authority, feedback, and relationality. For example, students from high-context cultures may interpret automated feedback as impersonal or disrespectful, while others may view algorithmic recommendations as more objective than human judgment (Hofstede et al., 2010; Cummings-Koether et al., 2024). Ethical AI design must therefore account for cultural variability in meaning-making, rather than assuming a universal learner model.

Taken together, these considerations suggest that hybrid pedagogy enabled by AI is inherently a moral endeavor. Decisions about data collection, model deployment, and pedagogical integration reflect values about efficiency, equity, and human development. Treating ethics as an afterthought or compliance requirement risks perpetuating harm under the guise of innovation. Instead, ethical reflection must be embedded into the very conception of hybrid learning environments, guiding how AI augments rather than replaces human judgment and cultural responsiveness.

This reframing positions educators and institutions as stewards of ethical practice rather than mere adopters of technology. It also demands that AI systems be evaluated not only in terms of learning outcomes but also in relation to their impact on learner agency, cultural identity, and trust. By situating algorithmic bias within a broader ethical and cultural analysis, this chapter lays the groundwork for a more holistic framework that aligns AI innovation with the fundamental purposes of education.

While ethical principles for artificial intelligence are now widely articulated in policy documents and academic literature, a persistent gap remains between abstract ethical commitments and their operationalization within educational practice. Hybrid learning environments intensify this challenge because they blend human judgment with algorithmic mediation, often in opaque ways. In such contexts, ethical AI cannot be reduced to compliance with regulatory standards or post hoc bias audits. Instead, it must be embedded across the entire lifecycle of AI adoption, from procurement and design to classroom enactment and institutional governance. This requires a shift from ethics as a constraint on innovation toward ethics as a constitutive element of pedagogical quality and cultural legitimacy (Floridi, 2019; Williamson & Eynon, 2020).

Educational institutions play a pivotal role in shaping how AI systems are interpreted and used. Research shows that identical AI tools can produce markedly different outcomes depending on institutional culture, educator agency, and governance structures (Prinsloo & Slade, 2017). When institutions adopt AI-driven analytics or assessment tools without clear ethical frameworks, responsibility for interpreting algorithmic outputs is often devolved to individual educators who may lack the training or authority to challenge system recommendations. This fragmentation of responsibility creates what Selbst et al. (2019) describe as a "responsibility gap," where harms occur without clear accountability. Addressing this gap requires institution-wide ethical alignment that integrates cultural sensitivity, pedagogical values, and shared governance.

Empirical controversies surrounding AI proctoring systems illustrate how ethical and cultural failures emerge in real educational contexts. During the global shift to online learning, many institutions rapidly deployed remote proctoring tools relying on facial recognition, gaze tracking, and behavioral analytics. Subsequent studies documented disproportionate misclassification of students with darker skin tones, neurodivergent behaviors, or culturally specific communication patterns (Buolamwini & Gebru, 2018; Swauger, 2020). Beyond technical inaccuracies, these systems imposed culturally narrow norms of "appropriate" test-taking behavior, often misinterpreting domestic learning environments common in non-Western or lower-income contexts as suspicious. Such practices reveal how AI can impose hidden cultural standards that conflict with principles of equity and dignity.

Automated essay scoring systems provide another instructive example. While proponents argue that such systems increase efficiency and consistency, extensive research has shown that they privilege surface-level linguistic features and standardized rhetorical structures aligned with dominant academic conventions (Perelman, 2014; Williamson et al., 2023). For multilingual learners and students from diverse cultural traditions, this can result in systematic undervaluation of ideas expressed through alternative narrative or argumentative forms. The ethical issue here is not solely algorithmic bias but epistemic injustice, wherein certain forms of expression are rendered less credible by design (Fricker, 2007). In hybrid pedagogy, where written interaction often replaces oral dialogue, such injustices can have amplified consequences for learner identity and participation.

Adaptive learning systems further complicate the ethical landscape. These platforms promise personalization by dynamically adjusting content based on learner behavior and performance. However, studies indicate that adaptivity often relies on narrow definitions of success and engagement, reinforcing path dependencies that limit learners' exposure to diverse knowledge pathways (Kizilcec & Lee, 2020; Holmes et al., 2022). When adaptivity is driven by historical performance data, students from marginalized backgrounds may be steered toward remedial content, reducing opportunities for intellectual challenge and growth. Such outcomes underscore the need for ethical scrutiny of how personalization intersects with cultural expectations, learner agency, and long-term educational trajectories.

Effective ethical AI governance in education requires institutional structures that support transparency, reflexivity, and participation. Governance frameworks must clarify who is responsible for evaluating AI systems, how ethical concerns are escalated, and how cultural impacts are assessed over time. Research in learning analytics governance emphasizes the importance of clear data stewardship policies, participatory oversight committees, and mechanisms for contestability that allow learners and educators to question algorithmic decisions (Prinsloo & Slade, 2017; Slade & Prinsloo, 2013). Without such mechanisms, ethical principles remain aspirational rather than actionable.

Transparency is a foundational requirement for accountability, yet transparency alone is insufficient if explanations are not intelligible or culturally meaningful. Explainable AI research highlights that explanations must be tailored to users' epistemic needs and contextual knowledge (Miller, 2019). In educational settings, this means that educators should be able to understand how AI recommendations align with pedagogical goals, while learners should receive explanations that support metacognition rather than compliance. Cultural responsiveness in explainability involves recognizing that different learners may interpret feedback through diverse cultural lenses, affecting motivation and trust. Ethical governance must therefore integrate explainability with pedagogical training and intercultural awareness.

Procurement processes represent another critical point of ethical intervention. Institutions often adopt AI tools developed by external vendors whose design assumptions and data practices may not align with local educational values. Scholars have warned that vendor-driven innovation risks entrenching commercial priorities over pedagogical and cultural considerations (Williamson, 2017). Ethical procurement requires rigorous evaluation of data sources, model limitations, and cultural applicability, as well as contractual provisions that allow institutions to audit, adapt, or withdraw systems that produce harm. Such practices position institutions as active moral agents rather than passive consumers of technology.

Educators occupy a central role in mediating the ethical impact of AI in hybrid pedagogy. Their professional judgment shapes how algorithmic outputs are interpreted, communicated, and acted upon in the classroom. However, studies consistently show that educators often feel underprepared to critically engage with AI systems, particularly regarding ethical and cultural implications (Celik et al., 2022; Holmes & Tuomi, 2022). This skills gap risks either overreliance on algorithmic authority or wholesale rejection of AI tools, neither of which supports responsible innovation.

Professional development is therefore essential to cultivating ethical literacy among educators. Such training should move beyond technical instruction to include critical examination of data ethics, cultural bias, and the limits of automation. Intercultural pedagogy offers valuable insights here, emphasizing reflexivity, dialogue, and relational ethics as foundations for teaching in diverse contexts (Deardorff, 2006). When educators are empowered to question AI recommendations and adapt them to local cultural realities, AI becomes a support for, rather than a substitute for, human judgment.

The educator agency also intersects with collective professional ethics. Codes of conduct and professional standards increasingly recognize the ethical responsibilities associated with digital technologies, including obligations to protect learner privacy, promote equity, and uphold academic integrity (Boddington, 2021). Embedding AI ethics within professional norms reinforces the idea that ethical practice is not an optional add-on but a core dimension of educational professionalism.

Drawing together the ethical principles, cultural insights, and practical considerations discussed above, this chapter advances a Culturally Responsive AI Ethics Framework for hybrid education. This framework conceptualizes ethical AI as a dynamic alignment between human dignity, cultural pluralism, and institutional accountability. Rather than prescribing fixed rules, it emphasizes processes of ongoing ethical deliberation informed by local contexts and stakeholder participation.

At its core, the framework affirms that AI systems should enhance, not diminish, learner agency. This entails designing systems that support reflective learning, provide meaningful choices, and respect learners' rights to understand and challenge algorithmic decisions. Cultural responsiveness is operationalized through inclusive data practices, participatory design involving diverse communities, and pedagogical flexibility that accommodates multiple ways of knowing and expressing understanding. Institutional accountability is realized through transparent governance structures, ethical impact assessments, and continuous monitoring of social and cultural effects.

Importantly, the framework situates ethics as integral to educational quality rather than as a trade-off against innovation. Empirical evidence suggests that ethically grounded AI systems foster greater trust, acceptance, and long-term sustainability within educational communities (Holmes et al., 2022). By aligning technological innovation with cultural respect and moral responsibility, institutions can harness AI's potential while safeguarding the human values at the heart of education.

Moving beyond algorithmic bias requires a reconceptualization of AI in education as a socio-technical and cultural phenomenon. Bias, while significant, represents only one dimension of a broader ethical landscape shaped by power, knowledge, and institutional choice. Hybrid pedagogy amplifies these dynamics by embedding AI deeply into learning relationships and decision-making processes. Addressing the ethical and cultural dimensions of AI therefore demands holistic frameworks that integrate philosophical ethics, intercultural sensitivity, and practical governance.

This chapter has argued that ethical AI in education is not merely about correcting flawed algorithms but about cultivating educational systems that honor diversity, agency, and human dignity. By adopting culturally responsive ethical frameworks, educators and institutions can ensure that AI serves as a tool for inclusion rather than exclusion, fostering hybrid learning environments grounded in fairness, trust, and respect for the plurality of human experience.

2.3. Framework Development: From Literature and Cases to CRAEF

The Culturally Responsive AI Ethics Framework (CRAEF) was developed through a critical interpretive synthesis of interdisciplinary literature spanning AI ethics, intercultural education, learning analytics governance, and responsible innovation. Rather than following a quantitative systematic review, this chapter adopts a conceptual synthesis approach that integrates normative ethical theory (Floridi, 2019; Fricker, 2007), policy frameworks (UNESCO, 2021; OECD, 2021), and documented empirical controversies in hybrid education environments (Prinsloo & Slade, 2017; Swauger, 2020; Williamson et al., 2023). This approach prioritizes conceptual coherence and explanatory depth over exhaustiveness, focusing on sources that illuminate the ethical and cultural dimensions of AI deployment in hybrid learning.

Three recurring ethical tensions emerged consistently across the literature and illustrative cases. First, ethical reflection was necessary to interrogate the normative assumptions embedded in AI systems, particularly those related to fairness, autonomy, and epistemic legitimacy. Second, intercultural awareness was required to recognize how algorithmic systems privilege certain cultural norms, linguistic patterns, and epistemologies while marginalizing others (Blodgett et al., 2020; Bhatt et al., 2023). Third, accountability mechanisms were essential to translate ethical commitments into institutional practice, ensuring that responsibility for AI-mediated decisions remained visible and contestable (Prinsloo & Slade, 2017). These three themes form the conceptual pillars of CRAEF.

Importantly, these pillars operate as an integrated system rather than independent components. Ethical reflection establishes the normative foundation by identifying what values should guide AI adoption. Intercultural awareness evaluates whether these values are enacted in ways that respect cultural diversity and epistemic plurality. Accountability mechanisms institutionalize these commitments by embedding them into governance, procurement, and pedagogical practice. Together, these pillars enable institutions to move beyond reactive bias correction toward proactive ethical design and governance.

3. EXPECTED CONTRIBUTIONS

The integration of artificial intelligence into education has accelerated dramatically in the past decade, reshaping hybrid and online learning environments through automated assessment, learning analytics, adaptive content delivery, and algorithmic decision-making. These systems increasingly influence not only how learners engage with knowledge but also how institutions define success, risk, and merit. While early educational technology research emphasized efficiency and personalization, recent scholarship has marked a decisive ethical turn, recognizing that AI-mediated education is deeply entangled with social values, cultural assumptions, and power relations (Williamson & Eynon, 2020; Holmes et al., 2022). Hybrid pedagogy, in particular, amplifies ethical complexity by situating AI at the intersection of human judgment and automated governance, where decisions are simultaneously pedagogical and political.

Much of the existing debate has centered on algorithmic bias, typically framed as a technical problem arising from skewed data or flawed model design. Although this focus has generated important insights, it remains insufficient for addressing the broader ethical and cultural implications of AI in education. Algorithmic bias does not emerge in a vacuum; it reflects historical inequities, epistemological hierarchies, and institutional priorities that shape how educational data are produced and interpreted (Barocas & Selbst, 2016; Noble, 2018). Consequently, ethical AI in hybrid education demands a more expansive framework that integrates ethical reflection, intercultural awareness, and mechanisms of accountability. This chapter argues that without such integration, AI risks reinforcing new forms of exclusion under the guise of innovation.

Empirical research has repeatedly demonstrated that AI systems used in educational contexts can disadvantage learners from marginalized backgrounds. Predictive analytics models designed to identify "at-risk" students often rely on historical performance data that encode socioeconomic disparities, resulting in higher risk classifications for students from under-resourced communities regardless of their actual learning potential (Baker & Hawn, 2022). Similarly, automated essay scoring systems have been shown to reward surface-level features such as sentence length and lexical complexity rather than substantive reasoning, disproportionately penalizing multilingual learners and those employing culturally distinct rhetorical styles (Perelman, 2014; Williamson et al., 2023). These outcomes reveal that bias is not merely an error to be corrected but a systemic feature of data-driven educational governance.

Attempts to address bias through technical fixes, such as fairness-aware algorithms or bias audits, often encounter fundamental limitations. Formal definitions of fairness are inherently normative and mutually incompatible, requiring value judgments that extend beyond computational optimization (Barocas et al., 2019). In education, where learning is a developmental and relational process, reducing fairness to statistical parity risks undermining pedagogical goals such as formative feedback, creativity, and critical thinking. Moreover, fairness metrics rarely capture cultural dimensions of learning, such as the legitimacy of diverse epistemologies or communication practices. As Kizilcec and Lee (2020) argue, algorithmic fairness in education must be evaluated in relation to educational values and cultural contexts, not solely mathematical criteria.

The persistence of bias despite technical interventions suggests that ethical challenges in AI-mediated education are rooted in deeper socio-technical dynamics. These include whose knowledge is represented in training data, whose values inform system design, and whose interests are prioritized in institutional adoption decisions. Addressing such questions requires moving beyond bias as an isolated concern toward a broader ethical analysis of AI's role in shaping educational futures.

Beyond bias, AI integration in hybrid education raises significant ethical concerns related to surveillance, autonomy, and trust. Learning analytics platforms and AI-driven monitoring tools often collect extensive data on student behavior, engagement, and affect, transforming learning environments into sites of continuous observation (Prinsloo & Slade, 2017). While proponents argue that such data enable early intervention and personalized support, critics warn that pervasive monitoring can erode learner autonomy and normalize surveillance as a pedagogical practice (Zuboff, 2019). These concerns are particularly acute in hybrid contexts, where digital traces often substitute for face-to-face interaction, amplifying the power asymmetry between institutions and learners.

Remote proctoring technologies exemplify the ethical risks associated with surveillance-oriented AI. During the COVID-19 pandemic, universities worldwide adopted AI-based proctoring systems to maintain assessment integrity in online settings. Subsequent investigations revealed widespread harms, including racial bias in facial recognition, misclassification of neurodivergent behaviors, and heightened anxiety among students required to expose their private living spaces to institutional scrutiny (Swauger, 2020; Gilliard, 2017). In the United States and Europe, student protests and legal challenges led several institutions to suspend or ban such tools, underscoring the ethical unsustainability of surveillance-driven assessment practices. These real-world cases illustrate that ethical failure often arises not from isolated algorithmic errors but from institutional decisions that prioritize control and efficiency over dignity and care.

Transparency and explainability further complicate ethical governance. Many AI systems used in education operate as black boxes, producing recommendations or risk scores without intelligible explanations. This opacity undermines educators' professional judgment and learners' ability to understand or contest decisions that affect their academic trajectories (Burrell, 2016; Selbst & Barocas, 2018). In culturally diverse classrooms, lack of explainability exacerbates mistrust, as learners may interpret algorithmic feedback through different cultural frames, leading to misalignment between system intent and learner experience. Ethical AI in hybrid education therefore requires transparency that is not only technical but pedagogically and culturally meaningful.

A critical yet often underexamined dimension of AI ethics in education concerns culture and epistemic justice. AI systems are predominantly developed in the Global North and trained on datasets reflecting Western educational norms, linguistic patterns, and epistemological assumptions. When deployed globally, these systems risk marginalizing local knowledge systems and reinforcing what scholars describe as digital or epistemic colonialism (Williamson, 2017; Bhatt et al., 2023). In hybrid education, where digital platforms mediate access to knowledge, such dynamics can profoundly shape whose voices are heard and whose ways of knowing are legitimized.

Natural language processing tools used for automated feedback and assessment illustrate this problem. Research shows that these systems struggle with non-standard dialects, code-switching, and culturally embedded metaphors, leading to systematic misinterpretation of learner intent (Blodgett et al., 2020). For students in multilingual contexts, particularly in regions such as Africa or Southeast Asia, this can result in persistent negative feedback that reflects linguistic difference rather than learning deficiency. These outcomes constitute forms of epistemic injustice, whereby certain forms of expression are rendered less credible by design (Fricker, 2007).

Intercultural communication research further highlights that perceptions of fairness, autonomy, and authority vary across cultural contexts. Studies comparing AI adoption in East Asia and Europe, for example, indicate that learners in collectivist cultures may be more accepting of automated guidance but less tolerant of surveillance, while learners in individualist contexts may value autonomy but resist opaque decision-making (Hofstede et al., 2010; Cummings-Koether et al., 2024). These findings challenge universalist ethical frameworks and underscore the need for culturally responsive approaches that recognize diversity in values and expectations.

The ethical challenges outlined above point to the necessity of a conceptual framework that integrates ethical reflection, intercultural awareness, and accountability mechanisms within hybrid education. Rather than treating ethics as a checklist or compliance requirement, such a framework conceptualizes ethical AI as an ongoing process of reflection and negotiation among stakeholders. Ethical reflection involves critically examining the values embedded in AI systems, including assumptions about learning, intelligence, and success. Intercultural awareness requires recognizing that these values are culturally situated and may conflict with local pedagogical traditions or learner identities. Accountability mechanisms ensure that ethical commitments are translated into institutional practices through transparent governance, participatory design, and avenues for contestation.

Figure 1. Conceptual Framework for Ethical AI in Hybrid Education. (Author's own work)

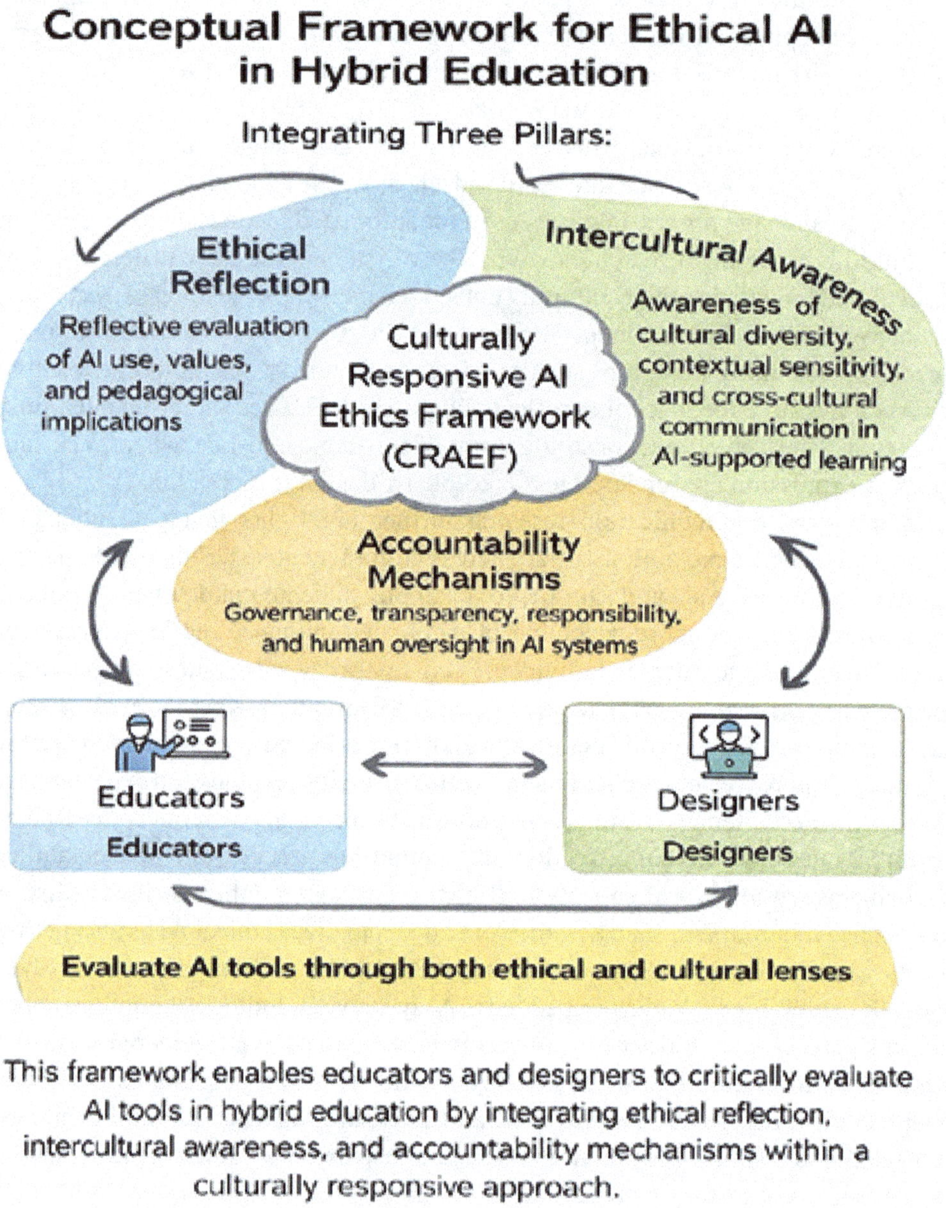

This Culturally Responsive AI Ethics Framework responds directly to gaps in existing AI ethics literature, which often prioritizes abstract principles without sufficient attention to educational practice or cultural diversity. By situating AI within hybrid pedagogy as a moral and cultural project, the framework enables educators and designers to evaluate AI tools through lenses that extend beyond technical performance. It emphasizes that ethical AI is not a static property of a system but a relational achievement shaped by how technologies are designed, interpreted, and governed within specific educational contexts.

A central contribution of this framework lies in its capacity to bridge ethical theory and pedagogical practice. Ethical principles such as justice, autonomy, and beneficence gain concrete meaning only when operationalized in classroom decisions, assessment practices, and institutional policies. In hybrid education, this translation is particularly complex because AI systems often mediate interactions invisibly, shaping learning pathways without explicit human intervention. The framework therefore foregrounds the role of educators as ethical agents whose professional judgment is essential to interpreting and contextualizing algorithmic outputs.

Research indicates that educators often feel ill-equipped to critically engage with AI tools, particularly regarding ethical and cultural implications (Celik et al., 2022). Without institutional support, this skills gap can lead either to uncritical reliance on algorithmic authority or to resistance that forecloses potential benefits. A culturally responsive ethical framework positions professional development as a core component of ethical AI adoption, emphasizing reflexivity, intercultural competence, and critical data literacy as essential pedagogical skills in hybrid environments.

While ethical principles for artificial intelligence in education are increasingly articulated at a global level, their practical interpretation and legitimacy remain deeply contingent on cultural context. Hybrid education, which blends physical and digital learning spaces, magnifies these contextual differences by embedding AI systems into everyday pedagogical interactions. As a result, perceptions of fairness, autonomy, and responsibility vary significantly across regions, challenging universalist approaches to ethical AI governance. Intercultural case studies demonstrate that ethical failures often arise not from technical malfunction but from cultural misalignment between AI systems and local educational values.

In East Asian contexts, such as China, South Korea, and Japan, AI-driven learning analytics and adaptive tutoring systems have been widely adopted within highly structured educational systems emphasizing performance optimization and standardized assessment. Research indicates that students in these contexts often express comparatively high trust in algorithmic recommendations, perceiving them as objective and authoritative extensions of institutional expertise (Zawacki-Richter et al., 2019). However, this trust coexists with ethical concerns related to surveillance and data sovereignty, particularly as large-scale student data collection is frequently centralized and opaque. In China, the deployment of AI-powered classroom monitoring systems that track facial expressions and attention levels has sparked public debate about the erosion of student privacy and the normalization of affective surveillance, even within cultures traditionally tolerant of institutional authority (Williamson & Hogan, 2020). These controversies reveal that cultural acceptance of authority does not equate to ethical consent, underscoring the need for accountability mechanisms that transcend assumptions about cultural compliance.

In contrast, European approaches to AI in education are strongly shaped by regulatory frameworks emphasizing individual rights, transparency, and data protection. The General Data Protection Regulation has significantly influenced how learning analytics and AI systems are designed and deployed within European higher education institutions. Empirical studies from countries such as Germany and the Netherlands indicate that educators and students exhibit greater skepticism toward opaque AI systems, particularly those involved in automated decision-making about assessment or progression (Kampylis et al., 2021). A notable case occurred in the United Kingdom, where the use of an algorithm to standardize A-level examination results during the COVID-19 pandemic disproportionately downgraded students from disadvantaged schools, leading to widespread public backlash and the eventual abandonment of the system. Subsequent analyses revealed that the algorithm embedded structural inequalities by privileging historical school performance over individual achievement, highlighting how algorithmic governance can conflict with societal norms of fairness and merit (Williamson, Eynon, & Potter, 2020). This case underscores the ethical necessity of aligning AI systems with culturally embedded conceptions of justice and educational purpose.

African contexts further complicate the ethical landscape by foregrounding issues of infrastructural inequality, linguistic diversity, and epistemic marginalization. In many sub-Saharan African countries, AI-enabled educational platforms are introduced through international development initiatives or private-sector partnerships, often without meaningful local participation in design or governance. Studies examining adaptive learning tools deployed in Kenya and South Africa have found that systems trained primarily on Western curricula and English-language data frequently fail to accommodate local pedagogical practices or indigenous knowledge systems (Adam & Groves, 2019). Learners using these platforms may encounter content that is culturally irrelevant or linguistically inaccessible, reinforcing perceptions of education as externally imposed rather than locally grounded. Such cases illustrate how ethical AI must address not only fairness within systems but also justice in the global distribution of epistemic authority.

The Culturally Responsive AI Ethics Framework introduced in Part 1 gains practical significance through its application to these intercultural realities. Operationalizing the framework requires translating ethical reflection, intercultural awareness, and accountability into concrete institutional practices that shape how AI systems are selected, implemented, and evaluated. Ethical reflection begins at the point of problem formulation, where institutions must interrogate why AI is being introduced and whose interests it serves. Research on responsible innovation emphasizes that many ethical harms originate from poorly defined problem spaces that conflate efficiency with educational quality (Stilgoe, Owen, & Macnaghten, 2013). In hybrid education, this reflection entails questioning whether AI-driven automation genuinely enhances learning or merely optimizes administrative convenience.

Intercultural awareness becomes operational when institutions actively involve diverse stakeholders in the design and evaluation of AI systems. Participatory design approaches, which include educators, learners, and community representatives, have been shown to improve both ethical outcomes and system effectiveness by surfacing culturally specific concerns that might otherwise remain invisible (Holstein et al., 2019). In multilingual contexts, participatory data practices can help ensure that language models and assessment tools reflect local linguistic norms rather than penalizing deviation from standardized forms. Such practices also challenge the dominance of Global North epistemologies by legitimizing local knowledge as a source of design insight.

Accountability mechanisms translate ethical commitments into enforceable structures. Institutional governance frameworks that include ethical review boards for educational AI, transparent procurement processes, and ongoing impact assessments are critical for sustaining ethical alignment over time. Research in learning analytics governance highlights the importance of clearly defined roles and responsibilities, particularly in hybrid environments where decision-making authority is distributed across human and algorithmic actors (Prinsloo & Slade, 2017). Without such structures, ethical responsibility becomes diffuse, increasing the risk that harms will be normalized or overlooked.

At the pedagogical level, the framework emphasizes human-in-the-loop approaches that preserve educator agency and contextual judgment. AI systems in hybrid education often generate recommendations about content sequencing, learner risk, or assessment outcomes. When these recommendations are treated as authoritative, educators may feel compelled to conform, even when algorithmic outputs conflict with their professional knowledge of learners' cultural backgrounds or personal circumstances. Studies indicate that such deference to algorithmic authority can undermine pedagogical responsiveness and exacerbate inequities (Holmes & Tuomi, 2022).

Human-in-the-loop pedagogy repositions AI as a decision-support tool rather than a decision-maker. This approach aligns with ethical theories emphasizing relational responsibility and care, which are particularly salient in culturally diverse learning environments. By retaining final decision-making authority, educators can contextualize algorithmic insights within broader understandings of learner identity, motivation, and social context. Professional development programs that cultivate critical data literacy and intercultural competence are essential to enabling this role.

Evidence from European teacher education initiatives suggests that educators trained in ethical AI interpretation are more likely to use analytics reflectively and less likely to reproduce deficit narratives about marginalized learners (Kampylis et al., 2021).

The ethical and cultural challenges identified in this chapter have significant implications for policy at institutional, national, and international levels. Ministries of education and accreditation bodies increasingly recognize the need to regulate AI in education, yet existing guidelines often focus narrowly on data protection or technical standards. A culturally responsive approach to policy requires embedding ethics and intercultural diversity into teacher training requirements, accreditation criteria, and funding frameworks for educational technology. Policies that mandate ethical impact assessments prior to large-scale AI deployment can help surface potential harms early, particularly those related to cultural misalignment or social inequity.

International organizations such as UNESCO and the OECD have begun to articulate such holistic approaches, emphasizing human-centered AI, cultural diversity, and inclusive governance (UNESCO, 2023; OECD, 2021). However, translating these principles into enforceable national policies remains uneven. Comparative policy analysis suggests that countries with strong participatory governance traditions are more likely to implement meaningful ethical oversight, while those relying on market-driven innovation risk prioritizing scalability over cultural responsiveness (Williamson & Hogan, 2020). Aligning policy with the Culturally Responsive AI Ethics Framework therefore requires not only regulatory instruments but also institutional cultures that value ethical deliberation and stakeholder engagement.

The intercultural cases and operational insights discussed in this part reinforce the central argument of the chapter: ethical AI in hybrid education cannot be achieved through technical solutions alone. Instead, it requires sustained attention to cultural context, power relations, and institutional accountability. The Culturally Responsive AI Ethics Framework offers a conceptual and practical pathway for navigating these complexities by integrating ethical reflection, intercultural awareness, and governance mechanisms across the AI lifecycle.

Future research should further examine how this framework operates in diverse educational systems, particularly in underrepresented regions where AI adoption is often mediated by global market forces. Longitudinal studies assessing the cultural and ethical impacts of AI over time would provide valuable evidence for refining policy and practice. Ultimately, ensuring that AI contributes to equitable and culturally respectful hybrid education is not a one-time achievement but an ongoing moral commitment.

3.1. Application Scenario: Applying CRAEF in Institutional AI Procurement and Deployment

To illustrate the practical application of CRAEF, consider a university evaluating an AI-driven automated feedback system used to support student writing in hybrid learning environments. Ethical reflection requires institutional stakeholders to examine whether the system's training data and evaluation criteria align with pedagogical goals that respect diverse rhetorical traditions and linguistic variation (Perelman, 2014; Williamson et al., 2023). Rather than assuming algorithmic outputs are neutral, educators and administrators must critically assess whether the system privileges dominant linguistic norms that may disadvantage multilingual or culturally diverse learners.

Intercultural awareness involves evaluating whether the system performs equitably across different learner populations and cultural contexts. For example, institutions must examine whether automated feedback accurately interprets culturally specific narrative structures or code-switching practices (Blodgett et al., 2020). This process may involve participatory evaluation with educators and students who can identify potential misinterpretations or culturally insensitive outputs.

Accountability mechanisms ensure that ethical concerns can be addressed through formal governance structures. Institutions must establish procedures allowing educators and learners to question algorithmic outputs, request clarification, and escalate concerns when necessary (Prinsloo & Slade, 2017). Procurement processes should include transparency requirements regarding training data sources, model limitations, and mechanisms for institutional oversight. This integrated application demonstrates how CRAEF translates abstract ethical principles into operational institutional practice.

3.2. Participatory Data Governance and Learner Agency

A culturally responsive approach to AI ethics requires moving beyond institutional oversight toward participatory governance involving educators, learners, and communities. Participatory data governance recognizes that those affected by AI systems should have a voice in how these systems are evaluated, interpreted, and refined. Research in learning analytics governance emphasizes the importance of mechanisms that allow stakeholders to question algorithmic decisions and participate in ethical oversight (Prinsloo & Slade, 2017).

Learner participation is particularly critical because students directly experience the consequences of algorithmic decisions. Providing students with opportunities to understand how AI systems operate, question algorithmic feedback, and report perceived bias strengthens ethical accountability and fosters critical digital literacy

(Bhatt et al., 2023). Rather than positioning learners as passive recipients of AI-mediated education, participatory governance enables them to function as active ethical stakeholders.

Educators similarly require institutional support to develop the skills necessary to interpret and evaluate AI outputs critically. Professional development programs focusing on ethical literacy, data interpretation, and intercultural competence can enhance educators' ability to identify potential bias and contextualize algorithmic recommendations (Celik et al., 2022). This participatory approach strengthens institutional accountability while aligning AI adoption with educational values grounded in cultural respect and human dignity.

Ethical Reflection:

- Educators: Evaluate whether AI recommendations align with pedagogical values and learner dignity.
- Institutions: Assess ethical implications during procurement and deployment decisions.
- Policymakers: Establish ethical guidelines and regulatory oversight mechanisms.

Intercultural Awareness:

- Educators: Interpret AI outputs within cultural and linguistic context.
- Institutions: Evaluate AI tools across diverse learner populations.
- Technologists: Design systems that reflect diverse epistemologies and linguistic variation.

Accountability Mechanisms:

- Educators: Provide feedback on AI performance and challenge inappropriate outputs.
- Institutions: Implement governance structures, ethical audits, and participatory review processes.
- Policymakers: Require transparency, explainability, and ethical impact assessment.

4. CONCERNS AND LIMITATIONS

The chapter concludes that ethical and cultural responsibility in AI education is not a static goal but a continuous process of moral learning where educators, technologists, and students co-evolve toward a shared vision of fairness. To move beyond algorithmic bias, institutions must embrace a human-centered pedagogy that sees technology not as a neutral agent but as a moral participant in the co-construction of global knowledge.

Despite the growing consensus that artificial intelligence holds transformative potential for hybrid and digital education, its integration raises profound ethical and cultural concerns that resist simple resolution. Ethical AI in education is often framed as a technical challenge, solvable through improved algorithms, better datasets, or enhanced transparency mechanisms. However, such framings underestimate the depth of the socio-cultural and epistemic tensions embedded in AI systems. These tensions are not peripheral obstacles but constitutive limitations that shape how AI is designed, interpreted, and enacted within educational institutions. Addressing them requires moving beyond surface-level compliance toward a deeper engagement with moral philosophy, cultural theory, and critical pedagogy.

One of the most persistent concerns relates to the tension between transparency and complexity in contemporary AI systems. While transparency is widely recognized as a foundational principle of ethical AI, many educational technologies rely on complex machine learning models, particularly deep neural networks, whose internal decision-making processes are difficult even for their creators to fully interpret. This opacity challenges traditional ethical frameworks that depend on explainability and accountability, especially in educational contexts where decisions can significantly affect learners' academic trajectories and self-perception. Research in algorithmic accountability has demonstrated that explainability is not merely a technical feature but a normative demand rooted in democratic and educational values (Burrell, 2016; Selbst & Barocas, 2018). When students and educators cannot understand how or why an AI system produces certain recommendations or assessments, trust becomes fragile, and the possibility of meaningful ethical scrutiny diminishes.

The problem of opacity is particularly acute in hybrid learning environments, where AI-mediated decisions are often embedded seamlessly into learning management systems, adaptive platforms, or analytics dashboards. These systems may influence grading, content access, or risk profiling without explicit visibility to learners. Studies in learning analytics ethics have shown that such invisibility can normalize algorithmic authority, leading educators to defer to data-driven insights even when they conflict with contextual knowledge or professional judgment (Prinsloo & Slade, 2017). The ethical risk here lies not only in incorrect outputs but in the gradual erosion of pedagogical agency, as educators and learners come to perceive algorithmic decisions as objective or inevitable. Transparency, therefore, must be understood not simply as model interpretability but as a relational practice that enables dialogue, contestation, and shared understanding within educational communities.

Closely connected to the issue of transparency is the concern of cultural bias embedded in AI training data. AI systems used in education are typically trained on large datasets that reflect dominant linguistic, cultural, and behavioral norms, often drawn from Global North contexts. As critical scholars have argued, data are never neutral representations of reality but socially produced artifacts that encode historical power relations and epistemic hierarchies (Noble, 2018; Blodgett et al., 2020). When such datasets underpin educational AI, they risk marginalizing learners whose ways of knowing, communicating, or demonstrating competence diverge from dominant norms. For example, natural language processing systems used for automated writing feedback may implicitly privilege standardized academic English, disadvantaging multilingual learners or those from oral knowledge traditions.

Empirical research has increasingly documented how cultural bias manifests in educational AI, not only through overt misclassification but through subtle forms of epistemic exclusion. Learners from marginalized backgrounds may be consistently flagged as "at risk," receive simplified content, or be steered toward less demanding learning pathways based on patterns that reflect systemic inequality rather than individual potential (Kizilcec & Lee, 2020). Such outcomes resonate with the concept of epistemic injustice, wherein individuals are wronged in their capacity as knowers due to prejudicial structures of credibility and interpretation (Fricker, 2007). In this sense, culturally biased AI does not merely replicate inequality but actively participates in its reproduction by shaping how knowledge, ability, and legitimacy are recognized within educational systems.

Another significant limitation arises from what has been termed ethics fatigue, a phenomenon in which institutions approach ethical responsibility as a finite compliance exercise rather than an ongoing moral practice. As AI governance frameworks proliferate, educational organizations may adopt ethical guidelines, conduct impact assessments, or establish review committees primarily to satisfy regulatory or reputational demands. While such measures are important, research in responsible innovation warns that proceduralization can lead to a hollowing out of ethical intent, where ethics becomes a checklist rather than a lived institutional value (Stilgoe, Owen, & Macnaghten, 2013). In educational settings already burdened by administrative pressures, ethics fatigue can result in superficial engagement with complex moral questions, leaving deeper cultural and pedagogical implications unexamined.

This fatigue is exacerbated by the rapid pace of technological change, which often outstrips institutions' capacity for reflective adaptation. Educators may experience ethical overload as they are expected to navigate data privacy, algorithmic bias, and intercultural sensitivity alongside their core teaching responsibilities. Without sustained professional development and institutional support, ethical AI risks being perceived as an external imposition rather than an integral dimension of educational quality. This perception undermines the possibility of cultivating ethical reflexivity, which scholars identify as essential for navigating uncertain and evolving technological landscapes (Floridi, 2019).

Underlying these concerns is a structural tension between innovation and regulation that shapes how AI is adopted in education. On one hand, proponents of educational innovation argue that excessive regulation stifles experimentation and limits the potential benefits of AI-enhanced learning. On the other hand, insufficient regulation creates conditions in which untested or ethically questionable systems can be deployed at scale, exposing learners to harm without adequate safeguards. Comparative studies of AI governance suggest that market-driven innovation environments are particularly prone to ethical lapses, as commercial imperatives prioritize scalability and efficiency over contextual sensitivity and long-term impact (Williamson & Hogan, 2020). In education, this tension is especially problematic because learners, unlike consumers, often cannot opt out of institutional technologies that shape their learning experiences.

Taken together, these concerns highlight the limitations of viewing ethical AI as a static target that can be achieved through technical fixes or policy declarations. Instead, they point to the need for a more dynamic and culturally grounded understanding of ethical responsibility, one that recognizes AI as a socio-technical system embedded within educational values, power relations, and cultural narratives. This understanding sets the stage for a deeper exploration of how institutions might move beyond algorithmic bias toward a more human-centered and morally responsive pedagogy.

Building on the conceptual limitations outlined above, the ethical and cultural responsibility of AI in education must be reframed as a continuous process of moral learning rather than a problem to be definitively solved. This reframing challenges dominant narratives of technological progress that assume linear improvement through innovation alone. Instead, it aligns with educational theories that emphasize learning as an iterative, relational, and value-laden practice. Within this perspective, ethical AI is not an endpoint but an evolving commitment that requires educators, technologists, policymakers, and learners to co-evolve in response to emerging challenges and insights.

Central to this process is the recognition that AI systems are not neutral tools but moral participants in educational ecosystems. This claim does not imply that AI possesses moral agency in the human sense, but rather that its design and deployment actively shape moral relations by influencing who is heard, who is valued, and who is given opportunities to learn. Scholars in science and technology studies have long argued that technologies mediate social relations and embed normative assumptions about desirable behavior and outcomes (Winner, 1980). In education, AI systems mediate pedagogical relationships by structuring attention, feedback, and evaluation, thereby participating in the co-construction of knowledge and identity.

A human-centered pedagogy that acknowledges this moral participation requires reasserting the primacy of human judgment, care, and contextual understanding. Rather than delegating pedagogical authority to algorithms, educators must remain critically engaged interpreters of AI-generated insights. Research on human-in-the-loop systems demonstrates that ethical outcomes improve when AI is positioned as a support for, rather than a replacement of, professional expertise (Holmes & Tuomi, 2022). In culturally diverse classrooms, this approach allows educators to contextualize data-driven recommendations within learners' social, linguistic, and cultural realities, mitigating the risk of reductive or deficit-oriented interpretations.

Such pedagogy also demands a shift in how institutions conceptualize fairness and inclusion. Traditional metrics of fairness in AI often focus on statistical parity or error rates across demographic groups. While these metrics are valuable, they are insufficient for capturing the lived experiences of learners navigating AI-mediated education. Critical scholars argue that fairness must be understood relationally, taking into account historical inequalities, power asymmetries, and the cultural meanings attached to educational success (Selbst et al., 2019). For example, an AI system that distributes resources evenly may still perpetuate injustice if it fails to address structural barriers faced by marginalized learners. Human-centered pedagogy thus requires integrating quantitative assessments with qualitative, culturally informed perspectives.

The process of continuous moral learning also extends to institutional governance. Ethical responsibility cannot rest solely on individual educators, particularly in large-scale hybrid education systems where AI infrastructure is centrally procured and managed. Institutions must cultivate governance structures that support ongoing ethical deliberation, including mechanisms for feedback, redress, and adaptation. Studies in learning analytics governance emphasize the importance of transparency not only toward users but within organizations, ensuring that decision-making processes around AI adoption are visible and contestable (Prinsloo & Slade, 2017). Such structures help prevent ethics fatigue by embedding ethical reflection into routine institutional practices rather than treating it as an exceptional task.

At the policy level, embracing continuous moral learning requires moving beyond prescriptive regulations toward adaptive frameworks that can respond to contextual variation. International guidelines, such as UNESCO's Recommendation on the Ethics of Artificial Intelligence, provide valuable normative foundations by emphasizing human rights, cultural diversity, and sustainability. However, their effectiveness depends on how they are translated into local educational contexts. Research on policy implementation suggests that top-down mandates are most effective when combined with bottom-up engagement, allowing institutions to interpret ethical principles in ways that resonate with local values and needs (OECD, 2021). In this sense, ethical AI governance becomes a dialogic process rather than a fixed rule set.

Importantly, students themselves must be recognized as active participants in this moral learning process. Too often, learners are positioned as passive recipients of AI-driven education, with little opportunity to question or influence the systems that shape their learning. Critical digital pedagogy advocates for involving students in discussions about data use, algorithmic decision-making, and the cultural assumptions embedded in educational technologies (Bhatt, MacKenzie, & Knox, 2023). Such engagement not only enhances transparency but fosters critical digital literacy, empowering learners to navigate AI-mediated environments with awareness and agency. When students are invited to reflect on how AI affects their learning, ethical responsibility becomes a shared educational outcome rather than an abstract institutional obligation.

The chapter ultimately argues that moving beyond algorithmic bias requires a fundamental shift in how educational institutions understand technology itself. Rather than viewing AI as a neutral amplifier of existing practices, institutions must acknowledge its role in shaping educational values and futures. This acknowledgment calls for humility in innovation, recognizing that not all educational problems are best solved through automation and that some forms of inefficiency may reflect essential human processes such as dialogue, mentorship, and care. As educational theorists have noted, the pursuit of efficiency can conflict with the moral aims of education, which include fostering critical thinking, empathy, and democratic participation (Biesta, 2015).

In conclusion, the ethical and cultural responsibility of AI in education is best understood as an ongoing moral project rather than a technical challenge with definitive solutions. Transparency, cultural sensitivity, and regulation are necessary but insufficient without a deeper commitment to human-centered pedagogy and continuous ethical learning. By embracing AI as a moral participant in the co-construction of global knowledge, educational institutions can move beyond narrow conceptions of algorithmic bias toward a more holistic vision of fairness, dignity, and inclusion. This vision demands not only better technologies but more reflective educational cultures, capable of adapting ethically as AI continues to reshape the landscape of learning.

REFERENCES

Adam, T., & Groves, C. (2019). Digital futures and the ethics of care. *Ethics and Information Technology*, *21*(3), 219–231. DOI: 10.1007/s10676-018-9466-1

Baker, R. S., & Hawn, A. (2022). Algorithmic bias in education. *International Journal of Artificial Intelligence in Education*, *32*(2), 252–277. DOI: 10.1007/s40593-021-00285-7

Barocas, S., Hardt, M., & Narayanan, A. (2019). Fairness and machine learning. https://doi.org//arXiv.1908.09635DOI: 10.48550

Barocas, S., & Selbst, A. D. (2016). Big data's disparate impact. *California Law Review*, *104*(3), 671–732. DOI: 10.15779/Z38BG31

Bhatt, I., MacKenzie, A., & Knox, J. (2023). AI, education, and epistemic justice. *Learning, Media and Technology*, *48*(1), 1–14. DOI: 10.4337/9781803928562.00031

Biesta, G. (2015). What is education for? On good education, teacher judgement, and educational professionalism. *European Journal of Education*, *50*(1), 75–87. DOI: 10.1111/ejed.12109

Blodgett, S. L., Barocas, S., Daumé, H.III, & Wallach, H. (2020). Language (technology) is power. *Proceedings of the ACL*, 485–504. DOI: 10.18653/v1/2020.acl-main.485

Boddington, P. (2021). *Towards a code of ethics for artificial intelligence*. Springer., DOI: 10.1007/978-3-319-60648-4

Buolamwini, J., & Gebru, T. (2018). Gender shades: Intersectional accuracy disparities in commercial gender classification. *Proceedings of Conference on Fairness, Accountability and Transparency*, 77–91. DOI: 10.1145/3287560.3287596

Burrell, J. (2016). How the machine "thinks": Understanding opacity in machine learning algorithms. *Big Data & Society*, *3*(1), 1–12. DOI: 10.1177/2053951715622512

Celik, I., Dindar, M., Muukkonen, H., & Järvelä, S. (2022). The promises and challenges of artificial intelligence for teachers. *Computers & Education*, *178*, 104352. DOI: 10.1016/j.compedu.2021.104352

Cummings-Koether, M., ... (2024). Cultural perceptions of AI in education. AI & Society. 10.48550/arXiv.2510.19743

Deardorff, D. K. (2006). Identification and assessment of intercultural competence as a student outcome of internationalization. *Journal of Studies in International Education, 10*(3), 241–266. DOI: 10.1177/1028315306287002

Floridi, L. (2019). Establishing the rules for building trustworthy AI. *Nature Machine Intelligence, 1*(6), 261–262. DOI: 10.1038/s42256-019-0055-y

Floridi, L., Cowls, J., Beltrametti, M., Chatila, R., Chazerand, P., Dignum, V., Luetge, C., Madelin, R., Pagallo, U., Rossi, F., Schafer, B., Valcke, P., & Vayena, E. (2018). AI4People An ethical framework for a good AI society: Opportunities, risks, principles, and recommendations. *Minds and Machines, 28*(4), 689–707. DOI: 10.1007/s11023-018-9482-5 PMID: 30930541

Fricker, M. (2007). *Epistemic injustice: Power and the ethics of knowing*. Oxford University Press., DOI: 10.1093/acprof:oso/9780198237907.001.0001

Gilliard, C. (2017). Pedagogy and the logic of platforms. EDUCAUSE Review. https://er.educause.edu/articles/2017/7/pedagogy-and-the-logic-of-platforms

Holmes, W., Porayska-Pomsta, K., Holstein, K., Sutherland, E., Baker, T., Shum, S. B., Santos, O. C., Rodrigo, M. T., Cukurova, M., Bittencourt, I. I., & Koedinger, K. R. (2022). Ethics of AI in education: Towards a community-wide framework. *International Journal of Artificial Intelligence in Education, 32*(4), 504–526. DOI: 10.1007/s40593-021-00239-1

Holmes, W., & Tuomi, I. (2022). State of the art and practice in AI in education. *European Journal of Education, 57*(4), 542–570. DOI: 10.1111/ejed.12533

Kampylis, P., Punie, Y., & Devine, J. (2021). AI in education: Ethical implications. *Computers and Education: Artificial Intelligence, 2*, 100018. DOI: 10.1016/j.caeai.2021.100018

Kizilcec, R. F., & Lee, H. (2020). Algorithmic fairness in education. *Proceedings of the Learning Analytics and Knowledge Conference*, 335–346. DOI: 10.1145/3375462.3375537

Miller, T. (2019). Explanation in artificial intelligence: Insights from the social sciences. *Artificial Intelligence, 267*, 1–38. DOI: 10.1016/j.artint.2018.07.007

Noble, S. U. (2018). *Algorithms of oppression: How search engines reinforce racism*. NYU Press., DOI: 10.18574/nyu/9781479833641.001.0001

O'Neil, C. (2016). *Weapons of math destruction: How big data increases inequality and threatens democracy*. Crown.

OECD. (2021). AI in education: Challenges and opportunities. DOI: 10.1787/589b283f-en

Perelman, L. (2014). When "the state of the art" is counting words. *Assessing Writing, 7*(1), 1–16. DOI: 10.1016/j.asw.2014.05.001

Prinsloo, P., & Slade, S. (2017). Ethics and learning analytics: Charting the (Un) Charted. In Lang, C., Siemens, G., Wise, A. F., & Gaevic, D. (Eds.), *Handbook of learning analytics* (2nd ed., pp. 49–57). Society for Learning Analytics and Research., DOI: 10.18608/hla17.004

Selbst, A. D., & Barocas, S. (2018). The intuitive appeal of explainable machines. *Fordham Law Review, 87,* •••. https://ir.lawnet.fordham.edu/flr

Stilgoe, J., Owen, R., & Macnaghten, P. (2013). Developing a framework for responsible innovation. *Research Policy, 42*(9), 1568–1580. Advance online publication. DOI: 10.1016/j.respol.2013.05.008

Swauger, S. (2020). Software that monitors students. Hybrid Pedagogy. https://hybridpedagogy.org/software-that-monitors-students/

UNESCO. (2021). Recommendation on the ethics of artificial intelligence. United Nations Educational, Scientific and Cultural Organization. SHS/BIO/REC-AIETHICS/2021

Williamson, B. (2017). Big data in education: The digital technologies of data, politics and school practice. *Sage (Atlanta, Ga.)*. Advance online publication. DOI: 10.4135/9781529714920

Williamson, B., Bayne, S., & Shay, S. (2023). The datafication of writing assessment. *Assessment & Evaluation in Higher Education*. Advance online publication. DOI: 10.1080/13562517.2020.1748811

Williamson, B., & Eynon, R. (2020). Historical threads, missing links and future directions: Historiography and the digital turn. *Learning, Media and Technology*. Advance online publication. DOI: 10.1080/17439884.2020.1798995

Williamson, B., Eynon, R., & Potter, J. (2020). Pandemic politics and examination algorithms. *Learning, Media and Technology*. Advance online publication. DOI: 10.1080/17439884.2020.1761641

Williamson, B., & Hogan, A. (2020). *Commercialisation and AI governance: The emerging digital platforms for learning*. Globalisation, Societies and Education.

Chapter 5
Reframing Teaching in the Age of AI: Educators and Intelligent Systems in Hybrid Learning

Hoang Anh Du
http://orcid.org/0009-0002-4294-0992
Leeds Beckett University, UK

Koi Jun Chee
National University of Singapore, Singapore

Sokthea Kim
Institute for International Studies and Public Policy, Royal University of Phnom Penh, Cambodia

ABSTRACT

The rise of artificial intelligence (AI) in education is redefining the role of teachers, shifting them from content transmitters to learning architects who collaborate with intelligent systems. This chapter examines how human–AI partnerships empower educators to design, facilitate, and assess hybrid learning experiences that are more personalized, inclusive, and globally connected. Rather than replacing educators, AI systems function as cognitive partners that augment teachers' analytical capacity, reduce administrative burdens, and enhance student engagement. Drawing on empirical studies, theories of human–machine collaboration, and global best practices, the chapter explores how hybrid education can harness AI to strengthen teacher agency. It also addresses ethical tensions, including algorithmic dependency, data privacy, and deprofessionalization risks. The chapter concludes by proposing

DOI: 10.4018/979-8-3373-7462-8.ch005

a pedagogical and institutional framework for re-skilling and repositioning teachers in AI-mediated hybrid ecosystems that foster creativity, critical thinking, and intercultural collaboration.

1. BACKGROUND AND RATIONALE

The integration of artificial intelligence (AI) into education has generated both optimism and concern. Early developments in intelligent tutoring systems and adaptive learning platforms led some scholars to suggest that automated systems might eventually rival or even surpass human instruction in efficiency and scalability. However, decades of research have consistently demonstrated that essential dimensions of education such as empathy, ethical judgment, contextual understanding, and mentorship cannot be replicated by algorithms alone. Consequently, recent scholarship increasingly emphasizes that the future of education lies not in replacing teachers with technology but in developing collaborative relationships between educators and intelligent systems (Luckin, 2018; Holmes et al., 2022).

In hybrid learning environments, AI technologies can support educators by automating routine tasks such as grading, data processing, and administrative coordination. This assistance may allow teachers to devote greater attention to higher-order pedagogical activities, including mentoring students, facilitating discussion, and designing creative learning experiences. AI-powered learning analytics can also help educators identify learning gaps, track student progress, and personalize feedback, while natural language processing tools may support multilingual learning environments and formative assessment practices. Nevertheless, the growing use of AI in education also raises important challenges. Overreliance on opaque algorithmic systems may weaken teacher autonomy, and uneven access to AI tools and training may exacerbate existing inequalities across institutions and regions.

Against this backdrop, the present chapter examines teacher–AI collaboration within the broader context of hybrid education, viewing AI not as a substitute for teachers but as a potential partner in pedagogical practice. Drawing on international policy frameworks such as the European Commission's DigCompEdu framework and the OECD's discussions on teacher readiness for digital transformation, the chapter highlights the importance of systemic capacity-building that supports educators in developing AI literacy, critical judgment, and pedagogical agency. Rather than focusing solely on technological adoption, this perspective emphasizes how educators can meaningfully integrate AI into teaching and learning processes while maintaining ethical responsibility and professional autonomy.

2. RESEARCH FOCUS

Teacher Empowerment and Transformative Human-AI Collaboration in Hybrid Learning Ecosystems

Methodologically, the chapter will synthesize current literature on human–AI collaboration, teacher professional development, and hybrid pedagogy, supported by case vignettes from universities and corporate learning organizations. It will adopt a theoretical lens combining activity theory (Engeström, 2015) and transformative learning theory (Mezirow, 2000) to explain how teachers learn *with* AI and evolve *through* it.

The rapid expansion of artificial intelligence in education (AIED) is reshaping teaching practices and learning environments. As AI systems increasingly support instructional design, assessment, and learning analytics, the boundaries between human expertise, algorithmic tools, and hybrid learning environments are becoming more intertwined. Rather than functioning merely as users of digital technologies, educators are increasingly positioned as orchestrators of sociotechnical learning systems in which AI plays a supportive yet influential role (Chiu, 2024; Holmes et al., 2019; Luckin et al., 2016; Miao & Holmes, 2021). This chapter therefore examines how teachers can be empowered through ethical and strategic collaboration with AI within hybrid teaching models.

Across higher education, professional programs, and corporate learning organizations, teachers are now encountering AI as both a source of cognitive augmentation and a trigger for professional uncertainty. Studies show that generative AI systems challenge educators' sense of expertise, authority, and pedagogical control, especially when these tools provide real-time feedback, automate assessments, or generate learning pathways once monopolized by teachers' professional judgments (Hadad et al., 2024; Wan et al., 2024; Lee, 2025). At the same time, research increasingly demonstrates that AI can enhance the reflective, analytical, and instructional capacities of educators if integrated thoughtfully into pedagogical design and teacher development (Holstein et al., 2019; Krumsvik & Jones, 2024; Zhuo et al., 2024). Hybrid models of teaching that blend synchronous and asynchronous learning, digital and face-to-face modalities, and human–AI co-orchestration create a unique opportunity to reconceptualize the teacher's role as a partner rather than a passive operator of technology (Dillenbourg & Jermann, 2010; Su & Yang, 2023). The notion of teacher–AI complementarity is becoming foundational, emphasizing how AI systems can support classroom orchestration and formative assessment, while teachers provide contextual judgment, socio-emotional presence, cultural mediation, and ethical oversight.

The first core objective of this chapter is to reconceptualize the teacher's role as an active collaborator with AI. This reconceptualization aligns with global conversations on AI literacy that view teachers not simply as technology adopters but as critical participants in shaping AI-enabled learning ecologies (Ng et al., 2021; Chiu et al., 2023). Research indicates that educators must cultivate new interpretive and design-oriented competencies such as prompt engineering, multimodal data interpretation, and ethical-critical reasoning to work productively with generative AI models (Chiu, 2024; Kasneci et al., 2023). These competencies are not technical add-ons but intrinsic to teaching in a world where AI continuously interacts with learners through recommendation engines, personalized feedback, and predictive analytics (Hwang et al., 2020; Valtonen et al., 2021). As hybrid classrooms become more data-rich, educators gain access to multimodal analytics that reveal learners' cognitive, emotional, and behavioral patterns (Järvelä et al., 2021). Yet these insights require pedagogical interpretation: teachers must decide when AI-generated signals are meaningful, when they risk bias, and how to integrate them into learning conversations without reducing students to data points (Tsai et al., 2020; Williamson & Eynon, 2020). This shift in role underscores a broader epistemological transition in the profession, echoing Schön's (1987) argument that educators are reflective practitioners whose expertise emerges not from following scripts but from navigating ambiguity, interpreting dynamic situations, and refining their decisions through experience.

The second mission of the chapter is to identify the pedagogical frameworks and competencies that enable teachers to harness AI for adaptive learning, intercultural dialogue, and inclusion in hybrid models. Hybrid learning is not merely a mode of delivery; it is an epistemic environment that blends distributed cognition across human and machine actors. Ouyang and Jiao's (2021) conceptualization of the three paradigms of AI in education AI-directed instruction, AI-supported human learning, and AI-teacher collaboration suggests that hybrid ecosystems increasingly favor the third paradigm, where AI augments rather than replaces pedagogical decision-making. Within such systems, teachers require competencies in computational thinking, data literacy, human–AI orchestration, and socio-emotional facilitation (Voskoglou & Buckley, 2012; Seufert et al., 2021). These competencies must also include intercultural awareness, as hybrid classrooms often involve diverse learners with different communication styles and digital literacies. Research on intercultural collaboration supported by AI demonstrates how AI-mediated translation, dialogic scaffolds, and multimodal communication tools can foster inclusive participation across linguistic and cultural boundaries but only if educators intentionally frame AI as a bridge rather than a gatekeeper (Su & Yang, 2023; Zhou et al., 2023).

Ethical and cultural integrity remains central to the competency framework. AI systems carry risks of algorithmic bias, opacity, and inequitable learning pathways, particularly in large-scale hybrid environments (Popenici & Kerr, 2017; Kasneci et al., 2023). Teachers must therefore learn to navigate these risks while advocating for transparency and fairness in AI design and procurement. Central to this is critical AI literacy, the ability not only to operate AI tools but also to critique their underlying assumptions, limitations, and potential impacts on learners' autonomy and identities (Ng et al., 2021; Krumsvik & Jones, 2024). Teachers' perceptions of AI tools also significantly shape adoption: research shows that educators are more likely to engage meaningfully with AI when they perceive it as enhancing rather than undermining creativity, professional judgment, and relational pedagogy (Kim & Kim, 2022; Latif et al., 2023). When AI is positioned as a partner, teachers report increased willingness to experiment with co-creation, personalized learning pathways, and reflective assessment dialogues with their students (Zhou et al., 2023; Tetzlaff et al., 2021).

The third aim of this chapter is to examine how institutions can design training systems and supportive policies that sustain teacher–AI partnerships over time. A consistent finding across the literature is that teacher readiness for AI is shaped less by individual motivation and more by organizational culture, professional development structures, and institutional support (Zawacki-Richter et al., 2019; Pellas & Kazanidis, 2022; Tuomi, 2018). Teacher education programs are increasingly experimenting with AI-enhanced training methods, such as AI-driven microteaching simulations, analytics-informed coaching, and reflective identity work in AI-enabled environments (Thurzo et al., 2023; Zhuo et al., 2024; Lee, 2025). These efforts highlight the importance of psychological readiness, not just technical skill. Integrating AI requires teachers to negotiate evolving identities, shifting power dynamics, and emotional uncertainties about their future professional relevance. Research by Lee (2025) and Wan et al. (2024) shows that anticipations of automation can generate both anxiety and curiosity among teachers, influencing adoption patterns in hybrid classrooms.

Institutional strategies must therefore address the socio-emotional dimension of AI integration. This includes enabling safe spaces for experimentation, promoting collaborative inquiry, and providing transparent communication about AI policies and data use. UNESCO's guidance for policymakers emphasizes the need for AI governance frameworks that uphold equity, accountability, and learner protection, while simultaneously strengthening teacher agency in technology decision-making (Miao & Holmes, 2021). Professional development programs must also model the hybrid pedagogies they hope teachers will adopt. Effective programs integrate hands-on practice, reflective cycles, design-thinking approaches, and opportunities for cross-cultural collaboration (Urbani et al., 2017; Tapalova & Zhiyenbayeva, 2022). Such systemic support helps educators not only to understand AI conceptually but to integrate it meaningfully into lesson planning, classroom orchestration, and learner engagement.

The guiding research questions of this chapter focus on three interconnected dimensions: the transformation of pedagogical identity, the competencies required for ethical and inclusive AI collaboration, and the institutional conditions necessary for sustainable professional growth. The first question: How does AI transform the pedagogical identity and autonomy of educators in hybrid settings? invites analysis of role renegotiation. As hybrid classrooms expand, AI increasingly co-defines learning content, pacing, assessment, and communication, thereby reshaping the locus of pedagogical authority. Teachers must negotiate the balance between automation and human judgment, between precision and openness, and between efficiency and relational meaning-making. Roll and Wylie's (2016) work on the evolution and revolution of AI in education underscores that while some tasks may be automated, the pedagogical essence interpreting meaning, fostering agency, enabling community remains distinctively human. Teachers become mediators of epistemic transparency, responsible for helping learners understand how AI-generated recommendations are produced and why certain pathways are suggested. This transparency is vital for maintaining trust within hybrid environments and aligns with research on learner agency and ethical learning analytics (Tsai et al., 2020; Valtonen et al., 2021).

The second research question: What competencies are necessary for teachers to effectively collaborate with AI while maintaining ethical and cultural integrity? emphasizes an emerging professional repertoire that blends cognitive, technical, cultural, and ethical expertise. Teachers must develop AI literacy that extends beyond functional operation toward conceptual understanding, critical evaluation, and socially responsible implementation (Chiu, 2024; Ng et al., 2021). They must also cultivate intercultural competencies that allow them to guide diverse learners through AI-mediated collaboration, particularly in global hybrid classrooms and multi-lingual corporate learning spaces (Su & Yang, 2023). Additionally, teachers must navigate culturally situated expectations around authority, autonomy, and educational purpose, recognizing that AI may interact differently with pedagogical norms across contexts. Ethical integrity becomes central: educators are increasingly accountable not only for what they teach, but for how algorithmic systems shape learning opportunities, identities, and trajectories (Popenici & Kerr, 2017; Kasneci et al., 2023).

The third research question: How can educational institutions design training systems and policies that sustain this partnership over time? requires an institutional perspective. Hybrid ecosystems place new demands on infrastructure, governance, and leadership vision. Schools and universities must adopt long-term strategies that include AI ethics guidelines, data governance protocols, and teacher-centered design processes (Timotheou et al., 2023; Miao & Holmes, 2021). Professional development must be continuous rather than episodic, responsive rather than prescriptive, and reflective rather than solely skill-based. Workplace learning environments must acknowledge teachers as co-designers of AI-enabled curricula, creating opportunities for iterative feedback, interdisciplinary collaboration, and shared inquiry. Corporate learning organizations, similarly, must integrate AI into leadership development, workforce upskilling, and cross-cultural team training, recognizing that hybrid environments increasingly blur boundaries between academic and professional learning.

Methodologically, this chapter synthesizes contemporary literature on human–AI collaboration, teacher professional identity, learning analytics, and hybrid pedagogy to construct a comprehensive framework for teacher empowerment. It draws on case vignettes from universities implementing AI-enhanced tutoring systems, teacher education programs exploring algorithmic feedback mechanisms, and corporate organizations leveraging generative AI for intercultural collaboration. The theoretical grounding combines activity theory (Engeström, 2015) and transformative learning theory (Mezirow, 2000). Activity theory situates teachers within a sociotechnical activity system influenced by tools, rules, community norms, and division of labor. It explains how AI becomes an artifact that reorganizes interactions and reshapes the collective practice of teaching. Transformative learning theory highlights how educators' frames of reference evolve through critical reflection, dissonance, and dialogue, particularly when encountering disruptive technologies such as generative AI. Together, these lenses illuminate the dynamic processes through which teachers learn with AI, confront ethical dilemmas, and reimagine their professional identities within hybrid spaces.

In summary, this chapter examines how teachers can collaborate with AI to create inclusive and adaptive hybrid learning environments. It argues that sustainable human-AI partnerships require an integrated approach that considers teacher identity, pedagogical competencies, and institutional support. By emphasizing AI literacy, reflective practice, and ethical responsibility, the chapter highlights how educators can maintain professional agency while working alongside intelligent technologies.

Case 1: Technology probe of hybrid human–AI orchestration tools (Middle-school classroom)

In a large U.S. middle-school classroom study, Echeverria et al. (2023) implemented a technology probe to test alternative designs for hybrid human–AI orchestration that dynamically transition learners between individual and collaborative activities. The probe explored "pairing policies" that combined teacher, student, and AI suggestions to form pairs for peer tutoring or small-group collaboration, surfaced AI suggestions through teacher dashboards, and solicited teacher reflection via interviews and workshops. The study foregrounded dynamic orchestration transitions that arise organically rather than being pre-scripted and intentionally probed how control over orchestration should be shared between human actors and algorithmic agents.

From an activity-theory perspective, the probe altered the activity system by introducing new tools (AI pairing policies and orchestration dashboards) and changing the division of labor (AI suggested pairings; teachers adjudicated and intervened). Teachers reported that the AI suggestions were useful for identifying students who needed help and potential peer helpers, especially during rapidly evolving lessons when human attention was stretched across multiple groups. The AI reduced cognitive load on teachers by triaging attention to where intervention might be most effective; this enabled teachers to focus on higher-order facilitation tasks rather than on moment-to-moment micro-management (Echeverria et al., 2023). Yet teachers also voiced concern that algorithmic pairing could overlook crucial contextual knowledge, classroom relationships, social dynamics, or cultural sensitivities that inform whether a pairing would be pedagogically wise. These concerns prompted teachers to negotiate hybrid control: they wanted AI suggestions but demanded final human authority to accept, adjust, or reject pairings.

Transformative learning processes were visible in teachers' reflections. Initially some educators felt uneasy about relinquishing any control to an algorithm; they experienced what Lan (2024) would describe as identity tension, questioning whether reliance on AI threatened their role. As teachers experimented, reflected in professional learning communities, and co-designed pairing criteria with researchers, many described a shift in perspective: rather than seeing AI as a replacement actor, they began to regard it as a scouting assistant that surfaces possibilities, freeing them for relational work (Echeverria et al., 2023). This identity reconfiguration moving from sole decision-maker to orchestrator who adjudicates AI-generated possibilities illustrates Mezirow's (2000) transformative learning: disorienting dilemmas (AI suggestions) triggered critical reflection (workshops), which led to new roles and practices (shared orchestration).

The probe also exposed limitations noted widely in the literature: teachers emphasized the need for transparency about how AI suggested pairings, forecasted adaptability for different classroom cultures, and safeguards to avoid reinforcing existing inequities when pairing lower-performing students together (Järvelä et al., 2023; Pillai et al., 2023). Practically, the probe's findings point toward design patterns: provide teachers with explainable AI outputs, allow easy override and tuning of algorithmic policies, and embed ethnographic classroom knowledge into pairing heuristics to preserve cultural nuance and equity.

Case 2: Multimodal STEM+C co-design: iterative teacher-researcher-AI collaboration (High-school STEM unit)

The second vignette draws on a multimodal co-design project reported by Cohn et al. (2024/2025), where secondary STEM teachers, researchers, and AI systems co-developed multimodal timelines and analytic artifacts to support inquiry projects in STEM+C (science, technology, engineering, mathematics + computing). In this project, AI processed multimodal student artifacts video, sensor data, and text to generate timelines and highlight moments of student strategy, difficulty, or collaboration. Teachers used AI-generated timelines as prompts for formative feedback, while researchers iteratively refined AI models based on teacher annotations and pedagogical priorities. This circular feedback loop produced gradually improved AI artifacts and sharpened teacher interpretive skill.

From an activity-theory lens, the multimodal timeline tool became a mediating artifact that reconfigured the activity system: researchers and AI assisted in data processing; teachers interpreted AI summaries to inform instruction; students received feedback that combined AI-derived observations with human interpretive commentary. The division of labor shifted: AI handled labor-intensive multimodal synthesis; teachers handled interpretation, ethical adjudication, and culturally sensitive feedback. In doing so, teachers reclaimed time for pedagogical reflection and for focusing on students' higher-order reasoning roles that machines could not perform.

Transformative learning occurred through cycles of experimentation and reflection. Teachers initially reported skepticism AI timelines sometimes prioritized different signals than teachers would and some feared the AI's reductive summaries might flatten students' complex activity. However, repeated co-design workshops allowed teachers to interrogate AI logic, ask for features that foregrounded context (e.g., social turns, rhetorical moves), and reframe their practice toward data-informed interpretation rather than data-driven instruction. Over time some teachers articulated a new professional stance: they were data-informed curators and interlocutors, using AI artifacts to initiate student reflection and to scaffold meta-cognitive conversation. This evolution mirrors Mezirow's transformative learning: teachers confronted disorienting evidence (AI summaries), engaged in critical reflection with peers and researchers, and altered their pedagogical practice accordingly.

The multimodal project also foregrounded equity and cultural concerns. Teachers cautioned that AI models trained on particular sensor signatures or discourse patterns might not adequately represent students from different linguistic or cultural backgrounds; they argued for participatory data practices in which students and teachers co-audit AI outputs (Cohn et al., 2024/2025). This aligns with broader calls in the literature to protect cultural diversity and ensure that AI supports, rather than homogenizes, diverse pedagogical traditions (Holmes et al., 2022; Zawacki-Richter et al., 2020).

Case 3: Corporate reskilling and AI-powered learning coaches: IBM SkillsBuild and enterprise practice

The third vignette examines a corporate/organizational example: IBM's SkillsBuild initiative and related enterprise efforts to integrate AI into workplace learning. IBM and other corporate actors have deployed AI-powered learning coaches, curated curricula on AI literacy and prompt engineering, and used adaptive learning pathways to reskill large cohorts of workers (IBM, 2023; Deloitte, 2022). Unlike classroom probes, corporate implementations emphasize scale, credentialing, and workforce alignment; they also foreground measurable outcomes (completion rates, credential attainment, placement).

From an activity theory perspective, corporate AI learning systems introduce new tools (adaptive learning platforms, AI coaches), alter rules (performance metrics, credentialing standards), and reshape the community (employees, managers, L&D teams). Crucially, corporate trainers and workplace educators play orchestration roles: they configure learning pathways, contextualize AI-generated recommendations to organizational goals, and mentor learners in applying AI insights to job tasks. These educators experience identity shifts analogous to classroom teachers: they move from content deliverers to workplace learning architects, responsible for aligning AI scaffolds with organizational workflows and for safeguarding learner equity (McKinsey, 2025; IBM, 2023).

Transformative learning processes are visible among workplace trainers who adopt AI coaching: trainers initially skeptical about AI's capacity to coach soft skills found that AI could handle routine practice and provide immediate micro-feedback, leaving trainers to focus on coaching complex judgment and on facilitating reflective debriefs. Over time, trainers described a new role as "AI supervisors" interpreting AI analytics, shaping the learning ecology, and designing scenarios in which AI feedback is discussed, contested, and applied to real work problems. This co-evolution of human and AI roles supports learning at scale while retaining human responsibility for meaning-making and ethical governance.

However, corporate contexts also highlight tensions of scale and equity. Large enterprises can procure advanced AI platforms and offer extensive professional learning; smaller organizations or underfunded public institutions may lack such capacity, thereby widening digital and professional divides (Deloitte, 2022). Moreover, corporate deployments raise concerns about surveillance, data governance, and worker autonomy when AI analytics are used for performance monitoring rather than purely formative learning. Ethical frameworks and participatory governance become essential in such contexts to prevent the instrumentalization of AI for managerial control (McKinsey, 2025; IBM, 2023).

Cross-Case Analysis: Common Patterns and Theoretical Interpretation

Across the three vignettes several cross-cutting patterns emerge. First, AI functions most productively when it reduces teachers' routine cognitive load (triage, data synthesis, micro-feedback) while leaving interpretive, relational, and ethical work to humans (Holstein et al., 2020). In each case, AI handled intensive signal-processing tasks, such as pairing algorithms in the technology probe, multimodal data synthesis in the STEM+C project, and adaptive sequencing in the corporate program, thereby freeing educators to focus on tasks that machines cannot easily perform, such as interpreting context, mediating cultural nuance, and fostering socio-emotional learning.

Second, the cases illustrate that teacher agency and identity are central determinants of whether AI supports or undermines pedagogy. When teachers participate in co-design, maintain veto power over AI decisions, and receive sustained professional development, they are more likely to adopt hybrid practices that augment their work. Conversely, when AI is deployed top-down without teacher involvement, educators report resistance, anxiety, and threats to professional identity (Lan, 2024; Chan & Tsi, 2024). This resonates with transformative learning theory: disorienting encounters with AI become opportunities for growth only when institutional structures invite reflection, dialogue, and experimentation.

Third, the role of explainability and shared control is crucial. Teachers demanded transparent AI suggestions and straightforward controls to adapt algorithmic behavior to classroom norms. The technology probe explicitly found that hybrid control shared across AI, teachers, and students worked best, but only when teachers could easily override and tailor algorithmic recommendations (Echeverria et al., 2023). This aligns with literature advocating for human-in-the-loop designs that keep teachers as decisive interpreters and safeguarders of equity (Järvelä et al., 2023; Martinez-Maldonado et al., 2023).

Fourth, each case demonstrates the importance of iterative professional learning and communities of practice. Teachers learned to use AI not only through formal training but also through iterative cycles of practice, reflection, co-design, and peer discussion. Professional development that blends technical skill (AI literacy, prompt engineering) with reflective practice and identity work fosters sustained adoption and ethical use (Kim, 2022; Zhang, 2024).

Finally, equity and cultural plurality must be centrally addressed. AI systems trained on biased corpora or designed with Western pedagogical assumptions risk marginalizing learners and eroding local traditions. All three cases highlighted the necessity of participatory design and localized datasets, and teachers advocated for mechanisms that allow contextual correction of AI outputs.

The cases suggest practical design and policy recommendations. First, designers should prioritize explainable AI and shared-control interfaces that make algorithmic reasoning visible and give teachers simple means to adjust behavior. Second, professional development should be continuous, practice-based, and identity-sensitive: it must create safe spaces for teachers to express fears, experiment, and reflect with peers. Third, institutions must embed ethical governance, data privacy, transparency, contestability into procurement and deployment processes. Fourth, participatory co-design between teachers, researchers, students, and vendors helps align AI affordances with pedagogical values and cultural contexts. Finally, funding and policy should address digital inequality by supporting resource-constrained schools and community organizations to access AI-enabled learning tools and training.

3. EXPECTED CONTRIBUTIONS

Teacher Identity, Agency, and Pedagogical Transformation in AI-Enhanced Hybrid Learning

The accelerating integration of artificial intelligence (AI) across global educational systems has catalyzed profound transformations in how teachers conceptualize pedagogy, navigate professional identity, and enact instructional decision-making within hybrid learning models. As generative AI, adaptive learning engines, teacher-bots, multimodal analytics, and algorithmically orchestrated learning platforms become increasingly embedded in higher education and teacher education, the field faces a pivotal question: How can educators be empowered and not diminished through strategic, ethical, and collaborative partnerships with AI? The central aim of this chapter is to construct a comprehensive and integrative understanding of how teachers can develop the agency, competencies, and relational capacities necessary to collaborate effectively with AI in hybrid learning environments. Rather than positioning AI as a technological add-on or a managerial force, this chapter frames AI as a cognitive and pedagogical partner whose value depends fundamentally on the teacher's interpretive, ethical, and cultural judgment. The research foregrounds three core missions: reconceptualizing the teacher's role from user to collaborator; identifying pedagogical frameworks and competencies that allow teachers to harness AI for adaptive, inclusive, and intercultural learning; and exploring institutional strategies that cultivate long-term professional readiness for sustainable teacher–AI partnership.

The first mission reconceptualizing the teacher's role responds to a significant shift in the literature. Early AI in Education scholarship focused primarily on intelligent tutoring systems and algorithmic optimization (Luckin et al., 2016), positioning teachers as beneficiaries rather than co-architects of AI systems. However, more recent research on generative models and large language models (LLMs) foregrounds a complementary relationship between humans and AI, in which the teacher's role becomes more not less central (Crompton & Burke, 2023). This shift is evident in studies demonstrating that AI cannot replicate contextualized human judgment, ethical discernment, socio-emotional sensitivity, or cultural mediation (Holmes et al., 2022). Teachers remain essential as relational anchors, ethical stewards, and interpretive guides who translate AI insights into meaningful learning experiences. Even in environments where teacher-bots provide immediate feedback or engage in dialogue with learners, students consistently indicate that the presence of a human educator is necessary for motivation, trust, and academic integrity (Wong et al., 2022). Across multiple empirical studies, teachers express both optimism about AI's potential and apprehension about losing professional autonomy, respect, or identity (Chan & Tsi, 2024). This chapter advances the argument that teacher empowerment depends not on resisting AI but on reshaping professional identity around what humans do uniquely well: emotional attunement, ethical reasoning, cultural judgment, narrative sense-making, and the orchestration of complex learning ecologies.

The pursuit of this reconceptualization is complicated by the profound tensions teachers experience when negotiating their identities in AI-enhanced ecosystems. Research exploring teacher professional identity in AI-supported training environments reveals that educators often feel caught between enthusiasm for innovation and fear of being evaluated, judged, or potentially replaced by the very systems they are encouraged to adopt (Lan, 2024). These identity tensions manifest as dilemmas associated with algorithmic authority, shifts in instructional labor, and the potential erosion of disciplinary expertise. For many educators, AI tools that generate lesson plans, assessments, or feedback can provoke anxiety about losing the creative, intellectual, and relational aspects of teaching that define their professional selves. From the perspective of transformative learning theory, these tensions can operate as disorienting dilemmas critical moments that stimulate reflective inquiry, perspective-taking, and professional growth (Mezirow, 2000). Teachers who engage in reflective dialogue about AI, explore its biases, examine its impact on equity, and experiment with co-design are more likely to develop expanded forms of identity that integrate AI as a productive partner rather than a threat. Therefore, this chapter cites identity transformation as a central component of teacher empowerment, arguing that hybrid teaching models must create reflective spaces that allow educators to renegotiate their roles, values, and practices.

Pedagogical Competencies, Institutional Readiness, and Sustainable Teacher-AI Partnership

To support this transformation, the second mission of this chapter focuses on mapping the pedagogical competencies required for effective and ethical teacher–AI collaboration. Recent scholarship identifies AI literacy as foundational, encompassing technical skills such as understanding how LLMs are trained, recognizing limitations of predictive models, and knowing how to evaluate AI outputs for accuracy and bias (Xie et al., 2024). However, AI literacy must also include ethical components, awareness of data privacy issues, algorithmic fairness, cultural bias, hallucinations, and the risks of over-reliance on machine-generated content (Zawacki-Richter et al., 2020). In teacher education, researchers note that preservice teachers often approach AI with naïve optimism, assuming that AI outputs are authoritative because of their fluency or speed (Shin et al., 2025). Educators frequently lack the critical evaluation skills necessary to analyze whether AI-generated feedback is pedagogically appropriate, culturally inclusive, or aligned with learning goals. Therefore, AI literacy must integrate critical judgment, reflective skepticism, and intercultural awareness.

Prompt engineering emerges in the literature as another essential competency. Teachers must learn to craft prompts that encourage generative models to support deep learning rather than superficial assistance. Effective prompting requires teachers to embed cognitive, ethical, and cultural scaffolds into queries, guiding AI systems to generate outputs that are contextualized, inclusive, and aligned with disciplinary epistemologies (Alabbasi & Tondeur, 2024). Prompt engineering is not simply a technical skill it is a pedagogical design practice. Through carefully constructed prompts, teachers can model inquiry, critical thinking, and disciplinary reasoning. They can also guide AI systems to generate multiple perspectives, simulate cross-cultural dialogue, and scaffold students' metacognitive reflection. In this sense, teachers orchestrate AI's cognitive capabilities to support dialogic, multimodal, and intellectually rigorous learning experiences.

Beyond technical and cognitive competencies, hybrid teaching models require teachers to cultivate relational, ethical, and intercultural competencies that cannot be automated. Studies demonstrate that AI systems often struggle with cultural nuance, emotional subtlety, or local knowledge, making the teacher essential for ensuring cultural sensitivity and inclusive pedagogy (Cukurova & Luckin, 2020). Teachers must understand how AI interacts with student identities, particularly for learners from linguistically diverse or marginalized backgrounds. AI-generated content may inadvertently reinforce stereotypes or erase cultural context, requiring teachers to mediate meaning, foster dialogue, and correct bias. This chapter therefore expands the concept of AI literacy to include intercultural digital literacy, a competency that combines cultural knowledge, ethical reasoning, and technological understanding to ensure inclusive and equitable AI-supported learning.

The literature also emphasizes the need for teachers to develop multimodal pedagogical design skills. A study on multimodal collaboration in STEM+C environments shows that teachers who integrate AI-based analytics, simulations, and visualizations with hands-on inquiry create more dynamic and responsive learning ecosystems (Gerard et al., 2023). However, these systems require teachers to orchestrate hybrid interactions thoughtfully, making decisions about when to intervene, when to scaffold, and when to allow AI tools to take the lead. Hybrid orchestration supported by dashboards, prediction tools, or adaptive feedback systems requires teachers to interpret real-time data and understand how AI perceives learning behaviors (Martinez-Maldonado et al., 2023). These competencies extend far beyond technical proficiency; they involve socio-pedagogical judgment, ecological awareness, and the ability to balance the roles of human facilitator and algorithmic partner.

The third mission of this chapter exploring institutional strategies responds to growing recognition that teacher empowerment cannot be achieved without organizational support. Institutions must design policies, training programs, and ethical frameworks that cultivate psychological readiness and sustainable professional development. Teachers consistently report that unclear policies related to AI usage, data privacy, and academic integrity generate anxiety and limit experimentation (Kim, 2023). Moreover, teachers often face pressure to adopt AI tools without receiving adequate training or time to reflect on pedagogical implications. Research on teacher leadership demonstrates that educators who feel supported by institutional leaders are more likely to assume proactive roles in AI innovation, mentor peers, and contribute to co-design processes that shape AI policy (Li et al., 2023). Conversely, when institutions adopt AI systems through top-down decision-making, teachers may experience a loss of agency, diminished trust, and reduced willingness to experiment.

Institutional readiness requires more than training workshops; it demands a systemic reconfiguration of learning ecosystems through the lens of activity theory (Engeström, 2015). Activity theory highlights the interconnectedness of tools, rules, community, and division of labor in shaping human activity. Applying this lens, institutions must redesign the structural elements of teaching workflow, assessment systems, resource allocation, evaluation metrics to support hybrid human–AI practice. When AI systems are introduced without addressing systemic tensions, teachers may find that AI increases labor rather than decreases it, or that AI decisions conflict with existing curricular or assessment structures. Therefore, this chapter argues that sustainable teacher–AI collaboration must involve institutional co-design, wherein teachers actively participate in shaping policies, selecting tools, and designing learning ecologies.

Professional development is essential to this systemic transformation. Research on AI in teacher education consistently demonstrates that educators require continuous, scaffolded, inquiry-driven professional learning experiences (Kim, 2023; Tondeur et al., 2024). One-off training sessions are insufficient. Teachers must be able to experiment with AI tools, reflect on their experiences, share strategies with colleagues, and receive coaching on ethical dilemmas or design challenges. Professional development should integrate case-based learning, collaborative inquiry, and design thinking approaches that position teachers as active researchers of their own practice. Studies in preservice teacher education reveal that reflective journals, AI-supported simulations, and peer-to-peer feedback facilitate deeper understanding of how AI affects pedagogy, identity, and power dynamics (Shin et al., 2025). Institutions that cultivate communities of practice around AI integration foster a culture of shared expertise, reducing isolation and empowering educators to navigate technological complexity collectively.

A critical dimension within institutional strategies relates to the emotional and psychological aspects of AI adoption. Teachers often experience fear of inadequacy, imposter syndrome, or uncertainty about judgment when confronting highly fluent AI systems (Chan & Tsi, 2024). Professional development must therefore address emotional resilience, build confidence, and support teachers in developing a growth mindset toward AI. Transformative learning theory suggests that identity-safe environment spaces where teachers can express vulnerability, ask questions, and share concerns are essential for enabling deep change (Mezirow, 2000). Institutions must cultivate cultures where experimentation is encouraged, mistakes are viewed as learning opportunities, and AI is framed as a tool that enhances rather than replaces human expertise.

Another dimension shaping the research focus is the evolving nature of teacher–student relationships in AI-mediated environments. Scholarship consistently shows that learners desire personalized feedback, immediate responses, and 24/7 availability features often associated with AI agents (Wong et al., 2022). Yet relational pedagogy remains central to learning motivation, belonging, and identity development. AI may support personalization, but it cannot replicate the embodied empathy, cultural understanding, and intuitive attunement that human educators provide (Holmes et al., 2022). Hybrid learning models thus require teachers to navigate a new relational landscape to understand when to delegate cognitive tasks to AI and when to foreground human presence. Teachers must also help students critically understand AI, challenge algorithmic bias, and engage in ethical reasoning about machine-generated information. This relational mediation forms a vital part of teacher competencies in hybrid ecosystems.

Parallel to these relational considerations is the question of student agency. In addition, students themselves must develop competencies for responsible engagement with AI systems. These include critical AI literacy, the ability to evaluate machine-generated outputs, recognize algorithmic bias, and maintain academic integrity when using generative tools. As hybrid learning environments become increasingly AI-mediated, learners must navigate new forms of autonomy and dependency. While AI can support personalized feedback and continuous learning, excessive reliance on AI-generated responses may weaken metacognitive development and independent problem-solving. Teachers therefore play a crucial role in guiding students to engage with AI as a learning partner rather than a cognitive shortcut, fostering reflective use of AI tools and encouraging deeper inquiry. Studies on student adoption of teacher-bots indicate that learners may adopt surface approaches to learning if AI tools provide overly convenient assistance (Lee et al., 2022). Students may rely on AI responses without developing metacognitive skills, critical thinking, or disciplinary reasoning. Teachers therefore play a crucial role in designing learning experiences that encourage students to use AI responsibly, question AI outputs, and cultivate discernment. The teacher must guide students in balancing AI-generated knowledge with human inquiry, ensuring that hybrid learning fosters deep learning rather than automated dependency. In addition, students may face new ethical and cognitive challenges when interacting with generative AI systems, including difficulties distinguishing between AI-generated and human-authored knowledge. Developing student AI literacy therefore becomes essential to ensure that learners can critically evaluate AI outputs, maintain academic integrity, and use AI tools in ways that support rather than undermine deep learning.

Another important dimension of the research agenda concerns the epistemological implications of AI in education. AI-enabled learning ecologies redistribute knowledge production, shifting from static content delivery to dynamic, co-constructed knowledge environments (Cukurova & Luckin, 2020). AI systems can synthesize vast amounts of information, identify patterns, and provide adaptive feedback. Yet humans remain responsible for contextualizing knowledge, interpreting meaning, and making ethical judgments about what counts as valid knowledge. Teachers thus serve as epistemic mediators, responsible for negotiating the boundaries between machine-generated knowledge and human-centered inquiry. This epistemic role requires teachers to develop sophisticated critical frameworks for understanding AI's influence on knowledge structures and learning processes.

Taken together, these intersecting themes of professional identity, pedagogical competencies, institutional readiness, relational pedagogy, student agency, and epistemic mediation compose the central research focus of this chapter. The literature makes clear that hybrid human–AI teaching models hold significant potential for enhancing creativity, reducing administrative burdens, supporting personalization, and fostering intercultural dialogue. However, these potentials can only be realized when teachers are empowered to collaborate with AI through robust professional development, reflective practice, ethical inquiry, and institutional support. AI cannot be understood as a neutral tool; it reshapes power dynamics, pedagogical relationships, and epistemic structures. Empowering teachers requires acknowledging these complexities and building ecosystems where teachers play central roles in orchestrating hybrid learning.

This chapter proposes an integrative research agenda that synthesizes insights from human–AI collaboration research, teacher professional development, AI literacy, hybrid pedagogy, and identity theory. It argues that the future of AI-enhanced education must be grounded in a human-centered vision that values teacher expertise, relational care, ethical stewardship, and cultural responsiveness. AI must function not as an instructional authority but as a partner in inquiry, a collaborator that supports teachers in creating adaptive, inclusive, and transformative learning environments. Ultimately, the research focus advances a conceptual and practical framework for understanding how teachers learn with AI and evolve through it, positioning educators as co-designers of hybrid futures in which human creativity and machine intelligence work together to support collective flourishing.

4. CONCERNS AND LIMITATIONS

Although the human-AI partnership in hybrid teaching presents significant opportunities for transformation, the emerging literature also highlights a range of ethical, pedagogical, cultural, and institutional concerns.

Although the human-AI partnership in hybrid teaching presents significant opportunities for transformation, the emerging literature underscores a complex constellation of ethical, pedagogical, cultural, and institutional concerns that must be critically examined. One of the most persistent limitations centers on the ethical dilemmas related to data usage, algorithmic bias, and the expanding surveillance capacities embedded in AI-assisted instructional systems. Much of the AI used in education relies on large-scale data extraction that tracks patterns of student behavior, engagement, and performance. This raises important questions about privacy, consent, transparency, and the extent to which students and teachers understand how their data are being used. Scholars caution that algorithmic processes are rarely neutral; they reproduce biases embedded in the datasets on which they were trained, disproportionately affecting marginalized students and perpetuating inequities across gender, race, language, and socioeconomic status (Cukurova & Luckin, 2020). Even generative AI systems designed to support creativity or provide instructional feedback may inadvertently reinforce stereotypes or misrepresent culturally diverse knowledge systems due to underrepresentation in training corpora (Holmes et al., 2022). Teachers report heightened anxiety about being evaluated through opaque data-driven systems, where algorithms can influence perceptions of teacher performance without contextual understanding of local classroom dynamics (Chan & Tsi, 2024). The ethical landscape grows more complicated when institutions adopt AI tools without establishing transparent guidelines, decision-making pathways, or mechanisms for contesting algorithmic judgments. As a result, the integration of AI into hybrid learning environments necessitates ongoing ethical scrutiny, culturally responsive data governance, and teacher empowerment in interpreting and challenging algorithmic outputs.

Another major concern pertains to technological dependency, where the convenience and efficiency of AI may inadvertently erode teachers' professional confidence, judgment, and creative autonomy. As LLMs and teacher-bots become more fluent, coherent, and pedagogically responsive, educators may begin to rely on them for lesson planning, assessment design, or feedback provision (Crompton & Burke, 2023). This reliance risks repositioning teachers as passive recipients of machine output rather than as critical decision-makers and pedagogical architects. Research on teacher identity in AI-enhanced training environments shows that some educators experience identity destabilization when AI performs tasks traditionally associated with teacher expertise, such as summarizing student misconceptions or generating instructional materials (Lan, 2024). Teachers report feelings of inadequacy or fear of being replaced, especially when institutional discourses frame AI as a solution to teacher shortages or instructional inefficiencies (Kim, 2023). Even preservice teachers who tend to be more digitally confident may internalize beliefs that AI can automatically provide authoritative responses, diminishing their motivation to cultivate disciplinary depth or pedagogical inventiveness (Shin et al., 2025). Over-reliance on AI also threatens reflective practice, as educators may defer too quickly to machine-generated suggestions rather than engaging in critical analysis, collaborative dialogue, or evidence-based inquiry. As AI systems become more embedded in instructional routines, the challenge is to ensure that educators retain epistemic agency, creative sovereignty, and the confidence needed to integrate AI as a partner without relinquishing human authority, interpretive judgment, or pedagogical imagination.

A third challenge concerns digital inequality, which manifests not only through unequal access to hardware and software but also through disparities in institutional capacity, digital literacy, and professional development support. Institutions with robust funding, advanced infrastructure, and strong research ecosystems are more likely to adopt sophisticated AI-enabled tools, cultivate AI literacy among staff, and offer high-quality professional learning experiences (Li et al., 2023). Meanwhile, under-resourced schools particularly in rural, Indigenous, or Global South contexts may struggle to integrate AI meaningfully into hybrid learning (Wong et al., 2022). Teachers in these environments often lack time, administrative support, or training to experiment with AI or understand its risks, reinforcing the digital divide between institutions with differing technological capacities (Xie et al., 2024). Even when AI tools are available, disparities in AI literacy can exacerbate inequality; educators who are less confident or experienced with AI may experience frustration, resistance, or exclusion from institutional decision-making processes (Tondeur et al., 2024). Students, too, experience uneven benefits, as those with access to AI-powered feedback, personalized learning analytics, or multimodal learning environments may outperform peers who rely on traditional instruction. The resulting inequalities raise significant justice concerns, particularly as hybrid learning becomes a norm rather than an exception. Without targeted policies, equity funding, and inclusive design frameworks, AI risks amplifying existing structural inequities rather than alleviating them.

Closely related to digital inequality is the often-overlooked issue of cultural homogenization, a phenomenon in which global AI systems risk marginalizing non-Western pedagogical practices, epistemologies, and ways of knowing. Most AI education systems are developed in Western contexts, trained on Western datasets, and reflect implicit assumptions about learning, cognition, communication, and knowledge (Holmes et al., 2022). As a result, widely adopted AI tools may propagate Western-centric pedagogical norms, individualism, direct instruction, textual reasoning while diminishing collective, oral, land-based, or culturally situated forms of learning prevalent in many parts of the world (Cukurova & Luckin, 2020). For instance, research on student–AI collaboration shows that AI-generated responses often exhibit rhetorical patterns and cognitive frames rooted in Anglo-American academic discourse, which can conflict with local cultural expectations for communication, politeness, hierarchy, or relational dynamics (Gerard et al., 2023). Teachers in non-Western settings report tensions when AI-generated content contradicts community values, spiritual knowledge systems, or culturally grounded teaching practices (Kim, 2023). Preservice teachers, especially in culturally diverse contexts, may internalize Western-centric AI outputs as normative, thus displacing local pedagogical traditions and eroding cultural sovereignty (Shin et al., 2025). This cultural flattening poses a significant threat to educational pluralism. It reinforces epistemic inequities, diminishes the diversity of global pedagogical knowledge, and risks universalizing Western notions of intelligence, learning, and academic excellence. As hybrid education becomes increasingly globalized, protecting cultural specificity and promoting intercultural dialogue must remain central to teacher–AI partnership.

The literature further highlights the tension between automation and augmentation, a tension that underscores the philosophical foundation of this chapter. While AI can streamline administrative tasks, grade assignments, generate learning materials, and provide adaptive feedback, its value in hybrid learning depends fundamentally on being used to expand, rather than replace, human capacities (Luckin et al., 2016). Research investigating students' perceptions of teacher-bots demonstrates that although learners appreciate the efficiency and immediacy of AI responses, they consistently prefer human teachers for emotional support, ethical guidance, and complex problem-solving (Lee et al., 2022). Studies examining teacher perceptions of AI support show that educators want AI to reduce workload, not undermine professional expertise or diminish relational engagement (Kim, 2023). Even when AI produces accurate suggestions, teachers argue that pedagogical decisions must remain grounded in contextual understanding, something AI cannot fully grasp (Crompton & Burke, 2023). Thus, the emphasis must remain on augmentation: AI should enhance teachers' creative, analytical, and relational capabilities rather than supplant them.

Furthermore, concerns arise regarding the interpretive opacity and unpredictability of AI systems. Black-box algorithms may generate outputs that appear fluent and convincing but are logically flawed, biased, or factually incorrect. Teachers must develop strong evaluative skills to recognize hallucinations, inaccuracies, or culturally insensitive responses produced by generative models (Xie et al., 2024). However, when teachers lack the training to understand model limitations, they may misinterpret AI-generated suggestions as authoritative, risking misguided instructional decisions. Research shows that preservice teachers often overestimate the accuracy of AI or struggle to identify subtle errors embedded in machine-generated explanations (Shin et al., 2025). Such misjudgments can have profound consequences for learning quality, assessment fairness, and student trust. Institutions must therefore establish systematic support mechanisms that enable teachers to critically interrogate AI outputs, design safeguards, and cultivate a shared culture of critical digital literacy.

Another limitation concerns the shifting emotional landscape of teaching. Teacher emotions, confidence, belonging, purpose, and self-efficacy play a critical role in shaping instructional quality and student learning. Yet the growing presence of AI in the classroom can disrupt these emotional dynamics, especially if teachers feel surveilled, undervalued, or uncertain about how AI evaluates their actions (Chan & Tsi, 2024). Teachers report feelings of vulnerability when interacting with AI systems that can instantly generate solutions they spent years mastering. Some experience emotional fatigue from balancing new hybrid responsibilities: learning AI tools, supporting students' AI usage, correcting AI errors, and managing institutional expectations (Li et al., 2023). Research on teacher identity in AI-enhanced training shows that emotional tensions, fear, skepticism, hope, curiosity shape how educators adopt or resist AI technologies (Lan, 2024). If institutions fail to support teachers emotionally, they risk undermining morale, professional commitment, and long-term willingness to innovate. Thus, the psychological dimensions of AI integration must be treated as a core pedagogical and institutional concern.

Finally, concerns arise regarding long-term sustainability and scalability of teacher–AI collaboration. Many AI tools introduced in educational settings are pilot projects, short-term grants, or commercial trials that lack continuity or institutional integration. Teachers often describe frustration when AI tools they have invested time into learning are discontinued, updated in ways that disrupt workflow, or replaced by new technologies with little warning (Martinez-Maldonado et al., 2023). The rapid pace of AI innovation raises questions about tool stability, financial sustainability, and alignment with long-term educational goals. Without long-term planning, institutions risk creating fragmented systems that overwhelm teachers, undermine coherence, and reduce trust in AI initiatives.

Despite these concerns, the literature converges on a central conclusion: The value of AI in hybrid education lies not in automation but in augmentation expanding human creativity, empathy, ethical judgment, and intercultural understanding. AI cannot replicate the emotional attunement, contextual reasoning, or cultural wisdom of educators. Instead, human-AI collaboration becomes most powerful when teachers are equipped to critically shape, interpret, and guide AI systems in ways that align with local pedagogical values and global equity principles. By acknowledging ethical dilemmas, mitigating technological dependency, addressing inequality, and safeguarding cultural plurality, educational systems can cultivate environments in which AI elevates rather than supplants teacher agency. True empowerment arises when educators leverage AI to enhance adaptive instruction, foster intercultural dialogue, design inclusive learning ecologies, and nurture human flourishing. In this vision, AI becomes a catalyst not a replacement for a more humane, ethical, and globally connected future of hybrid education.

By confronting these concerns, the chapter underscores that the value of AI in hybrid education lies not in automation but in augmentation expanding human creativity, empathy, and intercultural understanding. True empowerment emerges when educators are not replaced by technology but are elevated by it, leading hybrid education toward a more humane, ethical, and globally connected future.

REFERENCES

Chan, C. K. Y., & Tsi, L. H. (2024). Will generative AI replace teachers in higher education? A study of teacher and student perceptions. *Studies in Educational Evaluation, 83*, 101395. DOI: 10.1016/j.stueduc.2024.101395

Chiu, T. K. F. (2024). Embracing the future of Artificial Intelligence in the classroom: The relevance of AI literacy, prompt engineering, and critical thinking in modern education. *International Journal of Educational Technology in Higher Education, 21*(1), 14. Advance online publication. DOI: 10.1186/s41239-024-00448-3

Chiu, T. K. F., Xia, Q., Zhou, X., Chai, C. S., & Cheng, M. (2023). Systematic literature review on opportunities, challenges, and future research recommendations of artificial intelligence in education. *Computers and Education: Artificial Intelligence, 4*, 100118. Advance online publication. DOI: 10.1016/j.caeai.2022.100118

Cohn, C., Snyder, C., Horn Fonteles, J., Gerard, L., McElhaney, K., & Slotta, J. D. (2025). A multimodal approach to support teacher, researcher and AI collaboration in STEM+C learning environments. *British Journal of Educational Technology*. Advance online publication. DOI: 10.1111/bjet.13518

Crompton, H., & Burke, D. (2023). Large language models in education: A focus on the complementary relationship between human teachers and ChatGPT. *Education and Information Technologies, 28*(12), 15873–15892. DOI: 10.1007/s10639-023-11834-1

Cukurova, M., & Luckin, R. (2020). Artificial intelligence for education: Knowledge and its assessment in AI-enabled learning ecologies. *Educational Studies, 56*(2), 127–144. DOI: 10.1080/00131857.2020.1728732

Deloitte. (2022). *State of AI in the Enterprise* (5th ed.). Deloitte Insights.

Dillenbourg, P., & Jermann, P. (2010). Technology for classroom orchestration. In Khine, M. S., & Saleh, I. M. (Eds.), *New science of learning* (pp. 525–552). Springer., DOI: 10.1007/978-1-4419-5716-0_26

Echeverria, V., Yang, K., Lawrence, L. E. M., Shibani, A., Dash, S. K., & Martinez-Maldonado, R. (2023). Designing hybrid human–AI orchestration tools for individual and collaborative activities: A technology probe study. *IEEE Transactions on Learning Technologies, 16*(2), 191–205. DOI: 10.1109/TLT.2023.3248155

Gerard, L. F., McElhaney, K., Cohn, C., Slotta, J. D., & Tissenbaum, M. (2023). Supporting teacher—AI—researcher collaboration in multimodal STEM+C learning. *British Journal of Educational Technology*.

Hadad, S., Erturk, E., & Buzzetto-Hollywood, N. (2024). Generative AI and teachers' perspectives on its implementation in education. *Journal of Applied Learning and Teaching*, *7*(1). Advance online publication. DOI: 10.70725/815246mfssgp

Holmes, W., Bialik, M., & Fadel, C. (2019). *Artificial intelligence in education: Promises and implications for teaching and learning*. Center for Curriculum Redesign.

Holmes, W., Bialik, M., & Fadel, C. (2022). *Artificial Intelligence in Education: Promises and Implications for Teaching and Learning*. Center for Curriculum Redesign.

Holstein, K., Aleven, V., & Rummel, N. (2020). A conceptual framework for human–AI hybrid adaptivity in education. In Roll, I., McNamara, D., Sosnovsky, S., Luckin, R., & Dimitrova, V. (Eds.), *Artificial Intelligence in Education* (pp. 240–253). Springer., DOI: 10.1007/978-3-030-52237-7_20

Holstein, K., McLaren, B. M., & Aleven, V. (2019). Co-designing a real-time classroom orchestration tool to support teacher–AI complementarity. *Journal of Learning Analytics*, *6*(2), 27–52. DOI: 10.18608/jla.2019.62.3

Hwang, G. J., Xie, H., Wah, B. W., & Gašević, D. (2020). Vision, challenges, roles and research issues of Artificial Intelligence in Education. *Computers and Education: Artificial Intelligence*, *1*, 100001. Advance online publication. DOI: 10.1016/j.caeai.2020.100001

IBM. (2023). *IBM SkillsBuild Program Overview*. IBM Corporation. https://skillsbuild.org/

Järvelä, S., Malmberg, J., Haataja, E., Sobocinski, M., & Kirschner, P. A. (2021). What multimodal data can tell us about the students' regulation of their learning process? *Learning and Instruction*, *72*, 101203. Advance online publication. DOI: 10.1016/j.learninstruc.2019.04.004

Järvelä, S., Nguyen, A., & Hadwin, A. (2023). Human and artificial intelligence collaboration for socially shared regulation in learning. *British Journal of Educational Technology*, *54*(5), 1057–1076. DOI: 10.1111/bjet.13325

Kasneci, E., Sessler, K., Küchemann, S., Bannert, M., Dementieva, D., Fischer, F., Gasser, U., Groh, G., Günnemann, S., Hüllermeier, E., Krusche, S., Kutyniok, G., Michaeli, T., Nerdel, C., Pfeffer, J., Poquet, O., Sailer, M., Schmidt, A., Seidel, T., & Kasneci, G. (2023). ChatGPT for good? On opportunities and challenges of large language models for education. *Learning and Individual Differences*, *103*, 102274. Advance online publication. DOI: 10.1016/j.lindif.2023.102274

Kim, N. J., & Kim, M. K. (2022). Teacher's perceptions of using an artificial intelligence-based educational tool for scientific writing. *Frontiers in Education, 7*, 755914. Advance online publication. DOI: 10.3389/feduc.2022.755914

Krumsvik, R. J., & Jones, L. Ø. (2024). Generative AI in teacher education: Educators' perceptions of transformative potentials and the triadic nature of AI literacy explored through AI-enhanced methods. *Computers and Education: Artificial Intelligence, 7*, 100471. Advance online publication. DOI: 10.1016/j.caeai.2025.100471

Lan, Y. (2024). Through tensions to identity-based motivations: Exploring teacher professional identity in Artificial Intelligence-enhanced teacher training. *Teaching and Teacher Education, 137*, 104736. DOI: 10.1016/j.tate.2024.104736

Latif, S., Wu, Y., Huang, L., Khwaja, U. A., Diao, Z., & Wang, Q. (2023). Artificial intelligence in teaching and teacher professional development: A systematic review. *Computers and Education: Artificial Intelligence, 6*, 100355. Advance online publication. DOI: 10.1016/j.caeai.2024.100355

Lee, J., Pillai, R., Kaushik, N., & Sivathanu, B. (2022). Students' adoption of AI-based teacher-bots (T-bots) for learning in higher education. *Information Technology & People, 37*(1), 328–355. DOI: 10.1108/ITP-02-2021-0152

Lee, J. Y. (2025). Teaching with the algorithm: Anticipations of AI in teacher education. *European Journal of Teacher Education, 51*(1), 93–106. DOI: 10.1080/02619768.2025.2540793

Li, K. C., Wong, B. T. M., & Yang, Y. (2023). Exploring the impact of AI on teacher leadership: Regressing or expanding? *Education and Information Technologies, 28*, 21677–21695. DOI: 10.1007/s10639-023-12174-w

Luckin, R., Holmes, W., Griffiths, M., & Forcier, L. (2016). *Intelligence Unleashed: An argument for AI in Education.* Pearson.https://static.googleusercontent.com/media/edu.google.com/en//pdfs/Intelligence-Unleashed-Publication.pdf

Luckin, R., Holmes, W., Griffiths, M., & Forcier, L. B. (2016). *Intelligence unleashed: An argument for AI in education*. Pearson Education.

Martinez-Maldonado, R., Echeverria, V., & Shibani, A. (2023). Orchestrating collaborative learning with multimodal analytics: Challenges and opportunities. In Echeverria et al. (2023).

McKinsey & Company. (2025). *AI and the Future of Work: Global Workforce Trends 2025*. McKinsey Global Institute., DOI: 10.1145/3636555.3636857

Mezirow, J. (2000). *Learning as Transformation: Critical Perspectives on a Theory in Progress*. Jossey-Bass.ISBN-0-7879-4845-4

Miao, F., & Holmes, W. (2021). *AI and education: Guidance for policy-makers*. UNESCO.

Ng, D. T. K., Leung, J. K. L., Chu, S. K. W., & Qiao, M. S. (2021). Conceptualizing AI literacy: An exploratory review. *Computers and Education: Artificial Intelligence*, *2*, 100041. Advance online publication. DOI: 10.1016/j.caeai.2021.100041

Ouyang, F., & Jiao, P. (2021). Artificial intelligence in education: The three paradigms. *Computers and Education: Artificial Intelligence*, *2*, 100020. Advance online publication. DOI: 10.1016/j.caeai.2021.100020

Pellas, N., & Kazanidis, I. (2022). Artificial intelligence in teacher education: Knowledge and its assessment in AI-enabled learning ecologies. *Educational Philosophy and Theory*, *54*(8), 1145–1159. DOI: 10.1080/00131857.2020.1728732

Pillai, R., Sivathanu, B., Metri, B., & Kaushik, N. (2023). Students' adoption of AI-based teacher-bots (T-bots) for learning in higher education. *Information Technology & People*, *37*(1), 328–355. DOI: 10.1108/ITP-02-2021-0152

Popenici, S. A. D., & Kerr, S. (2017). Exploring the impact of artificial intelligence on teaching and learning in higher education. *Research and Practice in Technology Enhanced Learning*, *12*(1), 22. Advance online publication. DOI: 10.1186/s41039-017-0062-8 PMID: 30595727

Roll, I., & Wylie, R. (2016). Evolution and revolution in artificial intelligence in education. *International Journal of Artificial Intelligence in Education*, *26*(2), 582–599. DOI: 10.1007/s40593-016-0110-3

Schön, D. A. (1987). *Educating the reflective practitioner: Toward a new design for teaching and learning in the professions*. Jossey-Bass.

Seufert, S., Guggemos, J., & Sailer, M. (2021). Technology-related knowledge, skills, and attitudes of pre- and in-service teachers: The current situation and emerging trends. *Computers in Human Behavior*, *115*, 106552. Advance online publication. DOI: 10.1016/j.chb.2020.106552 PMID: 32921901

Shin, M., Abdelnour, S., & Tondeur, J. (2025). Applying artificial intelligence in teacher education: Preservice teachers' attitudes and reflections when using ChatGPT for teaching and learning. *European Journal of Teacher Education*, *48*(5), 934–963. Advance online publication. DOI: 10.1080/02619768.2025.2540791

Su, J., & Yang, W. (2023). A multimodal approach to support teacher, researcher and AI collaboration in STEM+C learning environments. *British Journal of Educational Technology*, *54*(2), 447–468. DOI: 10.1111/bjet.13518

Tapalova, O., & Zhiyenbayeva, N. (2022). Artificial intelligence in education: AIEd for personalised learning pathways. *Electronic Journal of e-Learning*, *20*(5), 639–653. DOI: 10.34190/ejel.20.5.2597

Tetzlaff, L., Schmiedek, F., & Brod, G. (2021). Developing personalized education: A dynamic framework. *Educational Psychology Review*, *33*(3), 863–882. DOI: 10.1007/s10648-020-09570-w

Thurzo, A., Strunga, M., Urban, R., Surovková, J., & Afrashtehfar, K. I. (2023). Impact of artificial intelligence on dental education: A review and guide for curriculum update. *Education Sciences*, *13*(2), 150. Advance online publication. DOI: 10.3390/educsci13020150

Timotheou, S., Miliou, O., Dimitriadis, Y., Sobrino, S. V., Giannoutsou, N., Cachia, R., Monés, A. M., & Ioannou, A. (2023). Impacts of digital technologies on education and factors influencing schools' digital capacity and transformation: A literature review. *Education and Information Technologies*, *28*(6), 6695–6726. DOI: 10.1007/s10639-022-11431-8 PMID: 36465416

Tsai, Y. S., Perrotta, C., & Gašević, D. (2020). Empowering learners with personalised learning approaches? Agency, equity and transparency in the context of learning analytics. *Assessment & Evaluation in Higher Education*, *45*(4), 554–567. DOI: 10.1080/02602938.2019.1676396

Tuomi, I. (2018). *The impact of artificial intelligence on learning, teaching, and education: Policies for the future*. Publications Office of the European Union., DOI: 10.2760/12297

Urbani, J. M., Roshandel, S., Michaels, R., & Truesdell, E. (2017). Developing and modeling 21st-century skills with preservice teachers. *Teacher Education Quarterly*, *44*(4), 27–50.

Valtonen, T., Leppänen, U., Hyypiä, M., Kokko, A., Manninen, J., Vartiainen, H., Sointu, E., & Hirsto, L. (2021). Learning analytics in higher education: A systematic literature review. *Computers and Education: Artificial Intelligence*, *2*, 100033. Advance online publication. DOI: 10.1016/j.caeai.2021.100033

Voskoglou, M. G., & Buckley, S. (2012). Problem solving and computational thinking in a learning environment. *Egyptian Computer Science Journal*, *36*(4), 28–46.

Wan, H., Huang, X., Huang, J., & Luo, H. (2024). Will generative AI replace teachers in higher education? A study of teacher and student perceptions. *Studies in Educational Evaluation, 83*, 101395. Advance online publication. DOI: 10.1016/j.stueduc.2024.101395

Williamson, B., & Eynon, R. (2020). Historical threads, missing links, and future directions in AI in education. *Learning, Media and Technology, 45*(3), 223–235. DOI: 10.1080/17439884.2020.1798995

Wong, B. T. M., Li, K. C., & Yang, Y. (2022). Exploring the impact of artificial intelligence on teaching and learning in higher education. *Smart Learning Environments, 9*(16). Advance online publication. DOI: 10.1186/s41039-017-0062-8

Xie, Y., Song, K., & Tondeur, J. (2024). In search of artificial intelligence (AI) literacy in teacher education: A scoping review. *Computers and Education Open, 5*, 100169. DOI: 10.1016/j.caeo.2024.100169

Zawacki-Richter, O., Marín, V., Bond, M., & Gouverneur, F. (2020). Systematic review of research on artificial intelligence applications in higher education. *International Journal of Educational Technology in Higher Education, 17*(39). Advance online publication. DOI: 10.1186/s41239-020-00218-x

Zawacki-Richter, O., Marín, V. I., Bond, M., & Gouverneur, F. (2019). Systematic review of research on artificial intelligence applications in higher education – where are the educators? *International Journal of Educational Technology in Higher Education, 16*(1), 39. Advance online publication. DOI: 10.1186/s41239-019-0171-0

Zhang, W. (2024). Teaching with the algorithm: Anticipations of AI in teacher education. *European Journal of Teacher Education*. Advance online publication. DOI: 10.1080/02619768.2025.2540793

Zhou, X., Chen, L., & Chen, C. H. (2023). Collaborative learning by teaching: An AI-embedded online learning system to support teacher–student co-creation. *Australasian Journal of Educational Technology, 39*(4), 57–75. DOI: 10.14742/ajet.8327

Zhuo, M., Zhou, X., & Chiu, T. K. F. (2024). Through tensions to identity-based motivations: Exploring teacher professional identity in Artificial Intelligence-enhanced teacher training. *Teaching and Teacher Education, 148*, 104736. Advance online publication. DOI: 10.1016/j.tate.2024.104736

Chapter 6
Intelligent Bridges: Designing Culturally Responsive Hybrid Pedagogies Through AI Collaboration

Sovanna Huot
http://orcid.org/0009-0006-8335-442X
Department of Education, National Institute of Education, Phnom Penh, Cambodia

Sovanna Loch
http://orcid.org/0000-0002-1211-1248
Department of English, Nava Nalanda Mahavihara, Bihar, India

Chheangkhy Hok
http://orcid.org/0009-0000-6431-527X
Department of Khmer Literature, University of Heng Samrin Thbongkhmum, Cambodia

Sovannaroth Chheang
http://orcid.org/0009-0007-3382-7169
Department of Education, Sovanna Elton Foreign Language School, Phnom Penh, Cambodia

Phearun Tep
http://orcid.org/0009-0000-2490-677X
Department of English, University of Delhi, New Delhi, India

ABSTRACT

This chapter analyses the use of Artificial Intelligence (AI) as a bridging tool between technology and culture through the lens of the design of Culturally Responsive

DOI: 10.4018/979-8-3373-7462-8.ch006

Hybrid Pedagogy (CRHP). The integration of the four pillars of the CRHP framework, cultural awareness, pedagogical adaptivity, collaborative intelligence, and ethical integrity, is presented to keep hybrid education inclusive and human centred. Through the lens of global case studies and ethical principles, the chapter posits that the most valuable innovations come not from automation of processes but, from the ethically guided human and machine partnership where co-agency is possible. The chapter ends with the assertion that the future of education is dependent on the construction of intelligent bridges, or learning ecosystems, that can integrate multiple dimensions of diversity and creativity with technology to sustain a sense of belonging and shared understanding within a digitally connected society.

1. INTRODUCTION

The 21st century is witnessing significant and multidimensional changes in higher education, primarily attributable to artificial intelligence (AI) and hybrid learning. Higher education institutions are redefining learning spaces that are physical and digital, and that interact and evolve continuously. The global crises, especially the COVID-19 pandemic, have triggered an era of enduring changes to the pedagogical approaches and to the priorities of educational institutions (Hodges et al., 2024). The most notable changes have come in the field of hybrid pedagogy. It signifies a shift from simply blended learning to an innovative and culturally responsive pedagogy that seeks to balance and integrate the technological with the interpersonal and relational.

Garrison and Vaughan (2008) have pioneered a conceptualization of blended learning as an educational paradigm that is integrative by design and attempts to combine online learning environments with face-to-face learning environments. They suggest that hybrid systems transcend merely mixing delivery modes by building communities of inquiry that foster critical reflection, collaboration, and sustained engagement. In a similar vein, Boelens et al. (2017) suggest that hybrid education is most valuable when it can bridge cognitive, social, and teaching presences, thereby promoting learner autonomy and inclusivity alongside meaningful social interactions. Collectively, these perspectives suggest that hybrid education is about bridging the gaps between modalities and meanings, combining the technological efficiency of digital tools and the emotional engagement and contextual sensitivity of human teaching. With hybrid learning systems, new ethical challenges arise along with potential positive outcomes. Zawacki-Richter et al. (2019) state that while transformative potential lies in each of the subfields such as adaptive feedback, predictive analytics, and automated assessment, the tools can entrench structural inequities and cultural biases in the absence of critical application. Similarly, most authors cite that the tools of AI in education are not all the same as the technical approaches; there are social and ethical and overall, morally adaptive approaches that must be taken (Holmes et al., 2019). With little thought put into the tools, the systems can somehow perpetually and rapidly marginalize whole communities of learners along the diverse continuum, as exemplified when the dominant data sets are Anglo, Western, middle class, and economically privileged.

In the case of rapid technological changes, the tension between cultural responsiveness and technological advancement must be resolved. Ecosystems of learning must be situated in such a way that this tension is resolved in a positive way (Huot & Em, 2025). Data driven education encompasses an inherent bias in the values and the political discourse that is framed in learning, intelligence, and success. With the AI tools, technology capacity must be built, but the purpose of the education must be to achieve a new narrative around inclusion, equity, and a culturally sustainable approach. This chapter proposes a new conception of intercultural understanding and AI collaboration to harness technological efficiency and empathy to bridge the gap in innovation through the AI intercultural collaboration pedagogy. AI collaboration is used as a new terminology to define the relationship and partnership of the human educators and human learners with intelligent systems in such a way that all parties engage in the relational co-partnership of knowledge construction and learning process. There has been a notable rise in advocacy for relational paradigms in education theorists. Instead of viewing AI as a technological fix as Selwyn (2019) suggests, educators should think of AI as a sociotechnical partner, a collaborator in a learning ecosystem involving a culturally and socially constructed ecosystem. Luckin (2018) similarly argues, AI should be designed to enhance human intelligence, not substitute it. This illustrates that successful integration of AI depends upon active human reasoning and ethical consideration. Hence, AI collaboration and integration should be seen as a winding pedagogy and a relational imperative for educational innovation, ensuring that innovation in technology in education facilitates and enhances human relations.

The 21st-century hybrid university must move the thinking frameworks of efficiency and automation toward what Razzouk and Shute (2012) call design thinking for education, a problem-solving approach which is iterative, empathetic, and context sensitive. In such a paradigm, AI is a facilitator of intercultural communication, providing mediation in translation, feedback, and personalized interaction. However, such mediation is to remain ethically constrained and subject to the scrutiny, the beneficence and explicability principle of Floridi and Cowls (2022) suggest that AI systems must serve the human good and leave users in a state of blindness and incomprehensibility. The need to balance technological accuracy with cultural intelligence drives the rationale for this chapter. The more globalized and data driven higher education becomes, the more the risk of homogenization, which occurs when a variety of ways of knowing are overridden by the algorithms (Huot & Loch, 2025b). This context is where responsive, culturally aware, AI collaboration becomes a viable option for innovation. In this context, it does not prioritize AI as a technological resource, but as a facilitator of intercultural communication and responsive collaboration, promoting mutual understanding, equitable involvement, and co-creation in global classrooms.

This chapter framing AI collaborations as a type of intelligent empathy addresses the co-creative partnership of human discernment and machine analytics in relation to the respect of cultural diversity and shared learning objectives. This has the potential to transform the educational paradigm from the Artificial Intelligence discourse to what some scholars now refer to as augmented humanity. It clarifies that the role of Artificial Intelligence in education should not seek an optimization of learning processes through a reduction of diversity in the creation of intercultural spaces of dialogue, but instead, focus on the enhancement of the moral and cultural dimensions of learning. This chapter primarily seeks to examine the potential of AI collaborations in building culturally responsive hybrid pedagogies that foster inclusivity, agency, and intercultural dialogue. It synthesizes contributions from the fields of AI ethics, digital pedagogy, and intercultural communication to support the claim that technological intelligence divorced from cultural intelligence serves no constructive purpose.

More specifically, the chapter has four main objectives that are interconnected:

1. To recast AI as not being an instructional design partner that replaces human curricula designers, but instead, a co-creative partner in the process.
2. To ensure cultural responsiveness and equity, particularly in relation to the pedagogical practices supported by AI.
3. To elaborate and defend the Culturally Responsive Hybrid Pedagogy (CRHP) Framework.
4. To promote changes in institutions from AI models based on efficiency to models based on ethics.

2. CONCEPTUAL FOUNDATIONS: HYBRID PEDAGOGY AND INTERCULTURAL RESPONSIVENESS

2.1 Defining Hybrid Pedagogy

Possibly the most constructive innovation in modern higher education is hybrid pedagogy. It is no longer strictly conceptualized as blended learning, as it begins to focus on other facets of education in addition to the simple logistical integration of in-person and online teaching (Huot & Loch, 2025b). It emphasizes flexibility, accessibility, and learner agency. It is no longer enough for blended learning to focus on the logistics of a learning environment that combines different modes of instructional delivery, face-to-face and online. Hybrid pedagogy operates on a different plane, viewing the intersection of different learning environments, face-to-face, online, and teaching modalities as a product of philosophical and cultural cross-fertilization (Huot & Hok, 2025a).

Stommel et al. (2020) argue that blended learning is less a method than a critical praxis. He advocates for teaching approaches that value human relationships, social context, and critical reflection in digitally mediated environments. Likewise, Stommel (2014) suggests that hybrid pedagogy should be a critical humanistic dialogue of educators, learners, and education technologies. It is, among other things, a practical recognition of social equity, critical cognition, and collaborative knowledge construction. Along with other theorists on hybrid pedagogy, Stommel et al. (2020) and Stommel (2014) reinforce the notion that hybrid pedagogy is not simply a rearrangement of teaching styles or methods. It is a philosophy, a conceptual framework that transforms the opportunities of digital pedagogy into constructive possible empowerment of learners as active meaning-makers.

Garrison and Vaughan (2008) introduce the Community of Inquiry model, which suggests that hybrid learning is successful when three intentional alignments, i.e., cognitive, social, and teaching are present. They state that deep and meaningful learning experiences through the purposeful integration of these presences is possible in well-structured hybrid learning environments. The hybrid classroom, therefore, is an adaptive cultural ecosystem, in which participants negotiate identity, language, social belonging, and the use of digital learning tools. This also reflects connectivism theory, which Siemens (2005) posits that learning in networked, and what he refers to as a symptom of advanced technology, is based on the ability to form and navigate connections to various information, people, and contexts, not just the simple acquisition of content. From this perspective, the relational and cultural aspects of hybrid pedagogy are the most prominent. It turns digital environments into negotiation spaces whereby learners' individual and cultural heritages are juxtaposed to the knowledge systems of globalization. The most successful hybrid learning environments, as Bonk and Graham (2006) stress, blend not just media but also cultures and pedagogical traditions, thereby providing a new opportunity to a responsive flexible learning design that attains a diverse set of beliefs. Hence, hybrid learning epitomizes cultural practices of adaptation with technology as a facilitator of intercultural dialogue and the knowledge transfer of inclusion.

Though Veletsianos and Houlden (2020) warn us about the danger of hybrid pedagogy falling into the trap of technological instrumentalism. Simply if innovation means improvement. They state that the digital turn in education is as much about power as it is about pedagogy. This suggests focusing more critically on hybrid education and the digital tools to employ facilitating it. More critically on digital infrastructures that mediate how people engage, how people are included or excluded, and how people are represented (or not represented). Therefore, the integration of AI into hybrid pedagogy, must be based on the premise that the designer(s) are (technologically and culturally) literate and that all students' voices and experiences are the focal point of the design.

2.2 Intercultural and Culturally Responsive Theories

The human aspect of hybrid pedagogy is further explained with the help of the intercultural communication theory and culturally responsive pedagogy. Both theories place diversity and empathy at the centre of transformative education. Deardorff (2006) defines intercultural communication competence as the ability to communicate effectively and appropriately in intercultural situations, (and) is the product of one's intercultural knowledge, skills and attitudes. Deardorff (2006) believes that such competence is achieved through self-awareness, cultural empathy and behavioural flexibility. Applying this to hybrid learning environments, it means that both educators and learners should focus on the development of digital intercultural sensitivity, which is the ability to engage and communicate in a respectful and reflexive way across different virtual cultures.

Gay (2018) describes culturally responsive pedagogy as the use of culturally diverse learners' knowledge, experiences, and performance styles to construct more effective and relevant educational experiences. Culturally responsive pedagogy, according to her, is also not supposed to be viewed as a luxury, but a necessity to restructure the educational system's inequitable practices. This, in the context of hybrids, means that digital tools and AI should not just communicate and disseminate learning content effectively, but should also be responsive to the varied cultural patterns of communication, diverse languages, and different ways of knowing and understanding. Ladson-Billings (1995) also states that culturally responsive pedagogy empowers students intellectually, socially, and emotionally, framing education as cultural affirmation and social justice. This describes the necessity of constructing pedagogies that affirm and validate the students' everyday lifeworld, while also preparing them to unmask and tackle the oppressive power structures. In the context of hybrid education, this means creating digital environments that appreciate and recognize multiplicity, where students' diverse cultural backgrounds are not stifled, but are utilized as valuable resources for inspiration and innovation.

The relationship between hybrid pedagogy and CRP provides a valuable theoretical foundation: hybrid pedagogy offers the structural flexibility for individualized responsive relationships, while CRP fills this relationship with equity, personhood, and contextual grounding. This relationship is also framed in Vygotsky (1978) sociocultural perspective, which attributes learning to social mediation, the integration of individual mental processes and social cultural resources. In digital and hybrid pedagogy, AI is one of those resources that provides the communication and support structures. Yet, as Kim et al. (2025) notes, this mediation must be culturally informed and dialogic, not mechanistic, so that the digital learning environments do not simply accommodate the students' cultural contexts but are framed and designed to be culturally responsive from the start.

In addition, theorists of intercultural relations, especially Hofstede (2001), remind us that communication styles, power distance, and preferred ways of learning fall under the sway of culture and its many manifestations. For instance, high-context cultures may be more reliant on relational and implicit cues, while low-context cultures tend to favour more direct and explicit forms of communication. In hybrid learning environments, AI-based systems that ignore these cultural nuances may misread learners and provide unfair feedback and inaccurate or inappropriate evaluations. Therefore, the design and evaluation of hybrid pedagogy need to incorporate cultural analytics, which is the study of the cultural dimensions that influence participation and performance. Finally, Alim and Paris (2017) defend the need for culturally sustaining pedagogy, which, in its further development, is an extension of critical race pedagogy (CRP) that goes beyond mere inclusion, but actively seeks to maintain and extend linguistic and cultural pluralism, and, in so doing, protect minority languages and ways of knowing and being from the homogenizing effects of technology. In hybrid learning, this perspective means that AI systems should be developed in ways that go beyond simply translating materials from one language to another.

2.3 Challenges in AI-Mediated Cultural Integration

D'Ignazio and Klein (2020) call attention to the data feminism gaps, which focuses on the systemic bias within the frameworks of data collecting, tagging, and interpreting processes that overlook the data from the non-Western, female, and minority groups. They state that data are not neutral; they are products of power and politics, and that means the algorithms that process the data reproduce inequities. In the same way, Noble (2018) demonstrates in Algorithms of Oppression how search engines and recommendation systems amplify the dominant Eurocentric narratives in the digital realm while also perpetuating the oppression of others in the form of race and gender.

As valuable as the personalization of services by AI systems might be, they are also likely to bypass human decision-making altogether. Holmes et al. (2019) mentioned that personalization should not be confused with understanding, adaptive learning systems may change because of interaction with a user, but this does not mean that the systems understand the user's intent, meaning or any of the participant's cultural context. The importance of this claim is evident in hybrid pedagogy, where the culture of meaning-making of the participant is critical. For example, systems generated using data from the West may misinterpret the absence of communication in participants (Anderson et al., 2025; Huot & Loch, 2025a).

Intentionality and design are also required for Cultural Responsiveness and cannot be a post-hoc solution. Eubanks (2018) notes that Automation, like AI, often reflects the social systems that construct it; without critical inspection, this reflects systems of inequality under the shield of fairness. As such, the addition of intercultural sensitivity and Cultural Responsiveness within AI education is framed by the need to Design for Diversity rather than Defaulting to Diversity. This calls for the holistic inclusion of cultural, multilingual, and ethical dimensions of care, not as an afterthought, but from the outset of the algorithm's design. More complexity must be added to the hierarchies of language and the hierarchies of knowledge present within the global AI systems. Language models, like Google Translate and DeepL, continue to be advanced but because of the global dominant language data and the data sources they still use, they continue to use and ignore many of the indigenous and local and regionally used languages. Because of the hegemony of English in digital communication, Canagarajah (2013) explains that it risks silencing alternative epistemologies and modes of reasoning.

The AI mediated learning systems keeps and stores massive amounts of student data which creates ethical concerns about the privacy of the student and about consent. Issues of trust, ownership and transparency are central to these concerns. UNESCO (2022) states that civil respect of ethics and the cultural side of things must be incorporated together when it comes to the ethics surrounding data collection.

To conclude, AI and hybrid pedagogy can potentially fully integrate the democratization and individualization of learning; however, their impact will be determined by the degree of cultural responsiveness they integrate. D'Ignazio and Klein (2020) remind us that to be equitable, there must be an innovation of the technologies that shifts from seeing data as neutral to recognizing data as situated, relational, and ethical, as demonstrated in the Figure 1.

Figure 1.

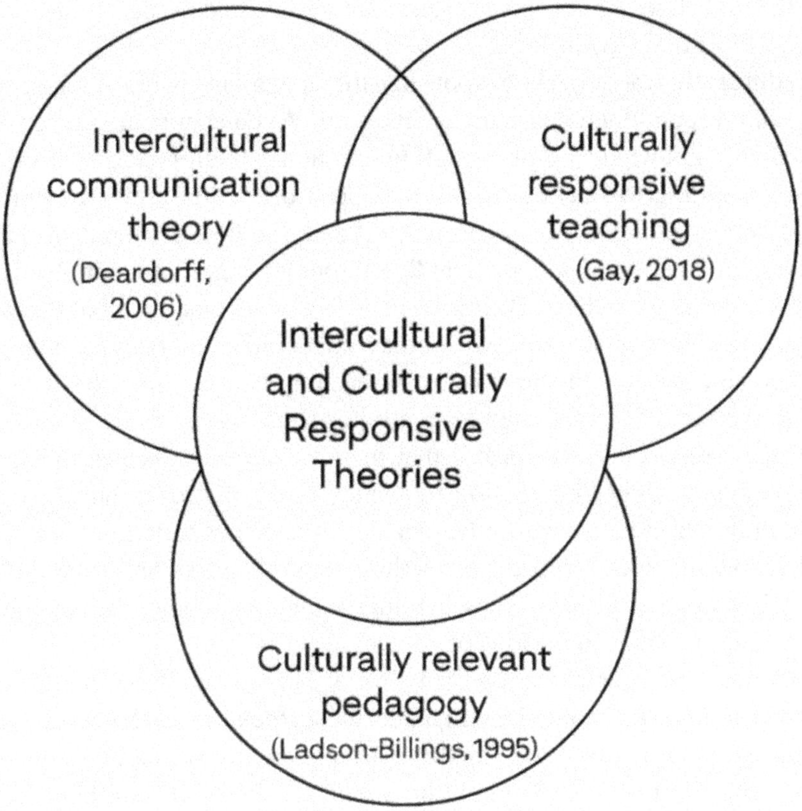

3. THE IMPACT OF AI PARTNERSHIP IN HYBRID PEDAGOGICAL DESIGN

3.1 AI as Co-Agent in Pedagogy

AI collaboration brings to the forefront a new branch in educational philosophy. Instead of viewing artificial intelligence as a tool of simple automation, AI systems can act as co-agents in the educational ecosystem. In this case, AI systems do not replace the teacher or the learner; AI becomes an interactive partner in the teaching and learning processes. In this case, the educational triad consists of a human teacher, an AI teaching partner, and a student or a learner. In a positive form of AI collaboration, Floridi and Cowls (2022) describe a possible collaboration where the entities work to achieve a shared and identifiable educational purpose. AI plays an ethically and algorithmically positive role in teaching when it collaborates with educational objectives of transparency, accountability, and human control over the AI system (Floridi & Cowls, 2022).

According to this model, AI is responsible for recognizing patterns, personalizing learning, and responding to learners' needs, while AI educators are responsible for contextualizing knowledge, demonstrating emotional intelligence, and mediating ethically. According to Luckin (2018), the speed of an AI system's computation is not the best potential of an AI system; instead, the best potential of AI lies in its ability to augment human understanding through insight into complex learning processes. In the same manner, Holmes et al. (2019) state that the art of meaningful, AI integration hinges on the ability to achieve an equilibrium between algorithmic intelligence and the humanistic aspects of teaching and learning. Selwyn (2019) challenges the view of technology as neutral or subservient. Systems of machine learning may propose to an educator that they accelerate a learner's progression because they have higher interaction frequency in the platform, but the educator may culturally understand that the learner's silence or hesitation is a sign of contemplation and not disengagement, something that AI cannot understand (Huot & Hok, 2025b; Kim et al., 2025). Thus, AI-augmented pedagogy relies on educators to preserve the cultural dimensions of education.

In hybrid environments, the combination of human and machine partnership creates what is called distributed intelligence, where the different levels of cognition of the various agents contribute to the formation of creativity and decision making. As Seldon and Abidoye (2018) put it, here is in the era of co-intelligence, where the unique human traits of empathy and moral reasoning are supplemented with the AI capacity of recognizing patterns in data. This collaborative perspective is also consistent with constructivism and connectivism. As Siemens (2005) explains, in a digital world, learning consists of the capacity to create connections between different nodes of information, which can be human or machine. If you consider the AI partnership as a learning extension of this theory, you can think of the intelligent algorithm as a new node within the learning ecosystem.

Fundamentally, when AI collaboration is framed as co-agency, it conceptualizes the role of the human educator as an ethical architect, balancing the affordances of AI and the realities of the learner, and reimagines education as an ecology of intelligence rather than a hierarchy of control. As Floridi (2013) states, ethics must be built into the architecture of information systems, and this holds true for education design, where a cultural lens and a relational dimension of care are critical for an ethical framework.

3.2 Applications and Innovations

DreamBox, CenturyTech, and Smart Sparrow, for instance, employ AI-powered adaptive systems. These systems provide individualized instruction based on real-time learner information. They create unique learning pathways that constantly change by assessing gaps in knowledge, learning styles, and the degree of active participation. VanLehn (2011) notes that such systems improve instructional efficiency by modifying the difficulty, pace, and format of learning activities. However, feedback is not the same as understanding, and as Williamson and Eynon (2020) point out, even though AI can produce a syntactically accurate response, it cannot understand the cultural and contextual nuances of a given response. Thus, the most effective collaboration with AI requires human interpretation. In AI feedback, the educator sees a tool to improve meaningful discourse and a way to prompt thoughtful debates to update the AI suggestions. This approach reinvents AI as a simple feedback tool to become a more complex partner that encourages higher levels of thinking (metacognition) and understanding across cultures.

Teachers and educators can utilize multilingual AI technology to connect with more students and develop culturally rich learning environments. DeepL and Microsoft Translator are examples of AI multilingual technology that students and teachers can utilize to communicate and collaborate in real time. As noted Anderson et al. (2025), while AI translators provide an unprecedented democratization of communication, they oversimplify communication in diverse contexts and lose important cultural nuances. Therefore, educators are encouraged to utilize the translators as tools that foster more global understanding, while still maintaining and respecting local cultural expressions. Educators can utilize translation in a variety of creative and culturally responsive ways (Huot & Hok, 2025a). In addition to the traditional translate this activity, they can design activities that make students consider and reflect in greater depth about the nuances in communication across different languages and the importance of different cultural contexts. As noted in the research, AI technology and multilingual concepts in teaching support the development of inclusive, plurilingual, and empathetic skill sets, rather than a reliance on a singular language standardization (Huot et al., 2025).

The use of new analytical dashboards for collaborative learning is another example of innovation in AI that analyses participation, groups, and culture within a hybrid classroom. These dashboards track and visualize patterns of interaction, showing who speaks and how often, in what language, etc. These systems provide what Ifenthaler and Yau (2020) call actionable insights for inclusive pedagogy, empowering educators to act when certain cultural representatives go unvoiced. The data-driven systems described must also remain ethically constrained. Slade and Prinsloo (2013) characterize analytics as for care, not control, which puts the focus on empowering rather than monitoring the learners. In the context of inter-cultural education, learning analytics serve the purpose of monitoring equity, helping educators and peers ensure that every individual in the hybrid setting is seen and heard.

3.3. Ethical and Epistemological Limits

The use of AI in education not only creates new possibilities. It also creates possible new fundamental epistemological and ethical challenges. A pertinent question as described by Williamson and Eynon (2020) is whether AI will ever possess the ability to understand and appreciate empathy, culture, or context? Most critical AI educators agree that, despite the new innovations, AI will only have performative intelligence as opposed to understanding the true meaning behind concepts and ideas. According to Bender et al. (2021), many of the Large Language Models (LLMs) as a result, the only output of a LLM is a statistically generated output that may or may not similarly align to the intended concepts of the input.

Additionally, the lack of knowledge surrounding AI highlights the importance of AI literacy, both for students and teachers. Knox et al. (2020) articulate that empowering critical literacy involves grappling with, not only what AI does, but how it frames knowledge and power. Certain types of knowledge, those which dictate the structure of the data, are always favoured by AI. What educational algorithms will capture, and what forms of reasoning they will exclude is unequivocally a function of the dominant discourse of Western education. Educational algorithms that get instructed on Western pedagogical practices will likely overlook indigenous and storytelling approaches to reasoning. In this respect, ethically using AI will require a form of cultural auditing, which is the practice of assessing algorithms to capture the cultural knowledge they exclude and reshape. D'Ignazio and Klein (2020) articulate this idea of data feminism, which is centred on empowering the voices of the marginalized and subverting the false neutrality of dominant power structures.

Lastly, the intersection of privacy and surveillance technologies is quite real. As AI educational technologies gather data on learners (e.g., behaviour, language, and even biometrics), the line between surveillance and personalization disappears. Eubanks (2018) is correct in observing that automated systems can reproduce social stratification under the guise of efficiency and are often making decisions that the people they affect cannot access. This highlights the need for hybrid education to operationalize algorithmic transparency and the use of data with consent.

To summarize, the use of AI in hybrid teaching is perhaps the most advanced and riskiest of all the suggested human-computer partnerships. The positive potential is in greater accessibility, empathy, and flexibility. The negative potential is in greater bias and reduced user agency. The challenge for teachers, then, is not to reject the use of AI, but to guide it to serve as a learning partner in the culturally relevant fabric of teaching, keeping agency, pluralism, and ethics at the centre. As Holmes et al. (2019) aptly state, AI will change education not by teaching us less about what it means to be human, but by requiring us to know it more deeply, as seen in Table 1.

Table 1.

AI Domain	Key Applications	Ethical and Cultural Notes
Adaptive Learning	DreamBox, CenturyTech	Ensure cultural context in data-driven personalization.
Generative Feedback	ChatGPT, GrammarlyGO	Combine AI feedback with human interpretation.
AI Translation	DeepL, Microsoft Translator	Preserve linguistic diversity and cultural nuance.
Collaborative Analytics	Learning Dashboards	Protect privacy; promote inclusion through ethical use.

4. THE CULTURALLY RESPONSIVE HYBRID PEDAGOGY (CRHP) FRAMEWORK

4.1 Core Principles and Rationale

The CRHP Framework stands out as the only framework that directly portable to practice and assesses the incorporation of artificial intelligence (AI) in higher education with a model that is explicitly inter- cultural and ethically oriented. The CRHP Framework is rooted in recognizing that hybrid education, in its most transformative sense, is not about the technology; it is about the culture. The assertion draws from the recognition that learning technologies (including AI) are embedded in specific social, cultural, and moral frameworks. Intercultural education theorists maintain that transformative pedagogy, in its most ideal form, focuses on pluralism (Deardorff, 2006; Hofstede, 2001). With the current push within universities to utilize AI to customize students' learning experiences, the CRHP Framework aims to integrate empathy, ethical care and educational equity to counter cultural embedding bias and techno-determinism.

The framework theorizes AI-human interactions as an ecosystem of cyclical and reflective practice, where cultural awareness, collaborative and adaptive pedagogy, collaborative intelligence, and ethical integrity, anchor and reinforce the cycle. Cultural awareness initiates this cycle and builds sensitivity to the ways in which culture shapes cognition, communication, and the varied ways individuals may participate in a learning process. Intercultural competence, as Deardorff (2006) describes, is not a competence and is rather a process which must be designed for educational experiences. This aligns with the CRHP emphasis on awareness as a continuing pedagogical position. From this foundation, cultural pedagogical insight and adaptive pedagogy design learning pathways in AI-moderated adaptive pathways and responsive feedback to the varying needs of individual students. Laurillard (2013) suggests that effective learning design must be grounded in dialogue, and this is the principle which drives adaptive hybrid pedagogy, where personalization draws from both learner and cultural data.

During this cycle, collaborative intelligence symbolizes a movement away from the perspective of AI being an adversary to humans, and instead, viewing AI as being an ally in the co-creative process. Levy and Murnane (2013) argue that the most effective educational uses of AI occur when technology supports (rather than replaces) human creativity, communication, and problem solving. Within the CRHP framework, collaborative intelligence facilitates intercultural engagement by increasing the possibility of dialogue, peer-to-peer learning, and global connections, while still prioritizing human agency and relational pedagogy. Finally, the framework's integrity operates as a stabilizing core and positions fairness, transparency, inclusivity, and accountability as the fundamental principles of design and deployment of AI. Bynum (2006) and UNESCO (2022) assert that ethics, particularly in the educational contexts at the intersection of power, access, and representation, should not be seen as after-the-fact constraints, but rather, as primary design elements.

As a whole, the CRHP framework shows the relationship between the cultural awareness and the rest of the framework's components, including the pedagogical adaptation and the synergistic refinement of the learning practice through collaboration, and how the ethical integrity of all the components sustains accountability throughout the entire hybrid ecosystem. The cyclical nature of the framework promotes constant feedback during the processes of design, implementation, and reflection, and this promotes the evolution of hybrid learning within the prism of culture and technology, all the while remaining human-centred and ethically grounded.

4.2 Implications for Practice

In the meanwhile, Using AI with clear ethical rules of CRHP: teaching AI literacy has teachers interpret AI feedback and redesign the evaluations that prioritise inclusion and student growth, not automation, as the three main following points:

1. **Curriculum Design:** Embedding modules on AI literacy and intercultural reflection is crucial to help learners understand the dynamics, including the

strengths and weaknesses, of intelligent systems. Such empowerment enables students to examine digital education's bias, representation, and ethics.

2. **Instructional Practice:** Balanced pedagogy that combines machine-generated feedback (e.g. language correction, analytics-based insights) with teacher interpretation is essential. Educators, as ethical mediators, contextualize AI outputs through cultural lenses and empathy.
3. **Assessment Strategies:** AI-supported analytics can be used to design assessments that are inclusive and formative, focusing on growth, not compliance. For instance, the coupled use of adaptive feedback and cultural participation observations can improve equity and fairness in assessing a diversity of learners.

The CRHP Framework embodies a technological shift from hybrid learning to culturally centric AI. It designates ethical human agency and cultural sensitivity as cornerstones of educational sustainability and innovation. CRHP constructs a digitally intelligent educational ecosystem that balances values and human innovation to offer a hybrid future university that is temporally advanced and permanently humane.

5. CASE STUDIES AND GLOBAL PERSPECTIVES

The world is experiencing an unequal integration of artificial intelligence (AI) into hybrid learning environments. This is a result of contextual innovation and cultural constraints. Scholars Holmes et al. (2019) and Zawacki-Richter et al. (2019) argue that, educational systems globally, must integrate AI not as a one-size-fits-all solution, but as a technologically contextualized fusion that is influenced by local pedagogy, language, and institutional frameworks. Likewise, Selwyn (2019) cautions that educational technology should be viewed through local lenses to avoid unnecessary replication of western-centred pedagogies.

5.1 Vietnam: Cross-Cultural AI Translation and Linguistic Inclusion

The incorporation of digital and hybrid teaching and learning practices into Vietnam's higher education system is one of the components of the country's educational modernization strategy (Nguyen & Hamid, 2021). However, varying urban and rural university Linguistic and Cultural inequities, especially in English-medium instruction, Further focuses the concern. A cross-cultural AI translation project was initiated to bridge this gap as a partnership between Can Tho University and the University of Social Sciences and Humanities (Hanoi). The project employed AI translation tools, such as DeepL, Google Translate API, and ChatGPT, to assist hybrid seminars with students from diverse regional and ethnic backgrounds in the bilingual and trilingual hybrid seminars. These AI translation tools alleviated the linguistic barriers and facilitated the participation of students from dominantly non-participating languages by providing online remote lectures and real-time translation and transcription.

Loan and Th y (2024) state that the use of multilingual AI not only widened the gap to access but also restructured the communicative hierarchies by giving power to previously language-excluded students. Canagarajah (2013) also notes that such plurilingual practices encourage translingual competence, the ability to fluidly maneuver and negotiate multiple linguistic codes in each global learning context.

Nevertheless, educators engaged in the initiative highlighted the need for critical human intervention. As Nguyen et al. (2024) indicated, automatic translation tools do not understand nuances of some idioms and culturally specific phrases, which can result in omission, distortion and even alteration of meanings. In response to these challenges, educators practiced the human-in-the-loop AI approach (Floridi & Cowls, 2022) and enlisted bilingual faculty members to review the AI translations with students. This initiative improved the accuracy of translations and turned translation reviews into educational exercises of cultural representation and cultural interpretation. In participation reports (UNESCO, 2025), the project recorded a positive change in the level of participation for students from rural and ethnic minority groups.

5.2 The Netherlands: Design-Based AI Collaboration and Intercultural Teamwork

Educational design research and project-based learning have long been major fields of interest for The Netherlands (De Laat & Prinsen, 2014; Laurillard, 2013). Utrecht University has launched a pilot project called "Designing Together" with AI aimed to understand the potential of AI collaboration tools for supporting intercultural collaboration and iterative learning in hybrid design studios. The project employed a range of AI-driven collaborative tools (e.g., generative writing assistants, feedback via algorithms, and analytics dashboards) to facilitate cross-continental design collaboration among students from Europe, Asia, and Africa. Participants worked in teams to develop digital prototypes to solve global challenges, such as sustainability and public health. AI tools used for collaboration evaluated team discussions and provided feedback on the balance of participation and the extent of cognitive diversity.

Levy and Murnane (2013) contend that in an AI environment, routine cognitive tasks will be automated, and this will mean a premium is placed on problem solving, creativity and collaboration. The Utrecht model exemplified this by setting AI as a reflective mirror, so students had to think about the group and decision-making processes. The project's findings (De Laat & Prinsen, 2014), AI-enabled feedback loops, fostered empathy at the intercultural level. Students from high-context communication cultures (e.g., Japan, India) started to participate more actively in discussions, while students from low-context cultures became better at reading and responding to indirect communication. This aligns with the cultural dimension model (Hofstede, 2001), which captures the communication style variations in the collectivist–individualist and high–low context cultural dimensions.

Additionally, the provision of AI-driven learning analytics facilitated meta-cognitive reflection. Pea and Linn (2020) argue that in reflective learning, there is more of a cognitive payoff when learners can see the patterns of their participation and engagement. In Utrecht, for example, AI dashboards showed which participants dominated or were silenced in discussions. This facilitated self-regulation of the group toward more balanced participation.

Even with the benefits, project coordinators described the ethical issues around data privacy and the transparency of the algorithms used. Following the plea for explainable AI in education of Williamson and Eynon (2020), Utrecht incorporated AI Workshops, where students had the opportunity to examine how their data was used for analysis and how algorithms applied to automated feedback. This exemplified the embodiment of AI literacy (Huot & Such, 2025; Knox et al., 2020) and enabled students to make an ethical stance around the construction of AI rather than being passive data objectives. Overall, the Dutch case showed that, when lightning the collaborative AI through participatory and transparent design, it can foster and intercultural understanding, collaboration, and reflective learning. The project illustrated the CRHP framework's insistence that the collaboration of human and machine intelligence be kept as dialogic rather than as a partnership one based on automation.

5.3 Australia: Hybrid Mentoring and Indigenous Epistemologies

Australia has exemplified the integration of Indigenous knowledge systems with AI-supported mentoring and analytics. Such an initiative is an alignment with the CRHP framework's integrity and cultural responsiveness, showing that technology is used to improve local epistemologies, rather than remove them. The project, from the University of Queensland and the National Centre for Indigenous Digital Education (NCIDE), consisted of developing equitable hybrid mentoring systems of AI analytics dashboards and Indigenous pedagogy yarning (story-based dialogue) and pedagogy relational learning (Bessarab & Ng'Andu, 2010).

To understand student mentoring needs, learning logs and engagement patterns were analysed through AI. While most predictive analytics models identify at-risk behaviours, the Australian model, influenced by relational ethics (Yunkaporta, 2020), referred to these notifications as strengthening relational invitations. Hero et al. (2024) recount Indigenous narratives as pedagogical tools emphasizing relationally, storytelling, and in-spirit, which operate in the community. Thus, the hybrid mentoring model framed cultural assets in supporting learners and pivoted from deficit narratives. With AI, Indigenous scholars designed data visualization tools to reflect non-Western epistemic logics (Battiste, 2019) and adopted a view of learning progression as cyclical instead of linear.

Integralists trained all sage AI-driven narrative analysis to enhance and support students' reflective journaling and storytelling to help them track themes of identity, belonging, and resilience. Such tools provided both a quantitative and qualitative perspective on learner experience. The project's most significant success was its epistemic pluralism, in this case, understanding that AI, in Indigenous pedagogy, can only be used in a positive way when it is based on Indigenous methodological ethics. The project operated within the bounds of the Australian AI Ethics Framework, Department of Industry, Science, Energy and Resources, (DISER, 2021) which focuses on fairness, privacy and accountability. Indigenous scholars were part of the governance board to ensure the data sovereignty principles, ownership, access, and control of cultural data, were respected (Kukutai & Taylor, 2016).

Successful outcomes included: strengthened student belonging, the creation of culturally attuned analytics, and increased retention of Indigenous students (NCIDE Report, 2023). However, beyond the metrics, the initiative reframed success to include relational wellbeing, in the spirit of the moral architecture of information systems (Bynum, 2006).

5.4 Comparative Insights: Toward a Global Ethic of AI Collaboration

The three case studies taken together illustrate the potential of AI collaboration in hybrid learning as a relational construct, rather than a singular model, and as a culturally attuned practice. Affirming the diversity of geography and the scale of the institutions involved, some common converging insights include:

1. **Cultural Situatedness is Critical:** The pedagogical benefits of AI are maximized when technology is integrated with the local cultural logics and linguistic ecologies (Deardorff, 2006; Gay, 2018). In Vietnam, the multilingual translation initiatives promoted equitable access to information; in Australia, Indigenous mentorship reframed the use of analytics for surveillance as relational.
2. **The Necessity of Participatory and Human-Centred Design:** In all cases, the educators and students collaboratively designed the AI tools. This is consistent

with principle of human-centred design (Norman, 2013). When users participate in the design process, the systems are designed to accommodate user diversity instead of a top-down approach.

3. **Ethics and Transparency Build Trust:** It is recommended by UNESCO (2022) that for AI to be integrated in an equitable way, there must be transparency. While participatory algorithm audits in AI in the Netherlands allowed students to speak about the interpretation of the data and the accountability of the data owners, transparency remained the key.
4. **Collaboration is Not Limited to Human-Machine Interactions:** As illustrated by the examples, real AI collaboration is more complex. It includes partnerships across educators, learners, communities, and AI. This is consistent with Seldon and Abidoye (2018) when they state that the purpose of education in the age of AI must be to foster the concept of "co-intelligence," the collaboration of human empathy and the machine's precision.
5. **Equity is Ethical and Epistemic:** Equity in the age of AI-enhanced hybrid learning cannot be limited to issues of access; it is about the recognition of different ways of knowing. The digital education of the disenfranchised cannot be divorced from the knowledge systems that are culturally specific, as stated by Battiste (2019), and Paris and Alim (2017).

This is why Selwyn (2019) insists that technological innovation in education should reflect diversity rather than dictate uniformity. The CRHP framework positions AI collaboration as a cultural act and a process of co-creation that donor's diversity and fosters a shared understanding, as illustrated in Figure 2.

Figure 2.

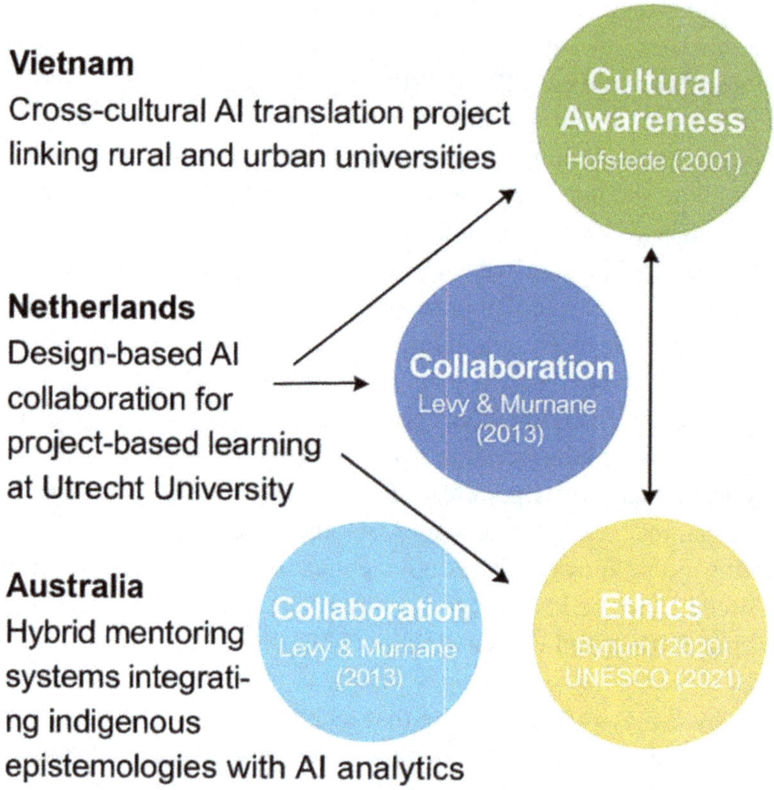

6. ETHICAL, EQUITY, AND POLICY CONSIDERATIONS

AI has the potential to transform hybrid education, but without strong ethical frameworks, the embedding of such technologies will threaten cultural diversity, the dignity of the individual, and the integrity of the academic process. While the value frameworks of educational technologies should be negatively defined with respect to the absence of certain values, it is essential that the embedding of AI technologies into learning design places a premium on positive values such as fairness, transparency, and inclusion as opposed to efficiency. Bynum (2006) and (Floridi, 2019) are some of those scholars that argue that AI should aim to support humanity and not reduce education to a method of extracting data from students. The considerations that follow illustrate the importance of culturally and ethically focused AI driven pedagogy. One of the primary ethical concerns in education supported by AI is still the culturally tending biases that affect algorithms. Machine learning algorithms trained on homogenous samples will reinforce hegemonic stereotypes, bias, and the absence of the marginalized. D'Ignazio and Klein (2020) argue that the absence of data, inclusive of a feminist perspective, is a primary cause of algorithmic inequity.

Zhang et al. (2022) study outlines various ways educational institutions can support efforts toward more accountability in the use of educational AI. Building inclusive data training and contextual assessments into curricula is one example, which involves the use of datasets representing various languages, regions, and cultures. A case in point, bias in testing and predictive analytics may be improved through the testing of localized AI algorithms, which are adapted to the norms of a particular community (i.e., community-centred algorithms). From a theorization perspective, an inclusive approach to predictive analytics and testing algorithms should be integrated into the design of AI systems to foster the accountability and ethical use of educational data. Trust and relational ethics are central to the 'beyond compliance' dimension of the ethical use of educational data. AI in Education operates under the premise that, per the recommendation, data collection in educational settings must be governed by the principles of informed consent, transparency, and cultural protection, which in this case, refers to the collection and use of learners' educational data (UNESCO, 2022).

Additionally, the use of data in a culturally sensitive manner requires an understanding of differing perceptions of privacy and ownership. For example, in some Indigenous and collectivist cultures, knowledge and data are viewed as a collective good, not the possession of individuals (Kukutai & Taylor, 2016). Therefore, educational institutions need to operationalize the principles of data sovereignty, which empowers communities to control the use, rights, and meaning of their cultural data. The digital divide continues to be a cross-domain inequity with both cultural and technological dimensions. The availability of AI-supported hybrid education tools is constrained not only by physical infrastructure, but also by financial resources, language proficiency, digital skills, and the availability of culturally relevant educational materials. Holmes et al. (2019) assert that to achieve equitable innovation, there must be a balance among accessibility of tools, multiple language support, and culturally relevant educational materials.

Increasing equity in access means building AI systems that require less bandwidth, regionally relevant open-source systems, and advocating for AI literacy as a basic right (UNESCO, 2022). Digital inclusion means focusing on both access and culture, so educational technology strengthens, rather than bypasses, local teaching methodologies. The primary responsibility lies with institutions for the ethical integration of AI. Universities need to set up AI ethics and intercultural inclusion boards that monitor technology integration and data governance. These boards should draw on a wide range of disciplines to achieve pluralism in decision-making (Williamson & Eynon, 2020), including education, technology, ethics, and culture.

Policy frameworks should go further by mandating that the teaching and learning AI systems perform ethical impact assessments with a focus on social, as well as technical, dimensions. Holmes et al. (2019) suggest that institutional governance of AI in education should change from reactive regulation to proactive stewardship, creating an anticipatory culture of accountability.

In AI-enriched education, leadership must also include ethical foresight and empathic governance. Educators and leaders need training that allows the development of AI literacy with an emphasis on justice, empathy, and accountability. As Seldon and Abidoye (2018) remark, preparing institutions for the future involves fostering co-intelligence, the integration of human discretion with the accuracy of machines.

Continuing education programs should prioritize:

- Critical AI literacy: significance of algorithmic processes in shaping what gets known and decided (Knox et al., 2020)
- Cultural empathy: the role of technology in shaping (and even, the absence of) cross-sectional communication and inclusion; and
- Ethical analysis: the impact of automation in education on society.

Such capacity-building efforts should allow institutions to position technology leaders as system builders and ethical guardians of the human-centred aspect of innovation.

Also, the use of AI in hybrid models of teaching and learning should be directed toward the enhancement of human dignity and ethical openness. Supporting the right to difference means education as more than cognition; it must be cultural. Ethical innovation, as Braidotti (2022) posits, calls for the creation of systems that, at the very least, increase empathy, relationally, and agency. Thus, the CRHP model best represents conceptions of UNESCO (2022) on AI that is culturally inclusive, one that learns alongside humanity, values diversity, and preserves the ethical essence of education in the digital age, as depicted in Table 2.

Table 2.

Dimension	Focus Area	Key Action and Principle
Algorithmic Bias	Inclusive training and contextual data testing	Ensure fairness and cultural representation in AI datasets.
Data Ethics	Transparency and consent in data use	Uphold privacy, cultural sensitivity, and informed participation.
Digital Equity	Access and localized technologies	Expand open, multilingual, and low-cost AI learning tools.
Institutional Policy	Governance and oversight	Establish AI ethics boards and inclusion taskforces.
Leadership & Development	Ethical and empathetic AI literacy	Train educators to integrate fairness, empathy, and accountability.

7. CONCLUSION

In this chapter, I embodied the 'intelligent bridges' metaphor as a redefined perceptive tool that envisions artificial intelligence (AI) as a connector of culture with code, diversity with data, and humanness with technology. AI here does not stand in for human connections; instead, I see it as a promoter of intercultural understanding, ethical imagination, and learning through dialogue. Integrating AI into Culturally Responsive Hybrid Pedagogy (CRHP) sees the technology as a co-creative partner with educators and learners in the productive design of ethically responsive educational ecosystems.

The CRHP model perceives hybrid pedagogy as an intricate cultural ecosystem with technology as the integrator. Human wisdom gets amplified with the addition of technological systems. Learning in this context goes beyond the cognitive and procedural and emphasizes the relational and interpretative dimensions of meaning-making. This activates a deal of emotional engagement and algorithmic imprecision. CRHP incorporates all four pillars of cultural awareness, pedagogical adaptivity, collaborative intelligence, and ethical integrity, as a result transforming hybrid learning spaces into energized intercultural communities of practice. In such spaces, the relational differences of diversity are not viewed as a hindrance to productivity, but rather, as a radical and positive enabler of collective innovation and advancement.

In the future's hybrid university, AI collaboration is culturally definable as a new form of dialogue where partnerships allow algorithms to learn from the diverse human spectrum, empathetic inclusive design from educators, and student active participation as knowledge co-creators across various languages, cultures, and disciplines. This indicates a paradigm shift from automation to ethical co-agency, leveraging the interdependence of human originality and artificial intelligence. This co-agency means education is no longer confined to procedural changes but rather to transformative learning, where adaptive digital systems foster a sense of community, critical thinking, and cultural awareness. Ultimately, the promise of innovative technology embeds intelligent bridges the opportunity to articulate a human-centred digital crossroads of minds, cultures, and technologies. Such bridges uphold the ethical imperative of educating for wisdom, justice, and empathy amidst the encroaching algorithms of the age. They remind us that the most significant metric of intelligence, whether human or artificial, is not in how fast and accurately tasks are completed, but rather in the ability to empathize, relate, and to collaboratively envision a world possible. The ever-evolving global education ecosystem with its hybrid and AI-enabled transformations presents us with an urgent and hopeful continuum.

Constructing intelligent bridges requires the ability to contest the standardizing grip of technology, the adaptive ability to craft supportive ecosystems, and the preservation of learning's intrinsic human values. In this way, educators and technology innovators can ensure that the digital transformation of learning is not an end in and of itself, but rather a route towards a world that is equitable, interculturally connected, and sufficiently integrated. A world wherein AI coexists with humans, rather than in isolation.

REFERENCES

Alim, H. S., & Paris, D. (2017). What is culturally sustaining pedagogies and why does it matter? In D. Paris & H. S. Alim (Eds.), *Culturally sustaining pedagogies: Teaching and learning for justice in a changing world* (pp. 1–24). Teachers College Press.

Anderson, J. E., Nguyen, C. A., & Moreira, G. (2025). Generative AI-driven personalization of the community of inquiry model: Enhancing individualized learning experiences in digital classrooms. *The International Journal of Information and Learning Technology*, *42*(3), 296–310. DOI: 10.1108/IJILT-10-2024-0240

Battiste, M. (2019). *Decolonizing education: Nourishing the learning spirit*. University of British Columbia Press. DOI: 10.59962/9781895830972

Bender, E. M., Gebru, T., McMillan-Major, A., & Shmitchell, S. (2021). On the dangers of stochastic parrots: Can language models be too big? *Proceedings of the 2021 ACM conference on fairness, accountability, and transparency*, 610–623. DOI: 10.1145/3442188.3445922

Bessarab, D., & Ng'Andu, B. (2010). Yarning about yarning as a legitimate method in indigenous research. *International Journal of Critical Indigenous Studies*, *3*(1), 37–50. DOI: 10.5204/ijcis.v3i1.57

Boelens, R., De Wever, B., & Voet, M. (2017). Four key challenges to the design of blended learning: A systematic literature review. *Educational Research Review*, *22*, 1–18. DOI: 10.1016/j.edurev.2017.06.001

Bonk, C. J., & Graham, C. R. (2006). *The handbook of blended learning: Global perspectives, local designs*. Pfeiffer.

Braidotti, R. (2022). *Posthuman feminism*. Polity Press.

Bynum, T. W. (2006). Flourishing ethics. *Ethics and Information Technology*, *8*(4), 157–173. DOI: 10.1007/s10676-006-9107-1

Canagarajah, S. (2013). *Translingual practice: Global Englishes and cosmopolitan relations*. Routledge. DOI: 10.4324/9780203120293

D'Ignazio, C., & Klein, L. F. (2020). *Data feminism*. MIT Press., DOI: 10.7551/mitpress/11805.001.0001

De Laat, M., & Prinsen, F. R. (2014). Social learning analytics: Navigating the changing settings of higher education. *Research & Practice in Assessment, 9*, 51–60. https://files.eric.ed.gov/fulltext/EJ1062691.pdf

Deardorff, D. K. (2006). Identification and assessment of intercultural competence as a student outcome of internationalization. *Journal of Studies in International Education, 10*(3), 241–266. DOI: 10.1177/1028315306287002

DISER. (2021). *Australia's AI ethics framework.* Australian Government, Department of Industry, Science, Energy and Resources, https://consult.industry.gov.au/australias-ai-ethics-framework

Eubanks, V. (2018). *Automating inequality: How high-tech tools profile, police, and punish the poor.* St. Martin's Press.

Floridi, L. (2013). *The Ethics of Information.* Oxford University Press., DOI: 10.1093/acprof:oso/9780199641321.001.0001

Floridi, L. (2019). *The logic of information: A theory of philosophy as conceptual design.* Oxford University Press. DOI: 10.1093/oso/9780198833635.001.0001

Floridi, L., & Cowls, J. (2022). A unified framework of five principles for AI in society. In Carta, S. (Ed.), *Machine learning and the city: Applications in architecture and urban design* (pp. 535–545). John Wiley & Sons. DOI: 10.1002/9781119815075.ch45

Garrison, D. R., & Vaughan, N. D. (2008). *Blended learning in higher education: Framework, principles, and guidelines.* John Wiley & Sons.

Gay, G. (2018). *Culturally responsive teaching: Theory, research, and practice* (3rd ed.). Teachers College Press.

Hero, J.-M., Wilson, C., Turner, B., Turner, C., Gibbes, B., & Phyland, R. (2024). Integrating Indigenous knowledges in higher education: Interdisciplinary approaches in science and humanities. *Journal of Australian Indigenous Issues, 27*(1-2), 24–40. DOI: 10.3316/informit.T2024080800004491551202171

Hodges, C., Moore, S., Lockee, B., Trust, T., & Bond, A. (2024). The difference between emergency remote teaching and online learning. In Martindale, T., Amankwatia, T. B., Cifuentes, L., & Piña, A. A. (Eds.), *Handbook of Research in Online Learning: Insights and Advances* (pp. 511–522). Brill., DOI: 10.1163/9789004702813_021

Hofstede, G. (2001). *Culture's consequences: Comparing values, behaviors, institutions and organizations across nations* (2nd ed.). Sage Publications.

Holmes, W., Bialik, M., & Fadel, C. (2019). *Artificial intelligence in education. Promise and implications for teaching and learning.* Center for Curriculum Redesign.

Huot, S., & Em, S. (2025). Effective strategies of English teaching in Cambodia's underserved communities: Bridging digital divide to access education quality. [JEILT]. *Journal of Education Innovation and Language Teaching*, *1*(1), 53–77. DOI: 10.63381/jeilt.v1i1.38

Huot, S., & Hok, C. (2025a). Enhancing English language teaching for multilingual learners: Leveraging heritage languages in the classroom. *Journal of Social and Educational Research*, *4*(1), 87–95. DOI: 10.5281/zenodo.15698964

Huot, S., & Hok, C. (2025b). Unpacking the struggle: Linguistic, pedagogical, and cognitive barriers in Cambodian students' English essay writing. *Context (Ibadan)*, *12*(4), 149–168. DOI: 10.5281/zenodo.15807401

Huot, S., & Loch, S. (2025a). Digital practices in Cambodian EFL classrooms: Teacher narratives from remote learning. In K. Khette & Tayade (Eds.), *Proceeding of one day national conference on English language, literature, cultural studies and media studies* (Vol. 2, pp. 19–31). Centre for Learning, Research and Development, Savda, Maharashtra. DOI: 10.5281/zenodo.16921807

Huot, S., & Loch, S. (2025b). Educating in the age of AI: Preparing Cambodian teachers and students for an AI-augmented learning future. *Journal of Educational Technology and E-Learning Innovations*, *1*(2), 31–38. DOI: 10.54536/jeteli.v1i2.5170

Huot, S., Loch, S., Nget, R., & Em, S. (2025). Exploring multiliteracies in the digital era: A framework for 21st-century learning. [CJESS]. *Cambodian Journal of Educational and Social Sciences*, *2*(1), 7–27. DOI: 10.69496/cjess.v2i1.50

Huot, S., & Such, C. (2025). Leveraging social media for language learning: Opportunities and challenges. [JEILT]. *Journal of Education Innovation and Language Teaching*, *1*(2), 10–29. DOI: 10.63381/jeilt.v1i2.56

Ifenthaler, D., & Yau, J. Y.-K. (2020). Utilising learning analytics to support success in higher education: A systematic review. *Educational Technology Research and Development*, *68*(4), 1961–1990. Advance online publication. DOI: 10.1007/s11423-020-09788-z

Kim, H., Hwang, J., Kim, T., Choi, M., Lee, D., & Ko, J. (2025). Impact of generative artificial intelligence on learning: Scaffolding strategies and self-directed learning perspectives. *International Journal of Human-Computer Interaction*, •••, 1–23. DOI: 10.1080/10447318.2025.2531267

Knox, J., Wang, Y., & Gallagher, M. (2020). *Artificial intelligence and education futures: Critical perspectives and alternative imaginaries*. Routledge., DOI: 10.4324/9780429286798

Kukutai, T., & Taylor, J. (2016). *Indigenous data sovereignty: Toward an agenda.* ANU press. DOI: 10.22459/CAEPR38.11.2016

Ladson-Billings, G. (1995). Toward a theory of culturally relevant pedagogy. *American Educational Research Journal, 32*(3), 465–491. DOI: 10.3102/00028312032003465

Laurillard, D. (2013). *Teaching as a design science: Building pedagogical patterns for learning and technology*. Routledge. DOI: 10.4324/9780203125083

Levy, F., & Murnane, R. J. (2013). *Dancing with robots: Human skills for computerized work.* Third Way.

Loan, T. T. T., & Th y, N. T. H. (2024). Vietnamese University lecturers apply AI in teaching. A case study in Thu Dau Mot university. *European Journal of Theoretical and Applied Sciences*, 2(6), 643–650. DOI: 10.59324/ejtas.2024.2(6).57

Luckin, R. (2018). *Machine learning and human intelligence. The future of education for the 21st century*. UCL institute of education press.

Nguyen, H. L., Dang, B., Hong, Y., & Nguyen, A. (2024). Digital transformation in Vietnamese higher education: An epistemic network analysis of policy documents. *Kokusai Kyoiku Kyoryoku Ronshu, 27*(2), 138–156. DOI: 10.1108/JICE-03-2024-0010

Nguyen, V. H., & Hamid, M. O. (2021). The CEFR as a national language policy in Vietnam: Insights from a sociogenetic analysis. *Journal of Multilingual and Multicultural Development, 42*(7), 650–662. DOI: 10.1080/01434632.2020.1715416

Noble, S. U. (2018). *Algorithms of oppression: How search engines reinforce racism.* New York university press., DOI: 10.18574/nyu/9781479833641.001.0001

Norman, D. (2013). *The design of everyday things*. Basic Books.

Paris, D., & Alim, H. S. (2017). *Culturally sustaining pedagogies: Teaching and learning for justice in a changing world.* Teachers College Press.

Pea, R., & Linn, M. C. (2020). Personal perspectives on the emergence of the learning sciences: 1970s–2005. Frontiers in Education, Razzouk, R., & Shute, V. (2012). What is design thinking and why is it important? *Review of Educational Research, 82*(3), 330–348. DOI: 10.3102/0034654312457429

Seldon, A., & Abidoye, O. (2018). *The fourth education revolution: Will artificial intelligence liberate or infantilise humanity*. University of Buckingham Press.

Selwyn, N. (2019). *Should robots replace teachers?: AI and the future of education.* John Wiley & Sons.

Siemens, G. (2005). Connectivism: A learning theory for the digital age. *International Journal of Instructional Technology & Distance Learning*, *2*(1), 3–10. http://www.itdl.org/Journal/Jan_05/Jan_05.pdf

Slade, S., & Prinsloo, P. (2013). Learning analytics: Ethical issues and dilemmas. *The American Behavioral Scientist*, *57*(10), 1510–1529. DOI: 10.1177/0002764213479366

Stommel, J. (2014). *Critical digital pedagogy: A definition*. Hybrid Pedagogy.

Stommel, J., Friend, C., & Morris, S. M. (2020). *Critical digital pedagogy: A collection*. Hybrid Pedagogy.

UNESCO. (2022). *Recommendation on the ethics of artificial intelligence*. UNESCO Paris. https://unesdoc.unesco.org/ark:/48223/pf0000381137

UNESCO. (2025). *Viet Nam: Artificial intelligence readiness assessment report*. UNESCO Paris. https://articles.unesco.org/sites/default/files/medias/fichiers/2025/10/Viet%20Nam%20Artificial%20Intelligence%20Readiness%20Assessment%20Report.pdf

VanLehn, K. (2011). The relative effectiveness of human tutoring, intelligent tutoring systems, and other tutoring systems. *Educational Psychologist*, *46*(4), 197–221. DOI: 10.1080/00461520.2011.611369

Veletsianos, G., & Houlden, S. (2020). Radical flexibility and relationality as responses to education in times of crisis. *Postdigital Science and Education*, *2*(3), 849–862. DOI: 10.1007/s42438-020-00196-3 PMID: 40477172

Vygotsky, L. S. (1978). *Mind in society: The development of higher psychological processes* (Cole, M., Ed.). Harvard University Press.

Williamson, B., & Eynon, R. (2020). Historical threads, missing links, and future directions in AI in education. *Learning, Media and Technology*, *45*(3), 223–235. DOI: 10.1080/17439884.2020.1798995

Yunkaporta, T. (2020). *Sand talk: How Indigenous thinking can save the world*. HarperCollins.

Zawacki-Richter, O., Marín, V. I., Bond, M., & Gouverneur, F. (2019). Systematic review of research on artificial intelligence applications in higher education–where are the educators? *International Journal of Educational Technology in Higher Education*, *16*(39), 1–27. DOI: 10.1186/s41239-019-0171-0

Zhang, X., Chan, F. T., Yan, C., & Bose, I. (2022). Towards risk-aware artificial intelligence and machine learning systems: An overview. *Decision Support Systems*, *159*(4), 1–13. DOI: 10.1016/j.dss.2022.113800

KEY TERMS AND DEFINITIONS

Artificial Intelligence (AI): Artificial Intelligence (AI) is the field of computer science where machines are programmed to complete tasks that would otherwise require human thinking, such as gaining knowledge, reasoning, understanding through language, and solving problems. Functions of AI within education include personalized learning, automatic response creation, and learning analytics. Nevertheless, as Floridi and Cowls (2022) note, AI operates within the boundaries of the rights of the individual, culture, and ethics, and therefore, deserves to be served with fairness, transparency, and respect.

Culturally Responsive Hybrid Pedagogy (CRHP): Culturally Responsive Hybrid Pedagogy (CRHP) is an approach to education that blends the use of technology in learning with in-class learning and focuses on culture, social equity, and the ethics of inclusion. It frames the use of AI within intercultural and inclusive pedagogy, assuring that technology enhances, rather than reduces, the value of context, the complexity of learners, and the social assets of the community.

Digital Inclusion: Refers to the equitable access, active participation, and empowerment of all learners in technology-mediated learning, as well as the removal of obstacles, be it infrastructural, digital literacy, or socio-cultural. According to UNESCO (2022), digital inclusion goes beyond connectivity to require culturally responsive design, so that all learners, regardless of their diversity or social identity, can use technology in a purposeful and meaningful way.

Ethical Co-Agency: Ensures the collaborative partnership of human and AI in the decision-making and learning process. Rather than placing AI systems as independent, co-agency emphasizes shared responsibility whereby the educator navigates the ethics of the AI, while the AI accommodates integration, personalization, and reflective practices.

Hybrid Learning: Combines various physical and digital learning frameworks for flexibility, engagement and accessibility. As Garrison and Vaughan (2008) state, hybrid learning should not just mean the merging of modalities, but should integrate social, cognitive and teaching presence for a community of personalization and supportive learning experience.

Intercultural Dialogue: Intercultural Dialogue is the process of the two-way exchange of ideas, beliefs, and knowledge of different cultures. In hybrid education, it is the use of digital technologies (AI facilitators, collaborative learning tools, and cross-border virtual exchanges) to support empathy and understanding at a global level and among participants and educators of different cultures.

Chapter 7

Advising Hybrid Pedagogies Through AI and Intercultural Collaboration:

Fostering Digital Literacy, Global Competence, and Ethical Practice

Nicole Simon
http://orcid.org/0009-0004-0678-1300
SUNY Nassau Community College, USA

ABSTRACT

Intersecting of Artificial Intelligence (AI) and hybrid pedagogies has redefined the landscape of higher education. As universities increasingly engage in Collaborative Online International Learning (COIL) and Virtual Exchange (VE) initiatives, the development of digital literacy, intercultural competence, and ethical awareness has become foundational for equitable global learning. When purposefully integrated, AI can scaffold intercultural dialogue, automate administrative processes, and provide adaptive feedback that enhances engagement and inclusivity. Ethical implications surrounding privacy, data governance, algorithmic bias, and equitable access present critical challenges. Conceptual and practical framework for employing AI as a mediating tool within hybrid pedagogies support intercultural collaboration exploring interconnections among digital literacy, global competence, and ethical AI practice, emphasizing transparency, cultural responsiveness, and data integrity.

DOI: 10.4018/979-8-3373-7462-8.ch007

1. INTRODUCTION

The intersection of artificial intelligence (AI) and hybrid pedagogies is reshaping higher education, particularly in intercultural learning contexts such as Collaborative Online International Learning (COIL) and Virtual Exchange (VE) programs (Deardorff, 2006; O'Dowd, 2021). Hybrid pedagogies combine asynchronous and synchronous learning environments, enabling students to engage flexibly while sustaining opportunities for real-time interaction and collaboration across institutional and national boundaries.

Within these settings, AI increasingly functions as a mediating layer that shapes how learners communicate, receive feedback, and interpret participation. Intelligent tutoring systems, automated translation tools, and learning analytics can reduce linguistic barriers and support student engagement, particularly in multilingual and transnational classrooms (Bin & Sun, 2025; Daher, 2025). When used deliberately, such tools can help students participate more confidently in collaborative tasks and navigate unfamiliar communicative norms.

At the same time, AI introduces tensions that are especially visible in intercultural learning environments. Algorithmic systems can privilege dominant linguistic patterns, misinterpret culturally situated forms of expression, or render certain contributions less visible through automated metrics (Bryson, 2019). These effects are rarely neutral. They influence whose voices are amplified, how participation is evaluated, and which forms of communication are recognized as legitimate.

This chapter advances a framework for integrating AI into hybrid pedagogies that foregrounds human judgment, cultural context, and ethical responsibility. Rather than treating AI as an instructional authority, the framework positions it as a tool whose outputs require interpretation, critique, and dialogue. By linking AI use to the development of digital judgment, intercultural awareness, and ethical reasoning, the chapter argues for a form of hybrid pedagogy in which technology supports—rather than displaces—relational and reflective learning.

2. HYBRID PEDAGOGIES AND AI IN INTERCULTURAL LEARNING

Hybrid pedagogies leverage both asynchronous and synchronous modalities to support learning across time zones, languages, and institutional contexts. Asynchronous activities allow students to engage with materials and peers at a measured pace, while synchronous sessions create spaces for immediacy, negotiation, and shared meaning-making. In COIL and VE programs, this combination is particularly important, as learners must navigate differences in communication styles, academic expectations, and cultural norms (O'Dowd & Ritter, 2006; Kern & Warschauer, 2000).

AI-supported tools extend these pedagogical possibilities by providing forms of feedback and analysis that are difficult to sustain at scale. Discourse analytics, for example, can surface patterns of participation that prompt reflection on turn-taking, authority, or silence within intercultural groups. Translation and transcription tools can support multilingual collaboration, reducing linguistic friction during both live and asynchronous interaction (Bin & Sun, 2025; Daher, 2025).

These affordances, however, require careful pedagogical framing. Automated analyses may flatten culturally nuanced communication or reproduce biases embedded in training data. Without contextual interpretation, AI-generated insights risk being treated as objective assessments rather than provisional indicators shaped by design choices and cultural assumptions. For this reason, educators remain central as interpreters and ethical guides, helping students situate AI feedback within social, linguistic, and relational contexts.

Effective integration therefore depends less on the sophistication of AI tools than on how they are introduced, explained, and discussed. When instructors make AI processes visible—clarifying what data are collected, how outputs are generated, and where limitations lie—students are better positioned to engage critically. In intercultural learning environments, this transparency supports not only technological understanding but also reflection on how power, representation, and voice are mediated through digital systems.

3. CONCEPTUAL FRAMEWORK FOR AI-SUPPORTED HYBRID PEDAGOGY

Table 1 illustrates the interaction between AI tools, educator facilitation, and desired learner outcomes across three domains: digital literacy, global competence, and ethical practice.

Table 1. Conceptual Framework for AI-Supported Hybrid Pedagogy

Domain	AI Role	Educator Role	Learner Outcome
Digital Literacy	Adaptive prompts, participation analytics, personalized learning pathways	Guide reflection, provide scaffolding, contextualize technology use	Enhanced self-directed learning and confidence in digital environments
Global Competence	Translation, collaborative platforms, discourse analytics	Facilitate intercultural dialogue, model cross-cultural communication, encourage reflection	Improved cross-cultural understanding, collaboration skills, and empathy
Ethical Practice	Bias monitoring, privacy alerts, responsible data use	Model ethical technology use, oversee equity and inclusion, address algorithmic bias	Awareness of ethical AI, responsible digital citizenship, and culturally responsive engagement

This framework demonstrates that AI is most effective when paired with intentional human facilitation, ensuring that hybrid learning environments are equitable, culturally responsive, and ethically grounded. By foregrounding both technological affordances and human oversight, educators can harness AI to support intercultural collaboration while maintaining the primacy of relational learning and reflective practice.

4. AI LITERACY IN INTERCULTURAL HYBRID LEARNING

Digital literacy in contemporary higher education extends beyond technical competence to include interpretive judgment about how digital systems shape communication, evaluation, and participation. In AI-mediated learning environments, students encounter automated feedback, analytics dashboards, and algorithmic recommendations that actively influence how learning is experienced. Developing AI literacy therefore involves learning to interpret these outputs critically rather than accepting them as neutral or authoritative (Daher, 2025).

In intercultural hybrid contexts, this interpretive dimension becomes especially significant. Tools such as automated translation, discourse analytics, or participation metrics often rely on training data and design assumptions that reflect dominant linguistic and cultural norms. As a result, indirect communication styles, strategic silence, or context-dependent expression may be misread or undervalued. AI literacy equips students to recognize these limitations and to situate algorithmic feedback within cultural, relational, and task-specific contexts rather than treating it as a definitive evaluation.

Hybrid pedagogy offers structural support for this kind of learning. Asynchronous environments provide time for students to review AI-generated feedback, compare it with peer or instructor input, and reflect on discrepancies. Synchronous sessions create opportunities for collective interpretation, where learners can discuss why an automated system may have produced a particular assessment and how cultural norms or language proficiency may have shaped the data being analyzed. Together, these modalities support a form of literacy grounded in dialogue and contextual reasoning rather than procedural compliance.

AI literacy is closely connected to learner agency and self-regulated learning. Students who understand how AI systems generate recommendations are better positioned to use those recommendations strategically—drawing on them as one source of information among others rather than as prescriptive guidance (Long et al., 2025). For example, participation analytics that flag low verbal contribution during live sessions may prompt reflection on time-zone constraints, linguistic confidence, or culturally preferred modes of engagement rather than being interpreted as evidence of disengagement. Faculty framing is crucial in supporting this reframing, particularly in intercultural settings where participation norms vary widely.

Instructor modeling plays a central role in cultivating this stance. When educators openly demonstrate how they question AI-generated insights, acknowledge uncertainty, or consider alternative explanations, they normalize critical engagement and epistemic humility. This modeling helps students develop a more nuanced relationship with AI systems—one that balances trust with skepticism and efficiency with reflection. In this way, AI literacy becomes not only an individual competency but a shared practice shaped through interaction and guided interpretation.

Ethical considerations are inseparable from AI literacy in hybrid intercultural learning. AI systems collect, process, and visualize learner data in ways that raise questions about privacy, consent, representation, and power. Students must understand not only how these systems function but also whose interests they serve and which forms of communication they privilege. Guided comparison of AI feedback with human evaluation can surface instances of bias or misrepresentation, prompting discussion about the cultural assumptions embedded in automated systems.

Structured reflective activities make these dynamics visible. Learners might examine how a translation tool renders culturally specific metaphors, or analyze why sentiment analysis misclassifies indirect critique as negativity. Such exercises encourage students to treat AI outputs as socially situated artifacts rather than objective truths. Linking these classroom practices to broader governance frameworks, such as UNESCO's human-centered AI guidance (UNESCO, 2025a), further situates AI literacy within global ethical debates and professional responsibility.

Importantly, AI literacy in intercultural hybrid learning is not developed in isolation. It emerges through observation of peers, negotiation of shared norms, and collective sense-making around technology use. When students discuss how different group members interpret AI feedback or respond to automated recommendations, literacy becomes relational and participatory. Faculty can support this process by designing activities that require collaborative reflection on AI mediation rather than individual compliance with algorithmic suggestions.

Ultimately, cultivating AI literacy within hybrid pedagogies prepares students to navigate environments where communication, evaluation, and decision-making are increasingly mediated by intelligent systems. In intercultural contexts, this preparation involves learning to interpret data with cultural sensitivity, to question automated authority, and to balance technological efficiency with ethical and relational judgment. By embedding AI literacy within reflective hybrid design, educators support learners in developing the critical capacity required for responsible participation in global, digitally mediated learning and work environments.

5. DEVELOPING DIGITAL LITERACY AND INTERCULTURAL COMPETENCE

Digital literacy encompasses not only operational proficiency but also critical engagement with the sociotechnical dimensions of digital systems. In AI-mediated learning environments, digital literacy includes understanding how algorithms shape communication, information access, and decision-making. Students must learn to interpret AI feedback, evaluate its reliability, and reflect on the ethical implications of data use and automation.

Intercultural competence emphasizes the affective, cognitive, and behavioral capacities required for effective communication across cultural boundaries. Within COIL and VE contexts, technology-mediated collaboration can deepen intercultural empathy when paired with structured reflection and guided dialogue. AI systems—such as adaptive writing assistants, discussion analyzers, and reflective journaling bots—can prompt learners to articulate assumptions, analyze discourse tone, and recognize cultural nuances in communication.

Together, digital literacy and intercultural competence form the foundation of global competence. When students critically engage with AI tools, they improve both digital fluency and awareness of how technology mediates cultural identity and representation. Integrating reflective activities around AI processes—such as bias detection, privacy evaluation, or ethical analysis—encourages learners to see technology as both a learning aid and a site of critical inquiry.

6. THE FOUNDATIONS OF INTERCULTURAL COMPETENCE

Intercultural competence extends beyond knowledge of other cultures; it involves recognizing and navigating cultural norms, values, and communication patterns while maintaining empathy, flexibility, and ethical responsibility. Scholars such as Deardorff (2006) emphasize the integration of attitudes (respect, openness, curiosity), skills (observation, interpretation, analysis), and knowledge (cultural frameworks, contextual understanding) in cultivating intercultural competence.

Hybrid pedagogies provide unique affordances for fostering these capacities by exposing students to diverse perspectives, collaborative tasks, and opportunities to reflect on communicative behaviors. Synchronous interactions, such as videoconferencing or live discussions, allow learners to observe verbal and non-verbal cues, negotiate meaning in real time, and develop empathy through direct engagement. Asynchronous spaces—including discussion boards, reflective journals, and collaborative documents—allow students time to analyze, reflect, and respond thoughtfully. The combination of these modalities supports experiential and reflective learning, enhancing the ability to navigate complexity in intercultural contexts.

7. AI AS A SCAFFOLD FOR REFLECTIVE PRACTICE

Artificial intelligence can enhance intercultural learning by providing structured reflection prompts, adaptive guidance, and analytic feedback. AI tools complement, rather than replace, human facilitation by offering insights that might otherwise be difficult to detect. AI-guided prompts, for instance, through adaptive writing tools or reflective journaling bots—encourage students to examine how their cultural backgrounds influence communication, problem-solving, or decision-making. These prompts help make implicit cultural dynamics explicit, guiding learners toward deeper reflection.

AI-driven discussion analytics can reveal participation patterns that may otherwise remain invisible, such as who speaks most frequently, who contributes indirectly, or which ideas spark the most engagement. In intercultural teams, these patterns often reflect culturally shaped communication preferences rather than individual ability or motivation. When faculty guide students in interpreting these analytics critically, learners gain awareness of how culture mediates interaction and how equitable participation can be promoted.

Automated sentiment analysis tools can also help instructors and students recognize points of tension, disagreement, or misunderstanding. For instance, a neutral statement in one cultural context may be perceived as impolite in another. By flagging such divergences, AI can prompt discussion about cultural interpretation while ensuring human judgment remains central.

8. FOSTERING EMPATHY THROUGH AI AND HYBRID LEARNING

Empathy, the capacity to understand and share the experiences of others, is a critical dimension of intercultural competence. Hybrid learning environments supported by AI can enhance empathy by making social and cultural dynamics visible. Adaptive AI feedback, combined with guided reflection, can highlight patterns of dominance, reticence, or miscommunication that may otherwise go unnoticed, prompting learners to step outside their own perspective.

For example, in a COIL project spanning multiple time zones, AI analytics might reveal that students from a particular cultural group participate less frequently in synchronous discussions. Rather than interpreting this as disengagement, reflective prompts can guide the group to consider explanations such as language proficiency, time zone constraints, or cultural communication norms. This structured inquiry fosters perspective-taking, emotional awareness, and ethical reasoning.

Scenario-based simulations, supported by AI, can provide controlled environments for practicing intercultural negotiation. Adaptive feedback on communication style, tone, and strategy enhances perspective-taking and strengthens intercultural competence while keeping ethical reflection central to learning.

9. DESIGNING AI-ENHANCED REFLECTIVE ACTIVITIES

Effective AI integration requires intentional instructional design. Reflection should be scaffolded across multiple stages, guiding students from self-observation toward critical analysis and informed action. AI-generated prompts can help learners identify patterns in communication, question assumptions, and plan adaptive strategies for future collaboration. Hybrid modalities enrich this reflective process: asynchronous engagement allows students time to process feedback and consider cultural context, while synchronous sessions provide collective sense-making and shared interpretation. To ensure ethical and pedagogical integrity, AI tools must be embedded within culturally contextualized frameworks that acknowledge the limits of automated interpretation. Faculty facilitation remains essential for interpreting

AI outputs responsibly, particularly when communication norms or participation styles vary across cultures.

Iterative feedback loops supported by AI analytics enable students to track changes in intercultural awareness over time, making development visible, continuous, and actionable. By combining automated insights with faculty-guided reflection, learners develop both metacognitive skills and intercultural sensitivity. Challenges include algorithmic bias, overreliance on automation, and inequitable access. Faculty must contextualize AI outputs, maintain relational depth in learning, and ensure equitable engagement. Transparency—explaining how AI tools function, what data they collect, and how they support learning objectives—is critical for fostering trust and ethical reflection.

10. TOWARD INTEGRATED GLOBAL COMPETENCE

When integrated into hybrid pedagogy, AI-supported reflective practices directly contribute to global competence. Sustained engagement with AI-mediated feedback and intercultural collaboration develops students' self-awareness, perspective-taking, adaptive communication, and ethical reasoning. By coupling AI-supported reflection with hybrid learning modalities, educators create environments that are technologically sophisticated, relationally rich, and ethically grounded, preparing students for global participation in complex, digitally mediated contexts.

11. HYBRID PEDAGOGIES AND AI IN INTERCULTURAL LEARNING

Hybrid pedagogies combine synchronous and asynchronous elements to create flexible, interactive, and relational learning environments. In intercultural contexts, these designs accommodate variation in time zones, language proficiency, communication styles, and access, while maintaining opportunities for meaningful dialogue and collaboration.

Grounded in constructivist and sociocultural learning theories, hybrid pedagogy emphasizes knowledge construction through interaction, reflection, and participation in communities of practice. Asynchronous components—discussion forums, collaborative documents, and reflective journals—allow learners to process ideas thoughtfully. Synchronous components—videoconferencing, live chat, and real-time group work—provide immediacy, co-presence, and relational connection. Together, these modalities support both cognitive and affective engagement.

Hybrid pedagogy enables students to engage with difference in ways that purely synchronous or asynchronous formats cannot sustain. Time-delayed communication reduces linguistic pressure and allows reflection on cultural norms. Live interaction supports spontaneity, emotional connection, and negotiation of meaning. This interplay creates a pedagogical rhythm supporting both cognitive and relational dimensions of intercultural learning.

Hybrid pedagogies are central to initiatives like COIL and VE, which connect students across institutions and countries through structured, curriculum-integrated collaboration. Asynchronous preparation (readings, recorded lectures, reflective prompts) combined with synchronous collaboration (team projects, case studies, joint research) foregrounds both task completion and the process of intercultural interaction. Learners reflect on communication, misunderstandings, and cultural perspectives in problem-solving.

Research highlights multimodal engagement as essential for supporting diverse learners. Hybrid designs align with cognitive preferences and sociocultural contexts, accommodating variation in prior educational experience, digital fluency, and participatory comfort. Challenges include differences in academic calendars, assessment practices, and institutional expectations, as well as potential power imbalances based on language dominance, technological access, or perceived institutional prestige. Faculty facilitation is critical in establishing norms of reciprocity, respect, and shared responsibility. Hybrid pedagogy provides structural flexibility to address these challenges, but success depends on intentional design and continuous instructor engagement.

12. ADVANCING INTERCULTURAL COMPETENCE THROUGH AI

Intercultural competence—the knowledge, skills, and dispositions required for effective cross-cultural interaction—is central to COIL and Virtual Exchange (VE) experiences. In hybrid learning environments, students must navigate linguistic diversity, cultural norms, communication styles, and educational expectations that differ across national and institutional contexts. AI, when thoughtfully integrated, can serve as a scaffolding tool that supports intercultural learning without replacing the relational, reflective processes that are foundational to competence development.

Hybrid pedagogies create multiple pathways for intercultural engagement. Asynchronous activities such as discussion forums, collaborative document editing, and reflective journaling allow students time to process cultural differences, experiment with language, and observe peer contributions in a low-pressure environment. Synchronous sessions, through video conferencing or shared digital workspaces, provide real-time opportunities for negotiation, dialogue, and co-construction of knowledge. AI enhances both modalities by providing adaptive support, feedback, and analytics that can help students monitor their engagement, recognize patterns in intercultural interactions, and identify potential misunderstandings.

AI-powered tools, including automated translation, discourse analysis, and sentiment recognition, can reduce barriers to communication and enable more inclusive participation. For instance, translation tools help students engage across language differences, while AI-driven discussion analytics highlight participation equity, prompting students to reflect on whose voices are most prominent and whose contributions may be underrepresented. These tools, however, must be introduced carefully: without critical framing, learners may treat AI outputs as neutral or definitive, overlooking embedded cultural assumptions or algorithmic bias. Educators play a critical role in modeling interpretive skills, demonstrating how AI outputs should be questioned, contextualized, and integrated into human judgment.

Reflective practices are particularly effective for developing intercultural competence in AI-mediated contexts. Students benefit from structured activities that compare AI feedback with peer and instructor input, analyze misinterpretations by automated systems, and explore alternative communicative strategies. For example, when AI sentiment analysis misclassifies indirect or context-dependent communication, learners can examine why these misreadings occurred and discuss culturally grounded approaches to expression. Such exercises foster metacognitive awareness, enabling students to recognize both the limits of AI and the complexities of intercultural interaction.

Moreover, AI can scaffold ethical and relational dimensions of intercultural competence. Automated prompts can encourage students to consider the perspectives, needs, and values of peers from different cultural backgrounds. Reflective journaling bots or discussion facilitators can guide learners to interrogate power dynamics, equity, and inclusion within collaborative projects. These interventions cultivate empathy, perspective-taking, and ethical sensitivity—essential components of global competence—while situating technology as a mediator rather than a replacement for human relational engagement.

Instructors themselves are central to developing intercultural competence. Hybrid and AI-enhanced learning requires deliberate pedagogical orchestration: faculty must design activities that balance AI facilitation with human guidance, provide culturally responsive feedback, and monitor the impact of automated systems on participation and equity. For example, faculty may review AI-generated analytics to identify students whose contributions are undervalued due to language proficiency or cultural communication styles, and then implement strategies to support more equitable engagement. Such integration ensures that technology enhances rather than constrains intercultural learning opportunities.

Finally, advancing intercultural competence through AI is inseparable from broader global competence development. Students who engage critically with AI while collaborating across cultures gain experience navigating technological complexity, cultural difference, and ethical tension simultaneously. They learn to interpret algorithmic outputs, question assumptions, and adapt strategies in culturally sensitive ways. By embedding reflection, discussion, and collaborative problem-solving into AI-mediated hybrid pedagogy, educators foster learners who are not only digitally literate but also interculturally competent, ethically aware, and prepared to participate effectively in global, technology-rich environments.

13. AI ENHANCEMENTS FOR INTERACTION AND INCLUSIVITY

AI introduces new layers of support and complexity into hybrid intercultural pedagogies. When aligned with pedagogical goals, AI tools can enhance interaction, promote inclusivity, and provide insights that support reflective learning. One of the most significant applications is adaptive learning analytics, where AI systems track participation patterns across discussion forums, collaborative documents, and synchronous sessions. These analytics can identify learners who may be less vocal or marginalized, revealing interaction imbalances that often reflect cultural communication norms rather than individual motivation. Visualization of these patterns allows both instructors and students to recognize inequities in participation, providing opportunities to adjust pedagogical strategies and foster a more inclusive learning environment.

Linguistic support further illustrates AI's potential to promote inclusivity. Automated translation, captioning, and transcription tools enable learners to engage in multilingual dialogue, reducing barriers for non-native speakers and increasing confidence in synchronous interactions. When framed as shared resources rather than accommodations for "deficient" learners, such tools normalize linguistic diversity and challenge monolingual assumptions. Similarly, AI-powered discourse and sentiment analysis tools can detect patterns of agreement, disagreement, or emotional tone in student interactions, offering a lens to examine intercultural misunderstandings and prompting reflective discussion. Importantly, these tools should serve as prompts for inquiry rather than authoritative judgments, since algorithms may misinterpret indirect communication, silence, or context-dependent expressions (Salas Pilco et al., 2022; UNESCO, 2025b).

Faculty play a critical role in mediating AI tools. By transparently explaining how AI systems generate outputs and encouraging students to question these outputs, educators transform potential limitations into opportunities for deeper learning. Discussions about why an AI system categorized a message in a particular way can stimulate reflection on cultural norms, linguistic variation, and algorithmic assumptions, reinforcing both digital literacy and intercultural competence.

14. BALANCING AUTOMATION AND HUMAN FACILITATION

A central tension in AI-supported hybrid pedagogy is the balance between automation and human facilitation. AI provides efficiency, scalability, and data-driven insights, but intercultural learning is fundamentally relational. Trust, empathy, and understanding arise from dialogue, shared experience, and reflective engagement, not algorithmic calculation. Hybrid pedagogies address this tension by pairing asynchronous spaces—which allow time for reflective engagement with AI-generated feedback—with synchronous sessions that support human interpretation, dialogue, and relational repair. Faculty can model critical engagement by highlighting both the benefits and limitations of AI, emphasizing that technology supports—but does not replace—human judgment.

15. ETHICAL CONSIDERATIONS: DESIGNING AI TO MITIGATE HARM IN INTERCULTURAL HYBRID PEDAGOGY

Ethical considerations in AI-mediated hybrid pedagogy must extend beyond awareness of potential risks to the deliberate design of safeguards that prevent harm in intercultural learning environments. Because AI systems actively shape how participation, communication, and learning are interpreted, ethical integration requires constraining how automated outputs are generated, interpreted, and acted upon. In transnational and intercultural contexts, where communication norms, linguistic practices, and access conditions vary widely, unmediated reliance on AI risks reinforcing inequities rather than supporting inclusion.

A central ethical risk arises when AI-generated analytics—such as participation metrics, sentiment classifications, or engagement scores—are treated as objective indicators of learning or contribution. In intercultural hybrid settings, these metrics often privilege dominant linguistic and cultural norms, misrepresenting indirect communication, silence, or asynchronous engagement as disengagement or deficiency. To mitigate this risk, AI analytics must be explicitly framed as provisional indicators rather than evaluative judgments. Participation data should not be used for grading or individual assessment; instead, they should function as prompts for guided reflection on access constraints, cultural communication styles, and group dynamics. Faculty mediation is essential in contextualizing these outputs and preventing deficit interpretations that can marginalize learners whose communicative practices differ from algorithmic norms.

Privacy and data governance constitute another critical ethical dimension requiring structural safeguards. AI-enhanced hybrid learning environments frequently collect extensive learner data, including behavioral analytics, linguistic patterns, and interaction histories, often across multiple national jurisdictions. Ethical mitigation requires transparency not only in principle but in practice: students must be informed in advance about what data are collected, how they are used, and who has access to them. Equally important, learners should be provided with meaningful opt-out options and non-AI alternatives that carry no academic penalty. Without such design constraints, participation in AI-mediated learning risks becoming coercive, undermining informed consent and learner autonomy.

Algorithmic bias presents a particularly acute ethical challenge in intercultural learning environments. AI systems trained on culturally homogeneous datasets may misclassify communication styles, rhetorical strategies, or affective expression that fall outside dominant norms. For example, sentiment analysis tools may interpret indirect critique or culturally normative restraint as negative or unclear, while automated translation systems may flatten culturally specific metaphors or relational cues. Ethical mitigation therefore requires positioning these tools not as neutral mediators of meaning but as objects of critical inquiry. Structured activities that examine misclassification, translation loss, or bias enable learners to recognize the limits of automation while developing both AI literacy and intercultural competence (UNESCO, 2025a).

Preserving learner agency is a core ethical safeguard in AI-supported hybrid pedagogy. Students should retain the capacity to question, contextualize, or override AI-generated feedback and recommendations. Encouraging reflective justification for accepting or rejecting automated guidance strengthens ethical reasoning and counters algorithmic determinism. When learners understand that AI outputs are one source of information among others—rather than authoritative prescriptions—they are better positioned to engage critically and responsibly with technology while maintaining autonomy in decision-making.

Faculty play a decisive role in operationalizing ethical mitigation. By modeling critical engagement with AI outputs—questioning assumptions, acknowledging uncertainty, and demonstrating how cultural context shapes interpretation—instructors normalize skepticism and reflective judgment. This modeling helps prevent over-automation and reinforces the principle that AI functions as a mediating tool rather than an instructional authority. Ethical pedagogy in AI-mediated environments thus depends not only on tool selection but on sustained human facilitation that foregrounds relational learning, cultural responsiveness, and interpretive judgment.

Finally, ethical mitigation must be embedded institutionally rather than treated as an individual instructor responsibility. Institutions have an obligation to establish policies that align AI deployment with principles of equity, accessibility, transparency, and human-centered design. This includes regular bias audits, participatory evaluation of AI tools, accessibility compliance, and professional development that equips faculty to mediate both technological and intercultural complexity. Ethical integration is not a static achievement but an ongoing process of monitoring, reflection, and adjustment in response to evolving contexts and learner experiences (UNESCO, 2025a).

By embedding ethical constraints, human interpretation, and learner agency into the design of AI-enhanced hybrid pedagogy, educators can actively mitigate the risks of cultural misrecognition, algorithmic bias, and over-automation. Ethical AI practice in intercultural learning environments thus becomes not merely a matter of compliance or awareness, but a pedagogical commitment to equity, relationality, and responsible global engagement.

16. ETHICAL AI AND RESPONSIBLE DIGITAL CITIZENSHIP

As AI becomes increasingly embedded in hybrid and intercultural learning environments, ethical considerations move from abstract concerns to central pedagogical responsibilities. Students must not only develop digital literacy and intercultural competence but also cultivate the capacity to engage ethically with AI systems, understanding their implications for privacy, equity, and societal impact. Responsible digital citizenship in AI-mediated contexts encompasses critical awareness of algorithmic decision-making, transparency, accountability, and cultural sensitivity.

AI systems are not neutral instruments; they encode assumptions, biases, and priorities into their functioning. Automated translation tools, adaptive feedback, and analytics dashboards may unintentionally privilege dominant linguistic, cultural, or epistemic norms. For example, indirect communication patterns common in some cultures may be misinterpreted as disengagement or lack of clarity, while AI-driven assessment metrics may inadvertently reinforce existing inequities. Students who critically interrogate these outputs develop ethical discernment and a capacity to question whose voices are amplified or marginalized by technology.

Hybrid pedagogy offers multiple entry points for ethical engagement. Asynchronous reflective activities allow learners to analyze AI outputs, compare them with peer and instructor feedback, and identify instances of bias, misrepresentation, or inequity. Synchronous collaborative sessions provide opportunities for dialogue about algorithmic ethics, cultural responsiveness, and data governance, enabling learners to discuss real-world scenarios, debate trade-offs, and co-construct shared norms for responsible AI use. For example, faculty can guide students through exercises that compare AI-generated language suggestions with culturally grounded communication practices, prompting discussion of the ethical dimensions of algorithmic mediation.

Faculty play a critical role in modeling ethical digital citizenship. By transparently explaining the capabilities, limitations, and underlying assumptions of AI tools, instructors demonstrate epistemic humility and critical reflection. They can scaffold decision-making by highlighting ethical trade-offs, questioning automated recommendations, and showing how context shapes the interpretation of AI outputs. This modeling fosters a learning culture where students recognize that technology is a cultural actor as well as a technical tool.

Integrating ethical AI practices also requires connecting classroom experiences to broader policy and societal frameworks. Referencing global guidance, such as UNESCO's human-centered AI recommendations for education (UNESCO, 2025a), helps students situate their learning within larger debates about privacy, equity, and accountability. Assignments and discussions can explicitly engage with questions such as: Who owns the data generated in a COIL project? How can AI support equitable participation without reproducing bias? What responsibilities do students and educators have in mitigating algorithmic harm? These questions reinforce the link between ethical awareness, digital literacy, and intercultural competence.

Ethical engagement with AI is inseparable from student agency and self-regulation. Encouraging learners to critically evaluate AI recommendations, reflect on their decision-making, and discuss ethical dilemmas with peers supports both autonomy and metacognition. When students understand the limitations and potential consequences of AI interventions, they are more likely to use technology intentionally and responsibly, balancing efficiency with empathy and inclusivity.

Finally, ethical AI practice in hybrid pedagogy strengthens global competence. Students who critically engage with AI-mediated interactions gain skills that transfer beyond the classroom: interpreting algorithmic outputs in context, navigating cultural differences sensitively, and advocating for equitable and responsible technology use. By linking AI literacy, intercultural competence, and ethical awareness in a cohesive framework, hybrid learning environments prepare learners to be not only proficient users of technology but also thoughtful, culturally responsive, and ethically grounded participants in global digital communities.

Practical recommendations for faculty emphasize the importance of intentional, transparent, and ethically grounded AI integration within hybrid and intercultural learning environments. Instructors should make AI processes explicit by clearly explaining their capabilities, limitations, and potential biases so that students understand how automated systems shape feedback and participation. Designing structured reflective activities that compare AI-generated feedback with peer and instructor evaluation can help surface ethical and intercultural considerations while reinforcing critical digital literacy. Faculty should also facilitate ongoing dialogue around data governance, privacy, and algorithmic bias, explicitly linking classroom practices to global policy frameworks to situate learning within broader societal contexts.

By modeling critical interpretation of AI outputs—questioning assumptions, contextualizing recommendations, and balancing efficiency with ethical judgment—educators demonstrate reflective and responsible technology use. Integrating ethical reflection with digital literacy and intercultural competence activities supports the development of a holistic framework for global competence, ensuring that AI functions as a pedagogical support rather than an unquestioned authority.

17. EQUITY AND ACCESS

Ethical AI integration in hybrid pedagogy cannot be separated from questions of equity and access. Global disparities in internet connectivity, device availability, and digital fluency create uneven learning conditions that can exacerbate existing inequities. Students in resource-limited contexts may struggle to participate fully in synchronous sessions, access AI-enhanced tools, or interpret automated feedback. These disparities have the potential to marginalize learners who are already underrepresented in higher education, undermining the democratic potential of AI-enhanced global learning initiatives.

Equity also extends to the cultural and linguistic assumptions embedded in AI systems. Many AI tools are developed using datasets that overrepresent certain languages, dialects, or communication norms. As a result, automated translation systems, sentiment analysis tools, and adaptive feedback mechanisms may misinterpret communication from students whose linguistic or cultural practices differ from the dominant model. For example, AI algorithms trained primarily on Western forms of argumentation may misclassify indirect reasoning or culturally specific rhetorical strategies as unclear or deficient.

To mitigate these inequities, institutions and educators can adopt multiple, complementary strategies:

1. **Algorithmic bias audits**: Regularly review AI tools to identify patterns of misclassification, exclusion, or skewed recommendations. Adjust datasets and model parameters to ensure broader representation.
2. **Participatory design**: Include students and faculty from diverse backgrounds in the selection, implementation, and evaluation of AI tools. Co-design ensures that learning technologies reflect the needs and values of the communities they serve.

3. **Accessibility standards**: Ensure that AI-mediated platforms are compatible with assistive technologies, follow international accessibility guidelines (e.g., WCAG 2.1), and accommodate learners with varying abilities.
4. **Alternative pathways**: Provide multiple ways for students to demonstrate learning or receive feedback, including non-AI-mediated options, so that technical limitations or personal preferences do not constrain participation.

These practices emphasize that equity is not solely a technical challenge; it is a pedagogical and ethical responsibility. Faculty and institutions must actively structure learning experiences to minimize disparities and cultivate an inclusive learning ecosystem.

18. ALGORITHMIC BIAS AND CULTURAL IMPLICATIONS

Algorithmic bias is one of the most insidious ethical challenges in AI-enhanced hybrid pedagogy. Bias can emerge at multiple stages: in the collection of training data, in the assumptions embedded within algorithms, or in the interpretation of outputs. In intercultural learning environments, biased AI systems can distort participation patterns, misrepresent communication styles, or inadvertently reinforce stereotypes.

For instance, a sentiment analysis tool may classify a student's culturally normative indirect communication as "negative" or "unclear," leading to automated feedback that misguides both students and facilitators. Similarly, automated translation tools may fail to convey culturally specific meanings or subtle emotional cues, affecting understanding and interpersonal trust. Without careful oversight, such biases can perpetuate structural inequities and undermine the development of intercultural competence.

Faculty play a crucial mediating role in identifying and addressing algorithmic bias. They can contextualize AI outputs for students, prompting reflection on where the system may misrepresent reality. In addition, ongoing dialogue with students about AI limitations encourages critical engagement and reinforces ethical literacy. Bias mitigation is thus both a technical and pedagogical responsibility, requiring coordination between faculty, instructional designers, and IT specialists.

19. INSTITUTIONAL RESPONSIBILITIES

Institutions have a central role in establishing ethical guardrails for AI-mediated hybrid learning. Ethical frameworks should extend beyond compliance with legal requirements to include principles such as fairness, inclusion, accountability, and human-centered design. Strategies may include:

- **Policy alignment**: Embed AI ethics within institutional policies, ensuring that learning technologies adhere to standards for transparency, inclusivity, and cultural sensitivity.
- **Professional development**: Provide faculty training in both AI literacy and ethical facilitation, emphasizing how to interpret AI outputs, scaffold reflection, and mediate intercultural dynamics.
- **Infrastructure investment**: Ensure that technical platforms are reliable, secure, and accessible, supporting equitable participation across diverse student populations.
- **Monitoring and evaluation**: Continuously assess the impact of AI tools on learning outcomes, engagement patterns, and equity indicators, adjusting practices in response to evidence.

Institutional commitment signals to students that ethical and intercultural considerations are integral to the learning environment, not peripheral concerns. It also supports faculty in navigating the often-ambiguous terrain of AI integration, providing guidance, resources, and accountability structures.

Ethical considerations must permeate all aspects of AI-enhanced hybrid pedagogy rather than being treated as peripheral concerns. Ethical integration involves recognizing and protecting learner agency, ensuring that students retain autonomy in how they engage with AI-mediated feedback and analytics. Transparency regarding data collection, analysis, and interpretation is essential for maintaining trust and informed consent, particularly in transnational learning environments governed by multiple regulatory frameworks. Educators and institutions must also actively address disparities in access, linguistic support, and technological fluency to prevent AI systems from reinforcing existing inequities. Ongoing efforts to identify and mitigate algorithmic bias are critical, especially when AI tools risk misrepresenting culturally situated communication styles. Finally, ethical pedagogy requires embedding intercultural awareness and reflective practice across both synchronous and asynchronous activities, ensuring that technology supports human learning, empathy, and critical inquiry rather than supplanting them.Faculty who foreground ethics cultivate not only responsible technology use but also critical thinking, empathy, and global citizenship. Ethical pedagogy in AI-mediated environments reinforces the humanistic principles that must remain central to higher education, even as technological sophistication grows.

20. TOWARD A RESPONSIBLE AND INCLUSIVE AI-ENHANCED HYBRID PEDAGOGY

In summary, ethical considerations in AI-mediated hybrid learning are multidimensional and interconnected. Privacy, security, equity, and algorithmic bias intersect with intercultural dynamics, access disparities, and pedagogical strategies. Successfully navigating these challenges requires collaboration between faculty, students, instructional designers, and institutional leaders. AI has the potential to enhance learning in powerful ways—supporting personalized feedback, equitable participation, and reflective practice—but only when deployed with human oversight, ethical vigilance, and cultural sensitivity. Faculty and institutions must cultivate a culture of critical engagement in which AI is understood as a tool for augmentation rather than authority, and in which learners are empowered to interrogate, question, and shape their experiences.

By embedding ethical principles into the design, implementation, and evaluation of AI-enhanced hybrid pedagogy, educators can create learning environments that are inclusive, transparent, and human-centered. This foundation not only protects student rights and promotes equitable access but also reinforces the broader goal of global competence, preparing learners to navigate complex, diverse, and technologically mediated environments with confidence, responsibility, and empathy.

21. GLOBAL PERSPECTIVES: CHALLENGES AND OPPORTUNITIES

AI-enhanced hybrid pedagogy holds transformative potential for global education but is shaped by uneven access to infrastructure, technology, and educational resources. Resource-rich institutions may leverage cloud-based AI platforms, high-speed internet, and advanced analytics, while institutions in under-resourced regions face limitations that affect synchronous engagement, AI tool accessibility, and participation equity. For example, COIL partnerships between universities in high- and low-bandwidth contexts may require asynchronous alternatives and flexible deadlines to mitigate disparities.

Cultural and linguistic diversity further complicates AI integration. Machine translation, sentiment analysis, and automated feedback can facilitate cross-linguistic interaction but are prone to misinterpret idioms, tone, or rhetorical conventions. Faculty mediation is essential to contextualize AI outputs, ensure intercultural respect, and prevent reinforcement of ethnocentric assumptions. Participatory co-design involving students from diverse backgrounds can enhance AI responsiveness, cultural relevance, and linguistic inclusivity, fostering learner agency and reinforcing the principle that technology should serve human learning rather than impose dominant norms.

Despite these challenges, AI-enabled hybrid pedagogy offers opportunities to democratize international education. Thoughtful deployment can expand access to intercultural experiences beyond traditional mobility programs, support equitable participation in collaborative projects, and provide data-driven insights that enhance reflective practice. The success of these initiatives depends on sustained institutional support, faculty expertise, and iterative evaluation of pedagogical outcomes.

22. EDUCATIONAL PHILOSOPHY AND INSTITUTIONAL READINESS

Beyond technological capability, the adoption of AI in hybrid learning environments is deeply shaped by institutional philosophy and readiness. Universities vary widely in their approach: some prioritize rapid, experimental integration of AI, investing heavily in tools without fully embedding pedagogical or ethical frameworks; others adopt a cautious, human-centered approach, focusing on faculty preparation, relational teaching, and ethical safeguards. Both approaches carry risks—rapid deployment may outpace faculty competence or ethical oversight, while overly cautious adoption can limit student access to transformative learning experiences.

Institutional readiness encompasses multiple dimensions: Faculty Expertise: Instructors must be trained in AI literacy, intercultural facilitation, and hybrid course design. Without competent faculty, even the most sophisticated AI tools cannot realize intended learning outcomes. Policy and Governance: Institutions require policies addressing data protection, accessibility, equity, and ethical AI use. Clear guidance ensures alignment with international standards, such as UNESCO's AI ethics frameworks (UNESCO, 2025a). Sustainability: AI platforms demand ongoing technical support, evaluation, and maintenance. Institutions must commit resources for long-term sustainability rather than treating AI as a one-off innovation.

Faculty professional development is critical. Training should combine technical literacy with reflective, scenario-based exercises that simulate intercultural and hybrid challenges. This approach empowers instructors to anticipate ethical, technological, and cultural complexities proactively, ensuring that AI enhances learning rather than inadvertently marginalizing students.

AI-supported hybrid pedagogy offers significant opportunities to democratize international education. Traditional global learning models, such as study abroad programs, are constrained by cost, travel, and visa restrictions—factors that disproportionately affect underrepresented learners. Thoughtfully implemented AI-mediated hybrid environments, however, can provide equitable access to cross-cultural experiences, multilingual collaboration, adaptive feedback, and participatory problem-solving, regardless of geographic location or language proficiency. AI analytics can highlight participation imbalances, inform faculty intervention, and track intercultural competence development, providing actionable insights at a scale previously unattainable.

Global partnerships can further leverage AI to co-create multilingual datasets, culturally contextualized resources, and adaptive learning exercises, distributing both the labor and benefits of innovation across institutions and regions. This collaborative approach strengthens intercultural understanding, enhances equitable access, and ensures that AI-mediated learning remains contextually grounded and inclusive.

23. NAVIGATING RISKS AND LEVERAGING SUCCESS

Effective AI-enhanced global pedagogy requires careful attention to both potential risks and strategic leverage points. A critical starting point is the evaluation of AI tools themselves: faculty and institutions should prioritize platforms that are transparent, reliable, and culturally sensitive, avoiding opaque "black-box" systems that obscure how outputs are generated or how data are used. Ethical oversight must be embedded directly into course design, ensuring that AI deployment aligns with principles of fairness, inclusivity, and learner autonomy rather than efficiency alone. Equally important is a commitment to iterative improvement. Ongoing feedback from students and faculty can inform refinements to tool usability, intercultural appropriateness, and alignment with learning outcomes, supporting responsive and contextually grounded implementation. Within this process, metacognitive framing plays a crucial role. Encouraging learners to reflect explicitly on the intersection of technology, culture, and collaboration fosters critical awareness of AI's affordances and limitations, positioning technology as an object of inquiry rather than a neutral authority.

Challenges that emerge in AI-mediated hybrid learning—such as technological disruptions, misinterpretations by automated systems, or intercultural misalignments—should be reframed as opportunities for learning rather than failures. With intentional reflective guidance, these moments can foster resilience, adaptability, and collaborative problem-solving, reinforcing both intercultural competence and global citizenship. Students learn to navigate uncertainty, negotiate meaning across difference, and critically assess the role of technology in shaping interaction. In this way, difficulty becomes pedagogically productive, deepening learners' capacity for reflection and ethical judgment in complex, technology-rich environments.

The overarching opportunity of AI-enhanced hybrid pedagogy lies in its capacity to balance technological innovation with humanistic principles. AI can facilitate collaboration, multilingual engagement, and analytics-driven insight at a scale previously unattainable, yet the relational, ethical, and empathetic dimensions of learning remain irreplaceable. When equity, cultural responsiveness, and ethical vigilance are foregrounded, institutions can create learning environments that amplify human capacities while responsibly leveraging technological affordances. Such environments affirm that AI serves as a mediator of learning—not a substitute for human connection, judgment, or care.

24. PRACTICAL RECOMMENDATIONS AND FUTURE DIRECTIONS

Operationalizing AI integration in hybrid intercultural pedagogy requires coordinated action across pedagogical, ethical, and institutional domains. AI should be introduced incrementally and aligned with clearly articulated learning objectives to avoid cognitive overload and superficial adoption. Priority should be given to ethical, transparent, and accessible tools that provide users with meaningful control over data and engagement. Structured reflection on AI mediation, algorithmic bias, and data ethics should be embedded throughout curricula rather than confined to isolated discussions, ensuring sustained critical engagement. Faculty development initiatives must integrate AI literacy with intercultural facilitation skills and reflective pedagogy, equipping instructors to mediate both technological and cultural complexity. At the institutional level, cross-departmental frameworks are needed to align infrastructure, pedagogy, and ethical commitments. Finally, future research should examine the longitudinal impacts of AI-supported hybrid learning on intercultural competence, collaborative practices, and the transfer of digital literacy to professional and global contexts.

AI-supported hybrid pedagogy represents an evolving paradigm that unites technological innovation with humanistic educational goals. When implemented thoughtfully, AI can enhance digital literacy, intercultural competence, and global collaboration—skills essential for navigating today's interconnected world. The challenge lies in ensuring AI amplifies rather than replaces human capacities such as creativity, empathy, and critical reflection. Faculty must act as mediators and facilitators, using AI to provide insight, scaffolding, and inclusivity rather than as an authoritative arbiter of learning. Institutions must provide infrastructure, ethical frameworks, and professional development to support responsible deployment.

By foregrounding equity, transparency, cultural responsiveness, and ethical engagement, hybrid pedagogy can transform global learning into a space where students: engage meaningfully across linguistic and cultural boundaries; critically reflect on AI's role in shaping communication, collaboration, and decision-making;

and develop the skills, awareness, and confidence to participate responsibly in digitally mediated societies.

AI, when thoughtfully integrated, is not merely a tool—it is a catalyst for reflective practice, critical inquiry, and global competence. Hybrid learning ecosystems that foreground faculty expertise, student participation, and ethical oversight can democratize international education, foster intercultural understanding, and cultivate globally competent citizens. By balancing technological innovation with humanistic principles, institutions can ensure AI supports learning ethically, inclusively, and culturally, preparing students to thrive in complex, interconnected, and diverse environments.

25. ETHICAL CONSIDERATIONS: PRIVACY, EQUITY, AND BIAS

AI integration raises critical ethical concerns: privacy, data protection, equity, and algorithmic bias. AI systems collect extensive learner data spanning international jurisdictions with varying regulations. Compliance with standards such as GDPR and institutional policies is essential, and transparency is critical to maintain trust. Students should understand data collection, usage, and access with informed consent as a core principle.

Equity remains central. Global digital divides in connectivity, device availability, and digital literacy can marginalize students. AI tools trained on culturally homogeneous data may reinforce dominant norms, misinterpreting or excluding underrepresented communication practices. Mitigation strategies include algorithmic bias audits, diverse training datasets, participatory design, accessibility compliance (WCAG 2.1), and alternative assessment pathways.

26. GLOBAL PERSPECTIVES AND INFRASTRUCTURE CHALLENGES

Implementation and impact of AI-enhanced hybrid pedagogy vary due to disparities in infrastructure, technological literacy, and policy frameworks. Resource-rich institutions adopt cloud-based AI platforms and advanced analytics, while less-resourced contexts face barriers to synchronous collaboration and AI tools. Global collaborations can address these challenges through co-designed multilingual resources, culturally responsive AI tools, and shared materials, foregrounding inclusion and co-construction.

27. INSTITUTIONAL READINESS AND EDUCATIONAL PHILOSOPHY

Effective AI integration requires alignment between institutional philosophy, policy frameworks, and pedagogical readiness. Faculty must have AI literacy, intercultural facilitation competence, and hybrid course design skills. Institutional policies must address data protection, accessibility, equity, and ethical AI deployment, supported by sustainable infrastructure and ongoing evaluation. AI-supported hybrid learning enables equitable access to cross-cultural dialogue, adaptive feedback, multilingual engagement, and analytics-informed reflection.

28. PRACTICAL RECOMMENDATIONS AND FUTURE DIRECTIONS

Operationalizing AI in hybrid pedagogy requires coordinated action across pedagogical, ethical, and institutional dimensions. AI should be introduced incrementally, aligned with clear learning objectives to avoid cognitive overload. Tools must demonstrate transparency, security, accessibility, and user control. Faculty professional development should integrate AI literacy, intercultural facilitation, and reflective instructional design. Structured reflection on AI mediation, algorithmic bias, and data ethics should be embedded throughout curricula. Institutional frameworks should align infrastructure, pedagogy, and ethical commitments. Future research should examine longitudinal impacts on intercultural competence, group dynamics, and digital literacy transfer.

CONCLUSION

AI-supported hybrid pedagogy unites technological innovation with humanistic goals. When implemented thoughtfully, AI enhances digital literacy, intercultural competence, and global collaboration. Faculty mediate AI tools to provide insight, scaffolding, and inclusion rather than replace human judgment. Ethical, culturally responsive, and equity-driven design ensures AI amplifies human capacities rather than supplanting them.

Hybrid pedagogy fosters reflection, critical inquiry, and empathy, transforming global education into an inclusive, interculturally rich, and ethically grounded ecosystem. AI becomes a catalyst for reflective practice and global competence, preparing learners to thrive technologically, ethically, and humanistically in a complex, interconnected world.

Ultimately, the convergence of human and artificial intelligence in hybrid learning environments offers a profound opportunity: to reimagine global education not as a set of standardized protocols but as a co-created, ethically grounded, and interculturally rich learning ecosystem. Students and faculty become collaborators in a dynamic process, navigating cultural differences, technological affordances, and ethical dilemmas together.

AI is not merely a tool—it is a catalyst for reflective practice, critical inquiry, and global competence. By integrating it thoughtfully into hybrid pedagogies, higher education institutions can prepare learners to thrive in complex, interconnected, and culturally diverse contexts, ensuring that the benefits of AI are realized not only technologically but humanistically, ethically, and globally. Globally, AI-supported hybrid pedagogy presents both formidable challenges and remarkable opportunities. Infrastructure gaps, linguistic diversity, institutional readiness, and algorithmic bias complicate implementation, yet carefully designed programs can democratize access to international learning experiences, promote intercultural understanding, and cultivate global competence. The key lies in integrating AI thoughtfully, ethically, and inclusively, ensuring that technology supports human learning rather than supplanting it. When global perspectives, faculty expertise, and student participation are foregrounded, hybrid pedagogies can become powerful platforms for equitable, interculturally rich, and transformative education in the digital age.

REFERENCES

Bin, Y., & Sun, L. (2025). AI-supported language learning for intercultural competence: Personalized feedback and adaptive collaboration. *Nature Human Behaviour, 9*(2), 234–248. PMID: 39747405

Bryson, J. J. (2019). The past decade and future of AI's impact on society. In *Towards a new enlightenment? A transcendent decade*. Turner.

Daher, W. (2025). *Digital literacy and AI: Interpreting algorithmic outputs in educational contexts*. Springer Link.

Deardorff, D. K. (2006). Identification and assessment of intercultural competence as a student outcome of internationalization. *Journal of Studies in International Education, 10*(3), 241–266. DOI: 10.1177/1028315306287002

Kern, R., & Warschauer, M. (2000). *Network-based language teaching: Concepts and practice*. Cambridge University Press.

Long, P., et al. (2025). Self-regulated learning and AI literacy: Enhancing autonomy in hybrid learning contexts. *arXiv preprint*.

O'Dowd, R. (2021). Virtual exchange: Moving forward into the next decade. *Computer Assisted Language Learning, 34*(3), 209–224. DOI: 10.1080/09588221.2021.1902201

O'Dowd, R., & Ritter, M. (2006). Understanding and working with "failed communication" in telecollaborative exchanges. *Computer Assisted Language Learning, 19*(1), 1–15.

Salas Pilco, S., Xiao, X., & Hu, B. (2022). AI in education: Ethical challenges and intercultural perspectives. *Journal of Learning Analytics, 9*(1), 45–67.

UNESCO. (2021). *AI in Education: Guidance for Policy-Makers*. UNESCO Publishing.

UNESCO. (2025a). *AI in education: Guidance for policy-makers*. UNESCO Publishing.

UNESCO. (2025b). *Ethics of AI in education: Policy recommendations and global perspectives*. UNESCO Publishing.

Chapter 8

Film, AI, and Hybrid Pedagogy:

Designing Intercultural Learning Experiences

Angeliki Ypsilanti
http://orcid.org/0000-0001-8333-4169
Ionian University, Greece

Ioannis Karras
http://orcid.org/0000-0002-1635-8192
Ionian University, Greece

ABSTRACT

This chapter examines the integration of artificial intelligence (AI) into hybrid pedagogical environments for Teaching English for Intercultural Communication (TEIC), with a focus on film-based learning. Using selected Disney films as cultural texts, it introduces the Intergenerational Sensitizer, a digital tool that adapts film-based critical incidents to prompt reflection, dialogue, and meaning-making across generational and cultural standpoints. Drawing on Bhabha's (1994) theory of hybridity, intercultural competence frameworks, and human-centered AI design, the chapter conceptualizes hybrid pedagogy as a "third space" where digital mediation and classroom interaction intersect. Methodologically, it follows a design-based approach, outlining the co-creation and application of AI-enhanced activities in hybrid Teaching English as a Foreign Language (TEFL) and TEIC settings. By treating AI as a mediator, the chapter shows how technology can support a model of hybrid language education that is ethically informed, culturally sensitive, and dialogically appropriate.

DOI: 10.4018/979-8-3373-7462-8.ch008

1. INTRODUCTION

This chapter proposes a design-oriented framework for integrating artificial intelligence (AI) into hybrid pedagogical environments for Teaching English for Intercultural Communication (TEIC), with particular emphasis on film-based learning in Greek EFL classrooms. As digital technologies are mediating shifts in educational practice, language educators face the challenge of using AI in ways that enrich rather than undermine the intercultural dimension of language learning. The present study responds to this challenge by conceptualizing AI not as a substitute for instruction but as a pedagogical mediator capable of supporting personalized feedback, guided reflection, and dialogic engagement across blended learning modalities. Building on the premise that linguistic competence develops in tandem with intercultural understanding (Byram, 1997), the chapter advances a commitment to ethically responsible and culturally responsive approaches to AI use in hybrid language education.

Despite growing interest in AI-supported language education, there remains limited guidance on how AI-based tools and systems used in language classrooms can be pedagogically integrated without reducing intercultural learning to automated feedback or static content delivery. In particular, the potential of AI to support dialogic, reflective, and culturally sensitive engagement in hybrid language classrooms remains under-theorized. This chapter addresses this gap through a design-oriented framework that positions AI as a mediating resource within intercultural pedagogy rather than as an instructional authority.

Conceptually, the chapter draws on Bhabha's (1994) notion of the "third space," Deardorff's (2009) model of intercultural competence, and applied research on human-centered AI in education (Holmes et al., 2019; Luckin et al., 2016). Together, these perspectives foreground learning as a dialogic, reflective, and socially situated process in which cultural meaning is actively negotiated rather than passively transmitted. Building on Garrison and Vaughan's (2008) model of blended learning, hybrid pedagogy is therefore understood not simply as a combination of online and in-person instruction, but as a pedagogical space where learners encounter to reinterpret and co-construct cultural meaning. Against this theoretical backdrop, AI functions as a mediating resource that augments human instruction by offering adaptive feedback, alternative perspectives, and real-time scaffolding. In this way, the hybrid classroom becomes an AI-supported intercultural arena that sustains dialogue, reflection, and perspective-taking.

Film pedagogy is integrated as a core component of the chapter's design logic, as narrative films offer culturally situated representations of conflict that lend themselves to critical-incident analysis in intercultural language education. The study draws on the screenplays of selected Disney films, i.e., *Coco* (2017), *Encanto* (2021), and

Moana (2016), which are treated as both linguistic artefacts and representational sites of cultural negotiation. These Disney narratives provide rich intercultural material through their portrayals of family relationships, value conflicts, and identity dilemmas that resonate with learners' lived experiences. Within these narratives, moments of tension or misunderstanding are construed as critical incidents that can be adapted for classroom use. When reframed through AI systems, such incidents are recast as structured prompts that invite learners to analyze language in context, consider multiple interpretations, and engage in reflective discussion. In this chapter, these incidents function as pedagogical design artefacts rather than records of learner interaction, serving to illustrate how intercultural and intergenerational meaning-making can be scaffolded in practice.

To operationalize the proposed framework, the chapter introduces the Intergenerational Sensitizer, an adaptation of Cushner and Brislin's (1996) Intercultural Sensitizer model. Whereas the original model uses critical incidents from cross-cultural encounters to expand trainees' attributional repertoires, the Intergenerational Sensitizer transposes this technique into the generational domain. The tool begins with the inciting incident that propels each protagonist's journey, such as Miguel defying his grandmother, Mirabel challenging Abuela, or Moana resisting her father, and guides learners through a consistent sequence of tasks. These include the presentation of film characters' perspectives on the causes of conflict and potential resolutions, the target learners' own interpretive standpoint, alternative generational explanations, and rationales for evaluating each attribution. Through AI-mediated simulations and reflective scaffolding, the Sensitizer encourages learners to view intergenerational friction as a process of cultural negotiation between tradition and modernity, authority and autonomy, and collective and individual aspirations.

Against this background, the chapter pursues the following objectives:

1. to conceptualize AI as a pedagogical mediator that supports dialogic, reflective, and culturally responsive learning in hybrid TEIC environments.
2. to propose the Intergenerational Sensitizer as a design-oriented pedagogical tool that adapts film-based critical incidents for intercultural and intergenerational inquiry.
3. to illustrate how film narratives and AI-mediated interaction can be combined to scaffold learners' linguistic development and intercultural awareness in hybrid classrooms.
4. to contribute to ongoing discussions on ethically grounded AI use in language education by foregrounding human facilitation, interpretive openness, and negotiated meaning-making.

The central research question emerging from this context is: How might AI-mediated, film-based activities in hybrid TEIC classrooms enhance learners' linguistic development and intercultural awareness through engagement with intergenerational and cultural narratives? This question rests on the conception of hybridity as an integral educational condition rather than a mere technological add-on, emphasizing how meaning is negotiated across digital and face-to-face learning modalities.

The chapter's original contribution lies in the design of the Intergenerational Sensitizer as an AI-mediated pedagogical tool that integrates film-based critical incidents as a reusable model for intercultural reflection and hybrid classroom interaction. By reframing generational conflict as a site of intercultural meaning-making, the chapter advances a design-oriented model for ethical and dialogic AI use in TEIC contexts.

The following sections review relevant scholarship on hybrid pedagogy and AI-enhanced intercultural learning, outline the proposed methodology, and examine anticipated applications, limitations, and implications for TEIC practice. By integrating theoretical perspectives with AI-mediated design considerations, specifically anchored in the Intergenerational Sensitizer, the chapter demonstrates how hybrid learning environments can leverage digital tools alongside face-to-face interaction to foster reflective, culturally responsive, and human-centered language education.

2. LITERATURE REVIEW

The Intergenerational Sensitizer

This study discusses the creation of an Intergenerational Sensitizer based on the critical incident technique initially developed by Flanagan (1954) and later used by Fiedler et al. (1971) for the purposes of compiling a Culture Assimilator or Intercultural Sensitizer. Within this tradition, a Culture Assimilator is defined as a "programmed learning experience" that uses critical incidents to showcase "divergencies in norms, customs, and values between two cultures" (Fiedler et al., 1971, p. 97). Research in intercultural training has demonstrated that such sensitizers can effectively expand learners' attributional repertoires by exposing them to alternative interpretations of culture-based misunderstandings (Albert & Triandis, 1985; Cushner & Brislin, 1996). However, this work has predominantly focused on national or ethnic cultures, leaving other social dimensions of difference comparatively underexplored. Against this background, it is proposed that intercultural sensitizer theory can be productively transferred to the compilation of an Intergenerational

Sensitizer, whose purpose is to showcase differences of opinion in norms, customs, and values between generations rather than between national groups.

More specifically, springing from the "individualism-collectivism divide" suggested by Triandis et al. (1988) for the purposes of intercultural training, the design of the present film-based Intergenerational Sensitizer is aimed at distinguishing between individualist and collectivist orientations as they emerge across generational positions. While the individualism–collectivism framework has traditionally been applied cross-culturally, more recent research suggests that generational cohorts within the same society may hold contrasting value systems shaped by historical context, educational experience, and exposure to global media. By bringing together traditionally collectivist cultures with a spirit of individualism due to present-day values and, more specifically, Mexican, Colombian, Polynesian and Greek attributional perspectives on intergenerational conflicts, the expectation is that the target learners, viz. Greek English as a Foreign Language (EFL) learners, will look for explanations and resolutions that resonate with their own generational experiences and sociocultural reference points, instead of defaulting to an oversimplified or essentialized notion of a "home culture."

It ought to be noted that the intergenerational conflicts used for generating, first, perspectives and, then, attributions, are practically the inciting incidents in *Coco*, *Encanto*, and *Moana*, whereas the pattern of attributions promoted is that of "teaching persons from one culture to interpret events as persons from another culture do" (Albert & Triandis, 1985, p. 330) and, by extension, that of teaching persons from one generation to interpret events as persons from another generation do. In the classic critical incident model, each intergenerational episode in narrative form is followed by three to four alternative explanations provided by "members of the other culture [...] to expand the trainee's conception of possible attributions in that situation" (Albert & Triandis, 1985, p. 330). In the present design, this model is AI-assisted in order to enhance accessibility and engagement, while retaining its fundamentally reflective and dialogic orientation.

As a further note, Leong and Kim (1991) contend that different perspectives lead to different "interpretive frameworks," which may result in "misunderstandings and conflicts." In sensitizer design, among all possible explanations generated, there is typically one preferred explanation that models a culturally appropriate interpretation. With regard to the present Intergenerational Sensitizer, it is important to clarify that the preferred explanation does not function as a prescriptive or corrective judgment. Instead, it draws on film characters' perspectives in order to teach the target cultural group, i.e., Greek EFL learners, how to distinguish between interpretations attributable to generational diversity, viz. different generational perspectives. In this configuration, possible explanations arise from generational differences, whereas the preferred explanation emerges from understanding the roots of these differences through the "interpretive frameworks" of the learners' own generation.

Although the Intergenerational Sensitizer claims to be culture-specific to the extent that collectivist cultures can be understood through a culture-specific lens, it is foremost generation-specific to the extent that cultural differences can be better understood when attributing the "individualism-collectivism" divide to generational positioning rather than to static national traits. This orientation aligns with contemporary intercultural scholarship that rejects essentialized, static views of culture in favor of perspectives that see culture as fluid, contextually enacted, and internally differentiated (Dervin, 2016; Holliday, 2011; Kramsch, 1998).

Building on this generation-sensitive reinterpretation of the intercultural sensitizer model, the study next turns to the pedagogical environment within which such interpretive work can be meaningfully enacted. In particular, it examines how hybrid pedagogy and AI-mediated learning design can extend the intergenerational sensitizer beyond a static analytical tool into a dynamic space for dialogue, reflection, and meaning-making in the language classroom. Situating the sensitizer within AI-supported hybrid learning environments allows for the integration of multiple perspectives, modes of engagement, and temporalities of learning, while foregrounding intercultural language education as a process of negotiation rather than transmission.

Building on this foundation, the next section examines how film-based pedagogy and AI-supported scaffolding can jointly foster intercultural and intergenerational learning in TEIC and TEFL contexts. Narrative films provide rich, contextually grounded scenarios, while AI-mediated prompts expand interpretive possibilities, guiding learners to reflect, negotiate meaning, and rehearse explanatory reasoning. Together, they translate abstract intercultural concepts into engaging learning experiences aligned with human-centered hybrid pedagogy.

Film-Based Pedagogy, AI, and Intercultural Meaning-Making

Film-based pedagogy has long served as a powerful resource in language education, particularly when intercultural understanding is a central objective. As multimodal cultural texts, films immerse learners in situated language use, socially embedded values, and culturally nuanced interactions that extend beyond decontextualized linguistic input. When combined with reflective tasks, they encourage learners to articulate assumptions, interpret character motivations, and engage in perspective-taking, fostering both empathy and intercultural awareness (Byram et al., 2001; Kramsch, 1993; Liddicoat & Scarino, 2013). Empirical research suggests that film-based tasks can foster perspective-taking and reflective dialogue when learners analyze characters' motivations, conflicts, and value systems rather than engage with films merely as illustrative cultural content (Herrero & Vanderschelden, 2019). Related research on intercultural language education further shows that reflective tasks can promote learners' development as intercultural mediators and citizens (Porto, 2016; Ypsilanti & Karras, 2025).

From an intercultural pedagogical perspective, film narratives are particularly productive because they foreground moments of tension, ambiguity, and misunderstanding which are features that closely align with the logic of critical incidents in intercultural training. Such moments invite learners to consider how meaning is shaped by social position, cultural norms, and lived experience, and to explore alternative explanations for conflict and behavior. When used pedagogically, films can therefore function as structured interpretive prompts that support learners in articulating assumptions, testing interpretations, and negotiating meaning. This orientation resonates with intercultural approaches in language education that conceptualize learning as an interpretive and dialogic process grounded in ambiguity, reflection, and perspective-taking rather than the acquisition of fixed cultural knowledge (Byram, 1997; Kramsch, 1998; Liddicoat & Scarino, 2013). Research on film in EFL further supports this view, highlighting narrative texts as productive mediational spaces in which learners articulate assumptions, negotiate meaning, and reflect on cultural misunderstandings (Herrero & Vanderschelden, 2019; Jackson, 2014).

Recent developments in AI-supported language education introduce new possibilities for extending this interpretive potential. While AI tools are increasingly used for feedback provision, conversational practice, and individualized learning support, their role in fostering reflective and intercultural engagement remains comparatively underexplored (Godwin-Jones, 2019; Kukulska-Hulme et al., 2024). Many applications prioritize efficiency and accuracy, often limiting opportunities for interpretive openness. At the same time, critical scholarship cautions that AI systems shape how learners conceptualize language, culture, and knowledge, highlighting the need for pedagogical designs that foreground transparency, ethical awareness, and human mediation (Holmes et al., 2019; Selwyn, 2019).

In this context, the Intergenerational Sensitizer is best understood as a structured pedagogical sequence that organizes learners' engagement with intercultural complexity over time. Film-based critical incidents supply concrete narrative situations through which generational conflict and value tension become visible and discussable, while AI-supported prompts widen the range of interpretive possibilities available to learners during initial engagement. Rather than deliver interpretations, this design encourages learners to rehearse explanatory reasoning, articulate provisional positions, and anticipate alternative viewpoints before these interpretations are taken up in collective classroom discussion. In this way, the Sensitizer translates intercultural and intergenerational learning into a process of guided interpretive work, where meaning emerges through successive stages of individual reasoning and socio-discursive negotiation.

The following section therefore explores how hybrid pedagogy and human-centered AI frameworks can support intercultural and intergenerational learning in TEIC and TEFL contexts with a view to enabling learners to navigate cultural difference through reflective, dialogic, and technologically mediated practices.

Hybrid Pedagogy, AI, and Intercultural Language Education

Research on hybrid pedagogy has moved well beyond early understandings of blended learning as the simple addition of online components to conventional classrooms. In applied linguistics and CALL research, hybrid pedagogy is increasingly conceptualized as an educational ecology in which modes of participation, temporalities of learning, and forms of cultural engagement are interdependent rather than sequential. Scholars such as Kern (2006) and Liddicoat and Scarino (2013) describe technology-mediated language learning as a context where learner identity, meaning-making, and cultural interpretation are continuously negotiated. Within TEFL and TEIC, hybrid environments are therefore viewed not merely as delivery modes but as dialogic spaces in which learners alternate between individual online engagement and collective in-class meaning-making (Guth & Helm, 2010; O'Dowd, 2018). This orientation is theoretically enriched by Bhabha's (1994) notion of the "third space," which conceptualizes cultural contact zones as sites of hybrid negotiation rather than assimilation to a dominant norm. In language education, this third space enables learners to encounter unfamiliar values, test interpretations, and reconstruct their understandings through dialogue with others.

Intercultural competence research provides further conceptual grounding for this view of hybridity. Deardorff (2009) models intercultural competence as a developmental process involving attitudes of openness and respect, skills of interpretation and evaluation, and the ability to communicate effectively and appropriately across difference. Empirical studies in intercultural language education suggest that these dimensions are fostered most effectively through pedagogies that encourage reflection, perspective-taking, and iterative interaction rather than through transmission-oriented instruction (Byram et al., 2002; Deardorff, 2006; Liddicoat & Scarino, 2013; O'Dowd & Ritter, 2006). These processes become particularly salient in hybrid classrooms, where learners must navigate not only new linguistic forms but also digitally mediated representations of culture. From this perspective, AI can be understood as a participant in the third space of learning, insofar as it provides scaffolding that supports the skills Deardorff (2006) identifies, namely reflection, empathy, and adaptive communication. Recent studies in applied linguistics and educational technology note that AI systems are capable of prompting alternative interpretations and sustaining reflective engagement in ways that complement teacher-led interaction rather than replace it (Godwin-Jones, 2019; Kukulska-Hulme et al., 2024).

At the same time, the emergence of human-centered AI design frameworks has reshaped discussions on how such technologies should be integrated into educational practice. Selwyn (2019) as well as Holmes et al. (2019) caution that AI tools influence how learners perceive language, identity, and cultural knowledge, and therefore must be employed transparently and ethically. Rather than treat AI as an autonomous tutor or evaluator, these scholars advocate designs that keep human interpretation and dialogue at the core of pedagogical activity. In intercultural language classrooms, this implies using AI to augment reflective and dialogic processes instead of providing automated judgments of correctness or cultural adequacy. Despite these insights, there remains limited work on how such human-centered principles can be operationalized in concrete pedagogical designs that address both intercultural and intergenerational dimensions of meaning-making.

Recent work on generative AI in language education has begun to explore how large language models can support dialogic interaction, adaptive scaffolding, and learner reflection rather than task automation (e.g. Godwin-Jones, 2023; Kukulska-Hulme et al., 2024; Zawacki-Richter et al., 2024). However, much of this literature remains focused on efficiency, feedback, or skills development, with comparatively limited attention to how generative AI can be pedagogically aligned with intercultural meaning-making and ethical classroom mediation. The present chapter responds to this gap by conceptualizing AI as a dialogic resource embedded within film-based critical incidents, offering a pedagogical pathway for integrating generative AI into intercultural language education without positioning it as an autonomous instructional agent.

Within AI-supported hybrid pedagogies, the Intergenerational Sensitizer functions as a pedagogical artefact uniquely suited to this human-centered vision. The tool invites learners to engage with AI-generated critical incidents in online spaces, where they formulate personal responses in English and explore the simulated viewpoints of film characters. These individually mediated reflections are then carried into face-to-face classroom discussion, enabling collective interrogation of the same incidents from multiple generational and cultural perspectives. This movement between modalities exemplifies Bhabha's third space as a dynamic process of negotiation rather than a fixed instructional setting. At the same time, it resonates with intercultural competence models that emphasize iterative cycles of interpretation and interaction (Byram et al., 2001; Liddicoat & Scarino, 2013), wherein understanding develops through repeated engagement with difference.

Hybrid pedagogy thus provides both the structural conditions and the pedagogical rationale for employing AI-mediated sensitizer activities that address generational diversity as an integral dimension of intercultural communication. In this respect, cultural meaning is negotiated not only across national or ethnic boundaries but also across age-based value systems, life experiences, and intergenerational relationships. By foregrounding generational positioning as a source of cultural interpretation, the study extends intercultural competence frameworks that conceptualize culture as negotiated across multiple social groupings rather than as a fixed national attribute (Byram, 1997).

Grounded in intersecting theoretical perspectives, i.e., hybridity as third space (Bhabha, 1994), intercultural competence as developmental practice (Deardorff, 2009), and AI as ethically designed digital mediation (Holmes et al., 2019; Selwyn, 2019), the chapter frames the Intergenerational Sensitizer as a tool for sustaining interpretive engagement in Greek EFL classrooms. The following discussion outlines how the sensitizer is pedagogically organized and how learners' linguistic and intercultural engagement can be examined in AI-supported hybrid TEIC environments, setting the stage for a consideration of the epistemological and ethical dimensions of AI use in intercultural learning.

Critical AI Literacy and Cultural Mediation

While the Intergenerational Sensitizer leverages AI to expand interpretive possibilities, it also raises important epistemological and ethical questions. Generative AI models may reproduce dominant narratives or simplified portrayals of culture, particularly when mediating globally circulated media texts. To address this, the sensitizer is explicitly designed for teacher-guided use as AI outputs function as provisional prompts rather than authoritative statements. Learners are encouraged to interrogate, contest, and reframe these AI-generated perspectives, fostering both critical AI literacy and intercultural awareness.

Building on this conceptual and ethical framing, the methodology outlines how the Intergenerational Sensitizer is structured. It details the selection of films, the design of AI-mediated critical incidents, and procedures for analyzing learners' interpretive and intercultural engagement in hybrid TEIC/EFL classrooms, emphasizing teacher mediation and reflective practice throughout.

3. METHODOLOGY OF THE STUDY

The study adopts a qualitative, design-oriented methodological framework that translates the principles of the Intergenerational Sensitizer into a pedagogical design rather than report outcomes from a completed classroom intervention. The methodology focuses on the systematic selection, structuring, and pedagogical framing of film-based critical incidents, defined here as key narrative moments that foreground intergenerational conflict, value tension, or misunderstanding between characters. These incidents are treated as design artefacts intended to model how intercultural and intergenerational meaning-making can be scaffolded in hybrid TEIC contexts.

Drawing on narrative moments of intergenerational conflict from selected Disney films, the methodological approach foregrounds perspective-taking, interpretive reasoning, and dialogic engagement as core pedagogical processes. A consistent analytical structure is applied across films to ensure comparability at the level of design, while allowing for nuanced exploration of how cultural and generational tensions are represented and can be pedagogically mobilized through AI mediation.

Design of the Intergenerational Sensitizer

The Intergenerational Sensitizer follows a replicable design sequence applied to each selected film-based critical incident:

Each critical incident follows a structured interpretive sequence: (a) presentation of the narrative conflict, (b) character-based generational perspectives on causes and resolutions, (c) target group perspective-taking tasks, (d) selection among alternative explanations, and (e) analytical rationales linked to intercultural and intergenerational constructs.

To illustrate the framework, the films *Coco*, *Encanto*, and *Moana* were chosen because their narratives foreground tensions between younger protagonists and family or community authorities, making them particularly suitable for modelling intergenerational critical incidents. Their global circulation and familiarity among learners further support shared interpretive engagement in classroom settings. The present chapter therefore draws on widely recognized Disney narratives for accessibility and shared cultural reference points. However, the proposed framework is adaptable to non-Western, independent, or locally produced films that foreground intergenerational or intercultural tensions, enabling contextualized implementation across diverse educational settings.

Overall, this methodological framework establishes a coherent and transferable design model for developing film-based intercultural learning tools. By structuring each critical incident around shared stages of interpretation, explanation, and reflective justification, the study proposes a pedagogical design that is both systematic and adaptable across TEIC and TEFL contexts.

Data Collection and Analysis

As a design-oriented study, the chapter outlines a prospective data collection and analysis framework intended for future empirical implementation of the Intergenerational Sensitizer.

Proposed data sources include:

- learners' written reflections on film-based critical incidents,
- recordings or transcripts of classroom interaction,
- AI-generated interaction logs documenting prompts and alternative explanations.

These sources are intended to document how learners engage with AI-mediated film narratives in hybrid TEIC environments. Unlike conventional TEFL approaches that prioritize discrete language forms or task completion, this design centers on narrative-driven episodes of cultural and generational tension, allowing for the integrated analysis of language use, perspective-taking, and reflective engagement.

Analytically, the study anticipates the use of interpretive thematic analysis to identify patterns in learners' language production, attributional reasoning, and intercultural reflection. By specifying these analytical procedures in advance, the chapter clarifies how the proposed design could be empirically examined while maintaining transparency about its current conceptual status.

AI Prompt Design and Replicability

To ensure transparency and replicability, the AI-mediated perspectives used in the Intergenerational Sensitizer were generated through a consistent prompt design strategy aligned with human-centered and pedagogically guided AI use. Prompts were formulated to position the AI not as an authoritative source of cultural knowledge, but as a dialogic mediator offering plausible character-based interpretations grounded in the film narratives.

Each prompt specified: (a) the film and critical incident under consideration, (b) the character perspective to be simulated (e.g., adolescent, parental, or elder figure), (c) the focus on intergenerational values, motivations, and conflict resolution, and (d) the instructional goal of encouraging reflection rather than evaluative judgment. The AI was instructed to provide multiple interpretive options, framed as perspectives rather than definitive explanations, using accessible language suitable for EFL learners.

An example prompt structure included instructions such as: "Using the script or narrative summary of the selected scene, identify the inciting incident and reformulate it as a critical incident that foregrounds an intergenerational or intercultural tension between characters." All AI-generated outputs were subsequently reviewed and, where necessary, refined by the researcher to ensure narrative accuracy, cultural sensitivity, pedagogical relevance, and alignment with intercultural learning objectives.

By documenting the prompt design principles rather than fixed outputs, the study emphasizes pedagogical control and adaptability. Educators and researchers may modify prompts to suit different films, cultural contexts, proficiency levels, or classroom goals, while maintaining the core design logic of the Intergenerational Sensitizer. This approach supports ethical AI use, critical literacy, and the reproducibility of the proposed framework across diverse TEFL/TEIC settings.

Participants

The anticipated participants are learners of English as a Foreign Language in public or private primary and secondary schools within the Greek educational context. These learners are expected to possess age-appropriate levels of English proficiency that enable engagement with selected film excerpts, guided discussion, and AI-supported reflective tasks. As members of contemporary Greek society, participants bring perspectives shaped by family relationships, cultural traditions, and evolving social values, which are central to the study's focus on intergenerational meaning-making.

Teachers are expected to act as pedagogical facilitators who integrate the Intergenerational Sensitizer into existing instructional practices. Far from requiring specialized training, the design assumes teachers' professional capacity to adapt materials to learners' developmental stages, contextualize AI-generated prompts, and guide reflective dialogue within hybrid learning environments. In this way, the methodology foregrounds human mediation and pedagogical judgment as integral to the effective use of AI-supported sensitizer activities.

Together, the methodological framework, documented prompt design principles, and proposed analytical procedures position the Intergenerational Sensitizer as a transparent, adaptable, and empirically examinable pedagogical model for hybrid TEIC contexts.

4. ILLUSTRATIVE OUTPUTS FROM THE DESIGN OF THE INTERGENERATIONAL SENSITIZER

This section presents illustrative outputs generated through the design and AI-mediated modelling of film-based critical incidents drawn from *Coco*, *Encanto*, and *Moana*. Rather than report empirical learner data, the section demonstrates how the Intergenerational Sensitizer operationalizes intercultural and intergenerational meaning-making through structured perspectives, alternative attributions, and reflective rationales. The materials presented here function as pedagogical exemplars that show how AI-generated prompts and interpretive pathways can be used in hybrid TEIC/EFL classrooms to scaffold perspective-taking, cultural comparison, and dialogic reflection. In this sense, the section provides a design-based illustration of the sensitizer's pedagogical logic rather than evaluative findings from classroom implementation.

Critical Incident 1 (from *Coco*): Design Illustration

The following critical incident in Table 1 illustrates how the Intergenerational Sensitizer structures an intergenerational conflict drawn from the inciting incident of *Coco*. Specifically, Table 1 presents a narrative reconstruction of the incident used as a pedagogical prompt. The description functions as a shared interpretive reference point from which alternative perspectives and explanations are generated.

Table 1. Critical Incident Based on the Conflict between Miguel, Abuelita and Papá

During an emotional confrontation in the family courtyard Miguel pleads for the right to play music. He argues that his family should guide him not restrict him and that de la Cruz being his ancestor means he is meant to be a musician. His father Papá dismisses this reinforcing the family's belief that music is dangerous and led to abandonment. His Abuelita the matriarch becomes furious declaring that music is a *curse* that tore their family apart. When Miguel insists on playing Abuelita physically destroys his guitar—a symbolic act of silencing his dreams. Shocked and heartbroken Miguel retaliates by rejecting the family's most sacred tradition: remembrance through the *ofrenda*. His defiant words — *"I don't care if I'm on some stupid ofrenda!"* — stun his elders crossing a cultural and emotional boundary. Feeling unheard and unsupported Miguel grabs the family photo and runs away rejecting not just their rules but their very identity.

Note. From *ChatGPT (May version)* by OpenAI, 2024. https://chat.openai.com/chat

Perspectives I (Why)

Table 2 presents AI-generated character perspectives produced in response to targeted prompts. These perspectives are not treated as authoritative interpretations, but as designed prompts intended to expose learners to contrasting attributional frames within the same cultural setting.

Table 2. Modelled Perspectives on the Causes of the Conflict

Miguel Rivera
I came into conflict with Abuelita because she sees music as a curse, while for me, it's my passion—it's who I am. My family believes music caused abandonment and pain, so they've banned it for generations. But to me, music is beautiful and brings people together.
When I learned Ernesto de la Cruz might be my ancestor, I felt like music was my destiny. But Abuelita got furious, refused to listen, and even smashed my guitar. It felt like she was erasing my dreams. I know she wants to protect me, but it hurt that she wouldn't understand. I didn't mean to reject my family—I just felt like they had already rejected me.
Abuelita
I came into conflict with Miguel because I was trying to protect him. Our family has suffered because of music—because of a man who chose his dreams over his family and abandoned them. I have worked hard to keep us strong so we never feel that pain again.
But Miguel doesn't understand. He sees music as his destiny, while I see it as a curse that could take him away from us. When I saw him with that guitar, idolizing Ernesto de la Cruz, I had to stop him. Smashing his guitar was meant to break music's hold on him, but instead, I broke his heart. And when he rejected the ofrenda, it felt like he was throwing away his family.
I only wanted to keep him safe, but now I fear I may have pushed him away.
Papá
I came into conflict with Miguel because I want what's best for him, and I don't believe music is the future he needs. Our family has always prioritized family first, and music tore us apart in the past. I don't want that for Miguel.
When Miguel said Ernesto de la Cruz was his ancestor and that meant he was destined to be a musician, I couldn't accept it. We don't even know if he was really part of our family, and even if he was, he abandoned his own. To me, music is a risk—one that could make Miguel forget where he comes from.
I know Miguel thinks I don't support him, but I just want to keep him close and safe. When he rejected the ofrenda, it felt like he was rejecting everything we believe in, and that hurt. I just wish he could see that we're trying to protect him. I don't want to lose him like we lost others to music. Maybe I need to find a way to show him we love him, no matter what.

Note. From *ChatGPT (May version)* by OpenAI, 2024. https://chat.openai.com/chat

Pedagogically, these perspectives are designed to:

- surface intergenerational value conflicts,
- model emotionally grounded reasoning,
- invite learners to compare protection-oriented and autonomy-oriented interpretations.

Perspectives II (How)

Table 3 presents alternative resolution pathways articulated from each character's standpoint. These responses exemplify how the sensitizer encourages learners to move beyond causal attribution toward negotiated meaning and reconciliation strategies.

Table 3. Modelled Perspectives on Conflict Resolution

Miguel To resolve this conflict, I know I can't just run away or yell. I need to help my family understand why music is so important to me and show them that playing music doesn't mean I'm abandoning them. I need to talk to Abuelita and Papá when we're calm. I want them to know that I respect our family and traditions, but that music is a way to express who I am. Maybe if I explain how I feel instead of arguing, they'll listen. I also need to prove that music can bring us together. Maybe I can show them that music can honor our traditions, just like the ofrenda. If they see that music helps us remember instead of erase our past, maybe they'll change their minds. Most of all, I need to show them that I'll always choose family first. I regret saying I didn't care about the ofrenda—I do care. I just want to follow my dreams without losing them. It won't be easy, but I won't give up. If they see that my music comes from love, maybe one day, they'll understand it like I do. **Abuelita** I want to resolve this conflict by understanding Miguel instead of shutting him down. I acted out of fear—fear of losing him the way we lost others—but I see now that in trying to protect him, I may have pushed him away. I only want what's best for my grandson. First, I need to listen to Miguel with an open heart. He's stubborn like me, but I know his love for music is real. If I want him to listen to me, I must also be willing to listen to him and understand why music means so much to him. Then, I need to make peace with music. I still fear what it could do, but maybe I've been too harsh. Instead of seeing it as a curse, I could try to see it as something that connects us, a way to honor our family. Finally, I need to show Miguel that he's loved, no matter what. I was hurt when he rejected the ofrenda, but I realize he said it out of pain. I don't want to lose him, and if accepting his love for music keeps our family together, then I need to open my heart to it. Family is everything, and maybe music doesn't have to take him away after all. **Papá** I want to resolve this conflict by truly listening to Miguel. I was so focused on protecting him that I didn't understand what music means to him. I see now that banning music isn't the answer—I just want to make sure he never forgets his family, no matter what path he takes. First, I need to talk to Miguel calmly and let him explain why music is so important. I need to show him I care about his happiness, while also helping him understand that my fears come from love and protection, not control. Then, I want to find a compromise. If music is part of who he is, maybe he can follow his passion without losing his connection to family. I want him to know he doesn't have to choose between his dreams and us. Maybe we can use music to honor our traditions. Most of all, I need to remind Miguel that he will always be my son, and I will always love him. Family comes first, but that doesn't mean ignoring who he is. If I can support him and keep our family strong, we can heal the wounds of the past—together. *Note.* From *ChatGPT (May version)* by OpenAI, 2024. https://chat.openai.com/chat

Anticipated Target Group Perspective (If you were…)

Table 4 illustrates how the sensitizer prompts cultural repositioning, inviting learners to reinterpret the conflict through a Greek cultural lens. This task is designed to scaffold intercultural comparison by drawing on concepts such as *philotimo* and family hierarchy.

Table 4. From the Target Viewer's Perspective

Miguel if you were Greek how would you react to conflict with Abuelita?
If I were Greek my reaction to the conflict with Abuelita would still revolve around the struggle between tradition and personal passion. Greek culture values family respect for elders and tradition so going against Abuelita's wishes would still feel like a betrayal. However Greek history is full of heroes defying fate and authority to pursue their destiny much like I'm trying to do with my music. I might view my struggle as a mythological challenge balancing duty to family with following my true calling. I would likely appeal to philotimo the Greek value of honor and doing what is right explaining that my music is for something greater than myself. I might also use storytelling like the ancient Greeks to connect my music with family traditions. If things got heated with Abuelita I could turn to filoxenia the value of hospitality and kindness to find common ground. Rather than storming off I'd try to show her through action—perhaps playing a song that honors our family—that music isn't a curse but a gift. In the end a Greek version of me would try to respect family while still pursuing my passion like many heroes and musicians in Greek stories have done.

Note. From *ChatGPT (May version)* by OpenAI, 2024. https://chat.openai.com/chat

Explanations

The following set of explanations invites learners to interpret the intergenerational conflict depicted in the Mexican family by adopting and evaluating different character perspectives. Rather than identify a single "correct" answer, learners are encouraged to consider how values, intentions, and emotional positions shape interpretations of conflict and its possible resolution. The final prompt extends this reflection by asking learners to transpose the scenario into their own sociocultural frame of reference, fostering empathetic engagement and intercultural comparison.

1. Why was there conflict in the Mexican family? Adopt the best perspective:
    a. Miguel felt rejected by his family when he realized that his dream of becoming a musician was not well received.
    b. Abuelita tried to protect Miguel against pain and adversity by banning music from his life.
    c. Papá believed that music was a risk not worth taking because it would tear their family apart.

2. How could conflict be resolved the Mexican way? Adopt the best method:
   a. Miguel: By showing the rest of the family that music can help them honor their cultural traditions.
   b. Abuelita: By listening with an open heart and making peace with music so that family stays connected.
   c. Papá: By making a conscious compromise to keep both ends satisfied.
3. What would a similar conflict in the family mean to a Greek teenager in a Mexican's shoes? Empathize with what feels like the best option.
   a. It would not keep them from fulfilling their destiny.
   b. It would inspire them to honor their family while pursuing their true passion.

Rationales

The rationales below model how perspectives can be read as expressions of intergenerational positioning, cultural norms, and moral reasoning. In this way, the rationales function as interpretive scaffolds that make visible the cultural logics underpinning different explanations, resolutions, and acts of empathy, while also inviting comparison across Mexican and Greek sociocultural contexts.

Question 1: You have adopted perspective a, which says the following: Miguel felt rejected by his family when he realized that his dream of becoming a musician was not well received. This reaction is indicative of an individualist mindset that prioritizes personal ambition over family tradition. However, disregarding the values and responsibilities that come with fostering a sense of collective identity may also be indicative of the younger generation of Mexicans or second-generation Mexican Americans born to immigrant parents who may have a skewed understanding of their culture including family roles, celebrations, and perspectives on history and heritage.

You have adopted perspective b, which says the following: Abuelita tried to protect Miguel against pain and adversity by banning music from his life. This perspective resonates with cultural values often associated with Mexican familismo that grants elders a central role in decision-making. Emotional support during hardship is also part of a sense of duty linked to family well-being.

You have adopted perspective c, which says the following: Papá believed that music was a risk not worth taking because it would tear their family apart. This reaction is indicative of a collectivist mindset that prioritizes family over personal goals, thus discouraging independence. It is also indicative of intergenerational solidarity in Mexican culture whereby younger generations are expected to seek advice from elders and honor their guidance and support.

Question 2: You have adopted Miguel's method of resolving the conflict, which says the following: By showing the rest of the family that music can help them honor their cultural traditions. This method is indicative of how a younger generation's actions may speak louder than words. At the same time, it shows adaptability and a growth mindset because conflict is viewed as a learning experience rather than a roadblock.

You have adopted Abuelita's method of resolving the conflict, which says the following: By listening with an open heart and making peace with music so that family stays connected. This method is indicative of recognizing the power of reconciliation. More specifically, reconciliation is about acknowledging conflict, addressing misunderstandings, and transforming past struggles into lessons that deepen bonds.

You have adopted Papá's method of resolving the conflict, which says the following: By making a conscious compromise to keep both ends satisfied. This method is indicative of showing willingness to make concessions to reach a resolution that honors everyone's needs. More specifically, conscious compromise entails focusing on long-term harmony rather than temporary conflict management that may leave unresolved tensions.

Question 3: You have empathized with option a, which says the following: It would not keep them from fulfilling their destiny. This highlights how Greek mythological heroes serve as strong examples when it comes to defying limitations and pursuing destiny despite immense challenges.

You have empathized with option b, which says the following: It would inspire them to honor their family while pursuing their true passion. This highlights the importance of honoring the institution of family to ensure the continuity of cultural values across generations and pursuing self-fulfillment from within a space of family support.

The concept of "familismo" is not exclusive to Mexican culture nor is it solely characteristic of Latino communities. In fact, familism applies to Greek culture, too as it refers to an inherent sense of duty to preserve cultural traditions and honor family heritage. To what extent adolescents may be impacted by familism, Piña-Watson et al. (2013, p. 206) explain that Mexican familismo is one of those cultural values that "form the lens through which the adolescent will interact with and organize his or her world" while Pnevmatikos and Bardos (2014, p. 1478) have discovered that when "serving family as a welfare provider, young people become more dependent on their family and thus their dependency on the family is maintained." If the difference between Mexican familismo and Greek familism could be characterized as one of interdependency versus dependency, then Mexican familismo could be construed as emphasizing reciprocity among family members in conjunction with personal autonomy whereas Greek familism could be construed as emphasizing the kind of hierarchy that prioritizes obedience and duty over individual independence. Clearly then, Greek EFL students receiving intercultural training through *Coco* might benefit more if they are not only introduced to the differences between Mexican and Greek familism but also guided through a concept more familiar to them – *philotimo*. This concept, which cannot be directly translated into any other language, reflects a commitment to doing what is right as well as a willingness to help others without expecting anything in return. Vassiliou and Vassiliou (1973, p. 331) underscore that aspect of *philotimo* which can be better understood in terms of "behaving properly according to in-group norms." Hence, the next question to be examined: Does Miguel trespass the boundaries of his ethnic identity by showing deviant behavior from "in-group norms?"

Critical Incident 2 (Encanto): Design Illustration

The following critical incident in Table 5 illustrates how the Intergenerational Sensitizer operationalizes intergenerational tension through the inciting incident of *Encanto*. Specifically, Table 5 presents a narrative reconstruction of the incident as a pedagogical trigger, providing a shared interpretive frame for subsequent reflection.

Table 5. Critical Incident Based on the Conflict between Mirabel and Abuela Alma

During a family celebration Mirabel urgently warns that their magical house Casita is in danger pointing out cracks and the flickering candle that sustains their family's power. However when she leads the family outside to show them the house appears perfectly fine making her warnings seem exaggerated. Abuela Alma embarrassed and eager to maintain the family's image dismisses Mirabel's concerns assuring everyone that the magic is intact and quickly redirects attention back to the celebration. This causes tension between Mirabel who feels ignored and powerless and Abuela who is focused on protecting the family's facade of perfection even if it means ignoring the issues at hand.

Note. From *ChatGPT (May version)* by OpenAI, 2024. https://chat.openai.com/chat

Perspectives I (Why)

Table 6 presents AI-generated character perspectives developed in response to structured prompts embedded in the sensitizer. These perspectives are designed to make visible how fear, responsibility, and invisibility are differently construed across generations within the same familial context.

Table 6. Modelled Perspectives on the Causes of the Conflict

Mirabel
I clashed with Abuela Alma because I tried to warn her that the house and magic were in danger, but she wouldn't listen. I was scared, and it hurt that she dismissed me instead of believing me.
I think she was scared too, but instead of facing the problem, she acted like everything was fine. She wants to protect the family's image, but it felt like she wasn't seeing or hearing me.
In this family, everyone has a place except me. I just wanted to help, but instead, I felt blamed. No matter how hard I try, it never seems like enough for her.
Abuela Alma
I clashed with Mirabel because I was afraid—afraid of losing the magic that holds our family together. The house, the miracle—it's everything to us. When Mirabel warned me that the house was in danger, I couldn't let that fear spread. If the family believed the magic was fading, everything could unravel.
I know she only wanted to help, but I couldn't show weakness. I've spent my life protecting our legacy, and the thought of losing it was unbearable. When she couldn't prove what she saw, I had to take control. If I acknowledged her fears, it would mean admitting that things weren't perfect.
But in shutting her down, I pushed her away. She felt unheard, invisible. I acted out of fear, not love. Now, I see that I need to truly listen—to stop pretending everything is fine and face the truth, together.

Note. From *ChatGPT (May version)* by OpenAI, 2024. https://chat.openai.com/chat

From a pedagogical standpoint, these perspectives model:

- emotionally grounded causal reasoning,
- the tension between authority and vulnerability,
- the impact of intergenerational expectations agency.

Perspectives II (How)

Table 7 outlines alternative resolution pathways articulated from Mirabel's and Abuela Alma's standpoints.

Table 7. Modelled Perspectives on Conflict Resolution

Mirabel
I know resolving my conflict with Abuela won't be easy, but I can't ignore the truth. I need to reach her without making her feel attacked—I'm not trying to break the family or the magic, I'm trying to protect it, just like she is. First, I need to be patient and listen. Abuela is so focused on holding everything together that she doesn't see how much we're all struggling. If I can show her that her fear is making us feel like we're not enough, maybe she'll understand why I won't stay silent. Then, I need to prove that our strength isn't just in the magic—it's in us. Our love and support keep us whole, even when things aren't perfect. Abuela needs to see that perfection isn't what holds this family together. Finally, I need her to see that I'm not a threat—I'm part of the family. I may not have a magical gift, but I love this family with everything I have. If she can see that, maybe we can start healing. It won't be easy, but I'm ready to face it—for her, for the family, and for myself.
Abuela Alma
I see now that I've hurt Mirabel, even though I was only trying to protect the family and our magic. My fear made me close off from her, and I need to fix that. She matters just as much as anyone else, gift or not. To make things right, I need to truly listen to Mirabel—her fears, her frustrations—rather than trying to control everything. I've spent so long protecting the family's image of strength that I forgot real strength comes from facing our struggles together. I must let go of my need for control and trust in my family. The magic and the house don't define us—our love does. That means admitting I was wrong, asking for forgiveness, and showing Mirabel that she belongs. This is my chance to be a better grandmother and leader. If I can listen to Mirabel, I can help heal our family, not just protect it. Only through honesty—about the magic, our hopes, and our fears—can we truly be whole again.

Note. From *ChatGPT (May version)* by OpenAI, 2024. https://chat.openai.com/chat

Rather than prescribe solutions, these perspectives are designed to invite learners to evaluate reconciliation strategies in relation to cultural norms, power relations, and emotional accountability.

Anticipated Target Group's Perspective (If you were…)

Table 8 illustrates how the sensitizer prompts learners to reposition the conflict within a Greek cultural framework. By drawing on culturally salient concepts such as *philotimo*, respect for elders, and expressive family interaction, the task supports intercultural comparison and reflexive interpretation.

Table 8. From the Target Viewer's Perspective

Mirabel if you were Greek how would you react to conflict with Abuela Alma?
If I were Greek my conflict with Abuela Alma would still be just as intense but my approach might be different. Greek culture like mine values family tradition and respect for elders so challenging my yiayia would feel just as shocking. However Greek families also embrace passionate debates so my outburst might be seen as part of a strong-willed discussion rather than outright disrespect. Family honor (philotimo) is key in Greek culture. Abuela sees herself as our protector much like Greek matriarchs do. Instead of just telling her she's wrong I might appeal to her sense of duty—explaining that even the strongest homes need care just as families need to listen to each other. Greek families also cherish storytelling and history. I could remind Abuela of times when our ancestors had to adapt to survive—how the ancient Greeks rebuilt after struggles—showing her that admitting something is wrong isn't weakness but strength. Still I'd struggle with feeling unseen. If Abuela kept ignoring me I'd likely stand my ground drawing inspiration from Greek tragedies—fighting for what's right even if misunderstood. But in the end whether in Colombia or Greece I'd still try to show her that true strength comes not from perfection but from love change and unity.

Note. From *ChatGPT (May version)* by OpenAI, 2024. https://chat.openai.com/chat

Explanations

The following set of explanations structures an intergenerational conflict drawn from *Encanto* around competing interpretations of responsibility, authority, and care within the family. This supports comparative reflection while foregrounding empathy and interpretive choice rather than evaluative judgment.

1. Why was there conflict in the Colombian family? Adopt the best perspective:
    a. Mirabel felt dismissed when she tried to raise concerns about the safety of the family house.
    b. Abuela Alma clung to the magic of the family legacy, refusing to face the truth about the house's cracks even at the cost of stifling Mirabel's concerns.
2. How could conflict be resolved the Colombian way? Adopt the best method:
    a. Mirabel: By letting go of rigid beliefs, expectations, or preconceived notions that may limit their perspective on how family unity can be preserved.
    b. Abuela Alma: By letting go of the need to control and realizing that real strength comes from facing their struggles together as a family.
3. What would a similar conflict in the family mean to a Greek teenager in a Colombian's shoes? Empathize with what feels like the best option.
    a. It would be construed as part of a strong-willed discussion rather than outright disrespect towards the elderly.
    b. It would call for readaptation for survival reasons.

Rationales

The rationales below make explicit the intercultural and intergenerational reasoning that underpins each possible response. They are intended to scaffold learners' interpretive processes by connecting individual choices to culturally situated value systems and patterns of intergenerational relations.

Question 1: You have adopted perspective a, which says the following: Mirabel felt dismissed when she tried to raise concerns about the safety of the family house. This reaction is indicative of a collectivist mindset that puts family security first but receives no acknowledgment by the matriarch of the multi-generational household, i.e., the grandmother, because her commitment to family unity is questioned.

You have adopted perspective b, which says the following: Abuela Alma clung to the magic of the family legacy refusing to face the truth about the house's cracks even at the cost of stifling Mirabel's concerns. This reaction is indicative of the embodiment of familismo by a Mexican matriarch who is determined to preserve cultural and family traditions and pass them down to younger generations without demonstrating openness to intergenerational dialogue.

Question 2: You have adopted Mirabel's method of resolving the conflict, which says the following: By letting go of rigid beliefs, expectations, or preconceived notions that may limit their perspective on how family unity can be preserved. This method is indicative of how younger generations can offer a fresh perspective on defining intergenerational solidarity, for example, through open communication and mutual respect.

You have adopted Abuela Alma's method of resolving the conflict, which says the following: By letting go of the need to control and realizing that real strength comes from facing their struggles together as a family. This method is indicative of how intergenerational solidarity can be redefined to ensure that each family member feels personally valued without compromising the family's cohesion.

Question 3: You have empathized with option a, which says the following: It would be construed as part of a strong-willed discussion rather than outright disrespect towards the elderly. This highlights the importance of speaking one's mind in the face of what is perceived as emotionally draining due to conflict environment while advocating for meaningful change in the way cohabiting family members interact.

You have empathized with option b, which says the following: It would call for readaptation for survival reasons. This highlights the importance of navigating changing circumstances driven by the need to guarantee survival, whether on an individual or collective level.

The concept of "intergenerational solidarity" is widely used and encompasses multiple dimensions (i.e., associational, affectual, consensual, functional, normative, structural) according to Bengtson and Schrader (1982). Which dimension takes precedence over the others in Colombian culture can be evidenced in Mazza (2007) who addresses the issue of intergenerational solidarity in relation to financial assistance, job opportunities, and shared resources within families, viz. pointing towards the structural dimension of intergenerational solidarity which is about cohabitation. Regarding Greek culture, Siatitsa and Dagkouli-Kyriakoglou (2024) address the issue of intergenerational support in relation to youth housing arrangements, highlighting the implications of the same dimension. Drawing thus on the crude reality of what intergenerational solidarity entails in terms of economic dependence, it becomes obvious that younger and older generations are expected to provide for one another both financially and emotionally because this is the essence of interfamilial support. Clearly then, Greek EFL students receiving intercultural training through *Encanto* are exposed to how intergenerational solidarity is rooted in cultural values and social expectations, particularly during times of need or transition. More specifically, they are expected to recognize that the instinct to persevere and sustain life ultimately guides the pursuit of stability, regardless of any culture-specific dictates. Hence, the next question to be examined: Does Mirabel hold the key to this stability because of her resolve to change the rules and prioritize the affectual dimension of intergenerational solidarity whereby family members are expected to nurture and reciprocate positive emotions while staying true to themselves?

Critical Incident 3 (Moana): Design Illustration

The critical incident in Table 9 demonstrates how the Intergenerational Sensitizer engages with conflicts rooted in leadership, tradition, and collective survival. Specifically, Table 9 presents the narrative episode as a pedagogical stimulus, positioning tradition and change as competing yet interdependent forces within intergenerational decision-making.

Table 9. Critical Incident Based on the Conflict between Moana and Chief Tui

In this pivotal moment Moana challenges her father Chief Tui by suggesting they venture beyond the reef to find fish as the lagoon's resources are running out. Moana believes the ocean holds the solution to their problems while Chief Tui staunchly defends the old rule that no one goes beyond the reef. His rule established for the safety of their people no longer seems relevant to Moana who argues that the old way isn't working.

Note. From *ChatGPT (May version)* by OpenAI, 2024. https://chat.openai.com/chat

Perspectives I (Why)

Table 10 presents AI-generated perspectives that articulate contrasting interpretations of the same situation. These perspectives foreground the divergence between protection-oriented leadership and future-oriented agency.

Table 10. Modelled Perspectives on the Causes of Conflict

Moana
I clashed with my dad because he wouldn't see the bigger picture. Our lagoon is running out of fish, and the rule about staying within the reef no longer makes sense. The ocean is vast—there has to be a way for our people to survive. But when I tried to show him a solution beyond our old boundaries, he was too afraid to listen.
He holds onto that rule like it's the only way to protect us, but I think he's just scared. I'm trying to help, to secure our future, but all he sees is danger. I know he loves me, but I can't let fear stop us from moving forward.
It was frustrating because I wasn't trying to run from responsibility—I was trying to do what's best for our people. But he saw my determination as defiance, not the courage to take risks for our family.
Father
I clashed with Moana because I was trying to protect her—and our village—from a dangerous idea. The rule about staying within the reef has kept us safe for generations, and I believed following it was the right thing. The ocean is unpredictable, and I've seen the dangers it holds. I couldn't just let Moana risk herself.
I know she wants to help, but the ocean isn't a place for adventure—it's a place where things can go wrong. If I let her go, she might not come back, and I couldn't bear that. As her father, my job is to keep her safe, even if she doesn't understand why.
It wasn't about not trusting her—it was about not trusting the ocean. I fought against her idea out of fear, not rejection. Sometimes, as a father, protecting your child means making hard choices, even when they don't see it that way.

Note. From *ChatGPT (May version)* by OpenAI, 2024. https://chat.openai.com/chat

Pedagogically, these perspectives are designed to:

- expose learners to collective rather than individualist value systems,
- highlight fear as a culturally mediated response,
- frame conflict as a site of ethical decision-making rather than disobedience.

Perspectives II (How)

Table 11 presents alternative resolution pathways that illustrate how intergenerational trust and leadership can be renegotiated through dialogue, shared responsibility, and adaptive change.

Table 11. Modelled Perspectives on Conflict Resolution

Moana
To resolve this conflict, I need to show my father that I'm not being reckless—I'm doing this for our people, not just for adventure. I understand he's trying to protect me, but fear can't hold us back. I must earn his trust by proving I can make my own decisions, even if they challenge tradition. The ocean isn't just a threat—it's a resource we can learn to work with. The best way to show this is by taking the first step and demonstrating that we can face the unknown together. I'll be patient and help him see that change doesn't mean abandoning tradition. If I can prove I'm not running away but working toward our future, maybe he'll see me differently. It won't be easy, but I'm ready to fight for what's right.
Father
To resolve this conflict, I need to see that Moana isn't defying me—she's fighting for our people. I've been so focused on my fears that I haven't recognized her determination. She's not a child anymore; she's a leader. I've clung to old rules out of fear, but she's right—we can't let fear control us. Protecting her doesn't mean shielding her from challenges but trusting her to face them. I must accept that change is necessary and let go of the past so we can move forward. I need to have faith in her choices and show her that I, too, can change. Together, as a family, we can overcome both the ocean's dangers and the fears that hold us back.

Note. From *ChatGPT (May version)* by OpenAI, 2024. https://chat.openai.com/chat

These perspectives encourage learners to reflect on how tradition can be honored while responding to ecological, social, and generational change.

Anticipated Target Group's Perspective (If you were...)

Table 12 illustrates how learners are invited to reinterpret the conflict through a Greek cultural lens, engaging with cultural concepts such as *philotimo* and *oikogeneia* alongside narrative traditions that foreground journeys, risk, and destiny. This task supports intercultural comparison by aligning Polynesian themes of collective survival with Greek historical and mythological frames.

Table 12. From the Target Viewer's Perspective

Moana if you were Greek how would you react to conflict with Chief Tui your Father?
If I were Greek my conflict with my father would still be about tradition vs. exploration but might carry even deeper cultural weight. In a patriarchal Greek family defying him would feel like challenging fate itself—almost like a Greek tragedy. His resistance would be rooted in philotimo (honor) and oikogeneia (family duty) seeing my desire to explore as hubris leading to ruin. But Greek history is also full of adventurers—Odysseus Jason Prometheus—who dared to seek the unknown. I might try to convince my father through stories of our ancestors showing him that true legacy isn't just about staying safe but about growing and evolving. Instead of outright rebellion I'd approach him with sophrosyne—wisdom and balance—earning his trust while proving that his fear is holding us back. I might seek guidance from an elder he respects. Still I wouldn't back down. Like Greek heroes I'd follow my path hoping he'd see my journey wasn't defiance but a way to save our people and restore our true identity.

Note. From *ChatGPT (May version)* by OpenAI, 2024. https://chat.openai.com/chat

Explanations

The questions below present the intergenerational conflict in *Moana* as a critical incident that invites learners to evaluate competing perspectives, explore culturally situated approaches to resolution, and relate the narrative to their own generational experiences.

1. Why was there conflict in the Polynesian family? Adopt the best perspective:
   a. Moana opposed her father's will in order to do what was best for their people.
   b. Father was adamant about staying within the reef because that rule had kept them safe for generations.
2. How could conflict be resolved in the Polynesian way? Adopt the best method:
   a. Moana: By challenging tradition and embracing change.
   b. Father: By trusting each other and overcoming dangers in unison.
3. What would a similar conflict in the family mean to a Greek teenager in a Polynesian's shoes? Empathize with what feels like the best option.
   a. It would be about breaking free from the constraints of fear of the unknown.
   b. It would be tied to both self-discovery and the restoration of a people's true identity.

Rationales

The following rationales unpack the interpretive choices associated with the *Moana* incident, connecting learners' perspectives to indigenous worldviews, intergenerational responsibility, and collective identity formation.

Question 1: You have adopted perspective a, which says the following: Moana opposed her father's will in order to do what was best for their people. This reaction is indicative of a community-oriented mindset that prioritizes long-term sustainability over holding onto traditional practices despite evolving circumstances.

You have adopted perspective b, which says the following: Father was adamant about staying within the reef because that rule had kept them safe for generations. This reaction is indicative of a community leader who is not ready to embrace new ideas or methods for making the community a better place for everyone.

Question 2: You have adopted Moana's method of resolving the conflict, which says the following: By challenging tradition and embracing change. This method is indicative of an indigenous worldview that approaches problem-solving holistically, considering the long-term effects of actions on the land for future generations.

You have adopted Father's method of resolving the conflict, which says the following: By trusting each other and overcoming dangers in unison. This method reflects an indigenous mindset in progress that balances honoring the past with shaping a sustainable future through strengthened communal ties.

Question 3: You have empathized with option a, which says the following: It would be about breaking free from the constraints of fear of the unknown. This highlights the importance of venturing into the unknown not only without disregarding the wisdom of past generations but also without fearing to embrace new sustainable practices.

You have empathized with option b, which says the following: It would be tied to both self-discovery and the restoration of a people's true identity. This highlights the importance of these two interconnected processes as the former involves unlearning restrictive beliefs that may have been passed down through generations while the latter involves restoring the community's identity to rebuild a collective sense of pride in its heritage.

United Nations (2006) have developed a general understanding of the term "indigenous people" based on their "strong link to territories and surrounding natural resources," their "distinct language, culture and beliefs," the "resolve to maintain and reproduce their ancestral environments and systems as distinctive peoples and communities," to name but a few. What is more, the process of building an indigenous identity is not only contingent upon rewriting the ancestral narrative to build a new one that incorporates changes in mindset as implied by *Moana* film but also upon incorporating collective memory of the past to counterpose the selective shaping of memory by official discourses. Kidman (2015) explored how Māori youth bring in their own version of how history memory is interpreted to reestablish their own sense of belonging. To achieve this, they tend to engage with "indigenous and/or tribal narratives which then become a form of counter-narrative or parallel story that speaks to a set of cultural and historical memories that [...] reinforce tribal youth identities" (Kidman, 2015, p. 645). The idea of renegotiating identity is then closely linked to renegotiating agency in contexts where hegemonic discourses take over. The suggested approach to familiarizing Greek EFL learners with the idea of indigeneity comes from Karatsareas et al. (2024) who define indigeneity either as a form of in-group identity deeply rooted in ancestral and historical connections to a land or as a form of in-group mentality that informs the sense of collective identity shared by ethnic communities who navigate cultural continuity and preservation. A case in point is the "Greek contexts of Istanbul, Albania, and Cyprus" where "these disparate communities have justifiable claims as indigenous to those regions due to longstanding history with the place" (Karatsareas et al., 2024, p. 14).

Summary

The illustrative critical incidents and associated modelled perspectives demonstrate how intergenerational conflicts in *Coco*, *Encanto*, and *Moana* can function as pedagogical catalysts for intercultural interpretation, perspective-taking, and reflective dialogue in hybrid TEIC/EFL contexts. By foregrounding alternative attributions, culturally grounded rationales, and guided comparison with Greek cultural frameworks, the Intergenerational Sensitizer exemplifies a design approach that integrates film-based pedagogy and AI mediation without displacing teacher facilitation or learner agency. The following discussion situates these design outputs within a hybrid language education framework and considers their theoretical and pedagogical implications.

5. DESIGN OUTCOMES AND PEDAGOGICAL IMPLICATIONS

The Intergenerational Sensitizer in the EFL/EIC Context

The design outcomes suggest that the adapted film-based Intergenerational Sensitizer can be meaningfully integrated into Greek EFL/EIC classrooms as an interactive, quiz-oriented pedagogical artefact. The Intergenerational Sensitizer builds on conceptual work originally developed in Ypsilanti's (2025) doctoral research, where it was theorized as a film-based critical incident framework for fostering intergenerational and intercultural reflection in EFL contexts. In line with earlier applications of the critical incident technique as a structured prompt for intercultural interpretation (Albert & Triandis, 1985; Flanagan, 1954), the recasting of inciting incidents from *Coco*, *Encanto*, and *Moana* into intergenerational critical incidents provides a principled way of foregrounding generational values, culturally embedded norms, and contrasting attributional perspectives. Rather than function as a test of cultural knowledge, the sensitizer is designed to expand learners' interpretive repertoires by engaging them in reflective evaluation of multiple explanations and resolutions.

Across the three illustrative cases, the sensitizer foregrounds learners' active engagement with meaning-making through language. By requiring learners to articulate explanations, justify preferred interpretations, and negotiate resolutions in English, the activity creates conditions for purposeful language use embedded in narrative contexts that resonate with learners' lived experiences and sociocultural concerns. This alignment between narrative engagement and reflective language use reflects a core principle of intercultural language learning, namely that intercultural understanding develops through interpretive work rather than the transmission of predefined cultural facts (Liddicoat & Scarino, 2013).

From a pedagogical perspective, the sensitizer supports oral interaction by structuring opportunities for extended discourse, peer negotiation, and conditional reasoning. Evaluating alternative explanations and adopting a preferred attribution encourages learners to practice argumentation and perspective-taking, echoing Deardorff's (2009) emphasis on adaptive communication as a central dimension of intercultural competence. The interactive, quiz-based format further lends itself to sustained engagement, particularly in instructional contexts where learner motivation may otherwise be limited by routine post-viewing activities. As Ypsilanti and Karras (2023, p. 44) observe, "a transformation in mindset happens when conceptualizing previous intercultural experiences to impart derived worldviews through open and constructive dialogue in class." Within this design, cinematic narratives prompt learners to relate fictional conflicts to their own family dynamics and generational experiences while developing intercultural self-awareness alongside communicative confidence.

For teachers, the Intergenerational Sensitizer offers a structured yet flexible means of embedding intercultural inquiry within everyday language instruction. Consistent with human-centered approaches to AI-mediated pedagogy (Luckin et al., 2016), the tool supports interpretation without prescribing authoritative readings. Linguistic objectives are integrated with narrative-based intercultural content, while classroom interaction is organized around reflective discussion attentive to cultural and generational implications. In this way, the sensitizer functions both as an analytic scaffold and as a pedagogical resource that facilitates negotiated meaning-making characteristic of hybrid and "third space" pedagogies (Bhabha, 1994), linking language development with intergenerational and intercultural learning.

Hybridity, AI, and Pedagogical Implications

A central implication emerging from the design concerns the role of AI within hybrid TEIC environments, conceptualized not merely as blended delivery modes but as dialogic and intercultural learning ecologies (Kern, 2006; Liddicoat & Scarino, 2013). Within the sensitizer, AI mediation enables critical incidents to be reframed through multiple viewpoints and adaptive prompts, supporting learners' engagement with alternative interpretations and culturally grounded reasoning. In this sense, chatbots such as ChatGPT function as mediational tools rather than instructional authorities, prompting reflection, modelling explanatory discourse, and stimulating learners' oral and written expression. This orientation aligns with prior research on digital mediation and intercultural reflection in language education (Guth & Helm, 2010; Godwin-Jones, 2019; Kukulska-Hulme et al., 2024).

Hybrid pedagogy operationalizes these processes through structured movement across digital and face-to-face modalities. Learners engage individually with AI-generated prompts and perspectives in asynchronous or semi-guided contexts before negotiating interpretations collectively in face-to-face classroom interaction. When situated within such hybrid configurations, the Intergenerational Sensitizer enacts hybridity as a "third space" of dialogue (Bhabha, 1994), where cinematic narratives, AI-mediated scaffolding, and teacher-guided discussion intersect. From this perspective, post-viewing activities of this kind "assess the student's quality of responsiveness to relatable movie themes and characters" (Ypsilanti & Karras, 2024, p. 168), while also supporting iterative cycles of interpretation, reflection, and interaction central to intercultural competence development (Byram et al., 2001; Deardorff, 2009).

Pedagogically, AI-assisted hybridity affords opportunities for differentiation by aligning tasks with learners' CEFR-related proficiency levels and cognitive readiness, while fostering emerging AI literacy alongside film literacy. This approach is consistent with human-centered AI frameworks that emphasize transparency, learner agency, and critical engagement with algorithmically generated content (Holmes et al., 2019; Selwyn, 2019). Within this framework, gamified hybrid formats are designed to encourage learner autonomy, initiative, and ethical reasoning, reinforcing the role of technology as a facilitator of reflective inquiry rather than a source of authoritative interpretation (Ypsilanti & Karras, 2025).

At the same time, teacher mediation remains pivotal. Educators play a crucial role in contextualizing AI-generated outputs, guiding discussion, and ensuring that intercultural reflection remains dialogic and critical. The discussion illustrates how

AI-mediated hybrid pedagogy can transform the Intergenerational Sensitizer into a dynamic pedagogical artefact that integrates language development, intercultural reflection, and digital literacy within contemporary TEIC/TEFL practice. This positioning resonates with emerging research on AI-supported film literacy, where interactive digital tools have been shown to scaffold interpretive reasoning and reflective dialogue when embedded within human-centered pedagogical designs (Ypsilanti & Karras, 2025).

6. CONCLUSIONS

Limitations of Study

As a design-oriented investigation, the present study does not report findings from classroom implementation, which limits empirical claims regarding the effectiveness of the Intergenerational Sensitizer in enhancing linguistic development, intercultural awareness, or learner engagement. The anticipated participants, learning processes, and outcomes are therefore grounded in theoretical modelling and AI-supported simulations rather than in observed classroom interaction. In addition, the use of animated film narratives and AI-mediated perspectives cannot fully represent the diversity of intergenerational and cultural experiences present in heterogeneous EFL classrooms, and the transferability of the proposed design beyond the Greek educational context remains tentative. Finally, while AI tools offer adaptive and dialogic affordances, their pedagogical value is contingent upon learners' digital literacy, institutional infrastructure, and teacher mediation, all of which may vary considerably across contexts. These limitations highlight the need for empirical validation through classroom trials, longitudinal observation, and cross-cultural comparison.

Implications

The proposed Intergenerational Sensitizer carries clear implications for teacher decision-making, curriculum design, and classroom orchestration in TEFL/TEIC contexts. At the level of pedagogical decision-making, it supports teachers in selecting and sequencing culturally meaningful film-based incidents that prompt reflection, dialogue, and empathetic engagement rather than surface-level comprehension. In terms of curriculum design, the sensitizer offers a flexible framework that can be embedded within CEFR-aligned syllabi, enabling the systematic integration of intercultural objectives alongside linguistic goals without requiring curricular overhaul. With respect to classroom orchestration, the model provides a structured yet adaptable interactional script through which teachers can coordinate AI-mediated exploration, small-group discussion, and whole-class reflection across hybrid learning environments. These implications foreground the role of the teacher as an intentional designer and mediator of intercultural learning, ensuring that AI and film function as pedagogical resources rather than instructional authorities.

Suggestions for Further Research

Future research should examine the classroom implementation of the Intergenerational Sensitizer across educational levels, including primary, secondary, and tertiary contexts, in order to explore developmental differences in learners' intercultural sensitivity and communicative engagement. Comparative studies across cultural settings could investigate how learners from different sociocultural backgrounds respond to intergenerational narratives and conflict scenarios. Longitudinal research would also be valuable in assessing the sustained impact of AI-mediated, film-based pedagogies on language development, intercultural competence, and learner motivation. In addition, further inquiry could explore the integration of emerging AI applications, such as adaptive learning systems or immersive environments, while critically addressing ethical considerations related to transparency, agency, and data use in digital pedagogy.

Concluding Remarks

Positioned as a design-oriented pedagogical framework rather than an empirical intervention study, the chapter offers a transferable model for integrating film pedagogy and human-centered AI in TEIC contexts. Drawing on critical incidents from films such as *Coco*, *Encanto*, and *Moana*, the sensitizer invites learners to explore generational perspectives, negotiate meaning across cultural contexts, and reflect on tensions between individual and collective values. Positioned within hybrid learning environments, the framework conceptualizes the classroom as a dialogic "third space" in which cinematic narratives, AI mediation, and teacher-facilitated interaction intersect.

While the study remains conceptual in nature, it suggests that such an approach can create conditions conducive to the development of communicative fluency, intercultural awareness, and empathetic understanding. By foregrounding empathy as a component of intercultural communication, the sensitizer encourages learners to engage constructively with difference and conflict through language. At the same time, it offers teachers a principled way of integrating film literacy and AI tools into intercultural language education. Future empirical research will be necessary to evaluate the model's effectiveness, refine its pedagogical design, and explore its broader applicability within evolving TEFL/TEIC contexts.

REFERENCES

Albert, R. D., & Triandis, H. C. (1985). Intercultural education for multicultural societies: Critical issues. *International Journal of Intercultural Relations*, *9*(3), 319–337. DOI: 10.1016/0147-1767(85)90032-X

Bengtson, V. L., & Schrader, S. S. (1982). Parent–child relations. In Mangen, D. J., & Peterson, W. A. (Eds.), *Research instruments in social gerontology: Social roles and social participation* (Vol. 2, pp. 115–185). University of Minnesota Press.

Bhabha, H. K. (1994). *The location of culture*. Routledge.

Byram, M. (1997). *Teaching and assessing intercultural communicative competence*. Multilingual Matters.

Byram, M., Gribkova, B., & Starkey, H. (2002). Developing the intercultural dimension in language teaching: A practical introduction for teachers. Language Policy Division, Directorate of School, Out-of-School and Higher Education, Council of Europe.

Byram, M., Nichols, A., & Stevens, D. (Eds.). (2001). *Developing intercultural competence in practice* (Vol. 1). Multilingual Matters. DOI: 10.21832/9781853595356

Cushner, K., & Brislin, R. W. (1996). *Intercultural interactions: A practical guide* (2nd ed.). Sage Publications, Inc. DOI: 10.4135/9781452204970

Deardorff, D. K. (2006). The Identification and assessment of intercultural competence. *Journal of Studies in International Education*, *10*(3), 241–266. DOI: 10.1177/1028315306287002

Deardorff, D. K. (2009). *The SAGE handbook of intercultural competence*. SAGE. DOI: 10.4135/9781071872987

Dervin, F. (2016). *Interculturality in education: A theoretical and methodological toolbox*. Springer. DOI: 10.1057/978-1-137-54544-2

Fiedler, F. E., Mitchell, T., & Triandis, H. C. (1971). The culture assimilator: An approach to cross-cultural training. *The Journal of Applied Psychology*, *55*(2), 95–102. DOI: 10.1037/h0030704

Flanagan, J. C. (1954). The critical incident technique. *Psychological Bulletin*, *51*(4), 327–358. DOI: 10.1037/h0061470 PMID: 13177800

Garrison, D. R., & Vaughan, N. D. (2008). *Blended learning in higher education: Framework, principles, and guidelines*. John Wiley & Sons.

Godwin-Jones, R. (2019). Emerging technologies and language learning: More than just one model. *Language Learning & Technology, 23*(1), 1–17.

Godwin-Jones, R. (2023). Emerging spaces for language learning: AI bots, ambient intelligence, and the metaverse. *Language Learning & Technology, 27*(2), 6–27. DOI: 10.64152/10125/73501

Guth, S., & Helm, F. (Eds.). (2010). *Telecollaboration 2.0: Language, literacies and intercultural learning in the 21st century* (Vol. 1). Peter Lang. DOI: 10.3726/978-3-0351-0013-6

Herrero, C., & Vanderschelden, I. (Eds.). (2019). *Using film and media in the language classroom: Reflections on research-led teaching* (Vol. 73). Multilingual Matters.

Holliday, A. (2011). Intercultural communication and ideology. *Sage (Atlanta, Ga.)*. Advance online publication. DOI: 10.4135/9781446269107

Holmes, W., Bialik, M., & Fadel, C. (2019). *Artificial intelligence in education promises and implications for teaching and learning*. Center for Curriculum Redesign.

Jackson, J. (2014). *Introducing language and intercultural communication*. Routledge. DOI: 10.4324/9781315848938

Karatsareas, P., Hadodo, M. J., & Ioannidou, E. (2024). Researching identities, authenticities, and institutions in minoritized settings: Insights from diverse Greek-speaking communities. In Hadodo, M. J., Katsareas, P., & Ioannidou, E. (Eds.), *Greek in minoritized contexts* (pp. 1–21). Routledge., DOI: 10.4324/9781003269694-1

Kern, R. (2006). Perspectives on technology in learning and teaching languages. *TESOL Quarterly, 40*(1), 183–210. DOI: 10.2307/40264516

Kidman, J. (2015). Indigenous youth, nationhood and the politics of belonging. In Wyn, J., & Cahill, H. (Eds.), *Handbook of children and youth studies* (pp. 637–649). Springer Singapore. DOI: 10.1007/978-981-4451-15-4_49

Kramsch, C. (1993). *Context and culture in language teaching*. Oxford University Press.

Kramsch, C. (1998). *Language and culture*. Oxford University Press.

Kukulska-Hulme, A., Wise, A. F., Coughlan, T., Biswas, G., Bossu, C., Burriss, S. K., Ferguson, R., Gaved, M., Herodotou, C., Holmes, W., & Whitelock, D. (2024). *Innovating pedagogy 2024* (Open University Innovation Report No. 12). The Open University.

Leong, F. T., & Kim, H. H. (1991). Going beyond cultural sensitivity on the road to multiculturalism: Using the Intercultural Sensitizer as a counselor training tool. *Journal of Counseling and Development, 70*(1), 112–118. DOI: 10.1002/j.1556-6676.1991.tb01570.x

Liddicoat, A. J., & Scarino, A. (2013). *Intercultural language teaching and learning*. John Wiley & Sons. DOI: 10.1002/9781118482070

Luckin, R., Holmes, W., Griffiths, M., & Forcier, L. B. (2016). *Intelligence unleashed: An argument for AI in education*. Pearson.

Mazza, J. (2007, October 23-25). *Labor markets and social inclusion in Latin America and the Caribbean: Perspectives for intergenerational solidarity* [Paper presentation]. UN Expert Group Meeting on Intergenerational Solidarity: Strengthening Economic and Social Ties, New York, USA.

O'Dowd, R. (2018). From telecollaboration to virtual exchange: State-of-the-art and the role of UNICollaboration in moving forward. *Research-publishing. net, 1*, 1-23.

O'Dowd, R., & Ritter, M. (2006). Understanding and working with 'failed communication' in telecollaborative exchanges. *CALICO Journal, 23*(3), 623–642. DOI: 10.1558/cj.v23i3.623-642

Piña-Watson, B., Ojeda, L., Castellon, N. E., & Dornhecker, M. (2013). Familismo, ethnic identity, and bicultural stress as predictors of Mexican American adolescents' positive psychological functioning. *Journal of Latina/o Psychology, 1*(4), 204–217. DOI: 10.1037/lat0000006

Pnevmatikos, D., & Bardos, A. N. (2014). Greek adolescents' intimate relations before their transition to adulthood. *Journal of Adolescence, 37*(8), 1475–1488. DOI: 10.1016/j.adolescence.2014.07.018 PMID: 25154545

Porto, M. (2016). Ecological and intercultural citizenship in the primary English as a foreign language (EFL) classroom: An online project in Argentina. *Cambridge Journal of Education, 46*(4), 395–415. DOI: 10.1080/0305764X.2015.1064094

Selwyn, N. (2019). *Should robots replace teachers? AI and the future of education*. Polity Press.

Siatitsa, D., & Dagkouli-Kyriakoglou, M. (2024). Youth housing trajectories: Gender and intergenerational solidarity in Greece. In Wyn, J., Cahill, H., & Cuervo, H. (Eds.), *Handbook of Children and Youth Studies* (pp. 1059–1071). Springer Nature Singapore., DOI: 10.1007/978-981-99-8606-4_106

Triandis, H. C., Brislin, R., & Hui, C. H. (1988). Cross-cultural training across the individualism-collectivism divide. *International Journal of Intercultural Relations, 12*(3), 269–289. DOI: 10.1016/0147-1767(88)90019-3

United Nations. (2006). Indigenous peoples, indigenous voices: Factsheet. *United Nations Permanent Forum on Indigenous Issues.* https://www.un.org/esa/socdev/unpfii/documents/5session_factsheet1.pdf

Vassiliou, V. G., & Vassiliou, G. (1973). The implicative meaning of the Greek concept of philotimo. *Journal of Cross-Cultural Psychology, 4*(3), 326–341. DOI: 10.1177/002202217300400305

Ypsilanti, A. (2025). *Critical incident representations in films: An intercultural framework* [Doctoral dissertation, Ionian University]. National Archive of PhD Theses (EADD). DOI: 10.12681/eadd/59879

Ypsilanti, A., & Karras, I. (2023). From TENOR to TEIC: The English teacher's final "say-so" in reformulating education policies. *European Journal of Education and Pedagogy, 4*(6), 41–46. DOI: 10.24018/ejedu.2023.4.6.761

Ypsilanti, A., & Karras, I. (2024). Introducing Pixar shorts in the Greek EFL classroom as a means to enhancing empathy among high school students. In *Proceedings of the IAFOR International Conference on Arts & Humanities in Hawaii (IICAH2024).* International Academic Forum (IAFOR). DOI: 10.22492/issn.2432-4604.2024.15

Ypsilanti, A., & Karras, I. (2025). Experiencing film literacy through Magic School AI. In Baba Khouya, Y., & Ismaili Alaoui, A. (Eds.), *Application of AI in the Teaching and Learning of English as a Foreign Language (EFL)* (pp. 275–330). IGI Global Scientific Publishing., DOI: 10.4018/979-8-3373-0969-9.ch008

Zawacki-Richter, O., Bai, J. Y., Lee, K., Slagter van Tryon, P. J., & Prinsloo, P. (2024). New advances in artificial intelligence applications in higher education? *International Journal of Educational Technology in Higher Education, 21*(1), 32. DOI: 10.1186/s41239-024-00464-3

Chapter 9
Designing Inclusive Hybrid Pedagogies in Physical Science With AI From Classroom to Cloud

V. Devaki
http://orcid.org/0000-0002-7109-0205
SASTRA University, India

Chinna Suresh
http://orcid.org/0000-0002-3389-1116
SASTRA University, India

V. Vidya
http://orcid.org/0000-0001-5167-6340
SASTRA University, India

B. Lalithabala
http://orcid.org/0009-0005-1152-0006
SASTRA University, India

ABSTRACT

This chapter discusses the change of Physical Science education in the time of Artificial Intelligence and hybrid learning. It theorizes the transition between the traditional classroom designs and inclusive technology enhanced learning ecologies incorporating physical and digital space. The chapter is based on constructivist, socio-cultural, inquiry based and intercultural theories of learning. It explains the use of AI based tools, including adaptive learning systems, virtual laboratories, intelligent tutoring systems and generative simulations as well as automated

DOI: 10.4018/979-8-3373-7462-8.ch009

assessment in Physical Science. The chapter also discusses the changing professional identity of educators, highlighting the fact that AI literacy and intercultural competence should be included in the teacher preparation programs. In the future, the chapter tells about the potential transformations of generative AI for a world scientific collaboration. In the end, it states that the suitable integration of AI into hybrid pedagogies developing scientifically literate, ethically informed and globally competent students.

1. INTRODUCTION

The Shifting Landscape of Science Education

In the 21st century, education is experiencing a radicalization process due to the progression of globalization, digitization and artificial intelligence (AI). In the conventional classroom, in-person teaching and a rigid time-space approach to learning is gradually being replaced by hybrid and online learning environments that combine both physical and digital modes of learning (Bozkurt et al., 2023). These new spaces make available to learners providing the opportunity to interact, collaborate and build knowledge on both geographical and cultural levels. In this paradigm shift, Physical Science education has its own niche. The depth of its concept, its focus on empirical experimentation and focus on visualization make it a challenge and opportunity in the digital age. The change of the classroom to the cloud is not only a technological modification but a radical change in pedagogy (Alenezi, 2023). It transforms the learning environment to become a holistic system in which there are no demarcations between formal and informal learning. Students can now visit laboratories online, communicate with peers around the globe and interact with smart digital tutors who can provide scaffolding on a one-on-one basis. This change is also in line with the larger objectives of Education 4.0, in which learning becomes dynamic, adaptive and interdisciplinary and prepares students to a future characterized by constant technological evolution (Oliveira & de Souza, 2021).

The Rise of Hybrid Pedagogy

Blended learning is also known as hybrid pedagogy and it represents the intersection between the physical and the virtual learning space. It takes into consideration both synchronous and asynchronous forms of interaction, using technology to expand the classroom interaction (Rasheed et al., 2020). In contrast to the entirely online or traditional models, hybrid pedagogy is highly designed. The deliberate combination of the face-to-face and digital learning experience in order to promote the conceptual learning and interactions. Hybrid pedagogy is also applicable to Physical Science, where the simulation with AI capabilities could be combined with practical experiences in laboratories to produce the effect of immersion, which does not rely on time, space, or resources (Almufarreh & Arshad, 2023).

The need to use hybrid pedagogy in science education is not just practical but philosophical. Inquiry, experimentation, collaboration as a part of curriculum component are now add to science and are most enhanced by digital augmentation. For example, online discussion groups allow argumentation and reasoning; virtual labs make experiments accessible to resource constrained settings; and AI-based devices encourage more personalized feedback, strengthening metacognition and self-managed learning. Therefore, the hybrid pedagogy in Physical Science is an agent of democratizing the process of learning without compromising the rigor and epistemic integrity of scientific inquiry (Schäfer et al., 2024).

AI as a Catalyst for Educational Transformation

Artificial Intelligence (AI) has become one of the most disruptive developments within the educational field. It is used in adaptive learning environments and intelligent tutoring systems (ITS) as well as predictive analytics and automated assessment systems. The potential of AI in the teaching of Physical Science is that it can represent the complex phenomena, customize the learning experience and provide real-time feedback that underpins the inquiry-based learning (Kim et al., 2022). As an example, a dynamic simulation enabled by AI can be used to visualize molecular dynamics or electromagnetic fields, which are more abstract or high speed that, can be observed under normal conditions. In the same manner, the natural language processing systems are capable of reading the written descriptions of physical concepts by students, detecting false notions and providing specific instructions.

However, the implementation of AI in education requires both ethical and critical consideration as well. Researchers are cautious of algorithmic bias, the issue of data privacy and excessive dependence on automation that could weaken human agency in learning (Yu, 2023). Thus, AI does not need to replace the teacher but rather be used to augment pedagogical processes in a manner that promotes equity and inclusion. Implemented correctly, AI can make science education more democratic, especially in situations with low resources or distance (Hagendorff, 2020).

Inclusivity and Intercultural Sensitivity in the AI Era

The concept of inclusiveness has become an important topic of discussion in education and in particular the design of digital and hybrid learning platforms. Not only it is difficult to guarantee access to technology but also create an inclusive environment in epistemology, the appreciation and inclusion of various cultural, linguistic and cognitive views in education. Physical Science which is commonly viewed as being universal and culture-neutral is in reality a construct of contextual knowledge practices and sociocultural values (Longo et al., 2020). Thus, hybrid pedagogy should be inclusive in order to appreciate different ways of knowing and enable students with diverse backgrounds to have significance in interacting with scientific ideas.

Artificial Intelligence may positively contribute to improving inclusivity by providing adaptive interfaces, the possibility of multiple languages and accessibility tools (Budhwar et al., 2023). However, inclusivity should always be a pedagogical decision and not a technical one. Educators should acquire technical, ethical and intercultural awareness of AI literacy. As such, teacher education programs are left with the burden of ensuring that future education professionals are prepared to adopt AI with a critical perspective and at the same time protect humanistic and equitable education values (MacKenzie et al., 2022).

Teacher Preparation in the Hybrid Paradigm

Physical Science pre-service teachers should be able to find their way in hybrid environments, which require digital skills and pedagogical flexibility. Studies have shown that beliefs, confidence and professional identity among teachers are essential factors in effective use of technology in classrooms. Therefore, the training programs must focus on reflective practice, design thinking and collaborative innovation. Teachers should not only know how to utilize AI tools, but why and when to do so, as they are meant to serve some pedagogical purpose and meet ethical expectations (Falloon, 2020). Any institution that trains science teachers must also be able to design hybrid and AI-based teaching practices. This entails encouraging intercultural cooperation amongst teacher apprentices by worldwide undertakings, virtual exchange schemes and co-teaching schemes. This type of experience fosters international scientific citizenship where teachers are able to reside out of localized paradigms and connect to the universal but culturally sensitive nature of science education.

From Transition to Transformation

The shift toward the cloud is not a short-term measure in response to the crisis like the COVID-19 pandemic, but a long-term reorganization of education. Augmented with AI, hybrid pedagogy can be used to provide more personalized, participatory and inclusive learning in science. But the realization of this vision would not come without technological investment, but systemic rethinking of curriculum, pedagogy, assessment and teacher preparation would be needed. The future classroom is not a physical location, but rather a pedagogical network, a school where learners, educators and smart systems will co-create knowledge in dynamic and equal ways (Onu et al., 2024).

This chapter thus, starts with conceptual discussion into the pedagogical basis of hybrid science education and then discusses more specifically the role of AI, inclusivity, intercultural collaboration and teacher preparation. It will combine theoretical, empirical and practical insights to shed light on how Physical Science pedagogy can change based on the transformational power of AI and hybrid learning. As the title implies, the process of leaving classroom and traveling to cloud is not a displacement but rather a re-invention of educational space- a movement of educational environments that are open, intelligent and inclusive. The Figure 1 interprets the whole journey of the chapter in transforming the traditional based to AI integrated hybrid pedagogy.

Figure 1. AI Integration in Hybrid Pedagogy: A Transformative Journey (Author's own work)

2. PEDAGOGICAL FOUNDATIONS OF HYBRID SCIENCE EDUCATION

Revisiting Pedagogical Paradigms for the Digital Era

The movement to hybrid education in the science field is not only a technological change but it is a radical reorganization of pedagogical thought. The idea of hybrid pedagogy is conceptually based on various learning theories that pre-empt active engagement, social interaction and situated cognition. Of these, constructivism, the socio-cultural theory and inquiry-based learning, have developed to have a significant impact on the design of hybrid learning in science teaching (Nguyen et al., 2020). Physical Science is interested in the study of the natural phenomena by experimentation and reasoning which naturally fits these paradigms. The hybrid model becomes a pedagogical interface between the old scientific inquiry and the new technology mediated innovation (Panyajamorn, 2022).

In the hybrid setting, the boundaries between teacher, learner and content are permeable. Students do not receive the knowledge but engage in building the understanding based on the interaction with the digital tools, peers and real-life issues. The teachers act as designers of learning experiences like organizing physical and virtual space to develop a more desirable interaction (Li et al., 2021). Such change requires the theoretical foundation that incorporates the cognitive and social aspects of learning to make sure that digitalization does not make learning an act of content delivery.

Constructivism and Meaning-Making in Hybrid Contexts

Constructivism theorizes that learners develop knowledge actively by experience and reflection and not passively through absorption of information. The constructivist principles are enhanced in the hybrid classroom through the digital affordances which enable students to manipulate simulations, visualize phenomena and collaboratively solve problems with each other. Physical Science Virtual labs, such as those that allow learners to design experiments, adjust variables and see the results in real-time, can facilitate greater conceptual learning (de Jong et al., 2013).

The constructivist focus on the autonomy of learners and contextual learning can be very close to the affordances of AI-based hybrid spaces (Kim et al., 2022). Individual misconceptions can be recognized and content customized through adaptive platforms that run machine learning algorithms. Such personalization is a constructivist method since learning is developed based on feedback, self-control and trial and error. Further, the hybrid model will help motivate students to use theoretical information to real-life problems, which is aligned with situated cognition, which states that knowledge cannot be constructed outside of a situation and an activity.

However, constructivism in mixed environments also requires special planning to avoid cognitive overload (Dwivedi et al., 2023). Learners can be overwhelmed by availability of various digital resources unless scaffolding of activities is done well. Thus science hybrid pedagogy must integrate structured inquiry guided exploration and reflective dialogue that provide the learners stay focused on conceptual coherence and not on fragmented experiences.

Socio-Cultural Theory: Collaboration and Contextual Learning

Socio-cultural view is mostly based on the work of (Kozulin & Wertsch, 1987) and puts more stress on the central role of social interaction and mediation of culture in learning. These principles are reflected in hybrid environments in the form of collaborative learning communities, which are not physically defined. Discussion forums, virtual whiteboards and AI-based collaboration platforms are some of the tools that allow learners to collaborate through shared inquiry and knowledge construction. As an example, learners in other places may collectively discuss experimental results of a virtual physics lab, with real-time AI feedback about interaction in the group and communication.

There is a distance between what learners can accomplish independently and assisted that is called the Zone of Proximal Development (ZPD) and it is discovered to be new in hybrid education. The ITS can also play the role of intelligent tutors that dynamically change their level of support according to the performance and engagement of a learner (Anderson & Dron, 2011). This type of scaffolding supports the ZPD development in the form of a symbiotic pedagogical collaboration, which combines human and machine instructions.

The socio-cultural theory also emphasizes the importance of language and cultural tools in the development of cognition. This would translate in hybrid Physical science pedagogy as designing multilingual, culturally sensitive educational resources which respect different epistemologies. Combined with intelligent reasoning, AI-powered translation and captioning technologies can make science education in the world more democratic (Zawacki-Richter et al., 2019). However, the socio-cultural lenses can warn the educators that technology needs to be contextualized were tools can only take meaning when they are built in the context of real human interactions and the shared purposes.

Inquiry-Based Learning and the Nature of Science

The epistemological nature of science itself, inquiry, questioning and systematic investigation, is present in inquiry-based learning (IBL). It changes the emphasis on memorizing facts and gives way to scientific reasoning and evidence-based argumentation processes (Gormally et al., 2009). In hybrid Physical Science education, AI and digital resources increase the range of possibilities of inquiry to go beyond the traditional laboratory limits. AI-assisted virtual experiments allow students to model complex phenomena, including electromagnetic wave propagation or chemical kinetics and analyze data in real-time to be able to formulate hypotheses and make conclusions (L. Wang et al., 2024).

The hybrid model will also encourage open inquiry, in which the students will ask their own questions, create investigations, with the assistance of digital materials. This goes in line with constructivist and socio-cultural principles of independence and cooperation (Kirschner et al., 2018). The AI analytics can also be used to fortify the inquiry process by detecting patterns in the problem-solving strategies of the students, thus informing both formative feedback and adaptive instruction.

However, the pedagogical issue is to maintain the authenticity of inquiry in structured hybrid systems. There is a danger of excessive automation that is degrading an inquiry into a procedural job that lacks exploration. In this way, teachers are required to make sure that AI is used as an augmentative collaborating entity and does not dictate the scientific process because it must keep students in charge and creative (Dwivedi et al., 2021).

Intercultural Pedagogy in Hybrid Science Education

Intercultural pedagogy goes beyond the cognition and involves cultural diversity and international interconnectedness (Granados-Beltrán, 2016). Science is generally described as a universal language but in a different cultural context, science is practiced and understood in various ways. The hybrid learning spaces enable opportunities never before seen in the world to connect the learners around the world with the use of collaborative online projects and also international partnerships, promoting intercultural scientific literacy.

Viewed in this context, hybrid Physical Science education must not only pass on canonical knowledge, but it must also encourage students to consider the impact of cultural values upon scientific inquiry and practice. To illustrate, when talking about energy conservation, one can take into consideration the native conception of sustainability and expand the epistemic foundation of science education (Reed & Rudman, 2023). Artificial intelligence can help in that it will filter the abundance of content sources and help the ideologies to communicate across cultures, but teachers have to mediate that process or face the risk of culture tokenism or superficial trade.

Another aspect of intercultural pedagogy in hybrid environments is the creation of global competence, i.e., the factor of being able to effectively and respectfully interact with a person who belongs to a different culture (Zidny et al., 2020). The models of Collaborative Online International Learning (COIL) are examples of such approaches, as they involve the element of intercultural collaboration into the curricular design. COIL projects when applied to the Physical Science can connect students studying around the world in order to co-investigate a phenomenon, compare environmental data, or co-create science communication resources that blend scientific inquiry with cultural understanding and digital literacy (Naicker et al., 2022).

Synthesizing the Pedagogical Framework

Combined, constructivism, socio-cultural theory, inquiry-based learning and intercultural pedagogy are the theoretical underpinnings of hybrid Physical Science education. All of these frameworks promote the ideas of learner-centeredness, collaboration, contextualization and inclusivity. The hybrid model realizes these concepts by means of digital technologies, which introduce flexibility, personalization and connectivity all over the world. Nonetheless, the pedagogical integrity of hybrid education is determined by the ability to cohere theory and design (Rata, 2021). Teachers have to be reflective professionals - to balance autonomy of AI tools with human judgment, empathy and ethical sensitivity.

Finally, hybrid science pedagogy does not imply substituting the traditional teaching but supplementing it. It is a didactical development that reflects the sophistication of modern science such as dynamic, interrelated and multiethnic. Based on the sound learning theories, grounding hybrid designs will help educators see that technology is not the driver of pedagogy but the reverse and AI can be used as a means to positively influence science learning by constructive, collaborative and culturally responsive learning.

3. ARTIFICIAL INTELLIGENCE AND HYBRID PEDAGOGY

Reframing Teaching and Learning with AI

Artificial Intelligence (AI) has graduated to the status of the thing of the present and the future of the educational process. In hybrid learning ecosystems, AI serves as a technological facilitator and pedagogical companion and promotes personalization, adaptability and inclusivity (Rata, 2021). The ground-breaking application of AI into the analysis of learning behaviors, the use of resources and feedback, is of significant benefit in hybrid pedagogy, which is based on the combination of face-to-face and online modes of interaction. In Physical Science education, where abstract ideas can be a thorn in the flesh of understanding of students, AI can serve as a catalyst that will help establish a balance between the theoretical and the practical knowledge (Choudhary et al., 2022).

Nevertheless, the effects of AI are not only efficiency and automation, but also epistemic and ethical aspects of pedagogy are redefined. It poses a challenge to the educators to think over what teaching, learning and assessment can be in the situations when machines are sharing the cognitive space that was traditionally regarded as human. The challenge of effective use of AI in the context of hybrid science pedagogy is to make a critical balance between automation and humanization. This is to ensure that intelligent systems enhance, but do not reduce, intellectual and ethical interactions of learners.

AI-Driven Personalization and Adaptive Learning

Adaptive learning, dynamic modification of the content, difficulty and feedback depending on the learner data, is one of the most transformative contributions of AI to hybrid pedagogy (Sweller et al., 2019). The adaptive learning systems use algorithms that compare the performance of students in real-time in order to customize the learning materials and activities. Adaptive platforms can be used in Physical Science to detect long-standing misunderstandings in subjects like Newtonian motion or thermodynamics and the use of individualized scaffolds to influence conceptual change.

As an example, ITS like ALEKS or Carnegie Learning use Bayesian networks and diagnose student comprehension and provide sequenced problems based on personal progress (H. Wang et al., 2023). This ability is in line with the constructivist beliefs that it enables learners to learn at their own speed thus encouraging mastery as opposed to memorization. Moreover, adaptive systems with AI can produce multimodal feedback including textual, graphical or auditory feedbacks to meet the needs of various learning styles and accessibility requirements (Shoaib et al., 2023).

However, personalization creates pedagogical dilemmas. Too much individualization can cause the isolation of learners and the erosion of the spirit of collaboration, which science teaching is all about. As such, hybrid pedagogy should be such that adaptive learning is possible within frameworks of social connections, in these instances, AI will customize cognitive directions but leave communal query intact. The role of teachers in mediating this balance is critical in the context of processing algorithmic insights through professional judgment and contextual awareness.

AI-Enabled Simulation and Visualization in Physical Science

Physical Science, in itself, deals with phenomena that tend to be invisible, instantaneous or conceptual in nature. Simulations and visualization tools based on AI can solve this issue by simulating complex systems in data-driven interactive settings. The virtual and augmented reality (VR/AR) laboratories, combined with AI algorithms, enable learners to handle variables, visualize the molecular interactions and visualize the electromagnetic fields (Cipresso et al., 2018). Such tools make laboratory experiences more democratic particularly in institutions with limited physical resources.

Machine learning also improves the reality of simulations by creating predictive systems on the basis of massive datasets (Carvalho et al., 2019). As an example, AI can model both planetary movement or material stress profiles based on real-world physics data, enabling students to be able to experiment with phenomena that would be challenging or dangerous to reproduce in a physical laboratory. These tools represent experiential constructivism, a combination of the abstract thinking with the manipulation in the safety, scalability and inclusiveness.

In addition, generative AI systems e.g. text-to-simulation or code-generation models can expand this capability by generating visualizations or experimental situations based on text input. A learner may enter the search query of simulating the interaction of two light waves and a real-time interactive demonstration will be created. This feature does not only make the process of learning faster but also makes the learners creative with what they are reading. Nevertheless, teachers should be more critical about the accuracy of these systems and make sure that the representations created by AI have scientific and epistemic integrity.

Automated Assessment and Feedback Systems

Evaluation has been an essential part of good instructional practice and AI is redefining the process of capturing and interpreting evidence of learning. There are automated assessment systems which analyze not only the structured information such as multiple choice questions but also the unstructured one such as a written explanation or a series of steps in solving a problem. In hybrid Physical Science classes, AI is able to not only evaluate final solutions, but also process data, which would give an idea of the reasoning pathways taken by students. These formative feedbacks enable the learners to develop their strategies, thus encouraging metacognitive development (Yang et al., 2024).

Natural language processing (NLP) models can be used to assess the conceptual description of physics problems by students to identify the misconceptions that actuaries of traditional grading could fail to detect. On the same note, digital lab notebooks or diagrams can be viewed using computer vision algorithms to ascertain the authenticity of the experimental setup. These innovations make assessment more of a diagnostic and continuous one rather than the summative and retrospective one (Young et al., 2018).

However, the educators should be aware of the ethical and interpretive shortcomings of algorithmic assessment. Discriminations on the training data may result in biased evaluation and a disadvantage to the selected groups of learners. Therefore, it is necessary to have clear AI design and human moderation in order to ensure fairness and accountability. Best hybrid pedagogies combine automated feedback as an addition to human assessment, that is, an enhancement of human assessment and not a substitute.

Teacher–AI Collaboration: Redefining Pedagogical Roles

When AI is introduced into hybrid pedagogy, it can only change the professional identity of teachers. Quite on the contrary, AI necessitates educators of a more sophisticated level. The educators are to be taught how to analyze algorithmic information, develop learning activities using AI and teach students to be aware of AI systems themselves. In this meaning, teachers will be transformed into AI-enhanced professionals who will coordinate human-machine work to learn something significant (Michel-Villarreal et al., 2023).

The organization of teacher in AI collaboration may also simplify administrative work like grading or attendance-record keeping and allow teachers to concentrate on mentoring and innovative facilitation. Nevertheless, in this partnership, AI literacy is needed for knowledge of the logic, affordances and constraints of intelligent systems. In the absence of such literacy, teachers will be mere consumers of black box technologies, which will erode pedagogical agency. Physical Science teacher training programs should thus include AI competence in their course content, which will then allow graduates to design, assess and ethically consider the application of AI tools in teaching.

This collaboration can thrive in hybrid pedagogy. Teachers can use AI analytics to find students who require more attention, help to set lesson time, or create group activities that would solve common misunderstandings. As an AI is used as a pedagogical co-agent and not a sub-agent, it improves the relational aspect of instruction and not eradicates it.

Recent studies demonstrate the tangible effect of AI-assisted hybrid learning in Physical Science. An AI-enhanced Case-Based Learning (AI-CBL) model that incorporates a chatbot used as a scaffolding system to provide guidance and real-time feedback yielded much greater learning gains (N-Gain = 0.98, High) with AI-CBL compared to conventional CBL alone (N-Gain = 0.52, Medium; $p < 0.001$). There was improved conceptual learning, metacognitive reflection and motivation among the students (Al Hasanah et al., 2025). A computer vision and Bayesian Knowledge Tracing-based AI-adaptive mixed-reality Intelligent Science Station was used at the elementary level to customize hands-on physics activities (Yannier et al., 2024). The adaptive condition learners performed better than their counterparts in randomized conditions (69% vs. 54; d = 0.66) without showing a lower level of enjoyment. Likewise, a chatbot based on the generative AI that supports self-regulated learning in secondary physics improved mastering content, motivation, and planning-reflection abilities (Ng et al., 2024). When combined, these instances demonstrate that AI can significantly supplement hybrid science pedagogy at all levels of education.

Ethical, Equity and Epistemological Considerations

Regardless of this potential, AI brings complicated ethical and equity issues that hybrid pedagogy should address. Algorithms systems are not neutral; they show the biases of the people who created them and the data. These biases may be present in education; they may be characterized by unequal predictive power between groups of people or thwarting of stereotypes. Also, AI relies on data gathering, which is a privacy issue as well as in cases where systems track the interaction of students of digital environments (Floridi et al., 2018).

Epistemologically, excessive dependence on AI will lead to science learning being more of algorithmic empiricism with one blindly accepting the outputs of the computations. Teachers should thus develop AI epistemic awareness in students; that is, the skills that allow them to doubt the way algorithms make predictions, categorize information and give scientific phenomena. The integration of such critical literacy would make sure that learners will not just be passive consumers of information produced by AI but active interpreters of information.

Equity also further applies to disparities in the global access to AI. The infrastructure and finances to implement advanced AI tools are not available in many institutions especially in developing regions. The hybrid pedagogy should encourage the open-source AI resources, low-bandwidth solutions and context-sensitive adaptation that will reflect the educational realities of the region to avert the occurrence of digital colonialism (Sethi & Sarangi, 2017). It is an ethical requirement that AI must be not only intelligent but inclusive, open and socially just.

Toward an AI-Infused Pedagogical Ecology

The integration of AI into hybrid pedagogy marks the point of the shift of the content transmission paradigm towards intelligent facilitation. AI systems are able to expand cognitive and affective abilities of learners and instructors when properly incorporated (Tapalova & Zhiyenbayeva, 2022). They facilitate rich-data experimentation, conceptual scaffolds and real-time formative feedback which are characteristic of deep learning and inquiry in Physical Science.

However, to be successful in AI in education requires the preservation of a pedagogical ecology that cherishes human bond, moral uprightness and cross-cultural comprehension. The hybrid model offers the flexibility to the structure to combine the human mastery with machine intelligence to make sure that technology is servant of pedagogy. With the development of AI to generative and conversational models, teachers will need to reconsider hybrid pedagogy as an ecosystem of collaboration with human and artificial intelligences to create collaborative, adaptive and reflective learning environments that are inclusive.

4. DESIGNING INCLUSIVE HYBRID PEDAGOGIES

Inclusion as the Core of Educational Transformation

The shift toward AI and hybrid learning is providing unprecedented chances of innovation and the ethical challenge of guaranteeing equity and inclusivity. Inclusivity in Physical Science education is more than access to digital tools and it is a design of pedagogical learning that acknowledges and supports the various cultural, linguistic, cognitive and socio-economic backgrounds of the learners. When rightly designed, the hybrid model can minimize obstacles to participation by incorporating different and adaptive technologies in flexible learning. However, inclusiveness should also be a pedagogical promise, as opposed to a technical deliverable.

This part examines ways of Artificial Intelligence (AI) to create greater inclusivity in hybrid Physical Science instruction which focuses on the concepts of universal design in learning (UDL), equality of access, linguistic and cultural responsiveness and support of learners with disabilities. It also explores how AI can be utilized by teachers to in-person learning to develop compassionate, contextual hybrid institutional settings, which enable every student to participate in scientific inquiry in a meaningful way.

Universal Design for Learning in Hybrid Science Contexts

Universal Design for Learning (UDL) provides the system of designing inclusive learning environments that embrace individual variability as opposed to regarding it as non-compliance with the norm. The three principles of UDL, which include the provision of various means of representation, engagement and expression, are perfectly aligned with the hybrid and AI-improved pedagogical affordances. These principles are applied in Physical Science education by multimodal instruction methods, which enables students to represent, engage and show comprehension in many forms (Capp, 2017).

To illustrate, a physics lesson related to energy conservation could be hybrid, i.e. full of video lecture (representation), a simulator of pendulum motion powered by AI (engagement) and a collaborative online lab report (expression). AI analytics will be able to determine the modality that will best suit the understanding of each learner, suggesting a personalized learning journey. In addition, AI that is generated can provide different explanations or images of the same thing, which fits the approach to flexibility and accessibility by UDL.

The UDL theory also encourages teachers to consider the diversity proactively instead of retrofitting accommodations to meet the needs of particular students. Hybrid pedagogy is therefore an inclusive design process of merging technology and pedagogy to foresee the diverse needs of the learners (Zawacki-Richter et al., 2019). Although it is possible to use AI to support differentiation, it is the responsibility of human educators to make sure that personalization does not undermine learner agency and does not reinforce stereotypes or ability labels.

AI and Accessibility: Supporting Learners with Disabilities

The potential of AI technologies in assisting learners who experience physical, sensory and cognitive disabilities has been enormous. Accessibility tools such as speech recognition, automatic captioning and text-to-speech, which are AI-powered, serve to support students with hearing, vision, or reading disabilities in Physical Science classes. On the same note, adaptive interfaces are able to adjust the complexity of content, show contrast or input options to individual needs.

When combined with AI, virtual and augmented reality (VR/AR) environments may also provide multisensory experiences that help students who may have learning problems with traditional representations to learn abstract scientific phenomena (Grewal et al., 2020). As an example, an AI-enhanced chemistry simulator can give tactile feedback to the interaction between molecules or sound data trends to learners with visual impairments.

But even inclusion with technology poses challenges of accessibility outside of disability, most especially in resource constrained settings where bandwidth, quality of devices and language barriers still exist. Educators are therefore required to come up with less techy and more adaptable solutions, including downloadable materials, asynchronous discussion boards and open-source AI tools, which will not create more digital gaps.

Cultural and Linguistic Inclusion in Science Pedagogy

Education in science is perceived to be culturally hegemonic, favouring western ways of epistemologies and languages. However, there is an opportunity to recontextualize science instruction as multilingual and culturally responsive provided by hybrid pedagogy. Students with diverse lingual backgrounds can be supported in terms of understanding content with the help of AI-supported translation, transcription and multilingual chatbots, thus being able to contribute to science discourse more (Grassini, 2023).

As an illustration, natural language translators, which are based on AI, can offer real-time captions in hybrid classes when students can collaborate in multilingual groups and represent various countries. Equally, production of speech in local language can enable teachers to develop culturally more familiar interpretations of scientific concepts that can overcome language breaks. However, cultural inclusion is not only language based, it is also about recognizing world diversity in the formulation of scientific issues.

Teachers in Physical Science have the ability to make lessons contextual in localized examples like renewable energy systems in rural India, indigenous ecological knowledge in climate science that learners can perceive science as being relevant to their real lives. The AI will be able to help by filtering collections of data about a region or proposing contextually relevant examples, but the critical intercultural action of an educator is the one that can make these integrations genuine and respectful instead of artificial.

Socio-Economic Equity and Digital Access

Although hybrid and AI-enhanced learning can be associated with an increased access, they also have the capacity to widen inequities in case digital resources are unevenly distributed. The digital divide, which includes the differences in terms of internet access, device access and digital literacy, is a significant obstacle to fair hybrid education. Students in most developing settings might not have access to the devices they can share or consistent connectivity, so they can take part in synchronous learning or simulate activities that require a lot of data.

In order to address these inequalities, teachers and institutions may adopt inclusive digital practices, including the provision of offline access, the use of open educational resources (OER) and the use of AI systems, which work effectively with low-bandwidth conditions. Micro-learning experience can be provided by low-cost AI chatbots or SMS-based learning assistants, such as those and no sophisticated infrastructure is needed (Mtebe & Raisamo, 2014).

Also, equity must consider the problem of algorithmic bias the inclination of AI systems to favor the information of the most dominant cultural or socio-economic groups. Predictive analytics and automated grading or content suggestion can be biased and marginalized learners may fall victim to it. Ethical hybrid pedagogy requires the transparency of the algorithm design, periodic audit of the AI-based tools and participatory co-design involving the voice of different learners.

Pedagogical Strategies for Inclusive Hybrid Design

Inclusive hybrid Pedagogy Designing Physical science Inclusion involves the matching of technology, content and pedagogy using deliberate frameworks (Maarof, M., & Jalaluddin, 2019). Some of such effective strategies are

1. **Inclusive Content Curation:** Use AI-powered recommendation systems to source diverse multimedia resources representing varied cultural and gender perspectives in science.
2. **Collaborative Problem-Based Learning:** Design hybrid inquiry tasks where students from different contexts collaboratively investigate phenomena, fostering intercultural dialogue and empathy.
3. **Scaffold Flexibility:** Combine synchronous interactions (e.g., virtual labs) with asynchronous discussions to accommodate time zone, connectivity and learning style differences.
4. **Accessible Design Audits:** Employ AI analytics to identify participation gaps (e.g., who speaks less in discussions) and redesign activities for equitable engagement.
5. **Reflective Praxis:** Encourage students to critically evaluate how AI tools shape their learning experiences, promoting meta-awareness of inclusion and ethics.

These approaches make inclusion not a post hoc but the design principle of all of pedagogical choices. With the introduction of inclusivity into AI-enhanced hybrid systems, education will be a step closer to the democratic notion of learning as 'learning to everyone, everywhere'.

The Teacher's Role: From Facilitator to Inclusion Architect

The teachers still play a central role in inclusive hybrid pedagogy. They are sensitive to the socio-cultural background of students, with the addition of AI literacy, which allows building balanced digital spaces. Education programs should, therefore, equip teachers as inclusion architects like professionals capable of creating and modifying learning experiences that can utilize AI to improve the social good (Ferri et al., 2020).

There must be critical reflection and lifelong learning. Teachers ought to be taught how to ascertain AI-generated learning analytics in an ethical perspective not merely what the information conveys, but what voices it is responding to or not. The collaboration between human empathy and algorithmic understanding allows teachers to make sure that AI supports, but not causes a replacement of inclusive pedagogy.

5. AI-SUPPORTED TOOLS AND STRATEGIES IN PRACTICE

Translating Theory into Action

The effectiveness of hybrid Physical Science pedagogy hinges on the effectiveness of artificial intelligence (AI) tools to be implemented in real-life teaching. Whereas the preceding sections examined both conceptual and intercultural aspects, the current section will examine practice, i.e., how AI can be used concretely to improve visualization, experimentation, problem-solving and assessment in hybrid environments (Vinayakumar et al., 2019). To be properly integrated, technology must have clear learning goals based on inquiry and collaboration, but not as a new thing or the automation of learning, for itself. The subsequent subsections introduce some of the chosen types of AI-enhanced tools and strategies that proved to have an educational benefit in science education.

Intelligent Tutoring and Adaptive Systems

Intelligent tutoring systems (ITS) are systems of learner feedback guided by learner analytics and cognitive modeling. Learning programs such as Cognitive Tutor, ALEKS and ASSISTments tailor instruction on subjects such as kinematics, thermodynamics, or optics through the diagnosis of misconceptions and provision of specific hints (Adiguzel et al., 2023). These systems can be used in hybrid environments as an addition to live mentoring, so that teachers can track conceptual progress via dashboards and then modify classroom delivery.

As an example, an ITS can detect chronic mistakes in the construction of force-diagrams and can cause the student scaffold visual displays or an explanatory animation. The analytics reviewed by teachers can be used to group learners with similar difficulties in pairs before laboratory sessions so that they can learn with each other. This synergy is a representation of the human-AI collaboration, as automated feedback improves the formative assessment segment, with teachers retaining the contextualized judgment.

AI-Enhanced Virtual and Remote Laboratories

Physical Science learning focuses on laboratory training which is sometimes prohibited due to cost, safety, or logistics. Virtual and remote labs that are based on AI can break these obstacles since they simulate real-time experiments. Virtual labs, including PhET AI Extensions or Labster SmartSim, use machine-learning algorithms to predict the result of manipulating the variables and provide dynamic and data-driven feedback (Park & Kim, 2022). AI contributes in two ways. For the first one, predictive modeling enables the simulations to act like in reality when unfamiliar conditions are introduced, enhancing conceptual knowledge of the cause-effect associations. Second, performance analytics determine the quality of the experimental design determining whether the learner manipulated the variables of the experiment in a correct or incorrect manner. Physical sensors are also connected to remote laboratories to combine real-life data with virtual experiments, promoting the real inquiry in distance learning as well (Yuen et al., 2011). These systems make laboratories accessible to schools that do not have the infrastructure, which is in line with the inclusive principles of hybrid pedagogy. However, learners should not be allowed to forget physical interaction in the process of learning as long as possible.

Visualization and Generative Modeling Tools

The scientific modeling has always been a part of science education. AI adds to it with generative and predictive modeling. There is a type of generative AI that can generate real-time simulations, diagrams, or explanatory animations based on textual inputs, which are large-scale transformer models trained on scientific data. A learner who asks to be illustrated magnetic field lines around a solenoid can immediately be shown an interactive model were they can adjust in real time by current or coil density (Kung et al., 2023).

Graphing and data-analysis applications with AI support (e.g., Google Colab AI Assistant or Wolfram Alpha Notebook Edition) help learners to plot experimental data, establish patterns and predict results through regression or neural-network fitting. These tools foster skills in quantitative reasoning and competence in experimental design. Notably, visualization helps the learners with different cognitive styles such as spatial learners understand the complex interactions with the help of visual images and verbal learners are able to combine simulations with textual elaboration.

Teachers have to, however, lead to critical reading. In its uncontrolled form, generative outputs can simplify or misrepresent phenomena. The epistemic rigor is preserved with the help of embedding explanation prompts, i.e., asking students to explain why the visualization of the AI acts in a specific way.

AI-Supported Inquiry and Problem-Based Learning

Problem-based learning (PBL) and inquiry frameworks are in line with AI-mediated hybrid pedagogy. The whole process of inquiry that is question formulation to reflection can be supported with the help of AI platforms, which can give resources of data, clues of diagnosis and modeling tools, which are automatic. As an illustration, AI can be used to recommend experimental designs or process sensor data on remote temperature probes by the students studying heat transfer (Argaw et al., 2016).

Examples of cognitive partners include conversational agents like ChatGPT style tutors or domain-specific bots, which prompt hypothesis generation, promote elaboration and demand metacognitive questions (What assumption are you making about energy loss here?). Studies show that properly crafted dialogue agents enhance rational thinking and conceptual memory as they take the form of Socratic questioning instead of telling people what to do.

Moreover, online collaboration analytics rooted in AI track group problem-solving and detects uneven interaction or the collapse of communication. The educators get practical feedback, e.g., what pupils take over the speaking floor or need facilitating and facilitating hybrid teamwork becomes equitable and evidence-grounded.

Assessment and Feedback Innovations

The use of AI-based analytics to deliver rapid, formative feedback is becoming more widespread in assessment in hybrid Physical Science education. Open-ended problem-solving can be assessed on automated systems, simulated code can be evaluated, or laboratory reports can be evaluated with natural language processing. These tools evaluate justification instead of correctness alone, reasoning steps, consistency and integration of concepts (Kamrowska-Załuska, 2021).

As an example, an AI essay-scorer may point out inconsistency in a student explaining electric potential by referring to textbooks or video. The follow-up activities can then be customized by the teachers instead of taking hours to grade. AI-assisted rubrics are transparent and indicate what criteria the feedback was prompted by, which helps prevent the issue of the black-box effect of opaque algorithms.

The analytics dashboards to visualize the longitudinal progress are also supported by AI. Students are able to trace their way through mastery of concepts and look back on the learning patterns. In conjunction with teacher reflection sessions, analytics facilitate assessment as learning, which strengthens metacognitive awareness instead of testing that is applicable by compliance.

Gamification and Motivation Systems

The issue of motivation has always been a challenge in learning science. The gamification systems based on AI are personalized to learners through the challenges, rewards and feedback loops, which are based on the learner profiles. Through engagement data, these systems alter the level of difficulty in tasks and narrative to maintain an optimal challenge (Shahzadi et al., 2025).

As an example, an AI-aided energy saving game can bring contextual missions (i.e., the design of efficient houses in various climates) scaled to the previous achievements of learners. In addition to fun, gamification leads to persistence and repetitive experimentation, which are fundamental qualities of scientific research. Nonetheless, teachers ought to make sure that extrinsic incentives do not outshine intrinsic interest.

Integrating AI into Lesson Design and Teacher Practice

To have real learning benefits, AI tools should be embedded in considered instructional design frameworks. According to the Technological Pedagogical Content Knowledge (TPACK) framework, an effective teaching practice is a result of the interaction among subject knowledge, pedagogy and technology (Koh et al., 2015). In Physical Science, it refers to the process of harmonizing AI abilities, i.e., data analysis, simulation, visualization, with curriculum objectives like conceptual knowledge and experimental logic.

Practical steps include:

- Incorporating AI tasks into 5E inquiry cycle (Engage-Explore-Explain-Elaborate-Evaluate).
- Informing differentiated grouping and focused remediation with the help of AI analytics.
- Reflection should be included as it works to motivate students to criticize AI explanations.
- Finding the right balance between the AI-mediated sessions and human-centered discussion to preserve the socio-emotional activity.

These practices should be modelled by teacher professional development in micro-teaching or design-thinking workshops and allow the educators to experimentally assess the pedagogical utility of AI.

The physical science education using AI-enhanced hybrid pedagogy allows merging individualized digital learning with physical classroom inquiry. An example would be the online activity with AI conversational tutors where students can discuss with them the concepts of Newton laws and in-person classes where students would also focus on the validation of their ideas through laboratory sessions. The AI systems can come up with problem sets that have been differentiated under electricity and magnetism, and educators can utilize classroom time to engage in collaborative thinking and correct misconceptions. AI-assisted virtual simulations also expand laboratory experiences under the conditions of scarcity of physical resources. Also, the formative feedback on the scientific explanations, which is assisted by AI, can guide the instructors to plan the specific interventions. These practices demonstrate that generative AI can be used as a pedagogical aids tool which can deepen conceptual knowledge, inquiry, and student interest in the context of a physical science blended learning.

Ethical and Practical Safeguards

Ethical guidelines on data privacy, transparency and inclusivity should be used to implement it. Such frameworks as the Recommendation on the Ethics of AI by UNESCO (2021) should be implemented in institutions. The teachers should explain the use of learner data clearly where possible offer the option of opting out and stress that AI feedback is an addition to, but not a replacement of, human feedback.

Ethical literacy means also assisting students in becoming aware of the shortcomings of algorithms, developing doubt of the automated authority and value of scientific skills as a human undertaking.

From Tools to Transformative Practice

The AI-based tools transform not only the traditional physical science pedagogy, where a teacher delivers information to the students. They also customize it into investigative eco-systems. At intelligent tutors, learning is individualized, simulations democratize experimentation, generative visualizations broaden imagination, analytics refine feedback and collaboration enabled by AI promotes inclusion. The role of the educator transforms to the one of learning designer and ethical curator, making sure every tool helps to gain deeper insight, involvement and equality. Finally, AI has the ability to empower hybrid pedagogy not through automation but through augmentation, that is, allowing both teachers and students to be more critically-minded, creative and inclusive in exploring the physical world continuously.

6. PREPARING FUTURE TEACHERS

Teacher Education in the Age of Hybrid and AI Pedagogies

The adoption of Artificial Intelligence (AI) and hybrid pedagogies in science education requires a change of the professional preparation of teachers. The teachers of physical sciences, especially, have to deal with the two-fold task of not only mastering the disciplinary knowledge but also acquiring the pedagogical and technological skills to reach the students in the digital, hybrid and intercultural learning environments. Programs in teacher education should thus include the tech adoption workshops to develop AI literacy, competence in designing digital pedagogies, cross-cultural awareness and moral responsibility.

In this section, the researchers look at the competencies that will be needed by the future teachers working in AI-enhanced hybrid classrooms, the models of competency development and approaches to maintaining reflective, inclusive and innovation-driven teacher education.

AI Literacy as a Core Professional Competence

The concept of AI literacy is becoming widely recognized as a necessary part of the teacher education. It covers the information about the functionalities of AI systems, their educational uses, the ethical and social consequences of their use. In the case of Physical Science teachers, AI literacy is spread to data analytics interpretation, creating AI-assisted learning activities and critical discussion of algorithmic reasoning and scientific investigation.

According to (Ng et al., 2021), AI literacy education takes the form of three dimensions: (1) conceptual knowledge of AI mechanisms, (2) practical skills in the use of AI-based educational products and (3) critical knowledge regarding bias, transparency and data ethics. Considering the importance of integrating such dimensions into pre-service teacher programs is to make sure that the graduates leave with the knowledge not of the technology consumer but of the intelligent designer of the AI-enhanced pedagogy.

AI literacy may also be introduced into the curriculum of teacher education through interdisciplinary courses taught collaboratively by faculty in computer science and education, which can allow teacher trainees to explore tools like ITS, virtual laboratories and data-driven formative assessment. The ethical situations that arise during the seminars such as the effects of student surveillance or automated grading can then be considered in reflective seminars to create ethical judgment in addition to technical ability.

Developing Digital Pedagogical Design Skills

Hybrid and AI-supported instruction demand teacher competence as teachers must be able to integrate content, pedagogy and technology, the conceptualization of which is provided by the Technological Pedagogical Content Knowledge (TPACK) framework (Mishra & Koehler, 2006). In Physical Science, it implies the creation of lessons, which would tie together the complex conceptual knowledge (e.g., electromagnetism) with inquiry-based pedagogies and digital tools, which allow conducting experiments, visualizing and collaborating.

Pre-service teachers should be trained to:

1. **Select and align AI tools** with learning objectives such as adaptive tutoring for conceptual reinforcement or simulations for hypothesis testing.
2. **Design multimodal resources** for hybrid delivery, ensuring accessibility and inclusion.
3. **Evaluate AI outputs** critically, assessing their pedagogical and epistemological accuracy.
4. **Integrate feedback analytics** to inform differentiated instruction and learner support.

Teacher trainees may also receive genuine experiences of designing and testing hybrid learning units in instructional design studios or design-thinking laboratories. These conditions promote cyclic reflection, peers critique and constant improvement-resembling the design cycles that they will participate in later at their classrooms.

Reflective and Ethical Professional Practice

Technology in hybrid and AI-supported education increases the role and responsibility of teachers. Educators need to be reflective practitioners who challenge assumptions either by asking questions about their teaching decisions or writing about them and modifying them according to the data about learners and based on ethics. AI analytics can provide an unprecedented understanding of the engagement of learners, but only in the case of ethical application, the task of a teacher is to analyze and interpret this information critically, not to use the power of algorithms.

Training programs about teacher education must prioritize data ethics and train trainees to work around privacy issues, informed consent and algorithmic bias (Mishra & Koehler, 2006). Pre-service teachers can be made aware of the possible harms, including unequal access or misuse of data, by case-based discussions and simulated ethical dilemmas and can devise mitigation measures. As an example, a study of anonymized classroom analytics would provoke a question on whether predictive models have an unwanted side effect of stigmatizing some groups of learners.

The same is true in the case of ethical reflection of teachers as to their digital identity and professionalism. Educators of the future would have to set good examples of responsible AI adoption and technology application, show transparency, fairness, as well as respect the independence of learners in online environments.

Intercultural Competence and Global Collaboration

Intercultural competence is a pedagogical and ethical necessity that has to be incorporated in the teacher preparation during the digital era. The hybrid education setting inherently transcends borders and Physical Science is very convenient to work on a global scale as the latter is universal, though with cultural interpretation. Pre-service teachers are thus supposed to be trained to create intercultural hybrid learning experiences which connect students with different contexts using common scientific enquiry (Tomozeiu & Kumpulainen, 2016).

Teacher trainees can receive the first-hand experience of intercultural collaboration with the assistance of Collaborative Online International Learning (COIL) projects, virtual exchange programs and joint scientific research. These experiences help them to learn how to handle linguistic diversity, promote respectful communication, as well as, appreciate culturally different ways of solving problems.

Artificial intelligence can also enhance intercultural cooperation through automatizing the translation process, summarizing a discussion in different languages and visualizing global data sets. Nevertheless, the teacher training should not rely blindly on AI mediation, but this branch of study should prioritize empathy, cultural humility and human facilitation.

Mentorship, Professional Learning Communities and Lifelong Growth

It is impossible to prepare teachers to work in hybrid and AI-rich classes within the framework of the initial training only. On-going professional growth and mentorship continue to be crucial to remain competent with the changing technologies and pedagogies. Forming professional learning communities local and virtual provides teachers with an opportunity to exchange the best practices, troubleshoot and co-create new pedagogical models (Harris & Jones, 2010).

Mentorship programs may match novice teachers with mentors who have experience in the field of AI and hybrid pedagogy and develop reflective dialogue and confidence. Professional learning platforms based on AI are also able to provide personalized learning journeys using teaching analytics, which supports self-directed lifelong learning.

Even teacher educators are called to be flexible learners, who will work with AI ethics, data interpretation and research on instruction design. Policymakers in the institutions are supposed to encourage teacher educators, technologists and scientists to work together in a bid to ensure consistence between technological innovation and pedagogical integrity.

Curricular and Institutional Reforms

To have teacher preparation in accordance with the requirements of hybrid AI-based learning, institutional and policy-level change is needed. Universities and institutions of teacher education must:

- Include the modules of AI and digital pedagogy as compulsory core courses.
- Offer virtual classroom and analytics dashboard-based simulation-based practicum experience.
- These should be in the form of ethics committees that lead to responsible AI integration during teacher training.
- Incubate pre-service teachers Support Research Pre-service teachers to design, implement and publish hybrid pedagogy innovations.

Teacher education programs must not be accredited based on their subject knowledge and pedagogy only; they must also be flexible in technology, intercultural and ethically competent (*UNESCO Science Report 2021*, 2021). These reforms will make sure that the next generation of teachers comes out as flexible, moral and professionals who are competent in the world.

The Teacher of the Future: Designer, Facilitator and Ethicist

The changing hybrid classroom makes the teacher a designer, facilitator and ethicist. Teachers create learning environments in which AI tools improve inquiry and visualization as designers. They, as the facilitators, coordinate interactions that would support collaboration and inclusivity. They, as ethicists, protect against the abuse of technology and make algorithm systems equitable.

This multi-dimensional role in the teaching of Physical Science education makes teaching an innovative and stewardship act. Through modeling responsible interaction with technological systems that are increasingly mediating that world, teachers encourage curiosity about the physical world. Therefore, the training of teachers needs to cultivate more than merely technical skills but moral and creative imagination needed to teach in an AI augmented age too.

7. FUTURE DIRECTIONS WITH GENERATIVE AI

The New Frontier of Human–AI Co-Creation

The most radical stage in the development of educational technology is Generative Artificial Intelligence (GenAI). Beyond the adaptive systems, which react to learners, generative models generate new content, text, visuals, simulations, or assessments, which allow dynamic, co-creative learning experiences. In the education of Physical Science, the evolution signifies a paradigm shift that is students no longer engage with passive data but create models with the help of AI, formulate hypotheses and visualize abstract ideas.

The development of large language models (LLMs) like GPT-4, Claude and Gemini and multimodal experience (DALL-E and Stable Diffusion) has provided new horizons to hybrid pedagogy. Such tools are able to generalize elaborate descriptions, model experiments and scaffold inquiry learning in a manner never seen before. Yet, their possibilities have to be utilized in the frames of the moral, didactical and epistemological constructs that preserve the human agency and scientific integrity (L. Wang et al., 2024).

Generative AI and Knowledge Construction in Physical Science

Traditional science education sees learners develop knowledge by observation, experimentation and reflection. Generative AI enhances this mechanism because it is an intelligent co-creator that can produce more than one representation of an idea, like energy transfer or quantum behavior, based on the prompts of the learners (Cazzaniga, 2024).

An example of this is when a student learning thermodynamics requests an AI system to create relative visualizations of the entropy in various processes, create step-by-step experiment configurations or simulate the pattern of molecular motion. Such interactions foster epistemic curiosity, which makes students pursue question and answer and validation.

The model based reasoning is another core thinking process in Physical Science that is also facilitated by the use of generative AI. When students create hypothetical models with AI tools and contrast them with empirical or simulated data, they provoke cycles of speculation and disproving the existence of real scientific investigations. This does not just give rise to conceptual mastery but an epistemological knowledge of science as a process of ever-refining.

Personalized Inquiry and Adaptive Creativity

Generative AI opens up new opportunities of personalized inquiry by modifying content and structure of problems to suit the cognitive peculiarities of a particular learner. GenAI is able to create explanations, analogies, or situations of problems adapted to the learning style and previous misconceptions of each individual learner, unlike earlier adaptive systems that could only respond to relatively fixed pre-programmed answers.

This individualization in hybrid Physical Science classrooms allows differentiated learning without disaggregating the learning community. An analogic comparison that forces the student with difficulty in the vector representation could be made to the real-life motion (i.e. sailing against wind currents) whereas an advanced learner could be tasked to model resultant forces with the help of AI-based modeling software (Salehi & Burgueño, 2018).

GenAI is also creative in nature, which encourages cross-disciplinary discovery, such as the combination of physics and art, design or storytelling. As an illustration, the students will be able to create artistic versions of electromagnetic fields or write narrative accounts of the scientific findings. This level of multimodal creativity facilitates not only a deeper comprehension but humanizes learning of science to enable it to be accessible to a variety of learners.

Generative Simulations and Virtual Experimentation

Physical Science education is successful on experimentation but access to laboratories is not even all over the world. With the use of virtual and augmented reality, generative AI will be able to simulate experimentation with complex experiments using realistic data and interactive control. In contrast to ordinary simulations, generative systems have the ability to generate new experimental configurations, such as being able to manipulate variables outside of fixed values, or to generate entirely new material properties in virtual settings (Salehi & Burgueño, 2018).

Such a type of generative experimentation even improves conceptual flexibility. To study extreme conditions of scientific laws, learners can experiment with impossible or unusually dangerous situations (e.g., extreme conditions or conditions of a vacuum). Reinforcement-driven generative physics engines are capable of modelling emergent behaviour in dynamic systems, including fluid dynamics, planetary dynamics or the exchange of energy within an ecosystem.

In addition, AI mediated data analysis enables students to practice the scientific reasoning directly; to define patterns, to calculate uncertainty and to make evidence-based conclusions based on simulated experiments. This democratizes access to real scientific investigation and serves to bridge the difference between theory and practice in blended contexts.

AI-Augmented Assessment and Feedback

Assessment is also redefined as generated AI can provide real-time and dialogic feedback. Written explanations, experimental designs, or solving problems can be checked through large language models, which can give instant and context-specific feedback, which goes beyond numerical grading.

As an example, the analysis of conceptual coherence of a student explaining the third law of Newton can be performed and the AI will produce corrective hints or questions. Generative systems allow teachers to create adaptive assessment systems, which increase the complexity of the assessment as the student advance swapping between computational problems to conceptual reasoning.

Moreover, AI-based rubrics and feedback summaries decrease the amount of grading but facilitate metacognitive reflection. The student is able to seek personalized overviews of their learning, which can be useful in highlighting the strengths and false beliefs. These systems support learning assessment instead of learning evaluation when applied in a transparent and ethical manner (Barrera Castro et al., 2024).

Ethical, Epistemological and Pedagogical Boundaries

Generative AI has enormous questions of ethics and epistemology, even with its potential. Among the essential issues, there are authorship, academic honesty, bias and epistemic trustworthiness. The former can be accurate in fact, or misleading in concept, yet sound authoritative because of AI-generated explanations or visualization, which is known as an algorithmic hallucination. Even in a physical science, where accuracy and empirical testing mostly dominate, uncontrolled AI outputs may reinforce myths.

Students should thus be trained by the teachers to develop critical AI literacy where the students are taught to analyze AI generated information using evidence based arguments. The work in the classroom procedures must mandate that learners validate AI results with empirical evidence or textbooks. This is in accordance with the pedagogical principle of AI as hypothesis generator but not as oracle.

Data transparency, intellectual property and inclusiveness should also be taught within the ethical education. Even in the fields of science, AI systems trained on biased data are capable of reproducing cultural or gender stereotypes. Therefore, teachers assume a significant role of ethical intermediaries, so the introduction of AI should not ignore the principles of fairness, equity and authenticity (Pangrazio & Sefton-Green, 2021).

Collaborative Intelligence: Humans and Machines as Partners

Hybrid pedagogy does not involve AI teacher replacement but instead the future of this methodology is a collaborative intelligence, a partnership in which humans and machines complement each other. Within this paradigm, curation of learning experiences is done by teachers, whereas adaptive scaffolds, analytical insights and creative augmentation are done by AI.

In this Physical Science education, group projects, scientific modeling and interdisciplinary exploration can be improved. As an example, AI has the ability to process data of student experiments real time, providing visualization assistance as teachers lead interpretation and discussion. It is an example of co-agency a pedagogical change in control to cooperation.

At the institutional level, collaborative intelligence may be carried out through teacher education, where novice teachers may expect AI mentors to support in lesson planning and human mentors to support them emotionally and contextually. Such hybrid mentorship ecosystems can eventually transform teacher professionalization and peer learning.

Research and Innovation Trajectories

Future research must address both opportunities and risks of generative AI integration. Key priorities include:

1. **Pedagogical Frameworks:** Developing instructional models that embed GenAI within inquiry, experimentation and reflection.
2. **Ethical Governance:** Establishing standards for transparency, data stewardship and algorithmic accountability in educational use.
3. **Cultural Responsiveness:** Designing multilingual, inclusive generative systems that reflect diverse epistemologies of science.
4. **Evaluation Metrics:** Creating tools to measure cognitive and affective outcomes of AI-augmented learning.
5. **Sustainability and Environmental Impact:** Investigating the ecological footprint of large-scale AI deployment and promoting green AI principles.

Interdisciplinary research collaborations among educators, computer scientists, cognitive psychologists and ethicists are crucial to shaping the next generation of hybrid learning systems grounded in human-centered values.

Toward Human-Centered Generative Pedagogy

Generative AI is the beginning of a stage whereby knowledge development is a collective affair between machines and humans. Within the context of hybrid Physical Science education, it can help to make abstract theories concrete, enable customized exploration and democratize access to superior modeling and experimentation (Pangrazio & Sefton-Green, 2021).

Nevertheless, the success of such transformation will be determined by the fact that human-centered design should be retained that is the generative systems should enhance critical thinking, creativity and empathy instead of automatizing them. Educators need to be central to pedagogical planning, to the ways they can teach people to be responsible towards AI, to be critical of what it delivers and to value science as a cognitive and moral endeavor.

It is not the level of intelligent machines that will determine the future of education, but rather how human beings will learn to work with intelligent machines. With ethical and non-discriminating pedagogy, generative AI can transform a hybrid classroom into a living laboratory of imagination- with all learners emerge as scientists and creators in the narrative of discovery being created.

8. CONCLUSION

The classroom to cloud is more than mere technological upgrade. It is a complex reorganization of the nature of knowledge construction, sharing and experience in Physical Science education. The chapter has shown that hybrid pedagogy, carefully combined with Artificial Intelligence, forms an effective educational ecosystem that increases access, enhances conceptual knowledge and supports meaningful scientific research. Combining the constructivist, socio-cultural, inquiry-based and intercultural approach, the chapter provides a coherent framework of the pedagogical design of the learning environment that is dynamic, participatory and inclusive. Artificial Intelligence is not the replacement of the teacher; it is an intellectual partner that helps in visualization, personalization, feedback and collaboration. On the adaptive tutoring and intelligent simulations to the generative modeling and real-time assessment AI benefits the cognitive and affective aspects of learning without compromising the epistemic rigor of science. Meanwhile, the chapter also stresses that technological innovation has to be based on the ethical responsibility, equity and human values. Devoid of a critical scrutiny, AI has the potential of strengthening the already existing inequalities and perverting the essence of scientific knowledge itself. The focal point of this change is the changing role of the teacher. The role of future teachers is envisioned as being that of constructors of learning experiences, inquiry facilitators, intercultural mediators and ethical guardians of technology. The teacher education would, consequently, be viewed as the basis of sustainable innovation, as it necessitated the implementation of AI literacy, digital pedagogical design, reflective practice and international collaboration into the professional training. With the on-going development of generative AI, new arenas of human-machine co-creation are emerging, allowing new levels of personalization, creativity and experimentation in Physical Science education. But it is not the cleverness of the tools that will result in the final achievement of this transformation but rather the discretion with which they are used. Human and equity-based philosophy means that technology will enhance curiosity, thinking and compassion and not eliminate them. The hybrid, AI-enhanced classroom represents in this way a living laboratory of discovery, a space that will enable all learners to engage in the scientific enterprise in the fullest way possible and equip future generations to function in an ever more complex, interconnected, ever more technologically mediated world.

REFERENCES

Adiguzel, T., Kaya, M. H., & Cansu, F. K. (2023). Revolutionizing education with AI: Exploring the transformative potential of ChatGPT. *Contemporary Educational Technology, 15*(3), ep429. DOI: 10.30935/cedtech/13152

Al Hasanah, H., Heru Iswanto, B., & Sugihartono, I. (2025). AI-CBL: A Technology-Enhanced Learning Model Combining Chatbot and Case-Based Pedagogy to Improve Critical Thinking in Physics Education. *Jurnal Penelitian & Pengembangan Pendidikan Fisika, 11*(1), 109–122. DOI: 10.21009/1.11108

Alenezi, M. (2023). Digital Learning and Digital Institution in Higher Education. *Education Sciences, 13*(1), 88. DOI: 10.3390/educsci13010088

Almufarreh, A., & Arshad, M. (2023). Promising Emerging Technologies for Teaching and Learning: Recent Developments and Future Challenges. *Sustainability (Basel), 15*(8), 6917. DOI: 10.3390/su15086917

Anderson, T., & Dron, J. (2011). Three generations of distance education pedagogy. *International Review of Research in Open and Distance Learning, 12*(3), 80. DOI: 10.19173/irrodl.v12i3.890

Argaw, A. S., Haile, B. B., Ayalew, B. T., & Kuma, S. G. (2016). The Effect of Problem Based Learning (PBL) Instruction on Students' Motivation and Problem Solving Skills of Physics. *Eurasia Journal of Mathematics, Science and Technology Education, 13*(3). Advance online publication. DOI: 10.12973/eurasia.2017.00647a

Barrera Castro, G. P., Chiappe, A., Becerra Rodriguez, D. F., & Sepulveda, F. G. (2024). Harnessing AI for Education 4.0: Drivers of Personalized Learning. *Electronic Journal of E-Learning, 22*(5), 01–14. DOI: 10.34190/ejel.22.5.3467

Bozkurt, A., Gjelsvik, T., Adam, T., Asino, T. I., Atenas, J., Bali, M., Blomgren, C., Bond, M., Bonk, C. J., Brown, M., Burgos, D., Conrad, D., Costello, E., Cronin, C., Czerniewicz, L., Deepwell, M., Deimann, M., DeWaard, H. J., Dousay, T. A., & Zawacki-Richter, O. (2023). Openness in Education as a Praxis: From Individual Testimonials to Collective Voices. *Open Praxis, 15*(2), 76–112. DOI: 10.55982/openpraxis.15.2.574

Budhwar, P., Chowdhury, S., Wood, G., Aguinis, H., Bamber, G. J., Beltran, J. R., Boselie, P., Lee Cooke, F., Decker, S., DeNisi, A., Dey, P. K., Guest, D., Knoblich, A. J., Malik, A., Paauwe, J., Papagiannidis, S., Patel, C., Pereira, V., Ren, S., & Varma, A. (2023). Human resource management in the age of generative artificial intelligence: Perspectives and research directions on ChatGPT. *Human Resource Management Journal, 33*(3), 606–659. DOI: 10.1111/1748-8583.12524

Capp, M. J. (2017). The effectiveness of universal design for learning: A meta-analysis of literature between 2013 and 2016. *International Journal of Inclusive Education, 21*(8), 791–807. DOI: 10.1080/13603116.2017.1325074

Carvalho, D. V., Pereira, E. M., & Cardoso, J. S. (2019). Machine Learning Interpretability: A Survey on Methods and Metrics. *Electronics (Basel), 8*(8), 832. DOI: 10.3390/electronics8080832

Cazzaniga, M. (2024). Gen-AI. *Staff Discussion Notes, 2024*(001), 1. DOI: 10.5089/9798400262548.006

Choudhary, K., DeCost, B., Chen, C., Jain, A., Tavazza, F., Cohn, R., Park, C. W., Choudhary, A., Agrawal, A., Billinge, S. J. L., Holm, E., Ong, S. P., & Wolverton, C. (2022). Recent advances and applications of deep learning methods in materials science. *npj Computational Materials, 8*(1), 59. DOI: 10.1038/s41524-022-00734-6

Cipresso, P., Giglioli, I. A. C., Raya, M. A., & Riva, G. (2018). The Past, Present, and Future of Virtual and Augmented Reality Research: A Network and Cluster Analysis of the Literature. *Frontiers in Psychology, 9*, 2086. Advance online publication. DOI: 10.3389/fpsyg.2018.02086 PMID: 30459681

de Jong, T., Linn, M. C., & Zacharia, Z. C. (2013). Physical and Virtual Laboratories in Science and Engineering Education. *Science, 340*(6130), 305–308. DOI: 10.1126/science.1230579 PMID: 23599479

Dwivedi, Y. K., Hughes, L., Ismagilova, E., Aarts, G., Coombs, C., Crick, T., Duan, Y., Dwivedi, R., Edwards, J., Eirug, A., Galanos, V., Ilavarasan, P. V., Janssen, M., Jones, P., Kar, A. K., Kizgin, H., Kronemann, B., Lal, B., Lucini, B., & Williams, M. D. (2021). Artificial Intelligence (AI): Multidisciplinary perspectives on emerging challenges, opportunities, and agenda for research, practice and policy. *International Journal of Information Management, 57*, 101994. DOI: 10.1016/j.ijinfomgt.2019.08.002

Dwivedi, Y. K., Hughes, L., Wang, Y., Alalwan, A. A., Ahn, S. J., Balakrishnan, J., Barta, S., Belk, R., Buhalis, D., Dutot, V., Felix, R., Filieri, R., Flavián, C., Gustafsson, A., Hinsch, C., Hollensen, S., Jain, V., Kim, J., Krishen, A. S., & Wirtz, J. (2023). Metaverse marketing: How the metaverse will shape the future of consumer research and practice. *Psychology and Marketing, 40*(4), 750–776. DOI: 10.1002/mar.21767

Falloon, G. (2020). From digital literacy to digital competence: The teacher digital competency (TDC) framework. *Educational Technology Research and Development, 68*(5), 2449–2472. DOI: 10.1007/s11423-020-09767-4

Ferri, F., Grifoni, P., & Guzzo, T. (2020). Online Learning and Emergency Remote Teaching: Opportunities and Challenges in Emergency Situations. *Societies (Basel, Switzerland), 10*(4), 86. DOI: 10.3390/soc10040086

Floridi, L., Cowls, J., Beltrametti, M., Chatila, R., Chazerand, P., Dignum, V., Luetge, C., Madelin, R., Pagallo, U., Rossi, F., Schafer, B., Valcke, P., & Vayena, E. (2018). AI4People—An Ethical Framework for a Good AI Society: Opportunities, Risks, Principles, and Recommendations. *Minds and Machines, 28*(4), 689–707. DOI: 10.1007/s11023-018-9482-5 PMID: 30930541

Gormally, C., Brickman, P., Hallar, B., & Armstrong, N. (2009). Effects of Inquiry-based Learning on Students' Science Literacy Skills and Confidence. *International Journal for the Scholarship of Teaching and Learning, 3*(2). Advance online publication. DOI: 10.20429/ijsotl.2009.030216

Granados-Beltrán, C. (2016). Critical Interculturality. A Path for Pre-service ELT Teachers. *Íkala. Revista de Lenguaje y Cultura, 21*(2). Advance online publication. DOI: 10.17533/udea.ikala.v21n02a04

Grassini, S. (2023). Shaping the Future of Education: Exploring the Potential and Consequences of AI and ChatGPT in Educational Settings. *Education Sciences, 13*(7), 692. DOI: 10.3390/educsci13070692

Grewal, D., Noble, S. M., Roggeveen, A. L., & Nordfalt, J. (2020). The future of in-store technology. *Journal of the Academy of Marketing Science, 48*(1), 96–113. DOI: 10.1007/s11747-019-00697-z

Hagendorff, T. (2020). The Ethics of AI Ethics: An Evaluation of Guidelines. *Minds and Machines, 30*(1), 99–120. DOI: 10.1007/s11023-020-09517-8

Harris, A., & Jones, M. (2010). Professional learning communities and system improvement. *Improving Schools, 13*(2), 172–181. DOI: 10.1177/1365480210376487

Kamrowska-Załuska, D. (2021). Impact of AI-Based Tools and Urban Big Data Analytics on the Design and Planning of Cities. *Land (Basel), 10*(11), 1209. DOI: 10.3390/land10111209

Kim, J., Lee, H., & Cho, Y. H. (2022). Learning design to support student-AI collaboration: Perspectives of leading teachers for AI in education. *Education and Information Technologies, 27*(5), 6069–6104. DOI: 10.1007/s10639-021-10831-6

Kirschner, P. A., Sweller, J., Kirschner, F., & Zambrano, R. J. (2018). From Cognitive Load Theory to Collaborative Cognitive Load Theory. *International Journal of Computer-Supported Collaborative Learning, 13*(2), 213–233. DOI: 10.1007/s11412-018-9277-y PMID: 30996713

Koh, J. H. L., Chai, C. S., Benjamin, W., & Hong, H.-Y. (2015). Technological Pedagogical Content Knowledge (TPACK) and Design Thinking: A Framework to Support ICT Lesson Design for 21st Century Learning. *The Asia-Pacific Education Researcher, 24*(3), 535–543. DOI: 10.1007/s40299-015-0237-2

Kozulin, A., & Wertsch, J. V. (1987). Vygotsky and the Social Formation of Mind. *The American Journal of Psychology, 100*(1), 123. DOI: 10.2307/1422646

Kung, T. H., Cheatham, M., Medenilla, A., Sillos, C., De Leon, L., Elepaño, C., Madriaga, M., Aggabao, R., Diaz-Candido, G., Maningo, J., & Tseng, V. (2023). Performance of ChatGPT on USMLE: Potential for AI-assisted medical education using large language models. *PLOS Digital Health, 2*(2), e0000198. DOI: 10.1371/journal.pdig.0000198 PMID: 36812645

Li, Q., Li, Z., & Han, J. (2021). A hybrid learning pedagogy for surmounting the challenges of the COVID-19 pandemic in the performing arts education. *Education and Information Technologies, 26*(6), 7635–7655. DOI: 10.1007/s10639-021-10612-1 PMID: 34220284

Longo, F., Padovano, A., & Umbrello, S. (2020). Value-Oriented and Ethical Technology Engineering in Industry 5.0: A Human-Centric Perspective for the Design of the Factory of the Future. *Applied Sciences (Basel, Switzerland), 10*(12), 4182. DOI: 10.3390/app10124182

Maarof, M., & Jalaluddin, N. S. (2019). The Implementation of Pedagogical Strategies in Inclusive Education Program for Pupils with Special Needs among Mainstream Teachers: A Case study. *Jurnal Pendidikan Bitara UPSI, 12*(12), 29–38. DOI: 10.37134/bitara.vol12.4.2019

MacKenzie, A., Bacalja, A., Annamali, D., Panaretou, A., Girme, P., Cutajar, M., Abegglen, S., Evens, M., Neuhaus, F., Wilson, K., Psarikidou, K., Koole, M., Hrastinski, S., Sturm, S., Adachi, C., Schnaider, K., Bozkurt, A., Rapanta, C., Themelis, C., & Gourlay, L. (2022). Dissolving the Dichotomies Between Online and Campus-Based Teaching: A Collective Response to The Manifesto for Teaching Online (Bayne et al. 2020). *Postdigital Science and Education, 4*(2), 271–329. DOI: 10.1007/s42438-021-00259-z PMID: 40477827

Michel-Villarreal, R., Vilalta-Perdomo, E., Salinas-Navarro, D. E., Thierry-Aguilera, R., & Gerardou, F. S. (2023). Challenges and Opportunities of Generative AI for Higher Education as Explained by ChatGPT. *Education Sciences, 13*(9), 856. DOI: 10.3390/educsci13090856

Mishra, P., & Koehler, M. J. (2006). Technological Pedagogical Content Knowledge: A Framework for Teacher Knowledge. *Teachers College Record*, *108*(6), 1017–1054. DOI: 10.1111/j.1467-9620.2006.00684.x

Mtebe, J. S., & Raisamo, R. (2014). Investigating perceived barriers to the use of open educational resources in higher education in Tanzania. *International Review of Research in Open and Distance Learning*, *15*(2). Advance online publication. DOI: 10.19173/irrodl.v15i2.1803

Naicker, A., Singh, E., & van Genugten, T. (2022). Collaborative Online International Learning (COIL): Preparedness and experiences of South African students. *Innovations in Education and Teaching International*, *59*(5), 499–510. DOI: 10.1080/14703297.2021.1895867

Ng, D. T. K., Leung, J. K. L., Chu, S. K. W., & Qiao, M. S. (2021). Conceptualizing AI literacy: An exploratory review. *Computers and Education: Artificial Intelligence*, *2*, 100041. DOI: 10.1016/j.caeai.2021.100041

Ng, D. T. K., Tan, C. W., & Leung, J. K. L. (2024). Empowering student self-regulated learning and science education through <scp>ChatGPT</scp> : A pioneering pilot study. *British Journal of Educational Technology*, *55*(4), 1328–1353. DOI: 10.1111/bjet.13454

Nguyen, T. P. L., Nguyen, T. H., & Tran, T. K. (2020). STEM Education in Secondary Schools: Teachers' Perspective towards Sustainable Development. *Sustainability (Basel)*, *12*(21), 8865. DOI: 10.3390/su12218865

Oliveira, K. K. de S., & de Souza, R. A. C. (2021). *Digital Transformation towards Education 4.0.* Informatics in Education., DOI: 10.15388/infedu.2022.13

Onu, P., Pradhan, A., & Mbohwa, C. (2024). Potential to use metaverse for future teaching and learning. *Education and Information Technologies*, *29*(7), 8893–8924. DOI: 10.1007/s10639-023-12167-9

Pangrazio, L., & Sefton-Green, J. (2021). Digital Rights, Digital Citizenship and Digital Literacy: What's the Difference? *Journal of New Approaches in Educational Research*, *10*(1), 15–27. DOI: 10.7821/naer.2021.1.616

Panyajamorn, T. (2022). Using MOOC and Gamification Hybrid Learning Models in Rural Public Schools in Thailand. *The Journal of Educators Online*, *19*(3). Advance online publication. DOI: 10.9743/JEO.2022.19.3.12

Park, S.-M., & Kim, Y.-G. (2022). A Metaverse: Taxonomy, Components, Applications, and Open Challenges. *IEEE Access : Practical Innovations, Open Solutions*, *10*, 4209–4251. DOI: 10.1109/ACCESS.2021.3140175

Rasheed, A., San, O., & Kvamsdal, T. (2020). Digital Twin: Values, Challenges and Enablers From a Modeling Perspective. *IEEE Access : Practical Innovations, Open Solutions*, *8*, 21980–22012. DOI: 10.1109/ACCESS.2020.2970143

Rata, E. (2021). The Curriculum Design Coherence Model in the Knowledge-Rich School Project. *Review of Education*, *9*(2), 448–495. DOI: 10.1002/rev3.3254

Reed, M. S., & Rudman, H. (2023). Re-thinking research impact: Voice, context and power at the interface of science, policy and practice. *Sustainability Science*, *18*(2), 967–981. DOI: 10.1007/s11625-022-01216-w PMID: 36119558

Salehi, H., & Burgueño, R. (2018). Emerging artificial intelligence methods in structural engineering. *Engineering Structures*, *171*, 170–189. DOI: 10.1016/j.engstruct.2018.05.084

Schäfer, M. T., van Es, K., & Lauriault, T. P. (Eds.). (2024). *Collaborative Research in the Datafied Society*. Amsterdam University Press., DOI: 10.1515/9789048555925

Sethi, P., & Sarangi, S. R. (2017). Internet of Things: Architectures, Protocols, and Applications. *Journal of Electrical and Computer Engineering*, *2017*, 1–25. DOI: 10.1155/2017/9324035

Shahzadi, A., Ishaq, K., Nawaz, N. A., Rosdi, F., & Khan, F. A. (2025). Unveiling personalized and gamification-based cybersecurity risks within financial institutions. *PeerJ. Computer Science*, *11*, e2598. DOI: 10.7717/peerj-cs.2598 PMID: 40062254

Shoaib, M., Fitzpatrick, D., & Pitt, I. (2023). Assistive technology-based solutions in learning mathematics for visually-impaired people: Exploring issues, challenges and opportunities. *Multimedia Tools and Applications*, *82*(29), 46153–46184. DOI: 10.1007/s11042-023-17409-z PMID: 38037570

Sweller, J., van Merriënboer, J. J. G., & Paas, F. (2019). Cognitive Architecture and Instructional Design: 20 Years Later. *Educational Psychology Review*, *31*(2), 261–292. DOI: 10.1007/s10648-019-09465-5

Tapalova, O., & Zhiyenbayeva, N. (2022). Artificial Intelligence in Education: AIEd for Personalised Learning Pathways. *Electronic Journal of e-Learning*, *20*(5), 639–653. DOI: 10.34190/ejel.20.5.2597

Tomozeiu, D., & Kumpulainen, M. (2016). Operationalising intercultural competence for translation pedagogy. *The Interpreter and Translator Trainer*, *10*(3), 268–284. DOI: 10.1080/1750399X.2016.1236558

UNESCO Science Report 2021. (2021). United Nations. DOI: 10.18356/9789210058575

Vinayakumar, R., Alazab, M., Soman, K. P., Poornachandran, P., Al-Nemrat, A., & Venkatraman, S. (2019). Deep Learning Approach for Intelligent Intrusion Detection System. *IEEE Access : Practical Innovations, Open Solutions, 7*, 41525–41550. DOI: 10.1109/ACCESS.2019.2895334

Wang, H., Tlili, A., Huang, R., Cai, Z., Li, M., Cheng, Z., Yang, D., Li, M., Zhu, X., & Fei, C. (2023). Examining the applications of intelligent tutoring systems in real educational contexts: A systematic literature review from the social experiment perspective. *Education and Information Technologies, 28*(7), 9113–9148. DOI: 10.1007/s10639-022-11555-x PMID: 36643383

Wang, L., Ma, C., Feng, X., Zhang, Z., Yang, H., Zhang, J., Chen, Z., Tang, J., Chen, X., Lin, Y., Zhao, W. X., Wei, Z., & Wen, J. (2024). A survey on large language model based autonomous agents. *Frontiers of Computer Science, 18*(6), 186345. DOI: 10.1007/s11704-024-40231-1

Yang, J., Jin, H., Tang, R., Han, X., Feng, Q., Jiang, H., Zhong, S., Yin, B., & Hu, X. (2024). Harnessing the Power of LLMs in Practice: A Survey on ChatGPT and Beyond. *ACM Transactions on Knowledge Discovery from Data, 18*(6), 1–32. DOI: 10.1145/3649506

Yannier, N., Hudson, S. E., Chang, H., & Koedinger, K. R. (2024). AI Adaptivity in a Mixed-Reality System Improves Learning. *International Journal of Artificial Intelligence in Education, 34*(4), 1541–1558. DOI: 10.1007/s40593-023-00388-5

Young, T., Hazarika, D., Poria, S., & Cambria, E. (2018). Recent Trends in Deep Learning Based Natural Language Processing [Review Article]. *IEEE Computational Intelligence Magazine, 13*(3), 55–75. DOI: 10.1109/MCI.2018.2840738

Yu, H. (2023). Reflection on whether Chat GPT should be banned by academia from the perspective of education and teaching. *Frontiers in Psychology, 14*, 1181712. Advance online publication. DOI: 10.3389/fpsyg.2023.1181712 PMID: 37325766

Yuen, S. C.-Y., Yaoyuneyong, G., & Johnson, E. (2011). Augmented Reality: An Overview and Five Directions for AR in Education. *Journal of Educational Technology Development and Exchange, 4*(1). Advance online publication. DOI: 10.18785/jetde.0401.10

Zawacki-Richter, O., Marín, V. I., Bond, M., & Gouverneur, F. (2019). Systematic review of research on artificial intelligence applications in higher education – where are the educators? *International Journal of Educational Technology in Higher Education, 16*(1), 39. DOI: 10.1186/s41239-019-0171-0

Zidny, R., Sjöström, J., & Eilks, I. (2020). A Multi-Perspective Reflection on How Indigenous Knowledge and Related Ideas Can Improve Science Education for Sustainability. *Science & Education*, *29*(1), 145–185. DOI: 10.1007/s11191-019-00100-x

Chapter 10
Design of Artificial Intelligence-Supported Education Module:
The Example of Environment and Climate Change

Nagihan Kadıoğlu
http://orcid.org/0000-0003-4911-8985
Hacettepe University, Turkey

Berna Çolak
http://orcid.org/0009-0006-1155-3358
Milli Eğitim Bakanlığı, Turkey

Özge Özyalçın Oskay
http://orcid.org/0000-0002-9368-5381
Hacettepe University, Turkey

ABSTRACT

With the rapid advancement of technology, access to information has also become easier. Artificial intelligence is one of the technologies that has come to the fore in recent years. As digital transformation occurs at such a rapid pace around the world, schools are also trying to keep up with this pace. However, one of the fundamental goals of education is to teach students how to cope with the rapid development of technologies and adapt to this situation. With the emergence of artificial intelligence, many traditional sustainability practices have been developed and enriched with innovations. One of these is course modules. In this context, the aim of this study is to design an AI-supported educational module that science teachers can

DOI: 10.4018/979-8-3373-7462-8.ch010

use in their Environmental Education and Climate Change courses. The course module comprehensively addresses environmental and climate change issues for middle school students, aiming to relate sustainable living concepts and recycling practices to artificial intelligence technologies and provide an interdisciplinary learning environment.

1. DIGITALIZATION IN EDUCATION

There are multiple examples of the definitions of education and learning in the literature. Education is the process of creating behavioral change in individuals through their own experiences, and the concept of "through their own experiences" in the definition emphasizes the active participation of individuals in the learning-teaching process (Yeşilyurt, 2020). Education, in its broadest sense, is the process of nurturing individuals according to specific goals, and it is expected that the personality of the individual undergoing this process will be positively influenced. Here, the term "positively influenced" should be understood as the individual's ability to perform the desired behavior. Education and teaching have been on a journey alongside human development throughout the ages. This journey has been greatly influenced by educational processes and events that have taken place in human life, groundbreaking discoveries, and new technologies. Some phenomena and concepts have found their place within education or have accompanied it in part of the educational process. However, the education and teaching process, the age group of the student body, their development, socio-economic, socio-cultural, religious, and historical processes, the technological development and processes of countries, and the philosophical views held within a country in short, all the differences that exist—have led to the creation of different curricula for each community. Although there are differences in the educational curricula of countries, digitalization in education has entered the educational agenda of almost every country, especially due to the presence of technology in all areas of life. The concept of digitalization in education has created a field for itself with the digital development and transformation in technology. The emergence of digital tools in technology and, in particular, the screen age have been very influential. At the end of the 19th century, technological developments led to the transition from an agricultural society to an industrial society. In the second half of the 20th century, rapid technological developments and the introduction of advanced technologies into human life led to the transition from an industrial society to an information society. Today, new technological products are being made available to people every day, and these products are making human life easier (Sarıhan, 1998). While these processes of development and transformation continue, education has interpreted and assimilated these developments within itself.

The reflections of this assimilation have found their place in the field of educational technologies. Educational content has become increasingly rich and updated day by day. These developments have brought education and educational processes in line with the times, contributing significantly to the transition to an information society and its development. Rapid changes in the digital sphere around the world have particularly shifted the classroom environment to a different point in terms of space. The traditional hierarchy between the teacher and the learner is now beginning to disappear. Learners' quick access to information is taking away the teacher's role as a transferor of knowledge. The abundance and accessibility of information have made teachers comparable to other teachers, learning resources, and others (Taşkıran, 2017). These comparisons indicate that keeping up with the times and continuously updating oneself has become a professional requirement for teachers in an educational role, playing an important role in the transformation of teacher qualifications in the modern era. In the early 2000s, overhead projectors (devices that use mirrors and light to project prepared texts onto a board) were replaced by screens in classrooms. Digitalization has taken the concept of space to different dimensions and even made education independent of the concept of space. In the past, the concept of space in education was limited to an area within a school or university, but now education is being transferred and accommodated wherever the individual is located. Face-to-face education is being replaced by digital education platforms. However, in order for digital transformation in education to be achieved, it must be accepted that learning is a lifelong process that is not limited to the time spent at school or in the classroom. Technology provides a much broader and more flexible learning tool than what is offered in classrooms, connecting all stakeholders in education (teachers, parents, experts, mentors). It is argued that a personalized, simulated education program will be more helpful to students in solving complex problems and in the context of social issues (Ataş & Gündüz, 2019). The integration of Artificial Intelligence Applications, which have developed in recent years, into the digitalization process is gaining momentum and enabling the process to evolve in a different direction. Especially in this period, Siri (smart personal assistant) and Gemini (chatbot supported by artificial intelligence), Chat GPT, etc., which are intensively used on mobile phones, are smart and artificial intelligence-supported applications that are integrated into our social life. These systems respond to needs, can make comments, give suggestions, and help individuals in their daily lives by analyzing needs and providing appropriate feedback. The period during which we transitioned to these processes so quickly and rapidly, and digitalization accelerated, was the COVID-19 pandemic period that swept the world between March 2019 and September 2021. This period, with its home quarantine processes and the realization of how humanity should actually behave in major pandemics, how all stages of life should be evaluated during the process, and the sudden shift of social environments to digital, has made digital transformation necessary for every aspect of all levels of education and has created an important critical period for the education community. It has been an important test of the necessity of using technology and the need to act in a solution-oriented manner during times of crisis. During this process, everyone spent approximately 1.5 years of their lives at home or in closed spaces. During this period, individuals discovered themselves and realized that they could manage their own learning processes, and the importance of social learning became apparent. The events that took place have highlighted the place of digitalization, especially in education, and the development of our adaptation processes on an individual level. In particular, the consequences of critical period deficiencies in individuals during childhood and adolescence have been observed and experienced by large groups of people. When looking at the issue of digitalization in education specifically in Turkey, the program and curriculum changes that took place in 2004 and 2005 in an effort to adapt to the learning requirements of the era, the establishment of computer classrooms in schools, and the preparation of instructors who would lead these classrooms or coordinate them through in-service training can be considered the first steps toward digitalization. With the start of this process, numerous new studies have been conducted on the topic of digitalization in education, and the education and teaching process continues to undergo transformation with new applications.

2. ARTIFICIAL INTELLIGENCE AND EDUCATION

Artificial intelligence (AI) is defined as the simulation of human intelligence through machines and enables the automation of mental processes such as problem solving, learning, pattern recognition, and decision making (Russell & Norvig, 2020). AI is a field of study that is based on human intelligence and can be replicated through computers, producing products in various areas of daily life. Today, special circumstances such as the pandemic have made it necessary to transition to digital education and training environments. The technical revolution in this field, consisting of high-speed internet networks, artificial intelligence, big data, and cloud services, is also of great importance in the transition to digital environments (Nabiyev & Erümit, 2020). In recent years, the use of artificial intelligence technologies has expanded considerably. In parallel with this, AI is now on the education agenda of many countries, and studies on the inclusion of AI in education are rapidly increasing. The focus of these studies is not to replace teachers with artificial intelligence technologies, but to enable teachers to be freed from routine tasks so that lessons can be presented in a more professional, engaging, and enjoyable manner, to identify the most appropriate teaching materials for different student profiles, and to facilitate learning processes and support lasting learning

(Nabiyev & Erümit, 2020). AI-supported learning environments are digital systems that automate teaching processes through algorithms that continuously improve themselves with data obtained from users and support active learning by providing personalized content based on students' learning history, speed, and interests (Chen et al., 2020). This type of learning experience, which is particularly beneficial for students with different learning speeds and styles, supports students in taking ownership of their own learning processes while also contributing to the development of their self-regulation skills. Artificial intelligence-supported learning environments have the potential to increase students' learning motivation and self-regulation skills due to these characteristics (OECD, 2021). A review of the literature reveals studies integrating various artificial intelligence tools into science education. For example, Torun and Mustafaoğlu (2024) used ChatGPT in a science lesson for sixth-grade students on the topic of "force." While students used ChatGPT during their brainstorming session, the teacher also utilized ChatGPT to explain the topic. The study reported that students' opinions about this application were positive. Ceylan and Çakır (2025) used artificial intelligence tools such as Merge Explorer and Sketchfab in science lessons for elementary school students and found that there was a significant increase in students' attitudes toward science lessons and their beliefs about their competence. Nguyen et al. (2025) used the GPT-4 model to simulate different communication tools for artificial intelligence and provided various prompts to generate solutions for local climate issues. The researchers stated that artificial intelligence is promising in reflecting different perspectives on climate issues. Okunade (2024), in a study conducted to gain insights into the development and impact of AI in science education in Nigerian middle schools, recommends the integration of artificial intelligence into the national curriculum, adequate funding and resources, and continuous professional development for teachers.

3. ENVIRONMENTAL EDUCATION

Environmental education is a learning process that develops individuals' ability to make informed decisions related to the environment and enhances environmental literacy (Simon et al., 2025). Environmental education encompasses efforts to ensure the sustainability of ecosystems by conserving natural resources, and its primary aim is to encourage individuals to participate actively and responsibly in environmental protection beyond merely informing them (UNESCO, 2015).

With the global increase in environmental issues, environmental education began to take its place on international agendas in the 1970s. It gained an institutional framework with the 1977 Tbilisi Conference, the relationship between sustainable development and education was clearly articulated at the 1992 Rio Summit, and from the 1990s onwards, sustainability-focused approaches came to the forefront. In the 2000s, environmental education was seen to be reshaped based on social participation and cooperation (Gülersoy & Gülersoy, 2023). In Turkey, a protocol signed in 1999 between the Ministry of Environment and Forestry and the Ministry of National Education aimed to include environmental topics at various educational levels and to organize in-service courses focused on environmental education for students and teachers nationwide (Gülersoy & Gülersoy, 2023). In 2015, an elective Environmental Education course curriculum was organized for middle schools, including units on "The Balance of Nature," "Matter Cycle and Natural Balance," "The Limitation of Resources and Ecological Footprint," "Global Environmental Issues," and "Environmentally Friendly Solutions and Technologies." The scope of the Environmental Education course includes "the delicate balance between living and non-living entities in the world, interactions between humans and the environment, the impacts of human activities on this delicate balance, the limitation of natural resources, global environmental issues, the sustainability of limited resources and the delicate balance, and the principle of 'think globally, act locally'" (MEB, 2015). In the curriculum published by the Ministry of National Education (MEB, 2015), this course has fifteen objectives, which are listed below:

1. "Students understanding nature and the relationship between nature and the living beings that exist in nature"
2. "Taking measures to protect the natural balance"
3. "Students recognizing the impact of human activities on the balance of nature"
4. "Students need to realize the importance of ensuring the continuity of material cycles for the preservation of the natural balance."
5. "Students understanding the importance of the continuity of biogeochemical cycles for life"
6. "Students' ability to establish a connection between human production and consumption activities and natural material cycles"
7. "Students taking responsibility for the protection of nature" "Students taking responsibility for the protection of nature"
8. "Students should primarily believe in the necessity of reducing waste production and ensuring the recycling of waste that must be produced."
9. "Students understanding that every person leaves a positive or negative mark in nature" "Students understanding that every person leaves a positive or negative mark on nature"
10. "Having students calculate their ecological footprint and relate it to natural resource consumption" "Students calculating their ecological footprints and establishing the relationship with natural resource consumption"

11. "Students understanding the importance of the sustainable and efficient use of natural resources" "The importance of students understanding the sustainable and efficient use of natural resources"
12. "Students recognizing global environmental issues and taking responsibility for solving these problems" "Students recognizing global environmental issues and taking responsibility for their solutions"
13. "Students should be aware of the need to leave a clean environment for future generations." "Students should be aware that a clean environment needs to be left for future generations."
14. "Establishing a connection between sustainable development and the sustainable use of natural resources" "Establishing a connection between sustainable development and the sustainable use of natural resources"
15. "Students should be knowledgeable about recycling technologies" "Students should have knowledge about recycling technologies"

In the 2022-2023 academic year, the environmental education course was updated to "Environmental Education and Climate Change," reflecting the policy decisions taken in line with the Paris Climate Agreement and the Ministry of National Education's Strategic Plan (MEB, 2022b). This development is also supported by internationally recognized environmental agreements such as the United Nations Framework Convention on Climate Change, the Kyoto Protocol, and the Paris Agreement, which present climate change as a serious global threat. The units included in the course have been updated and renamed as "Human and Nature Count," "Cyclical Nature," "Environmental Issues," "Global Climate Change," "Climate Change and Turkey," and "Sustainable Development and Environmentally Friendly Technologies." With this change, it is observed that the concept of "sustainability" is also being focused on. The objectives of the Environmental and Climate Change course, which has undergone a name change, are as follows;

With the Environmental Education and Climate Change Course Curriculum, students,

- "having interest and curiosity about events occurring in nature and the immediate environment, developing a positive attitude,"
- "realizing that every person around them leaves a positive or negative mark,"
- "establishing a relationship between the use of natural resources and production and consumption activities,"
- "in the process of discovering nature and understanding the relationship between humans and the environment, they use scientific process skills and life skills,"

- "believing in the necessity of leaving a livable environment for future generations by gaining awareness of sustainable development,"
- "understanding the importance of efficient resource use and sustainability in solving environmental issues and climate change from a local, national, and global perspective,"
- "to be knowledgeable about the impacts of environmental issues and global climate change on the environment, society, and economy,"
- "taking responsibility for preventing and mitigating the problems caused by climate change,"
- "being knowledgeable about the effects of climate change in Turkey,"
- "Gaining awareness about national/international agreements related to climate change and the environment, as well as institutions and organizations working on this issue,"
- "being knowledgeable about environmentally friendly technologies,"
- "to raise awareness of environmental careers and to familiarize themselves with related professional fields,"
- "using dilemmas related to environmental issues to develop scientific reasoning and decision-making skills,"
- "It is aimed that they adopt national, cultural, universal moral values and principles of environmental ethics" (MEB, 2022a).

Climate change education holds an important place in the education provided in schools, aiming to improve the education system (Oversby, 2015).

4. ENVIRONMENTAL EDUCATION AND ARTIFICIAL INTELLIGENCE

Environmental education plays a crucial role in overcoming challenges such as air and water pollution, unsustainable waste management, and habitat destruction by shaping individuals' knowledge, attitudes, and behaviors towards the environment (Doğan et al., 2025). With environmental education, it is possible to change people's attitudes by developing their environmental knowledge and values; it encourages people to naturally care about environmental issues, behave responsibly towards the environment, exhibit environmentally beneficial behaviors, and especially ensures that future generations acquire environmental knowledge and the habit of protecting the environment (Huang, 2018).

With the emergence of artificial intelligence, many traditional sustainability practices have evolved and been enriched with innovations. For example, Koyuncuoğlu (2023) evaluated the use of Artificial Intelligence in the field of sustainability at the higher education level and noted that AI has caused changes in dimensions such as education, AI-supported research, curriculum development, energy consumption, AI strategies, digital transformation, and community initiatives.

The increase in global environmental pollution and ecological degradation necessitates the enhancement of environmental literacy and awareness in line with sustainable development goals. However, issues such as traditional, teacher-centered approaches, the lack of personalized learning, and the shortage of qualified educators lead to inconsistencies in students' environmental knowledge, attitudes, and behaviors, deepening the gap between theoretical knowledge and practical application (Xiaoyu et al., 2025). Language models like ChatGPT can assist in areas such as analyzing large amounts of data in climate change research, communicating information in an understandable manner to broader audiences, supporting decision-makers in combating climate change, and creating climate scenarios (Biswas, 2023).

Beyond the traditional approach in education, language-based AI applications like ChatGPT can provide instant and personalized answers to students' questions about environmental concepts such as recycling, climate change, and ecological balance; at the same time, they encourage students to create creative content, offering a rich learning experience supported by multimedia.

AI-based text generation tools contribute to students' better understanding of environmental risks and scientific data by simplifying and making complex topics like climate change more comprehensible, but they also harbor some logical and scientific depth deficiencies (Cheung et al., 2024). For example, these language models may not fully grasp scientific concepts, may be inadequate in evaluating context, may be influenced by biases in training data, and may lack up-to-date expert knowledge (Biswas, 2023). Therefore, the competence of teachers who will use artificial intelligence technology is of great importance.

Artificial intelligence offers significant opportunities in combating climate change; however, these opportunities also come with sacrifices such as ethical risks and an increased carbon footprint (Cowls, et al., 2021). While various studies support predictions regarding the high carbon footprint potential of AI applications, the European Commission's (2020) White Paper states that these technologies can contribute to all sustainable development goals; however, it emphasizes that to prevent these contributions from being overshadowed by negative environmental impacts, the environmental effects of AI systems must be reduced throughout their entire lifecycle, from production to data processing and machine learning (cited in Tuğaç, 2023). Therefore, robust ethical frameworks and policies are needed for the responsible development, implementation, and monitoring of artificial intelligence (Temur, 2025). The challenges of addressing the interpretability of AI-generated recommendations and concerns related to accountability and transparency, especially in the context of climate change, require careful consideration of ethical issues regarding the privacy, security, and potential misuse of AI technologies (Rane et al., 2024).

Considering the ethical and societal dimensions of artificial intelligence technology; questioning its areas of use, decision-making processes, and impacts is of great importance for the future use of this technology in a more sustainable, reliable, and fair manner. In this regard, it is necessary to establish a strong regulatory framework and to effectively monitor the development and application of artificial intelligence with the participation of trained experts (Koyuncuoğlu, 2023).

5. PURPOSE OF THE STUDY

In science education, students are expected not only to learn abstract scientific concepts but also to actively participate in class, offer creative solutions to global problems, and develop new products. It is important for students to develop environmental awareness, become conscious of issues such as environmental problems and sustainable development, internalize these issues, and propose solutions. At the same time, it is important for students, who are digital natives born into advanced technology, to know how to use current technology in the process of creating products in order to develop their 21st century skills such as collaboration, communication, critical thinking, and problem solving. Pedagogical features such as personalized learning, instant feedback, and interactive experiences show that the use of AI-based chatbots in science education enables students to better understand abstract and complex topics and supports their learning processes by providing quick answers (Torun & Karamustafaoğlu, 2025). The integration of artificial intelligence aims to improve the quality of education while also eliminating unique obstacles encountered in science education, such as the shortage of competent science teachers and the need for practical, experiential learning opportunities for students (Okunade, 2024). In light of all this information, this study proposes a lesson design for middle school students on the topic of "Sustainable Development and Environmentally Friendly Technologies" in science classes.

6. COURSE MODULE DEVELOPMENT

Educational Informatics Network (EBA) was established in 2012 by the Ministry of National Education as part of the FATİH Project. It is managed by the General Directorate of Innovation and Educational Technologies. As a social education platform, EBA allows users to share content and interact, and it is an online learning platform that offers course materials, video lectures, interactive activities, and assessment tools for students and teachers. The digital content available on EBA consists of educational materials presented in various formats such as e-books, videos, audio files, visual materials, interactive applications, and e-exams, and these contents are continuously updated in line with technological developments and pedagogical needs (Erensayın & Güler, 2017). The use of EBA has significantly increased, especially during the pandemic period. On March 16, 2020, all schools in Turkey were closed by the decision of the Ministry of National Education (MEB), and subsequently, distance education was implemented in state schools through both EBA TV and the EBA internet platform (MEB, 2020). With EBA, teachers and students have been able to access accurate and reliable e-content after being reviewed, and it is aimed to ensure the highest level of interaction between students and teachers through EBA and to create an environment close to face-to-face education conditions during the distance education process (Türker & Dündar, 2020).

Thanks to the EBA Course module within the EBA platform, teachers can share their work in a virtual environment with other teachers and students, assign homework and track progress, create exams, and generate reports. This situation strengthens the interaction between teachers and students.

In teaching modules developed for interdisciplinary themes such as sustainable living, it is essential to include not only activities that enhance cognitive levels but also experiences that foster affective awareness. In this process, content that encourages active student participation and is enriched with digital tools strengthens the student-centered learning approach of the Maarif Model (MEB, 2023). Therefore, while developing this module, an environment was designed where students could work together collaboratively, and the aim was to develop 21st-century skills such as critical thinking, problem-solving, collaboration, and digital literacy that students should possess.

This lesson module, designed within the scope of the study, has been prepared for middle school students. The topic of "Sustainable Development and Environmentally Friendly Technologies" addressed within the course module aims for "students to understand that sustainable development is dependent on the interaction between environmental, economic, and social systems; to recognize the relationship between the individual and societal well-being of today's generation and future generations with these systems, and to develop solutions to environmental issues" (MEB, 2022b). The course module aims to comprehensively address environmental and climate change issues for middle school students, while associating sustainable living concepts and recycling practices with artificial intelligence technologies and providing an interdisciplinary learning environment. Through AI-supported activities, it is aimed for students to analyze environmental data, generate creative ideas for sustainability, and develop innovative perspectives in the field of recycling. This approach not only supports students in acquiring theoretical knowledge but also enables them to identify real-world problems and develop technology-based solution strategies.

The module is structured in a student-centered manner; artificial intelligence has been integrated into this process as an auxiliary tool to enable students to work in groups collaboratively, produce original products, and take an active role in the learning process. During the module design process, criteria such as the course's objectives, duration, and learning outcomes were taken into account.

Students' use of artificial intelligence in the product development process is directly related to their AI literacy. Therefore, teachers need to raise students' awareness about the use of artificial intelligence within ethical frameworks. Informing students about AI hallucinations, in particular, will help them develop the habit of verifying the answers suggested by AI with other reliable sources. This way, students can approach the product they have created critically and identify any logical and scientific shortcomings. Furthermore, during the product creation process, students are asked to provide information about the stages and methods of AI usage. This helps determine whether AI is being used as an auxiliary tool. All of this is crucial for students to become digitally native individuals with high AI awareness and literacy, rather than just ordinary users of AI.

Teachers must also be competent in artificial intelligence in order to guide and evaluate students' use of artificial intelligence. UNESCO (2024) has addressed this issue in detail by preparing a guide on teacher competencies related to the use of artificial intelligence. Teachers can effectively use artificial intelligence as a tool in the learning process if they are proficient in understanding what artificial intelligence is and its limitations, recognizing and using different artificial intelligence tools, using different commands, and questioning the outputs of artificial intelligence.

7. RECOMMENDATIONS

This study focuses on a proposed lesson plan and is limited solely to the topic of “Sustainable Development and Environmentally Friendly Technologies” as covered in the middle school Science curriculum. The effectiveness of this lesson design is directly linked to the technology and artificial intelligence literacy of both the teacher, in their role as the implementer, and the students. Students’ and teachers’ proficiency in using artificial intelligence, their ability to critically evaluate the products created, and technical and infrastructure issues encountered when accessing artificial intelligence tools are also significant factors in achieving the lesson’s objectives. For this reason, to make this lesson plan more generalizable and subject to in-depth analysis, it is recommended that it be implemented through experimental studies involving experimental and control groups with students from different technical backgrounds, and that the results be discussed.

REFERENCES

Arslan, K. (2020). Eğitimde yapay zekâ ve uygulamaları [Artificial intelligence in education and its applications]. *Batı Anadolu Eğitim Bilimleri Dergisi, 11*(1), 71–88.

Ataş, H., & Gündüz, S. (2019). *Yükseköğretimde dijital dönüşüm* [Digital transformation in higher education]. Dijital Dönüşüm Ekonomik ve Toplumsal Boyutuyla. Gazi Kitabevi.

Batal, M. S. (2016). *Yapay zeka uygulamaları ve yapay zekanın geleceği.* [Artificial intelligence applications and the future of artificial intelligence]. Unpublished institutional report. Uluslararası Sunhıll Üniversitesi, 1-9.

Biswas, S. S. (2023). Potential use of chat GPT in global warming. *Annals of Biomedical Engineering, 51*(6), 1126–1127. DOI: 10.1007/s10439-023-03171-8 PMID: 36856927

Ceylan, İ., & Çakır, R. (2025). Yapay zekâ destekli araçların ilkokul öğrencilerinin fen bilimleri dersine yönelik yeterlilik inançları, tutumları ve başarısına etkisi [The effect of artificial intelligence-supported tools on elementary school students' self-efficacy beliefs, attitudes, and achievement in science lessons] [TUJPED]. *Turkish Journal of Primary Education, 10*(2), 71–90. DOI: 10.52797/tujped.1797585

Chen, X., Xie, H., Zou, D., & Hwang, G. J. (2020). Application and theory gaps during the rise of artificial intelligence in education. *Computers & Education, 146*, 103751. DOI: 10.1016/j.compedu.2019.103751

Cheung, K. K. C., Pun, J. K., & Li, W. (2024). Students' holistic reading of socio-scientific texts on climate change in a ChatGPT scenario. *Research in Science Education, 54*(5), 957–976. DOI: 10.1007/s11165-024-10177-2

Cowls, J., Tsamados, A., Taddeo, M., & Floridi, L. (2021). The AI gambit: Leveraging artificial intelligence to combat climate change—opportunities, challenges, and recommendations. *AI & Society*, •••, 1–25. PMID: 34690449

Doğan, Y., Simsar, A., & Konca, A. S. (2025). Preservice teachers' perceptions of environmental issues. *Journal of Baltic Science Education, 24*(3), 399–412. DOI: 10.33225/jbse/25.24.399

Dong, S. W., Wu, J. J., & Li, Z. G. (2014). Study on the framework of environmental education curriculum system. *Advanced Materials Research, 962-965*, 590–593.

Erensayın, E., & Güler, Ç. (2017). EBA platformundaki ders materyallerinin eğitsel yazılım değerlendirme ölçütlerine göre değerlendirilmesi [Evaluation of instructional materials on the EBA platform according to educational software evaluation criteria] [KEFAD]. *Ahi Evran Üniversitesi Kırşehir Eğitim Fakültesi Dergisi, 18*(1), 657–678.

Gülersoy, A. E., & Gülersoy, Ö. (2023). Çevre eğitimi ve iklim değişikliği dersi (6, 7 veya 8. sınıflar) öğretim programı kazanımlarının yenilenmiş Bloom taksonomisi bilişsel alan basamaklarına göre değerlendirilmesi [An Evaluation of the Learning Outcomes of the Environmental Education and Climate Change Course (Grades 6, 7, or 8) According to the Revised Bloom Taxonomy's Cognitive Domain Levels]. *Jass Studies-The Journal of Academic Social Science Studies, 16*(97), 1–16.

Huang, S. P. (2018). Effects of using artificial intelligence teaching system for environmental education on environmental knowledge and attitude. *Eurasia Journal of Mathematics, Science and Technology Education, 14*(7), 3277–3284. DOI: 10.29333/ejmste/91248

Koyuncuoğlu, D. (2023). Yükseköğretimde yapay zekâ tabanlı sürdürülebilirlik yaklaşımı ve karşılaştırmalı bir inceleme [An AI-Based Approach to Sustainability in Higher Education and a Comparative Study]. *Journal of Academic Value Studies, 9*(3), 182–194. DOI: 10.29228/javs.72130

MEB. (2015). *Ortaokul çevre eğitimi dersi öğretim programı [Middle School Environmental Education Curriculum].*

MEB. (2020). Millî Eğitim Bakanı Ziya Selçuk YEĞİTEK'te EBA kontrol merkezini ziyaret etti [Minister of National Education Ziya Selçuk visited the EBA control center at YEĞİTEK]. https://yegitek.meb.gov.tr/www/mill-egitim-bakani-ziya-selcukyegitekte-eba-kontrol-merkezini-ziyaret-etti/icerik/3036

MEB. (2022a). Çevre Eğitimi ve İklim Değişikliği Dersinin Müfredatı Tamamlandı [The Curriculum for the Environmental Education and Climate Change Course Has Been Finalized]. https://www.meb.gov.tr/cevre-egitimi-ve-iklim-degisikligi-dersinin-mufredati-tamamlandi/haber/25946/tr

MEB. (2022b). *Çevre eğitimi ve iklim değişikliği dersi öğretim programı (Ortaokul 6, 7 veya 8. sınıflar). [Curriculum for the Environmental Education and Climate Change Course (6th, 7th, or 8th Grade Middle School)].*

MEB. (2023). *Türkiye yüzyılı maarif modeli tanıtım kitapçığı [Brochure Introducing the "Century of Turkey" Education Model].* Ankara: MEB Yayınları. https://www.meb.gov.tr

Nabiyev, V., & Erümit, A. K. (2020). Yapay zekanın temelleri. [The Fundamentals of Artificial Intelligence] In Nabiyev, V., & Erümit, A. K. (Eds.), *Eğitimde yapay zeka: Kuramdan uygulamaya* [Artificial Intelligence in Education: From Theory to Practice]. (pp. 2–37). Pegem Akademi Yayınları. DOI: 10.14527/9786257052986.01

Nguyen, H., Nguyen, V., Ludovise, S., & Santagata, R. (2025). Misrepresentation or inclusion: Promises of generative artificial intelligence in climate change education. *Learning, Media and Technology, 50*(3), 393–409. DOI: 10.1080/17439884.2024.2435834

OECD. (2021). *AI and the Future of Skills, Volume 1: Capabilities and Assessments.* OECD Publishing.

Okunade, A. I. (2024). The role of artificial ıntelligence in teaching of science education in secondary schools in Nigeria. *European Journal of Computer Science and Information Technology, 12*(1), 57–67. DOI: 10.37745/ejcsit2013/vol12n15767

Oversby, J. (2015). Teachers' learning about climate change education. *Procedia: Social and Behavioral Sciences, 167*, 23–27. DOI: 10.1016/j.sbspro.2014.12.637

Rane, N., Choudhary, S., & Rane, J. (2024). Contribution of ChatGPT and similar generative Artificial Intelligence for enhanced climate change mitigation strategies. *Available at SSRN* 4681720. http://dx.doi.org/DOI: 10.2139/ssrn.4681720

Russell, S., & Norvig, P. (2020). *Artificial Intelligence: A Modern Approach* (4th ed.). Pearson.

Sarıhan, H. İ. (1998). *Rekabette başarının yolu: Teknoloji yönetimi* [The Key to Success in Competition: Technology Management]. Desnet Yayınları.

Simon, P. D., Zhong, Y., Cruz, I. C. D., & Fryer, L. K. (2025). Scoping Review of Research on Augmented Reality in Environmental Education. *Journal of Science Education and Technology, 34*(4), 919–935. Advance online publication. DOI: 10.1007/s10956-025-10218-z

Taşkıran, A. (2017). Dijital çağda yükseköğretim [Higher education in the digital age]. *Açıköğretim Uygulamaları ve Araştırmaları Dergisi, 3*(1), 96–109.

Temur, S. (2025). Eğitimde yapay zekâ kullanımı: Etik sorunlar ve çözümler [Ethical Issues and Solutions]. *Mehmet Akif Ersoy Üniversitesi Eğitim Fakültesi Dergisi*, (74), 568–595. DOI: 10.21764/maeuefd.1516576

Torun, B., & Karamustafaoğlu, O. (2025). Fen öğretiminde ChatGPT kullanımı hakkında öğrenci görüşleri [Student opinions on the use of ChatGPT in science education]. *Cumhuriyet International Journal of Education, 14*(1), 240–249. DOI: 10.30703/cije.1609145

Tuğaç, Ç. (2023). Birleşmiş milletler sürdürülebilir kalkınma amaçlarının gerçekleştirilmesinde yapay zekâ uygulamalarının rolü [The role of artificial intelligence applications in achieving the United Nations sustainable development goals]. *Sayıştay Dergisi, 34*(128), 73–99. DOI: 10.52836/sayistay.1245051

Türker, A., & Dündar, E. (2020). COVID-19 pandemi sürecinde eğitim bilişim aği (eba) üzerinden yürütülen uzaktan eğitimlerle ilgili lise öğretmenlerinin görüşleri [High school teachers' views on distance learning conducted via the Education Information Network (EBA) during the COVID-19 pandemic]. *Milli Eğitim Dergisi, 49*(1), 323–342.

UNESCO. (2015). Not just hot air: putting climate change education into practice. https://unesdoc.unesco.org/ark:/48223/pf0000233083

UNESCO. (2024). *AI competency framework for teachers.* United Nations Educational, Scientific and Cultural Organization., DOI: 10.54675/ZJTE2084

Xiaoyu, W., Zainuddin, Z., Leng, C. H., Wenting, D., & Li, X. (2025). Evaluating the efficacy of ChatGPT in environmental education: findings from heuristic and usability assessments. *On the Horizon: The International Journal of Learning Futures*, (ahead-of-print).

Yeşilyurt, E. (2020). Öğretmenin pusulası: Genel öğretim ilkeleri [The teacher's guide: General principles of teaching]. *EKEV Akademi Dergisi*, (83), 263–288. DOI: 10.17753/Ekev1525

APPENDIX: MODULE / COURSE PLAN TEMPLATE

"Practical Course Module Protect Our Planet – Sustainable Living and Smart Future"

- **Main themes:**
- Sustainable Development
- Efficient Use of Natural Resources
- Recycling and Upcycling
- Environmental Responsibility
- Climate Change and Global Impacts
- Sustainability with Artificial Intelligence
- Smart Technologies and Future Vision

Guiding question(s): "What smart practices should individuals and societies adopt for a sustainable future?"

Developed science concepts and discussed dimensions:

- Scientific concepts
    - o Biodiversity
    - o Ecosystem
    - o Climate change
    - o Greenhouse effect
    - o Global warming

Objectives of the module

*(Environment and Climate Change: ÇEİD)

ÇEİD.6.1. S/He realizes that while meeting his desires and needs in daily life, he should also consider the needs of future generations.
ÇEİD.6.2. Recognizes the importance of the sustainable use of water resources.
ÇEİD.6.3. Discusses the impact of the sustainable use of resources on development based on research data.
ÇEİD.6.4. Explains the importance of recycling and recovery in terms of sustainable development.
ÇEİD.6.5. Designs an upcycled product using waste materials.
ÇEİD.6.6. It presents examples that support sustainable development in Turkey and the world.

ÇEİD.6.7. Designs a project that includes a solution based on sustainable development awareness for a real-life problem.
ÇEİD.6.8. Provides examples of different career fields related to the environment, climate, and sustainable development.

Evaluation

- Classroom worksheets and/or activity forms
- Quiz (one or two times during the process)
- Synthesis activity documents (e.g., posters, presentations, application examples by students, proposed solution plans, etc.)

Lesson Plan-1 (2 x 40 min) Introduction to the Focus Problem – Introduction

Course outcomes/achievements:

ÇEİD.6.1. He realizes that while meeting his daily desires and needs, he should also consider the needs of future generations.
ÇEİD.6.2. Recognizes the importance of the sustainable use of water resources.
ÇEİD.6.3. Discusses the impact of sustainable resource use on development based on research data.

At the end of this course, students;

It relates the concepts of waste and conscious consumption to daily life.
S/He understands that water resources are limited and valuable.
Develops applicable individual and societal measures for water and energy conservation.
Discusses the economic and environmental impacts of resource use.

Guiding question (Module)

"For a sustainable future, what smart practices should individuals and societies adopt?" "Which smart applications should individuals and societies adopt for a sustainable future?"

Guiding sub-question(s) (Lesson plan)

1. If you were to make a prediction about your life in the future world, 10 or 20 years from now, what would the outcome of that prediction be?
   1) What could be the consequences of water being a limited resource?
   2) How does energy and water waste affect society?
   3) What individual measures can be taken to use resources more efficiently?

Evaluation

Individual and Group Performances
Classroom observation forms
In-process quiz and activity checklists
Presentation of projects created with Canva, ChatGPT, and DALL-E
Project report + Oral presentation
Reflective learning journals
Evaluation of visuals and texts created using artificial intelligence
Presentation of group discussions

Course Flow and Content

Course Content and Activities

1- As the class begins.....

The lesson plan should be reviewed before the class, and the necessary resources and literature for the lesson content should be read. If deemed necessary, adjustments can be made to the prepared plan. Subsequently, the plan can be uploaded to applications like ChatGPT or Gemini to request ideas, suggestions, or corrections. When the class starts, preliminary information about the lesson content can be provided. In the provided preliminary information, topics, concepts, and definitions can be included.

A brief overview of the technique to be used in the class;

In the brainstorming technique, the topic to be discussed is first turned into a question and displayed in a place where all group members can see it.

In the second stage, individuals in the group are asked to answer the question in the most free and unrestricted manner.

One of the people in the group is tasked with leading the meeting, and this person is the moderator. The moderator guides the meeting according to the rules.

The ideas and suggestions presented by the group members are not criticized. It should be noted that the aim of this technique is not to evaluate, but to develop and elevate suggestions and thoughts to the highest level. At this point, the moderator must be very well aware of where to intervene.

After freely expressed opinions are collected without criticism, the stage of rational evaluation begins. This is the part where the main ideas mature.

Brainstorming techniques today:

• Face-to-face brainstorming: This is the type of brainstorming that most people are familiar with. It involves face-to-face discussions and idea generation. However, face-to-face brainstorming can have its disadvantages. For example, groupthink, which causes people to accept ideas to avoid tension in the environment, and strong personalities dominating discussions (whether intentionally or not).

• Online brainstorming: These types of brainstorming sessions have become more common with the increase in remote and hybrid work. To conduct a successful online brainstorming session, a collaborative online platform like Canva's Whiteboard feature is required. Thanks to this feature, facilitators can prepare visual guides for more efficient sessions and play music to set the atmosphere. The Whiteboard feature also allows participants to write their ideas in real-time without any concerns.

• It is important to have a good facilitator in both methods. In face-to-face sessions, a good facilitator can mediate discussions to encourage everyone to speak and reduce groupthink. In online brainstorming, facilitators are there to prevent discussions from stagnating, save time, and change the course of discussions.

1. If you were to make a prediction about your life 10 or 20 years from now in the future world, what would be the outcome of that prediction?

An activity plan is prepared using the question above.

Lecture: Science

Subject: The Future World and the Impact of Technology on Our Lives

Duration: 2 class hours

Grade Level: Middle School

Technique: Brainstorming + AI-Supported Creative Thinking

Generates creative ideas about future life.

Uses AI tools for idea development and content creation.

Analyzes scientific and technological developments by adapting them to the future.

It develops collaboration and problem-solving skills.

Materials to be Used:

https://dogmprojeler.meb.gov.tr/upload/feyza/YapayZeka.pdf

https://tubitak.gov.tr/sites/default/files/25506/yapay_zeka_ortaokul.pdf

Arslan, 2020

Batal, 2016

https://polen.itu.edu.tr/items/c89dda55-f49c-49fa-9e26-a8981ef3e2fa

2- As the lesson progresses...

A. The teacher asks the question: “What will the world be like in 10 or 20 years?” An inspiring short video/digital content is watched.
B. Rule reminder: Think freely, criticize, generate bold ideas.
C. Students gather ideas by asking questions to AI tools:
    - Ask ChatGPT: “What will transportation be like in 20 years?” Ask ChatGPT: “How will transportation be in 20 years?”
    - Create an image of “A future city design” with Bing/DALL-E.
    - Design a poster with Canva AI.

(Here, students are first asked to imagine these scenarios. Then, examples are provided on how to instruct artificial intelligence to turn these ideas into designs. Sample prompts might include:

- Design an urban transportation vehicle that can travel by land, air, and sea 20 years from now
- Design a fully glass transportation capsule that will be used in Ankara in 2050
- Design an eco-friendly transportation vehicle
- Think like the owner of a transportation company and design an eco-friendly, low-fuel-consumption vehicle for students’ use).

D. Groups present their ideas. Shares visuals/prototypes with the class.
    - Discussion: Which ideas are more feasible? Which technologies seem feasible?
    - Each student answers the question: “What was the most interesting thing I learned while using AI?”

Materials to be Used

A video created with Sora / Synthesia / Runway is watched: Future cities, technologies, etc.

ChatGPT (idea and story generation)

DALL-E / Canva (visual design)

Perplexity (research support)

Canva / Prezi (presentation preparation)

Writing a mini reflection text with ChatGPT
Example AI-Supported Question Titles
1. Ask ChatGPT:
How will education be in 20 years?
In which areas does artificial intelligence work in human life?
What technologies will be in the cities of the future?
2. Visual Production (DALL-E / Canva):
A school in the future
A living space on Mars
A factory that operates with robots

3- At the End of the Lesson

Classification of Ideas

- Technology
- Health
- Environment
- Education
- Social Life

*The teacher helps students make their projects more realistic by providing verbal feedback during the project development process.

Presentation and Discussion

- Students share the ideas and visuals they have created with the class.
- Discussion: Which ideas are more feasible? Which technologies seem possible?

**Teachers can use an AI-powered assessment rubric to evaluate the work prepared by their groups. Below, in the section titled "Guidelines for Teachers When Applying the Brainstorming Technique," you will find an example of a rubric created with the assistance of Google Gemini and Microsoft Copilot.

Closure and Reflection

- Students are asked to share what they have learned and their experiences during the event process.

The Section That Can Guide the Teacher While Applying the Brainstorming Technique;

The teacher asks the students the question:

What will the world be like in 10 or 20 years? What will change in our lives? "How will the world be in 10 or 20 years? What will change in our lives?"

An inspiring video, a short news clip, or an image related to the topic (for example, flying cars, smart cities, AI-supported living spaces) is shown.

The rules of brainstorming are reminded:

- Every idea is valuable, no criticism.
- The more creative, the better.
- It's free to be inspired by others' ideas.

Students generate ideas individually or in groups.

- What could change in 10 years?
- What technologies could exist in 20 years?
- What would be different in daily life?
- How will education, health, transportation, environment, and social life be?

Ideas are written on a board or a digital platform. (For example: Padlet, Jamboard)

Ideas are categorized by themes:

- Technology
- Health
- Environment
- Education
- Social Life, etc.

Students are asked to share the ideas that most interest or surprise them.

A mini discussion is held on the question, “Is it possible for these ideas to come true?”

The teacher emphasizes the importance of brainstorming and the power of creative thinking.

Table 1. An example of a rubric that can be used to evaluate students' work (created using Google Gemini and Microsoft Copilot)

Evaluation Criteria	Excellent (4 Points)	Average (3 Points)	Needs Improvement (2 Points)	Poor (1 Point)	Score
Prompt Quality	Detailed, context-rich, and creative prompts were used. Clear boundaries were set for the AI.	Clear prompts were used, but details and "role definition" were lacking.	Very general or superficial, single-sentence prompts were used.	Prompts were vague, off-topic, or too short.	
Content	The product is clear and meaningful, and fully aligned with the theme of "future transportation / cities."	It is aligned with the theme, but some ideas are superficial.	It is partially relevant to the theme, but the connections are weak.	It is not aligned with the theme or contains very limited information.	
Sustainability and Environmental Awareness	Environmentally friendly transportation, energy conservation, and harmony with nature are clearly emphasized.	There are environmentally conscious elements, but details are scarce.	The environment is mentioned only indirectly or to a limited extent.	The environmental dimension is not included.	
Innovation, Originality, and Creativity	Surprising and original transportation solutions were developed that go beyond current technologies.	Reasonable additions were made to known future scenarios (such as flying cars).	Current technologies were merely replicated; no innovative ideas were presented.	The ideas are illogical or completely unrelated to the topic.	
Technical Consistency	Details such as the system's power source, speed, and security have been grounded in a logical framework.	The system's operation has been explained only superficially; there are some logical gaps.	The technology's operating principle or infrastructure has not been explained at all.	The proposed solution is physically or logically impossible.	
Interaction with Artificial Intelligence	They questioned the AI output and revised the result at least 2–3 times by saying, "Change this."	They made minor adjustments to the AI output but did not question it in depth.	They accepted the AI's initial response as is, without giving it any thought.	They were unable to use AI tools effectively or generate any output.	

continued on following page

Table 1. Continued

Evaluation Criteria	Excellent (4 Points)	Average (3 Points)	Needs Improvement (2 Points)	Poor (1 Point)	Score
Using AI Tools Responsibly	The AI output has been interpreted, and the student's own ideas have been incorporated.	The AI output has been used, with limited personal input.	The AI output has been copied verbatim, and the interpretation is weak.	The AI output has been copied verbatim, and the interpretation is weak.	
Visual and Verbal Presentation	Ideas were presented in an engaging and organized manner using both text and AI-generated visuals.	Ideas were conveyed in an organized manner, with basic visual support.	The presentation was disorganized, and visual or tabular support was insufficient.	The presentation was unclear, with no coherence between content and visuals.	

Lesson Plan-2- Synthesis and Analysis Section (8 X 40 Min): Development of Targeted Concepts and Skills

Guiding question(s): "What smart practices should individuals and societies adopt for a sustainable future?" "Which smart practices should individuals and societies adopt for a sustainable future?"

Developed science concepts and discussed dimensions:

- Scientific concepts
  - Sustainable Development
  - Efficient Use of Natural Resources
  - Recycling and Upcycling
  - Environmental Responsibility
  - Climate Change and Global Impacts
  - Sustainability with Artificial Intelligence
  - Smart Technologies and Future Vision

Module's target outcomes:

ÇEİD.6.1. He realizes that while meeting his desires and needs in daily life, he should also consider the needs of future generations.
ÇEİD.6.2. Recognizes the importance of the sustainable use of water resources.
ÇEİD.6.3. Discusses the impact of sustainable resource use on development based on research data.

ÇEİD.6.4. Explains the importance of recycling and recovery in terms of sustainable development.
ÇEİD.6.5. Designs an upcycled product using waste materials.
ÇEİD.6.6. It presents examples that support sustainable development in Turkey and the world.
ÇEİD.6.7. Designs a project that includes a solution based on sustainable development awareness for a real-life problem.
ÇEİD.6.8. Gives examples of different career fields related to the environment, climate, and sustainable development.

Evaluation:

- Classroom worksheets and/or activity forms
- Quiz (one or two times during the process)
- Synthesis activity documents (e.g., posters, presentations, application examples by students, proposed solution plans, etc.)

Course Flow and Content

Course Content and Activities

1. At the beginning of the lesson, from this week onwards, the subsequent lessons will continue with the stages of exploration, deepening, and explanation. In the introduction section, we will inform students about the objective, and in the continuation of the process, we will address this event as if it were a real-life problem, allowing them to identify and notice the points to be considered during the solution stages. Below, the lesson stages and contents will be provided in table form.
2. (2 x 40 min = 2 classes) SNOWBALL ACTIVITY
   - In this activity, students can use various AI tools during the idea-generation process. They can refine their ideas by gathering with their group members to discuss them. Additionally, since groups will create concept maps during the final product development phase, they are encouraged to use AI tools in stages such as concept mapping and data visualization.
   - The teacher distributes news papers prepared on a topic but containing different perspectives related to the topic to the students and presents them as preliminary information. Students read the provided materials and first think about what they will say. They can take notes on what comes to their mind or what they want to share.

- Then, the student forms a pair with their closest friend. The students take turns sharing what they want with their friend. Common sentences are extracted from the shared ones, and the thoughts or information of both students are combined.
- The pair group merges with the other pair group sitting nearby to form a single quartet group. The pairs take turns sharing the thoughts or information they wish to convey. As in the previous step, common sentences are extracted from the shared thoughts or information, and each group's thoughts or information are combined.
- The quartet group merges with another quartet group to form an octet group. The quartet groups take turns sharing the thoughts or information they want to convey. As in the previous step, common sentences are extracted from the shared thoughts or information, and the ideas or information of each group are combined.
- The students are informed that the information and thoughts derived from this will be presented to the entire class. Therefore, the students need to choose a spokesperson to give the presentation.
- If the teacher wishes, they can skip the step where groups of eight are formed and complete the activity with groups of four.
- The spokesperson stands up and shares the information and thoughts that emerged from the group with the class.
- Students may be asked to transform the information or thoughts they wish to share into a product using a concept map. At each stage, these concept maps can be combined or one can be selected and further developed. In the final step, a single concept map is created, and this product is shared with other groups.
- The teacher can support every student being active by stating that they will choose the spokesperson who will share this common product with the class.
- The teacher assigns another group to comment on and ask questions about the presentation of the group that is presenting.
- In this way, while conducting a study aimed at high-level cognitive skills such as providing feedback by commenting on the presentation, attention will also be drawn to the sensitivity regarding listening.

  At the end of the lesson, students are given a role-playing activity that corresponds to the angles they have studied.

3. (2 x 40 min = 2 classes) ROLE PLAYING ACTIVITY
   - The main purpose of the role-playing technique is to help students understand their own feelings and thoughts regarding certain situations

and to enable them to create meaning about the social world surrounding them.

POINTS TO CONSIDER AT THE ACTIVITY:

- For the success of the role-playing method, students must also have a say in the selection of the situation or event to be simulated.
- At the end of the role play, a discussion environment regarding the game must be created in the classroom.
- Each scene should generally not last more than 5-10 minutes.
- If necessary, the required sections can be repeated.
- A free and safe atmosphere should be created in the classroom.
- ROLES TO BE SELECTED FOR THE ROLE-PLAYING TECHNIQUE TO BE USED:
- Roles to be Used (Example):
- Environmental Engineer
- Mayor
- Sustainable Agriculture Specialist
- Recycling Factory Worker
- Climate Activist
- City Planner
- Smart Home Designer
- Energy Expert
- Water Policies Advisor
- Waste Management Specialist
- A Citizen of the Future (for example: a child or young person from 20 years in the future)
- Artificial Intelligence Assistant (a character that supports the student's idea generation process) These roles allow students to stimulate and discuss different perspectives.
- Role Play Review Discussion Questions Suggestion:
- Which issue did the role you portrayed highlight?
- What ideas have been generated to solve this problem?
- What was the contribution of different professions and roles to the solution?
- Which idea did you find the most creative or the most feasible?
- How can these ideas be implemented in real life?
- Creative Drama Post-Evaluation Proposal:
- What were the strengths of the group work?
- Did you encounter any difficulties during the process? How were they overcome?

- How did it feel to come up with a solution to a real-life problem?
- Have you thought about what you can do for a sustainable future?
- What new ideas and perspectives did this course provide you with?

Assessment Tools (Visual / Written):

Creating posters with Canva / Google Slides
Writing solution proposals with ChatGPT
Creating a visual of a sustainable city with DALL-E
Creating a brainstorming board with Padlet / Jamboard
Quick quiz competition with Kahoot / Quizizz (sample questions can be added)
Mini video presentations with Flipgrid

4. (4 x 40 min = 4 classes) CREATIVE DRAMA METHOD

Creative drama has many effects, such as helping students think critically, evaluate and analyze events, observe various events and situations, make organizational decisions in group or individual work, and generate new solutions. For this reason, it is thought that applying creative drama in this context will help students internalize the subject better.

- After the snowball technique and role-playing technique are applied to the students, the creative drama method is implemented. Thus, it is observed how the various outcomes of the lessons drawn from the events discussed in the snowball and role-playing techniques are understood by the students.
- Students are divided into groups of 4 or 8 (the number of people in the groups is left to the teacher's discretion). After the groups are formed, an unfinished scenario is given, and the students are asked to complete this scenario by making decisions within their groups.
- 20 minutes are given for the groups to discuss and plan this scenario among themselves.
- At the end of the allotted time, students are asked to enact the given story, which was left unfinished, based on their planning and task distribution.

As a result of the simulations, a general evaluation is conducted in the class, and the conclusions drawn are separately noted on the board with their main ideas. After each group's simulation is completed, the results are discussed in general, and the lesson is concluded.

Example of an Unfinished Script for the Creative Drama Method: Scenario Beginning (example):

"The year is 2045… The world is feeling the effects of climate change more intensely. People living in a city are struggling to access clean water. At a meeting organized by the municipality, citizens come together to find a solution to the water problem. An environmental engineer, a farmer, a student, a municipal official, and a scientist also participate in the meeting. The discussion is escalating: What should the solution be? How can we protect water resources? How can recycling be increased?..."

Task: Students create and enact the continuation of this scenario.

Figure 1. Poster for a course module created by artificial intelligence (This figure was created by ChatGPT and has not been corrected for spelling errors.)

Chapter 11

Preparing Higher Education for the Era of Artificial Intelligence: A Multidimensional Framework for Institutional Readiness

Ngo Tinh Giang Nguyen
http://orcid.org/0000-0001-6838-8951
Ho Chi Minh City University of Economics and Finance, Vietnam

Agustinus Bandur
Binus University, Indonesia

ABSTRACT

This chapter conceptualizes institutional readiness as a multidimensional organizational capability that extends beyond technology to include strategy, governance, human capacity, infrastructure, and culture. Drawing on change management theory, digital maturity frameworks, educational governance, and ethical AI scholarship, it introduces an Institutional Readiness Framework (IRF) for AI-integrated hybrid education structured around five interdependent dimensions. The IRF is designed as a diagnostic and developmental framework rather than a ranking or compliance tool, supporting institutional reflection and capacity building across diverse contexts. Through synthesis of empirical research, policy analysis, and comparative insights from digitally mature and emerging systems, the chapter demonstrates how readiness develops over time through governance alignment, cultural mediation of AI, and iterative change processes. It further outlines practical approaches to evaluating readiness that prioritize learning and strategic planning.

DOI: 10.4018/979-8-3373-7462-8.ch011

1. INTRODUCTION: WHY INSTITUTIONAL READINESS MATTERS

The rapid expansion of artificial intelligence and hybrid learning models is reshaping higher education systems worldwide. Universities and training institutions increasingly deploy AI driven tools to support teaching, assessment, administration, student advising, and research activities. At the same time, hybrid education combining digital and face-to-face modalities has shifted from an emergency response to a core mode of educational delivery. While these developments signal accelerated innovation, growing evidence suggests that technological adoption alone does not equate to institutional readiness. Instead, the integration of AI within hybrid education has revealed persistent gaps in governance, capability, and organizational alignment.

Recent empirical and policy oriented research highlights this disconnect. Drawing on large scale survey evidence, KPMG LLP (2025) reports widespread use of generative AI among students and employees in higher education, particularly for productivity enhancement, research support, and administrative efficiency. However, the report also identifies limited institutional guidance on ethical use, academic integrity, and data governance, indicating that individual level adoption has progressed more rapidly than organizational preparedness. Similarly, Molina et al. (2024) emphasize that while AI driven innovations offer significant opportunities to personalize learning, reduce administrative burden, and optimize education management, their effectiveness depends on institutional readiness across infrastructure, human capacity, governance, and ethical oversight.

This chapter advances the argument that AI integrated hybrid education does not automatically produce institutional readiness. Rather, readiness should be understood as a multidimensional condition that extends beyond technological infrastructure to encompass leadership vision, policy coherence, faculty capability, organizational culture, and ethical accountability. Without alignment across these dimensions, AI initiatives risk becoming fragmented, reactive, or misaligned with educational missions. The following sections situate institutional readiness within the post-pandemic transformation of higher education, conceptualize readiness as a multi-level construct, and outline the aims and contributions of this chapter.

1.1. The Post-Pandemic Shift: From Rapid Adoption to Strategic Readiness

The COVID-19 pandemic marked a turning point in the digital transformation of higher education. Institutions worldwide were compelled to transition rapidly to online and hybrid delivery models with limited preparation and long term planning. During this period, AI-powered systems, including learning analytics platforms, automated assessment tools, and generative AI applications, were increasingly introduced to sustain teaching and administrative functions. While these measures enabled institutional continuity, they were largely driven by crisis response rather than strategic design.

Evidence suggests that the effects of this rapid adoption phase have persisted beyond the pandemic. According to KPMG LLP (2025), students now routinely rely on generative AI for tasks such as research, idea generation, and content summarization, while academic and professional staff increasingly use AI to streamline administrative workflows and enhance efficiency. However, institutional policies governing acceptable use, assessment integrity, and ethical deployment remain underdeveloped in many contexts. Molina et al. (2024) similarly observe that AI innovations have often been implemented in fragmented ways, without sufficient attention to institutional capacity, regulatory clarity, or long-term sustainability.

This post-pandemic context has shifted the central challenge facing higher education. The issue is no longer whether AI-enhanced and hybrid education should be adopted, but whether institutions are strategically ready to sustain these models in ways that are pedagogically sound, ethically responsible, and organizationally coherent. Strategic readiness therefore entails a qualitative transition from short term problem solving to long term capacity building. Institutions that fail to make this transition risk entrenching inconsistent practices, intensifying faculty resistance, and undermining trust among students and staff.

1.2. Beyond Technology: Institutional Readiness as a Multi Level Construct

A key limitation of many digital transformation initiatives lies in their narrow focus on technological infrastructure. While access to digital platforms and AI tools is a necessary foundation, it is insufficient to ensure meaningful and sustainable educational transformation. Institutional readiness must instead be conceptualized as a multi level construct encompassing individual, organizational, and governance dimensions alongside technology.

At the individual level, faculty readiness plays a decisive role in shaping how AI and hybrid education are enacted in practice. Ali (2025) demonstrates that faculty AI readiness varies significantly across higher education institutions, with differences in AI literacy, pedagogical confidence, and perceptions of institutional support influencing educators willingness to integrate AI into teaching and assessment. Even in technologically advanced environments, limited faculty readiness can constrain effective implementation and generate resistance, suggesting that institutional readiness depends on sustained investment in professional development and academic engagement rather than technical provision alone.

Student readiness constitutes another critical dimension. Rahman et al. (2025) find that students' adoption of AI chatbots in higher education is strongly influenced by their level of technological readiness, with institutional trust and guidance moderating adoption behavior. In the absence of clear institutional norms, students may simultaneously depend on AI tools while perceiving their use as academically risky or ethically ambiguous. This tension underscores the importance of governance frameworks that provide clarity, legitimacy, and consistency in AI use across learning contexts.

At the organizational and policy level, readiness is shaped by broader governance environments. Kundu and Bej (2025), in their comparative analysis of AI policies in China, Singapore, Finland, and the United States, illustrate how national regulatory traditions and strategic priorities influence institutional approaches to AI integration. Their findings highlight that institutional readiness is deeply embedded within policy ecosystems and cultural contexts, and cannot be reduced to a standardized or universally transferable model.

Across these levels, readiness emerges through alignment rather than accumulation. Leadership vision, policy coherence, human capability, and organizational culture must evolve together within a shared institutional strategy. Institutional readiness should therefore be understood as a dynamic and relational process rather than a static condition.

1.3. Aim, Scope, and Contribution

Building on these perspectives, the aim of this chapter is to conceptualize and operationalize institutional readiness for AI integrated hybrid education. The chapter seeks to support higher education leaders, policymakers, and administrators in assessing their organizational capacity to design, implement, and sustain hybrid learning environments that incorporate AI in ethical, inclusive, and pedagogically meaningful ways.

The chapter makes three primary contributions. First, it synthesizes empirical and policy insights from research on faculty AI readiness, student adoption behavior, institutional governance, and AI innovation in education to develop a holistic understanding of institutional readiness. Second, it introduces a structured Institutional Readiness Framework that identifies key dimensions of readiness across strategy, governance and policy, capability development, infrastructure, and organizational culture. Third, it situates this framework within diverse global contexts, recognizing that readiness manifests differently depending on governance systems, resource conditions, and cultural norms.

Rather than proposing a universal model of best practice, the chapter adopts a developmental and diagnostic perspective. Institutional readiness is framed as an ongoing process of organizational learning and adaptation rather than a fixed endpoint. By foregrounding readiness as a strategic, cultural, and ethical challenge, this chapter contributes to emerging debates on how higher education institutions can navigate AI driven transformation while maintaining educational integrity and institutional legitimacy.

2. CONCEPTUAL FOUNDATIONS OF INSTITUTIONAL READINESS

Institutional readiness for AI-integrated hybrid education cannot be understood solely through the lens of technological innovation. Rather, it is grounded in theories of organizational change, learning, and governance that explain how institutions adapt to complex and sustained transformation. This section outlines the conceptual foundations informing the Institutional Readiness Framework proposed in this chapter. Drawing selectively from change management theory, digital maturity and educational governance models, and ethical and intercultural approaches to AI, the section establishes readiness as a dynamic organizational process rather than a static condition.

Unlike traditional software adoption, AI introduces the unique challenge of algorithmic opacity. Institutional readiness must involve "Explainability Protocols." This means leaders must be ready to explain exactly how an AI system reached a specific recommendation especially in high-stakes areas like admissions, grading, or student support alerts. Readiness is not just about having the technological tool; it is about having the human capacity and governance structures to audit the tool's logic to prevent "Black Box Bias."

2.1. Change Management and Learning Organizations

The integration of artificial intelligence into hybrid education constitutes a form of deep organizational change rather than a discrete technological intervention. It reshapes pedagogical practices, professional identities, governance routines, and institutional norms. As such, institutional readiness for AI-integrated hybrid education is best understood through theories of change management that emphasize process, learning, and collective sense-making rather than linear implementation.

A foundational point of reference in this literature is Kotter's 8-Step Change Model, which conceptualizes organizational change as a staged process involving creating urgency, developing guiding coalitions, articulating a shared vision, and embedding new practices into organizational culture (Kotter and Cohen, 2014). While originally developed in corporate contexts, the model has been widely adapted to public and educational institutions undergoing complex reform.

Figure 1. Kotters' 8-Step Change Model - the 08 accelerators (Kotter and Cohen, 2014)

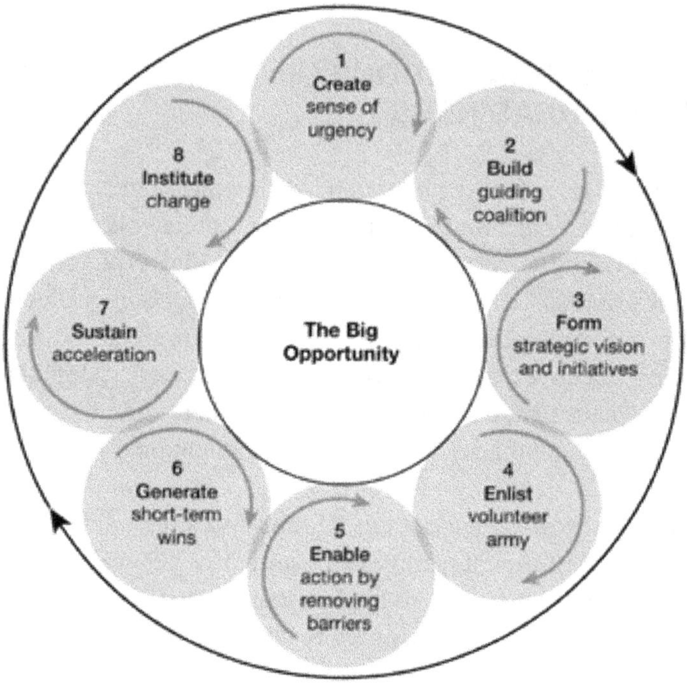

In higher education, however, change rarely follows a linear or top down trajectory. Empirical work by Kang et al. (2022) demonstrates that the application of Kotter's model in universities is often emergent and iterative rather than sequential. Their study shows that institutions revisit stages of vision building, coalition formation, and consolidation multiple times as change unfolds, particularly in environments characterized by professional autonomy, collegial governance, and disciplinary diversity. This insight is critical for understanding institutional readiness, as it suggests that readiness is not a prerequisite to change but an outcome that evolves through engagement with change itself.

Recent studies on AI adoption further reinforce this process-oriented view. Tursunbayeva (2024) argues that AI-driven transformation challenges traditional change management approaches by introducing uncertainty, opacity, and ethical ambiguity. Unlike conventional digital tools, AI systems continuously evolve through data, feedback, and algorithmic refinement, requiring organizations to adapt dynamically rather than stabilize quickly. From this perspective, readiness is not achieved once AI is implemented, but is sustained through ongoing learning, monitoring, and recalibration.

Within higher education specifically, Al Sabbagh and Elgeddawy (2025) highlight that successful AI adoption depends on how institutions manage human responses to change, including trust, perceived control, and professional identity. Their study of higher education institutions in Oman illustrates that resistance to AI often stems less from technical limitations than from concerns about transparency, workload, and the redistribution of decision making authority. Change management processes that emphasize participation, communication, and capability development are, therefore, central to building readiness over time.

Strategic responses to generative AI further underscore the importance of learning oriented change. Gering et al. (2025) find that leading universities responding effectively to generative AI adoption adopt adaptive strategies characterized by experimentation, cross-functional coordination, and incremental institutionalization. Rather than pursuing comprehensive AI strategies from the outset, these institutions develop readiness through pilot initiatives, feedback loops, and gradual policy alignment. This approach reflects a shift from control-oriented change toward adaptive governance, where readiness is cultivated through practice rather than prescribed in advance.

Taken together, these perspectives support a conceptualization of institutional readiness as a processual and developmental phenomenon. Readiness emerges through cycles of experimentation, reflection, and organizational learning as institutions engage with AI-integrated hybrid education. Leadership plays a critical role in framing AI as a pedagogical and strategic opportunity rather than a purely technical disruption, while governance structures must enable learning across institutional levels.

In this chapter, change management theory is therefore not treated as a prescriptive blueprint, but as an analytical lens that foregrounds readiness as an evolving organizational capability. The Institutional Readiness Framework developed later builds on this foundation by emphasizing progression, alignment, and learning rather than static benchmarks. By situating readiness within theories of change and learning organizations, the framework avoids treating AI integration as a one time reform and instead recognizes it as a continuous institutional journey.

2.2. Digital Maturity and Educational Governance

While change management theory explains how institutions navigate transformation over time, the concept of digital maturity provides insight into what capacities institutions have developed to support digital and AI enabled education. In higher education, digital maturity frameworks have been widely used to assess institutional progress in areas such as leadership, governance, infrastructure, and engagement. However, digital maturity alone does not fully capture institutional readiness for AI integrated hybrid education.

One of the most influential governance oriented tools in this space is HEInnovate, developed by the OECD and the European Commission. HEInnovate conceptualizes institutional development across multiple dimensions, including leadership and governance, organizational capacity, digital transformation, and external engagement. Rather than focusing solely on technological capability, the framework emphasizes strategic alignment, governance processes, and institutional culture as key drivers of sustainable innovation.

HEInnovate is particularly valuable for understanding how digital transformation is embedded within institutional governance. Its emphasis on leadership commitment, cross functional coordination, and organizational learning aligns closely with contemporary understandings of higher education as a complex and loosely coupled system. Empirical work by Patricio and Ferreira (2023) demonstrates that HEInnovate dimensions are most effective when treated as interdependent rather than sequential, reinforcing the idea that digital transformation requires coherence across governance, strategy, and institutional practices.

Despite these strengths, it is important to distinguish digital maturity from institutional readiness. Digital maturity refers to the extent to which institutions have developed formal structures, processes, and resources to support digital innovation. It captures accumulated capacity, such as established governance mechanisms, digital infrastructure, and innovation oriented leadership. Readiness, by contrast, reflects an institution's current ability to mobilize those capacities effectively in response to specific transformations, such as the integration of AI into hybrid education.

This distinction is evident in recent empirical studies. KPMG LLP (2025) reports that many higher education institutions demonstrate high levels of digital maturity, evidenced by widespread AI usage among students and staff and significant investment in digital platforms. However, the same institutions often lack coherent policies on ethical AI use, assessment integrity, and data governance, indicating limited readiness to manage AI as a systemic pedagogical transformation. Similarly, Molina et al. (2024) emphasize that digital infrastructure and tools do not automatically translate into effective outcomes unless supported by institutional capacity for governance, monitoring, and adaptation.

At the human level, readiness gaps further complicate maturity assessments. Ali (2025) shows that faculty AI readiness varies considerably even within digitally mature institutions, suggesting that organizational maturity does not guarantee readiness at the level of academic practice. From the student perspective, Rahman et al. (2025) demonstrate that adoption of AI tools is shaped not only by access but also by perceived institutional trust and guidance, reinforcing the role of governance and communication in translating maturity into readiness.

Governance context also plays a critical role in shaping the relationship between maturity and readiness. Comparative analysis by Kundu and Bej (2025) illustrates how national policy environments influence institutional approaches to AI integration. In systems with strong centralized guidance, digital maturity may be achieved through compliance and standardization, while readiness depends on how institutions interpret and enact policies locally. Conversely, in more decentralized systems, maturity may develop unevenly, with readiness emerging through experimentation and institutional autonomy. These findings suggest that readiness is inherently contextual and cannot be inferred directly from maturity indicators alone.

Building on change management insights, readiness should therefore be understood as a dynamic governance capability rather than a static level of digital advancement. As shown in studies of AI driven organizational transformation, institutions that respond effectively to generative AI do not necessarily exhibit the highest levels of formal digital maturity, but rather the ability to align governance structures, human capabilities, and strategic intent in real time (Gering et al., 2025). Change management research further supports this view by highlighting that readiness emerges through iterative alignment between leadership, policy, and practice rather than through the accumulation of technological assets (Kotter and Cohen, 2014; Kang et al., 2022).

In this chapter, HEInnovate is therefore used as a foundational governance lens, not as a readiness model in itself. Its dimensions inform the Institutional Readiness Framework by identifying key organizational domains that matter for AI integrated hybrid education. However, the IRF extends beyond maturity assessment by focusing explicitly on how institutions activate, coordinate, and sustain these domains in response to AI driven pedagogical change. This distinction allows readiness to be conceptualized as an adaptive and developmental capacity, complementing rather than duplicating existing digital maturity frameworks.

2.3. Ethics, Equity, and Intercultural Governance of AI in Education

As artificial intelligence becomes increasingly embedded in hybrid education systems, ethical considerations move from the periphery of institutional decision making to its core. Ethical issues related to AI use in education are often discussed in terms of compliance, risk mitigation, or technical safeguards. However, such an approach is insufficient for addressing the systemic implications of AI for equity, inclusion, and cultural diversity. Institutional readiness for AI integrated hybrid education therefore requires a shift from viewing ethics as a set of rules to be enforced toward understanding ethics as a form of governance embedded in institutional structures, policies, and practices.

A governance oriented approach to AI ethics is strongly articulated in the work of UNESCO. UNESCO (2023) emphasizes that AI in education must be guided by principles of human rights, social justice, and cultural diversity, with particular attention to equity, transparency, and accountability. Rather than prescribing narrow technical standards, UNESCO frames ethical AI as a collective institutional responsibility involving policymakers, educational leaders, educators, learners, and technology providers. This perspective underscores that ethical readiness depends on an institution's capacity to anticipate social consequences, engage stakeholders, and adapt governance mechanisms as technologies evolve.

Framing ethics as governance highlights the importance of institutional agency in shaping how AI systems are selected, implemented, and evaluated. Decisions about data collection, algorithmic transparency, assessment practices, and learning analytics are not merely technical choices, but normative ones that reflect institutional values and priorities. Without explicit governance structures to guide these decisions, ethical principles risk remaining symbolic rather than operational. UNESCO's emphasis on participatory governance and context sensitivity is particularly relevant in higher education, where institutional missions and student populations are diverse and often internationally connected.

Scholarly work in AI in education further reinforces the need for a governance based ethical framework. Holmes et al. (2022) argue that ethical challenges in AI enabled learning environments cannot be addressed solely through compliance driven codes of conduct or technical fixes. Instead, they advocate for a community wide approach that integrates ethical reflection into the design, deployment, and evaluation of AI systems. Their framework highlights issues such as fairness, learner agency, explainability, and accountability as ongoing concerns that must be negotiated within institutional and professional communities.

Equity and intercultural considerations add further complexity to institutional readiness. AI systems used in education are often developed within specific cultural and linguistic contexts, which may not align with local pedagogical traditions or learner needs. UNESCO (2023) cautions that without deliberate governance attention, AI tools may reproduce existing inequalities or marginalize underrepresented groups through biased data, standardized pedagogical assumptions, or language limitations. Ethical readiness therefore requires institutions to critically evaluate whether AI applications support inclusive learning environments and respect cultural diversity, rather than assuming neutrality or universality.

From this perspective, ethics becomes inseparable from institutional governance capacity. Readiness involves the ability to establish clear ethical principles, translate them into policy and practice, and revisit them as technologies and contexts change. This includes developing institutional guidelines for AI use, mechanisms for stakeholder consultation, and processes for monitoring unintended consequences. Importantly, ethical readiness is not achieved once such measures are introduced, but is sustained through continuous institutional learning and reflection.

In this chapter, ethics, equity, and intercultural responsibility are therefore treated as integral components of institutional readiness rather than external constraints on innovation. By framing ethics as governance, the Institutional Readiness Framework positions ethical accountability as a dynamic and embedded organizational capability. This approach aligns ethical considerations with strategic decision making, reinforcing the argument that readiness for AI integrated hybrid education depends not only on what institutions can do technologically, but on how they govern change in ways that uphold educational values and social responsibility.

3. INSTITUTIONAL READINESS FRAMEWORK (IRF) FOR AI-INTEGRATED HYBRID EDUCATION

Institutional Readiness Framework (IRF) constitutes the central intellectual contribution of this chapter. The framework is designed to help higher education institutions assess, reflect on, and strengthen their capacity to implement AI-integrated hybrid education in ways that are strategic, ethical, inclusive, and sustainable. Unlike technology-centered maturity models, the IRF conceptualizes readiness as an organizational capability that emerges from the alignment of strategy, governance, people, infrastructure, and culture.

The IRF responds to a critical gap identified in both research and practice. While many institutions demonstrate high levels of digital adoption, fewer possess the institutional coherence required to govern AI as a pedagogical and organizational transformation. The framework therefore shifts attention from isolated initiatives toward systemic readiness, recognizing that AI integration reshapes institutional missions, professional roles, governance norms, and learning cultures.

3.1. Rationale and Design Principles of the Institutional Readiness Framework

The Institutional Readiness Framework is grounded in three design principles that reflect the realities of organizational change in higher education. These principles ensure that the framework supports reflection and capacity building rather than prescriptive evaluation.

Diagnostic Rather Than Ranking

The IRF is designed as a diagnostic framework rather than a ranking or benchmarking tool. It does not assign scores, maturity levels, or comparative labels to institutions. Ranking based approaches risk reducing complex organizational dynamics to simplified indicators and may encourage compliance oriented behavior rather than meaningful transformation.

Instead, the IRF enables institutions to identify strengths, gaps, and tensions across multiple readiness dimensions. It acknowledges that readiness may be uneven, with progress in some areas coexisting alongside constraints in others. This diagnostic orientation supports strategic prioritization and informed decision making without positioning readiness as a competitive outcome.

Context Sensitive

Institutional readiness is deeply shaped by contextual factors, including governance structures, regulatory environments, resource availability, institutional missions, and cultural norms. The IRF is therefore designed to be adaptable rather than universal.

Rather than prescribing fixed standards, the framework allows institutions to interpret each dimension in relation to their own strategic objectives and constraints. This context sensitivity is particularly important in global higher education systems, where institutions in emerging economies, teaching focused universities, and research intensive institutions face distinct readiness challenges. Readiness is thus understood as situated and relational, not transferable through standardized models.

Developmental and Process Oriented

The IRF conceptualizes readiness as a developmental process rather than a static state. Institutions are not expected to achieve readiness across all dimensions simultaneously. Instead, readiness evolves through experimentation, learning, and adaptation as institutions engage with AI-integrated hybrid education over time.

This developmental orientation encourages institutions to revisit readiness periodically, reflecting on how changes in technology, policy, and pedagogy reshape organizational needs. By framing readiness as an ongoing journey, the framework supports continuous institutional learning rather than one-time evaluation.

3.2. The Five Dimensions of Institutional Readiness

The Institutional Readiness Framework conceptualizes readiness for AI-integrated hybrid education as a multidimensional organizational capability. The five dimensions outlined below capture the strategic, governance, human, infrastructural, and cultural conditions required for sustainable and ethical AI integration. While analytically distinct, these dimensions are interdependent and must be understood as mutually reinforcing rather than sequential.

Figure 2. Institutional Readiness Framework for AI-Integrated Hybrid Education (Author's own work)

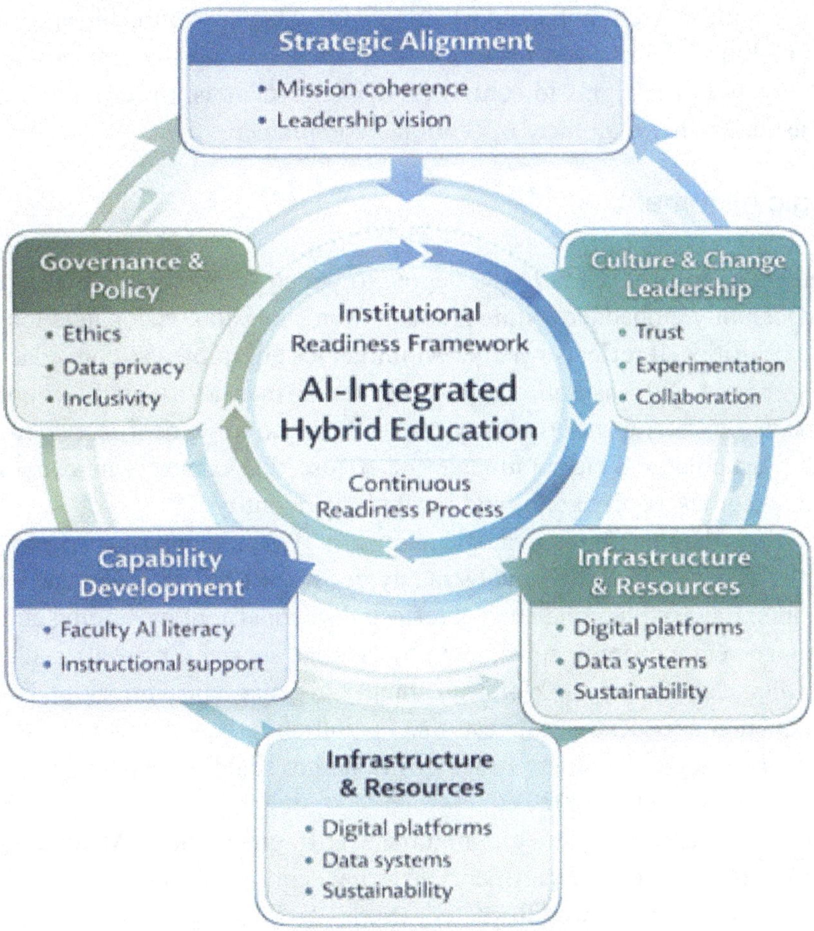

The Institutional Readiness Framework conceptualizes readiness for AI-integrated hybrid education as a multidimensional organizational capability. The five dimen-sions outlined below capture the strategic, governance, human, infrastructural, and cultural conditions required for sustainable and ethical AI integration. While analytically distinct, these dimensions are interdependent and must be understood as mutually reinforcing rather than sequential.

Institutional readiness is often incorrectly viewed as a top-down administrative task; however, true readiness requires "Student-in-the-Loop" governance. Students are not merely passive recipients of AI-driven personalization; they are active agents who must co-create the readiness ecosystem. Readiness in this domain involves the co-design of policies, where students are included in the drafting of Academic Integrity guidelines to ensure they are realistic and culturally sensitive. It also requires leveraging student "tech-ambassadors" to provide AI peer mentorship and bridging the digital divide. Ultimately, readiness includes educating students on their data sovereignty and their rights to contest AI-driven decisions, fostering a culture of "Data Justice" rather than mere institutional compliance.

Strategic Alignment

Strategic alignment refers to the degree to which AI-integrated hybrid education is coherently embedded within an institution's mission, vision, and long-term strategic priorities. It reflects whether AI initiatives are framed as core educational enablers aligned with institutional purpose, rather than as isolated technological experiments or short-term efficiency tools. Strategic alignment is evident when leadership articulates a clear rationale for AI use that connects innovation with learning outcomes, equity goals, and institutional identity.

Institutions demonstrating strategic alignment typically integrate AI and hybrid learning explicitly into institutional strategy documents and teaching and learning frameworks. Leadership coherence is reflected in consistent messaging across senior management, academic units, and professional services, as well as alignment between digital strategies, workforce planning, and pedagogical priorities. Evidence from global higher education suggests that institutions where AI adoption is guided by a shared strategic vision are better positioned to scale innovation and manage ethical risk (Molina et al., 2024).

A common barrier to strategic alignment is fragmentation. AI initiatives are often driven by individual departments, external vendors, or innovation units without institutional coordination. In such cases, leadership endorsement may remain rhetorical, with limited translation into resource allocation or policy support. This misalignment can result in pilot fatigue, duplication of effort, and limited institutional learning, undermining readiness despite high levels of experimentation.

Governance and Policy

Governance and policy readiness refers to an institution's capacity to regulate, guide, and oversee AI use through coherent and transparent frameworks that address ethics, data privacy, inclusivity, academic integrity, and accountability. This dimension captures the extent to which institutions move beyond ad hoc decision making toward systematic governance of AI-enabled educational practices.

Institutions with strong governance readiness typically establish institution-wide guidelines for ethical AI use, clarify responsibilities for data stewardship, and define accountability structures for decision making related to algorithmic systems. Such governance arrangements help legitimize AI use among faculty and students by reducing uncertainty and providing shared norms. Comparative policy research demonstrates that governance capacity is strongly shaped by national regulatory environments, but institutional interpretation and enactment remain critical determinants of readiness (Kundu and Bej, 2025).

Governance barriers often arise from policy lag, where AI technologies are adopted faster than institutional rules can be developed or updated. This can result in inconsistent practices, confusion regarding acceptable use, and heightened ethical risk. Conversely, overly restrictive governance may discourage pedagogical experimentation if policies are framed primarily in terms of risk avoidance rather than responsible innovation. Effective readiness therefore requires governance that is both principled and enabling (UNESCO, 2023; Holmes et al., 2022).

Capability Development

Capability development refers to the institution's ability to equip faculty and staff with the skills, knowledge, and pedagogical support required to integrate AI into hybrid teaching and learning in meaningful ways. This dimension emphasizes human capacity as a central component of readiness, recognizing that AI adoption ultimately depends on professional competence and confidence.

Empirical evidence highlights significant variation in faculty AI readiness within and across institutions. Ali (2025) shows that differences in AI literacy, pedagogical confidence, and perceived institutional support strongly influence educators' willingness to adopt AI tools. Institutions that invest in professional development, instructional design support, and peer learning communities are more likely to translate AI potential into pedagogical innovation. Capability development is further strengthened when AI-related teaching efforts are recognized within workload models and promotion criteria.

A key barrier to capability development is uneven engagement. Early adopters may advance rapidly while others remain hesitant or resistant, creating internal divides. Faculty may also perceive AI integration as an additional workload or a threat to professional autonomy if support structures are insufficient. Without sustained investment in human capability, even well-designed strategies and technologies are unlikely to produce lasting readiness.

Infrastructure and Resources

Infrastructure and resource readiness refers to the availability, quality, and sustainability of the technological and financial foundations that support AI-integrated hybrid education. This includes digital platforms, data systems, technical support, and long-term investment capacity.

Institutions demonstrating infrastructure readiness typically maintain reliable learning management systems, secure data architectures, and access to AI-enabled tools that are interoperable and scalable. Sustainable funding models and dedicated support units further enable institutions to move beyond short-term pilots toward institutionalized practice. Global analyses indicate that infrastructure readiness is a necessary but insufficient condition for effective AI integration, as its impact depends on alignment with governance and human capability (Molina et al., 2024).

Barriers in this dimension often relate to resource asymmetry and sustainability. Institutions may rely on project-based funding or external vendors without long-term planning, leading to fragmentation and dependency. Challenges related to system interoperability, escalating maintenance costs, and data security can further constrain readiness, particularly in resource-limited contexts.

Culture and Change Leadership

Culture and change leadership refer to the extent to which institutional norms, values, and leadership practices support trust, experimentation, collaboration, and shared ownership of change. This dimension captures the social and relational foundations of readiness, which shape how AI initiatives are perceived and enacted across the institution.

Institutions with strong cultural readiness foster open dialogue about AI, encourage experimentation without fear of punitive consequences, and promote collaboration across academic and professional boundaries. Leadership plays a crucial role in building trust by communicating transparently about AI use, addressing concerns related to surveillance or job displacement, and involving stakeholders in decision making. Studies of AI-driven organizational transformation indicate that adaptive and participatory leadership is a key differentiator between superficial adoption and sustained readiness (Gering et al., 2025; Kotter and Cohen, 2014).

Cultural barriers are often the most persistent. Change fatigue, lack of trust, and fear of loss of professional autonomy can undermine engagement even when strategic and technical conditions are favorable. Research in higher education change management shows that without inclusive leadership and opportunities for collective sense making, resistance may become entrenched, limiting institutional learning and adaptation (Kang et al., 2022; Al Sabbagh and Elgeddawy, 2025).

3.3. Practical Application: The IRF Readiness Diagnostic Checklist

To transition the Institutional Readiness Framework (IRF) from a theoretical construct into an actionable organizational management tool, it is necessary to operationalize its five dimensions through a systematic evaluative process. While the framework is intentionally designed to be diagnostic and developmental rather than a prescriptive ranking system, institutional leaders require concrete markers to assess their baseline capabilities and identify systemic gaps (HEInnovate, 2023; Deogaonkar, 2025). This process of "readiness auditing" allows for the identification of misalignments between technological ambition and organizational reality, ensuring that AI integration is grounded in the institution's unique sociocultural and strategic context (Gering et al., 2025; Karan & Angadi, 2025). The following diagnostic synthesis translates the conceptual dimensions of the IRF into strategic inquiries designed for higher education administrators and governance committees.

At the level of Strategic Alignment, readiness is determined by the degree to which AI initiatives are coherently embedded within the institution's core mission rather than operating as isolated experiments. Leaders must critically evaluate whether the institutional mission statement and long-term strategic plans explicitly articulate a pedagogical and ethical rationale for digital transformation (Capano et al., 2025; Nguyen et al., 2025). This involves ensuring that there is a dedicated, sustainable budget allocated specifically for AI experimentation and capability building distinct from standard IT maintenance and that senior leadership communications consistently link AI adoption to broader educational goals such as equity and enhanced learning outcomes to prevent strategic fragmentation (Al Sabbagh & Elgeddawy, 2025; Deogaonkar, 2025).

In the domain of Ethical Governance, readiness requires moving beyond mere legal compliance toward a proactive framework for community-wide accountability (Holmes et al., 2022). A ready institution is characterized by the establishment of multidisciplinary AI ethics committees that include technical experts, ethicists, and student representatives (Schiff, 2022). Furthermore, governance maturity is evidenced by the existence of transparent, "plain-language" guidelines that demystify acceptable generative AI use for students, thereby safeguarding academic integrity while mitigating ambiguity in a rapidly shifting policy landscape (Kundu & Bej, 2025; Nguyen et al., 2025). This also necessitates established protocols for verifying the algorithmic transparency and data privacy standards of third-party educational technology vendors prior to procurement (Molina et al., 2024).

Regarding Capability Development, or Human Capacity, the IRF posits that AI adoption ultimately depends on the professional competence and psychological readiness of the academic workforce (Ali, 2025; Verano-Tacoronte et al., 2025). Institutions must diagnose whether they provide a tiered, ongoing professional development program that addresses both foundational AI literacy and advanced pedagogical integration (Hoang, 2025; Liu, 2025). A key indicator of readiness in this area is the formal identification of "AI Champions" or digital leaders within non-STEM disciplines to lead context-sensitive, peer-to-peer training (Harsanti et al., 2025; Hoang, 2025). Moreover, readiness is signaled when faculty efforts to redesign curricula for the AI era are formally recognized and incentivized within institutional workload models and promotion criteria (Tursunbayeva, 2024).

The Technological Infrastructure dimension requires a shift toward interoperable and secure data architectures that support long-term pedagogical objectives (Roll et al., 2021). Institutional leaders should evaluate whether the university possesses a centralized data architecture that facilitates cross-departmental analytics while strictly adhering to data sovereignty and student privacy regulations (Kuleto et al., 2021; UNESCO, 2023). Readiness also involves assessing the scalability of currently deployed AI-enabled platforms and learning management systems, ensuring that the institution is not overly reliant on precarious, short-term project funding that might compromise the continuity of the digital learning environment (Sârb, 2024).

Finally, the Organizational Culture of a ready institution is defined by trust, shared ownership, and a commitment to psychological safety during periods of uncertainty (Ng, 2025). This is operationalized through protocols that encourage faculty to pilot AI tools and transparently report pedagogical failures without fear of punitive consequences (Kang et al., 2022). Institutional readiness further demands inclusive forums where the impact of AI on faculty autonomy and student belonging can be openly negotiated (KPMG LLP, 2025). By integrating student voices particularly regarding their perceptions of usefulness and adoption behaviors the institution ensures that its digital transformation is not merely a technical exercise but a relational journey grounded in organizational capability and ethical responsibility (Homer et al., 2025; Rahman et al., 2025).

4. CHANGE MANAGEMENT PATHWAYS FOR AI AND HYBRID TRANSFORMATION

Institutional readiness for AI-integrated hybrid education does not emerge instantaneously; it develops through iterative processes of negotiation, learning, and adaptation. Even institutions with strong strategic intent and technological capacity often encounter resistance as AI reshapes professional identities, pedagogical norms, and governance arrangements. Understanding and addressing these sources of resistance is therefore a central component of change management.

This section conceptualizes change management pathways as dynamic processes through which institutions move from initial experimentation to sustained integration. Rather than treating resistance as a deficit or failure, the chapter frames it as a diagnostic signal that reveals misalignments between institutional structures, professional values, and emerging technological practices. By addressing resistance explicitly, institutions can transform tension into a resource for organizational learning and capacity building.

4.1. Sources of Institutional Resistance

Resistance to AI-integrated hybrid education arises from multiple sources operating at individual, organizational, and systemic levels. While technological challenges are often foregrounded, research consistently shows that resistance is more strongly shaped by human, cultural, and governance factors. Three recurrent sources of resistance are particularly salient in higher education contexts: concerns over faculty autonomy, digital fatigue, and policy uncertainty.

Faculty autonomy remains a central axis of resistance in AI-driven transformation. Academic work is historically grounded in professional discretion, disciplinary expertise, and pedagogical independence. The introduction of AI tools into teaching, assessment, and curriculum design can therefore be perceived as encroaching on professional judgment or standardizing pedagogical practices. Empirical studies reveal that faculty anxiety is not primarily rooted in technical incapacity, but in concerns about loss of control, deskilling, and diminished academic identity. Verano-Tacoronte et al. (2025) show that uncertainty around generative AI, particularly tools such as ChatGPT, heightens anxiety among university teachers when institutional expectations are unclear or perceived as top-down mandates. Similarly, Liu (2025) demonstrates that confidence and perceived readiness mediate faculty adoption of AI, suggesting that resistance often reflects psychological and professional concerns rather than outright opposition to innovation.

From a change management perspective, resistance related to autonomy signals the need for participatory governance and co-design. When faculty are positioned as passive recipients of AI initiatives rather than active contributors, resistance is likely to intensify. Conversely, institutions that frame AI as augmentative rather than substitutive of academic work are more likely to cultivate engagement and trust (Kuleto et al., 2021). Addressing autonomy concerns therefore requires leadership approaches that respect disciplinary differences and recognize professional expertise as central to AI integration.

A second major source of resistance is digital fatigue, particularly in post-pandemic higher education environments. The rapid expansion of online and hybrid learning during the COVID-19 period accelerated digital adoption but also generated exhaustion among educators and students. As institutions shift from emergency digitalization to strategic AI integration, many stakeholders experience change saturation, perceiving AI initiatives as an additional burden rather than a meaningful improvement. Student-focused research in Southeast Asia highlights that acceptance of AI technologies is strongly influenced by perceived usefulness and effort expectancy, both of which decline when digital overload is high (Homer et al., 2025). These findings align with broader adoption studies showing that readiness is contingent on whether individuals perceive technological change as supportive of their goals rather than disruptive.

Digital fatigue also interacts with organizational rhythms and workload structures. When AI initiatives are layered onto existing responsibilities without adjustments to time allocation, training, or support, resistance may manifest as disengagement or superficial compliance. Studies of school and university readiness indicate that digital readiness alone does not predict adoption unless supported by leadership practices that manage pace, sequencing, and workload expectations (Karan and Angadi, 2025; Harsanti et al., 2025). Change management pathways must therefore account for temporal and emotional dimensions of readiness, not only technical capacity.

A third source of resistance lies in policy uncertainty and governance ambiguity. In many institutions, AI adoption has outpaced the development of clear policies on data use, assessment integrity, intellectual property, and ethical responsibility. This lack of clarity creates risk aversion among faculty and administrators, who may avoid experimentation to protect themselves from potential compliance or reputational consequences. Comparative research demonstrates that uncertainty regarding acceptable AI use is a significant inhibitor of adoption, particularly in contexts where national or institutional guidelines are fragmented or evolving (Kuleto et al., 2021).

Policy uncertainty is further exacerbated when institutional leadership communicates inconsistent messages about AI. Deogaonkar (2025) finds that digital leadership and strategic resource allocation play a critical role in shaping institutional readiness, particularly in post-pandemic contexts. Where leadership signals commitment without providing policy clarity or resource support, resistance may emerge as skepticism rather than overt opposition. This underscores the importance of aligning governance development with change communication, ensuring that policies are framed as enabling responsible experimentation rather than merely enforcing compliance.

These sources of resistance highlight that readiness is not simply a function of willingness to adopt AI, but of institutional capacity to manage change in ways that respect professional identity, address fatigue, and reduce uncertainty. Effective change management pathways therefore require institutions to engage resistance explicitly, using it as a diagnostic lens to identify misalignments and recalibrate strategy, governance, and support structures accordingly.

4.2. A Three-Phase Change Pathway for AI and Hybrid Transformation

Institutional readiness for AI-integrated hybrid education develops through a gradual and iterative change process rather than a single moment of adoption. Evidence from higher education systems suggests that successful transformation unfolds across identifiable phases, each associated with distinct leadership tasks, stakeholder concerns, and organizational learning dynamics. Drawing on change management theory and empirical studies on AI adoption in education, a three-phase pathway can be observed: sense-making and trust building, pilot innovation and feedback loops, and institutionalization and scaling.

Phase 1: Sense-Making and Trust Building

The initial phase of AI and hybrid transformation is characterized by sense-making, during which institutions seek to interpret the meaning, implications, and legitimacy of AI within their educational mission. At this stage, uncertainty is high, and perceptions of AI are shaped as much by narratives and emotions as by technical understanding. Faculty concerns regarding professional autonomy, assessment integrity, and surveillance are particularly salient, while students may express ambivalence shaped by perceived usefulness and trust in institutional guidance (Verano-Tacoronte et al., 2025; Homer et al., 2025).

Research consistently shows that readiness at this stage is strongly influenced by confidence, perceived institutional support, and clarity of purpose. Studies of faculty AI adoption indicate that educators' willingness to engage with AI tools depends not only on technical competence but also on whether they perceive AI as aligned with pedagogical values and institutional priorities (Ali, 2025; Liu, 2025). Similarly, student adoption is moderated by institutional signals regarding appropriate use, ethical boundaries, and learning expectations (Rahman et al., 2025).

Leadership plays a central role in this phase by framing AI as a shared institutional concern rather than a managerial mandate. Effective sense-making involves transparent communication, acknowledgment of uncertainty, and opportunities for dialogue across academic and professional groups. Rather than promoting AI as inevitable or disruptive, leaders who emphasize agency, experimentation, and ethical responsibility are more likely to foster trust and psychological safety. This emphasis on trust building aligns with change leadership research, which highlights the importance of emotional engagement and shared understanding in the early stages of transformation (Kotter and Cohen, 2014; Kang et al., 2022).

Phase 2: Pilot Innovation and Feedback Loops

Once a basic level of trust and shared understanding is established, institutions typically move into a phase of pilot innovation. This stage involves small-scale experimentation with AI-enabled tools and hybrid pedagogies within controlled contexts, such as specific courses, programs, or support units. The purpose of piloting is not rapid scaling, but learning: identifying pedagogical value, surfacing ethical concerns, and understanding organizational implications.

Empirical studies suggest that pilot initiatives are most effective when accompanied by structured feedback loops that include faculty, students, instructional designers, and governance actors. Faculty readiness research demonstrates that hands-on experimentation, supported by peer learning and instructional design expertise, significantly enhances confidence and pedagogical integration of AI (Ali, 2025; Al Sabbagh and Elgeddawy, 2025). From the student perspective, perceived usefulness and responsiveness to feedback increase acceptance of AI-supported learning environments (Rahman et al., 2025).

At this stage, institutions begin translating abstract principles into operational practices. Governance frameworks are tested, ethical guidelines are refined, and support structures are adjusted based on lived experience. Comparative policy research shows that institutions operating in diverse regulatory environments often rely on pilot projects as a means of localizing national or international AI principles into contextually appropriate practices (Kundu and Bej, 2025). This iterative adaptation reflects a broader pattern observed in digitally transforming universities, where experimentation precedes formalization (Gering et al., 2025).

However, this phase also carries risks. Without clear boundaries and learning mechanisms, pilot initiatives may remain isolated, reinforcing fragmentation rather than readiness. Change management research emphasizes that pilot innovation must be intentionally connected to institutional learning processes, ensuring that insights inform strategy, policy, and capability development rather than remaining confined to innovation enclaves (Kang et al., 2022; Tursunbayeva, 2024).

Phase 3: Institutionalization and Scaling

The final phase involves the gradual institutionalization and scaling of AI-integrated hybrid practices. At this point, AI moves from experimental activity toward normalized practice embedded within institutional systems, policies, and cultures. Institutionalization does not imply uniform adoption across all contexts, but rather the establishment of stable structures that support responsible and adaptive use over time.

Evidence from global higher education suggests that scaling is most sustainable when supported by aligned governance, resourcing, and leadership practices. Digital leadership research highlights the importance of strategic resource allocation and coordination across units in consolidating transformation gains (Deogaonkar, 2025). Similarly, studies of AI-driven organizational transformation emphasize that scaling requires integration into existing quality assurance processes, professional development pathways, and decision-making routines (Gering et al., 2025).

Importantly, institutionalization also involves ethical normalization. As Holmes et al. (2022) argue, ethical AI in education cannot rely solely on initial compliance measures but must be embedded into everyday professional judgment and institutional accountability structures. This requires ongoing review of data practices, transparency mechanisms, and inclusivity outcomes as AI systems evolve. At the same time, institutions must remain attentive to change fatigue and inequitable workload distribution, which can undermine long-term readiness if not addressed (Kuleto et al., 2021).

Rather than representing an endpoint, institutionalization marks a transition toward continuous adaptation. As AI technologies, regulatory expectations, and pedagogical models continue to change, institutions must revisit earlier phases of sense-making and experimentation. In this way, the three-phase pathway should be understood as cyclical rather than linear, reinforcing the view of readiness as an ongoing developmental process rather than a final state.

4.3. Leadership Roles in Sustaining Readiness

Leadership plays a decisive role in sustaining institutional readiness for AI-integrated hybrid education beyond initial adoption phases. While strategy, governance, and infrastructure establish the formal conditions for readiness, leadership practices determine whether these conditions are translated into shared commitment, trust, and continuous organizational learning. In contexts characterized by uncertainty, ethical ambiguity, and rapid technological change, readiness depends less on directive authority and more on how leaders communicate, involve stakeholders, and distribute responsibility across the institution.

Communication as Sense-Giving Rather Than Promotion

Effective leadership communication in AI and hybrid transformation is not limited to promoting innovation or announcing new initiatives. Instead, it involves sustained sense-giving that helps faculty, staff, and students understand why AI is being introduced, how it aligns with educational values, and what implications it holds for professional roles and learning practices. Research consistently shows that anxiety and resistance surrounding AI adoption are closely linked to uncertainty and perceived loss of control (Verano-Tacoronte et al., 2025; Liu, 2025).

Leaders who sustain readiness communicate transparently about both opportunities and risks, acknowledging ethical concerns, limitations of AI systems, and unresolved questions. Such communication fosters trust by signaling that AI integration is not being imposed as a technical inevitability, but approached as a collective institutional choice. Empirical studies in higher education suggest that when leadership narratives frame AI as a pedagogical support rather than a replacement for academic judgment, faculty confidence and willingness to engage increase significantly (Ali, 2025; Homer et al., 2025).

Importantly, communication must be continuous rather than episodic. As AI tools evolve and policies adapt, leaders play a critical role in updating institutional narratives, clarifying expectations, and reinforcing shared purpose. In this sense, communication sustains readiness by stabilizing meaning amid ongoing change.

Participation and Co-Creation of Change

Sustaining readiness also depends on the extent to which leadership enables meaningful participation in AI and hybrid transformation. Higher education institutions are characterized by professional autonomy and distributed expertise, making participatory approaches particularly important. Studies of AI adoption consistently indicate that faculty and staff are more likely to engage when they perceive AI initiatives as co-created rather than imposed (Al Sabbagh and Elgeddawy, 2025; Harsanti et al., 2025).

Participatory leadership practices include involving academic staff in the design of AI use guidelines, inviting feedback from students on AI supported learning experiences, and creating cross functional working groups that bridge academic, technical, and administrative perspectives. Such practices not only improve the quality of decision making, but also contribute to psychological ownership of change. Evidence from organizational change research suggests that participation mitigates resistance by transforming AI adoption from an external demand into a shared institutional project (Kang et al., 2022; Tursunbayeva, 2024).

Participation is particularly important in addressing ethical and intercultural dimensions of AI use. When institutions create spaces for dialogue around fairness, inclusivity, and cultural relevance, ethical governance becomes embedded in everyday practice rather than confined to formal policy documents. This participatory approach aligns with broader recommendations for community-based ethical governance of AI in education (Holmes et al., 2022; UNESCO, 2023).

Distributed Leadership and Collective Capability

Finally, sustaining readiness requires a shift from centralized leadership toward distributed leadership models. AI-integrated hybrid education spans teaching, assessment, student support, data governance, and infrastructure, making it unrealistic for readiness to be sustained solely through senior leadership roles. Instead, readiness is reinforced when leadership is enacted across multiple levels of the institution, including department heads, program leaders, instructional designers, and digitally skilled faculty.

Research on strategic responses to generative AI shows that institutions demonstrating sustained readiness rely on networks of internal champions who translate strategic intent into local practice (Gering et al., 2025). These actors play a mediating role, adapting institutional goals to disciplinary contexts and supporting peers through informal mentoring and experimentation. Distributed leadership thus enhances institutional learning by allowing innovation to emerge from practice while remaining aligned with overarching strategy.

From a practical perspective, distributed leadership involves recognizing and legitimizing these roles through workload allocation, professional recognition, and access to decision making forums. Digital leadership research further suggests that when resource allocation and authority are aligned with distributed leadership structures, institutions are better able to sustain AI readiness over time (Deogaonkar, 2025). Without such alignment, readiness risks becoming dependent on individual enthusiasm rather than institutional capability.

Together, communication, participation, and distributed leadership form a reinforcing set of leadership practices that sustain readiness beyond initial transformation phases. By fostering shared understanding, collective ownership, and locally embedded leadership, institutions can maintain adaptive capacity in the face of evolving AI technologies. Sustaining readiness, therefore, is less about controlling change and more about enabling conditions under which institutions continue to learn, adjust, and act responsibly.

5. COMPARATIVE INSIGHTS FROM GLOBAL AND EMERGING CONTEXTS

5.1. Digitally Mature Systems: The UK and Finland

Digitally mature education systems provide valuable insight into how institutional readiness for AI-integrated hybrid education can be cultivated over time. However, maturity should not be conflated with completeness or universal applicability. Examining contexts such as the United Kingdom and Finland is useful not because they represent ideal models, but because they illustrate how policy coherence, ethical governance, and institutional learning can evolve through sustained engagement with digital transformation.

In both contexts, readiness for AI in education has emerged gradually, shaped by long-standing investments in digital education, professional autonomy, and public sector governance. Rather than pursuing rapid technological expansion, these systems have emphasized alignment between national policy, institutional governance, and pedagogical values. This alignment has created conditions under which AI integration is framed as an extension of educational purpose rather than a disruptive add-on.

In the United Kingdom, AI governance in education has developed through a combination of sector-level guidance, institutional autonomy, and professional debate. Universities operate within a relatively flexible regulatory environment that allows experimentation, yet this flexibility is balanced by increasing attention to ethics, academic integrity, and data governance. Nguyen et al. (2025) show that UK policy discourse around generative AI has moved from broad organizing visions toward more explicit institutional guidelines, reflecting a shift from exploration to normalization. This transition has required universities to clarify acceptable use, redesign assessment practices, and articulate ethical boundaries, rather than relying solely on individual discretion.

What is notable in the UK context is not the presence of uniform rules, but the way governance capacity is distributed across institutions. Readiness is supported by internal policy mechanisms, cross-functional committees, and professional development structures that enable institutions to interpret national guidance in locally meaningful ways. This reinforces the idea that institutional readiness depends less on centralized control than on the ability to translate policy signals into coherent institutional practice.

Finland presents a different but equally instructive trajectory. Finnish education policy has long emphasized equity, trust, and teacher professionalism, which has shaped the way digital and AI technologies are approached. As Sârb (2024) documents, Finland's digital education evolution has been characterized by incremental development, strong public sector coordination, and sustained investment in teacher capacity. AI integration is framed not primarily as a productivity tool, but as a means of supporting inclusive, learner-centered education.

In Finland, ethical considerations are embedded early in policy design rather than introduced as corrective measures. This approach aligns with broader Nordic governance traditions that prioritize transparency, social trust, and public accountability. The result is a form of institutional readiness in which ethical governance is not experienced as external regulation, but as an extension of professional norms. However, this does not imply the absence of tension. Finnish institutions continue to grapple with questions of data use, algorithmic transparency, and the balance between innovation and equity, particularly as commercial AI tools become more prominent.

Across both contexts, several common patterns emerge. First, digitally mature systems tend to treat AI integration as a governance challenge as much as a technological one. Policy coherence does not eliminate uncertainty, but it provides institutions with interpretive frameworks that reduce ambiguity and support coordinated action. Second, readiness is sustained through professional capacity building rather than technological acceleration alone. Investments in teacher education, institutional support units, and reflective practice are central to maintaining alignment over time.

Importantly, these cases also reveal the limits of transferability. The governance capacity, resource base, and cultural conditions that support readiness in the UK and Finland cannot be assumed elsewhere. As Roll et al. (2021) caution, AI in education is deeply shaped by institutional context, disciplinary traditions, and socio-political environments. Attempting to replicate policy instruments or governance structures without attending to these conditions risks superficial adoption without substantive readiness.

For institutions in less digitally mature or resource-constrained contexts, the relevance of these cases lies not in emulation, but in principle. The UK and Finland demonstrate that institutional readiness is strengthened when AI integration is approached as a long-term, values-driven process, supported by governance mechanisms that encourage learning, dialogue, and adaptation. These insights provide a comparative lens through which other systems can reflect on their own readiness trajectories, without assuming convergence toward a single model of AI-integrated hybrid education.

5.2. Adaptive and Emerging Contexts: Singapore and Vietnam

While digitally mature systems illustrate how long-term policy coherence can support institutional readiness, adaptive and emerging contexts reveal how readiness develops under conditions of strong state steering, uneven institutional capacity, and constrained resources. Singapore and Vietnam provide instructive contrasts in this regard. Both countries have articulated national ambitions around digital transformation and artificial intelligence, yet institutions operate within different governance traditions, levels of autonomy, and readiness baselines. Examining these contexts highlights how institutional readiness is shaped not only by resources, but by governance arrangements, leadership practices, and cultural mediation.

Singapore: State Steering and Strategic Coherence

Singapore represents a highly coordinated policy environment in which AI and digital transformation are strongly shaped by state vision and long-term planning. National education strategies emphasize lifelong learning, adaptability, and skills renewal in response to economic uncertainty and technological disruption (Ng, 2025). Within this context, higher education institutions operate with relatively clear policy direction, benefiting from alignment between national AI strategies, education policy, and workforce development priorities.

Comparative analyses of AI policy show that Singapore has developed comparatively coherent frameworks linking ethical considerations, innovation goals, and capacity development, particularly in contrast to more fragmented systems (Kundu and Bej, 2025; Capano et al., 2025). This coherence supports institutional readiness by reducing uncertainty and providing legitimacy for AI integration initiatives. Institutions are able to frame AI-enhanced hybrid education as a strategic response to national priorities rather than as isolated institutional experiments.

However, strong state steering also shapes the nature of institutional readiness. While policy clarity supports strategic alignment and governance readiness, it may limit bottom-up experimentation if institutions rely heavily on compliance rather than institutional learning. Research on Asian higher education policy cautions that AI adoption in such contexts risks prioritizing implementation speed over pedagogical reflection, unless institutions actively cultivate internal capability and change leadership (Schiff, 2022; Molina et al., 2024). Readiness in Singapore therefore depends not only on policy coherence, but on the ability of institutional leaders to translate national visions into locally meaningful practices that engage faculty and students.

Empirical studies of technology adoption in Southeast Asia suggest that faculty and student readiness remains a critical mediating factor. Acceptance of AI tools is influenced by perceived usefulness, confidence, and institutional support rather than policy mandates alone (Ali, 2025; Rahman et al., 2025). This underscores that even in highly steered systems, institutional readiness must be actively developed across the human and cultural dimensions of the IRF.

Vietnam: Innovation under Constraint

Vietnam presents a contrasting adaptive context characterized by rapid digitalization, expanding higher education participation, and uneven institutional capacity. National policy discourse increasingly emphasizes digital transformation and AI, yet regulatory frameworks and institutional resources remain in development (Molina et al., 2024; Capano et al., 2025). As a result, institutional readiness for AI-integrated hybrid education often emerges through localized innovation rather than systemic alignment.

Empirical evidence from Vietnam highlights significant variation in AI adoption and readiness across institutions and disciplines. Studies of AI-based learning behaviors indicate that students' engagement with AI tools is shaped by digital literacy, learning culture, and perceived relevance, rather than uniform institutional guidance (Duong et al., 2025). Similarly, research on Vietnamese teachers points to the central role of digital and e-leadership in mediating AI integration, particularly in the absence of robust institutional support structures (Hoang, 2025).

Cultural and contextual factors further shape readiness. Research on AI-enhanced education in Southeast Asia emphasizes the importance of cultural integration, pedagogical traditions, and relational norms in shaping how AI tools are interpreted and used (Payadnya et al., 2025). In Vietnam, where respect for teacher authority and examination-oriented practices remain influential, AI adoption may generate tensions related to autonomy, assessment integrity, and trust. These dynamics reinforce the importance of governance and culture as readiness dimensions, even where technological access is improving.

From a change management perspective, Vietnam illustrates how readiness develops incrementally through experimentation and informal networks rather than formalized strategies. Institutions often rely on motivated individuals or small units to pilot AI-supported practices, creating pockets of readiness that may or may not scale. Research on organizational change in higher education suggests that such bottom-up innovation can be a strength if supported by adaptive leadership and learning-oriented governance, but a liability if left disconnected from institutional strategy (Kotter and Cohen, 2014; Kang et al., 2022; Gering et al., 2025).

Implications for Transferability

Comparing Singapore and Vietnam demonstrates that institutional readiness cannot be reduced to a single developmental pathway. In Singapore, readiness is facilitated by policy coherence and state coordination, yet depends on institutional capacity to foster participation and pedagogical ownership. In Vietnam, readiness emerges under constraint, shaped by uneven resources, cultural mediation, and leadership at the meso and micro levels.

These cases reinforce the value of the Institutional Readiness Framework as a context-sensitive diagnostic rather than a prescriptive model. Strategic alignment, governance, capability development, infrastructure, and culture manifest differently across these settings, but each remains essential. Transferability therefore lies not in replicating policy instruments or institutional designs, but in applying the IRF to surface locally relevant readiness challenges and pathways.

By foregrounding adaptation rather than convergence, the framework allows institutions in diverse contexts to recognize readiness as a developmental process shaped by governance conditions, cultural norms, and leadership practices. This perspective avoids universalist claims while offering a structured lens through which institutions can navigate AI-integrated hybrid education in ways that are both locally grounded and globally informed.

5.3. What These Cases Reveal About Institutional Readiness

Taken together, the comparative insights from digitally mature systems and adaptive or emerging contexts reveal that institutional readiness for AI-integrated hybrid education is neither linear nor uniform. Instead, readiness is shaped by the interaction between governance structures, cultural mediation, and the alignment or misalignment between policy intent and institutional practice. These cases underscore that readiness cannot be inferred solely from levels of technological advancement or regulatory sophistication, but must be understood as a situated and negotiated organizational capability.

Governance Diversity and Path-Dependent Readiness

One of the most salient insights across contexts is the diversity of governance arrangements shaping AI readiness. Digitally mature systems such as Finland and the United Kingdom demonstrate high levels of policy coherence, ethical framing, and institutional autonomy, enabling universities to interpret national AI strategies in ways that align with institutional missions and pedagogical traditions (Nguyen et al., 2025; Sârb, 2024). In these settings, readiness is often supported by stable governance frameworks that provide clarity without prescribing uniform implementation models.

By contrast, adaptive and emerging contexts such as Singapore and Vietnam illustrate more centralized and state-steered approaches, where national strategies play a stronger role in shaping institutional priorities (Capano et al., 2025; Kundu and Bej, 2025). While such governance structures can accelerate infrastructure development and policy alignment, they may also constrain institutional flexibility, particularly when local capacity or professional readiness lags behind policy ambition. These differences highlight that readiness evolves along path-dependent trajectories shaped by historical governance traditions, rather than converging toward a single model.

Cultural Mediation of AI Integration

Across all contexts, cultural factors emerge as a critical mediator of readiness. The cases demonstrate that AI tools are never pedagogically neutral; they are interpreted, adapted, and sometimes resisted through local educational values, professional norms, and learner expectations. Research from Southeast Asia shows that educators' and students' willingness to engage with AI is strongly influenced by cultural understandings of authority, assessment, and the role of technology in learning (Payadnya et al., 2025; Duong et al., 2025).

In digitally mature systems, cultural mediation often takes the form of deliberate ethical reflection and participatory dialogue, enabling institutions to negotiate tensions between innovation and academic integrity (Roll et al., 2021). In emerging contexts, cultural mediation may be more implicit, with educators adapting AI use pragmatically within existing pedagogical traditions rather than through formal ethical frameworks (Hoang, 2025). These patterns reinforce the argument that institutional readiness depends not only on governance and resources, but also on the capacity to translate AI into culturally meaningful educational practices.

Persistent Policy-Practice Gaps

A third recurring theme across cases is the persistence of policy–practice gaps. Even in systems with well-articulated AI strategies and ethical guidelines, institutional implementation often lags behind policy intent. Faculty readiness, student confidence, and organizational capability frequently emerge as limiting factors, shaping how policies are enacted on the ground (Ali, 2025; Rahman et al., 2025).

In emerging contexts, these gaps are often amplified by resource constraints and uneven professional development, leading to selective or informal adoption of AI tools despite ambitious national visions (Molina et al., 2024). In digitally mature systems, gaps may manifest in subtler ways, such as inconsistent faculty engagement or uncertainty around acceptable pedagogical uses of generative AI. Across contexts, these dynamics suggest that readiness cannot be achieved through policy design alone, but requires sustained investment in institutional learning, capability development, and change leadership.

Implications for the Institutional Readiness Framework

Collectively, these cases reinforce the central premise of the Institutional Readiness Framework: readiness for AI-integrated hybrid education is multidimensional, context-sensitive, and developmental. Governance diversity demonstrates that there is no single pathway to readiness. Cultural mediation highlights the importance of aligning AI integration with local educational values. Persistent policy–practice gaps underscore the need to view readiness as an ongoing organizational process rather than a compliance outcome.

Rather than identifying transferable best practices, the comparative analysis illustrates transferable questions for institutions to ask: How do governance structures enable or constrain ethical experimentation? How are AI tools culturally interpreted by educators and learners? Where do policy ambitions outpace institutional capacity? By foregrounding these questions, the framework supports institutions in navigating AI transformation in ways that are reflective, adaptive, and aligned with their specific contexts.

6. EVALUATING AND BENCHMARKING INSTITUTIONAL READINESS

As artificial intelligence becomes embedded in hybrid education, the question facing institutional leaders is no longer whether AI should be adopted, but how readiness for its sustained and responsible use can be understood, monitored, and strengthened over time. Evaluation and benchmarking play a critical role in this process, not as mechanisms of control or ranking, but as tools for reflection, strategic planning, and organizational learning. This section outlines how institutional readiness can be assessed in ways that support development rather than compliance, drawing on the Institutional Readiness Framework as a guiding structure.

6.1. Why Readiness Assessment Matters

Readiness assessment matters because AI-integrated hybrid education introduces risks and opportunities that extend beyond technology. Institutions that invest heavily in digital tools without understanding their organizational readiness often encounter unintended consequences, including faculty resistance, ethical controversy, uneven student experiences, and policy incoherence. Evidence from global higher education suggests that gaps between technological adoption and institutional capacity are a major source of implementation failure (Molina et al., 2024; KPMG LLP, 2025).

From a leadership perspective, readiness assessment provides a structured way to surface misalignments between strategy, governance, human capability, and culture. Rather than assuming readiness based on infrastructure or usage metrics, institutions benefit from examining whether AI initiatives are supported by coherent policies, professional development, and shared norms. Research on faculty AI readiness demonstrates that even technologically advanced institutions may struggle to integrate AI pedagogically when confidence, trust, and institutional support are weak (Ali, 2025; Verano-Tacoronte et al., 2025).

Readiness assessment is also essential for navigating policy uncertainty. Comparative studies show that higher education institutions operate within diverse regulatory environments, where national AI policies may be evolving, fragmented, or ambiguous (Kundu and Bej, 2025; Capano et al., 2025). In such contexts, institutional assessment helps leaders anticipate governance gaps and align internal practices with emerging external expectations. Importantly, assessment supports proactive rather than reactive governance, enabling institutions to identify risks before they escalate into crises.

Finally, readiness assessment matters because AI adoption is not static. Faculty confidence, student acceptance, and ethical expectations change over time as technologies evolve. Longitudinal assessment allows institutions to track developmental progress, revisit assumptions, and recalibrate strategies, reinforcing readiness as an ongoing organizational capability rather than a one-time achievement (Kotter and Cohen, 2014; Kang et al., 2022).

6.2. Diagnostic Indicators Across IRF Dimensions

To remain aligned with its diagnostic and developmental orientation, the Institutional Readiness Framework does not prescribe standardized instruments or scoring systems. Instead, it encourages the use of indicative markers that help institutions reflect on their current position across the five readiness dimensions.

In the area of strategic alignment, institutions may examine whether AI-integrated hybrid education is explicitly referenced in institutional strategies and teaching and learning frameworks, and whether leadership communication consistently links AI use to educational purpose. Studies indicate that where AI is framed primarily as an efficiency tool, strategic coherence tends to be weak, whereas institutions that articulate pedagogical and societal rationales demonstrate stronger readiness (KPMG LLP, 2025; Deogaonkar, 2025).

Governance and policy readiness can be explored through indicators such as the presence of institution-wide ethical guidelines, clarity of data governance arrangements, and mechanisms for stakeholder consultation. UNESCO (2023) and Holmes et al. (2022) emphasize that ethical readiness is reflected not only in policy existence, but in institutional capacity to operationalize principles through governance structures. Comparative research suggests that institutions in fragmented policy environments benefit from internal diagnostics that clarify accountability and decision-making authority (Kundu and Bej, 2025).

Capability development indicators focus on human readiness. Institutions may assess faculty AI literacy, access to instructional design support, and the extent to which AI-related innovation is recognized within workload and promotion systems. Empirical evidence consistently shows that faculty confidence and perceived institutional support mediate AI adoption more strongly than access to tools alone (Ali, 2025; Liu, 2025; Harsanti et al., 2025). Student readiness indicators, such as trust in AI systems and clarity of guidance on acceptable use, further complement this assessment (Rahman et al., 2025; Homer et al., 2025).

Infrastructure and resource readiness can be examined through the reliability and interoperability of digital platforms, sustainability of funding models, and availability of technical support. Global analyses indicate that infrastructure is often unevenly distributed, with project-based investments limiting scalability and long-term readiness (Molina et al., 2024; Kuleto et al., 2021).

Cultural and leadership readiness is more difficult to quantify, yet critical. Institutions may reflect on levels of trust between leadership and faculty, openness to experimentation, and opportunities for cross-unit collaboration. Change management research highlights that institutions with participatory leadership and transparent communication are better able to sustain readiness over time, even amid uncertainty and resistance (Kotter and Cohen, 2014; Gering et al., 2025).

6.3. Using Readiness Data for Strategic Planning

The value of readiness assessment lies not in data collection itself, but in how insights are used. When treated as an audit or compliance exercise, assessment risks reinforcing defensive behavior and superficial reporting. By contrast, when embedded within strategic planning processes, readiness data can support capacity building and informed decision making.

Effective use of readiness data begins with collective sense making. Rather than delegating assessment to technical units alone, institutions benefit from involving academic leaders, faculty representatives, professional staff, and students in interpreting findings. This participatory approach aligns with research showing that shared ownership of change increases trust and reduces resistance (Kang et al., 2022; Al Sabbagh and Elgeddawy, 2025).

Readiness insights can then inform prioritization. Institutions rarely have the resources to address all gaps simultaneously. Diagnostic assessment helps leaders identify leverage points, such as strengthening governance before scaling infrastructure, or investing in faculty capability before introducing new AI tools. Studies of strategic responses to generative AI suggest that institutions that sequence interventions thoughtfully are more likely to achieve sustainable outcomes (Gering et al., 2025).

Importantly, readiness assessment should avoid punitive evaluation. The IRF is designed to support learning rather than judgment. Using readiness data to rank departments or penalize individuals risks undermining trust and reinforcing resistance. Instead, assessment should be framed as a developmental baseline against which progress can be reviewed periodically. This approach aligns with UNESCO's emphasis on ethical governance and institutional responsibility in AI adoption (UNESCO, 2023).

Over time, readiness assessment can also support benchmarking in a non-competitive sense. Institutions may compare patterns rather than scores, learning from peer institutions operating in similar contexts. Comparative insights from Finland, Singapore, and Vietnam demonstrate that meaningful benchmarking focuses on governance approaches and capacity development strategies rather than replicating so-called best practices (Sârb, 2024; Ng, 2025; Duong et al., 2025).

Table 1. Illustrative Diagnostic Indicators Across IRF Dimensions

IRF Dimension	Example Diagnostic Focus
Strategic Alignment	Clarity of AI's educational purpose in strategy
Governance and Policy	Ethical guidelines, accountability clarity
Capability Development	Faculty AI confidence and support structures
Infrastructure and Resources	Platform reliability and sustainability
Culture and Leadership	Trust, participation, experimentation

Evaluating institutional readiness is ultimately about enabling better decisions. When assessment is framed as a tool for learning, dialogue, and strategic alignment, it strengthens rather than constrains institutional autonomy. By integrating diagnostic evaluation within the Institutional Readiness Framework, higher education leaders are better equipped to navigate AI-integrated hybrid education as a long-term organizational transformation grounded in purpose, ethics, and human capacity.

7. CHALLENGES, LIMITATIONS, AND ETHICAL TENSIONS

Despite its integrative intent, the Institutional Readiness Framework is not without limitations. Institutional transformation in the context of AI-integrated hybrid education unfolds within structural, regulatory, and cultural constraints that shape how readiness can be developed and sustained. Recognizing these challenges is essential not only for analytical rigor, but also for avoiding overly optimistic or universal claims about institutional change.

7.1. Structural and Resource Constraints

One of the most persistent challenges to institutional readiness lies in uneven access to resources. Financial capacity, digital infrastructure, and human expertise vary widely across higher education systems and within institutions themselves. While digitally mature universities may invest in AI platforms, data systems, and professional development, smaller or teaching-focused institutions often operate under conditions of scarcity. These constraints limit the pace and scope of readiness development, particularly in capability building and infrastructure sustainability.

Importantly, such constraints do not imply institutional failure. Rather, they highlight that readiness is shaped by structural conditions and must be pursued incrementally. The framework therefore treats readiness as a developmental process that adapts to resource realities, rather than as a standard to be achieved uniformly across contexts.

7.2. Governance and Legal Uncertainty

Governance and legal ambiguity represent another significant limitation. Regulatory frameworks for AI in education remain fragmented and uneven across jurisdictions, creating uncertainty around data protection, accountability, and ethical responsibility. Institutions often find themselves navigating overlapping or incomplete guidance while responding to rapid technological change.

This uncertainty complicates readiness by making governance a moving target. Policies developed today may quickly become outdated, and risk-averse approaches may inadvertently constrain pedagogical innovation. The framework acknowledges this tension by framing governance readiness as adaptive and iterative, emphasizing institutional capacity to revise policies, engage stakeholders, and respond to emerging risks rather than relying on fixed regulatory solutions.

7.3. Faculty Agency and Digital Well-Being

Faculty agency and well-being pose another critical challenge. AI integration can generate anxiety related to professional identity, surveillance, workload intensification, and loss of pedagogical autonomy. Digital fatigue, intensified by post-pandemic hybrid work patterns, further complicates engagement with AI initiatives.

If not addressed explicitly, these concerns can undermine readiness even in institutions with strong strategic intent and infrastructure. The framework therefore treats faculty agency as central to readiness, linking capability development and cultural leadership to well-being, trust, and meaningful participation. Readiness, in this sense, depends on institutions' ability to balance innovation with care for academic labor and professional autonomy.

7.4. Intercultural and Contextual Misalignment

Finally, intercultural and contextual misalignment presents a deeper ethical tension. Many AI tools are developed within specific linguistic, cultural, and pedagogical assumptions that may not align with local educational traditions or learner needs. When institutions adopt global AI solutions without critical adaptation, they risk reinforcing epistemic inequality or marginalizing local knowledge systems.

This challenge reinforces the importance of cultural humility within institutional readiness. Rather than assuming technological neutrality, the framework emphasizes reflective governance and contextual mediation, positioning readiness as the capacity to interrogate how AI reshapes educational values across diverse settings.

Taken together, these challenges underscore that readiness is neither linear nor uncontested. Structural limits, governance uncertainty, human concerns, and cultural complexity do not negate readiness efforts; they define the conditions under which readiness must evolve. The Institutional Readiness Framework responds to these realities by framing readiness as a continuous learning process shaped by constraint as much as by opportunity.

8. READINESS AS A CONTINUOUS LEARNING JOURNEY

This chapter has argued that institutional readiness for AI-integrated hybrid education cannot be reduced to technological capacity or digital maturity. Readiness is not synonymous with equipment, infrastructure, or access to advanced tools. Rather, it emerges through the alignment of governance, strategy, human capability, and institutional culture over time.

By conceptualizing readiness as an organizational capability, the chapter advances a shift in perspective. Readiness is not a destination to be reached, but a continuous learning journey shaped by adaptation, reflection, and ethical deliberation. Institutions that treat AI integration as a technical upgrade risk reinforcing fragmentation, resistance, and inequity. In contrast, institutions that approach readiness as adaptive governance are better positioned to navigate uncertainty and sustain innovation.

Three elements stand out as central to this conception of readiness. First, adaptive governance enables institutions to respond to evolving technological and regulatory landscapes without relying on static rules or compliance driven approaches. Second, ethical innovation ensures that AI integration remains aligned with educational values, equity, and social responsibility rather than efficiency alone. Third, cultural humility allows institutions to mediate global technologies through local contexts, respecting diversity in pedagogical traditions and learner experiences.

Viewed through this lens, higher education institutions function less as delivery systems and more as learning ecosystems. They learn not only through formal evaluation, but through experimentation, dialogue, and collective sense making. The Institutional Readiness Framework contributes to this understanding by offering a diagnostic and developmental tool that supports reflection rather than prescription.

Ultimately, readiness for AI-integrated hybrid education is not about being prepared once and for all. It is about cultivating the institutional capacity to learn continuously in the face of technological, social, and ethical change. Institutions that embrace readiness as an ongoing process will be better equipped to shape AI not as a disruptive force, but as a meaningful contributor to inclusive and transformative education.

REFERENCES

Al Sabbagh, M., & Elgeddawy, M. (2025). Change management and AI adoption for enhancing employee experience in higher education institutions, Oman. In *AI and IoT: Driving business success and sustainability in the digital age* (Vol. 1, pp. 307–315). Springer Nature Switzerland., DOI: 10.1007/978-3-031-92240-4_28

Ali, A. M. (2025). Evaluating artificial intelligence readiness within faculty in the higher education sector. *Higher Education Quarterly*, *79*(4), e70061. DOI: 10.1111/hequ.70061

Capano, G., He, A. J., & McMinn, S. (2025). Riding the tide of generative artificial intelligence in higher education policy: An Asian perspective. *Journal of Asian Public Policy*, *18*(2), 1–15. DOI: 10.1080/17516234.2025.2450571

Deogaonkar, A. (2025). Digital leadership, AI readiness and strategic resource allocation in education: A configurational approach to post-pandemic transformation. *International Journal of Educational Management*, *39*(5), 1105–1119. DOI: 10.1108/IJEM-06-2025-0438

Duong, N. T., Pham Thi, T. D., & Pham, V. K. (2025). A comparative study on AI-based learning behaviours: Evidence from Vietnam. *International Journal of Human-Computer Interaction*, *41*(16), 10007–10023. DOI: 10.1080/10447318.2024.2430433

Gering, Z., Feher, K., Harmat, V., & Tamassy, R. (2025). Strategic organisational responses to generative AI-driven digital transformation in leading higher education institutions. *The International Journal of Organizational Analysis*, *33*(12), 132–152. DOI: 10.1108/IJOA-09-2024-4850

Harsanti, H. R., Sudibjo, N., Riady, S., & Yu, P. (2025). 'Exploring Indonesian teachers' intention to use artificial intelligence in schools: The impact of digital leadership, digital readiness, and perceived usefulness'. *Cogent Social Sciences*, *11*(1), 2593596. DOI: 10.1080/23311886.2025.2593596

HEInnovate. (2023) *HEInnovate: A self-assessment tool for higher education institutions*. Available at: https://www.heinnovate.eu/en (Accessed: Day Month Year).

Hoang, N. H. (2025). 'E-leadership in the AI era: Exploring Vietnamese EFL teachers' digital leadership development in AI integration'. *Education and Information Technologies*, *30*(12), 1–34. DOI: 10.1007/s10639-025-13451-6

Holmes, W., Porayska-Pomsta, K., Holstein, K., Sutherland, E., Baker, T., Shum, S. B., Santos, O. C., Rodrigo, M. T., Cukurova, M., Bittencourt, I. I., & Koedinger, K. R. (2022). Ethics of AI in education: Towards a community-wide framework. *International Journal of Artificial Intelligence in Education, 32*(3), 504–526. DOI: 10.1007/s40593-021-00239-1

Homer, S. T., Chuen, P. W., & Chuah, C. (2025). The role of AI in education: A Southeast Asian student perspective through a unified theory of acceptance and use of technology lens. *Asia Pacific Journal of Education*, •••, 1–28. DOI: 10.1080/02188791.2025.2564138

Kang, S. P., Chen, Y., Svihla, V., Gallup, A., Ferris, K., & Datye, A. K. (2022). Guiding change in higher education: An emergent, iterative application of Kotter's change model. *Studies in Higher Education, 47*(2), 270–289. DOI: 10.1080/03075079.2020.1741540

Karan, B., & Angadi, G. R. (2025). Understanding school readiness factors in relation to the incorporation of artificial intelligence using TOE framework: Empirical evidence from India. *TechTrends, 69*(1), 38–59. DOI: 10.1007/s11528-024-01020-6

Kotter, J. P., & Cohen, D. (2014). *Change leadership*. Harvard Business Review Press.

KPMG LLP. (2025) *Generative AI and the future of education: how higher education institutions, their employees and students are using AI to drive success.* Toronto: KPMG Canada. Available at: https://kpmg.com/ca/AI

Kuleto, V., Ilić, M., Dumangiu, M., Ranković, M., Martins, O. M. D., Păun, D., & Mihoreanu, L. (2021). Exploring opportunities and challenges of artificial intelligence and machine learning in higher education institutions. *Sustainability (Basel), 13*(18), 10424. DOI: 10.3390/su131810424

Kundu, A. and Bej, T. (2025) 'AI policies in school education: a comparative study on China, Singapore, Finland, and the US', *Journal of Science and Technology Policy Management*. Available at: DOI: 10.1108/JSTPM-06-2024-0218

Liu, N. (2025). Exploring the factors influencing the adoption of artificial intelligence technology by university teachers: The mediating role of confidence and AI readiness. *BMC Psychology, 13*(1), 311. DOI: 10.1186/s40359-025-02620-4 PMID: 40148913

Molina, E., Cobo, C., Pineda, J., & Rovner, H. (2024) *AI revolution in education: what you need to know*. Digital Innovations in Education Brief No. 1. Washington, DC: World Bank. Available at: https://documents1.worldbank.org/curated/en/099734306182493324/pdf/IDU152823b13109c514ebd19c241a289470b6902.pdf

Ng, P. T. (2025). Learning in an era of uncertainty in Singapore: Diversity, lifelong learning, inspiration and paradigm shift. *Educational Research for Policy and Practice*, *24*(1), 121–127. DOI: 10.1007/s10671-023-09348-1 PMID: 38625282

Nguyen, A., Kishore, S., Hong, Y., Qutab, S., & Dang, B. (2025). Generative artificial intelligence in education: From organizing visions to official guidelines. *Information Technology & People*, *38*(8), 172–199. DOI: 10.1108/ITP-08-2024-1026

Patricio, L. D., & Ferreira, J. J. (2023). 'Aligning entrepreneurial universities' HEInnovate dimensions with entrepreneurs' needs: A graduate entrepreneur-centred perspective'. *International Journal of Management Education*, *21*(3), 100882. DOI: 10.1016/j.ijme.2023.100882

Payadnya, I. P. A. A., Putri, G. A. M. A., Suwija, I. K., Saelee, S., & Jayantika, I. G. A. N. T. (2025). Cultural integration in AI-enhanced mathematics education: Insights from Southeast Asian educators. *Journal for Multicultural Education*, *19*(1), 58–72. DOI: 10.1108/JME-09-2024-0119

Rahman, M. K., Hossain, M. A., Ismail, N. A., Hossen, M. S., & Sultana, M. (2025). 'Determinants of students' adoption of AI chatbots in higher education: The moderating role of tech readiness'. *Interactive Technology and Smart Education*, *22*(3), 448–480. Advance online publication. DOI: 10.1108/ITSE-12-2024-0312

Roll, I., McNamara, D., Sosnovsky, S., Luckin, R., & Dimitrova, V. (2021). *Artificial intelligence in education*. Springer International Publishing.

Sârb, C. (2024) *Digital education evolution: investigating Finland's past and future directions*. Available at: https://urn.fi/URN:NBN:fi:amk-2024111628412

Schiff, D. (2022). Education for AI, not AI for education: The role of education and ethics in national AI policy strategies. *International Journal of Artificial Intelligence in Education*, *32*(3), 527–563. DOI: 10.1007/s40593-021-00270-2

Tursunbayeva, A. (2024). Artificial intelligence adoption and change management. In *Augmenting human resource management with artificial intelligence: towards an inclusive, sustainable, and responsible future* (pp. 113–126). Springer Nature Switzerland., DOI: 10.1007/978-3-031-75266-7_9

UNESCO. (2023) *Artificial intelligence in education*. Paris: United Nations Educational, Scientific and Cultural Organization. Available at: https://www.unesco.org/en/digital-education/artificial-intelligence

Verano-Tacoronte, D., Bolívar-Cruz, A., & Sosa-Cabrera, S. (2025). Are university teachers ready for generative artificial intelligence? unpacking faculty anxiety in the ChatGPT era. *Education and Information Technologies*, *30*(14), 1–28. DOI: 10.1007/s10639-025-13585-7

Chapter 12
Sustainability, AI, and Hybrid Pedagogy:
Building Eco-Responsible, Culturally Inclusive Learning Systems

Aryan Yadav
http://orcid.org/0009-0008-4022-3045
Christ University, Delhi NCR, India

Shivani Thapliyal
http://orcid.org/0000-0002-7285-2830
Christ University, India

ABSTRACT

Artificial Intelligence (AI), Hybrid Education Models, and Sustainable Development have transformed the education systems of the world. Hybrid models also involve digital learning and in-person learning, whereas AI provides opportunities to experience learning on a personal, scaled, and interactive level. Regardless of these benefits, there are still ethical issues of governance, environmental sustainability, cultural inclusivity, and equity that are of essence. The chapter discusses the development of AI-based hybrid education models that will facilitate the environmentally friendly practices, intercultural cooperation, and sustainable educational objectives. Based on interdisciplinary studies in Intelligent Tutoring Systems, Technology-Enhanced Learning, Education for Sustainable Development, and culture-driven Sustainable Development Goals (SDGs), the chapter suggests a model of developing inclusive, ethical and future-oriented hybrid learning space, and explains the implications on educators, institutions, and policy makers.

DOI: 10.4018/979-8-3373-7462-8.ch012

1. INTRODUCTION

Due to the advancements in technology and the increasing recognition of environmental issues, technology-based communication is now available for interaction between different cultures. The primary factors in global education's transition to a new way of educating are Hybrid Pedagogy (a combination of face-to-face instruction and online learning) and the rapid development of Artificial Intelligence (AI) (using technological tools to meet the individual needs of learners by personalizing their learning experiences and evaluation.). In its early days, Hybrid Pedagogy was conceived to address the urgent need of educators and students to continue their educational activities during times of crisis. As Hybrid Pedagogy has gained traction across the globe as an effective method of educating students, the use of AI will continue to transform how learners access educational content, how we assess their learning outcomes, and how we personalize learning for each student.

The new possibilities that these technologies may bring, as well as their potential for creating new options, also present some very serious issues that go beyond just the technological implementation of these tools. There are important issues such as sustainability, equity, cultural representation and ethical responsibility emerging as key themes in discussions of AI-enabled hybrid learning and the use of educational institutions' digital infrastructure will continue to include AI-driven technologies. The increasing emphasis being placed on environmental impact, data privacy, algorithmic bias and lack of access shows that educational institutions must create pedagogical practices that integrate AI into their hybrid learning environments in a manner that is socially responsible, environmentally sustainable and culturally inclusive.

In defining global education policies, the concept of sustainability is a key motivating force for the United Nations' Sustainable Development Goals (SDGs) and the implementation of SDG 4 that emphasizes access to both inclusive and equitable quality education and to lifelong learning for all, therefore, education is considered a significant contributor to sustainable development and an end goal of sustainable development will be achieved by means of education. The sustainability of education extends beyond the curriculum. It encompasses the pedagogies that are used to instruct students in addition to the culture of the institution and the ethical use of technology in the classroom. The recent body of literature focused on sustainable education has indicated that all of the elements of sustainable education should support environmental stewardship, social equity, cultural diversity and economic responsibility. Therefore, as we are integrating artificial intelligence (AI) into hybrid pedagogy, it is essential for all of us to consider the impact from a sustainability standpoint.

AI has great potential to enhance sustainable education in terms of individualized learning experiences, increased efficiency when learning and also the possibility of informing learning decisions using data. Intelligent tutoring system research has shown that AI technologies can predict how a learner behaves, define an adaptive learning path, and provide immediate feedback that allows for learner independence and interaction. These features are especially important in hybrid learning situations, where learners need customized attention due to the wide array of available learning approaches and differences in learning styles. However, implementing AI systems will create ecological impacts, including increased consumption of electricity, increased demand for digital infrastructure and Creating electronic waste, which will contribute negatively to the environment. Additionally, AI systems may be designed to operate in a particular sociocultural and linguistic environment, which raises the issue of Inclusivity and the way AI systems can be used for inequitable interactions among learners from multiple cultures and languages.

One challenge of hybrid pedagogy is that it changes the way learners, instructors and schools interact with one another. The hybrid model of Pedagogy also offers greater access to learning opportunities, as well as greater flexibility. However, if there is not equitable access to digital resources and AI technology, Hybrid Pedagogies may continue to create inequalities already present in society. Historically underrepresented groups or emerging economies may be the greatest impact of using Hybrid Pedagogies due to their lower levels of connectivity and digital literacy and their decreased representation within the educational materials provided. Therefore, as more and more hybrids leverage AI Technology to advance the understanding of Hybrid Pedagogy, it is vital that this technology be used responsibly so that issues surrounding equity/social justice, and cultural diversity are not compromised with the technological advancements that will be made.

Cultural values help to shape the relationship between students and knowledge, how they make sense of technology, and their participation within their educational community. Using hybrid/digital learning platforms allows for intercultural collaboration through cross-cultural exchange, emotional awareness and partnerships, co-creation of knowledge and development of global citizenship. Only through appropriate pedagogical design do we have the potential to avoid the risk that digital/AI-enhanced learning programs will simply recreate the dominant cultural narratives while simultaneously marginalizing local knowledge systems and multiple/various perspectives.

Increased focus has been placed on Intercultural Pedagogy. As such, we require new education models that address these issues while providing a means to integrate and encourage cultural inclusion, multilingual education and support, and contextual relevance to place. When developing hybrid learning systems that leverage the use of AI, these models should be flexible to accommodate varying cultural attitudes; responsive to local culture and community; and transparent in how AI is used in its decision-making process. Therefore, the ethical use of AI in education should take into account not only the technological accuracy of an AI model and its underlying algorithms but also include aspects such as: the cultural responsiveness of the system; fairness; and valuing and respecting the cultural identity of the learner. Institutions and educators will continue to face increasing pressure to be able to create a level of digital literacy that incorporates an understanding of ethics, sustainability, and intercultural awareness.

As the trend of using AI in Hybrid Education continues to grow, many educational institutions will increasingly begin to use AI as part of their curriculum and in preparing students for success in today's workforce. There are still many challenges that must be addressed in addition to the integration of AI into Hybrid Education. The majority of the research done on Hybrid Education has primarily focused on individual studies rather than comprehensive overviews or frameworks combining AI, Sustainability and International Collaboration, meaning that researchers focus on each area separately from one another. Researchers are looking at how each area is being used and how to develop sustainable practices in Hybrid Education as well as how to take advantage of cultural differences to enhance the learning experience, but the inability to view these areas together has created barriers to the development of hybrid education practice learning ecosystems, which provide learners with the skills they need for future 21st Century challenges within the global economy.

The chapter also builds a framework for understanding the factors affecting the convergence of Sustainability, AI, and Hybrid Pedagogy, which leads to consideration of Practice and Future Research Implications. The chapter synthesizes research findings from the globe, across multiple fields, and aims to advance the conversation on Hybrid Pedagogies using AI and Intercultural Collaboration. Finally, this chapter will support Educational Professionals, Institutional Leadership, and Policy Makers in developing technology-enhanced, Eco-Responsible, Ethically Sound, Culturally Responsive Learning Systems.

Rapid advancements in digital technologies, artificial intelligence (AI) and pedagogical paradigms throughout the world are creating a deep and complex Revolution within the Global Education System. Hybrid pedagogy (Hybrid learning) combines traditional classroom and internet-based learning experiences to create an effective way for students to learn today (Garrison et al., 2008). Hybrid Pedagogy has transitioned from being an add-on to being a strategic methodology to meet the need of worldwide educators for a response to their need for creative flexibility, growth potential, and the ability to be resilient within their educational systems (Allen et al., 2017).

The introduction of Hybrid Educational Systems and Hybrid Education Methods has led to many more educational uses for AI Technology due to Technology advancements. The types of AI technologies used in education can be classified as; Intelligent Tutoring Systems (ITS), Adaptive Learning Systems, Automated Assessment Tools (AAT's) and Learning Analytics. The introduction of these technologies and their widespread use will significantly improve the quality and effectiveness of the delivery and assessment processes for student learning. More specifically, AI Technology will allow for students to receive more individualised, immediate and personalised feedback about their academic performance. In addition, AI Technology provides teachers with access to Predictive Analytics on student behaviour. In conclusion, AI Technology will assist educational institutions in making Data-Based (evidence) decisions when creating Hybrid Education Delivery Systems.

One of the many principal elements of the Global Education Policies and Practices that drive Sustainability is the framework provided by the United Nations Sustainable Development Goals (UN SDGs). One of the goals, (UN SDG 4) focuses on inclusive, equitable, and quality education, but also provides pathways to sustainable development of all types, both now and in the future.

Sustainability is not just about Environmental Content being taught in Schools; it includes Pedagogical Activities, Institutional Governance, Technology, and the way that Innovation is shaped in Education.

Within this larger definition of education for sustainability, it aims to prepare students to think critically, act responsibly, and participate positively in relation to global issues through the use of hybrid teaching methods with support from Artificial Intelligence (AI). Hybrid methods provide better access to learning opportunities in different ways; allow learners to build their individual education pathways; and provide opportunities for global collaboration. In addition, creating and maintaining these systems will require a commitment from all levels of education, including the design, implementation, and management of technology. In addition, the production of digital platforms, cloud computing, and AI technologies consumes a significant amount of energy and materials and produces carbon emissions, electronic waste and other negative impacts to the environment (Yigitcanlar et al., 2021; Regona et al., 2024).

The subject matter of artificial intelligence occupies a unique position within the broader context of sustainability. On one side of the equation, AI supports sustainable education through the application of recent studies and discoveries. AI helps make learning more efficient by significantly improving the educational process by reducing inefficiencies, aiding in real-time analysis of sustainability, and allowing institutions to implement sustainability practices based on an actual dataset or record. An actual case in point is the use of personalized learning systems by utilizing data records from previous years to allow students to retain more information; furthermore, AI provides equitable access to educational resources, thereby resulting in a more efficient manner of using educational resources overall. Conversely, AI requires a lot of resources; these resources include vast amounts of data, power, and updates to keep AI relevant. These two factors provide further reason as to why critical assessments should be performed as to how AI fits into sustainable hybrid education.

Equally important, yet often overlooked, is the cultural aspect regarding how AI impacts hybrid pedagogy. Although education is defined as the transmission of knowledge, it should also be noted that education is also very much a cultural process. Education transcends being just the transfer of information; education has cultural ramifications based upon an individual's wealth, language, and beliefs (Banks, 2015). New hybrid learning models are being created to connect learners from a variety of social, linguistic, and cultural backgrounds. While there are opportunities for cross-cultural collaboration and global education, there are also many issues associated with the intercultural nature of hybrid educational environments, such as cultural homogenization resulting from the use of AI systems, algorithmic bias, and epistemic domination associated with AI.

Many of the educational technologies that use artificial intelligence have been designed for specific societies and institutions, and consequently have a Western perspective regarding pedagogy, language, and assessment. In addition, these systems can create boundaries around local knowledge systems, diminish the value of indigenous knowledge perspectives, and limit the development of culturally relevant pedagogy when they are implemented throughout the world. In sustainable education, cultural inclusion must be considered a foundational element rather than an added benefit. As such, Sustainable Education is based on the idea that it is essential to incorporate and respect the different ways of knowing, learning, and existing to enhance social cohesion and create global citizens (UNESCO, 2017).

In addition, hybrid pedagogy introduces another layer of complexity to this issue in that it provides an opportunity to merge the traditional classroom with online environments. The combination of face-to-face and digital learning creates opportunities for context-based learning and relational pedagogy; however, students may lose connection to their peers and educators in hybrid environments if technology is not integrated in a manner that enhances their human connections, relationships, and ethical judgments (Selwyn, 2019).

To reimagine AI-enabled hybrid pedagogy, it is important to integrate sustainability principles and perspectives on ethics with respect to culture. Whereas most authors have suggested looking at AI simply as a neutral tool to create greater efficiencies and automate, this chapter suggests viewing AI as an increasingly important socio-technological agent whose design and implementation can be expected to have significant, long-term consequences on educational systems, ecological systems, and cultural systems. The chapter draws on inter-disciplinary research in such areas as the development of Artificial Intelligence in education, Education for Sustainable Development, Ethical Governance of Artificial Intelligence, and Intercultural Pedagogy to develop a broader view of Sustainable Hybrid Learning Systems.

There are a number of key considerations that are impacting the convergence of AI with Hybrid Pedagogy and Sustainability. These include Intelligent Tutoring Systems, sustainable digital practices, Ethical Governance of AI, and cross-cultural collaboration. All of these areas, as well as other potential areas of interest will need to be integrated into a Sustainable Development Goals framework to ensure stakeholder actions align with the goals of Sustainable Development. Finally, future research directions are outlined to continue contributing to the empirical, theoretical, and policy knowledge base of the rapidly evolving field of Hybrid Pedagogy.

Three areas, AI, Hybrid Pedagogy and Sustainability, represent three fast growing interconnected fields that require conceptual frameworks to provide educational paradigms to validate and link these once separate domains into an integrated educational model. The Eco-Cultural AI-Enabled Hybrid Learning Model is provided here to fulfil this requirement. The Eco-Cultural AI Enablement Hybrid Learning Model to then establish Sustainable Hybrid Education as a continually occurring dynamic or situational interplay of the three foundational pillars of education defined by the disciplines of AI, Hybrid Pedagogy and Sustainability, with Artificial Intelligence being the product of the enabling technologies supporting the technologically enabled infrastructures of AI systems including adaptive learning, intelligent tutoring systems and learning analytics.

Hybrid Pedagogy is defined as Designing for how to integrate both Face-to-Face (F2F) Instruction and Digital Learning Environments, in order to offer flexible access to learners and improve the degree of Learner Engagement through an effective Instructional Design Process. Finally, Sustainability establishes the foundation of the institution's Normative and Ethical Principles based on Environmental Sustainability, Social Equity, and Long-Term Viable Institutional Functioning.

The Three Foundational Pillars are on a Critical Socio-Cultural Layer that encompasses all aspects of Inclusion of Intercultural and/or International students, Digital Ethics, Governance, and the Alignment of the Faculty with the United Nations Sustainable Development Goal #4 - Universal Education.

Figure 1. Eco-Cultural AI-Enabled Hybrid Learning Model (Author's own work)

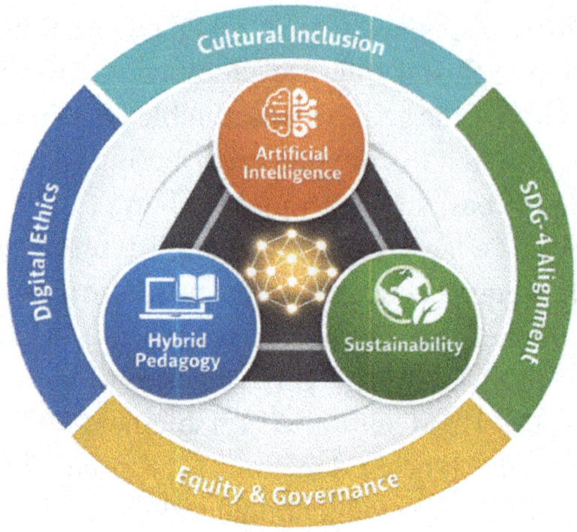

2. FACTORS RELATED TO THE TOPIC

Artificial Intelligence in Hybrid Pedagogy

Hybrid education includes both classroom traditional method and online technology-based learning, thus it provides a very different way of viewing education than what was previously assumed. Hybrid education offers benefits from local courses, but it also provides additional online flexibility and availability to enable students to continue their education through ongoing learning.Hybrid educators can create and implement instructional strategies that are tailored to meet individual student needs through the application of Artificial Intelligence technology to hybrid education models. Some of the methods employed to enhance hybrid education methods include the creation of personalized Adaptive Data-Driven Instructional Models, the use of Intelligent Tutoring Systems (ITS), the use of Adaptive Learning Platforms (ALP), the provision of AI-Based Tutoring and Conversational Chatbots, and the application of Learning Analytics. These applications enable hybrid instructors to track student engagement when interacting with instructional materials and measure the effectiveness of the instructional materials used with each student. In addition, the ability of hybrid education to allow students to pursue individualized pathways would provide much more motivation and independence for students.

In addition to the environmental factors associated with AI use in hybrid pedagogy, there are several ethical and social issues associated with the use of AI systems in learning environments as well. Issues such as algorithmic bias, data privacy, transparency, and accountability are major challenges faced by organisations related to building trust among their learners, as well as promoting equity. Moreover, as hybrid learning environments comprise many different cultural populations spread across the globe, the AI systems developed to support these hybrid pedagogy systems must not favor dominant culture norms and languages. Therefore, when creating ethical AI frameworks to support hybrid pedagogy, organisations must ensure that the principles of equity, fairness, and cultural understanding frame the decision-making about all learners in those systems.

Within Hybrid Pedagogy, the use of AI (artificial intelligence) is meant to be an additional resource to aid in supporting educational functions as opposed to being viewed as a substitute for face-to-face interactions between teachers and students. Historically, educators and students have interacted through a series of meaningful conversations through dialogue, mentoring, coaching, and developing mutual respect by establishing relationships with one another. Therefore, there should never be a single teaching method used in place of these types of teaching and learning opportunities. Therefore, the best outcome for educators would be to create synergy by combining technology with human interactions through AI to continue enhancing the use of human-centered instructional design through AI-based tools, which provide data-driven insights, support, and real-time feedback to allow for collaboration between educators and students as they work through their educational experiences. With AI-Enabled Learning Systems, educators in Hybrid Learning environments can offer multiple instructional designs/models for their learners, rather than offering a single one-size-fits-all design. Furthermore, by providing personalized learning opportunities, students are more motivated to achieve success, therefore decreasing their potential to leave the learning environment, and are more likely to be fully engaged in their educational experience, especially within large or heterogeneous learning environments (Pane et al., 2014).

AI-Powered Personalization from a Sustainability Perspective. AI-Powered Personalization is Based on Principle of Efficiency in Education, Support of Reduction in Redundant Activities and Optimization of Instructional Paths, Thus Reducing the Amount of Time and Resource Wasted in Instructional Activities and Maximising the Use of Institutional Resources. However, The Trade-Offs Must Be Made Regarding The Environmental Impact Associated With The Environmental Costs Of The AI Infrastructure (Power, Data Storage, Continual Updates). From An Ethical Perspective, The Role Of AI In Hybrid Pedagogy Is Influenced By Ethics.

Algorithmic Decision Making, In Addition To Affecting What Students See, Affect Students' Assessment, And The Way In Which Their Progress Is Represented. If These Systems Are Not Transparent, Hold Some Degree Of Accountability, They May Reinforce Bias And Inhibit Students' Ability To Make Decisions About Their Learning Process. Thus, In Order To Be Sustainable In The Hybrid Pedagogical Environment, Use of AI Should Be Based Upon Human-Centred Educational Values, and Should Be Verifiable And Auditable.

Intelligent Tutoring Systems and Personalized Learning

Intelligent Tutoring Systems (ITS) are one of the most advanced areas of application of AI in education. Intelligent tutoring systems help in the simulation of the tutoring process conducted by a human by adapting to the specific requirements of the learners. Intelligent tutoring systems function using artificial intelligence tools like machine learning, natural language processing, and learning models. In a hybrid learning system, Intelligent Tutoring Systems have a critical role to play in performing the role of bridging the gap between classroom learning and self-paced internet-based learning.

Studies on ITS prove their use can be highly beneficial to efficiency of learning by improving the adaptation of IS to the characteristics of learners and promoting sustainable education. By simulating the mental state, pre-existing knowledge, emotional state, and attitude of learners, ITS can offer learning that is responsive and centred on the individual. This characteristic of ITS aligns very well with the need to focus on sustainable education. With ITS, there will be fewer dropouts.

With hybrid pedagogy, the role of ITS becomes flexible, as it can be used for different types of learning activities. When it comes to the online components, the role of ITS includes sustaining learning support, either through adaptive learning activities, assessment, or feedback systems. When it comes to the offline components, it is the data or insights that the system can offer, such as learning progress or engagement, that can be used in teaching activities.

Despite their advantages, however, intelligent tutoring systems face some sustainability and ethics-based challenges. This is because the development and delivery of ITS require high levels of digital infrastructure energy consumption. Additionally, the data-intensive processes that occur in ITS raise various potential issues related to privacy, surveillance, and informed consent. These should be addressed in the successful sustainability of intelligent tutoring systems by adopting responsible data practice principles.

Another important factor that needs consideration in ITS design is cultural inclusiveness. Many AI-powered learning platforms are trained on data that is based on a certain cultural framework. However, these platforms may not serve everyone well when used on a global level. In this regard, an ITS that is used with an online or offline hybrid learning system that facilitates intercultural collaboration will require consideration with regards to handling cultural diversity. This requires that an ITS is capable of handling multiple languages. Furthermore, an ITS requires consideration based on different cultural contexts.

In support of an eco-responsible approach to tutoring that also deliberately incorporates the benefits of different cultures, there have to be intelligent tutoring system design standards that recognize the emphasis on optimization of computational efficiency, an avoidance of the unnecessary collection of data, and the promotion of tutoring value over technology. Only then can ITS act as a facilitator of sustainable hybrid tutoring.

The pedagogical strength of the ITS system is in their ability to promote master learning and self-directed learning, both of which are important in the sustainability of learning paradigms. Master learning entails allowing the learner to proceed at their own pace, and the ITS system promotes this by allowing the learner to revisit concepts at their own pace, thereby allowing them to gain a deeper level of understanding and retention of those concepts (Pane et al., 2014).

Despite such benefits, ITS also pose challenges from a sustainability perspective. One of the key aspects of ITS is their reliance on data regarding learners, such as behavioural and performance data, and in some cases, biometric data. Handling such data entails effective mechanisms for ensuring issues of privacy and integrity of data (Williamson & Eynon, 2020). Data-driven ITS add to sustainability issues arising from the usage of technology in teaching and learning.

Culturally responsive design can be seen as an important element that can affect the sustainability of the ITS. Most of these applications have been built in particular linguistic and cultural settings that could preclude them from being universally useful. It was found that there could be adverse effects on the engagement level of students stemming from the mismatch between instruction feedback and the criteria of assessment from the students' cultural background (Banks, 2015). Hence, sustainable blended teaching practices demand culture-sensitive ITS.

Digital Sustainability and Eco-Responsible Learning

Digital sustainability has increasingly become one of the key dimensions of educational innovation, especially in the context of AI-enabled hybrid pedagogy. As institutions extend digital infrastructures and introduce advanced technologies, there is an urgent need for critical consideration of environmental consequences of digital learning systems. Eco-responsible learning involves designing and implementing practices that minimize environmental impact, support long-term educational goals.

Eco-responsible learning with the use of AI in a hybrid learning environment requires the adoption of digital minimalist approaches when utilizing technology. In other words, the use of AI applications that have meaning in a pedagogical sense, preventing the unnecessary multiplication of platforms, and maximizing the use of the installed systems to function in a more energy-efficient manner. Then again, the educators can play a positive role in the implementation of learning tasks that emphasize the responsible use of technology and raise environmental awareness.

Another way to view sustainability within online education, aside from its ecological foundation, might be in terms of equity and justice on the social front. "The digital divide problem will worsen due to inequalities in the distribution of online resources, particularly within highly technology-intensive blended classes." A sustainable and eco-friendly approach to hybrid education would have to take account of the problem of the digital divide to make sustainable and eco-friendly approaches to hybrid online education inclusive, rather than shutting people out because of a lack of technology.

Thus, AI-infer hybrid pedagogy can make eco-responsible learning possible by ensuring the efficiency of resource utilization as well as adaptive learning. For example, using AI analytics, an institution can learn which online resources are not being utilized to the fullest potential and thus make learning pathways more effective by reducing redundancy once and for all. Adding the force of sustainability to the efficiency of learning, it can make both effective learning as well as responsible resource management possible.

In regard to issues of sustainability, learning analytics has the potential to enhance the efficiency and effectiveness of learning. The early detection of students at risk of not completing their learning can assist in lowering student dropout levels. It also has the potential to assist in curriculum design, learning assessment, and organizational learning.

However, learning analytics has to be supported by responsible data governance in order to be sustainable. The magnitude of learning data collected to perform learning analytics has ignited debates in several domains, such as privacy, autonomy, and asymmetry in learning between institutions and learners (Selwyn, 2019). Another consideration is environmental issues when large-scale learning systems are concerned due to processing and preservation of learning data.

Best practices in learning analytics inform a sustainable approach. This approach promotes data minimization, purposefully limiting data and being transparent. Data collection by institutions of higher learning will need to be justifiable from a teaching perspective. Finally, institutions of higher learning will need to ensure student involvement in data-dependent teaching.

Recent studies have proven that large-scale artificial intelligence systems leave a huge amount of waste on the planet. The emissions from training large language models can be enormous and depending on the energy source and scale, a single training session may produce an amount of CO2 equivalent to hundreds of tons. AI data centre operations consume about 1–1.5% of the world's total energy and as we continue to adopt AI at an ever-increasing rate, this number will only continue to grow. In addition to the large amounts of energy consumed, there is considerable water required to cool AI infrastructure and that creates another call for more electronic waste streams. These research results reveal a need to focus on embedding eco-responsible principles within AI-enabled hybrid education systems.

Many colleges and universities are starting to search for eco-friendly digital learning infrastructure options. Higher-education institutions have made use of energy-efficient cloud computing based on renewable energy, in support of AI-enhanced platforms for learning. Universities have also implemented various strategies that will lead to digital minimalism by eliminating unnecessary education technologies while using fewer overall learning platforms which reduces computing load. All these attempts show how schools could introduce eco-conscious learning and at the same time offer technologically advanced choices of their education to students.

Figure 2.

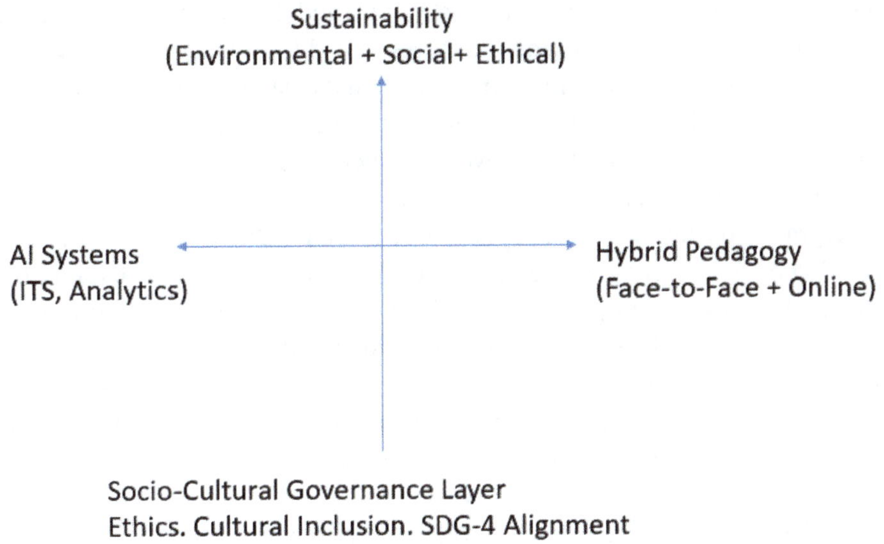

Intercultural Collaboration and Culture and the Sustainable Development Goals.

Culture has been found to be a significant yet overlooked foundation of sustainable development and learning. Beyond the confines of artistic or symbolic expressions, culture informs value, identity, knowledge, and social relations that directly implicate the process of learning itself. Within the framework of hybrid pedagogy and AI-based learning, culture has an important basis in determining whether the learning context itself will be inclusive, meaningful, and socially sustainable or not. The integration of culture into hybrid pedagogy has an important basis in light of the aim of SDG 4 on inclusive and equitable quality education.

The modern discourse of sustainability is increasingly marked by the emergence of a "fourth pillar" of sustainability, that of culture, alongside the environmental, social, and economic pillars. In this vein, culture is underlined as a promoter of social cohesion, ethical sensitivity, and communitarian responsibility. For education, cultural inclusiveness involves the identities, languages, and epistemologies of the world constituted by learners. Hybridized learning spaces enabled by information technologies and artificial intelligence open up new opportunities for intercultural collaboration, bringing together learners from all over the world in unprecedented ways.

However, there are also some challenges in intercultural collaboration in a hybrid setting. The digital platforms and artificial intelligence systems may mirror and reproduce the cultural patterns in their structure and discourse. If left unaddressed, these systems are apt to be left on the margins, and local discourses may be stifled in the process, resulting in cultural hegemony in the name of authentic intercultural interaction and collaboration, issues that a sustainable concept of a hybrid learning environment may address: the uneven production of digital knowledge and the embedding of diverse cultural perspectives.

Integrating the hybrid pedagogy approach and the SDGs is achieved by designing a learning model in a way where the concerns and aspects of sustainability become an integral part of learning. Project learning and problem learning approaches could become highly beneficial in this scenario as they will enable the students to learn about the cultural concerns of sustainability in the real world. Technologies such as AI can become highly helpful in increasing the engagement of the students and make them more cultural in their responsibilities.

Ethical and Culturally Responsive Artificial Intelligence

The role of ethics in bringing about responsible and successful assimilation of AI in the concept of hybrid pedagogy cannot be ignored. The growing impact of

AI on decisions and processes in learning and assessment, among others, gives rise to a growing number of ethical dilemmas such as bias, accountability, and privacy in a learning set-up. Moreover, this is not a problem in cross-cultural learning and training communities either.

A culturally responsive AI in education is achieved through systems that are capable of adapting to the cultural settings in which learners are found without any imposition of standards or assumptions along those lines. Such systems will employ AI algorithms that are trained in consideration of diverse learning bases as well as systems that are capable of adapting to learning within different cultural settings. A hybrid learning platform supports culturally responsive AI to encourage participation.

Bias in algorithms is still a pressing issue that affects AI integration in education. Bias may occur when the data sets used to train algorithms favour a specific group or when developers unknowingly translate their culture norms into algorithmic systems. The impact of bias may be particularly devastating when developing a learning system that is a combination of online and offline learning. This is particularly true when it comes to developing AI systems that target a global audience.

Data privacy issues and surveillance are some of the issues that come with AI-assisted hybrid pedagogy. It is important to note that intelligent environments of learning, including learning analytics, operate through large amounts of data. Even though data is a great enhancer of learning results, its collection is seen as an invasion of privacy. It is, therefore, important that learner privacy is respected through data security alignment with ethical principles.

On the theme of sustainability, ethical usage of AI must be considered inseparable from sustainability. Optimizing for computational efficiency, eliminating unnecessary data processing, and curtailing energy use are all involved in responsible AI design. By synchronizing ethics and sustainability, it becomes possible for institutions to foster a positive impact of AI-enabled hybrid education on both educational and sustainability fronts.

Equity, Inclusion, and Global Hybrid Learning Contexts

Equity and inclusivity are a number of the values that underpin sustainable education, and feature as some of the concerns in AI-supported hybrid learning approaches. While hybrid learning does indeed present an opportunity to offer ease of access and flexibility to many learners, if not well-designed, it is likely to entrench already existing inequalities in society. Digital divides, regarding access to technology, are some of the important barriers to a number of learners in developing economies.

AI-based hybrid learning environments must, therefore, be analyzed next with an equity lens that examines who is able to reap the benefits of innovation in technology and who is left out in this endeavour. Intelligent tutoring systems, adaptive learning platforms, and data analytics-based support for decision-making include inclusive learning environments through the identification of learners who are at risk, thus offering them support. This shall be possible only with equitable technology access guarantees and appropriate design that is culturally compliant.

Within the learning environment that is global in nature due to hybrid learning, both positives and negatives are present at once. For example, collaboration on a global level through hybrid learning makes it possible to achieve global classrooms and learning. The challenge in working within a global learning environment provided by hybrid learning is posed by language, practice, and technology differences.

There is a need to develop faculties in such a way that equity and inclusion in AI-enabled hybrid learning environments are facilitated. Teachers should be helped in terms of their digital and intercultural competency development so that they can create an efficient learning system. Apart from this, it is required that a facility be developed in an institution that is related to accessibility, affordability, and sustainability in the context of online learning.

The experiences of implementing and using hybrid learning with AI tools in education differ greatly all over the world. While institutions in the Global North may have access to better digital infrastructures, reliable internet access, and the finances needed to develop new technologies, institutions in the Global South will more often struggle with access to technology, such as connectivity or cost, as well as the capacity of their institutions to implement the advanced Ai supported systems. Therefore, it is vital when designing hybrid learning environments to address global inequalities in access to technology and access to educational resources.

Implications

The inclusion of artificial intelligence into hybrid models of education has significant repercussions within the realm of education. The future trends encompass the educational paradigm, educational administration, educational policies, educational accountability, and technological development. With the idea of sustainability in mind, the AI-based education and hybrid pedagogy should have a paradigm shift in terms of educational responsibility. The paradigm should include innovativeness and sustainability, equity, and inclusiveness.

Pedagogical Implications

The integration of AI and hybrid pedagogy has several implications for education. Hybrid learning enabled by AI means that teachers must become accustomed to different approaches, from those associated by tradition with classroom teaching to those based on mutual collaboration between the learner and AI. The focus of the teaching profession shifts from knowledge transmission to acting as a catalyst, guide, or mediator.

One of the significant implications of education with respect to pedagogy is the need to personalize and adapt to individualized approaches to learning. Intelligent tutoring tools and analytics powered by AI offer educators tools to personalize education according to individual needs and preferences of students. However, in a hybrid setup where students traverse different modes of education and different environments of learning, personalization will be important to promote overall connectivity of the continuum of education. Personalization can happen in education with respect to its principles of developing sustainable education, yet it cannot become a consequence of algorithmic optimizations within auto-learning episodes.

AI-powered hybrid pedagogies shall continue to enhance the possibilities of experiential/projecd-based learning. Group projects, feedback functions, and reflection analysis capacities of AI will enable the students to handle real-word sustainability challenges. This will go a long way in enhancing the critical thinking skills, problem solving skills and intercultural skills in addressing global issues.

The learning designs, which include sustainability issues and intercultural cooperation, will motivate the students to relate the subject matter to the areas of sustainability related to the society and environment.

Another critical implication of pedagogy in the digital age is that of assessment. Through the implementation of artificial intelligence, it is possible that assessment systems will be able to provide students with continuous or formative assessment and support student learning capabilities in a self-directed manner. Further, in a blended learning environment, these systems are also able to provide teachers with student learning processes in both online and classroom learning as a whole. However, in applying artificial intelligence to assessment systems, there are critical aspects relating to fairness and transparency to be considered in implementing sustainable pedagogy.

Sustainable hybrid pedagogy would also call for a different level of assessment literacy. Even though AI-assessment technologies would provide rapid responses or inline assessments, these would primarily concentrate on results rather than processes. Alternatively, educators would need to assess AI-assessment practices that truly serve the ideals of results in a sustainable development fashion—system thinking, values attributes, or competencies with an intercultural orientation (Sterling, 2011). Combining formative assessment activity, reflection, or projects using AI technology would constitute an attractive combination of effectiveness with a learning process.

Institutional Implications

From an organizational perspective, the implementation of hybrid learning through AI-enabled pedagogy translates to organizational change. Here, institutions need to shift from piece-meal approaches to the integration of technologies into their strategies in a manner that addresses both organizational sustainability and interconnected learning. This calls for organizational transformation in aspects such as mission and organizational policies.

One of the most important institutional outcomes in this matter is the need to focus on sustainable digital infrastructure. The development of a hybrid learning model using artificial intelligence depends on having a strong digital infrastructure with data and connectivity capabilities and a focus on sustainable infrastructure to reduce the negative impact on the environment through energy-efficient infrastructure and a green approach to information and communication technology.

Institutional governance structures and policies should also have a significant role in the appropriate use of AI. Data privacy transparency guidelines concerning AI should be in place to safeguard the rights of the learner. There should be a mechanism put in place to analyze the AI systems used in the institution to engage the entire stakeholder in decision-making in the institution. The policies in a culturally rich environment should be inclusive to safeguard the values of diversity in the hybrid learning environment facilitated by AI.

The other significant implication of the case study for the institution would be the development of the faculty. It would be paramount for the faculty members to receive training on how they can apply AI in the teaching processes they undertake. The faculty development that the institution would undertake would be significant since they would be ready for the task of applying the teaching that fits the concept of the hybrid approach.

Finally, the implications of institutions include the concepts of collaboration and partnership. Integrations and combinations of institutions and locations and sectors are fostered by AI hybrid learning approaches. Partnerships with industry, culture, and international bodies could offer improvements to the learning experience and become part of sustainability and agendas for the preservation of environments and settings where educations take place.

Hybrid learning environments also add to the effect of social interactions and community building. Online learning systems, apart from having flexibility, can also bring about isolation if they are designed in a manner that hinders interactions. The sustainable use of hybrid learning systems would emphasize cooperation and dialogic experiences inside the hybrid learning environment. Using AI tools would add to the process of social learning, not replace it.

Most importantly, it is necessary to ensure learners are helped to ensure critical AI literacy. It is vital to understand AI system workings and implications so learners can be empowered as responsible digital citizens. Including AI ethics, sustainability concepts in curricula helps learners have informed perspectives about technology in society and in nature (Floridi et al., 2018).

Policy and Practice Implications

Models of policies at the local, national, and international levels have important impacts on the application and implementation of AI-powered hybrid pedagogy. It is important to note that policymakers have an important role to play in fostering an enabling environment to facilitate the future of sustainable and inclusive digital learning and education, primarily aligned to ethics and values.

A key policy implication would be to ensure integration between educational policies and the agendas for sustainability. It has to be recognized in educational policies that the use of AI and hybrid learning has been important in achieving SDG-4 and that educational policies must support digital access initiatives. The digital divide also needs to be addressed by educational policymakers to ensure fair access to technology.

The other critical area of interest is AI ethical governance. Data regulation, data protection, and algorithmic accountability are just some of the norms which need to be developed. The ethical norms of AI need to be dynamic and responsive to cultural differences. Sharing of best practices would be enabled through global cooperation, which would be of aid in making the norms more global.

From the practice perspective, it is significant to implement the principles of policies in practical terms. This necessitates motivating inclusive learning, make choices concerning the application of AI tools on suitable ethical and sustainability drivers, as well as involve learners in digital learning spaces as active participants. Guidelines and toolkits derived in practice could assist the teachers in managing the intricacy associated with hybrid learning through the implementation of AI technologies.

It has multiple implications, and it affects learning, institutions, and policies. However, if a holistic method of dealing with these issues is adopted, resilient and globally appropriate learning systems can be the end result.

Specifically, for AI-based education to attain sustainability, there are demands for policy structures to be in place to ensure the complementary role of digital innovation in the pursuit of environmental as well as social values. This is because the role of policymakers is to formulate policies around the use of AI in education from the perspective of environmental values, which may even offer a push for sustainable technology practices.

However, the collaborative effort in the international space is quite significant in the hybrids and AI-powered learning systems, as in most instances, it encompasses more than one national boundary. There will be a capacity to enable cross-border learning initiatives in the event the standards on Ethical AI, data, and sustainability are aligned in a manner that protects the interests of learners. The policymakers need to facilitate research and innovation projects directed at ensuring sustainable uses of AI in the learning space.

Institutions of higher education should establish reasonable practices for using multiple forms of artificial intelligence and hybrid teaching methodologies. Institutions of higher education (IHE) need to develop environmentally-friendly (green) metrics for their use of artificial intelligence technologies and align their requirements with their environmental sustainability policies.

Through the following specific activities, IHE can implement the environmental sustainability practices recommended for their use of artificial intelligence.

1. Develop a standard environmental sustainability policy for IHEs to acquire green artificial intelligence systems and require that they use energy efficient (green) technology in all of their artificial intelligence acquisition.
2. Conduct regular environmental sustainability assessments of all artificial intelligence systems.
3. Develop and implement Data Minimisation and Privacy by Design principles for processing information through artificial intelligence systems.
4. Create and maintain an Ethical Review Board to review the design of, and implementation of, IHE's AI technology.
5. Require manufacturers of AI technologies to disclose energy consumption and carbon emissions associated with their products.
6. Ensure that shared cloud computing resources are managed with IHEs' entire energy supply from renewable resources.
7. Develop a process for auditing the decision-making algorithms for bias in order to reduce bias and discrimination in instruction supported by artificial intelligence.

Through the application of these governance mechanisms, IHEs will be better positioned to provide assurance regarding the ethical and environmental sustainability of all artificial intelligence products developed, produced and/or acquired by their institutions.

Implications for Cultural Inclusion and Global Learning

Inclusion of culture, therefore, represents a highly significant factor with respect to the sustainability of AI-based hybrid pedagogy on the one hand and the global approach to education on the other. It should be noted that as education slowly became a global phenomenon, hybrid educational settings allow people to interlink across different cultures and socio-economic settings.

The AI systems, which are a feature of the hybrid model, need to be investigated from a critical standpoint regarding their possible biases along cultural and epistemic lines. The language processing systems, systems that evaluate students, and content systems are most reflective of the prevailing culture, which may suppress other ideologies. Furthermore, it is assumed that education for sustainability requires adopting a thoughtful strategy regarding the development of culturally sensitive AI systems.

Educators and institutions can make use of hybrid pedagogies for supporting dialogue and teamwork for solving sustainability problems. Online exchange programs, projects, and research activities across different cultures represent some of the potential applications of AI-enabled hybrid education for global citizenship and responsibility for sustainable development.

One of the major areas of future research will pertain to the importance of longitudinal research studies to enable an understanding of the outcomes of AI-integrated hybrid learning and the effect of the same on learning outcomes and the accomplishment of sustainability goals. Most of the existing research in the area of AI-integrated learning in higher education is focused on cross-sectional studies or short-term interventions to measure the outcomes of learning in the short term in respect to learning outcomes, and studies of the same nature lack relevance to understand the impact of learning in respect to the important aspects of the same, which include educational autonomy, ethics, and intercultural knowledge (Dwivedi et al., 2021).

Another relevant avenue of research involves the environmental impact associated with AI systems in educational settings. While sustainability has been often cited as one of the justifications underpinning hybrid learning, little has been found in existing bodies of research to quantify environmental impact in AI-supported learning systems and infrastructures (Yigitcanlar et al., 2021; Regona et al., 2024). There is considerable value in performing learning system lifecycle assessments to gather information that is relevant to higher education institutions attempting to harmonize environmental sustainability with innovation in learning technologies.

Ethical frameworks of governance of AI in hybrid learning environments is an area of research that is an added priority. Even though issues of transparency, accountability, or ethics have received wide consideration, much less work is being done on an empirical investigation of these issues within an institution. Future research could explore governance frameworks that ensure institution-based policies, involvement of stakeholders, and an ongoing assessment of AI practices (Floridi et al., 2018). Research based on comparative studies in different nations across cultures could also illuminate ethical frameworks to ensure sustained legitimacy of AI-based learning.

Another area which has been under researched relates to the development of culturally responsive AI. Indeed, quite a large number of the AI systems designed with an eye on educational use come from particular cultural, linguistic, and didactic traditions, making them less transferable to different learning ecologies. Furthermore, there needs to be an exploration of how AI systems can be developed to meet the demands of epistemic diversity, multilingualism, and learning ecologies. Techniques of participatory design with educators and learners from a very different cultural background can offer some very useful strategies to advance a hybrid AI-enabled pedagogy that meets different cultural ecologies.

The future studies may also concentrate on the significance of AI-enriched hybrid pedagogy to contribute to ESD. Experiential learning, project-based learning, and problem-based learning in the learning spaces provided by hybrid learning are opened; nonetheless, research on data linking the contribution of AI-enriched pedagogy to sustainability competency development is sparse, as noted by Wals in 2015. Moreover, studies on sustainability issues in reality, interdisciplinary collaboration, and community-based learning may prove to be helpful in establishing a strong stance on sustainable hybrid learning.

At last, there is the need for research that will highlight learner views regarding AI, data governance, and sustainability. The importance of learning how learners view algorithmic decision-making approaches, data gathering, and sustainability concerns related to digital learning cannot be overemphasized, as this is relevant to the development of ethical educational systems that focus on learners (Williamson & Eynon, 2020).

3. FUTURE RESEARCH DIRECTIONS

Rapid developments in artificial intelligence and hybrid pedagogy offer a live and constantly developing field of study with many opportunities for further study and analysis in the years to come. A key trend that will become increasingly important for further study in the years to come will be the integration of AI with hybrid settings within the field of education and related sectors.

One promising area that may emerge in future work entails sustainability studies related to AI-supported educational systems. Although the idea of a mixed approach to learning is portrayed as ecologically sustainable when contrasted to other educational systems, the current pattern of AI computing has yet to be assessed from a sustainability prospective. Hence, further research is warranted that thoroughly investigates the energy consumption and lifecycle assessment associated with AI-supported educational systems.

One of the important regions that can be explored further in the realm of AI research is the cultural adaptability of AI systems used in the education sector. Current research pertaining to AI has mostly been concentrated on technological aspects of performance and learning outcomes rather than the engagement between AI-based systems and culture. There arises a need for research that can study the differences between various cultures associated with AI-based hybrid modes of learning. The development of multilingual AI-based systems can help achieve this objective.

There is also a need to investigate the ethics of AI in hybrid pedagogies in future studies. This will involve the analysis of organizational policies on data privacy in relation to AI transparency in various institutions. Longitudinal studies will be helpful in understanding how these ethics will be developed in time and their impact on teaching performance as well as community acceptance. Such studies should be carried out in consultation with teaching professionals to ensure that these ethics find roots in practice.

The function of educators in AI-facilitated hybrid learning is another area of research that has promising potential. Research that focuses on the experience of educators and the decisions that they make in terms of education can have important insights that can reveal the reaction of educators toward the integration of AI in facilitated learning. The impact of competency levels of educators in digital and intercultural environments can also be explored.

In conclusion, future studies should concentrate on an integrated approach to pedagogy on how to link AI, hybrid learning, and sustainability and inter-cultural collaboration. Design research and case studies should inform how an integrated approach to pedagogy can be successfully executed at different levels. Future studies will assist in the adaptation of hybrid learning pedagogy in different parts of the world by highlighting areas of improvement.

Another significant field of research is the environmental impact of AI systems used within the education sector. Despite sustainability being a popular paradigm in the hybrid reality of learning, the scientific literature lacks studies evaluating the environmental implications of education enabled by AI. In the years to come, research efforts should investigate the energy use, CO_2 emissions, data storage requirements, and e-waste generated due to the environmental sustainability of education AI systems (Regona et al., 2024; Yigitcanlar et al., 2021).

Ethical framework studies on AI governance within the context of hybrid learning are an additional area of high priority. Whereas the aspects of transparency, accountability, and justice are well-pondered norms, very few studies are available that examine the operationalization of these norms within the context of an institution of learning. Future research should explore the kind of governance framework that includes the alignment of an institution's policies with the engagement of various stakeholders and monitoring the use of AI (Floridi et al., 2018). Comparative studies can also help to explore the kind of influence that ethical norms are having on the sustainability of AI-influenced learning.

Culturally responsive design for AI is yet another research avenue that is not well investigated. Current AI systems employed in learning are often engineered in a particular cultural, language-based, and learning framework that is not universal in nature. Researchers should investigate ways in which AI technology can be utilized to promote epistemological diversity and multilingual learning as well as culturally responsive learning paradigms (Banks, 2015). A participatory design paradigm with educators and learners coming from diverse cultural settings is one promising pathway to develop culturally responsive AI-based hybrid learning paradigms.

Furthermore, it is recommended that future studies investigate the application of AI-supported hybrid pedagogy in terms of its sustainability function within education for sustainable development (ESD) in particular. Although hybrid learning spaces provide capacities for experiential, project-based, and problem-based learning, evidence of a sustainability focus in AI-supported pedagogy is still scant (Wals, 2015). Empirical studies in support of theoretical sustainability concepts within sustainability-focused hybrid education can help establish a theoretical basis within this context.

Finally, there is a call for research that critically investigates learners' views on AI, data governance, and sustainability. It is important that researchers not only learn about algorithmic decision-making but also explore learners' views on data collection practices and environmental factors that relate to digital learning. It is necessary that research is utilized that can facilitate pedagogics that engage learners in shaping a positive digital learning future.

4. CONCLUSION

The convergence between sustainability, artificial intelligence (AI), and hybrid education is one of the crucial milestones of the development of the international educational systems. With the challenges of high-speed technological development, environmental and cultural globalization (among others) affecting societies, there is a need to address these issues within the education system in a responsible and ingenious way. Here, both opportunities and responsibilities are presented by rolling AI into the hybrid model of learning. The educational strategies must be not only oriented to the improvement of the efficiency and the learning results but also must serve to achieve the ethical responsibility, environmental sustainability, and social inclusion. This chapter has discussed relevance of the AI-supported hybrid learning in contributing to building the sustainable learning systems that can solve the modern challenges of the world.

Relying on interdisciplinary research in other areas, including artificial intelligence in education, intelligent tutoring systems, education and sustainable development, technology-enhanced learning, and cultural studies, the chapter has considered the opportunities and challenges that are connected with AI-assisted hybrid learning. Artificial intelligence will play a huge role in transforming the face of education by providing personalized learning, adapting instructions, and decision making based on data. This being said, AI implementation should be informed by the ethics and sustainability values to make sure that technological innovation does not negatively affect the well-being of the environment and social justice. The responsible implementation process implies the focus on the problems of environmental impact, the governance, and the long-term implication on society.

The other important theme that was raised in this chapter is the role culture plays in influencing sustainable education. The cultural diversity should not be regarded as the minor aspect of the educational technology, but as the main factor of the sustainable learning environments. The hybrid learning models that incorporate digital technologies with the face-to-face interaction are associated with the opportunities to collaborate with intercultural partners and exchange knowledge, as well as acquire the global citizenship. Such rooms will enable students with various backgrounds to have fruitful conversations and mutual learning. To attain such results, careful pedagogical planning and culturally sensitive AI technologies are needed that will enhance inclusion and respect towards other points of view.

This discussion has implication at the level of pedagogy, institutions and policies. Teachers have to acquire new skills to be able to use AI tools and retain human-focused pedagogies. The role of the teacher is to mediate between the AI systems and the learner to make sure that the technology does not substitute meaningful learning relations between a teacher and learners. To establish a control system that guarantees ethical and responsible application of AI technologies, institutions should invest in sustainable digital infrastructure and create control mechanisms. Governments and international organizations at the policy level are increasingly important in formulating regulatory environments which will bring technological innovation to the country in line with societal and environmental objectives.

Lastly, this chapter demonstrates the need to consider AI as a component of a larger socio-technical system and not just a technical instrument. AI has an impact on the educational practice, environmental sustainability, and social values. The acknowledgment of this view prompt to more responsible and thoughtful methods of AI usages in education. With proper alignment, with sustainability, ethical governance, and intercultural knowledge, AI-based hybrid education can help to create stronger and more inclusive educational delivery frameworks in the future.

REFERENCES

Allen, I. E., Seaman, J., Poulin, R., & Straut, T. T. (2017). *Online report card: Tracking online education in the United States*. Babson Survey Research Group.

Banks, J. A. (2015). *Cultural diversity and education: Foundations, curriculum, and teaching* (6th ed.). Routledge. DOI: 10.4324/9781315622255

Dwivedi, Y. K., Hughes, L., Ismagilova, E., Aarts, G., Coombs, C., Crick, T., Duan, Y., Dwivedi, R., Edwards, J., Eirug, A., Galanos, V., Ilavarasan, P. V., Janssen, M., Jones, P., Kar, A. K., Kizgin, H., Kronemann, B., Lal, B., Lucini, B., & Williams, M. D. (2021). Artificial intelligence (AI): Multidisciplinary perspectives on emerging challenges, opportunities, and agenda for research, practice and policy. *International Journal of Information Management*, *57*, 101994. DOI: 10.1016/j.ijinfomgt.2019.08.002

Floridi, L., Cowls, J., Beltrametti, M., Chatila, R., Chazerand, P., Dignum, V., Luetge, C., Madelin, R., Pagallo, U., Rossi, F., Schafer, B., Valcke, P., & Vayena, E. (2018). AI4People—An ethical framework for a good AI society: Opportunities, risks, principles, and recommendations. *Minds and Machines*, *28*(4), 689–707. DOI: 10.1007/s11023-018-9482-5 PMID: 30930541

Garrison, D. R., & Kanuka, H. (2008). Blended learning: Uncovering its transformative potential in higher education. *The Internet and Higher Education*, *7*(2), 95–105. DOI: 10.1016/j.iheduc.2004.02.001

Pane, J. F., Steiner, E. D., Baird, M. D., & Hamilton, L. S. (2014). *Continued progress: Promising evidence on personalized learning*. RAND Corporation.

Regona, M., Yigitcanlar, T., Xia, B., & Li, R. Y. M. (2024). Artificial intelligence and the environment: A review of the environmental implications of AI. *Sustainable Cities and Society*, *101*, 104989. DOI: 10.1016/j.scs.2023.104989

Selwyn, N. (2019). *Should robots replace teachers? AI and the future of education*. Polity Press.

Sterling, S. (2011). *Transformative learning and sustainability: Sketching the conceptual ground*. Learning and Teaching in Higher Education.

UNESCO. (2017). *Education for sustainable development goals: Learning objectives*. UNESCO.

Williamson, B., & Eynon, R. (2020). Historical threads, missing links, and future directions in AI in education. *Learning, Media and Technology*, *45*(3), 223–235. DOI: 10.1080/17439884.2020.1798995

Yigitcanlar, T., Desouza, K. C., Butler, L., & Roozkhosh, F. (2021). Contributions and risks of artificial intelligence in building smarter cities: Insights from a systematic review. *Sustainability*, *13*(4), 2073. DOI: 10.3390/su13042073

Chapter 13
AI for Trust and Social Interaction:
A Social Capital Perspective on Knowledge Sharing in Vietnam's Higher Education

Thi-Trang Tran
http://orcid.org/0000-0001-9790-6009
HUTECH University, Vietnam

Thi-Thuy-Trang Ha
http://orcid.org/0009-0006-9204-8854
HUTECH University, Vietnam

Thi-Bich-Diep Le
HUTECH University, Vietnam

Ngoc Hong Truong
University of Economics Ho Chi Minh City, Vietnam

Linh Tran Khanh Do
RMIT International University, Vietnam

Hiep Pham
RMIT International University, Vietnam

Truong Huy
http://orcid.org/0000-0002-0063-5335
RMIT International University, Vietnam

Dung Truong Quang
http://orcid.org/0000-0002-5108-5062
RMIT International University, Vietnam

ABSTRACT

Knowledge sharing is critical to learning and innovation in higher education but is often constrained by hierarchy, competition, and limited trust and social interaction, particularly in emerging systems such as Vietnam. As artificial intelligence (AI) becomes increasingly integrated into universities, it reshapes how academic knowledge is exchanged. Drawing on Social Capital Theory, this study examines the effects of trust and social interaction on faculty knowledge sharing and the role of AI-enabled platforms in strengthening these relationships. Using a mixed-methods

DOI: 10.4018/979-8-3373-7462-8.ch013

design, data were collected from discussion groups with 15 faculty members and surveys of 244 faculty members across 11 universities in Ho Chi Minh City. The findings show that trust and social interaction positively influence knowledge sharing, while AI platforms act as relational amplifiers by enhancing transparency, security, and interaction. The study offers insights for developing human-centered, trust-building AI strategies in higher education.

1. INTRODUCTION: OVERVIEW OF KNOWLEDGE SHARING IN HIGHER EDUCATION

Knowledge sharing is widely recognized as the cornerstone of organizational learning, innovation, and sustainable performance, particularly in higher education institutions, where knowledge creation and dissemination are core missions (Tan & Ramayah, 2014). Universities are expected to function as knowledge-intensive institutions, where faculty collaboration, interdisciplinary exchange, and collective learning are fundamental to research quality, teaching innovation, and societal impact. Despite these expectations, ongoing evidence suggests that knowledge sharing among academics remains uneven, fragmented, and often lacks institutionalization (Al-Kurdi et al., 2018).

A persistent barrier to effective knowledge sharing in universities lies in the relational dynamics of academic work. Faculty members frequently operate in silos, with limited incentives to share expertise, teaching materials, or research insights beyond close networks. Knowledge withholding may also be strategic and rational in the workplace environment. Connelly et al. (2012) distinguish between different forms of knowledge hiding, including playing dumb, evasive hiding, and rationalized hiding. Such behaviors often emerge in competitive environments where authorship recognition, grant success, and professional reputation are at stake (Peng, 2013; Ramayah et al., 2014; Serenko & Bontis, 2016; Zacharewicz et al., 2019). These conditions slow the flow of information, hinder collaboration, and weaken an institution's overall ability to adapt to the changing demands of higher education.

At the heart of these challenges lie deficiencies in trust and social interaction. Trust is critical for creating psychological safety, enabling individuals to share tentative ideas, unfinished work, and experiential knowledge without fear of exploitation or reputational harm (Edmondson, 2018; Nahapiet & Ghoshal, 1998). When trust is low, teachers are more inclined to withhold their knowledge or limit exchanges to small, familiar networks. Similarly, a lack of opportunities for meaningful social interaction—formal or informal—hinders the development of relationships that foster ongoing collaboration and mutual learning (Cross, 2021). In a hierarchical and competitive academic environment, these relational deficiencies can significantly impede knowledge sharing.

These challenges are particularly prominent in Vietnamese higher education, where institutional and cultural factors intersect, limiting open knowledge exchange. Vietnamese universities operate within governance structures influenced by Confucian traditions, emphasizing hierarchy, seniority, and respect for authority (Bond & Hwang, 1986; Hallinger & Truong, 2014) where harmony preservation and respect for hierarchy shape communication norms. Hofstede (2001) cultural dimensions of power distance further illuminate this context. Vietnam scores relatively high on power distance, indicating acceptance of hierarchical order and uneven power distribution. In such an environment, young scholars may hesitate to question senior colleagues or openly share differing viewpoints, limiting horizontal knowledge flow. Vietnam also reflects a collectivist tendency, where group loyalty may encourage knowledge sharing within close networks but restrict broader exchange between departments. Veteran faculty may view knowledge as personal assets accumulated through experience rather than a shared resource. Markus and Kitayama (2014) argue that in collectivist cultures, individuals tend to adopt an interdependent self-construal, prioritizing relational harmony over self-assertion. In academic environments, it may collectively reduce willingness to share ideas or challenge established perspectives. Simultaneously, rapid higher education reforms, internationalization pressures, and intense competition for rankings, research funding, and prestige have increased pressure for individual performance. These dynamics may further diminish the incentive for collaborative knowledge sharing, making it more risky than beneficial. Research recently highlights how centralized management, competitive evaluation systems, and ongoing internationalization reforms influence academic collaboration and autonomy in Vietnamese high education institutions (Tran et al., 2020; Van Quyet & Hai, 2023; Vuong et al., 2020).

Against this backdrop, digital transformation, particularly the increasing adoption of AI, presents new opportunities to reshape how academic knowledge is shared. AI-powered systems such as intelligent knowledge repositories, adaptive learning platforms, recommendation engines, and AI-mediated communication tools can create alternative interactive spaces less constrained by physical distance, time, or rigid organizational hierarchies (Holmes et al., 2019; Hughes et al., 2025; Sure et al., 2025). By facilitating access to relevant resources, suggesting potential collaborators, and reducing the workloads in teaching and administrative tasks, AI can lower practical and social barriers to collaboration. In contexts where direct interaction is limited by hierarchy or workload, AI-powered platforms can provide a more neutral and inclusive environment for exchange.

Moreover, it is notable that AI alone cannot solve the challenges of knowledge sharing. The effectiveness of AI in supporting collaboration depends primarily on how it interacts with existing social structures, norms, and trust relationships (Mooradian et al., 2006). Without sufficient trust, transparency, and opportunities for social interaction, AI systems risk becoming underutilized or reinforcing existing inequalities rather than alleviating them (Zhou & Lu, 2024). In recent years, the increasing prevalence of algorithms and their potential to reproduce and amplify biases inherent in training data have become a central topic of discussion. For example, algorithms can favor established researchers over emerging researchers, seasoned researchers over lesser-known researchers, research conducted in dominant languages over minority languages, or researchers in certain fields, thereby excluding young researchers, researchers from minority groups, or those conducting interdisciplinary research (Eubanks, 2018; Noble, 2018). However, Iliadis and Russo (2016) emphasize that data systems are not neutral repositories, but structured representations shaped by power relations, institutional priorities, and design choices. When AI algorithms are used to recommend collaborators, citations ranking, or performance analytics, they can create and reinforce power dynamics that benefit some groups while limiting the opportunities for advancement for others like young scholars if not carefully designed and governed. Therefore, it is crucial to study the impacts of AI on knowledge sharing through the creation of collaborative opportunities and relationships by enhancing trust and social interaction.

However, the majority of existing empirical studies on AI in higher education primarily focus on pedagogical outcomes, analysis of student learning outcomes, or the technical effectiveness of AI-assisted teaching systems (Chen et al., 2020; Zawacki-Richter et al., 2019). While these studies demonstrate the increasing role of AI in education, they rarely consider how AI interacts with relational dynamics—such as trust and social interaction—that underpin knowledge sharing among faculty. In particular, little attention has been paid to how AI-assisted collaborative infrastructures influence knowledge exchange in hierarchical and culturally specific academic environments, especially in developing higher education systems like Vietnam. This creates a crucial research gap: although AI technologies are increasingly integrated into university workflows, their role in shaping the relational conditions for knowledge sharing remains largely unexplored.

To theorize these dynamics, this chapter integrates Social Capital Theory (SCT) with Cognitive Load Theory (CLT). SCT conceptualizes knowledge exchange as embedded within networks of relationships characterized by trust, shared norms, and mutual understandings (Nahapiet & Ghoshal, 1998). Its structural, relational, and cognitive dimensions explain how social interaction and trust enable collective learning. However, knowledge sharing also involves cognitive processes. CLT complements that individuals have limited cognitive capacity; thus, the accessibility and organization of information influence learning and collaboration (Sweller, 1988). AI-powered platforms may reduce extraneous cognitive load by filtering information, recommending relevant resources, and structuring communication. By combining SCT and CLT, this chapter conceptualizes AI as both a relational and cognitive infrastructure that shapes how faculty connect, process knowledge, and engage in knowledge-sharing behavior within Vietnamese higher education. Accordingly, AI is conceptualized as a context shaping academic collaboration, rather than a variable explicitly tested in this study. Guided by this framework, the chapter addresses the following research questions:

In the AI integration context, how does trust influence knowledge-sharing behaviors among lecturers in Vietnamese universities?
In the AI integration context, how does social interaction influence knowledge-sharing behaviors among lecturers in Vietnamese universities?

To answer these questions, the study adopted a mixed-methods approach, combining focus group discussions with 15 teachers and a questionnaire survey of 244 teachers from 11 universities in Ho Chi Minh City. The qualitative phase explored teachers' perceptions of trust, social interactions, and barriers to knowledge sharing, while the quantitative phase empirically tested the proposed relationships and the moderating role of AI platform use.

2. RESEARCH BACKGROUND AND THEORETICAL FOUNDATION

2.1 Knowledge Sharing Behaviors

Knowledge-sharing behavior refers to the intentional exchange of information, skills, experiences, and insights among individuals to support learning and collective problem-solving. Knowledge exchange occurs through both formal mechanisms, such as institutional archives, formal collaboration platforms, structured research groups, and informal channels, including hallway conversations, break-time discussions, and interactions on professional social media. Informal exchange is particularly important for tacit knowledge transfer and spontaneous idea development, while formal systems provide transparency, documentation, and accountability. Contemporary research conceptualizes knowledge sharing as a socially embedded and context-dependent behavior shaped by the interaction of individual motivations, organizational structures, and broader cultural norms (Fauzi et al., 2023; Zaremohzzabieh & Mohd Rasdi, 2023).

At the individual level, motivation is a primary driver of knowledge-sharing behavior. A substantial body of evidence indicates that intrinsic motivations—such as enjoyment in helping others, intellectual curiosity, professional identity development, and the perceived meaningfulness of contribution—are often more influential than extrinsic rewards, including monetary incentives or formal recognition (Gerhart & Fang, 2015; Lin, 2007). Expectations of reciprocity are also crucial; individuals are more willing to contribute knowledge when they believe others will reciprocate in the future, reinforcing the social exchange cycle that sustains cooperative behavior (Wasko & Faraj, 2005). However, motivation alone is not sufficient to guarantee knowledge sharing. Individuals frequently face psychological and practical barriers, including time constraints, low self-esteem, fear of negative judgment, and concerns about losing uniqueness or competitive advantage (Riege, 2005). These barriers are particularly prominent in academic settings, where expertise and reputation are closely tied to career advancement.

At the organisational level, knowledge-sharing behaviours are strongly influenced by institutional culture, leadership practices, and structural arrangements. Organisations that promote collaborative values, emphasise collective success, and frame knowledge as a shared organisational resource tend to foster higher levels of voluntary knowledge exchange (McDermott & O'Dell, 2001). The role of leaders is particularly influential: when they adopt collaborative behavior, demonstrate openness to learning, and create a psychologically safe environment, employees feel more comfortable sharing their knowledge (Srivastava et al., 2006). Structural mechanisms, such as cross-functional groups, digital knowledge management systems, and clearly defined intellectual property policies, can facilitate the flow of knowledge by reducing ambiguity and coordination costs (Faraj et al., 2018; Wenger et al., 2002). Conversely, systems that prioritize individual competition can inadvertently reduce the incentive to share knowledge, encouraging individuals to hoard it as a form of personal capital (Bock et al., 2005).

Cultural dimensions also add a critical layer of complexity to knowledge-sharing behaviors. Power distance influences an individual's comfort level when sharing knowledge with superiors; in environments with high power distance, hierarchical barriers can hinder the upward flow of knowledge (Ardichvili et al., 2006). Foucault (1977) and Lukes (2012) supports that knowledge sharing is shaped by both visible hierarchy and subtle forms of power that control access and influence norms and perceptions. Secondly, cultural orientations toward individualism and collectivism also influence whether knowledge is perceived as personal intellectual property or a collective good. While collectivist cultures may encourage sharing within trusted in-groups, they may also restrict knowledge exchange across organizational or disciplinary boundaries due to strong in-group–out-group distinctions (Chmielecki, 2013). Furthermore, aversion to uncertainty determines tolerance for ambiguity and willingness to share uncertain or incomplete knowledge. Cultures with high levels of aversion to uncertainty may favor formal and structured mechanisms over informal forms of exchange (Michailova & Hutchings, 2006).

2.2 Knowledge Sharing in Higher Education

Knowledge sharing plays a more vital role in sustaining the academic mission of higher education institutions, where the exchange of ideas, teaching materials, research results, and professional experience continuously shapes the development of both individuals and organizations (Chyi Lee & Yang, 2000). They encompass not only explicit knowledge that can be easily recorded and shared, but also tacit knowledge embedded in personal experience and professional judgment (Nonaka, 2009). When faculty actively participate in these exchanges, the benefits are enormous: pedagogical quality is improved as educators learn from each other, innovation is accelerated as diverse perspectives converge, and the organization strengthens its collective intellectual capacity, helping to better meet evolving educational needs (Tan & Ramayah, 2014).

Despite these relational foundations, knowledge sharing in academic environments is often constrained. Faculty members may view their knowledge as a personal asset tied to career advancement, where success in promotions, appointment evaluations, and grant competitions depends on demonstrating personal expertise and academic independence (Davenport et al., 1998). This can foster a protective attitude toward teaching innovations, research ideas, and methodological approaches. Concerns about intellectual property rights also hinder sharing, especially in areas where research findings may have commercial value or patent potential (Henkel, 2006). For instance, when researchers share their research ideas too early, they may face criticism or appropriation, potentially undermining their competitive edge in the funding or publication process (Henkel, 2006). Similarly, some people may take advantage of free-riding opportunities without reciprocity (Wasko & Faraj, 2005). In an academic context, scholars may share marginal findings while protecting core ideas valuable for publication, funding, or commercialization. These dynamics are further amplified by the rise of academic capitalism, where universities increasingly compete for external funding, patents, and industry partnerships (Slaughter & Leslie, 1997). As a result, knowledge sharing in higher education institutions that could benefit the entire academic community often remains siloed.

As Vietnamese higher education increasingly orients itself towards market demands and international competition, the motivation to protect intellectual property may overshadow the motivations for promoting open exchange. Currently, Vietnam has over 230 higher education institutions, most operating under the centralized management of the Ministry of Education and Training (MOET), although recent reforms have gradually expanded their autonomy (Tran & Marginson, 2018).

Since major reforms such as the Higher Education Reform Program of 2005 and subsequent autonomy policies in 2014 and 2018, universities have faced increasing pressure to improve research productivity, the number of international publications, and partnerships with industry. Faculty evaluation and promotion criteria primarily emphasize individual research outcomes, competition for grants, and heavy teaching workloads—often exceeding 250-300 teaching hours per year—diminishing the incentive for collaborative knowledge sharing (Le et al., 2024; Nguyen et al., 2022). Institutional reward systems remain largely performance-oriented, which may encourage faculty to strategically protect valuable knowledge rather than share it publicly.

Taken together, this research focuses on trust and social interaction because rather than a purely rational or transactional act, knowledge sharing involves risk, vulnerability, and relational judgement (Albaram & Lim, 2023; De Felice et al., 2023), particularly in professional and academic settings where expertise is closely tied to status and identity (van Houten, 2023; Wen & Ma, 2021). In Vietnam's hierarchical academic system, senior lecturers often hold the majority of symbolic and status, giving them legitimacy as collaborative experts which complicates the knowledge sharing behaviors among faculty. In such academic environments characterized by hierarchy, professional autonomy, and competitive pressure for performance, low levels of trust often lead to individuals retaining knowledge even when formal knowledge-sharing systems have been established (Bock et al., 2005; Serenko & Bontis, 2016). Social interaction further reinforces this process by facilitating the development of relationships, informal networks, and shared understanding, through which knowledge—especially tacit and experiential knowledge—can be effectively communicated (Cross & Sproull, 2004; Faraj et al., 2018). Despite these risks, research consistently shows that well-managed knowledge sharing enhances innovation, collaboration, and institutional adaptability when supported by trust and appropriate governance mechanisms (Wang & Noe, 2010). Therefore, focusing on trust and social interaction is particularly important in the context of higher education, where collaboration relies less on formal authority and more on voluntary participation and peer relationships (Dismore et al., 2024; Shaikh et al., 2023).

2.3 The Emergence of AI in Higher Education

AI has become an increasingly influential force in higher education, reshaping how teaching, research, and academic collaboration are organized. Beyond its teaching applications, AI is gaining prominence due to its potential to address persistent challenges in knowledge sharing, particularly those arising from hierarchical structures, heavy workloads, and fragmented academic networks. AI-powered platforms – such as adaptive learning systems, intelligent knowledge repositories, and AI-assisted communication tools – are now integrated into many universities, providing new infrastructure for interaction and collaboration (Holmes et al., 2019; Zawacki-Richter et al., 2019). In the context of knowledge sharing, these technologies hold immense potential by supporting collaboration, opening up new spaces for interaction, and enabling faculty to exchange knowledge more effectively.

For example, AI-powered systems are increasingly enhancing knowledge sharing and collaboration among faculty in higher education by identifying complementary expertise and suggesting potential collaborators (Li et al., 2024; Shiddiqi et al., 2025) making individual contributions more apparent and valued. By analyzing scholarly outputs, research interests, and teaching activities, AI enables connections that may not emerge through traditional academic networks, thereby expanding opportunities for collaboration across disciplines and career stages. Moreover, AI supports knowledge sharing indirectly by reducing the administrative burdens that frequently constrain academic collaboration. Automated assessment tools, AI-assisted feedback systems, and virtual teaching assistants handle routine and repetitive tasks, allowing faculty to reallocate time and cognitive resources toward collaborative research, curriculum development, and mentorship (Rozputnia et al., 2025). By alleviating workload pressures, AI increases faculty capacity to engage in sustained interaction with colleagues and participate in collective knowledge-building processes. Besides, drawing on weak ties theory, connections beyond close circles often provide access to new information and interdisciplinary opportunities, extending academic collaboration beyond immediate circles (Granovetter, 1973). AI can facilitate weak-tie connections across departments or institutions through algorithmic recommendations. Ultimately, these efficiencies can contribute to a shift in academic practice away from isolated individual performance toward more collaborative and collectively oriented goals. When faculty experience greater temporal and cognitive flexibility, they are more likely to engage in voluntary knowledge exchange, joint problem-solving, and peer learning (Sijbom et al., 2025).

Knowledge sharing is not only relational but also closely linked to organizational learning processes. Argyris and Schön (1997) distinguished between single-loop learning (improving efficiency within existing norms) and double-loop learning (questioning and transforming underlying assumptions). AI can facilitate single-loop learning by simplifying information retrieval and coordination, but their transformative potential depends on their ability to foster double-loop reflection on academic practices. March (1991) further developed this perspective with exploration–exploitation framework. AI can facilitate knowledge utilization by optimizing existing expertise and reinforcing dominant research areas through algorithmic recommendations. It can also facilitate exploration by connecting previously isolated researchers and generating new interdisciplinary knowledge. AI's ability to foster exploration or reinforce existing hierarchies depends on the interplay between relational capital and algorithmic design.

In Vietnamese universities, AI-powered digital platforms are frequently integrated with learning management systems and internal collaboration tools such as Google Workspace, Microsoft Teams, Moodle, and Canvas. These platforms saw widespread adoption following the rapid digital transformation brought about by the COVID-19 pandemic and are now commonly used for teaching management and administrative communication (Quy et al., 2023). Many systems incorporate AI-based features such as plagiarism detection (e.g., Turnitin), intelligent content recommendations, and collaborative document editing. Surveys of Vietnamese education institutions reveal that over 76% of faculty members regularly use AI for teaching, resource sharing, and communication with colleagues (Vietnam Pictorial, 2026). Beyond their pedagogical role, these platforms constitute an increasingly essential infrastructure for academic collaboration, enabling resource sharing, virtual meetings, and knowledge management with AI support.

2.4 Overview of Social Capital Theory

SCT offers a strong conceptual lens for understanding how knowledge sharing is influenced by the quality of relationships, network structures, and shared norms within an organization (Nahapiet & Ghoshal, 1998). They defined social capital as the actual and potential resources embedded within, available through, and derived from networks of relationships. These resources-trust, norms of reciprocity, shared understanding, and social ties-collectively enable individuals to access and exchange knowledge more effectively. SCT comprises three interrelated dimensions: structural (network ties and interaction patterns), relational (trust, norms, obligations), and cognitive (shared language and interpretive frameworks). Together, these dimensions shape individuals' ability and willingness to exchange knowledge (Tsai & Ghoshal, 1998). In higher education, where collaboration is largely voluntary and collegial rather than hierarchical, social capital is particularly critical in enabling knowledge exchange.

2.5 Overview of Cognitive Load Theory

From a learning science perspective, knowledge sharing through AI can be better understood through CLT (Sweller, 1988) which distinguishes between intrinsic, extraneous, and germane cognitive load. AI systems can reduce extrinsic loads by organizing information, suggesting relevant articles, and filtering large datasets, thereby making knowledge more accessible and supporting effective collaboration. However, poorly designed AI platforms can increase cognitive overload through excessive notifications, algorithmic suggestions, or information saturation, potentially hindering meaningful engagement (Eppler & Mengis, 2004). Beyond cognitive loads,

AI also influences metacognitive processes—instructors' perceptions of what they know, what others know, and when to seek further expertise (Schraw & Dennison, 1994). AI-powered systems can enhance metacognitive awareness by visualizing collaborative patterns and knowledge gaps. From a cognitive perspective (Hutchins, 1995), knowledge is not limited to individuals but is distributed among people, objects, and technological systems. Thus, AI becomes part of cognitive systems, reshaping how knowledge is coordinated, distributed, and utilized within academic networks.

2.6 Social Capital, Organizational Learning, and AI

Trust and social interaction are central to understanding how AI can either support or undermine knowledge sharing in higher education. Trust reduces perceived risk and creates the psychological safety necessary for faculty to engage in open exchanges (Edmondson, 1999; Rousseau et al., 1998). This is particularly important in hierarchical academic cultures where individuals may hesitate to challenge established norms or share unfinished ideas for fear of criticism or face-loss (Titi Amayah, 2013). In digitalized contexts, trust extends beyond interpersonal relationships to include confidence in algorithmic fairness, data governance, and transparency. AI platforms that emphasize transparency, data protection, and clear communication protocols can reinforce this sense of safety by providing faculty with a trustworthy and secure environment for collaboration (Treve, 2021). When it is perceived as reliable and ethically governed, it can strengthen relational capital-trust.

Meanwhile, social interaction forms the relational foundation upon which knowledge sharing is built. Frequent and meaningful interactions whether informal conversations, collaborative teaching, or peer discussions help faculty develop familiarity and mutual understanding, thereby encouraging the free exchange of expertise (Seibert et al., 2001). AI-powered tools enabling synchronous and asynchronous communication, virtual teamwork, and efficient knowledge retrieval can enhance opportunities for interaction, making collaboration easier and more convenient, especially across geographical or institutional boundaries (Chen et al., 2020). Consistent with Polanyi (2009) distinction and Nonaka (2009) SECI model, tacit knowledge transfer remains dependent on the socialization process — shared experience and depth of relationships, which cannot be fully automated. Therefore, AI may enhance efficiency and connectivity, but its contribution to deeper organizational learning depends on how it supports sustained interaction and reflective dialogue.

2.7 Research Gaps

Although previous research has explored knowledge sharing and the application of AI in higher education, these research areas remain quite fragmented (Holstein

& Doroudi, 2021; Serenko & Bontis, 2016; Zawacki-Richter et al., 2019). Existing work often views AI as a technologically efficient tool, prioritizing automation or performance outcomes over relational impacts (Zawacki-Richter et al., 2019). Meanwhile, research on social capital emphasizes trust and interaction but rarely examines how AI reshapes these mechanisms. Furthermore, very few studies analyze these dynamics within a hierarchical and high context like that of Vietnam. This study aims to fill this gap by combining SCT and CLT with an AI usage context and to understand how AI influences faculty's knowledge-sharing behaviors from relational and cognitive perspectives.

3. HYPOTHESIS DEVELOPMENT

3.1 Trust and Knowledge Sharing

Trust is consistently identified as one of the strongest predictors of knowledge-sharing behavior in any organizational context. Knowledge sharing carries inherent risks, including fear of criticism, loss of intellectual property rights, and the potential for misuse of shared ideas. Trust mitigates these risks by fostering expectations of fairness, competence, and reciprocity among collaborators, thereby enhancing individuals' willingness to contribute knowledge (Chowdhury, 2005). When individuals trust their colleagues, they expect to be treated fairly and reciprocally, perceive others as competent and trustworthy, and feel psychologically safe disclosing incomplete, implicit, or sensitive knowledge (Levin & Cross, 2004). Meta-analytic evidences further confirm that trust is consistently and positively associated with knowledge sharing across cultural and organizational contexts (Holste & Fields, 2010; Huang et al., 2011), underscoring its generalizability. Within higher education, trust plays a particularly salient role because academic collaboration is largely voluntary and embedded in professional norms rather than hierarchical control. Faculty members rely on trust developed through formal mechanisms—such as peer review processes, collaborative research practices, and institutional safeguards for intellectual property—as well as informal mechanisms, including collegial interactions, mentoring relationships, and repeated collaboration within teaching and research teams (Abrams et al., 2003). These interactions help establish shared identity and mutual respect, reinforcing the belief that contributions will be appropriately recognized. Conversely, a lack of trust, particularly among novice scholars or those with limited networks, can restrict participation in collaborative networks and significantly hinder knowledge exchange.

Trust remains equally important in an AI-integrated academic environment. While early studies suggested trust developed more slowly in virtual contexts (Jarvenpaa et al., 1998), later research demonstrated that digital trust can be effectively formed when platforms provide reliability, transparency, and clear communication norms (Bergquist & Ljungberg, 2001). In AI-powered systems, trust is further shaped by technological features that signal the integrity and fairness of the system (Felzmann et al., 2019). For instance, explainable AI mechanisms, transparent data-use policies, and robust data-protection mechanisms can reduce uncertainty and concerns about bias or intellectual property misuse, thereby supporting knowledge sharing (Felzmann et al., 2019; Shin, 2021). However, some academic critics have pointed out the potential impact of AI on trust; if people view AI as a tool for monitoring or tracking their performance, this could lead to distrust. Zuboff (2023) discusses surveillance capitalism as a framework for understanding the ability of digital systems to extract behavioral data for monitoring and control, leading to the "panopticon effect," where people adjust their behavior based on how they perceive that others will always be watching them. The lack of transparency, fairness, or faculty involvement in governing AI-based analytics systems used to measure productivity, identify collaborative networks, and evaluate teaching effectiveness can reduce anxiety, decrease psychological safety, and hinder open knowledge sharing (Ball, 2010; Zuboff, 2023). Thus, AI can either strengthen or erode trust depending on its design and institutional implementation, which thereby necessitates more discussion on how trust can be improved to promote knowledge sharing among academics in the AI-integrated context.

Taking together, the literature suggests that AI does not replace the role of trust but rather amplifies its importance by embedding trust within both interpersonal relationships and institutional infrastructures. In AI-integrated higher education environments, lecturers' willingness to share knowledge depends not only on interpersonal trust but also on confidence in the fairness, transparency, and ethical governance of AI systems. Accordingly, higher levels of trust are expected to significantly enhance lecturers' knowledge-sharing behavior.

> H1: Trust positively influences knowledge sharing among lecturers in the AI-integrated context in higher education

3.2 Social Interaction and Knowledge Sharing

Social interaction is widely recognised as a central driver of knowledge-sharing behaviour, as it provides the relational channels through which familiarity, shared understanding, and collaborative norms are developed. Through repeated interaction, individuals gain awareness of one another's expertise, communication styles, and expectations, which facilitates the effective exchange of knowledge (Hansen, 1999). Both the frequency and quality of social interaction are important. While frequent interaction maintains intimacy in relationships and creates opportunities for regular communication, high-quality interaction—characterized by genuine engagement, mutual respect, and meaningful dialogue—is particularly important for the transfer of complex and implicit knowledge, requiring context and shared interpretation (Reagans & McEvily, 2003). In higher education, social interaction is particularly important because knowledge sharing among scholars is largely voluntary and tied to collegial relationships rather than hierarchies. Collaborative research, joint teaching, mentoring, and informal academic exchange all depend on sustained interaction among faculty. University practice communities illustrate mutual engagement, shared goals, and common problem-solving—developed through ongoing interaction—supporting collective learning and innovation (Wenger, 1999). However, the academic context also presents unique challenges. Divisions of specialization, heavy workloads, competitive performance evaluation systems, and hierarchical norms can limit opportunities for interaction, especially for entry-level scholars or those outside established networks. Furthermore, relying solely on face-to-face interaction can constrain collaboration due to time and geographical constraints. Although face-to-face communication remains valuable in building relationship depth and conveying tacit knowledge, it is often insufficient to sustain interaction in an increasingly fragmented academic environment (Baltes et al., 2002).

AI is redefining the influence of social interactions on knowledge sharing and highlighting its impact on both explicit and tacit knowledge in higher education. AI platforms particularly facilitate the exchange of explicit knowledge, notably by recommending relevant research articles, identifying potential collaborators, organizing datasets, and promoting the sharing of educational resources. For instance, intelligent recommendation systems and digital repositories can improve the integration and dissemination of encoded information, in line with the externalization and combination stages of Nonaka (2009) SECI mode. AI lowers barriers to the acquisition and dissemination of formalized knowledge by reducing research costs and increasing the visibility of academic achievements. However, much academic expertise remains tacit, rooted in experience, judgment, and contextual understanding which cannot be captured or encoded by algorithms (Collins, 2019). Tacit knowledge also remains "sticky," requiring sustained interaction and trust to move across individuals and contexts (Leonard & Sensiper, 1998). In the SECI approach, the transfer of tacit knowledge is highly dependent on socialization, including mentoring, sharing experiences, observation, and informal dialogue (Nonaka, 2009). AI tools can indirectly support this process by multiplying interaction opportunities through intelligent scheduling systems (Chen et al., 2020), machine translation tools (Zawacki-Richter et al., 2019), and recommendation algorithms that facilitate interpersonal networks (Holstein & Doroudi, 2021). While AI can contribute to coordination and knowledge acquisition, it cannot replace deep interactive connections essential for the transfer of tacit knowledge. Therefore, in environments integrating AI, high-quality social interaction can be reinforced to enable effective knowledge sharing.

H2: Social interaction positively influences knowledge sharing among lecturers in the AI-integrated context in higher education

Figure 1. Conceptual framework (Author's own work)

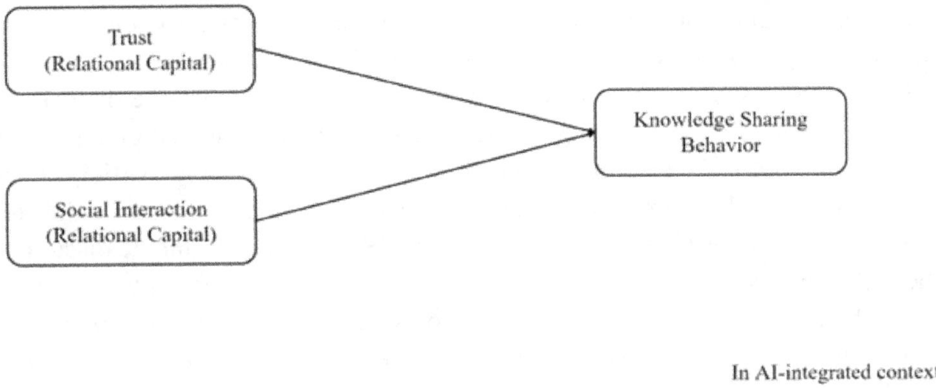

4. RESEARCH METHODOLOGY

4.1 Research Design

This study used a sequential exploratory mixed-methods design to investigate how trust and social interactions influence knowledge sharing behavior among university faculty in Ho Chi Minh City, Vietnam, specifically in the context of AI-enabled platforms. A mixed-methods approach was chosen to capture both the contextual depth and statistical generalizability needed to understand this complex phenomenon (Creswell & Clark, 2017; Tashakkori & Teddlie, 2021). Following Greene (2007) integrative framework, the qualitative phase generated culturally grounded insights that informed survey development, while the quantitative phase tested hypothesized relationships across a larger sample. Hence, the qualitative phase explored faculty experiences, perceptions, and culturally specific factors influencing knowledge sharing, providing insights to guide the development of culturally appropriate measurement tools. The subsequent quantitative phase examined the assumed relationships between constructs with a larger sample, allowing for statistical validation of the qualitatively defined models. Integrating these methods strengthens both the intrinsic validity of structures through the development of culturally grounded constructs and external validity through broader empirical testing across multiple organizations.

4.2 Qualitative Phase

Focus group discussions were conducted with 15 experienced faculty members from diverse fields (humanities, social sciences, natural sciences, engineering) and career stages (from teaching assistant to associate professor) at universities in Ho Chi Minh City. Participants were purposefully selected to ensure diversity in institutional background, teaching experience, and familiarity with digital technology (Patton, 2002). Focus groups were chosen because they allow participants to build upon each other's experiences and generate collective reflections on shared professional practices (Krueger, 2014; Morgan, 1997). Each 90-minute discussion followed a semi-structured process, exploring issues such as: perceptions of trust within the academic community, patterns of social interaction with colleagues, barriers and drivers of knowledge sharing, experiences using AI-powered platforms for collaboration, and knowledge sharing behaviors. The discussions were recorded with participants' consent, transcribed verbatim, and analyzed thematically. These insights were then used directly to refine the survey entries, ensuring linguistic clarity, cultural appropriateness, and relevance to faculty experiences within the Vietnamese context.

4.3 Quantitative Phase

Based on qualitative insights, the quantitative phase utilized a refined questionnaire with 14 items measuring trust (5 items), social interaction (4 items), and knowledge sharing (5 items), using a five-point Likert scale from "strongly disagree" to "strongly agree". Data were collected from 244 faculty members at 11 universities in Ho Chi Minh City using convenience sampling. Although convenience sampling limits statistical generalizability, it is widely used in organizational research where access to respondents is constrained (Etikan et al., 2016) which allows this paper for effective access to a wide range of disciplines. Given reliance on self-reported data, potential social desirability bias was addressed by ensuring anonymity, clarifying that no individual responses would be shared with institutions, and emphasizing the absence of right or wrong answers (Podsakoff et al., 2003). Moreover, to mitigate common method variance (CMV), procedural remedies included separating predictor and outcome items within the survey and using clear, psychologically neutral wording. Data was analyzed using statistical software: reliability was confirmed through Cronbach's alpha coefficient and exploratory factor analysis (EFA) confirmed the unidimensionality of the structure. Subsequently, the hypotheses were tested using SEM to examine the direct impact of trust and social interaction on knowledge sharing. By relying on qualitative findings to quantify the metrics, this study captured cultural understandings of relational dynamics in Vietnamese higher education while ensuring empirical rigor.

4. 4 Measurement development

Key constructs were operationalized based on established literature. Trust was assessed in terms of faculty members' confidence in their colleagues' competence, integrity, and goodwill (Levin & Cross, 2004; Rousseau et al., 1998). Social interaction captured both how often lecturers engage with one another and the quality of those exchanges, drawing on established measures of structural social capital (Cross & Sproull, 2004; Tsai & Ghoshal, 1998). Knowledge sharing was measured through items reflecting lecturers' willingness and intention to share information, expertise, and professional experience (Bock et al., 2005; Wang & Noe, 2010). To ensure the measures resonated with the Vietnamese higher education context, the items were carefully adapted to reflect AI-supported collaboration practices. Considering cultural characteristics such as respect for hierarchy and indirect communication styles, qualitative pretesting was conducted to ensure the wording was clear, culturally appropriate, and meaningful to participants. This approach helped maintain theoretical consistency while ensuring contextual relevance.

4.5 Methodological Limitations

To increase transparency, several limitations must be acknowledged. First, the quantitative phase relies on a convenient sampling method, which may lead to sampling bias and limit the ability to generalize results beyond the scope of the study sample (Etikan et al., 2016). Second, data collection is concentrated in Ho Chi Minh City; although this context provides a suitable and diverse higher education environment, results may differ in other regions of Vietnam, where institutional resources, governance dynamics, and digital infrastructure vary. Third, the survey relies on self-reporting measures, which may be influenced by societal desires or cognitive biases despite procedural safeguards (Podsakoff et al., 2003). Future research could address these issues by using probabilistic sampling across multiple regions, incorporating behavioral indicators of knowledge sharing (e.g., platform logs or contributions to archives), and employing a longitudinal research design to strengthen causal inferences.

5. RESULTS

5.1 Descriptive Analysis

As shown in Table 1, a total of 244 faculty members participated in the survey. Regarding gender distribution, the sample was relatively balanced, with 48.4% male and 51.6% female. In terms of educational qualifications, over half of the faculty held a Master's degree (52.9%), while 24.6% had completed a PhD. Regarding teaching experience, the majority of participants had 4 to 9 years of experience (66.8%). This was followed by faculty members with 10 to 20 years of experience (23.0%), indicating a significant presence of mid-level academics in the sample. A smaller proportion reported having 20 years of experience or more (7.8%). Only 2.5% of respondents had three years of experience, representing newly graduated teachers. Overall, the study sample comprises a diverse group of teachers in terms of gender, education, and seniority, thus providing a broad overview of the perspectives of teachers in the selected Vietnamese universities.

Table 1. Sample description (Author's own work)

	Number of lectures	Percentage (%)
Gender		
Male	118	48.4
Female	126	51.6
Education level		
Masters	129	52.9
PhD	60	24.6
Other	55	22.5
Teaching experience		
Up to 3 years	6	2.5
4 – 9 years	163	66.8
10 – 20 years	56	23.0
20 years or more	19	7.8

5.2 Reliability and Validity

The reliability and validity of the three focal constructs—trust, social interaction, and knowledge sharing—were rigorously assessed to ensure measurement quality. Reliability analysis using Cronbach's alpha demonstrated strong internal consistency across all three constructs. As shown in table 2, trust ($\alpha = 0.763$), social interaction ($\alpha = 0.729$), and knowledge sharing ($\alpha = 0.870$) all exceeded the commonly accepted threshold of 0.70, indicating that the items within each scale consistently measured their respective constructs. The particularly high alpha coefficient for knowledge sharing reflects excellent item cohesion, suggesting a robust underlying construct.

Table 2. Result of reliability (Author's own work)

Scale	Number of Items	Cronbach's Alpha
Social interaction	4	0.729
Trust	5	0.763
Knowledge sharing	5	0.870

Construct validity was examined through EFA. Illustrated in table 3, EFA results confirmed expected factor structure, with all items loading strongly (> 0.50) on their respective constructs. Trust items loaded between 0.666 and 0.731, social interaction items ranged from 0.556 to 0.797, and knowledge-sharing items loaded between 0.649 and 0.782, demonstrating clear construct separation and supporting unidimensionality. Kaiser–Meyer–Olkin (KMO) measure of sampling adequacy was high (0.875), and Bartlett's test of sphericity was significant, confirming suitability for factor analysis.

Table 3. Factor analysis (Author's own work)

Factor	Items	Factor loadings	KMO	Eigenvalue	Variance explained (%)
Knowledge sharing	5	0.649-0.782		6.410	35.609
Trust	4	0.666-0.731	0.875	1.763	45.405
Social interaction	4	0.556-0.797		1.351	52.912

Because the measurement items were adapted to the context of Vietnamese higher education and AI-enabled practices, an exploratory approach was necessary to verify the validity of the anticipated factor structure. Therefore, we used EFA in validating constructs, rather than assuming measure equivalence from previous studies. EFA revealed strong measurement quality (KMO = 0.875, a significant Bartlett's test, and factor loadings > 0.50 for all items) confirming unidimensionality and a discriminant structure. While confirmatory factor analysis (CFA) allows for more rigorous validation, this study prioritized establishing a culturally appropriate measurement structure by the insights taken from the qualitative phase.

5.3 Hypothesis Testing

Multiple regression analysis was conducted to test the influence of trust and social interaction on knowledge sharing. The model was significant, and both predictors contributed positively to knowledge-sharing behavior. In table 4, trust showed a strong, significant effect on knowledge sharing ($\beta = 0.333$, $p < 0.001$), indicating that higher levels of trust among lecturers were associated with greater willingness to share knowledge. Thus, H1 was supported. Social interaction also had a significant positive effect on knowledge sharing ($\beta = 0.214$, $p < 0.001$), demonstrating that more frequent and meaningful collegial interactions led to higher levels of knowledge sharing. Thus, H2 was supported. Collinearity diagnostics indicated no multicollinearity concerns, with tolerance values above 0.70 and VIF values below 2.

Table 4. Coefficients (Author's own work"/"Data analysis result)

	Std. Error	Beta	t	Sig.	Collinearity Statistics	
					Tolerance	VIF
Trust	0.052	0.333	6.290	0.000	0.737	1.357
Social Interaction	0.047	0.214	4.368	0.000	0.861	1.161

6. DISCUSSION

The research findings reveal that trust and social interaction are important predictors of faculty knowledge-sharing behavior, while highlighting the role of AI in strengthening these relational mechanisms. Consistent with SCT, the results show that knowledge sharing is driven not only by the availability of technology or individual motivation, but also by the quality of the relational conditions in which academic work is integrated. More importantly, the findings suggest that even in culturally hierarchical contexts such as Vietnamese higher education, AI can still function as a supportive infrastructure, strengthening trust and facilitating collaboration, rather than replacing interpersonal relationships. This extends prior research on AI-supported collaboration by showing how AI interacts with social and cultural dynamics to shape knowledge-sharing behaviors.

6.1 Trust, Knowledge Sharing, and AI

The strong positive effect of trust on knowledge sharing (H1) reinforces prior literature where trust reduces perceived risks and encourages the knowledge sharing behavior of both explicit and tacit knowledge (Holste & Fields, 2010; Levin & Cross, 2004). When lecturers trust their colleagues, they are more willing to share preliminary ideas, innovative teaching practices, and experiential insights without fear of misappropriation, negative evaluation, or reputational damage (Chowdhury, 2005; Titi Amayah, 2013). This finding is particularly salient in Vietnamese higher education, where hierarchical norms, respect for seniority, and face-saving practices can constrain open dialogue and horizontal knowledge exchange. In such settings, trust plays a compensatory role by mitigating concerns related to power asymmetry and occupational vulnerability, especially for early-career academics or those outside dominant networks. The results therefore extend prior trust–knowledge sharing research by demonstrating its heightened importance in hierarchical and collectivist academic cultures.

AI-enabled platforms appear to strengthen this trust–knowledge sharing relationship by embedding trust-supporting mechanisms within digital infrastructures. Features such as transparent data use policies, version control, automatic attribution, and traceable contribution history help reduce ambiguity and address concerns about intellectual property and fairness (Felzmann et al., 2019; Shin, 2021). By making contributions clear and verifiable, AI systems can supplement trust between individuals with institutionally backed trust. This finding is consistent with previous studies showing that AI can enhance trust in collaborative environments when systems are perceived as trustworthy, transparent, and ethically governed (Zawacki-Richter et al., 2019). Instead of simply facilitating information exchange, AI in this context actively contributes to the conditions for maintaining trust and making knowledge sharing less risky.

6.2 Social Interaction, Knowledge Sharing, and AI

The significant influence of social interaction on knowledge sharing (H2) supports previous studies emphasizing that frequent and high-quality interactions foster mutual understanding, reciprocity, and depth of relationships—critical prerequisites for effective knowledge exchange (Cross & Sproull, 2004; Reagans & McEvily, 2003). In academic context, sustained engagement through both formal and informal interactions enables collaboration and knowledge sharing (Gannon-Leary & Fontainha, 2007; Wenger, 1999). However, in the Vietnamese context, opportunities for sustained interaction are often constrained by institutional fragmentation, heavy teaching workloads, limited cross-departmental coordination, and reliance on formal communication channels. These structural constraints can weaken academic networks and reduce informal exchanges, even when faculty are motivated to collaborate. The findings therefore highlight the importance of creating interactional infrastructures that enable continuous engagement despite organizational and temporal limitations.

AI-supported platforms appear to amplify the positive effects of social interaction by lowering communication barriers and expanding opportunities for engagement. Technologies such as AI-based recommendation systems, intelligent scheduling tools, and asynchronous collaboration platforms facilitate more frequent and sustained interaction among lecturers (Chen et al., 2020). Moreover, AI enables interaction across time zones and geographical boundaries, reducing dependence on face-to-face meetings while maintaining continuity of collaboration. Features such as real-time feedback, automated summaries, and shared digital workspaces enhance both the efficiency and richness of interaction. These findings are consistent with research on social presence in digital environments, which shows that well-designed platforms can reduce isolation, strengthen connectedness, and increase willingness to share knowledge (Lowenthal & Dunlap, 2018; Richardson et al., 2017). Similar patterns are also observed in South Africa and Romanian universities where AI-supported teaching systems reduce routine instructional tasks and allow faculty to focus more on collaborative academic activities (Mulaudzi & Hamilton, 2025; Pisica et al., 2023). In this way, AI supports not only the quantity but also the quality of social interaction, reinforcing the relational pathways through which knowledge sharing occurs.

In Vietnamese higher education, it is widely characterized as a highly contextual culture where communication relies heavily on implicit signals and hierarchical sensitivities (Hall, 1976), hindering open dialogue. Meanwhile, AI systems typically operate through low-contextual logic—explicit rules, standardized processes, and coded communication. This cultural mismatch initially seemed to limit the effectiveness of AI in facilitating both explicit and tacit knowledge exchange. However, the findings reveal an insightful dynamic. By formalizing communication channels, clarifying contribution records, and reducing ambiguity in interactions, AI can mitigate hierarchical constraints embedded in high-context environments and bridge the tension between formality and collaboration. Crucially, the findings reaffirm that AI is not a substitute for human relationships, but a tool that supports trust-building and interaction in complex cultural contexts. When thoughtfully implemented, AI can contribute to more inclusive, collaborative, and sustainable knowledge-sharing practices, thereby strengthening organizational learning and innovation in higher education institutions.

7. IMPLICATIONS

7.1 Theoretical implications

This study advances SCT by demonstrating that trust and social interaction remain powerful predictors of knowledge-sharing behavior even within AI-supported academic environments. While traditional SCT emphasizes human relationships as the foundation of knowledge exchange (Nahapiet & Ghoshal, 1998), these findings suggest that AI act as a relationship-enhancing tool rather than a neutral technology class. AI tools—through transparent attribution, secure data management, and structured communication—enhance the structural, relational, and cognitive aspects of social capital by making networks more visible, interactions easier to initiate, and shared meanings more collectively constructed. This expands SCT by showing that, in modern universities, social capital is increasingly co-created through the interaction between people and technology, rather than simply through the interaction between individuals.

Secondly, this study challenges the technology-centric view of AI in education. While much of the literature on AI focuses on its technical capabilities such as personalization, automation, and resource management, this study emphasizes that the success of AI tools in fostering collaboration depends on existing relational conditions within the academic community. The study indicates that AI is not a standalone solution for fostering collaboration or knowledge sharing. Instead, trust and social interaction, key elements of SCT, act as boundary variables determining whether AI positively influences knowledge-sharing behavior. In hierarchical environments where trust and social interaction are weak, AI may exacerbate these problems or help overcome them, depending on the degree to which AI tools integrate with existing relational dynamics. This research contributes to the study of AI in education by advocating for AI systems that enhance relational capital, ensuring that AI serves as a tool to support human connection, not to replace it.

7.2 Practical Implications

At the institutional level, these findings provide crucial guidance for universities seeking to enhance knowledge sharing through AI-powered systems. The results suggest that AI should be strategically integrated into organizational operations in a way that strengthens trust and social interaction, rather than simply deployed to increase efficiency. Universities can utilize AI platforms to make collaborative activities clearer, more transparent, and more formally recognized. By adopting AI systems that record contributions, support equitable recognition, and provide a safe space for collaboration, organizations can alleviate faculty concerns particularly prominent for entry-level academics and those working in hierarchical environments. Furthermore, organizations can leverage AI-generated insights to better understand faculty interaction and collaboration patterns. Analytics from AI-powered collaborative platforms can help identify isolated individuals or entities, reveal underutilized expertise, and inform the design of mentoring programs, interdisciplinary research teams, or teaching practice communities. By using AI not only as a technological tool but also as a diagnostic and developmental resource, universities can create more inclusive and collaborative academic cultures, supporting sustainable knowledge sharing.

Furthermore, universities should establish clear governance structures regarding intellectual property, data ownership, and authorship in an AI-powered environment. Practical guidance from organizations like EDUCAUSE emphasizes that transparent data governance and clear policies on digital collaboration are crucial for building trust and encouraging faculty engagement in technology-assisted knowledge sharing. By utilizing AI not only as a technological tool but also as a diagnostic and developmental resource through analytics revealing collaboration patterns, identifying isolated scholars, and highlighting underutilized expertise, universities can design mentoring initiatives, interdisciplinary research teams, and faculty learning communities to foster sustainable knowledge exchange.

At the policy level, these findings provide valuable insights for educational authorities responsible for guiding the adoption of AI across the entire higher education sector. The results suggest that effective AI integration requires governance frameworks that clearly address relational and ethical aspects, including trust, transparency, and equity. Policymakers can use these insights to develop national or sector-wide guidelines requiring universities to implement AI systems consistent with principles of interpretability, data protection, and intellectual property protection. Clear guidance on data governance, algorithmic transparency, and intellectual property protection would mitigate ambiguity surrounding ownership of AI-mediated outputs. Such policies can mitigate uncertainty and build trust among faculty, encouraging knowledge sharing and collaboration among educational institutions. In addition, policymakers can leverage this evidence to guide broader higher education reforms related to learning performance assessment and human resource development. By recognizing collaborative knowledge sharing as a key driver of innovation and quality, policy frameworks can encourage universities to move beyond narrow, individualistic measures. For example, national funding programs or accreditation criteria could incorporate indicators related to collaborative teaching, interdisciplinary research, and joint innovation supported by AI. In this way, policymakers can help ensure that the adoption of AI contributes not only to the effectiveness of institutions but also to the long-term sustainability and inclusiveness of the higher education system.

8. CONCLUSION

This chapter examined how trust and social interaction shape knowledge-sharing behavior among faculty members in Vietnamese higher education, and how AI can strengthen these relational mechanisms. The research findings highlight that, despite rapid digital transformation, knowledge sharing remains fundamentally relational. Trust emerges as the strongest predictor of knowledge sharing, underscoring the importance of psychological safety and confidence in the integrity of colleagues when exchanging ideas, teaching materials, or research insights. Social interaction also significantly influences knowledge sharing, demonstrating that meaningful participation whether direct or digitally mediated helps establish familiarity, reciprocity, and shared understanding.

Importantly, the role of AI in this study is primarily understood as part of the technological context in which academic collaboration takes place. AI tools offer the ability to record transparent origins, securely store data, and create structured collaboration spaces that can strengthen the trust faculty have in each other. Similarly, AI-powered communication and recommendation systems can expand and enrich social interactions, particularly in Vietnam's hierarchical and fragmented academic environment. By integrating social capital dynamics with AI-powered pedagogy, this chapter contributes a new perspective on how universities can build more collaborative, inclusive, and knowledge-rich academic communities.

In summary, the findings affirm that the success of AI in education depends not only on technical capability, but also on how well those tools support the relational platforms that enable knowledge dissemination. For Vietnamese universities – and organizations in similar cultural contexts – using AI strategies to enhance trust and foster peer interaction can be crucial to fostering a sustainable knowledge-sharing culture and advancing the broader goals of inclusive, collaborative pedagogy.

Limitations and Future Research

Beside the implications, this study still has three limitations that open up avenues for future research. First, while it highlights the Vietnamese cultural context like hierarchy, collectivistm power-distance, it does not compare Vietnam with other Southeast Asian systems (e.g., Thailand, Malaysia, Indonesia), which limits the generalizability of its findings. International comparative studies would provide a better understanding of how cultural variations influence trust, social interactions, and AI-facilitated knowledge sharing. Second, the study does not examine disciplinary "epistemic cultures" within universities; since knowledge-sharing norms can vary considerably between faculties or departments, future work should compare disciplines to verify whether the observed relationships hold true across fields. Third, the cross-sectional design of the study does not allow for capturing the evolution of perceptions and behaviors after prolonged AI use. Longitudinal studies would make it possible to assess whether the relational effects of AI strengthen, diminish, or evolve over time.

REFERENCES

Abrams, L. C., Cross, R., Lesser, E., & Levin, D. Z. (2003). Nurturing interpersonal trust in knowledge-sharing networks. *The Academy of Management Perspectives, 17*(4), 64–77. DOI: 10.5465/ame.2003.11851845

Al-Kurdi, O., El-Haddadeh, R., & Eldabi, T. (2018). Knowledge sharing in higher education institutions: A systematic review. *Journal of Enterprise Information Management, 31*(2), 226–246. DOI: 10.1108/JEIM-09-2017-0129

Albaram, B. M., & Lim, Y. M. (2023). Conceptualization social influence from the need to belong perspective on psychological needs' satisfaction to share knowledge. *Heliyon, 9*(2), e13764. DOI: 10.1016/j.heliyon.2023.e13764 PMID: 36852045

Ardichvili, A., Maurer, M., Li, W., Wentling, T., & Stuedemann, R. (2006). Cultural influences on knowledge sharing through online communities of practice. *Journal of Knowledge Management, 10*(1), 94–107. DOI: 10.1108/13673270610650139

Argyris, C., & Schön, D. A. (1997). Organizational Learning: A Theory of Action Perspective. *Revista Española de Investigaciones Sociológicas*, (77/78), 345–348. DOI: 10.2307/40183951

Ball, K. (2010). Workplace surveillance: An overview. *Labor History, 51*(1), 87–106. DOI: 10.1080/00236561003654776

Baltes, B. B., Dickson, M. W., Sherman, M. P., Bauer, C. C., & LaGanke, J. S. (2002). Computer-Mediated Communication and Group Decision Making: A Meta-Analysis. *Organizational Behavior and Human Decision Processes, 87*(1), 156–179. https://doi.org/https://doi.org/10.1006/obhd.2001.2961. DOI: 10.1006/obhd.2001.2961

Bergquist, M., & Ljungberg, J. (2001). The power of gifts: Organizing social relationships in open source communities. *Information Systems Journal, 11*(4), 305–320. https://doi.org/https://doi.org/10.1046/j.1365-2575.2001.00111.x. DOI: 10.1046/j.1365-2575.2001.00111.x

Bock, G.-W., Zmud, R. W., Kim, Y.-G., & Lee, J.-N. (2005). Behavioral Intention Formation in Knowledge Sharing: Examining the Roles of Extrinsic Motivators, Social-Psychological Forces, and Organizational Climate. *Management Information Systems Quarterly, 29*(1), 87–111. DOI: 10.2307/25148669

Bond, M. H., & Hwang, K.-k. (1986). *The social psychology of Chinese people*. Oxford University Press.

Chen, L., Chen, P., & Lin, Z. (2020). Artificial Intelligence in Education: A Review. *IEEE Access : Practical Innovations, Open Solutions, 8*, 75264–75278. DOI: 10.1109/ACCESS.2020.2988510

Chmielecki, M. (2013). Culture as a barrier of knowledge sharing. *Journal of Intercultural Management, 5*(2), 101–111. DOI: 10.2478/joim-2013-0013

Chowdhury, S. (2005). The Role of Affect- and Cognition-based Trust in Complex Knowledge Sharing. *Journal of Managerial Issues, 17*(3), 310–326.

Chyi Lee, C., & Yang, J. (2000). Knowledge value chain. *Journal of Management Development, 19*(9), 783–794. DOI: 10.1108/02621710010378228

Collins, H. (2019). *Tacit and explicit knowledge.* University of Chicago press.

Connelly, C. E., Zweig, D., Webster, J., & Trougakos, J. P. (2012). Knowledge hiding in organizations. *Journal of Organizational Behavior, 33*(1), 64–88. https://doi.org/ https://doi.org/10.1002/job.737. DOI: 10.1002/job.737

Creswell, J. W., & Clark, V. L. P. (2017). *Designing and conducting mixed methods research.* Sage publications.

Cross, R. (2021). *Beyond collaboration overload: How to work smarter, get ahead, and restore your well-being*. Harvard Business Press.

Cross, R., & Sproull, L. (2004). More Than an Answer: Information Relationships for Actionable Knowledge. *Organization Science, 15*(4), 446–462. DOI: 10.1287/orsc.1040.0075

Davenport, T. H., De Long, D. W., & Beers, M. C. (1998). Successful knowledge management projects. *MIT Sloan Management Review, 39*(2), 43.

De Felice, S., Hamilton, A. F. C., Ponari, M., & Vigliocco, G. (2023). Learning from others is good, with others is better: the role of social interaction in human acquisition of new knowledge. *Philos Trans R Soc Lond B Biol Sci, 378*(1870), 20210357. DOI: 10.1098/rstb.2021.0357

Dismore, H., Campbell-Barr, V., Manning, R., & Warwick, P. (2024). A relational approach to knowledge exchange in higher education. *Studies in Higher Education, 49*(12), 2534–2545. DOI: 10.1080/03075079.2024.2312404

Edmondson, A. (1999). Psychological Safety and Learning Behavior in Work Teams. *Administrative Science Quarterly, 44*(2), 350–383. DOI: 10.2307/2666999

Edmondson, A. C. (2018). *The fearless organization: Creating psychological safety in the workplace for learning, innovation, and growth.* John Wiley & Sons.

Eppler, M. J., & Mengis, J. (2004). The Concept of Information Overload: A Review of Literature from Organization Science, Accounting, Marketing, MIS, and Related Disciplines. *The Information Society*, *20*(5), 325–344. DOI: 10.1080/01972240490507974

Etikan, I., Musa, S. A., & Alkassim, R. S. (2016). Comparison of convenience sampling and purposive sampling. *American Journal of Theoretical and Applied Statistics*, *5*(1), 1–4. DOI: 10.11648/j.ajtas.20160501.11

Eubanks, V. (2018). *Automating inequality: How high-tech tools profile, police, and punish the poor*. Macmillan+ ORM.

Faraj, S., Pachidi, S., & Sayegh, K. (2018). Working and organizing in the age of the learning algorithm. *Information and Organization*, *28*(1), 62–70. https://doi.org/https://doi.org/10.1016/j.infoandorg.2018.02.005. DOI: 10.1016/j.infoandorg.2018.02.005

Fauzi, M. A., Nguyen, M., & Malik, A. (2023). Knowledge sharing and theory of planned behavior: A bibliometric analysis. *Journal of Knowledge Management*, *28*(2), 293–311. DOI: 10.1108/JKM-11-2022-0933

Felzmann, H., Villaronga, E. F., Lutz, C., & Tamò-Larrieux, A. (2019). Transparency you can trust: Transparency requirements for artificial intelligence between legal norms and contextual concerns. *Big Data & Society*, *6*(1), 2053951719860542. DOI: 10.1177/2053951719860542

Foucault, M. (1977). *Discipline and punish: The birth ofthe prison*. Allen Lane.

Gannon-Leary, P., & Fontainha, E. (2007). Communities of Practice and virtual learning communities: benefits, barriers and success factors.

Gerhart, B., & Fang, M. (2015). Pay, intrinsic motivation, extrinsic motivation, performance, and creativity in the workplace: Revisiting long-held beliefs. *Annual Review of Organizational Psychology and Organizational Behavior*, *2*(1), 489–521. DOI: 10.1146/annurev-orgpsych-032414-111418

Granovetter, M. S. (1973). The strength of weak ties. *American Journal of Sociology*, *78*(6), 1360–1380. DOI: 10.1086/225469

Greene, J. C. (2007). *Mixed methods in social inquiry*. John Wiley & Sons.

Hall, E. (1976). *Beyond Culture*. Anchor Books.

Hallinger, P., & Truong, D. T. (2014). Exploring the contours of context and leadership effectiveness in Vietnam [Journal Article]. *Leading and Managing*, *20*(2), 43–59.

Hansen, M. T. (1999). The Search-Transfer Problem: The Role of Weak Ties in Sharing Knowledge across Organization Subunits. *Administrative Science Quarterly, 44*(1), 82–111. DOI: 10.2307/2667032

Henkel, J. (2006). Selective revealing in open innovation processes: The case of embedded Linux. *Research Policy, 35*(7), 953–969. https://doi.org/https://doi.org/10.1016/j.respol.2006.04.010. DOI: 10.1016/j.respol.2006.04.010

Hofstede, G. (2001). *Culture's consequences: Comparing values, behaviors, institutions and organizations across nations*. Sage publications.

Holmes, W., Bialik, M., & Fadel, C. (2019). *Artificial intelligence in education promises and implications for teaching and learning*. Center for Curriculum Redesign.

Holste, J. S., & Fields, D. (2010). Trust and tacit knowledge sharing and use. *Journal of Knowledge Management, 14*(1), 128–140. DOI: 10.1108/13673271011015615

Holstein, K., & Doroudi, S. (2021). Equity and artificial intelligence in education: will" aied" amplify or alleviate inequities in education? *arXiv preprint arXiv:2104.12920.*

Huang, Q., Davison, R. M., & Gu, J. (2011). The impact of trust, guanxi orientation and face on the intention of Chinese employees and managers to engage in peer-to-peer tacit and explicit knowledge sharing. *Information Systems Journal, 21*(6), 557–577. DOI: 10.1111/j.1365-2575.2010.00361.x

Hughes, L., Dwivedi, Y. K., Malik, T., Shawosh, M., Albashrawi, M. A., Jeon, I., Dutot, V., Appanderanda, M., Crick, T., De', R., Fenwick, M., Gunaratnege, S. M., Jurcys, P., Kar, A. K., Kshetri, N., Li, K., Mutasa, S., Samothrakis, S., Wade, M., & Walton, P. (2025). AI Agents and Agentic Systems: A Multi-Expert Analysis. *Journal of Computer Information Systems, 65*(4), 489–517. DOI: 10.1080/08874417.2025.2483832

Hutchins, E. (1995). *Cognition in the Wild.* MIT press. DOI: 10.7551/mitpress/1881.001.0001

Iliadis, A., & Russo, F. (2016). Critical data studies: An introduction. *Big Data & Society, 3*(2), 2053951716674238. DOI: 10.1177/2053951716674238

Jarvenpaa, S. L., Knoll, K., & Leidner, D. E. (1998). Is Anybody out There? Antecedents of Trust in Global Virtual Teams. *Journal of Management Information Systems, 14*(4), 29–64. DOI: 10.1080/07421222.1998.11518185

Krueger, R. A. (2014). *Focus groups: A practical guide for applied research*. Sage publications.

Le, A. T. T., Tran, T. V., Tran, T. M., & Phan, T. H. (2024). Intrinsic and Extrinsic Factors as Motivation Roles in Scientific Research Activities of Professors at Several Vietnamese Universities. *SAGE Open*, *14*(1), 21582440241230838. DOI: 10.1177/21582440241230838

Leonard, D., & Sensiper, S. (1998). The Role of Tacit Knowledge in Group Innovation. *California Management Review*, *40*(3), 112–132. DOI: 10.2307/41165946

Levin, D. Z., & Cross, R. (2004). The Strength of Weak Ties You Can Trust: The Mediating Role of Trust in Effective Knowledge Transfer. *Management Science*, *50*(11), 1477–1490. DOI: 10.1287/mnsc.1030.0136

Li, L., Dinh, L., Hu, S., & Hemphill, L. (2024). Academic collaboration on large language model studies increases overall but varies across disciplines. *arXiv preprint arXiv:2408.04163*. DOI: 10.21203/rs.3.rs-4887385/v1

Lin, H. F. (2007). Knowledge sharing and firm innovation capability: An empirical study. *International Journal of Manpower*, *28*(3-4), 315–332. DOI: 10.1108/01437720710755272

Lowenthal, P. R., & Dunlap, J. C. (2018). Investigating students' perceptions of instructional strategies to establish social presence. *Distance Education*, *39*(3), 281–298. DOI: 10.1080/01587919.2018.1476844

Lukes, S. (2012). Power: A radical view [2005]. *Contemporary sociological theory*, *266*(3), 1–22.

March, J. G. (1991). Exploration and Exploitation in Organizational Learning. *Organization Science*, *2*(1), 71–87. DOI: 10.1287/orsc.2.1.71

Markus, H. R., & Kitayama, S. (2014). Culture and the self: Implications for cognition, emotion, and motivation. In *College student development and academic life* (pp. 264–293). Routledge.

McDermott, R., & O'Dell, C. (2001). Overcoming cultural barriers to sharing knowledge. *Journal of Knowledge Management*, *5*(1), 76–85. DOI: 10.1108/13673270110384428

Michailova, S., & Hutchings, K. (2006). National Cultural Influences on Knowledge Sharing: A Comparison of China and Russia. *Journal of Management Studies*, *43*(3), 383–405. https://doi.org/https://doi.org/10.1111/j.1467-6486.2006.00595.x. DOI: 10.1111/j.1467-6486.2006.00595.x

Mooradian, T., Renzl, B., & Matzler, K. (2006). Who Trusts? Personality, Trust and Knowledge Sharing. *Management Learning*, *37*(4), 523–540. DOI: 10.1177/1350507606073424

Morgan, D. L. (1997). *Focus groups as qualitative research* (Vol. 16). Sage. DOI: 10.4135/9781412984287

Mulaudzi, L. V., & Hamilton, J. (2025). Lecturer's Perspective on the Role of AI in Personalized Learning: Benefits, Challenges, and Ethical Considerations in Higher Education. *Journal of Academic Ethics*, *23*(4), 1571–1591. DOI: 10.1007/s10805-025-09615-1

Nahapiet, J., & Ghoshal, S. (1998). Social Capital, Intellectual Capital, and the Organizational Advantage. *Academy of Management Review*, *23*(2), 242–266. DOI: 10.2307/259373

Nguyen, A. T., Truong, T. H., Luong, T. L., Luu, H. V., Hoang, T. T. N., & Luu, Q. D. (2022). Management factors influencing lecturers' research productivity in Vietnam National University, Hanoi, Vietnam: A structural equation modeling analysis. *Heliyon*, *8*(9), e10510. Advance online publication. DOI: 10.1016/j.heliyon.2022.e10510 PMID: 36120496

Noble, S. U. (2018). Algorithms of oppression: How search engines reinforce racism. In *Algorithms of oppression*. New York university press.

Nonaka, I. (2009). The knowledge-creating company. In *The economic impact of knowledge* (pp. 175–187). Routledge.

Patton, M. Q. (2002). Qualitative research and evaluation methods. Thousand Oaks. *Cal.: Sage Publications, 4*(10.4135), 9781452226058.

Peng, H. (2013). Why and when do people hide knowledge? *Journal of Knowledge Management*, *17*(3), 398–415. DOI: 10.1108/JKM-12-2012-0380

Pictorial, V. (2026). Purpose-driven AI education prepares students for digital, people-centred future. *Vietnam Pictorial*. https://vietnam.vnanet.vn/english/tin-van/purpose-driven-ai-education-prepares-students-for-digital-people-centred-future-430842.html

Pisica, A. I., Edu, T., Zaharia, R. M., & Zaharia, R. (2023). Implementing Artificial Intelligence in Higher Education: Pros and Cons from the Perspectives of Academics. *Societies (Basel, Switzerland)*, *13*(5), 118. DOI: 10.3390/soc13050118

Podsakoff, P. M., MacKenzie, S. B., Podsakoff, N. P., & Lee, J. Y. (2003). The mismeasure of man(agement) and its implications for leadership research. *The Leadership Quarterly, 14*(6), 615–656. https://doi.org/https://doi.org/10.1016/j.leaqua.2003.08.002. DOI: 10.1016/j.leaqua.2003.08.002

Polanyi, M. (2009). The tacit dimension. In *Knowledge in organisations* (pp. 135–146). Routledge.

Quy, V. K., Thanh, B. T., Chehri, A., Linh, D. M., & Tuan, D. A. (2023). AI and Digital Transformation in Higher Education: Vision and Approach of a Specific University in Vietnam. *Sustainability (Basel), 15*(14), 11093. DOI: 10.3390/su151411093

Ramayah, T., Yeap, J. A. L., & Ignatius, J. (2014). Assessing Knowledge Sharing Among Academics: A Validation of the Knowledge Sharing Behavior Scale (KSBS). *Evaluation Review, 38*(2), 160–187. DOI: 10.1177/0193841X14539685 PMID: 25015259

Reagans, R., & McEvily, B. (2003). Network Structure and Knowledge Transfer: The Effects of Cohesion and Range. *Administrative Science Quarterly, 48*(2), 240–267. DOI: 10.2307/3556658

Richardson, J. C., Maeda, Y., Lv, J., & Caskurlu, S. (2017). Social presence in relation to students' satisfaction and learning in the online environment: A meta-analysis. *Computers in Human Behavior, 71*, 402–417. https://doi.org/https://doi.org/10.1016/j.chb.2017.02.001. DOI: 10.1016/j.chb.2017.02.001

Riege, A. (2005). Three-dozen knowledge-sharing barriers managers must consider. *Journal of Knowledge Management, 9*(3), 18–35. DOI: 10.1108/13673270510602746

Rousseau, D. M., Sitkin, S. B., Burt, R. S., & Camerer, C. (1998). Not So Different After All: A Cross-Discipline View Of Trust. *Academy of Management Review, 23*(3), 393–404. DOI: 10.5465/amr.1998.926617

Rozputnia, B., Shevchenko, L., Umanets, V., Sabadosh, Y., Kushnir, A., & Voitsekhivska, N. (2025, September 17–19). 2025). Future Trends of AI in Higher Education: Google Workspace and Gemini. 2025 15th International Conference on Advanced Computer Information Technologies (ACIT), Schraw, G., & Dennison, R. S. (1994). Assessing Metacognitive Awareness. *Contemporary Educational Psychology, 19*(4), 460–475. DOI: 10.1006/ceps.1994.1033

Seibert, S. E., Kraimer, M. L., & Liden, R. C. (2001). A Social Capital Theory of Career Success. *Academy of Management Journal, 44*(2), 219–237. DOI: 10.2307/3069452

Serenko, A., & Bontis, N. (2016). Understanding counterproductive knowledge behavior: Antecedents and consequences of intra-organizational knowledge hiding. *Journal of Knowledge Management*, *20*(6), 1199–1224. DOI: 10.1108/JKM-05-2016-0203

Shaikh, S. A., Lämsä, A.-M., & Heikkinen, S. (2023). Collaborative Leadership in the Institution of Higher Education: A Sociocultural Context of Pakistan. *South Asian Journal of Business and Management Cases*, *12*(1), 65–80. DOI: 10.1177/22779779231154646

Shiddiqi, A. M., Alzamzami, M. N., Adillion, I. G., Budiman, M. I. A., Supriyanto, R., & Machmud, M. (2025). Findme-scholar: A contextual researcher recommender system for enhancing research collaboration using adaptive topic interest area modelling. *MethodsX*, *15*, 103583. https://doi.org/https://doi.org/10.1016/j.mex.2025.103583. DOI: 10.1016/j.mex.2025.103583 PMID: 40896715

Shin, D. (2021). The effects of explainability and causability on perception, trust, and acceptance: Implications for explainable AI. *International Journal of Human-Computer Studies*, *146*, 102551. https://doi.org/https://doi.org/10.1016/j.ijhcs.2020.102551. DOI: 10.1016/j.ijhcs.2020.102551

Sijbom, R. B. L., Emanuel, E. S., Koen, J., Baas, M., & De Schutter, L. (2025). Daily knowledge sharing at work: The role of daily knowledge sharing expectations, learning goal orientation and task interdependence. *European Journal of Work and Organizational Psychology*, *34*(2), 298–314. DOI: 10.1080/1359432X.2025.2458343 PMID: 40144200

Slaughter, S., & Leslie, L. L. (1997). *Academic capitalism: Politics, policies, and the entrepreneurial university*. Johns Hopkins University Press.

Srivastava, A., Bartol, K. M., & Locke, E. A. (2006). Empowering Leadership in Management Teams: Effects on Knowledge Sharing, Efficacy, And Performance. *Academy of Management Journal*, *49*(6), 1239–1251. DOI: 10.5465/amj.2006.23478718

Sure, T. A. R., Saigurudatta, P. V., Kapoor, S., Kandula, S. T. R., Choudhury, A., & Devendran, P. D. (2025, July 3–5). 2025). The Role of Natural Language Processing in Developing Intelligent Knowledge Repositories. 2025 IEEE International Conference on Industry 4.0, Artificial Intelligence, and Communications Technology (IAICT), Sweller, J. (1988). Cognitive load during problem solving: Effects on learning. *Cognitive Science*, *12*(2), 257–285. https://doi.org/https://doi.org/10.1016/0364-0213(88)90023-7

Tan, C. N.-L., & Ramayah, T. (2014). The role of motivators in improving knowledge-sharing among academics. *Information Research*, *19*(1), n1.

Tashakkori, A., & Teddlie, C. (2021). *Sage handbook of mixed methods in social & behavioral research.* SAGE publications.

Titi Amayah, A. (2013). Determinants of knowledge sharing in a public sector organization. *Journal of Knowledge Management, 17*(3), 454–471. DOI: 10.1108/JKM-11-2012-0369

Tran, L. T., & Marginson, S. (2018). Internationalisation of Vietnamese Higher Education: An Overview. In Tran, L. T., & Marginson, S. (Eds.), *Internationalisation in Vietnamese Higher Education* (pp. 1–16). Springer International Publishing., DOI: 10.1007/978-3-319-78492-2_1

Tran, T., Trinh, T.-P.-T., Le, C.-M., Hoang, L.-K., & Pham, H.-H. (2020). Research as a Base for Sustainable Development of Universities: Using the Delphi Method to Explore Factors Affecting International Publishing among Vietnamese Academic Staff. *Sustainability (Basel), 12*(8), 3449. DOI: 10.3390/su12083449

Treve, M. (2021). What COVID-19 has introduced into education: Challenges Facing Higher Education Institutions (HEIs). *Higher Education Pedagogies, 6*(1), 212–227. DOI: 10.1080/23752696.2021.1951616

Tsai, W., & Ghoshal, S. (1998). Social Capital and Value Creation: The Role of Intrafirm Networks. *Academy of Management Journal, 41*(4), 464–476. DOI: 10.2307/257085

van Houten, M. M. (2023). Professional tacit knowledge sharing in practice. Agency, boundaries, and commitment. *Journal of Workplace Learning, 35*(9), 197–217. DOI: 10.1108/JWL-02-2023-0025

Van Quyet, P., & Hai, P. T. T. (2023). Autonomy Governance Transformation in the Higher Education Institutions Towards the Typical Models in Vietnam. *Journal of Higher Education Theory and Practice, 23*(20), 1–14.

Vuong, T.-T., Ho, M.-T., Nguyen, M.-H., Nguyen, T.-H. T., Nguyen, T.-D., Nguyen, T.-L., Luong, A.-P., & Vuong, Q.-H. (2020). Adopting open access in the social sciences and humanities: Evidence from a developing nation. *Heliyon, 6*(7), e04522. Advance online publication. DOI: 10.1016/j.heliyon.2020.e04522 PMID: 32743103

Wang, S., & Noe, R. A. (2010). Knowledge sharing: A review and directions for future research. *Human Resource Management Review, 20*(2), 115–131. https://doi.org/https://doi.org/10.1016/j.hrmr.2009.10.001. DOI: 10.1016/j.hrmr.2009.10.001

Wasko, M. M., & Faraj, S. (2005). Why Should I Share? Examining Social Capital and Knowledge Contribution in Electronic Networks of Practice. *Management Information Systems Quarterly, 29*(1), 35–57. DOI: 10.2307/25148667

Wen, J., & Ma, R. (2021). Antecedents of knowledge hiding and their impact on organizational performance. *Frontiers in Psychology, 12*, 796976. DOI: 10.3389/fpsyg.2021.796976 PMID: 34987455

Wenger, E. (1999). *Communities of practice: Learning, meaning, and identity.* Cambridge university press.

Wenger, E., McDermott, R. A., & Snyder, W. (2002). *Cultivating communities of practice: A guide to managing knowledge*. Harvard business press.

Zacharewicz, T., Lepori, B., Reale, E., & Jonkers, K. (2019). Performance-based research funding in EU Member States—A comparative assessment. *Science & Public Policy*, *46*(1), 105–115. DOI: 10.1093/scipol/scy041

Zaremohzzabieh, Z., & Mohd Rasdi, R. (2023). Revisiting the determinants of knowledge-sharing behavior in organizations: A meta-analytic structural equation model application. *Global Knowledge, Memory and Communication*, *74*(1-2), 1–22. DOI: 10.1108/GKMC-02-2022-0034

Zawacki-Richter, O., Marín, V. I., Bond, M., & Gouverneur, F. (2019). Systematic review of research on artificial intelligence applications in higher education – where are the educators? *International Journal of Educational Technology in Higher Education, 16*(1), 39. DOI: 10.1186/s41239-019-0171-0

Zhou, T., & Lu, H. (2024). The effect of trust on user adoption of AI-generated content. *The Electronic Library*, *43*(1), 61–76. DOI: 10.1108/EL-08-2024-0244

Zuboff, S. (2023). The age of surveillance capitalism. In *Social theory re-wired* (pp. 203–213). Routledge. DOI: 10.4324/9781003320609-27

Compilation of References

Abrams, L. C., Cross, R., Lesser, E., & Levin, D. Z. (2003). Nurturing interpersonal trust in knowledge-sharing networks. *The Academy of Management Perspectives*, *17*(4), 64–77. DOI: 10.5465/ame.2003.11851845

Adam, T., & Groves, C. (2019). Digital futures and the ethics of care. *Ethics and Information Technology*, *21*(3), 219–231. DOI: 10.1007/s10676-018-9466-1

Adiguzel, T., Kaya, M. H., & Cansu, F. K. (2023). Revolutionizing education with AI: Exploring the transformative potential of ChatGPT. *Contemporary Educational Technology*, *15*(3), ep429. DOI: 10.30935/cedtech/13152

Al Hasanah, H., Heru Iswanto, B., & Sugihartono, I. (2025). AI-CBL: A Technology-Enhanced Learning Model Combining Chatbot and Case-Based Pedagogy to Improve Critical Thinking in Physics Education. *Jurnal Penelitian & Pengembangan Pendidikan Fisika*, *11*(1), 109–122. DOI: 10.21009/1.11108

Al Sabbagh, M., & Elgeddawy, M. (2025). Change management and AI adoption for enhancing employee experience in higher education institutions, Oman. In *AI and IoT: Driving Business Success and Sustainability in the Digital Age* (Vol. 1, pp. 307–315). Springer Nature Switzerland., DOI: 10.1007/978-3-031-92240-4_28

Albaram, B. M., & Lim, Y. M. (2023). Conceptualization social influence from the need to belong perspective on psychological needs' satisfaction to share knowledge. *Heliyon*, *9*(2), e13764. DOI: 10.1016/j.heliyon.2023.e13764 PMID: 36852045

Albert, R. D., & Triandis, H. C. (1985). Intercultural education for multicultural societies: Critical issues. *International Journal of Intercultural Relations*, *9*(3), 319–337. DOI: 10.1016/0147-1767(85)90032-X

Alenezi, M. (2023). Digital Learning and Digital Institution in Higher Education. *Education Sciences*, *13*(1), 88. DOI: 10.3390/educsci13010088

Ali, A. M. (2025). Evaluating artificial intelligence readiness within faculty in the higher education sector. *Higher Education Quarterly*, *79*(4), e70061. DOI: 10.1111/hequ.70061

Alim, H. S., & Paris, D. (2017). What is culturally sustaining pedagogies and why does it matter? In D. Paris & H. S. Alim (Eds.), *Culturally sustaining pedagogies: Teaching and learning for justice in a changing world* (pp. 1–24). Teachers College Press.

Al-Kurdi, O., El-Haddadeh, R., & Eldabi, T. (2018). Knowledge sharing in higher education institutions: A systematic review. *Journal of Enterprise Information Management*, *31*(2), 226–246. DOI: 10.1108/JEIM-09-2017-0129

Allen, I. E., Seaman, J., Poulin, R., & Straut, T. T. (2017). *Online report card: Tracking online education in the United States.* Babson Survey Research Group.

Almufarreh, A., & Arshad, M. (2023). Promising Emerging Technologies for Teaching and Learning: Recent Developments and Future Challenges. *Sustainability (Basel)*, *15*(8), 6917. DOI: 10.3390/su15086917

Anderson, J. E., Nguyen, C. A., & Moreira, G. (2025). Generative AI-driven personalization of the community of inquiry model: Enhancing individualized learning experiences in digital classrooms. *The International Journal of Information and Learning Technology*, *42*(3), 296–310. DOI: 10.1108/IJILT-10-2024-0240

Anderson, T., & Dron, J. (2011). Three generations of distance education pedagogy. *International Review of Research in Open and Distance Learning*, *12*(3), 80. DOI: 10.19173/irrodl.v12i3.890

Ang, S., & Van Dyne, L. (2015). *Handbook of cultural intelligence: Theory, measurement, and applications*. Routledge. DOI: 10.4324/9781315703855

An, Y., Yu, J. H., & James, S. (2025). 'Investigating the higher education institutions' guidelines and policies regarding the use of generative AI in teaching, learning, research, and administration'. *International Journal of Educational Technology in Higher Education*, *22*(1), 10. DOI: 10.1186/s41239-025-00507-3

Ardichvili, A., Maurer, M., Li, W., Wentling, T., & Stuedemann, R. (2006). Cultural influences on knowledge sharing through online communities of practice. *Journal of Knowledge Management*, *10*(1), 94–107. DOI: 10.1108/13673270610650139

Argaw, A. S., Haile, B. B., Ayalew, B. T., & Kuma, S. G. (2016). The Effect of Problem Based Learning (PBL) Instruction on Students' Motivation and Problem Solving Skills of Physics. *Eurasia Journal of Mathematics, Science and Technology Education*, *13*(3). Advance online publication. DOI: 10.12973/eurasia.2017.00647a

Argyris, C., & Schön, D. A. (1997). Organizational Learning: A Theory of Action Perspective. *Revista Española de Investigaciones Sociológicas*, (77/78), 345–348. DOI: 10.2307/40183951

Arslan, K. (2020). Eğitimde yapay zekâ ve uygulamaları [Artificial intelligence in education and its applications]. *Batı Anadolu Eğitim Bilimleri Dergisi, 11*(1), 71–88.

Ataş, H., & Gündüz, S. (2019). *Yükseköğretimde dijital dönüşüm* [Digital transformation in higher education]. Dijital Dönüşüm Ekonomik ve Toplumsal Boyutuyla. Gazi Kitabevi.

Baker, R. S., & Hawn, A. (2022). Algorithmic bias in education. *International Journal of Artificial Intelligence in Education*, *32*(2), 252–277. DOI: 10.1007/s40593-021-00285-7

Ball, K. (2010). Workplace surveillance: An overview. *Labor History*, *51*(1), 87–106. DOI: 10.1080/00236561003654776

Baltes, B. B., Dickson, M. W., Sherman, M. P., Bauer, C. C., & LaGanke, J. S. (2002). Computer-Mediated Communication and Group Decision Making: A Meta-Analysis. *Organizational Behavior and Human Decision Processes*, *87*(1), 156–179. https://doi.org/https://doi.org/10.1006/obhd.2001.2961. DOI: 10.1006/obhd.2001.2961

Banks, J. A. (2015). *Cultural diversity and education: Foundations, curriculum, and teaching* (6th ed.). Routledge. DOI: 10.4324/9781315622255

Barocas, S., Hardt, M., & Narayanan, A. (2019). Fairness and machine learning. https://doi.org//arXiv.1908.09635DOI: 10.48550

Barocas, S., & Selbst, A. D. (2016). Big data's disparate impact. *California Law Review, 104*(3), 671–732. DOI: 10.15779/Z38BG31

Barrera Castro, G. P., Chiappe, A., Becerra Rodriguez, D. F., & Sepulveda, F. G. (2024). Harnessing AI for Education 4.0: Drivers of Personalized Learning. *Electronic Journal of E-Learning, 22*(5), 01–14. DOI: 10.34190/ejel.22.5.3467

Batal, M. S. (2016). *Yapay zeka uygulamaları ve yapay zekanın geleceği.* [Artificial intelligence applications and the future of artificial intelligence]. Unpublished institutional report. Uluslararası Sunhıll Üniversitesi, 1-9.

Battiste, M. (2019). *Decolonizing education: Nourishing the learning spirit.* University of British Columbia Press. DOI: 10.59962/9781895830972

Bauer, E., Greiff, S., Graesser, A. C., Scheiter, K., & Sailer, M. (2025). Looking beyond the hype: Understanding the effects of AI on learning. *Educational Psychology Review, 37*(2), 45. DOI: 10.1007/s10648-025-10020-8

Becker, G. S. (1975). *Human capital: A theoretical and empirical analysis*. National Bureau of Economic Research.

Bender, E. M., Gebru, T., McMillan-Major, A., & Shmitchell, S. (2021). On the dangers of stochastic parrots: Can language models be too big? *Proceedings of the 2021 ACM conference on fairness, accountability, and transparency*, 610–623. DOI: 10.1145/3442188.3445922

Bengtson, V. L., & Schrader, S. S. (1982). Parent–child relations. In Mangen, D. J., & Peterson, W. A. (Eds.), *Research instruments in social gerontology: Social roles and social participation* (Vol. 2, pp. 115–185). University of Minnesota Press.

Bergquist, M., & Ljungberg, J. (2001). The power of gifts: Organizing social relationships in open source communities. *Information Systems Journal, 11*(4), 305–320. https://doi.org/https://doi.org/10.1046/j.1365-2575.2001.00111.x. DOI: 10.1046/j.1365-2575.2001.00111.x

Bessarab, D., & Ng'Andu, B. (2010). Yarning about yarning as a legitimate method in indigenous research. *International Journal of Critical Indigenous Studies, 3*(1), 37–50. DOI: 10.5204/ijcis.v3i1.57

Bhabha, H. K. (1994). *The location of culture*. Routledge.

Bhatt, I., MacKenzie, A., & Knox, J. (2023). AI, education, and epistemic justice. *Learning, Media and Technology, 48*(1), 1–14. DOI: 10.4337/9781803928562.00031

Biesta, G. (2015). What is education for? On good education, teacher judgement, and educational professionalism. *European Journal of Education, 50*(1), 75–87. DOI: 10.1111/ejed.12109

Bin, Y., & Sun, L. (2025). AI-supported language learning for intercultural competence: Personalized feedback and adaptive collaboration. *Nature Human Behaviour, 9*(2), 234–248. PMID: 39747405

Biswas, S. S. (2023). Potential use of chat GPT in global warming. *Annals of Biomedical Engineering, 51*(6), 1126–1127. DOI: 10.1007/s10439-023-03171-8 PMID: 36856927

Blodgett, S. L., Barocas, S., Daumé, H.III, & Wallach, H. (2020). Language (technology) is power. *Proceedings of the ACL*, 485–504. DOI: 10.18653/v1/2020.acl-main.485

Bock, G.-W., Zmud, R. W., Kim, Y.-G., & Lee, J.-N. (2005). Behavioral Intention Formation in Knowledge Sharing: Examining the Roles of Extrinsic Motivators, Social-Psychological Forces, and Organizational Climate. *Management Information Systems Quarterly*, *29*(1), 87–111. DOI: 10.2307/25148669

Boddington, P. (2021). *Towards a code of ethics for artificial intelligence*. Springer., DOI: 10.1007/978-3-319-60648-4

Bodily, R., Ikahihifo, T. K., Mackley, B., & Graham, C. R. (2018). The design, development, and implementation of student-facing learning analytics dashboards. *Journal of Computing in Higher Education*, *30*(3), 572–598. DOI: 10.1007/s12528-018-9186-0

Boelens, R., De Wever, B., & Voet, M. (2017). Four key challenges to the design of blended learning: A systematic literature review. *Educational Research Review*, *22*, 1–18. DOI: 10.1016/j.edurev.2017.06.001

Bond, M. H., & Hwang, K.-k. (1986). *The social psychology of Chinese people*. Oxford University Press.

Bonk, C. J., & Graham, C. R. (2006). *The handbook of blended learning: Global perspectives, local designs*. Pfeiffer.

Bozkurt, A., Gjelsvik, T., Adam, T., Asino, T. I., Atenas, J., Bali, M., Blomgren, C., Bond, M., Bonk, C. J., Brown, M., Burgos, D., Conrad, D., Costello, E., Cronin, C., Czerniewicz, L., Deepwell, M., Deimann, M., DeWaard, H. J., Dousay, T. A., & Zawacki-Richter, O. (2023). Openness in Education as a Praxis: From Individual Testimonials to Collective Voices. *Open Praxis*, *15*(2), 76–112. DOI: 10.55982/openpraxis.15.2.574

Bozkurt, A., & Sharma, R. C. (2020). Emergency remote teaching in a time of global crisis due to Corona Virus pandemic. *Asian Journal of Distance Education*, *15*(1), i–vi. http://asianjde.com/ojs/index.php/AsianJDE/article/view/447

Braidotti, R. (2022). *Posthuman feminism*. Polity Press.

Bryson, J. J. (2019). The past decade and future of AI's impact on society. In *Towards a new enlightenment? A transcendent decade*. Turner.

Buckingham Shum, S., & Crick, R. D. (2012, April). Learning dispositions and transferable competencies: pedagogy, modelling and learning analytics. In *Proceedings of the 2nd international conference on learning analytics and knowledge* (pp. 92-101). DOI: 10.1145/2330601.2330629

Buckingham Shum, S., & Ferguson, R. (2012). Social learning analytics. *Journal of Educational Technology & Society*, *15*(3), 3–26.

Buckingham Shum, S., & Luckin, R. (2019). Learning analytics and AI: Politics, pedagogy and practices. *British Journal of Educational Technology*, *50*(6), 2785–2793. DOI: 10.1111/bjet.12880

Budhwar, P., Chowdhury, S., Wood, G., Aguinis, H., Bamber, G. J., Beltran, J. R., Boselie, P., Lee Cooke, F., Decker, S., DeNisi, A., Dey, P. K., Guest, D., Knoblich, A. J., Malik, A., Paauwe, J., Papagiannidis, S., Patel, C., Pereira, V., Ren, S., & Varma, A. (2023). Human resource management in the age of generative artificial intelligence: Perspectives and research directions on ChatGPT. *Human Resource Management Journal*, *33*(3), 606–659. DOI: 10.1111/1748-8583.12524

Buolamwini, J., & Gebru, T. (2018). Gender shades: Intersectional accuracy disparities in commercial gender classification. *Proceedings of Conference on Fairness, Accountability and Transparency*, 77–91. DOI: 10.1145/3287560.3287596

Burrell, J. (2016). How the machine "thinks": Understanding opacity in machine learning algorithms. *Big Data & Society*, *3*(1), 1–12. DOI: 10.1177/2053951715622512

Bynum, T. W. (2006). Flourishing ethics. *Ethics and Information Technology*, *8*(4), 157–173. DOI: 10.1007/s10676-006-9107-1

Byram, M., Gribkova, B., & Starkey, H. (2002). Developing the intercultural dimension in language teaching: A practical introduction for teachers. Language Policy Division, Directorate of School, Out-of-School and Higher Education, Council of Europe.

Byram, M. (1997). *Teaching and assessing intercultural communicative competence*. Multilingual Matters.

Byram, M. (2020). *Teaching and assessing intercultural communicative competence: Revisited*. Multilingual Matters.

Byram, M., Nichols, A., & Stevens, D. (Eds.). (2001). *Developing intercultural competence in practice* (Vol. 1). Multilingual Matters. DOI: 10.21832/9781853595356

Canagarajah, S. (2013). *Translingual practice: Global Englishes and cosmopolitan relations*. Routledge. DOI: 10.4324/9780203120293

Capano, G., He, A. J., & McMinn, S. (2025). Riding the tide of generative artificial intelligence in higher education policy: An Asian perspective. *Journal of Asian Public Policy*, *18*(2), 1–15. DOI: 10.1080/17516234.2025.2450571

Capp, M. J. (2017). The effectiveness of universal design for learning: A meta-analysis of literature between 2013 and 2016. *International Journal of Inclusive Education, 21*(8), 791–807. DOI: 10.1080/13603116.2017.1325074

Carvalho, D. V., Pereira, E. M., & Cardoso, J. S. (2019). Machine Learning Interpretability: A Survey on Methods and Metrics. *Electronics (Basel), 8*(8), 832. DOI: 10.3390/electronics8080832

Cazzaniga, M. (2024). Gen-AI. *Staff Discussion Notes, 2024*(001), 1. DOI: 10.5089/9798400262548.006

Cechinel, C., Ochoa, X., Lemos dos Santos, H., Carvalho Nunes, J. B., Rodés, V., & Marques Queiroga, E. (2020). Mapping learning analytics initiatives in Latin America. *British Journal of Educational Technology, 51*(4), 892–914. DOI: 10.1111/bjet.12941

Celik, I., Dindar, M., Muukkonen, H., & Järvelä, S. (2022). The promises and challenges of artificial intelligence for teachers. *Computers & Education, 178*, 104352. DOI: 10.1016/j.compedu.2021.104352

Ceylan, İ., & Çakır, R. (2025). Yapay zekâ destekli araçların ilkokul öğrencilerinin fen bilimleri dersine yönelik yeterlilik inançları, tutumları ve başarısına etkisi [The effect of artificial intelligence-supported tools on elementary school students' self-efficacy beliefs, attitudes, and achievement in science lessons] [TUJPED]. *Turkish Journal of Primary Education, 10*(2), 71–90. DOI: 10.52797/tujped.1797585

Chan, C. K. Y., & Tsi, L. H. (2024). Will generative AI replace teachers in higher education? A study of teacher and student perceptions. *Studies in Educational Evaluation, 83*, 101395. DOI: 10.1016/j.stueduc.2024.101395

Chen, L., Chen, P., & Lin, Z. (2020). Artificial Intelligence in Education: A Review. *IEEE Access : Practical Innovations, Open Solutions, 8*, 75264–75278. DOI: 10.1109/ACCESS.2020.2988510

Chen, X., Xie, H., Zou, D., & Hwang, G. J. (2020). Application and theory gaps during the rise of artificial intelligence in education. *Computers & Education, 146*, 103751. DOI: 10.1016/j.compedu.2019.103751

Cheung, K. K. C., Pun, J. K., & Li, W. (2024). Students' holistic reading of socio-scientific texts on climate change in a ChatGPT scenario. *Research in Science Education, 54*(5), 957–976. DOI: 10.1007/s11165-024-10177-2

Chiu, T. K. F. (2024). Embracing the future of Artificial Intelligence in the classroom: The relevance of AI literacy, prompt engineering, and critical thinking in modern education. *International Journal of Educational Technology in Higher Education, 21*(1), 14. Advance online publication. DOI: 10.1186/s41239-024-00448-3

Chiu, T. K. F., Xia, Q., Zhou, X., Chai, C. S., & Cheng, M. (2023). Systematic literature review on opportunities, challenges, and future research recommendations of artificial intelligence in education. *Computers and Education: Artificial Intelligence, 4*, 100118. Advance online publication. DOI: 10.1016/j.caeai.2022.100118

Chmielecki, M. (2013). Culture as a barrier of knowledge sharing. *Journal of Intercultural Management, 5*(2), 101–111. DOI: 10.2478/joim-2013-0013

Choudhary, K., DeCost, B., Chen, C., Jain, A., Tavazza, F., Cohn, R., Park, C. W., Choudhary, A., Agrawal, A., Billinge, S. J. L., Holm, E., Ong, S. P., & Wolverton, C. (2022). Recent advances and applications of deep learning methods in materials science. *npj Computational Materials, 8*(1), 59. DOI: 10.1038/s41524-022-00734-6

Chowdhury, S. (2005). The Role of Affect- and Cognition-based Trust in Complex Knowledge Sharing. *Journal of Managerial Issues, 17*(3), 310–326.

Chyi Lee, C., & Yang, J. (2000). Knowledge value chain. *Journal of Management Development, 19*(9), 783–794. DOI: 10.1108/02621710010378228

Cipresso, P., Giglioli, I. A. C., Raya, M. A., & Riva, G. (2018). The Past, Present, and Future of Virtual and Augmented Reality Research: A Network and Cluster Analysis of the Literature. *Frontiers in Psychology, 9*, 2086. Advance online publication. DOI: 10.3389/fpsyg.2018.02086 PMID: 30459681

Cohn, C., Snyder, C., Horn Fonteles, J., Gerard, L., McElhaney, K., & Slotta, J. D. (2025). A multimodal approach to support teacher, researcher and AI collaboration in STEM+C learning environments. *British Journal of Educational Technology*. Advance online publication. DOI: 10.1111/bjet.13518

Collins, H. (2019). *Tacit and explicit knowledge*. University of Chicago press.

Connelly, C. E., Zweig, D., Webster, J., & Trougakos, J. P. (2012). Knowledge hiding in organizations. *Journal of Organizational Behavior, 33*(1), 64–88. https://doi.org/https://doi.org/10.1002/job.737. DOI: 10.1002/job.737

Cowls, J., Tsamados, A., Taddeo, M., & Floridi, L. (2021). The AI gambit: Leveraging artificial intelligence to combat climate change—opportunities, challenges, and recommendations. *AI & Society*, •••, 1–25. PMID: 34690449

Creswell, J. W., & Clark, V. L. P. (2017). *Designing and conducting mixed methods research*. Sage publications.

Crompton, H., & Burke, D. (2023). Large language models in education: A focus on the complementary relationship between human teachers and ChatGPT. *Education and Information Technologies*, *28*(12), 15873–15892. DOI: 10.1007/s10639-023-11834-1

Cross, R. (2021). *Beyond collaboration overload: How to work smarter, get ahead, and restore your well-being*. Harvard Business Press.

Cross, R., & Sproull, L. (2004). More Than an Answer: Information Relationships for Actionable Knowledge. *Organization Science*, *15*(4), 446–462. DOI: 10.1287/orsc.1040.0075

Cukurova, M., & Luckin, R. (2020). Artificial intelligence for education: Knowledge and its assessment in AI-enabled learning ecologies. *Educational Studies*, *56*(2), 127–144. DOI: 10.1080/00131857.2020.1728732

Cummings-Koether, M., ... (2024). Cultural perceptions of AI in education. AI & Society. 10.48550/arXiv.2510.19743

Cushner, K., & Brislin, R. W. (1996). *Intercultural interactions: A practical guide* (2nd ed.). Sage Publications, Inc. DOI: 10.4135/9781452204970

D'Ignazio, C., & Klein, L. F. (2020). *Data feminism*. MIT Press., DOI: 10.7551/mitpress/11805.001.0001

Daher, W. (2025). *Digital literacy and AI: Interpreting algorithmic outputs in educational contexts*. Springer Link.

Daniel, J. (2013). *Mega-universities and knowledge media*. Routledge. DOI: 10.4324/9780203045978

Davenport, T. H., De Long, D. W., & Beers, M. C. (1998). Successful knowledge management projects. *MIT Sloan Management Review*, *39*(2), 43.

De Felice, S., Hamilton, A. F. C., Ponari, M., & Vigliocco, G. (2023). Learning from others is good, with others is better: the role of social interaction in human acquisition of new knowledge. *Philos Trans R Soc Lond B Biol Sci*, *378*(1870), 20210357. DOI: 10.1098/rstb.2021.0357

de Jong, T., Linn, M. C., & Zacharia, Z. C. (2013). Physical and Virtual Laboratories in Science and Engineering Education. *Science*, *340*(6130), 305–308. DOI: 10.1126/science.1230579 PMID: 23599479

De Laat, M., & Prinsen, F. R. (2014). Social learning analytics: Navigating the changing settings of higher education. *Research & Practice in Assessment, 9*, 51–60. https://files.eric.ed.gov/fulltext/EJ1062691.pdf

Deardorff, D. K. (2006). Identification and assessment of intercultural competence as a student outcome of internationalization. *Journal of Studies in International Education, 10*(3), 241–266. DOI: 10.1177/1028315306287002

Deardorff, D. K. (2009). *The SAGE handbook of intercultural competence*. SAGE. DOI: 10.4135/9781071872987

Deardorff, D. K. (2020). *Manual for developing intercultural competencies: Story circles*. Taylor & Francis.

Deloitte. (2022). *State of AI in the Enterprise* (5th ed.). Deloitte Insights.

Deogaonkar, A. (2025). Digital leadership, AI readiness and strategic resource allocation in education: A configurational approach to post-pandemic transformation. *International Journal of Educational Management, 39*(5), 1105–1119. DOI: 10.1108/IJEM-06-2025-0438

Dervin, F. (2016). *Interculturality in education: A theoretical and methodological toolbox*. Springer. DOI: 10.1057/978-1-137-54544-2

Dillenbourg, P., & Jermann, P. (2010). Technology for classroom orchestration. In Khine, M. S., & Saleh, I. M. (Eds.), *New science of learning* (pp. 525–552). Springer., DOI: 10.1007/978-1-4419-5716-0_26

DISER. (2021). *Australia's AI ethics framework*. Australian Government, Department of Industry, Science, Energy and Resources, https://consult.industry.gov.au/australias-ai-ethics-framework

Dismore, H., Campbell-Barr, V., Manning, R., & Warwick, P. (2024). A relational approach to knowledge exchange in higher education. *Studies in Higher Education, 49*(12), 2534–2545. DOI: 10.1080/03075079.2024.2312404

Doğan, Y., Simsar, A., & Konca, A. S. (2025). Preservice teachers' perceptions of environmental issues. *Journal of Baltic Science Education, 24*(3), 399–412. DOI: 10.33225/jbse/25.24.399

Dong, S. W., Wu, J. J., & Li, Z. G. (2014). Study on the framework of environmental education curriculum system. *Advanced Materials Research, 962-965*, 590–593.

Downes, S. (2012). *Connectivism and connective knowledge: Essays on meaning and learning networks*. National Research Council Canada.

Drachsler, H., & Greller, W. (2016, April). Privacy and analytics: it's a DELICATE issue a checklist for trusted learning analytics. In *Proceedings of the sixth international conference on learning analytics & knowledge* (pp. 89-98). DOI: 10.1145/2883851.2883893

Duong, N. T., Pham Thi, T. D., & Pham, V. K. (2025). A comparative study on AI-based learning behaviours: Evidence from Vietnam. *International Journal of Human-Computer Interaction, 41*(16), 10007–10023. DOI: 10.1080/10447318.2024.2430433

Dwivedi, Y. K., Hughes, L., Ismagilova, E., Aarts, G., Coombs, C., Crick, T., Duan, Y., Dwivedi, R., Edwards, J., Eirug, A., Galanos, V., Ilavarasan, P. V., Janssen, M., Jones, P., Kar, A. K., Kizgin, H., Kronemann, B., Lal, B., Lucini, B., & Williams, M. D. (2021). Artificial Intelligence (AI): Multidisciplinary perspectives on emerging challenges, opportunities, and agenda for research, practice and policy. *International Journal of Information Management, 57*, 101994. DOI: 10.1016/j.ijinfomgt.2019.08.002

Dwivedi, Y. K., Hughes, L., Wang, Y., Alalwan, A. A., Ahn, S. J., Balakrishnan, J., Barta, S., Belk, R., Buhalis, D., Dutot, V., Felix, R., Filieri, R., Flavián, C., Gustafsson, A., Hinsch, C., Hollensen, S., Jain, V., Kim, J., Krishen, A. S., & Wirtz, J. (2023). Metaverse marketing: How the metaverse will shape the future of consumer research and practice. *Psychology and Marketing, 40*(4), 750–776. DOI: 10.1002/mar.21767

Dwivedi, Y. K., Kshetri, N., Hughes, L., Slade, E. L., Jeyaraj, A., Kar, A. K., Baabdullah, A. M., Koohang, A., Raghavan, V., Ahuja, M., Albanna, H., Albashrawi, M. A., Al-Busaidi, A. S., Balakrishnan, J., Barlette, Y., Basu, S., Bose, I., Brooks, L., Buhalis, D., & Wright, R. (2023). Opinion Paper:"So what if ChatGPT wrote it?" Multidisciplinary perspectives on opportunities, challenges and implications of generative conversational AI for research, practice and policy. *International Journal of Information Management, 71*, 102642. DOI: 10.1016/j.ijinfomgt.2023.102642

Echeverria, V., Yang, K., Lawrence, L. E. M., Shibani, A., Dash, S. K., & Martinez-Maldonado, R. (2023). Designing hybrid human–AI orchestration tools for individual and collaborative activities: A technology probe study. *IEEE Transactions on Learning Technologies, 16*(2), 191–205. DOI: 10.1109/TLT.2023.3248155

Edmondson, A. (1999). Psychological Safety and Learning Behavior in Work Teams. *Administrative Science Quarterly, 44*(2), 350–383. DOI: 10.2307/2666999

Edmondson, A. C. (2018). *The fearless organization: Creating psychological safety in the workplace for learning, innovation, and growth.* John Wiley & Sons.

Engeström, Y. (2001). Expansive learning at work: Toward an activity theoretical reconceptualization. *Journal of Education and Work, 14*(1), 133–156. DOI: 10.1080/13639080020028747

Eppler, M. J., & Mengis, J. (2004). The Concept of Information Overload: A Review of Literature from Organization Science, Accounting, Marketing, MIS, and Related Disciplines. *The Information Society*, *20*(5), 325–344. DOI: 10.1080/01972240490507974

Erensayın, E., & Güler, Ç. (2017). EBA platformundaki ders materyallerinin eğitsel yazılım değerlendirme ölçütlerine göre değerlendirilmesi [Evaluation of instructional materials on the EBA platform according to educational software evaluation criteria] [KEFAD]. *Ahi Evran Üniversitesi Kırşehir Eğitim Fakültesi Dergisi*, *18*(1), 657–678.

Etikan, I., Musa, S. A., & Alkassim, R. S. (2016). Comparison of convenience sampling and purposive sampling. *American Journal of Theoretical and Applied Statistics*, *5*(1), 1–4. DOI: 10.11648/j.ajtas.20160501.11

EU in ASEAN. (2024). *EU–ASEAN Sustainable Connectivity Package – Higher Education Programme (SCOPE-HE) 2024–2028* (2024–2028, Issue. EU-ASEAN – Global Gateway. https://euinasean.eu/scope-he

Eubanks, V. (2018). *Automating inequality: How high-tech tools profile, police, and punish the poor*. Macmillan+ ORM.

Eubanks, V. (2018). *Automating inequality: How high-tech tools profile, police, and punish the poor*. St. Martin's Press.

Falloon, G. (2020). From digital literacy to digital competence: The teacher digital competency (TDC) framework. *Educational Technology Research and Development*, *68*(5), 2449–2472. DOI: 10.1007/s11423-020-09767-4

Faraj, S., Pachidi, S., & Sayegh, K. (2018). Working and organizing in the age of the learning algorithm. *Information and Organization*, *28*(1), 62–70. https://doi.org/https://doi.org/10.1016/j.infoandorg.2018.02.005. DOI: 10.1016/j.infoandorg.2018.02.005

Fauzi, M. A., Nguyen, M., & Malik, A. (2023). Knowledge sharing and theory of planned behavior: A bibliometric analysis. *Journal of Knowledge Management*, *28*(2), 293–311. DOI: 10.1108/JKM-11-2022-0933

Felzmann, H., Villaronga, E. F., Lutz, C., & Tamò-Larrieux, A. (2019). Transparency you can trust: Transparency requirements for artificial intelligence between legal norms and contextual concerns. *Big Data & Society*, *6*(1), 2053951719860542. DOI: 10.1177/2053951719860542

Ferguson, R., Coughlan, T., Egelandsdal, K., Gaved, M., Herodotou, C., Hillaire, G., Jones, D., Jowers, I., Kukulska-Hulme, A., & McAndrew, P. (2019). *Innovating pedagogy 2019: Open university innovation report 7*. The Open University.

Ferguson, R., Hoel, T., Scheffel, M., & Drachsler, H. (2016). Guest editorial: Ethics and privacy in learning analytics. *Journal of Learning Analytics, 3*(1), 5–15. DOI: 10.18608/jla.2016.31.2

Ferri, F., Grifoni, P., & Guzzo, T. (2020). Online Learning and Emergency Remote Teaching: Opportunities and Challenges in Emergency Situations. *Societies (Basel, Switzerland), 10*(4), 86. DOI: 10.3390/soc10040086

Fiedler, F. E., Mitchell, T., & Triandis, H. C. (1971). The culture assimilator: An approach to cross-cultural training. *The Journal of Applied Psychology, 55*(2), 95–102. DOI: 10.1037/h0030704

Flanagan, J. C. (1954). The critical incident technique. *Psychological Bulletin, 51*(4), 327–358. DOI: 10.1037/h0061470 PMID: 13177800

Floridi, L. (2013). *The Ethics of Information*. Oxford University Press., DOI: 10.1093/acprof:oso/9780199641321.001.0001

Floridi, L. (2019). Establishing the rules for building trustworthy AI. *Nature Machine Intelligence, 1*(6), 261–262. DOI: 10.1038/s42256-019-0055-y

Floridi, L. (2019). *The logic of information: A theory of philosophy as conceptual design*. Oxford University Press. DOI: 10.1093/oso/9780198833635.001.0001

Floridi, L. (2023). *The ethics of artificial intelligence: Principles, challenges, and opportunities*. Oxford University Press. DOI: 10.1093/oso/9780198883098.001.0001

Floridi, L., & Cowls, J. (2022). A unified framework of five principles for AI in society. In Carta, S. (Ed.), *Machine learning and the city: Applications in architecture and urban design* (pp. 535–545). John Wiley & Sons. DOI: 10.1002/9781119815075.ch45

Floridi, L., Cowls, J., Beltrametti, M., Chatila, R., Chazerand, P., Dignum, V., Luetge, C., Madelin, R., Pagallo, U., Rossi, F., Schafer, B., Valcke, P., & Vayena, E. (2018). AI4People An ethical framework for a good AI society: Opportunities, risks, principles, and recommendations. *Minds and Machines, 28*(4), 689–707. DOI: 10.1007/s11023-018-9482-5 PMID: 30930541

Foucault, M. (1977). *Discipline and punish: The birth ofthe prison*. Allen Lane.

Fricker, M. (2007). *Epistemic injustice: Power and the ethics of knowing*. Oxford University Press., DOI: 10.1093/acprof:oso/9780198237907.001.0001

Gannon-Leary, P., & Fontainha, E. (2007). Communities of Practice and virtual learning communities: benefits, barriers and success factors.

Garrison, D. R., & Kanuka, H. (2008). Blended learning: Uncovering its transformative potential in higher education. *The Internet and Higher Education*, *7*(2), 95–105. DOI: 10.1016/j.iheduc.2004.02.001

Garrison, D. R., & Vaughan, N. D. (2008). *Blended learning in higher education: Framework, principles, and guidelines*. John Wiley & Sons.

Gašević, D., Dawson, S., & Siemens, G. (2015). Let's not forget: Learning analytics are about learning. *TechTrends*, *59*(1), 64–71. DOI: 10.1007/s11528-014-0822-x

Gay, G. (2018). *Culturally responsive teaching: Theory, research, and practice* (3rd ed.). Teachers College Press.

Gerard, L. F., McElhaney, K., Cohn, C., Slotta, J. D., & Tissenbaum, M. (2023). Supporting teacher—AI—researcher collaboration in multimodal STEM+C learning. *British Journal of Educational Technology*.

Gerhart, B., & Fang, M. (2015). Pay, intrinsic motivation, extrinsic motivation, performance, and creativity in the workplace: Revisiting long-held beliefs. *Annual Review of Organizational Psychology and Organizational Behavior*, *2*(1), 489–521. DOI: 10.1146/annurev-orgpsych-032414-111418

Gering, Z., Feher, K., Harmat, V., & Tamassy, R. (2025). Strategic organisational responses to generative AI-driven digital transformation in leading higher education institutions. *The International Journal of Organizational Analysis*, *33*(12), 132–152. DOI: 10.1108/IJOA-09-2024-4850

Gilliard, C. (2017). Pedagogy and the logic of platforms. EDUCAUSE Review. https://er.educause.edu/articles/2017/7/pedagogy-and-the-logic-of-platforms

Godwin-Jones, R. (2019). Emerging technologies and language learning: More than just one model. *Language Learning & Technology*, *23*(1), 1–17.

Godwin-Jones, R. (2023). Emerging spaces for language learning: AI bots, ambient intelligence, and the metaverse. *Language Learning & Technology*, *27*(2), 6–27. DOI: 10.64152/10125/73501

Goldie, J. (2016). Connectivism: A learning theory fir the digital age. *Medical Teacher*, *38*(10), 1–6. DOI: 10.3109/0142159X.2016.1173661 PMID: 27128290

Gormally, C., Brickman, P., Hallar, B., & Armstrong, N. (2009). Effects of Inquiry-based Learning on Students' Science Literacy Skills and Confidence. *International Journal for the Scholarship of Teaching and Learning*, *3*(2). Advance online publication. DOI: 10.20429/ijsotl.2009.030216

Granados-Beltrán, C. (2016). Critical Interculturality. A Path for Pre-service ELT Teachers. *Íkala. Revista de Lenguaje y Cultura*, *21*(2). Advance online publication. DOI: 10.17533/udea.ikala.v21n02a04

Granovetter, M. S. (1973). The strength of weak ties. *American Journal of Sociology*, *78*(6), 1360–1380. DOI: 10.1086/225469

Grassini, S. (2023). Shaping the Future of Education: Exploring the Potential and Consequences of AI and ChatGPT in Educational Settings. *Education Sciences*, *13*(7), 692. DOI: 10.3390/educsci13070692

Greene, J. C. (2007). *Mixed methods in social inquiry*. John Wiley & Sons.

Grewal, D., Noble, S. M., Roggeveen, A. L., & Nordfalt, J. (2020). The future of in-store technology. *Journal of the Academy of Marketing Science*, *48*(1), 96–113. DOI: 10.1007/s11747-019-00697-z

Gülersoy, A. E., & Gülersoy, Ö. (2023). Çevre eğitimi ve iklim değişikliği dersi (6, 7 veya 8. sınıflar) öğretim programı kazanımlarının yenilenmiş Bloom taksonomisi bilişsel alan basamaklarına göre değerlendirilmesi [An Evaluation of the Learning Outcomes of the Environmental Education and Climate Change Course (Grades 6, 7, or 8) According to the Revised Bloom Taxonomy's Cognitive Domain Levels]. *Jass Studies-The Journal of Academic Social Science Studies*, *16*(97), 1–16.

Guth, S., & Helm, F. (Eds.). (2010). *Telecollaboration 2.0: Language, literacies and intercultural learning in the 21st century* (Vol. 1). Peter Lang. DOI: 10.3726/978-3-0351-0013-6

Hadad, S., Erturk, E., & Buzzetto-Hollywood, N. (2024). Generative AI and teachers' perspectives on its implementation in education. *Journal of Applied Learning and Teaching*, *7*(1). Advance online publication. DOI: 10.70725/815246mfssgp

Hagendorff, T. (2020). The Ethics of AI Ethics: An Evaluation of Guidelines. *Minds and Machines*, *30*(1), 99–120. DOI: 10.1007/s11023-020-09517-8

Haidemariam, T., & Gran, A. B. (2025). On the problems of training generative AI: Towards a hybrid approach combining technical and non-technical alignment strategies. *AI & Society*. Advance online publication. DOI: 10.1007/s00146-025-02445-0

Hall, E. (1976). *Beyond Culture*. Anchor Books.

Hallinger, P., & Truong, D. T. (2014). Exploring the contours of context and leadership effectiveness in Vietnam [Journal Article]. *Leading and Managing, 20*(2), 43–59.

Hansen, M. T. (1999). The Search-Transfer Problem: The Role of Weak Ties in Sharing Knowledge across Organization Subunits. *Administrative Science Quarterly, 44*(1), 82–111. DOI: 10.2307/2667032

Harris, A., & Jones, M. (2010). Professional learning communities and system improvement. *Improving Schools, 13*(2), 172–181. DOI: 10.1177/1365480210376487

Harsanti, H. R., Sudibjo, N., Riady, S., & Yu, P. (2025). 'Exploring Indonesian teachers' intention to use artificial intelligence in schools: The impact of digital leadership, digital readiness, and perceived usefulness'. *Cogent Social Sciences, 11*(1), 2593596. DOI: 10.1080/23311886.2025.2593596

HEInnovate. (2023) *HEInnovate: A self-assessment tool for higher education institutions.* Available at: https://www.heinnovate.eu/en (Accessed: Day Month Year).

Helm, F. (2024). *Intercultural communication in virtual exchange.* Cambridge University Press. DOI: 10.1017/9781009385589

Henkel, J. (2006). Selective revealing in open innovation processes: The case of embedded Linux. *Research Policy, 35*(7), 953–969. https://doi.org/https://doi.org/10.1016/j.respol.2006.04.010. DOI: 10.1016/j.respol.2006.04.010

Hero, J.-M., Wilson, C., Turner, B., Turner, C., Gibbes, B., & Phyland, R. (2024). Integrating Indigenous knowledges in higher education: Interdisciplinary approaches in science and humanities. *Journal of Australian Indigenous Issues, 27*(1-2), 24–40. DOI: 10.3316/informit.T2024080800004491551202171

Herrero, C., & Vanderschelden, I. (Eds.). (2019). *Using film and media in the language classroom: Reflections on research-led teaching* (Vol. 73). Multilingual Matters.

Hoang, N. H. (2025). 'E-leadership in the AI era: Exploring Vietnamese EFL teachers' digital leadership development in AI integration'. *Education and Information Technologies, 30*(12), 1–34. DOI: 10.1007/s10639-025-13451-6

Hodge, S. R. HAEGELE, J., HODGE, S., & SHAPIRO, D. (2020). *Routledge handbook of adapted physical education.* Routledge.

Hodges, C., Moore, S., Lockee, B., Trust, T., & Bond, A. (2024). The difference between emergency remote teaching and online learning. In Martindale, T., Amankwatia, T. B., Cifuentes, L., & Piña, A. A. (Eds.), *Handbook of Research in Online Learning: Insights and Advances* (pp. 511–522). Brill., DOI: 10.1163/9789004702813_021

Hofstede, G. (2001). *Culture's consequences: Comparing values, behaviors, institutions and organizations across nations* (2nd ed.). Sage Publications.

Holliday, A. (2011). Intercultural communication and ideology. *Sage (Atlanta, Ga.)*. Advance online publication. DOI: 10.4135/9781446269107

Holmes, W. (2025, November). AI, education, and children's rights. [). Frontiers Media SA.]. *Frontiers in Education, 10*, 1656736. DOI: 10.3389/feduc.2025.1656736

Holmes, W., Bialik, M., & Fadel, C. (2019). *Artificial intelligence in education promises and implications for teaching and learning*. Center for Curriculum Redesign.

Holmes, W., Bialik, M., & Fadel, C. (2019). *Artificial intelligence in education. Promise and implications for teaching and learning*. Center for Curriculum Redesign.

Holmes, W., Bialik, M., & Fadel, C. (2019). *Artificial intelligence in education: Promises and implications for teaching and learning*. Center for Curriculum Redesign.

Holmes, W., Bialik, M., & Fadel, C. (2022). *Artificial Intelligence in Education: Promises and Implications for Teaching and Learning*. Center for Curriculum Redesign.

Holmes, W., Bialik, M., & Fadel, C. (2023). *Artificial intelligence in education*. Globethics Publications.

Holmes, W., Porayska-Pomsta, K., Holstein, K., Sutherland, E., Baker, T., Shum, S. B., Santos, O. C., Rodrigo, M. T., Cukurova, M., Bittencourt, I. I., & Koedinger, K. R. (2022). Ethics of AI in education: Towards a community-wide framework. *International Journal of Artificial Intelligence in Education, 32*(4), 504–526. DOI: 10.1007/s40593-021-00239-1

Holmes, W., & Tuomi, I. (2022). State of the art and practice in AI in education. *European Journal of Education, 57*(4), 542–570. DOI: 10.1111/ejed.12533

Holstein, K., & Doroudi, S. (2021). Equity and artificial intelligence in education: will" aied" amplify or alleviate inequities in education? *arXiv preprint arXiv:2104.12920.*

Holstein, K., Aleven, V., & Rummel, N. (2020). A conceptual framework for human–AI hybrid adaptivity in education. In Roll, I., McNamara, D., Sosnovsky, S., Luckin, R., & Dimitrova, V. (Eds.), *Artificial Intelligence in Education* (pp. 240–253). Springer., DOI: 10.1007/978-3-030-52237-7_20

Holstein, K., McLaren, B. M., & Aleven, V. (2019). Co-designing a real-time classroom orchestration tool to support teacher–AI complementarity. *Journal of Learning Analytics, 6*(2), 27–52. DOI: 10.18608/jla.2019.62.3

Holste, J. S., & Fields, D. (2010). Trust and tacit knowledge sharing and use. *Journal of Knowledge Management, 14*(1), 128–140. DOI: 10.1108/13673271011015615

Homer, S. T., Chuen, P. W., & Chuah, C. (2025). The role of AI in education: A Southeast Asian student perspective through a unified theory of acceptance and use of technology lens. *Asia Pacific Journal of Education*, •••, 1–28. DOI: 10.1080/02188791.2025.2564138

Huang, Q., Davison, R. M., & Gu, J. (2011). The impact of trust, guanxi orientation and face on the intention of Chinese employees and managers to engage in peer-to-peer tacit and explicit knowledge sharing. *Information Systems Journal, 21*(6), 557–577. DOI: 10.1111/j.1365-2575.2010.00361.x

Huang, S. P. (2018). Effects of using artificial intelligence teaching system for environmental education on environmental knowledge and attitude. *Eurasia Journal of Mathematics, Science and Technology Education, 14*(7), 3277–3284. DOI: 10.29333/ejmste/91248

Hughes, L., Dwivedi, Y. K., Malik, T., Shawosh, M., Albashrawi, M. A., Jeon, I., Dutot, V., Appanderanda, M., Crick, T., De', R., Fenwick, M., Gunaratnege, S. M., Jurcys, P., Kar, A. K., Kshetri, N., Li, K., Mutasa, S., Samothrakis, S., Wade, M., & Walton, P. (2025). AI Agents and Agentic Systems: A Multi-Expert Analysis. *Journal of Computer Information Systems, 65*(4), 489–517. DOI: 10.1080/08874417.2025.2483832

Huot, S., & Loch, S. (2025a). Digital practices in Cambodian EFL classrooms: Teacher narratives from remote learning. In K. Khette & Tayade (Eds.), *Proceeding of one day national conference on English language, literature, cultural studies and media studies* (Vol. 2, pp. 19–31). Centre for Learning, Research and Development, Savda, Maharashtra. DOI: 10.5281/zenodo.16921807

Huot, S. (2025). Digital tutors in the kingdom: Exploring ChatGPT's influence on Cambodian students' academic and cognitive growth. In Pandya, J. D., & Patel, K. C. (Eds.), *Interdisciplinary insights: Exploring multiple perspectives* (Vol. 2, pp. 36–54). Meadow Publication.

Huot, S. (2026a). Digital diplomacy in Cambodia: Embracing artificial intelligence for strategic engagement and national development. In Turan, A., & Ucuzal, H. (Eds.), *Diplomacy in the age of artificial intelligence* (pp. 307–330). IGI Global Scientific Publishing., DOI: 10.4018/979-8-3373-4937-4.ch013

Huot, S. (2026b). Emerging voices from Cambodia: International student journeys and educational aspirations in a globalized academic landscape. In Irham, I., Huda, M., & Yaqin, L. N. (Eds.), *International student narratives in globalized higher education* (pp. 365–400). IGI Global Scientific Publishing., DOI: 10.4018/979-8-3373-4212-2.ch014

Huot, S., & Em, S. (2025). Effective strategies of English teaching in Cambodia's underserved communities: Bridging digital divide to access education quality. [JEILT]. *Journal of Education Innovation and Language Teaching*, *1*(1), 53–77. DOI: 10.63381/jeilt.v1i1.38

Huot, S., & Hok, C. (2025a). Enhancing English language teaching for multilingual learners: Leveraging heritage languages in the classroom. *Journal of Social and Educational Research*, *4*(1), 87–95. DOI: 10.5281/zenodo.15698964

Huot, S., & Hok, C. (2025b). Unpacking the struggle: Linguistic, pedagogical, and cognitive barriers in Cambodian students' English essay writing. *Context (Ibadan)*, *12*(4), 149–168. DOI: 10.5281/zenodo.15807401

Huot, S., & Loch, S. (2025b). Educating in the age of AI: Preparing Cambodian teachers and students for an AI-augmented learning future. *Journal of Educational Technology and E-Learning Innovations*, *1*(2), 31–38. DOI: 10.54536/jeteli.v1i2.5170

Huot, S., & Loch, S. (2025c). From rote to reflective: Integrating ChatGPT to transform learning outcomes in Cambodian education. *International Journal of Language and Literary Studies*, *7*(4), 1–15. DOI: 10.36892/ijlls.v7i4.2188

Huot, S., Loch, S., Nget, R., & Em, S. (2025). Exploring multiliteracies in the digital era: A framework for 21st-century learning. [CJESS]. *Cambodian Journal of Educational and Social Sciences*, *2*(1), 7–27. DOI: 10.69496/cjess.v2i1.50

Huot, S., Sam, R., & Nguon, T. (2024). Influencing factors in teaching career choices in Cambodia in teacher education colleges: A conceptual framework. *European Journal of Arts. Humanities and Social Sciences*, *1*(6), 97–108. DOI: 10.59324/ejahss.2024.1(6).11

Huot, S., & Such, C. (2025). Leveraging social media for language learning: Opportunities and challenges. [JEILT]. *Journal of Education Innovation and Language Teaching*, *1*(2), 10–29. DOI: 10.63381/jeilt.v1i2.56

Huot, S., & Tep, P. (2025). Advancing ChatGPT for pedagogical innovation in Cambodia: Insight from global evidence and local implications. *The Context: Journal of English Studies*, *12*(4), 115–135. DOI: 10.5281/zenodo.15806972

Hutchins, E. (1995). *Cognition in the Wild*. MIT press. DOI: 10.7551/mitpress/1881.001.0001

Hwang, G. J., Xie, H., Wah, B. W., & Gašević, D. (2020). Vision, challenges, roles and research issues of Artificial Intelligence in Education. *Computers and Education: Artificial Intelligence*, *1*, 100001. Advance online publication. DOI: 10.1016/j.caeai.2020.100001

IBM. (2023). *IBM SkillsBuild Program Overview*. IBM Corporation. https://skillsbuild.org/

Ifenthaler, D., & Schumacher, C. (2016). Student perceptions of privacy principles for learning analytics. *Educational Technology Research and Development*, *64*(5), 923–938. DOI: 10.1007/s11423-016-9477-y

Ifenthaler, D., & Yau, J. Y. K. (2020). Utilising learning analytics to support study success. *Educational Technology Research and Development*, *68*(4), 1961–1988. DOI: 10.1007/s11423-020-09788-z

Iliadis, A., & Russo, F. (2016). Critical data studies: An introduction. *Big Data & Society*, *3*(2), 2053951716674238. DOI: 10.1177/2053951716674238

Jackson, J. (2014). *Introducing language and intercultural communication*. Routledge. DOI: 10.4324/9781315848938

Jandrić, P., Knox, J., Besley, T., Ryberg, T., Suoranta, J., & Hayes, S. (2018). Postdigital science and education. *50*(10), 893–899. DOI: 10.1080/00131857.2018.1454000

Järvelä, S., Malmberg, J., Haataja, E., Sobocinski, M., & Kirschner, P. A. (2021). What multimodal data can tell us about the students' regulation of their learning process? *Learning and Instruction*, *72*, 101203. Advance online publication. DOI: 10.1016/j.learninstruc.2019.04.004

Järvelä, S., Nguyen, A., & Hadwin, A. (2023). Human and artificial intelligence collaboration for socially shared regulation in learning. *British Journal of Educational Technology*, *54*(5), 1057–1076. DOI: 10.1111/bjet.13325

Jarvenpaa, S. L., Knoll, K., & Leidner, D. E. (1998). Is Anybody out There? Antecedents of Trust in Global Virtual Teams. *Journal of Management Information Systems*, *14*(4), 29–64. DOI: 10.1080/07421222.1998.11518185

Jivet, I., Scheffel, M., Drachsler, H., & Specht, M. (2017). Awareness is not enough: Pitfalls of learning analytics dashboards in the educational practice. In *European conference on technology enhanced learning* (pp. 82-96). Springer, Cham. DOI: 10.1007/978-3-319-66610-5_7

Kampylis, P., Punie, Y., & Devine, J. (2021). AI in education: Ethical implications. *Computers and Education: Artificial Intelligence*, *2*, 100018. DOI: 10.1016/j.caeai.2021.100018

Kamrowska-Załuska, D. (2021). Impact of AI-Based Tools and Urban Big Data Analytics on the Design and Planning of Cities. *Land (Basel)*, *10*(11), 1209. DOI: 10.3390/land10111209

Kang, S. P., Chen, Y., Svihla, V., Gallup, A., Ferris, K., & Datye, A. K. (2022). Guiding change in higher education: An emergent, iterative application of Kotter's change model. *Studies in Higher Education*, *47*(2), 270–289. DOI: 10.1080/03075079.2020.1741540

Karan, B., & Angadi, G. R. (2025). Understanding school readiness factors in relation to the incorporation of artificial intelligence using TOE framework: Empirical evidence from India. *TechTrends*, *69*(1), 38–59. DOI: 10.1007/s11528-024-01020-6

Karatsareas, P., Hadodo, M. J., & Ioannidou, E. (2024). Researching identities, authenticities, and institutions in minoritized settings: Insights from diverse Greek-speaking communities. In Hadodo, M. J., Katsareas, P., & Ioannidou, E. (Eds.), *Greek in minoritized contexts* (pp. 1–21). Routledge., DOI: 10.4324/9781003269694-1

Kasneci, E., Seßler, K., Küchemann, S., Bannert, M., Dementieva, D., Fischer, F., Gasser, U., Groh, G., Günnemann, S., Hüllermeier, E., Krusche, S., Kutyniok, G., Michaeli, T., Nerdel, C., Pfeffer, J., Poquet, O., Sailer, M., Schmidt, A., Seidel, T., & Kasneci, G. (2023). ChatGPT for good? On opportunities and challenges of large language models for education. *Learning and Individual Differences*, *103*, 102274. DOI: 10.1016/j.lindif.2023.102274

Kern, R. (2006). Perspectives on technology in learning and teaching languages. *TESOL Quarterly*, *40*(1), 183–210. DOI: 10.2307/40264516

Kern, R., & Warschauer, M. (2000). *Network-based language teaching: Concepts and practice*. Cambridge University Press.

Kidman, J. (2015). Indigenous youth, nationhood and the politics of belonging. In Wyn, J., & Cahill, H. (Eds.), *Handbook of children and youth studies* (pp. 637–649). Springer Singapore. DOI: 10.1007/978-981-4451-15-4_49

Kim, H., Hwang, J., Kim, T., Choi, M., Lee, D., & Ko, J. (2025). Impact of generative artificial intelligence on learning: Scaffolding strategies and self-directed learning perspectives. *International Journal of Human-Computer Interaction*, •••, 1–23. DOI: 10.1080/10447318.2025.2531267

Kim, J., Lee, H., & Cho, Y. H. (2022). Learning design to support student-AI collaboration: Perspectives of leading teachers for AI in education. *Education and Information Technologies, 27*(5), 6069–6104. DOI: 10.1007/s10639-021-10831-6

Kim, N. J., & Kim, M. K. (2022). Teacher's perceptions of using an artificial intelligence-based educational tool for scientific writing. *Frontiers in Education, 7*, 755914. Advance online publication. DOI: 10.3389/feduc.2022.755914

Kirschner, P. A., Sweller, J., Kirschner, F., & Zambrano, R. J. (2018). From Cognitive Load Theory to Collaborative Cognitive Load Theory. *International Journal of Computer-Supported Collaborative Learning, 13*(2), 213–233. DOI: 10.1007/s11412-018-9277-y PMID: 30996713

Kizilcec, R. F. (2016). How much information? Effects of transparency on trust in an algorithmic interface. In *Proceedings of the 2016 CHI Conference on Human Factors in Computing Systems (CHI '16)* (pp. 2390–2395). ACM.

Kizilcec, R. F., & Lee, H. (2020). Algorithmic fairness in education. *Educational Technology Research and Development, 68*, 1–20. DOI: 10.48550/arXiv.2007.05443

Kizilcec, R. F., & Lee, H. (2020). Algorithmic fairness in education. *Proceedings of the Learning Analytics and Knowledge Conference*, 335–346. DOI: 10.1145/3375462.3375537

Kizilcec, R. F., Pérez-Sanagustín, M., & Maldonado, J. J. (2017). Self-regulated learning strategies predict learner behavior and goal attainment in Massive Open Online Courses. *Computers & Education, 104*, 18–33. DOI: 10.1016/j.compedu.2016.10.001

Knaflic, C. N. (2025). *Storytelling with data: A data visualization guide for business professionals*. John Wiley & Sons.

Knight, J. (2022). Differentiating Knowledge Diplomacy from Soft Power and Cultural, Science, Education and Public Forms of Diplomacy. In Knight, J. (Ed.), *Knowledge diplomacy in international relations and higher education* (pp. 113–125). Springer., DOI: 10.1007/978-3-031-14977-1_9

Knox, J. (2019). What does the 'postdigital' mean for education? Three critical perspectives on the digital, with implications for educational research and practice. *Postdigital Science and Education, 1*(2), 357–370. DOI: 10.1007/s42438-019-00045-y

Knox, J. (2020). Artificial intelligence and education in China. *Learning, Media and Technology, 45*(3), 298–311. DOI: 10.1080/17439884.2020.1754236

Knox, J., Wang, Y., & Gallagher, M. (2020). *Artificial intelligence and education futures: Critical perspectives and alternative imaginaries*. Routledge., DOI: 10.4324/9780429286798

Koh, J. H. L., Chai, C. S., Benjamin, W., & Hong, H.-Y. (2015). Technological Pedagogical Content Knowledge (TPACK) and Design Thinking: A Framework to Support ICT Lesson Design for 21st Century Learning. *The Asia-Pacific Education Researcher, 24*(3), 535–543. DOI: 10.1007/s40299-015-0237-2

Kotter, J. P., & Cohen, D. (2014). *Change leadership*. Harvard Business Review Press.

Koyuncuoğlu, D. (2023). Yükseköğretimde yapay zekâ tabanlı sürdürülebilirlik yaklaşımı ve karşılaştırmalı bir inceleme [An AI-Based Approach to Sustainability in Higher Education and a Comparative Study]. *Journal of Academic Value Studies, 9*(3), 182–194. DOI: 10.29228/javs.72130

Kozulin, A., & Wertsch, J. V. (1987). Vygotsky and the Social Formation of Mind. *The American Journal of Psychology, 100*(1), 123. DOI: 10.2307/1422646

KPMG LLP. (2025) *Generative AI and the future of education: how higher education institutions, their employees and students are using AI to drive success*. Toronto: KPMG Canada. Available at: https://kpmg.com/ca/AI

Kramsch, C. (1993). *Context and culture in language teaching*. Oxford University Press.

Kramsch, C. (1998). *Language and culture*. Oxford University Press.

Krueger, R. A. (2014). *Focus groups: A practical guide for applied research*. Sage publications.

Krumsvik, R. J., & Jones, L. Ø. (2024). Generative AI in teacher education: Educators' perceptions of transformative potentials and the triadic nature of AI literacy explored through AI-enhanced methods. *Computers and Education: Artificial Intelligence, 7*, 100471. Advance online publication. DOI: 10.1016/j.caeai.2025.100471

Kukulska-Hulme, A., Wise, A. F., Coughlan, T., Biswas, G., Bossu, C., Burriss, S. K., Ferguson, R., Gaved, M., Herodotou, C., Holmes, W., & Whitelock, D. (2024). *Innovating pedagogy 2024* (Open University Innovation Report No. 12). The Open University.

Kukutai, T., & Taylor, J. (2016). *Indigenous data sovereignty: Toward an agenda*. ANU press. DOI: 10.22459/CAEPR38.11.2016

Kuleto, V., Ilić, M., Dumangiu, M., Ranković, M., Martins, O. M. D., Păun, D., & Mihoreanu, L. (2021). Exploring opportunities and challenges of artificial intelligence and machine learning in higher education institutions. *Sustainability (Basel), 13*(18), 10424. DOI: 10.3390/su131810424

Kundu, A. and Bej, T. (2025) 'AI policies in school education: a comparative study on China, Singapore, Finland, and the US', *Journal of Science and Technology Policy Management*. Available at: DOI: 10.1108/JSTPM-06-2024-0218

Kung, T. H., Cheatham, M., Medenilla, A., Sillos, C., De Leon, L., Elepaño, C., Madriaga, M., Aggabao, R., Diaz-Candido, G., Maningo, J., & Tseng, V. (2023). Performance of ChatGPT on USMLE: Potential for AI-assisted medical education using large language models. *PLOS Digital Health, 2*(2), e0000198. DOI: 10.1371/journal.pdig.0000198 PMID: 36812645

Ladson-Billings, G. (1995). Toward a theory of culturally relevant pedagogy. *American Educational Research Journal, 32*(3), 465–491. DOI: 10.3102/00028312032003465

Lan, Y. (2024). Through tensions to identity-based motivations: Exploring teacher professional identity in Artificial Intelligence-enhanced teacher training. *Teaching and Teacher Education, 137*, 104736. DOI: 10.1016/j.tate.2024.104736

Latif, S., Wu, Y., Huang, L., Khwaja, U. A., Diao, Z., & Wang, Q. (2023). Artificial intelligence in teaching and teacher professional development: A systematic review. *Computers and Education: Artificial Intelligence, 6*, 100355. Advance online publication. DOI: 10.1016/j.caeai.2024.100355

Laurillard, D. (2013). *Teaching as a design science: Building pedagogical patterns for learning and technology*. Routledge. DOI: 10.4324/9780203125083

Le, A. T. T., Tran, T. V., Tran, T. M., & Phan, T. H. (2024). Intrinsic and Extrinsic Factors as Motivation Roles in Scientific Research Activities of Professors at Several Vietnamese Universities. *SAGE Open, 14*(1), 21582440241230838. DOI: 10.1177/21582440241230838

Leal Filho, W., Kim, E., Borsatto, J. M. L. S., & Marcolin, C. B. (2025). Using artificial intelligence in sustainability teaching and learning. *Environmental Sciences Europe, 37*(1), 124. DOI: 10.1186/s12302-025-01159-w

Lee, J. Y. (2025). Teaching with the algorithm: Anticipations of AI in teacher education. *European Journal of Teacher Education, 51*(1), 93–106. DOI: 10.1080/02619768.2025.2540793

Lee, J., Pillai, R., Kaushik, N., & Sivathanu, B. (2022). Students' adoption of AI-based teacher-bots (T-bots) for learning in higher education. *Information Technology & People*, *37*(1), 328–355. DOI: 10.1108/ITP-02-2021-0152

Leonard, D., & Sensiper, S. (1998). The Role of Tacit Knowledge in Group Innovation. *California Management Review*, *40*(3), 112–132. DOI: 10.2307/41165946

Leong, F. T., & Kim, H. H. (1991). Going beyond cultural sensitivity on the road to multiculturalism: Using the Intercultural Sensitizer as a counselor training tool. *Journal of Counseling and Development*, *70*(1), 112–118. DOI: 10.1002/j.1556-6676.1991.tb01570.x

Levin, D. Z., & Cross, R. (2004). The Strength of Weak Ties You Can Trust: The Mediating Role of Trust in Effective Knowledge Transfer. *Management Science*, *50*(11), 1477–1490. DOI: 10.1287/mnsc.1030.0136

Levy, F., & Murnane, R. J. (2013). *Dancing with robots: Human skills for computerized work*. Third Way.

Li, L., Dinh, L., Hu, S., & Hemphill, L. (2024). Academic collaboration on large language model studies increases overall but varies across disciplines. *arXiv preprint arXiv:2408.04163*. DOI: 10.21203/rs.3.rs-4887385/v1

Liddicoat, A. J., & Scarino, A. (2013). *Intercultural language teaching and learning*. John Wiley & Sons. DOI: 10.1002/9781118482070

Li, K. C., Wong, B. T. M., & Yang, Y. (2023). Exploring the impact of AI on teacher leadership: Regressing or expanding? *Education and Information Technologies*, *28*, 21677–21695. DOI: 10.1007/s10639-023-12174-w

Lin, H. F. (2007). Knowledge sharing and firm innovation capability: An empirical study. *International Journal of Manpower*, *28*(3-4), 315–332. DOI: 10.1108/01437720710755272

Li, Q., Li, Z., & Han, J. (2021). A hybrid learning pedagogy for surmounting the challenges of the COVID-19 pandemic in the performing arts education. *Education and Information Technologies*, *26*(6), 7635–7655. DOI: 10.1007/s10639-021-10612-1 PMID: 34220284

Liu, M., Zhao, G., Zhong, Z., Ma, J., & Wang, W. (2024). Theoretical foundations for blended learning. In Li, M., Han, X., & Cheng, J. (Eds.), *Handbook of educational reform through blended learning* (pp. 1–44). Springer., DOI: 10.1007/978-981-99-6269-3_1

Liu, N. (2025). Exploring the factors influencing the adoption of artificial intelligence technology by university teachers: The mediating role of confidence and AI readiness. *BMC Psychology*, *13*(1), 311. DOI: 10.1186/s40359-025-02620-4 PMID: 40148913

Loan, T. T. T., & Th y, N. T. H. (2024). Vietnamese University lecturers apply AI in teaching. A case study in Thu Dau Mot university. *European Journal of Theoretical and Applied Sciences*, *2*(6), 643–650. DOI: 10.59324/ejtas.2024.2(6).57

Long, P., et al. (2025). Self-regulated learning and AI literacy: Enhancing autonomy in hybrid learning contexts. *arXiv preprint*.

Longo, F., Padovano, A., & Umbrello, S. (2020). Value-Oriented and Ethical Technology Engineering in Industry 5.0: A Human-Centric Perspective for the Design of the Factory of the Future. *Applied Sciences (Basel, Switzerland)*, *10*(12), 4182. DOI: 10.3390/app10124182

Lowenthal, P. R., & Dunlap, J. C. (2018). Investigating students' perceptions of instructional strategies to establish social presence. *Distance Education*, *39*(3), 281–298. DOI: 10.1080/01587919.2018.1476844

Luckin, R. (2018). *Machine learning and human intelligence. The future of education for the 21st century*. UCL institute of education press.

Luckin, R., & Holmes, W. (2016). *Intelligence unleashed: An argument for AI in education*. Pearson. https://www.pearson.com/content/dam/corporate/glob

Luckin, R., Holmes, W., Griffiths, M., & Forcier, L. (2016). *Intelligence Unleashed: An argument for AI in Education*. Pearson.https://static.googleusercontent.com/media/edu.google.com/en//pdfs/Intelligence-Unleashed-Publication.pdf

Luckin, R., Holmes, W., Griffiths, M., & Forcier, L. B. (2016). *Intelligence unleashed: An argument for AI in education*. Pearson Education.

Lukes, S. (2012). Power: A radical view [2005]. *Contemporary sociological theory*, *266*(3), 1–22.

Maarof, M., & Jalaluddin, N. S. (2019). The Implementation of Pedagogical Strategies in Inclusive Education Program for Pupils with Special Needs among Mainstream Teachers: A Case study. *Jurnal Pendidikan Bitara UPSI*, *12*(12), 29–38. DOI: 10.37134/bitara.vol12.4.2019

MacKenzie, A., Bacalja, A., Annamali, D., Panaretou, A., Girme, P., Cutajar, M., Abegglen, S., Evens, M., Neuhaus, F., Wilson, K., Psarikidou, K., Koole, M., Hrastinski, S., Sturm, S., Adachi, C., Schnaider, K., Bozkurt, A., Rapanta, C., Themelis, C., & Gourlay, L. (2022). Dissolving the Dichotomies Between Online and Campus-Based Teaching: A Collective Response to The Manifesto for Teaching Online (Bayne et al. 2020). *Postdigital Science and Education*, *4*(2), 271–329. DOI: 10.1007/s42438-021-00259-z PMID: 40477827

Makhija, R., Aggarwal, S., & Jain, S. (2025). Hybrid learning, artificial Intelligence, and Indian indigenized values. In Makhija, R., Aggarwal, S., & Jain, S. (Eds.), *Indigenous Teaching Disciplines and Perspectives for Higher Education* (pp. 267–284). IGI Global Scientific Publishing. DOI: 10.4018/979-8-3693-9296-6.ch013

March, J. G. (1991). Exploration and Exploitation in Organizational Learning. *Organization Science*, *2*(1), 71–87. DOI: 10.1287/orsc.2.1.71

Marginson, S. (2010). Higher education in the global knowledge economy. *Procedia: Social and Behavioral Sciences*, *2*(5), 6962–6980. DOI: 10.1016/j.sbspro.2010.05.049

Marginson, S. (2016). *The dream is over: The crisis of Clark Kerr's California idea of higher education*. University of California Press.

Marginson, S., & Rhoades, G. (2002). Beyond national states, markets, and systems of higher education: A glonacal agency heuristic. *Higher Education*, *43*(3), 281–309. DOI: 10.1023/A:1014699605875

Markus, H. R., & Kitayama, S. (2014). Culture and the self: Implications for cognition, emotion, and motivation. In *College student development and academic life* (pp. 264–293). Routledge.

Martinez-Maldonado, R., Echeverria, V., & Shibani, A. (2023). Orchestrating collaborative learning with multimodal analytics: Challenges and opportunities. In Echeverria et al. (2023).

Martinez-Maldonado, R., Echeverria, V., Fernandez Nieto, G., & Buckingham Shum, S. (2020, April). From data to insights: A layered storytelling approach for multimodal learning analytics. In *Proceedings of the 2020 chi conference on human factors in computing systems* (pp. 1-15). DOI: 10.1145/3313831.3376148

Mazza, J. (2007, October 23-25). *Labor markets and social inclusion in Latin America and the Caribbean: Perspectives for intergenerational solidarity* [Paper presentation]. UN Expert Group Meeting on Intergenerational Solidarity: Strengthening Economic and Social Ties, New York, USA.

McDermott, R., & O'Dell, C. (2001). Overcoming cultural barriers to sharing knowledge. *Journal of Knowledge Management, 5*(1), 76–85. DOI: 10.1108/13673270110384428

McKinsey & Company. (2025). *AI and the Future of Work: Global Workforce Trends 2025*. McKinsey Global Institute., DOI: 10.1145/3636555.3636857

MEA. (2025). *Brief on India–Cambodia bilateral relations*. Ministry of External Affairs Government of India. https://www.mea.gov.in/Portal/ForeignRelation/Cambodia-2025.pdf

MEB. (2015). *Ortaokul çevre eğitimi dersi öğretim programı [Middle School Environmental Education Curriculum].*

MEB. (2020). Millî Eğitim Bakanı Ziya Selçuk YEĞİTEK'te EBA kontrol merkezini ziyaret etti [Minister of National Education Ziya Selçuk visited the EBA control center at YEĞİTEK]. https://yegitek.meb.gov.tr/www/mill-egitim-bakani-ziya-selcukyegitekte-eba-kontrol-merkezini-ziyaret-etti/icerik/3036

MEB. (2022a). Çevre Eğitimi ve İklim Değişikliği Dersinin Müfredatı Tamamlandı [The Curriculum for the Environmental Education and Climate Change Course Has Been Finalized]. https://www.meb.gov.tr/cevre-egitimi-ve-iklim-degisikligi-dersinin-mufredati-tamamlandi/haber/25946/tr

MEB. (2022b). *Çevre eğitimi ve iklim değişikliği dersi öğretim programı (Ortaokul 6, 7 veya 8. sınıflar)*. [*Curriculum for the Environmental Education and Climate Change Course (6th, 7th, or 8th Grade Middle School)].*

MEB. (2023). *Türkiye yüzyılı maarif modeli tanıtım kitapçığı [Brochure Introducing the "Century of Turkey" Education Model].* Ankara: MEB Yayınları. https://www.meb.gov.tr

Mezirow, J. (2000). *Learning as Transformation: Critical Perspectives on a Theory in Progress*. Jossey-Bass.ISBN-0-7879-4845-4

Miao, F., & Holmes, W. (2021). *AI and education: Guidance for policy-makers.* UNESCO.

Miao, F., Holmes, W., Huang, R., & Zhang, H. (2021). *AI and education: Guidance for policy-makers. United Nations Educational, Scientific and Cultural Organization.* UNESCO., https://unesdoc.unesco.org/ark:/48223/pf0000376709

Michailova, S., & Hutchings, K. (2006). National Cultural Influences on Knowledge Sharing: A Comparison of China and Russia. *Journal of Management Studies*, *43*(3), 383–405. https://doi.org/https://doi.org/10.1111/j.1467-6486.2006.00595.x. DOI: 10.1111/j.1467-6486.2006.00595.x

Michel-Villarreal, R., Vilalta-Perdomo, E., Salinas-Navarro, D. E., Thierry-Aguilera, R., & Gerardou, F. S. (2023). Challenges and Opportunities of Generative AI for Higher Education as Explained by ChatGPT. *Education Sciences*, *13*(9), 856. DOI: 10.3390/educsci13090856

Microsoft. (2025) *AI in Education Report 2025*. Redmond, WA: Microsoft. Available at: https://cdn-dynmedia-1.microsoft.com (accessed: 3 January 2026).

Miller, T. (2019). Explanation in artificial intelligence: Insights from the social sciences. *Artificial Intelligence*, *267*, 1–38. DOI: 10.1016/j.artint.2018.07.007

Mishra, P., & Koehler, M. J. (2006). Technological Pedagogical Content Knowledge: A Framework for Teacher Knowledge. *Teachers College Record*, *108*(6), 1017–1054. DOI: 10.1111/j.1467-9620.2006.00684.x

Molina, E., Cobo, C., Pineda, J., & Rovner, H. (2024) *AI revolution in education: what you need to know*. Digital Innovations in Education Brief No. 1. Washington, DC: World Bank. Available at: https://documents1.worldbank.org/curated/en/099734306182493324/pdf/IDU152823b13109c514ebd19c241a289470b6902.pdf

Mooradian, T., Renzl, B., & Matzler, K. (2006). Who Trusts? Personality, Trust and Knowledge Sharing. *Management Learning*, *37*(4), 523–540. DOI: 10.1177/1350507606073424

Morgan, D. L. (1997). *Focus groups as qualitative research* (Vol. 16). Sage. DOI: 10.4135/9781412984287

Mtebe, J. S., & Raisamo, R. (2014). Investigating perceived barriers to the use of open educational resources in higher education in Tanzania. *International Review of Research in Open and Distance Learning*, *15*(2). Advance online publication. DOI: 10.19173/irrodl.v15i2.1803

Mulaudzi, L. V., & Hamilton, J. (2025). Lecturer's Perspective on the Role of AI in Personalized Learning: Benefits, Challenges, and Ethical Considerations in Higher Education. *Journal of Academic Ethics*, *23*(4), 1571–1591. DOI: 10.1007/s10805-025-09615-1

Nabiyev, V., & Erümit, A. K. (2020). Yapay zekanın temelleri. [The Fundamentals of Artificial Intelligence] In Nabiyev, V., & Erümit, A. K. (Eds.), *Eğitimde yapay zeka: Kuramdan uygulamaya* [Artificial Intelligence in Education: From Theory to Practice]. (pp. 2–37). Pegem Akademi Yayınları. DOI: 10.14527/9786257052986.01

Nahapiet, J., & Ghoshal, S. (1998). Social Capital, Intellectual Capital, and the Organizational Advantage. *Academy of Management Review*, *23*(2), 242–266. DOI: 10.2307/259373

Naicker, A., Singh, E., & van Genugten, T. (2022). Collaborative Online International Learning (COIL): Preparedness and experiences of South African students. *Innovations in Education and Teaching International*, *59*(5), 499–510. DOI: 10.1080/14703297.2021.1895867

Ng, D. T. K., Leung, J. K. L., Chu, S. K. W., & Qiao, M. S. (2021). Conceptualizing AI literacy: An exploratory review. *Computers and Education: Artificial Intelligence*, *2*, 100041. Advance online publication. DOI: 10.1016/j.caeai.2021.100041

Ng, D. T. K., Tan, C. W., & Leung, J. K. L. (2024). Empowering student self-regulated learning and science education through <scp>ChatGPT</scp> : A pioneering pilot study. *British Journal of Educational Technology*, *55*(4), 1328–1353. DOI: 10.1111/bjet.13454

Ng, P. T. (2025). Learning in an era of uncertainty in Singapore: Diversity, lifelong learning, inspiration and paradigm shift. *Educational Research for Policy and Practice*, *24*(1), 121–127. DOI: 10.1007/s10671-023-09348-1 PMID: 38625282

Nguyen, A. T., Truong, T. H., Luong, T. L., Luu, H. V., Hoang, T. T. N., & Luu, Q. D. (2022). Management factors influencing lecturers' research productivity in Vietnam National University, Hanoi, Vietnam: A structural equation modeling analysis. *Heliyon*, *8*(9), e10510. Advance online publication. DOI: 10.1016/j.heliyon.2022.e10510 PMID: 36120496

Nguyen, A., Kishore, S., Hong, Y., Qutab, S., & Dang, B. (2025). Generative artificial intelligence in education: From organizing visions to official guidelines. *Information Technology & People*, *38*(8), 172–199. DOI: 10.1108/ITP-08-2024-1026

Nguyen, H. L., Dang, B., Hong, Y., & Nguyen, A. (2024). Digital transformation in Vietnamese higher education: An epistemic network analysis of policy documents. *Kokusai Kyoiku Kyoryoku Ronshu*, *27*(2), 138–156. DOI: 10.1108/JICE-03-2024-0010

Nguyen, H., Nguyen, V., Ludovise, S., & Santagata, R. (2025). Misrepresentation or inclusion: Promises of generative artificial intelligence in climate change education. *Learning, Media and Technology*, *50*(3), 393–409. DOI: 10.1080/17439884.2024.2435834

Nguyen, T. P. L., Nguyen, T. H., & Tran, T. K. (2020). STEM Education in Secondary Schools: Teachers' Perspective towards Sustainable Development. *Sustainability (Basel)*, *12*(21), 8865. DOI: 10.3390/su12218865

Nguyen, T. V., Cong Pham, H., Nhat Nguyen, M., Zhou, L., & Akbari, M. (2023). Data-driven review of blockchain applications in supply chain management: Key research themes and future directions. *International Journal of Production Research*, *61*(23), 8213–8235. DOI: 10.1080/00207543.2023.2165190

Nguyen, V. H., & Hamid, M. O. (2021). The CEFR as a national language policy in Vietnam: Insights from a sociogenetic analysis. *Journal of Multilingual and Multicultural Development*, *42*(7), 650–662. DOI: 10.1080/01434632.2020.1715416

Noble, S. U. (2018). Algorithms of oppression: How search engines reinforce racism. In *Algorithms of oppression*. New York university press.

Noble, S. U. (2018). *Algorithms of oppression: How search engines reinforce racism*. NYU Press., DOI: 10.18574/nyu/9781479833641.001.0001

Nonaka, I. (2009). The knowledge-creating company. In *The economic impact of knowledge* (pp. 175–187). Routledge.

Norman, D. (2013). *The design of everyday things*. Basic Books.

Nussbaum, M. C. (2016). *Not for profit: Why democracy needs the humanities* (Updated ed.). Princeton University Press.

Nye, J. S. (2004). *Soft power: The means to success in world politics*. Public Affairs.

O'Dowd, R. (2018). From telecollaboration to virtual exchange: State-of-the-art and the role of UNICollaboration in moving forward. *Research-publishing. net, 1*, 1-23.

O'Dowd, R. (2021). Virtual exchange: Moving forward into the next decade. *Computer Assisted Language Learning*, *34*(3), 209–224. DOI: 10.1080/09588221.2021.1902201

O'Dowd, R., & Ritter, M. (2006). Understanding and working with 'failed communication' in telecollaborative exchanges. *CALICO Journal*, *23*(3), 623–642. DOI: 10.1558/cj.v23i3.623-642

O'Dowd, R., & Ritter, M. (2006). Understanding and working with "failed communication" in telecollaborative exchanges. *Computer Assisted Language Learning, 19*(1), 1–15.

O'Neil, C. (2016). *Weapons of math destruction: How big data increases inequality and threatens democracy*. Crown.

O'Dowd, R. (2018). From telecollaboration to virtual exchange: State-of-the-art and the role of UNICollaboration in moving forward. *Research-publishing. net, 1*, 1–23. DOI: 10.14705/rpnet.2018.jve.1

OECD. (2019) *OECD Learning Compass 2030*. Available at: https://www.oecd.org/education/2030-project/

OECD. (2019). *OECD Principles on Artificial Intelligence*. Paris: Organisation for Economic Co-operation and Development. https://oecd.ai/en/ai-principles

OECD. (2021). *21st-century readers: Developing literacy skills in a digital world.* Organisation for Economic Co-operation and Development Publishing., DOI: 10.1787/a83d84cb-

OECD. (2021). *AI and the Future of Skills, Volume 1: Capabilities and Assessments.* OECD Publishing.

OECD. (2021). AI and the future of skills, Volume 1: Capabilities and assessments. OECD Publishing. DOI: 10.1787/5ee71f34-en

OECD. (2021). AI in education: Challenges and opportunities. DOI: 10.1787/589b283f-en

OECD. (2023a). *OECD digital education outlook 2023: Towards an effective digital education ecosystem*. OECD Publishing., DOI: 10.1787/c74f03de-

OECD. (2023b). *Public governance review: Southeast Asia 2023*. OECD Publishing. https://www.oecd.org/en/publications/serials/oecd-public-governance-reviews_g1g1190c.html

Okunade, A. I. (2024). The role of artificial ıntelligence in teaching of science education in secondary schools in Nigeria. *European Journal of Computer Science and Information Technology, 12*(1), 57–67. DOI: 10.37745/ejcsit2013/vol12n15767

Oliveira, K. K. de S., & de Souza, R. A. C. (2021). *Digital Transformation towards Education 4.0*. Informatics in Education., DOI: 10.15388/infedu.2022.13

Onu, P., Pradhan, A., & Mbohwa, C. (2024). Potential to use metaverse for future teaching and learning. *Education and Information Technologies, 29*(7), 8893–8924. DOI: 10.1007/s10639-023-12167-9

Ouyang, F., & Jiao, P. (2021). Artificial intelligence in education: The three paradigms. *Computers and Education: Artificial Intelligence, 2*, 100020. Advance online publication. DOI: 10.1016/j.caeai.2021.100020

Oversby, J. (2015). Teachers' learning about climate change education. *Procedia: Social and Behavioral Sciences, 167*, 23–27. DOI: 10.1016/j.sbspro.2014.12.637

Pane, J. F., Steiner, E. D., Baird, M. D., & Hamilton, L. S. (2014). *Continued progress: Promising evidence on personalized learning*. RAND Corporation.

Pangrazio, L., & Sefton-Green, J. (2021). Digital Rights, Digital Citizenship and Digital Literacy: What's the Difference? *Journal of New Approaches in Educational Research, 10*(1), 15–27. DOI: 10.7821/naer.2021.1.616

Panyajamorn, T. (2022). Using MOOC and Gamification Hybrid Learning Models in Rural Public Schools in Thailand. *The Journal of Educators Online, 19*(3). Advance online publication. DOI: 10.9743/JEO.2022.19.3.12

Paris, D., & Alim, H. S. (2017). *Culturally sustaining pedagogies: Teaching and learning for justice in a changing world.* Teachers College Press.

Park, S.-M., & Kim, Y.-G. (2022). A Metaverse: Taxonomy, Components, Applications, and Open Challenges. *IEEE Access : Practical Innovations, Open Solutions, 10*, 4209–4251. DOI: 10.1109/ACCESS.2021.3140175

Patricio, L. D., & Ferreira, J. J. (2023). 'Aligning entrepreneurial universities' HEInnovate dimensions with entrepreneurs' needs: A graduate entrepreneur-centred perspective'. *International Journal of Management Education, 21*(3), 100882. DOI: 10.1016/j.ijme.2023.100882

Patton, M. Q. (2002). Qualitative research and evaluation methods. Thousand Oaks. *Cal.: Sage Publications, 4*(10.4135), 9781452226058.

Payadnya, I. P. A. A., Putri, G. A. M. A., Suwija, I. K., Saelee, S., & Jayantika, I. G. A. N. T. (2025). Cultural integration in AI-enhanced mathematics education: Insights from Southeast Asian educators. *Journal for Multicultural Education, 19*(1), 58–72. DOI: 10.1108/JME-09-2024-0119

Pea, R., & Linn, M. C. (2020). Personal perspectives on the emergence of the learning sciences: 1970s–2005. Frontiers in Education, Razzouk, R., & Shute, V. (2012). What is design thinking and why is it important? *Review of Educational Research, 82*(3), 330–348. DOI: 10.3102/0034654312457429

Peng, H. (2013). Why and when do people hide knowledge? *Journal of Knowledge Management, 17*(3), 398–415. DOI: 10.1108/JKM-12-2012-0380

Perelman, L. (2014). When "the state of the art" is counting words. *Assessing Writing, 7*(1), 1–16. DOI: 10.1016/j.asw.2014.05.001

Peters, G. P. (2008). From production-based to consumption-based national emission inventories. *Ecological Economics, 65*(1), 13–23. DOI: 10.1016/j.ecolecon.2007.10.014

Piaget, J. (1970). Science of education and the psychology of the child. Trans. D. Coltman.

Piaget, J. (1952). *The origins of intelligence in children.* International Universities Press. DOI: 10.1037/11494-000

Pictorial, V. (2026). Purpose-driven AI education prepares students for digital, people-centred future. *Vietnam Pictorial.* https://vietnam.vnanet.vn/english/tin-van/purpose-driven-ai-education-prepares-students-for-digital-people-centred-future-430842.html

Piña-Watson, B., Ojeda, L., Castellon, N. E., & Dornhecker, M. (2013). Familismo, ethnic identity, and bicultural stress as predictors of Mexican American adolescents' positive psychological functioning. *Journal of Latina/o Psychology, 1*(4), 204–217. DOI: 10.1037/lat0000006

Pisica, A. I., Edu, T., Zaharia, R. M., & Zaharia, R. (2023). Implementing Artificial Intelligence in Higher Education: Pros and Cons from the Perspectives of Academics. *Societies (Basel, Switzerland), 13*(5), 118. DOI: 10.3390/soc13050118

Pnevmatikos, D., & Bardos, A. N. (2014). Greek adolescents' intimate relations before their transition to adulthood. *Journal of Adolescence, 37*(8), 1475–1488. DOI: 10.1016/j.adolescence.2014.07.018 PMID: 25154545

Podsakoff, P. M., MacKenzie, S. B., Podsakoff, N. P., & Lee, J. Y. (2003). The mismeasure of man(agement) and its implications for leadership research. *The Leadership Quarterly, 14*(6), 615–656. https://doi.org/https://doi.org/10.1016/j.leaqua.2003.08.002. DOI: 10.1016/j.leaqua.2003.08.002

Polanyi, M. (2009). The tacit dimension. In *Knowledge in organisations* (pp. 135–146). Routledge.

Popenici, S. A. D., & Kerr, S. (2017). Exploring the impact of artificial intelligence on teaching and learning in higher education. *Research and Practice in Technology Enhanced Learning, 12*(1), 22. Advance online publication. DOI: 10.1186/s41039-017-0062-8 PMID: 30595727

Porayska-Pomsta, K., Holmes, W., & Nemorin, S. (2024). The Ethics of AI in Education. In du Boulay, B., Mitrović, A., & Yacef, K. (Eds.), *Handbook of Artificial Intelligence in Education*. Edward Elgar Publishing.

Porto, M. (2016). Ecological and intercultural citizenship in the primary English as a foreign language (EFL) classroom: An online project in Argentina. *Cambridge Journal of Education, 46*(4), 395–415. DOI: 10.1080/0305764X.2015.1064094

Prinsloo, P., & Slade, S. (2017). An elephant in the learning analytics room: The obligation to act. *Proceedings of the 7th International Learning Analytics & Knowledge Conference*, 46–55. DOI: 10.1145/3027385.3027406

Prinsloo, P., & Slade, S. (2017). Ethics and learning analytics: Charting the (Un) Charted. In Lang, C., Siemens, G., Wise, A. F., & Gaevic, D. (Eds.), *Handbook of learning analytics* (2nd ed., pp. 49–57). Society for Learning Analytics and Research., DOI: 10.18608/hla17.004

Prinsloo, P., Slade, S., & Khalil, M. (Eds.). (2022). *Learning analytics in open and distributed learning: Potential and challenges*. Springer Nature. DOI: 10.1007/978-981-19-0786-9

Punziano, G. (2025). Adaptive epistemology: Embracing generative AI as a paradigm shift in social science. *Societies (Basel, Switzerland), 15*(7), 205. DOI: 10.3390/soc15070205

Quy, V. K., Thanh, B. T., Chehri, A., Linh, D. M., & Tuan, D. A. (2023). AI and Digital Transformation in Higher Education: Vision and Approach of a Specific University in Vietnam. *Sustainability (Basel), 15*(14), 11093. DOI: 10.3390/su151411093

Rahman, M. K., Hossain, M. A., Ismail, N. A., Hossen, M. S., & Sultana, M. (2025). 'Determinants of students' adoption of AI chatbots in higher education: The moderating role of tech readiness'. *Interactive Technology and Smart Education, 22*(3), 448–480. Advance online publication. DOI: 10.1108/ITSE-12-2024-0312

Ramayah, T., Yeap, J. A. L., & Ignatius, J. (2014). Assessing Knowledge Sharing Among Academics: A Validation of the Knowledge Sharing Behavior Scale (KSBS). *Evaluation Review, 38*(2), 160–187. DOI: 10.1177/0193841X14539685 PMID: 25015259

Rane, N., Choudhary, S., & Rane, J. (2024). Contribution of ChatGPT and similar generative Artificial Intelligence for enhanced climate change mitigation strategies. *Available at SSRN* 4681720. http://dx.doi.org/DOI: 10.2139/ssrn.4681720

Rasheed, A., San, O., & Kvamsdal, T. (2020). Digital Twin: Values, Challenges and Enablers From a Modeling Perspective. *IEEE Access : Practical Innovations, Open Solutions, 8*, 21980–22012. DOI: 10.1109/ACCESS.2020.2970143

Rata, E. (2021). The Curriculum Design Coherence Model in the Knowledge-Rich School Project. *Review of Education, 9*(2), 448–495. DOI: 10.1002/rev3.3254

Reagans, R., & McEvily, B. (2003). Network Structure and Knowledge Transfer: The Effects of Cohesion and Range. *Administrative Science Quarterly, 48*(2), 240–267. DOI: 10.2307/3556658

Reed, M. S., & Rudman, H. (2023). Re-thinking research impact: Voice, context and power at the interface of science, policy and practice. *Sustainability Science, 18*(2), 967–981. DOI: 10.1007/s11625-022-01216-w PMID: 36119558

Regona, M., Yigitcanlar, T., Xia, B., & Li, R. Y. M. (2024). Artificial intelligence and the environment: A review of the environmental implications of AI. *Sustainable Cities and Society, 101*, 104989. DOI: 10.1016/j.scs.2023.104989

Richardson, J. C., Maeda, Y., Lv, J., & Caskurlu, S. (2017). Social presence in relation to students' satisfaction and learning in the online environment: A meta-analysis. *Computers in Human Behavior, 71*, 402–417. https://doi.org/https://doi.org/10.1016/j.chb.2017.02.001. DOI: 10.1016/j.chb.2017.02.001

Riege, A. (2005). Three-dozen knowledge-sharing barriers managers must consider. *Journal of Knowledge Management, 9*(3), 18–35. DOI: 10.1108/13673270510602746

Roll, I., & Wylie, R. (2016). Evolution and revolution in artificial intelligence in education. *International Journal of Artificial Intelligence in Education, 26*(2), 582–599. DOI: 10.1007/s40593-016-0110-3

Ross, J., & Collier, A. (2016). Complexity, mess, and not-yetness teaching online with emerging technologies. In Veletsianos, G. (Ed.), *Emergence and innovation in digital learning: Foundations and applications* (Vol. 80, pp. 50–70). ACUP.

Rousseau, D. M., Sitkin, S. B., Burt, R. S., & Camerer, C. (1998). Not So Different After All: A Cross-Discipline View Of Trust. *Academy of Management Review, 23*(3), 393–404. DOI: 10.5465/amr.1998.926617

Rozputnia, B., Shevchenko, L., Umanets, V., Sabadosh, Y., Kushnir, A., & Voitsekhivska, N. (2025, September 17–19). 2025). Future Trends of AI in Higher Education: Google Workspace and Gemini. 2025 15th International Conference on Advanced Computer Information Technologies (ACIT), Schraw, G., & Dennison, R. S. (1994). Assessing Metacognitive Awareness. *Contemporary Educational Psychology, 19*(4), 460–475. DOI: 10.1006/ceps.1994.1033

Russell, S., & Norvig, P. (2020). *Artificial Intelligence: A Modern Approach* (4th ed.). Pearson.

Ryan, R. M., & Deci, E. L. (2020). Intrinsic and extrinsic motivation from a self-determination theory perspective: Definitions, theory, practices, and future directions. *Contemporary Educational Psychology, 61*, 101860. DOI: 10.1016/j.cedpsych.2020.101860

Salas Pilco, S., Xiao, X., & Hu, B. (2022). AI in education: Ethical challenges and intercultural perspectives. *Journal of Learning Analytics, 9*(1), 45–67.

Salehi, H., & Burgueño, R. (2018). Emerging artificial intelligence methods in structural engineering. *Engineering Structures, 171*, 170–189. DOI: 10.1016/j.engstruct.2018.05.084

Sârb, C. (2024) *Digital education evolution: investigating Finland's past and future directions.* Available at: https://urn.fi/URN:NBN:fi:amk-2024111628412

Sarıhan, H. İ. (1998). *Rekabette başarının yolu: Teknoloji yönetimi* [The Key to Success in Competition: Technology Management]. Desnet Yayınları.

Schäfer, M. T., van Es, K., & Lauriault, T. P. (Eds.). (2024). *Collaborative Research in the Datafied Society.* Amsterdam University Press., DOI: 10.1515/9789048555925

Schiff, D. (2022). Education for AI, not AI for education: The role of education and ethics in national AI policy strategies. *International Journal of Artificial Intelligence in Education, 32*(3), 527–563. DOI: 10.1007/s40593-021-00270-2

Schön, D. A. (1987). *Educating the reflective practitioner: Toward a new design for teaching and learning in the professions.* Jossey-Bass.

Secretariat, A. S. E. A. N. (2022). *Digital policy action areas for a connected ASEAN: ASEAN best practice benchmarking and an action plan for regional harmonization.* ITU Publications Asia-Pacific Region. https://asean.org/wp-content/uploads/2024/03/Digital-Policy-Action-Areas-for-a-Connected-ASEAN.pdf

Secretariat, A. S. E. A. N. (2021). *AADMER work programme 2021-2025.* ASEAN Secretariat., https://asean.org/wp-content/uploads/2021/08/AADMER-Work-Programme-2021-2025.pdf

Seibert, S. E., Kraimer, M. L., & Liden, R. C. (2001). A Social Capital Theory of Career Success. *Academy of Management Journal, 44*(2), 219–237. DOI: 10.2307/3069452

Selbst, A. D., & Barocas, S. (2018). The intuitive appeal of explainable machines. *Fordham Law Review, 87*, •••. https://ir.lawnet.fordham.edu/flr

Seldon, A., & Abidoye, O. (2018). *The fourth education revolution: Will artificial intelligence liberate or infantilise humanity.* University of Buckingham Press.

Seligman, M. (2018). PERMA and the building blocks of well-being. *The Journal of Positive Psychology, 13*(4), 333–335. DOI: 10.1080/17439760.2018.1437466

Seligman, M. E. P. (2011). *Flourish.* Free Press., DOI: 10.1007/978-94-017-9088-8

Selwyn, N. (2019). *Should robots replace teachers? AI and the future of education.* Polity Press.

Selwyn, N. (2019). *Should robots replace teachers?: AI and the future of education.* John Wiley & Sons.

Selwyn, N. (2019). What's the problem with learning analytics? *Journal of Learning Analytics, 6*(3), 11–19. DOI: 10.18608/jla.2019.63.3

Selwyn, N. (2020). Re-imagining 'learning analytics'… a case for starting again? *The Internet and Higher Education, 46*, 100745. DOI: 10.1016/j.iheduc.2020.100745

Selwyn, N. (2021). *Education and technology: Key issues and debates.* Bloomsbury Publishing.

Selwyn, N. (2022). The future of AI and education: Some cautionary notes. *European Journal of Education, 57*(4), 620–631. DOI: 10.1111/ejed.12532

Serenko, A., & Bontis, N. (2016). Understanding counterproductive knowledge behavior: Antecedents and consequences of intra-organizational knowledge hiding. *Journal of Knowledge Management, 20*(6), 1199–1224. DOI: 10.1108/JKM-05-2016-0203

Sethi, P., & Sarangi, S. R. (2017). Internet of Things: Architectures, Protocols, and Applications. *Journal of Electrical and Computer Engineering, 2017*, 1–25. DOI: 10.1155/2017/9324035

Seufert, S., Guggemos, J., & Sailer, M. (2021). Technology-related knowledge, skills, and attitudes of pre- and in-service teachers: The current situation and emerging trends. *Computers in Human Behavior, 115*, 106552. Advance online publication. DOI: 10.1016/j.chb.2020.106552 PMID: 32921901

Shahzadi, A., Ishaq, K., Nawaz, N. A., Rosdi, F., & Khan, F. A. (2025). Unveiling personalized and gamification-based cybersecurity risks within financial institutions. *PeerJ. Computer Science, 11*, e2598. DOI: 10.7717/peerj-cs.2598 PMID: 40062254

Shaikh, S. A., Lämsä, A.-M., & Heikkinen, S. (2023). Collaborative Leadership in the Institution of Higher Education: A Sociocultural Context of Pakistan. *South Asian Journal of Business and Management Cases, 12*(1), 65–80. DOI: 10.1177/22779779231154646

Shiddiqi, A. M., Alzamzami, M. N., Adillion, I. G., Budiman, M. I. A., Supriyanto, R., & Machmud, M. (2025). Findme-scholar: A contextual researcher recommender system for enhancing research collaboration using adaptive topic interest area modelling. *MethodsX, 15*, 103583. https://doi.org/https://doi.org/10.1016/j.mex.2025.103583. DOI: 10.1016/j.mex.2025.103583 PMID: 40896715

Shin, D. (2021). The effects of explainability and causability on perception, trust, and acceptance: Implications for explainable AI. *International Journal of Human-Computer Studies, 146*, 102551. https://doi.org/https://doi.org/10.1016/j.ijhcs.2020.102551. DOI: 10.1016/j.ijhcs.2020.102551

Shin, M., Abdelnour, S., & Tondeur, J. (2025). Applying artificial intelligence in teacher education: Preservice teachers' attitudes and reflections when using ChatGPT for teaching and learning. *European Journal of Teacher Education, 48*(5), 934–963. Advance online publication. DOI: 10.1080/02619768.2025.2540791

Shoaib, M., Fitzpatrick, D., & Pitt, I. (2023). Assistive technology-based solutions in learning mathematics for visually-impaired people: Exploring issues, challenges and opportunities. *Multimedia Tools and Applications, 82*(29), 46153–46184. DOI: 10.1007/s11042-023-17409-z PMID: 38037570

Siatitsa, D., & Dagkouli-Kyriakoglou, M. (2024). Youth housing trajectories: Gender and intergenerational solidarity in Greece. In Wyn, J., Cahill, H., & Cuervo, H. (Eds.), *Handbook of Children and Youth Studies* (pp. 1059–1071). Springer Nature Singapore., DOI: 10.1007/978-981-99-8606-4_106

Siemens, G. (2005). Connectivism: A learning theory for the digital age. *International Journal of Instructional Technology & Distance Learning*, *2*(1), 3–10. http://www.itdl.org/Journal/Jan_05/Jan_05.pdf

Sijbom, R. B. L., Emanuel, E. S., Koen, J., Baas, M., & De Schutter, L. (2025). Daily knowledge sharing at work: The role of daily knowledge sharing expectations, learning goal orientation and task interdependence. *European Journal of Work and Organizational Psychology*, *34*(2), 298–314. DOI: 10.1080/1359432X.2025.2458343 PMID: 40144200

Simon, P. D., Zhong, Y., Cruz, I. C. D., & Fryer, L. K. (2025). Scoping Review of Research on Augmented Reality in Environmental Education. *Journal of Science Education and Technology*, *34*(4), 919–935. Advance online publication. DOI: 10.1007/s10956-025-10218-z

Slade, S., & Prinsloo, P. (2013). Learning analytics: Ethical issues and dilemmas. *The American Behavioral Scientist*, *57*(10), 1510–1529. DOI: 10.1177/0002764213479366

Slaughter, S., & Leslie, L. L. (1997). *Academic capitalism: Politics, policies, and the entrepreneurial university*. Johns Hopkins University Press.

Spelda, P., & Stritecky, V. (2020). The future of human–artificial intelligence nexus and its environmental costs. *Futures*, *117*, 102531. DOI: 10.1016/j.futures.2020.102531

Srivastava, A., Bartol, K. M., & Locke, E. A. (2006). Empowering Leadership in Management Teams: Effects on Knowledge Sharing, Efficacy, And Performance. *Academy of Management Journal*, *49*(6), 1239–1251. DOI: 10.5465/amj.2006.23478718

Sterling, S. (2011). *Transformative learning and sustainability: Sketching the conceptual ground*. Learning and Teaching in Higher Education.

Stilgoe, J., Owen, R., & Macnaghten, P. (2013). Developing a framework for responsible innovation. *Research Policy*, *42*(9), 1568–1580. Advance online publication. DOI: 10.1016/j.respol.2013.05.008

Stommel, J. (2014). *Critical digital pedagogy: A definition*. Hybrid Pedagogy.

Stommel, J., Friend, C., & Morris, S. M. (2020). *Critical digital pedagogy: A collection*. Hybrid Pedagogy.

Sure, T. A. R., Saigurudatta, P. V., Kapoor, S., Kandula, S. T. R., Choudhury, A., & Devendran, P. D. (2025, July 3–5). 2025). The Role of Natural Language Processing in Developing Intelligent Knowledge Repositories. 2025 IEEE International Conference on Industry 4.0, Artificial Intelligence, and Communications Technology (IAICT), Sweller, J. (1988). Cognitive load during problem solving: Effects on learning. *Cognitive Science, 12*(2), 257–285. https://doi.org/https://doi.org/10.1016/0364-0213(88)90023-7

Suryanarayana, K. S., Kandi, V. P., Pavani, G., Rao, A. S., Rout, S., & Krishna, T. S. R. (2024). Artificial intelligence enhanced digital learning for the sustainability of education management system. *The Journal of High Technology Management Research, 35*(2), 100495. DOI: 10.1016/j.hitech.2024.100495

Swauger, S. (2020). Software that monitors students. Hybrid Pedagogy. https://hybridpedagogy.org/software-that-monitors-students/

Sweller, J., van Merriënboer, J. J. G., & Paas, F. (2019). Cognitive Architecture and Instructional Design: 20 Years Later. *Educational Psychology Review, 31*(2), 261–292. DOI: 10.1007/s10648-019-09465-5

Tan, C. N.-L., & Ramayah, T. (2014). The role of motivators in improving knowledge-sharing among academics. *Information Research, 19*(1), n1.

Tapalova, O., & Zhiyenbayeva, N. (2022). Artificial intelligence in education: AIEd for personalised learning pathways. *Electronic Journal of e-Learning, 20*(5), 639–653. DOI: 10.34190/ejel.20.5.2597

Tashakkori, A., & Teddlie, C. (2021). *Sage handbook of mixed methods in social & behavioral research.* SAGE publications.

Taşkıran, A. (2017). Dijital çağda yükseköğretim [Higher education in the digital age]. *Açıköğretim Uygulamaları ve Araştırmaları Dergisi, 3*(1), 96–109.

Temur, S. (2025). Eğitimde yapay zekâ kullanımı: Etik sorunlar ve çözümler [Ethical Issues and Solutions]. *Mehmet Akif Ersoy Üniversitesi Eğitim Fakültesi Dergisi*, (74), 568–595. DOI: 10.21764/maeuefd.1516576

Tetzlaff, L., Schmiedek, F., & Brod, G. (2021). Developing personalized education: A dynamic framework. *Educational Psychology Review, 33*(3), 863–882. DOI: 10.1007/s10648-020-09570-w

Thurzo, A., Strunga, M., Urban, R., Surovková, J., & Afrashtehfar, K. I. (2023). Impact of artificial intelligence on dental education: A review and guide for curriculum update. *Education Sciences, 13*(2), 150. Advance online publication. DOI: 10.3390/educsci13020150

Tilak, J. B., Tilak, J. B., & Ghosh. (2018). *Education and development in India*. Springer. DOI: 10.1007/978-981-13-0250-3

Timotheou, S., Miliou, O., Dimitriadis, Y., Sobrino, S. V., Giannoutsou, N., Cachia, R., Monés, A. M., & Ioannou, A. (2023). Impacts of digital technologies on education and factors influencing schools' digital capacity and transformation: A literature review. *Education and Information Technologies*, *28*(6), 6695–6726. DOI: 10.1007/s10639-022-11431-8 PMID: 36465416

Titi Amayah, A. (2013). Determinants of knowledge sharing in a public sector organization. *Journal of Knowledge Management*, *17*(3), 454–471. DOI: 10.1108/JKM-11-2012-0369

Tomozeiu, D., & Kumpulainen, M. (2016). Operationalising intercultural competence for translation pedagogy. *The Interpreter and Translator Trainer*, *10*(3), 268–284. DOI: 10.1080/1750399X.2016.1236558

Torun, B., & Karamustafaoğlu, O. (2025). Fen öğretiminde ChatGPT kullanımı hakkında öğrenci görüşleri [Student opinions on the use of ChatGPT in science education]. *Cumhuriyet International Journal of Education*, *14*(1), 240–249. DOI: 10.30703/cije.1609145

Tran, L. T., & Marginson, S. (2018). Internationalisation of Vietnamese Higher Education: An Overview. In Tran, L. T., & Marginson, S. (Eds.), *Internationalisation in Vietnamese Higher Education* (pp. 1–16). Springer International Publishing., DOI: 10.1007/978-3-319-78492-2_1

Tran, T., Trinh, T.-P.-T., Le, C.-M., Hoang, L.-K., & Pham, H.-H. (2020). Research as a Base for Sustainable Development of Universities: Using the Delphi Method to Explore Factors Affecting International Publishing among Vietnamese Academic Staff. *Sustainability (Basel)*, *12*(8), 3449. DOI: 10.3390/su12083449

Treve, M. (2021). What COVID-19 has introduced into education: Challenges Facing Higher Education Institutions (HEIs). *Higher Education Pedagogies*, *6*(1), 212–227. DOI: 10.1080/23752696.2021.1951616

Triandis, H. C., Brislin, R., & Hui, C. H. (1988). Cross-cultural training across the individualism-collectivism divide. *International Journal of Intercultural Relations*, *12*(3), 269–289. DOI: 10.1016/0147-1767(88)90019-3

Trilling, B., & Fadel, C. (2009). *21st century skills: Learning for life in our times*. John Wiley & Sons.

Tsai, W., & Ghoshal, S. (1998). Social Capital and Value Creation: The Role of Intrafirm Networks. *Academy of Management Journal, 41*(4), 464–476. DOI: 10.2307/257085

Tsai, Y. S., Perrotta, C., & Gašević, D. (2020). Empowering learners with personalised learning approaches? Agency, equity and transparency in the context of learning analytics. *Assessment & Evaluation in Higher Education, 45*(4), 554–567. DOI: 10.1080/02602938.2019.1676396

Tsai, Y. S., Whitelock-Wainwright, A., & Gašević, D. (2021). More than figures on your laptop:(Dis) trustful implementation of learning analytics. *Journal of Learning Analytics, 8*(3), 81–100. DOI: 10.18608/jla.2021.7379

Tuğaç, Ç. (2023). Birleşmiş milletler sürdürülebilir kalkınma amaçlarının gerçekleştirilmesinde yapay zekâ uygulamalarının rolü [The role of artificial intelligence applications in achieving the United Nations sustainable development goals]. *Sayıştay Dergisi, 34*(128), 73–99. DOI: 10.52836/sayistay.1245051

Tuomi, I. (2018). *The impact of artificial intelligence on learning, teaching, and education: Policies for the future*. Publications Office of the European Union., DOI: 10.2760/12297

Türker, A., & Dündar, E. (2020). COVID-19 pandemi sürecinde eğitim bilişim aği (eba) üzerinden yürütülen uzaktan eğitimlerle ilgili lise öğretmenlerinin görüşleri [High school teachers' views on distance learning conducted via the Education Information Network (EBA) during the COVID-19 pandemic]. *Milli Eğitim Dergisi, 49*(1), 323–342.

Tursunbayeva, A. (2024). Artificial intelligence adoption and change management. In *Augmenting human resource management with artificial intelligence: towards an inclusive, sustainable, and responsible future* (pp. 113–126). Springer Nature Switzerland., DOI: 10.1007/978-3-031-75266-7_9

UNDP. (2023) *Human Development Report 2023/24: Breaking the Gridlock*. Available at: https://hdr.undp.org

UNESCO Science Report 2021. (2021). United Nations. DOI: 10.18356/9789210058575

UNESCO. (2015). Not just hot air: putting climate change education into practice. https://unesdoc.unesco.org/ark:/48223/pf0000233083

UNESCO. (2015). *Quality physical education (QPE): Guidelines for policy-makers*. UNESCO. https://unesdoc.unesco.org/images/0023/002311/231101E.pdf

UNESCO. (2017). *Education for sustainable development goals: Learning objectives*. UNESCO.

UNESCO. (2021). *AI in Education: Guidance for Policy-Makers*. UNESCO Publishing.

UNESCO. (2021). Recommendation on the ethics of artificial intelligence. United Nations Educational, Scientific and Cultural Organization. SHS/BIO/REC-AIETHICS/2021

UNESCO. (2021a). *AI and education: Guidance for policymakers*. United Nations Educational, Scientific and Cultural Organization., DOI: 10.54675/PCSP7350

UNESCO. (2021b). *Futures of education: Learning to become*. Paris: UNESCO. https://unesdoc.unesco.org/ark:/48223/pf0000370801

UNESCO. (2021c). *Recommendation on the ethics of artificial intelligence*. Paris: UNESCO. https://unesdoc.unesco.org/ark:/48223/pf0000381137

UNESCO. (2022) *Reimagining Our Futures Together*. Available at: https://www.unesco.org/en/futures-education

UNESCO. (2022). *Recommendation on the ethics of artificial intelligence*. UNESCO Paris. https://unesdoc.unesco.org/ark:/48223/pf0000381137

UNESCO. (2023) *Artificial intelligence in education*. Paris: United Nations Educational, Scientific and Cultural Organization. Available at: https://www.unesco.org/en/digital-education/artificial-intelligence

UNESCO. (2024). *AI competency framework for teachers*. United Nations Educational, Scientific and Cultural Organization., DOI: 10.54675/ZJTE2084

UNESCO. (2025). *Viet Nam: Artificial intelligence readiness assessment report*. UNESCO Paris. https://articles.unesco.org/sites/default/files/medias/fichiers/2025/10/Viet%20Nam%20Artificial%20Intelligence%20Readiness%20Assessment%20Report.pdf

UNESCO. (2025a). *AI in education: Guidance for policy-makers*. UNESCO Publishing.

UNESCO. (2025b). *Ethics of AI in education: Policy recommendations and global perspectives*. UNESCO Publishing.

United Nations Educational, Scientific and Cultural Organization [UNESCO]. (2021). AI and Education: Guidance for Policy-Makers. (UNESCO Digital Library, https://unesdoc.unesco.org/ark:/48223/pf0000376709)

United Nations. (2006). Indigenous peoples, indigenous voices: Factsheet. *United Nations Permanent Forum on Indigenous Issues*. https://www.un.org/esa/socdev/unpfii/documents/5session_factsheet1.pdf

Urbani, J. M., Roshandel, S., Michaels, R., & Truesdell, E. (2017). Developing and modeling 21st-century skills with preservice teachers. *Teacher Education Quarterly*, *44*(4), 27–50.

Valtonen, T., Leppänen, U., Hyypiä, M., Kokko, A., Manninen, J., Vartiainen, H., Sointu, E., & Hirsto, L. (2021). Learning analytics in higher education: A systematic literature review. *Computers and Education: Artificial Intelligence*, *2*, 100033. Advance online publication. DOI: 10.1016/j.caeai.2021.100033

van Houten, M. M. (2023). Professional tacit knowledge sharing in practice. Agency, boundaries, and commitment. *Journal of Workplace Learning*, *35*(9), 197–217. DOI: 10.1108/JWL-02-2023-0025

Van Quyet, P., & Hai, P. T. T. (2023). Autonomy Governance Transformation in the Higher Education Institutions Towards the Typical Models in Vietnam. *Journal of Higher Education Theory and Practice*, *23*(20), 1–14.

VanLehn, K. (2011). The relative effectiveness of human tutoring, intelligent tutoring systems, and other tutoring systems. *Educational Psychologist*, *46*(4), 197–221. DOI: 10.1080/00461520.2011.611369

Vassiliou, V. G., & Vassiliou, G. (1973). The implicative meaning of the Greek concept of philotimo. *Journal of Cross-Cultural Psychology*, *4*(3), 326–341. DOI: 10.1177/002202217300400305

Veletsianos, G., & Houlden, S. (2020). Radical flexibility and relationality as responses to education in times of crisis. *Postdigital Science and Education*, *2*(3), 849–862. DOI: 10.1007/s42438-020-00196-3 PMID: 40477172

Verano-Tacoronte, D., Bolívar-Cruz, A., & Sosa-Cabrera, S. (2025). Are university teachers ready for generative artificial intelligence? Unpacking faculty anxiety in the ChatGPT era. *Education and Information Technologies*, *30*(14), 1–28. DOI: 10.1007/s10639-025-13585-7

Viberg, O., Khalil, M., & Baars, M. (2020, March). Self-regulated learning and learning analytics in online learning environments: A review of empirical research. In *Proceedings of the tenth international conference on learning analytics & knowledge* (pp. 524-533). DOI: 10.1145/3375462.3375483

Vinayakumar, R., Alazab, M., Soman, K. P., Poornachandran, P., Al-Nemrat, A., & Venkatraman, S. (2019). Deep Learning Approach for Intelligent Intrusion Detection System. *IEEE Access : Practical Innovations, Open Solutions*, *7*, 41525–41550. DOI: 10.1109/ACCESS.2019.2895334

Voskoglou, M. G., & Buckley, S. (2012). Problem solving and computational thinking in a learning environment. *Egyptian Computer Science Journal*, *36*(4), 28–46.

Vuong, T.-T., Ho, M.-T., Nguyen, M.-H., Nguyen, T.-H. T., Nguyen, T.-D., Nguyen, T.-L., Luong, A.-P., & Vuong, Q.-H. (2020). Adopting open access in the social sciences and humanities: Evidence from a developing nation. *Heliyon*, *6*(7), e04522. Advance online publication. DOI: 10.1016/j.heliyon.2020.e04522 PMID: 32743103

Vygotsky, L. S. (1978). *Mind in society: The development of higher psychological processes* (Cole, M., Ed.). Harvard University Press.

Wang, H., Tlili, A., Huang, R., Cai, Z., Li, M., Cheng, Z., Yang, D., Li, M., Zhu, X., & Fei, C. (2023). Examining the applications of intelligent tutoring systems in real educational contexts: A systematic literature review from the social experiment perspective. *Education and Information Technologies*, *28*(7), 9113–9148. DOI: 10.1007/s10639-022-11555-x PMID: 36643383

Wang, L., Ma, C., Feng, X., Zhang, Z., Yang, H., Zhang, J., Chen, Z., Tang, J., Chen, X., Lin, Y., Zhao, W. X., Wei, Z., & Wen, J. (2024). A survey on large language model based autonomous agents. *Frontiers of Computer Science*, *18*(6), 186345. DOI: 10.1007/s11704-024-40231-1

Wang, S., & Noe, R. A. (2010). Knowledge sharing: A review and directions for future research. *Human Resource Management Review*, *20*(2), 115–131. https://doi.org/https://doi.org/10.1016/j.hrmr.2009.10.001. DOI: 10.1016/j.hrmr.2009.10.001

Wasko, M. M., & Faraj, S. (2005). Why Should I Share? Examining Social Capital and Knowledge Contribution in Electronic Networks of Practice. *Management Information Systems Quarterly*, *29*(1), 35–57. DOI: 10.2307/25148667

Webster, J. (2024). Updating digital citizenship education for a postdigital society. *New Zealand Journal of Educational Studies*, *59*(1), 109–124. DOI: 10.1007/s40841-023-00305-3

Wenger, E., McDermott, R. A., & Snyder, W. (2002). *Cultivating communities of practice: A guide to managing knowledge*. Harvard business press.

Wenger, E. (1999). *Communities of practice: Learning, meaning, and identity*. Cambridge university press.

Wen, J., & Ma, R. (2021). Antecedents of knowledge hiding and their impact on organizational performance. *Frontiers in Psychology, 12*, 796976. DOI: 10.3389/fpsyg.2021.796976 PMID: 34987455

West, D., Tasir, Z., Luzeckyj, A., Na, K. S., Toohey, D., Abdullah, Z., & Price, R. (2018). Learning analytics experience among academics in Australia and Malaysia: A comparison. *Australasian Journal of Educational Technology, 34*(3). Advance online publication. DOI: 10.14742/ajet.3836

Williamson, B., Macgilchrist, F., & Potter, J. (2023). Re-examining AI, automation and datafication in education. *48*(1), 1–5. DOI: 10.1080/17439884.2023.2167830

Williamson, B. (2017). Big data in education: The digital future of learning, policy and practice. *Sage (Atlanta, Ga.)*. Advance online publication. DOI: 10.4135/9781529714920

Williamson, B., Bayne, S., & Shay, S. (2023). The datafication of writing assessment. *Assessment & Evaluation in Higher Education*. Advance online publication. DOI: 10.1080/13562517.2020.1748811

Williamson, B., & Eynon, R. (2020). Historical threads, missing links and future directions: Historiography and the digital turn. *Learning, Media and Technology*. Advance online publication. DOI: 10.1080/17439884.2020.1798995

Williamson, B., Eynon, R., & Potter, J. (2020). Pandemic politics and examination algorithms. *Learning, Media and Technology*. Advance online publication. DOI: 10.1080/17439884.2020.1761641

Williamson, B., & Hogan, A. (2020). *Commercialisation and AI governance: The emerging digital platforms for learning*. Globalisation, Societies and Education.

Wise, A. F., & Shaffer, D. W. (2015). Why theory matters. *Journal of Learning Analytics, 2*(2), 5–9. DOI: 10.18608/jla.2015.22.2

World Bank. (2023) *Digital transformation in education: Evidence and policy implications*. Washington, DC: World Bank. Available at: https://documents1.worldbank.org (accessed: 3 January 2026).

Wu, C. H., Chien, Y. C., Chou, M. T., & Huang, Y. M. (2025). Integrating computational thinking, game design, and design thinking: A scoping review on trends, applications, and implications for education. *Humanities & Social Sciences Communications, 12*(1), 1–12. DOI: 10.1057/s41599-025-04502-x

Xiaoyu, W., Zainuddin, Z., Leng, C. H., Wenting, D., & Li, X. (2025). Evaluating the efficacy of ChatGPT in environmental education: findings from heuristic and usability assessments. *On the Horizon: The International Journal of Learning Futures*, (ahead-of-print).

Xie, Y., Song, K., & Tondeur, J. (2024). In search of artificial intelligence (AI) literacy in teacher education: A scoping review. *Computers and Education Open*, *5*, 100169. DOI: 10.1016/j.caeo.2024.100169

Yang, J., Jin, H., Tang, R., Han, X., Feng, Q., Jiang, H., Zhong, S., Yin, B., & Hu, X. (2024). Harnessing the Power of LLMs in Practice: A Survey on ChatGPT and Beyond. *ACM Transactions on Knowledge Discovery from Data*, *18*(6), 1–32. DOI: 10.1145/3649506

Yannier, N., Hudson, S. E., Chang, H., & Koedinger, K. R. (2024). AI Adaptivity in a Mixed-Reality System Improves Learning. *International Journal of Artificial Intelligence in Education*, *34*(4), 1541–1558. DOI: 10.1007/s40593-023-00388-5

Yan, Y., & Liu, H. (2025). Ethical framework for AI education based on large language models. *Education and Information Technologies*, *30*(8), 10891–10909. DOI: 10.1007/s10639-024-13241-6

Yeşilyurt, E. (2020). Öğretmenin pusulası: Genel öğretim ilkeleri [The teacher's guide: General principles of teaching]. *EKEV Akademi Dergisi*, (83), 263–288. DOI: 10.17753/Ekev1525

Yigitcanlar, T., Desouza, K. C., Butler, L., & Roozkhosh, F. (2021). Contributions and risks of artificial intelligence in building smarter cities: Insights from a systematic review. *Sustainability*, *13*(4), 2073. DOI: 10.3390/su13042073

Young, T., Hazarika, D., Poria, S., & Cambria, E. (2018). Recent Trends in Deep Learning Based Natural Language Processing [Review Article]. *IEEE Computational Intelligence Magazine*, *13*(3), 55–75. DOI: 10.1109/MCI.2018.2840738

Ypsilanti, A. (2025). *Critical incident representations in films: An intercultural framework* [Doctoral dissertation, Ionian University]. National Archive of PhD Theses (EADD). DOI: 10.12681/eadd/59879

Ypsilanti, A., & Karras, I. (2024). Introducing Pixar shorts in the Greek EFL classroom as a means to enhancing empathy among high school students. In *Proceedings of the IAFOR International Conference on Arts & Humanities in Hawaii (IICAH2024)*. International Academic Forum (IAFOR). DOI: 10.22492/issn.2432-4604.2024.15

Ypsilanti, A., & Karras, I. (2023). From TENOR to TEIC: The English teacher's final "say-so" in reformulating education policies. *European Journal of Education and Pedagogy*, *4*(6), 41–46. DOI: 10.24018/ejedu.2023.4.6.761

Ypsilanti, A., & Karras, I. (2025). Experiencing film literacy through Magic School AI. In Baba Khouya, Y., & Ismaili Alaoui, A. (Eds.), *Application of AI in the Teaching and Learning of English as a Foreign Language (EFL)* (pp. 275–330). IGI Global Scientific Publishing., DOI: 10.4018/979-8-3373-0969-9.ch008

Yuen, S. C.-Y., Yaoyuneyong, G., & Johnson, E. (2011). Augmented Reality: An Overview and Five Directions for AR in Education. *Journal of Educational Technology Development and Exchange*, *4*(1). Advance online publication. DOI: 10.18785/jetde.0401.10

Yu, H. (2023). Reflection on whether Chat GPT should be banned by academia from the perspective of education and teaching. *Frontiers in Psychology*, *14*, 1181712. Advance online publication. DOI: 10.3389/fpsyg.2023.1181712 PMID: 37325766

Yunkaporta, T. (2020). *Sand talk: How Indigenous thinking can save the world.* HarperCollins.

Zacharewicz, T., Lepori, B., Reale, E., & Jonkers, K. (2019). Performance-based research funding in EU Member States—A comparative assessment. *Science & Public Policy*, *46*(1), 105–115. DOI: 10.1093/scipol/scy041

Zaremohzzabieh, Z., & Mohd Rasdi, R. (2023). Revisiting the determinants of knowledge-sharing behavior in organizations: A meta-analytic structural equation model application. *Global Knowledge, Memory and Communication*, *74*(1-2), 1–22. DOI: 10.1108/GKMC-02-2022-0034

Zawacki-Richter, O., Bai, J. Y., Lee, K., Slagter van Tryon, P. J., & Prinsloo, P. (2024). New advances in artificial intelligence applications in higher education? *International Journal of Educational Technology in Higher Education*, *21*(1), 32. DOI: 10.1186/s41239-024-00464-3

Zawacki-Richter, O., Marín, V. I., Bond, M., & Gouverneur, F. (2019). Systematic review of research on artificial intelligence applications in higher education–where are the educators? *International Journal of Educational Technology in Higher Education*, *16*(1), 1–27. DOI: 10.1186/s41239-019-0171-0

Zawacki-Richter, O., Marín, V., Bond, M., & Gouverneur, F. (2020). Systematic review of research on artificial intelligence applications in higher education. *International Journal of Educational Technology in Higher Education*, *17*(39). Advance online publication. DOI: 10.1186/s41239-020-00218-x

Zhang, Q., Mohammad Ismail, M. I. R., & Zakaria, A. R. B. (2025). Enhancing intercultural competence in technical higher education through AI-driven frameworks. *Scientific Reports*, *15*(1), 1–15. DOI: 10.1038/s41598-025-03303-1 PMID: 40594064

Zhang, X., Chan, F. T., Yan, C., & Bose, I. (2022). Towards risk-aware artificial intelligence and machine learning systems: An overview. *Decision Support Systems*, *159*(4), 1–13. DOI: 10.1016/j.dss.2022.113800

Zhou, T., & Lu, H. (2024). The effect of trust on user adoption of AI-generated content. *The Electronic Library*, *43*(1), 61–76. DOI: 10.1108/EL-08-2024-0244

Zhou, X., Chen, L., & Chen, C. H. (2023). Collaborative learning by teaching: An AI-embedded online learning system to support teacher–student co-creation. *Australasian Journal of Educational Technology*, *39*(4), 57–75. DOI: 10.14742/ajet.8327

Zidny, R., Sjöström, J., & Eilks, I. (2020). A Multi-Perspective Reflection on How Indigenous Knowledge and Related Ideas Can Improve Science Education for Sustainability. *Science & Education*, *29*(1), 145–185. DOI: 10.1007/s11191-019-00100-x

Zuboff, S. (2019). *The age of surveillance capitalism*. PublicAffairs., DOI: 10.2307/j.ctvbnm3gz

Zuboff, S. (2023). The age of surveillance capitalism. In *Social theory re-wired* (pp. 203–213). Routledge. DOI: 10.4324/9781003320609-27

About the Contributors

Thi-Phuong Nguyen (Nguyen, T. P.) is a research fellow of Department of Science, Technology, and International Projects, Ho Chi Minh City University of Economics and Finance, Ho Chi Minh City, Vietnam. Dr Nguyen received her PhD (Management) from RMIT University. Her research interests span a wide array of fields, including leadership, corporate governance, strategic management, sustainability, supply chain management, and marketing, etc. With over a decade of experience in the higher education sector, Dr. Nguyen has cultivated a diverse skill set encompassing international program franchise, academic research, fundraising for research projects, and teaching at both undergraduate and postgraduate levels in global institutions such as RMIT University, Birmingham City University, Leipzig University, Liverpool John Moores University, Western Sydney University, and others. She has held various management roles in higher education projects within both for-profit and non-profit sectors.

Jiaming Zhang (Zhang, J.) is a PhD candidate researcher in Cross-Cultural Management at Vrije Universiteit Amsterdam, The Netherlands. He has over 15 years of professional experience working and managing in multicultural environments across China, Israel, Cambodia, and Vietnam. His expertise lies in developing and managing supply chains, expanding international business operations, and fostering cross-cultural collaboration in global contexts. Mr. Zhang has held senior leadership positions, including Director of Business Development at Innolux Group, where he played a pivotal role in transforming a startup into a leading enterprise in Vietnam's footwear manufacturing industry. His research and practice emphasize the intersections of cross-cultural management, business development, and sustainable leadership in emerging markets. His academic and professional contributions focus on helping organizations navigate cultural complexity while pursuing growth, innovation, and sustainability. Through his research and industry engagement, Jiaming Zhang brings valuable insights into the dynamic relationship between global business practices, intercultural communication, and organizational leadership in transnational contexts.

Anna Loseva (Loseva, A.) holds an MA in Teaching English as a Foreign Language from Moscow City Pedagogical University, Russia, and a Master of Education in Leadership and Management from Western Sydney University, Australia. She is currently a Lecturer and Course Coordinator for Business Academic Skills for a range of programs delivered at International Education Institute of UEH, where she specializes in academic language skills, academic writing, research, and business communication. Since 2010, Ms. Loseva has taught English and academic skills to university students in Russia, Japan, and Vietnam. She has presented her work at numerous international conferences in Europe and Asia, contributed as an editor for the iTDi blog, and organized professional development workshops for teachers globally. Her research interests focus on higher education, hybrid learning environments, teacher professional development, and the design of innovative curricula in cross-cultural contexts. With extensive international teaching experience and a strong background in academic skills development, Anna Loseva brings unique expertise in linking pedagogy, research, and intercultural education to the discourse on global higher education and sustainable teaching practices.

* * *

Lalithabala Boopathi is a distinguished Tamil scholar and academic with over 12 years of experience in teaching and research, encompassing Tamil literature, language, grammar, and education. She currently serves as an Assistant Professor in the Department of Education at SASTRA University, Thanjavur, and holds a PhD in Tamil Literature from Tamil University. Her educational journey includes multiple postgraduate qualifications, Education, UGC-NET, and specialised training in manuscriptology and digital competencies. Dr. Lalitha Bala has presented and published extensively at national and international forums, earning numerous awards for her contributions to Tamil research, literary criticism, pedagogy, and poetry. Known for her student-centric teaching approach, leadership, and commitment to lifelong learning, her work bridges classical Tamil traditions with contemporary educational perspectives, particularly in areas such as food culture, medicine, ethics, and society in Tamil literature.

Sovannaroth Chheang earned her bachelor's degree in English from Build Bright University, Phnom Penh, in 2016, where she built a solid foundation in language studies, communication, and pedagogy. She began her teaching career in 2013 as a Tutor at the Kindergarten Association, conducting both part-time and full-time English programs. Since 2018, she has served as a Teacher of English and General Assistant at Sovanna Elton Foreign Language School. Through these roles, she has developed broad expertise in classroom management, language instruction, curriculum design, and student engagement, supporting the school's mission of advancing foreign language learning. Ms. Chheang's academic interests center on pursuing a master's degree in English education or related fields within the humanities and social sciences. Passionate about integrating global research methodologies into her practice, she aims to enhance pedagogy, foster classroom innovation, and promote effective, research-informed teaching. Her commitment lies in bridging academic research with real-world practice to advance English education in Cambodia and beyond.

Berna Çolak completed an associate degree in Opticianry at the same university in 2018. I started my teaching career in 2019 at Malazgirt Secondary School in Istanbul. Since 2023, I have been working as a Science Teacher at Nasrettin Hoca Secondary School. Throughout my career, I have always valued learning, self-improvement, and sharing knowledge. During this time, I took part in various TÜBİTAK projects, hands-on science education programs, and scientific workshops. In addition to teaching, I worked as a table official for the Turkish Basketball Federation. I also continued my academic journey and graduated on July 1, 2025, from Hacettepe University, Institute of Educational Sciences, with a non-thesis Master's degree in Chemistry Education with a focus on Technology and Environmental Education. I am currently continuing my studies in the Philosophy Department at Anadolu University. I have always been open to growth and producing in the fields of science, environment, and education.

Devaki V serves as an Assistant Professor at the Department of Education (SASHE), SASTRA Deemed to be University, Thanjavur. She holds a Master of Science in Physics from Alagappa University, Karaikudi, graduating with the distinction of second rank in the university. Additionally, she completed her Master of Education at Sri Sarada College of Education, Salem, Tamil Nadu. She qualified for the position of Assistant Professor in Physics and Education, having successfully cleared the Tamil Nadu State Eligibility Test and also passed the Central Teacher Eligibility Test. She has completed her doctoral studies in the Department of Education at Bharathidasan University, Tiruchirappalli. Her research interests encompass metacognition, neurocognition, the pedagogy of science, and experiential learning.

Frederic Gautier is a graduate in Management Sciences and a Sciences-Po Paris laureate, Frédéric GAUTIER is a professor of industrial and logistics management.

He is academic director of the Sorbonne Business School and co-director of the Risk Chair.

Muhammad Hasan is a professor of entrepreneurship education at the Department of Economic Education, Faculty of Economics and Business, Universitas Negeri Makassar, Indonesia. His research interests encompass entrepreneurship education, women's entrepreneurship, gendered financial literacy, digital literacy and technology adoption in SMEs, innovation capability, entrepreneurial cognition, and sustainable entrepreneurial performance. His work is theoretically grounded in the Resource-Based View (RBV), Knowledge-Based View (KBV), Social Cognitive Theory (SCT), Job Demands–Resources (JD-R) Model, Transformative Learning Theory (TLT), Technology Acceptance Model (TAM), Diffusion of Innovation (DOI), and inclusive and gender-responsive development perspectives, particularly within emerging economy contexts.

Hok Chheangkhy is a lecturer at the Department of Khmer Literature, University of Heng Samrin Thbongkhmum. With a strong dedication to the study and preservation of Khmer language, literature, and culture, he has contributed to advancing literary education and research in Cambodia. His academic interests include classical and modern Khmer literature, linguistic analysis, and cultural studies. Mr. Chheangkhy is passionate about inspiring students to explore Cambodia's rich literary heritage and promoting the value of Khmer identity through education. In addition to teaching, he actively engages in academic writing and community cultural initiatives, aiming to strengthen the role of literature in contemporary Cambodian society.

Sovanna Huot is a PhD candidate in Political Science at the University of Delhi, New Delhi, India. He is a vice principal at a Government Public High School of Cambodia and is responsible for the school academic and institutional leadership. He is a very proficient academic across many disciplines. He has completed a two-year teacher training program from 2010-2012 and has obtained bachelor's degrees in English and in Educational Administration. He also has two master's degrees in law and in TEFL obtained through a very competitive scholarship, and a Master of Education, specialized in School Leadership, Upper Secondary School Principalship, from the National Institute of Education (NIE), Phnom Penh, 2021. He specializes in educational reform and in the practice-policy nexus of digit pedagogy and in glonacal (global–national–local) education systems. He has formal academic training in political science and education and has published scholarly work in both disciplines, including articles indexed in Scopus (Author ID: 59316244400).

Huy Truong Quang serves as a Senior Lecturer and Research Cluster Lead of Logistics & Supply Chain Management, at RMIT International University, Vietnam. He holds important management positions such as Purchasing Manager cum Warehouse Manager at the Nipro Vietnam Co. Ltd. - a Japanese leading medical device manufacturer. He got a Ph.D. degree in Kyoto University, Japan with research interests including but not limited to digital transformation, sustainability, risk management, quality, and supply chain management. He has published on these topics in high-quality academic journals such as International Journal of Production Research, Business Strategy and Environment, Journal of Cleaner Production, International Journal of Logistics Management, Journal of Manufacturing Technology Management, Business Process Management Journal, Engineering, Construction and Architectural Management, International Journal of Quality & Reliability Management, Operations Management Research, Journal of Enterprise Information Management, etc. He has also conducted some research projects on these topics in (1) Kyoto University (2) University of Minho, Portugal, (3) University of Girona, Spain, (5) Reutlingen University, Germany, (6) Vienna University, Austria and (7) Ho Chi Minh City University of Technology, Vietnam.

Ioannis Karras is a Professor at Ionian University, Greece. Ioannis studied applied linguistics and intercultural communication at various universities in Canada, the United Kingdom, and Greece. He has extensive experience (over 27 years) at all levels (Bachelor's, Master's, PhD). Moreover, he has lectured as a visiting professor/ invited speaker at several universities around the world. He has delivered numerous talks at international conferences and has conducted seminars and workshops with national and international audiences. Ioannis has authored and edited several books, book chapters and articles in peer-reviewed journals and conference proceedings in the areas of his specialization.

Sovanna Loch is a prominent figure at the Cambodian Monastery Rajgir, serving as a deputy in charge. He is also a PhD research scholar and ICCR Fellow in the Dept. of English at Nava Nalanda Mahavihara (Deemed University), an institution under the Ministry of Culture, Govt. of India. His academic background includes a bachelor's degree in Pāli and a master's in English, both obtained from NNM. His research primarily focuses on Cambodian classical and Buddhist English literature.

Kimyut Phin is an educator and emerging scholar. He is currently pursuing a Ph.D. in English at the University of Delhi, India. He holds bachelor's and master's degrees in English (TEFL and TESOL). He serves as the Director of the Institute of Foreign Languages of the University of Heng Samrin Thbongkhmum, Cambodia. He actively engages with academic management, leadership, innovation, institutional development, curriculum development, instructional design, assessment, projects, and research. He has involved in many Erasmus+ projects, such as the REACT, SICA, BALANCE, IND4.0, and UNICATION projects. He has also had teaching experiences in linguistics, applied linguistics, teaching methodology, second language acquisition, grammar for writing, academic writing skills, global studies, core English, and literature studies for years. Further, he has experience in lesson planning, classroom management, assessment and evaluation, and technology for teaching and learning. His research centers on teaching and learning approaches and methods, English language education, education quality, educational reform, digital pedagogy, literary theory and criticism, and learning motivation in Cambodia and beyond.

Chinna Suresh serving as Assistant Professor since July, 2018 in the Department of Education at the School of Arts, Sciences, Humanities, and Education (SASHE), SASTRA Deemed to be University, Thanjavur, Tamil Nadu, India. He earned his Ph.D. in Education from Sri Venkateswara University, Tirupati, Andhra Pradesh, in March,2018, and his M.Sc. in Mathematics from Sri Krishnadevaraya University, Anantapur, Andhra Pradesh, in 2010. In addition, he holds M.Sc (Psychology) from Tamil Nadu Open University, Chennai. His research interests include ICT in Education, Mathematics Pedagogy, Gender Studies, and Teaching Strategies.

Phearun Tep, originally from Cambodia, holds a degree in English from the Department of English at the University of Delhi. With experience teaching English literature, working as a translator, and authoring scholarly works in Cambodia, he is a committed researcher with interests in South Asian literature, Translation Studies, Indian Literary Theory & Criticism, fiction, cultural and post-conflict studies, and identity representation. His research examines how historical trauma, cultural memory, and narrative imagination inform human experience, contributing to literary scholarship and interdisciplinary studies.

Le Anh Duy Tran holds a Ph.D. in Management from Sorbonne Panthéon University in France. His educational background includes a Master of Science (MSc) in Logistics and Supply Chain Management from Manchester Metropolitan University, United Kingdom (UK).

Linh Tran Khanh Do serves as a Research Assistant at RMIT International University, Vietnam. She got a Master degree in University of Nottingham, United Kingdom with specialisation in sustainability, AI applications, and strategic management. With hands-on experience in both academic and industry projects, she focuses on integrating digital tools and data-driven insights to support sustainable business transformation. Linh's research background also includes leveraging advanced technologies to optimize decision-making processes. She is committed to developing forward-thinking, responsible strategies that balance technological advancement with long-term sustainability goals.

Dung Truong Quang is a Lecturer in Logistics and Supply Chain Management at RMIT International University, Vietnam. He got a Ph.D. from the University of Tasmania, Australia, in agricultural supply chains and has published in high-quality journals such as Journal of Business Research and Supply Chain Management: An International Journal. He has conducted research projects on various topics, including supply chain risk management, supply chain innovation, and supply chain collaboration.

Ngan Tuyet Truong is a researcher at University of Economics and Finance, HCMC, Vietnam. Her current research activities include sustainable business practices, service innovation management and service quality management in emerging countries. She has published research in distinguished journals such as Service Business, Journal of Hospitality and Tourism Technology, International Journal of Culture, Tourism and Hospitality Research, and Operations and Supply chain Management: An International Journal.

V Vidya, an articulate qualified English teacher who is able to effectively communicate with students, from diverse backgrounds or varying degrees of abilities, in English, Hindi, Tamil and Marathi. A committed and dedicated professional with a proven ability to teach, motivate and direct students towards optimum performance by inducing positive and energetic environment. Fully conversant with the English National Curriculum at school and college levels and experienced in employing ICT in the classroom to impart delightful and comprehensible learning experiences by creating conducive environment.

Vu Hai Nam holds a Master's degree from the UK and is a PhD candidate at UCSI University, Malaysia. With a decade of experience in the educational field, he currently holds the position of Vice Dean of the Institute of International Training and Cooperation at Ba Ria - Vung Tau University. His research focus lies in business, digital transformation, and sustainable development.

Index

A

C

D

E

F

G

H

V

www.ingramcontent.com/pod-product-compliance
Lightning Source LLC
La Vergne TN
LVHW062332300926
849161LV00007B/1668